Routledge History of Philosophy
Volume X

Volume X of the *Routledge History of Philosophy* presents a historical survey of the central topics in twentieth-century Anglo-American philosophy. It chronicles what has been termed the 'linguistic turn' in analytic philosophy and traces the influence the study of language has had on the main problems of philosophy. Each chapter contains an extensive bibliography of the major writings in the field.

In keeping with the importance of the linguistic turn, the introduction and the first two essays in the book deal with the philosophy of language. A subsequent series of essays concentrates on the central areas of metaphysics, ethics and epistemology. The book also covers the traditional, related topics of aesthetics, political philosophy and the philosophy of religion. Then there are essays on domains that have only become prominent in this century, namely, applied ethics, feminist philosophy and the philosophy of law. One chapter is devoted to the later Wittgenstein.

The book's authors have contributed to the on-going discussions they cover, some of them prominently. All the essays present their large and complex topics in a clear and well organized way. The reader will find a helpful Chronology of major events in philosophy, logic and science in the twentieth century and an extensive Glossary of technical terms.

John V. Caulfield lives in Toronto. He has taught philosophy at Cornell University and the University of Toronto, and is the author of *Wittgenstein: Language and World* (1981) and *The Looking-Glass Self* (1990). He is currently working on a book of essays on Wittgenstein.

Routledge History of Philosophy
General Editors – G. H. R. Parkinson and S. G. Shanker

The *Routledge History of Philosophy* provides a chronological survey of the history of Western philosophy, from its beginnings in the sixth century BC to the present time. It discusses all the major philosophical developments in depth. Most space is allocated to those individuals who, by common consent, are regarded as great philosophers. But lesser figures have not been neglected, and together the ten volumes of the *History* include basic and critical information about every significant philosopher of the past and present. These philosophers are clearly situated within the cultural and, in particular, the scientific context of their time.

The *History* is intended not only for the specialist, but also for the student and general reader. Each chapter is by an acknowledged authority in the field. The chapters are written in an accessible style and a glossary of technical terms is provided in each volume.

I   *From the Beginning to Plato*
C. C. W. Taylor

II   *From Aristotle to Augustine*
David Furley

III *Medieval Philosophy*
John Marenbo

IV   *The Renaissance and 17th-century Rationalism*
G. H. R. Parkinson

V   *British Philosophy and the Age of Enlightenment*
Stuart Brown

VI   *The Age of German Idealism*
Robert Solomon and Kathleen Higgins

VII *The Nineteenth Century*
C. L. Ten

VIII *Continental Philosophy in the 20th Century*
Richard Kearney

IX   *Philosophy of Science, Logic and Mathematics in the 20th Century*
S. G. Shanker

X   *Philosophy of Meaning, Knowledge and Value in the 20th Century*

Each volume contains 10–15 chapters by different contributors.

Routledge History of Philosophy
Volume X

Philosophy of Meaning,
Knowledge and Value in
the Twentieth Century

EDITED BY
John V. Canfield

Routledge
Taylor & Francis Group

LONDON AND NEW YORK

First published 1997
by Routledge
11 New Fetter Lane, London EC4P 4EE

Simultaneously published in the USA and Canada
by Routledge
29 West 35th Street, New York, NY 10001

First published in paperback 2003

Reprinted 2004

Routledge is an imprint of the Taylor & Francis Group

Selection and editorial matter © 1997 John Canfield

Individual chapters © 1997 the contributors

Typeset in Garamond by RefineCatch Ltd, Bungay, Suffolk
Printed and bound in Great Britain by
TJ International Ltd, Padstow, Cornwall

British Library Cataloguing in Publication Data
A catalogue record for this book is available from the British Library

Library of Congress Cataloging in Publication Data

ISBN 0–415–05605–5 hbk
ISBN 0–415–30882–8 pbk

Contents

CONTENTS

Preface to the
paperback edition

The success of the first edition of the **Routledge History of Philosophy**, which has led to the publication of this new paperback edition, fully justifies the thinking behind this project. Our view at the time that we planned this collection was that the history of philosophy has a special importance for contemporary philosophers and philosophy students. For the discipline demands that one develop the rigorous techniques required to grasp the significance of a philosopher's ideas within their historical framework, while constantly assessing the relevance of the problems or theories discussed to contemporary issues. The very persistence of these 'perennial problems in philosophy' is an indication, not just of their enduring relevance, but equally, of how important it is to be thoroughly grounded in their history in order to grasp their full complexity. We would like to take this opportunity to thank once again all of the authors involved, each of whom has produced such a lasting contribution to the history of philosophy, and also, our editors Richard Stoneman and Muna Khogali, for their role in making the **History** such an indispensable resource.

G. H. R. P. Reading, 2002
S. G. S. Toronto, 2002

General editors' preface

The history of philosophy, as its name implies, represents a union of two very different disciplines, each of which imposes severe constraints upon the other. As an exercise in the history of ideas, it demands that one acquire a 'period eye': a thorough understanding of how the thinkers whom it studies viewed the problems which they sought to resolve, the conceptual frameworks in which they addressed these issues, their assumptions and objectives, their blind spots and miscues. But as an exercise in philosophy, we are engaged in much more than simply a descriptive task. There is a crucial critical aspect to our efforts: we are looking for the cogency as much as the development of an argument, for its bearing on questions which continue to preoccupy us as much as the impact which it may have had on the evolution of philosophical thought.

The history of philosophy thus requires a delicate balancing act from its practitioners. We read these writings with the full benefit of historical hindsight. We can see why the minor contributions remained minor and where the grand systems broke down: sometimes as a result of internal pressures, sometimes because of a failure to overcome an insuperable obstacle, sometimes because of a dramatic technological or sociological change and, quite often, because of nothing more than a shift in intellectual fashion or interests. Yet, because of our continuing philosophical concern with many of the same problems, we cannot afford to look dispassionately at these works. We want to know what lessons are to be learnt from the inconsequential or the glorious failures; many times we want to plead for a contemporary relevance in the overlooked theory or to reconsider whether the 'glorious failure' was indeed such or simply ahead of its time: perhaps even ahead of its author.

We find ourselves, therefore, much like the mythical 'radical translator' who has so fascinated modern philosophers, trying to understand an author's ideas in his and his culture's eyes, and at the same time, in our own. It can be a formidable task. Many times we fail in the historical undertaking because our philosophical interests are so strong, or lose sight of the latter because we are so enthralled by the former. But the nature of philosophy is such that we are compelled to master both techniques. For learning about the history of philosophy is not just a challenging and engaging pastime: it is an essential element in learning about the nature of philosophy – in grasping how philosophy is intimately connected with and yet distinct from both history and science.

The *Routledge History of Philosophy* provides a chronological survey of the history of Western philosophy, from its beginnings up to the present time. Its aim is to discuss all major philosophical developments in depth, and with this in mind, most space has been allocated to those individuals who, by common consent, are regarded as great philosophers. But lesser figures have not been neglected, and it is hoped that the reader will be able to find, in the ten volumes of the *History*, at least basic information about any significant philosopher of the past or present.

Philosophical thinking does not occur in isolation from other human activities, and this *History* tries to situate philosophers within the cultural, and in particular the scientific, context of their time. Some philosophers, indeed, would regard philosophy as merely ancillary to the natural sciences; but even if this view is rejected, it can hardly be denied that the sciences have had a great influence on what is now regarded as philosophy, and it is important that this influence should be set forth clearly. Not that these volumes are intended to provide a mere record of the factors that influenced philosophical thinking; philosophy is a discipline with its own standards of argument, and the presentation of the ways in which these arguments have developed is the main concern of this *History*.

In speaking of 'what is now regarded as philosophy', we may have given the impression that there now exists a single view of what philosophy is. This is certainly not the case; on the contrary, there exist serious differences of opinion, among those who call themselves philosophers, about the nature of their subject. These differences are reflected in the existence at the present time of two main schools of thought, usually described as 'analytic' and 'continental' philosophy. It is not our intention, as general editors of this *History*, to take sides in this dispute. Our attitude is one of tolerance, and our hope is that these volumes will contribute to an understanding of how philosophers have reached the positions which they now occupy.

One final comment. Philosophy has long been a highly technical subject, with its own specialized vocabulary. This *History* is intended not only for the specialist but also for the general reader. To this end, we have tried to ensure that each chapter is written in an accessible style; and since technicalities are unavoidable, a glossary of technical terms is provided in each volume. In this way these volumes will, we hope, contribute to a wider understanding of a subject which is of the highest importance to all thinking people.

G. H. R. Parkinson
S. G. Shanker

Notes on contributors

Robert L. Arrington is Professor Emeritus of Philosophy at Georgia State University in Atlanta, Georgia. He is the author of *Rationalism, Realism and Relativism* (1989) and *Western Ethics* (1997) and editor of *A Companion to Philosophers* (1998). He is also co-editor of *Wittgenstein's Philosophical Investigations* (1991), *Wittgenstein and Quine* (1996), and *Wittgenstein and the Philosophy of Religion* (2000).

John V. Canfield is Professor Emeritus at the University of Toronto. He is the author of *Wittgenstein: Language and World* (1981), *The Looking-Glass Self* (1990), and papers on Wittgenstein and the philosophy of language. He is the editor (with Frank Donnell) of *The Theory of Knowledge* (1964), *Purpose in Nature* (1966), *The Philosophy of Wittgenstein* (in fifteen volumes, 1986) and (with Stuart Shanker) *Wittgenstein's Intentions* (1993).

Nino B. Cocchiarella is Professor Emeritus of Philosophy at Indiana University. He is the author of *Logical Investigations of Predication Theory and the Problem of Universals* (1986), *Logical Studies in Early Analytic Philosophy* (1987), and numerous articles including 'Conceptualism, Realism, and Intensional Logic' and 'Conceptual Realism versus Quine on Classes and Higher-Order Logic'.

William James DeAngelis is Associate Professor of Philosophy at Northeastern University in Boston, Massachusetts, where he has been the recipient of a Presidential Excellence-in-Teaching Award. His publications have been in the area of metaphysics and Wittgenstein studies; currently he is preparing a book on the philosophy of religion.

George Dickie lives in Chicago; he is the author of *Art and the Aesthetic* (1974), *The Art Circle* (1984), *Evaluating Art* (1988), *The Century of Taste* (1996) and *Art and Value* (2001). He is co-editor of *Aesthetics: A Critical Anthology* (2nd edn, 1988) and *Introduction to Aesthetics* (1997).

Marilyn Frye is Professor of Philosophy at Michigan State University. Her essays are collected in *The Politics of Reality* (1983) and *Willful Virgin* (1992).

Sarah Lucia Hoagland is Professor of Philosophy and Women's Studies at Northeastern Illinois University, in Chicago. She is author of *Lesbian Ethics* (1988), and co-editor of *For Lesbians Only: A Separatist Anthology* (1992).

Bernard Linsky is Professor of Philosophy of the University of Alberta. He has written articles on philosophical logic, modal metaphysics and Bertrand Russell, interests similar to those of his father, Leonard Linsky.

A. P. Martinich is Roy Allison Vaughan Professor of Philosophy and Professor of History and Government at the University of Texas at Austin. He is the author of *Hobbes: A Biography* (1999), *Thomas Hobbes: Perspectives on British History* (1997), *Philosophical Writing* (2nd edn, 1996), *Hobbes: A Dictionary* (1995) and *The Two Gods of Leviathan: Thomas Hobbes on Religion and Politics* (1991). He is also editor of *The Philosophy of Language* (4th edn, 2001), and co-editor of *A Companion to Analytic Philosophy* (2001).

Paul K. Moser is Professor and Chairperson of Philosophy at Loyola University of Chicago. He has authored *Philosophy after Objectivity; Knowledge and Evidence*; and *Empirical Justification*; co-authored *The Theory of Knowledge;* edited *Empirical Knowledge; A Priori Knowledge; Rationality in Action*; and *The Oxford Handbook of Epistemology*; co-edited *Human Knowledge* (3rd edn); *Morality and the Good Life; Moral Relativism; Divine Hiddenness*; and *The Rationality of Theism.* He is the general editor of four book series in philosophy, including *The Oxford Handbooks of Philosophy; Routledge Contemporary Introductions to Philosophy*; and *Routledge Contemporary Readings in Philosophy.*

Calvin G. Normore is Professor of Philosophy at University of California, Los Angeles. He has published and and lectured widely in a variety of areas including medieval philosophy, social and political philosophy, history of logic and decision theory.

Justin Oakley is Director of the Centre for Human Bioethics, Monash University, Australia. He is the author of *Morality and the Emotions* (1992) and co-author of *Virtue Ethics and Professional Roles* (2001). He has published articles on ethical theory, medical ethics and bioethics.

Arthur Ripstein is Professor of Law and Philosophy at the University of Toronto. He is the author of *Equality, Responsibility and the Law* (1998) and co-editor of *Law and Morality* (2nd edn, 2001), *Philosophy and Criminal Law* (1998) and *Practical Reason and Principle: Essays for David Gauthier* (2001). He is also an Associate Editor of Ethics.

Michael Stingl teaches philosophy at the University of Lethbridge. His research interests include ethical naturalism and various applied issues in biomedical ethics. He is currently editing a book on reforming the Canadian health system.

Edward R. Wierenga is Professor of Religion at the University of Rochester (NY). He is the author of *The Nature of God* (1989) and numerous articles.

Chronology

The dates assigned to books or articles are the dates of publication. The titles of works not written in English have been translated, unless they are better known in their original form.

	Philosophy (general)	Logic
1873		
1877	Peirce, *The Fixation of Belief*	
1879		Frege, *Begriffschrift*
1881		
1883		Bradley, *Principles of Logic*
1884		Frege, *The Foundations of Arithmetic*
1891		Frege, 'Function and Concept'
1892	Frege, 'On Sense and Reference'	Frege, 'Concept and Object'
1893	Bradley, *Appearance and Reality*	Frege, *The Basic Laws of Arithmetic* (vol. 2: 1903)
1895		
1897		
1898		
1899		Hilbert, *Foundations of Geometry*
1900	Husserl, *Logical Investigations*	Hilbert's address to the International Congress of Mathematicians: 'Mathematical Problems'
1901		
1902		Russell's paradox
1903	Moore, 'Refutation of Idealism' Moore, *Principia Ethica*	Russell, *The Principles of Mathematics* Frege, *Basic Laws of Arithmetic*
1904		
1905	Russell, 'On Denoting' Mach, *Knowledge and Error*	Meinong, 'Theory of Objects'

Philosophy of Science	Science and technology	
Jevons, *The Principles of Science*		1873
		1877
		1879
Helmholtz, *Popular Lectures*	Michelson – Morley experiment (speed of light found to be the same in perpendicular directions)	1881
Mach, *The Science of Mechanics*		1883
		1884
	Ehrlich's diphtheria antitoxin establishes field of immunology	1891
Pearson, *The Grammar of Science*	Lorentz – Fitzgerald contraction (contraction of objects at high speeds)	1892
Mach, *Popular Scientific Lectures* Hertz, *The Principles of Mechanics*		1893
	Discovery of x-rays (Roentgen) Cloud chamber developed (Thomson)	1895
	Discovery of electron (Thomson) Charge of electron measured (Thomson)	1897
	Term 'radioactivity' coined (M. Curie) Alpha and beta rays (radioactivity from uranium) discovered (Rutherford)	1898
		1899
	Quantum theory initiated: substances can emit light only at certain energies (Planck) Rediscovery of Mendel's 1860s work on genetics	1900
	First trans-Atlantic telegraphic transmission (Marconi)	1901
Poincaré, *Science and Hypothesis*	Rutherford and Soddy: 'The Cause and Nature of Radioactivity'	1902
	First successful airplane flight (Wright brothers)	1903
Duhem, *The Aim and Structure of Physical Theory*	Thomson's model of the atom: electrons embedded in sphere of positive electricity	1904
Boltzmann, *Popular Writings*	Einstein explains Brownian motion (motion of small particles suspended in liquid); seen as first proof of existence of atoms Einstein's papers on the special theory of relativity Einstein postulates light quantum (term 'photon' coined 1926) for particle-like behaviour of light	1905

	Philosophy (general)	Logic
1906		
1907	James, *Pragmatism* Bergson, *Creative Evolution*	
1908		
1909		
1910		Russell and Whitehead, *Principia Mathematica* (1910–13)
1911		
1912		Brouwer, *Intuitionism and Formalism*
1913	Husserl, *Ideas*	
1914	Russell, *Our Knowledge of the External World* Bradley, *Essays on Truth and Reality*	
1915		
1917		
1918	Russell, *The Philosophy of Logical Atomism* Schlick, *General Theory of Knowledge*	Lewis, *Survey of Symbolic Logic*
1919		Russell, *Introduction to Mathematical Philosophy*
1920	Whitehead, *The Concept of Nature*	
1921	Wittgenstein, *Tractatus Logico-Philosophicus*	Keynes, *A Treatise on Probability*
1922	Moore, *Philosophical Papers*	
1923		Skolem, 'Some Remarks on Axiomatic Set Theory'

Philosophy of Science	Science and technology	
	Existence of 'vitamins' (term coined 1912) postulated (Hopkins); discovered 1928	1906
		1907
Driesch, *The Science and Philosophy of the Organism*	Minkowski, *Space and Time* (proposes 4–dimensional universe)	1908
	Term 'gene' coined (Johannsen)	1909
	M. Curie, *Treatise on Radioactivity*	1910
	Rutherford's atomic theory: positively charged nucleus surrounded by negative electrons	1911
C. L. Morgan, *Instinct and Experience*	Theory of continental drift proposed (Wegener)	1912
	Bohr's model of the atom: electrons revolve around nucleus in fixed orbits, give off fixed quanta of energy by jumping orbit Henry Ford's assembly line	1913
Broad, *Perception, Physics, and Reality* Driesch, *The History and Theory of Vitalism*	Discovery of proton (Rutherford)	1914
	Einstein's general theory of relativity	1915
Schlick, *Space and Time in Contemporary Physics*	Existence of black holes predicted (Schwarzschild)	1917
		1918
		1919
Campbell, *Physics: The Elements*	Existence of neutron (uncharged particle) proposed (Harkins); discovered 1932 Red shift in spectra of galaxies reported (Slipher) Copenhagen Institute of Theoretical Physics founded (Bohr)	1920
	Insulin discovered (Banting, Best, McLeod, Collip)	1921
		1922
Broad, *Scientific Thought* C. L. Morgan, *Emergent Evolution*	Particle-wave duality of matter proposed (de Broglie); confirmed 1927 (Davisson)	1923

	Philosophy (general)	Logic
1924		
1925	Broad, *The Mind and Its Place in Nature*	
1926		
1927	Heidegger, *Being and Time* McTaggart, *The Nature of Existence*	
1928	Carnap, *The Logical Structure of the World*	Hilbert, *Principles of Mathematical Logic* von Mises, *Probability, Statistics and Truth*
1929	Carnap, Hahn and Neurath, *The Scientific World View: The Vienna Circle* Dewey, *Experience and Nature* Lewis, *Mind and the World Order*	
1930		Godel's proof of completeness of first-order redicate calculus

Philosophy of Science	Science and technology	
	Bose statistics for light quanta (Bose)	1924
	Galaxies shown to be independent systems (Hubble)	
	First use of insecticides	
Whitehead, *Science and the Modern World*	Electron spin hypothesized (Goudsmit, Uhlenbeck)	
	Pauli's exclusion principle (electrons of same quantum number cannot occupy same state)	
	Quantum mechanics given first comprehensive formulation (Born, Heisenberg, Jordan)	
	'Scopes Monkey Trial' (high-school teacher prosecuted for teaching evolution)	
	First analog computer (Bush)	
C. L. Morgan, *Life, Mind, and Spirit*	Probability interpretation of quantum mechanics (Born)	1926
	Fermi–Dirac statistics	
	Planck's law derived from first principles (Dirac)	
	First paper on wave mechanics (Schrödinger); Schrödinger's equation	
	Morgan, *The Theory of the Gene*	
Russell, *The Analysis of Matter* Weyl, *Philosophy of Mathematics and Natural Science* Bridgman, *The Logic of Modern Physics*	Heisenberg's uncertainty principle (cannot determine simultaneously position and momentum of electron)	1927
	First version of 'Big Bang' theory of origins of universe (Lemaître)	
Eddington, *The Nature of the Physical World* Reichenbach, *The Philosophy of Time and Space* Campbell, *Measurement and Calculation*	Dirac's equation combines quantum mechanics with special relativity	1928
	Discovery of penicillin (Fleming); production and clinical use not until 1940s	
Woodger, *Biological Principles*	Heisenberg and Pauli's quantum field theory	1929
	Hubble's law (more distant a galaxy, faster it is receding from Earth)	
	Discovery of deoxyribose nucleic acids (DNA)	
Heisenberg, *The Physical Principles of Quantum Theory*	Dirac, *Principles of Quantum Mechanics*	1930
	'Neutrino' postulated (Pauli); term coined 1932 (Fermi); discovered 1955	
	Discovery of planet Pluto (Tombaugh)	
	Immunization against typhus developed (Zinsser)	

	Philosophy (general)	Logic
1931	Tarski, 'The Concept of Truth in Formalized Languages'	Godel's incompleteness theorem Ramsey, *The Foundations of Mathematics* Carnap, 'The Logicist Foundations of Mathematics' Heyting, 'The Intuitionist Foundations of Mathematics' von Neumann, 'The Formalist Foundations of Mathematics'
1932	Price, *Perception*	
1933		
1934	Carnap, *The Logical Syntax of Language*	Hilbert, *Foundations of Mathematics* (vol.2: 1939)
1935		Reichenbach, *The Theory of Probability*
1936	Husserl, *The Crisis of European Sciences and Transcendental Phenomenology* Ayer, *Language, Truth, and Logic* Schlick, 'Meaning and Verification'	
1937		Turing, 'On Computable Numbers' ('Turing machine')
1938		Godel's proof of consistency of continuum hypothesis with basic axioms of set theory Dewey, *Logic: The Theory of Inquiry*
1939	Blanshard, *The Nature of Thought*	Nagel, *Principles of the Theory of Probability* Carnap, *Foundations of Logic and Mathematics*

Philosophy of Science	Science and technology	
Haldane, *The Philosophical Basis of Biology* Neurath, 'Physicalism' Schlick, 'Causality in Contemporary Physics' Carnap, 'Die physikalische Sprache als Universalsprache der Wissenschaft' (*The Unity of Science*, 1934)	'Positron' (positively charged electron) postulated (Dirac); discovered 1932 (Anderson); first form of anti-matter discovered	1931
Joad, *Philosophical Aspects of Modern Science*	Particle accelerator first used to split lithium atom (Cockcroft, Walton) Heisenberg's model of atomic nucleus: neutrons and protons held together by exchanging electrons Discovery of neutron (Chadwick) Morgan, *The Scientific Basis of Evolution*	1932
	Fermi's theory of beta decay (first suggestion of weak interaction) Vitamin C synthesized)	1933
Bachelard, *The New Scientific Spirit*		1934
Popper, *The Logic of Discovery* Eddington, *New Pathways in Science*	'Exchange particle' causing attraction between particles in atomic nucleus (strong force) proposed (Yukawa); called 'meson' (1939), now 'pion' Richter scale developed (Richter) First radar developed (Watson, Watt)	1935
Bridgman, *The Nature of Physical Theory* Inauguration of *The International Encyclopedia of Unified Sciences* (Neurath, Carnap, Morris)	Isolation of DNA in pure state (Belozersky) Primitive digital computer (Zuse) ABC (Atanasoff-Berry Computer), first electronic computer begun; completed 1939, operational version 1942.	1936
Stebbing, *Philosophy and the Physicists* Woodger, *The Axiomatic Method in Biology*	'Muon' discovered (Anderson); initial claim to be Yukawa meson shown false 1945 (Conversi, Puncini, Picconi) Concept of 'charge conjugation' introduced for particle interactions (Kramers); in 1958 is shown to be invalid for some interactions	1937
Oparin, *The Origin of Life* Reichenbach, *Experience and Prediction* Carnap, 'Logical Foundations of the Unity of Science'	Uranium atom first split (Hahn)	1938
Eddington, *The Philosophy of Physical Science*	Einstein's letter to Roosevelt: first step in US effort to build atomic bomb Method of calculating properties of material objects from quantum principles developed (Herring) DDT insecticide synthesized (Muller)	1939

	Philosophy (general)	Logic
1940	Russell, *An Inquiry into Meaning and Truth* Collingwood, *An Essay on Metaphysics*	
1941		Tarski, *Introduction to Logic and to the Methodology of the Deductive Sciences*
1942		
1943	Sartre, *Being and Nothingness*	Carnap, *Formalization of Logic*
1944	Stevenson, *Ethics and Language*	
1945		Waismann, 'Are There Alternative Logics?' Carnap, 'The Two Concepts of Probability'
1946		
1947	Carnap, *Meaning and Necessity*	
1948		
1949	Schlick, *Philosophy of Nature* Ryle, *The Concept of Mind*	Reichenbach, *The Theory of Probability* Kneale, *Probability and Induction*

Philosophy of Science	Science and technology	
	Penicillin developed as antibiotic (term 'antibiotic' coined 1941)	1940
	Zuse's Z2 computer: electromagnetic relays and punched tape for data entry	1941
	Two-meson theory (Sakata, Inoue) First controlled chain reaction (Fermi) First radio map of universe	1942
	Quantum electrodynamics (QED) developed (Tomonaga) First operational nuclear reactor (Oak Ridge, Tenn.) First all-electronic computer, 'Colossus', developed to crack codes (Turing)	1943
Reichenbach, *Philosophical Foundations of Quantum Mechanics*	DNA determined as hereditary material for almost all living beings (Avery) Jet-engine (V-1) and rocket-propelled (V-2) bombs	1944
Lillie, *General Biology and Philosophy of Organism*	Atomic bombs dropped on Hiroshima and Nagasaki ENIAC: first all-purpose, stored-program electronic computer	1945
Frank, *Foundations of Physics*	Term 'lepton' introduced for light particles not affected by strong force (Pais, Moller) 'V particle' discovered (Rochester and Butler) Radioactive carbon-14 method developed for dating objects (Libby)	1946
	'Pion' (Yukawa meson) discovered (Powell and team) Lamb Shift discovered; independent development of quantum electrodynamics (QED) 4 years after similar theory of Tomonaga Two-meson theory developed independently 5 years after similar theory of Sakata and Inoue (Marshak, Bethe)	1947
Woodger, *Biological Principles*	Opposed theories of the universe formulated: steady-state theory (Bond, Gold, Hayle) and 'Big Bang' theory (Gamow, Alpher, Harmon) Discovery of transistor (Shockley, Brattain, Bardeen); will replace vacuum tubes	1948
	Atomic nucleus not necessarily spherical (Rainwater)	1949

	Philosophy (general)	Logic
1950	Strawson, 'On Referring' Hempel, 'Problems and Changes in the Empiricist Criterion of Meaning'	Quine, *Methods of Logic* Carnap, *The Logical Foundations of Probability*
1951	Quine, 'Two Dogmas of Empiricism' Goodman, *The Structure of Appearance*	von Wright, *An Essay in Modal Logic*
1952	Hare, *The Language of Morals* Wisdom, *Other Minds*	Strawson, *Introduction to Logical Theory* Carnap, *The Continuum of Inductive Methods*
1953	Wittgenstein, *Philosophical Investigations* Quine, *From a Logical Point of View*	
1954	Ryle, *Dilemmas*	Goodman, *Fact, Fiction and Forecast* Savage, *The Foundations of Statistics*
1955		
1956	Reichenbach, *The Direction of Time* Wittgenstein, *Remarks on the Philosophy of Mathematics*	
1957	Chisholm, *Perceiving* Chomsky, *Syntactic Structures*	von Wright, *The Logical Problem of Induction*
1958	Polanyi, *Personal Knowledge* Baier, *The Moral Point of View* Geach, *Mental Acts*	
1959	Strawson, *Individuals* Hart and Honore, *Causation in the Law*	

Philosophy of Science	Science and technology	
Sommerhoff, *Analytical Biology*		1950
Bernal, *The Physical Basis of Life*	Heart-lung machine developed (Gibson) UNIVAC I, first commercially available computer	1951
Wisdom, *Foundations of Inference in Natural Science* Hempel, *Fundamentals of Concept Formation in Empirical Science* Woodger, *Biology and Language*	Plasmid (structure containing genetic material exchanged by bacteria) discovered (Lederberg) Bubble chamber for study of subatomic particles developed (Glaser) Thermo-nuclear bomb ('H Bomb') developed (Teller) First nuclear reactor accident (Chalk River, Canada) Polio vaccine developed (Salk); mass inoculation in 1954; superseded by new vaccine in 1957 (Sabine) 'Piltdown Man' revealed as fake	1952
Toulmin, *The Philosophy of Science* Braithwaite, *Scientific Explanation*	'Strangeness' quantum number introduced (Gell-Mann; Nakano, Nishijina) Double-helix structure of DNA determined (Crick, Watson)	1953
Reichenbach, *Nomological Statements and Admissible Operations*	European Centre for Nuclear Research (CERN) founded	1954
	Neutrinos observed (Cowen, Reines) FORTRAN, first computer-programming language (Backus, IBM) LISP, computer language of artificial intelligence, developed (McCarthy)	1955
	Anti-neutron discovered (Cook, Lambertson, Picconi, Wentzel)	1956
Bohm, *Causality and Chance in Modern Physics*	Parity not conserved for weak interactions (Yang, Lee, Wu) 'Boson' (W particle) proposed as mediator of weak interactions (Schwinger) Spuntnik I, first artificial satellite, launched by USSR	1957
Hanson, *Patterns of Discovery* Bohr, *Atomic Physics and Human Knowledge*		1958
Bunge, *Causality*		1959

	Philosophy (general)	Logic
1960	Quine, *Word and Object* Malcolm, 'Anselm's Ontological Arguments'	
1961	Austin, *Philosophical Papers* Grice, 'The Causal Theory of Perception' Malcolm, *Dreaming*	
1962	Black, *Models and Metaphors* Hart, *The Concept of Law*	
1963	Davidson, 'Actions, Reasons, and Causes' Hart, *Law, Liberty and Morality* Katz and Fodor, 'The Structure of a Semantic Theory' Popper, *Conjectures and Refutations* Shoemaker, *Self-knowledge and Self-identity*	Independence of Cantor's continuum hypothesis from axioms of set theory demonstrated (Cohen) von Wright, *The Logic of Preference* Quine, *Set Theory and Its Logic*
1964	Scheffler, *The Anatomy of Inquiry*	
1965	Chomsky, *Aspects of the Theory of Syntax* Devlin, *The Enforcement of Morals*	Hacking, *Logic of Statistical Inference*
1966		
1967	Davidson, 'Truth and Meaning' Frankena, *The Concept of Morality* Plantinga, *God and Other Minds*	Putnam, 'Mathematics without Foundations'
1968	Armstrong, *A Materialist Theory of the Mind* Fodor, *Psychological Explanation*	

Philosophy of Science	Science and technology	
	Mossbauer effect discovered (Mossbauer); used to confirm Einstein's general theory of relativity (Pound, Reblan) 'Resonances' (short-lived particles) discovered (Alvarez) First laser (Maiman); precursors are Townes' maser (1954), Kastler's 'optical pumping' (1950)	1960
Nagel, *The Structure of Science* Harre, *Theories and Things* Capek, *Philosophical Impact of Contemporary Physics*	First human being to orbit the Earth (Gagarin)	1961
Kuhn, *The Structure of Scientific Revolutions* Sellars, *Science, Perception and Reality* Maxwell, 'The Ontological Status of Theoretical Entities' Hesse, *Models and Analogies in Science*		1962
Smart, *Philosophy and Scientific Realism* Grunbaum, *Philosophical Problems of Space and Time*	First recognition of a quasar (Schmidt)	1963
	Concept of 'quark' introduced (Gell-Mann) 'Green Revolution' inaugurated with strain of rice generating double yield given sufficient fertilizer	1964
Hempel, *Aspects of Scientific Explanation*	Confirmation of 'Big Bang' theory with accidental discovery of radio-wave remnants of 'Big Bang' (Penzias, Wilson)	1965
Hempel, *Philosophy of Natural Science*		1966
Scheffler, *Science and Subjectivity*	Strong nuclear force shown to violate parity conservation (Lobashov) 'Electroweak theory' unifies weak and electromagnetic forces (Weinberg, Salam, Glashow) First pulsar discovered Keyboards used for computer data entry	1967
Becker, *The Biological Way of Thought*	Discovery of restrictive enzymes (can cut DNA of virus at particular point); would become a basic tool of genetic engineering	1968

	Philosophy (general)	Logic
1969	Quine, *Ontological Relativity* Searle, *Speech Acts*	Lewis, *Convention*
1970	Davidson, 'Semantics for Natural Languages'	Quine, *Philosophy of Logic* Cohen, *The Implications of Induction*
1971	Rawls, *A Theory of Justice* Judith Jarvis Thompson, 'A Defense of Abortion'	Salman, *Statistical Explanation and Statistical Relevance*
1972	Popper, *Objective Knowledge*	Kripke, 'Naming and Necessity'
1973		Lewis, *Counterfactuals* Hintikka, *Logic, Language Games and Information*
1974	Nozick, *Anarchy, State and Utopia*	Hacking, *The Emergence of Probability* Haack, *Deviant Logic*
1975	Singer, *Animal Liberation*	
1976		
1977	Dworkin, *Taking Rights Seriously* Malcolm, *Memory and Mind*	
1978	Goodman, *Ways of Worldmaking* Dummett, *Truth and other Enigmas*	
1979		
1980	Kripke, *Naming and Necessity* Rorty, *Philosophy and the Mirror of Nature*	

Philosophy of Science	Science and technology	
	First human beings on the moon (Armstrong, Aldrin) First artificial heart used in a human being Single gene first isolated (Beckwith)	1969
Monod, *Chance and Necessity*		1970
	Microprocessor (chip) introduced	1971
	Quantum chromodynamics (QCD) initiated (Gell-Mann) Biblical accounts of creation should receive equal attention as evolutionary theory: California State Board of Education	1972
	Creation of the universe from absolutely nothing under probabilistic laws of quantum mechanics proposed (Tyron) First Skylab launched Beginning of genetic engineering (Cohen, Boyer)	1973
Sklar, *Space, Time and Spacetime* Barnes, *Scientific Knowledge and Sociological Theory*	First of GUTs (grand unified theories) unifies strong, weak and electro-magnetic forces (Georgi, Glashow) J/psi particle discovered (Richter, Trug); confirmation of charm theory of quarks	1974
Feyerabend, *Against Method*	Personal computers introduced (Altair 8800)	1975
Bloor, *Knowledge and Social Imagery*	Functional synthetic gene constructed (Khorana)	1976
Lauden, *Progress and its Problems*	Upsilon particle discovered (Lederman): confirms quark theory of baryons Apple II personal computer introduced Earliest known cases of AIDS; disease not recognized until 1981	1977
Feyerabend, *Science in a Free Society*	First 'test-tube' baby	1978
Latour and Woolger, *Laboratory Life* Lakatos, *The Methodology of Scientific Research Programs*	Partial meltdown of nuclear reactor at Three Mile Island	1979
van Fraassen, *The Scientific Image* Bohm, *Wholeness and the Implicate Order*	Neutrinos may have tiny mass, thus representing 'missing mass' thought to hold galaxies together 'Inflationary universe' model: universe expands rapidly for short time before 'Big Bang' (Guth)	1980

	Philosophy (general)	Logic
1980		
1981	Putnam, *Reason, Truth and History* MacIntyre, *After Virtue*	
1982		
1983		
1984	Feinberg, *The Moral Limits of the Criminal Law* Armstrong and Macolm, *Consciousness and Causality*	
1985	Dworkin, *A Matter of Principle*	
1986	Malcolm, *Nothing is Hidden*	
1987	Feyerabend, *Farewell to Reason* Lakoff, *Women, Fire and Dangerous Things*	
1988		
1989	Grice, *Studies in the Way of Words*	

Philosophy of Science	Science and technology	
	Revival of 'catastrophism': collision between Earth and large body results in mass extinctions, including extinction of dinosaurs (W. and L. Alvarez)	1980
	First transference of genes from one animal to another of a different species 'New inflationary universe' theory of the origins of the universe (Linde, Albrecht, Steinhardt) First flight of space shuttle *Columbia*	1981
	First commercial product of genetic engineering (human insulin)	1982
Cartwright, *How the Laws of Physics Lie* Hacking, *Representing and Intervening*	Discovery of W and Z particles; further confirms electroweak theory (CERN)	1983
	Sheep successfully cloned (Wilkinson)	1984
Fox-Keller, *Reflections on Gender and Science*	Hole in ozone layer over Antarctica discovered	1985
Harding, *The Feminist Question in Science*	Individual quantum jumps in individual atoms observed Fifth fundamental force, hypercharge, discovered (Fishbach); not universally accepted Discovery of 'Great Attractor', a point towards which a number of galaxies (including ours) are moving Explosion of space shuttle *Challenger* First field trials of genetically engineered organisms (tobacco) Chernobyl nuclear reactor explosion	1986
Latour, *Science in Action* Putnam, *The Many Faces of Realism*	US Supreme Court rejection of equal-time concept of teaching for creationism	1987
Hawking, *A Brief History of Time*		1988
		1989

Introduction
John V. Canfield

This volume presents a chronological survey of some central topics in twentieth-century philosophy in the English-speaking world. A companion volume focuses on logic, the philosophy of science and related subjects, while another covers recent continental philosophy.[1] By way of a broad introduction to the essays printed here I shall discuss some characteristic features of modern Anglo-American philosophy.

Above all what distinguishes that way of thought is its passion for clarity. The attitude is reflected, for example, in Wittgenstein's remark that, 'People who have no need for transparency in their argumentation are lost to philosophy.'[2] The urge towards clarity is itself a concomitant of the so-called 'linguistic turn' that is the distinctive feature of twentieth-century Anglo-American philosophy. The phrase 'the linguistic turn' refers to a change from a relatively small concern with questions about language to a major one. It's not just that by and large, in this century, writers spend more time investigating the nature of language and allied problems, though that is true: compare, for example, the percentage of text devoted to such issues in Locke's *Essay* and Wittgenstein's *Philosophical Investigations*. It is rather that in various ways issues about language become the fundamental ones. This can be seen for instance in A. J. Ayer's famous book *Language, Truth, and Logic* where the first order of business is to establish the bounds of sensible language, and where pretty much everything else is said to follow from that alleged achievement.

The involvement with language that I am discussing has several distinct foci, and in what follows I shall consider three of them: *logical form*, *meaninglessness* and its opposite, *meaning*. A sentence as it appears in some natural language like English may not show forth its correct, underlying structure or form, which must rather be uncovered by the philosopher. Thus a statement's surface form – the form it appears to have – is contrasted with its real or *logical* form. The notion of logical form presupposes our having some way of characterizing those hidden or disguised structures. Historically, and as the term itself indicates, early characterizations of logical form employed the vocabulary of modern logic.

Modern logic was developed by Frege and Russell in the context of an attempt to prove the consistency of mathematics by deriving it from logic. To carry out that programme logic itself had first to be revamped. Here Frege made the essential contribution, by introducing the so called 'quantifiers'.[3] In a radical departure from classical or Aristotelian subject-predicate logic he originated the notion of the universal quantifier 'for all x' and the existential quantifier 'there exists an x'. Given those tools he was able to analyse sentences like 'All men are mortal' and 'Socrates is a man' in a more perspicuous way than the old logic could. It is the apparatus and vocabulary of the new logic that first inspired the search in recent philosophy for logical form.

Bertrand Russell's original and highly influential essay of 1905, 'On Denoting', applied ideas like those just mentioned from modern or mathematical logic to the discovery of logical form. Thus Russell's paper marks a key point in the development of Anglo-American philosophy. The particular issue he addresses has a technical or arcane air, but understanding it is essential to grasping the use subsequent thinkers made of his ideas, and thus necessary for understanding one central aspect of the philosophy discussed in this volume. (For a fuller discussion, see Professor Martinich's essay in this volume, 'Philosophy of language'.)[4] In Russell's well-known example the sentence, 'The present King of France is bald' appears to be of subject-predicate form with 'The present King of France' filling the subject role. On this reading the sentence has the same form as 'Jones is bald'. It *seems* that in each case something picked out by a singular referring expression (one that, like a proper name, picks out one individual) is said to have a certain property. This reading of the sentence causes trouble. The present King of France, like the unicorn in my garden, does not exist, so there is nothing for Russell's sentence to be about. If it is about nothing it must, apparently, be senseless. Yet we understand it. In response to that puzzle, Russell argued that when we correctly analyse the statement, and thus get to the level of its true or logical form, the phrase 'the present King of France' disappears; the sentence's true form is quite different from its apparent one. In the analysis we find only variables such as 'x' and 'y', the logical functions 'for all x' and 'there exists an x such that', and the *predicates* 'is presently King of France' and 'is bald'. Rendered in English, the statement's logical form is: there is at least one thing that is presently King of France, and any thing that is presently King of France is identical to that one thing, and that thing is bald. Since in fact there is nothing that is presently King of France, the statement in question is merely false, not senseless.

The idea of a hidden logical form underlying the propositions of ordinary or natural language was taken by Wittgenstein as a basic presupposition of his enormously influential book the *Tractatus Logico-Philosophicus* (1921). Wittgenstein thought that it was not necessary for the logician to describe the exact logical form of propositions; it was enough if he could come to know in general terms what that form is. Every proposition, he believed, could be analysed into a collection of elementary propositions linked by the so-called truth-functions *and*, *not*, *or* and *if . . . then*. Elementary propositions are those that cannot be analysed further. In the *Tractatus*, they consist solely of names of simple objects. The 'molecular propositions' that express ordinary language statements are formed by joining elementary propositions by means of the truth-functions. All meaningful propositions have the logical form just described; all would-be propositions lacking it are meaningless. A sentence can be meaningless even though we think it has sense; it is a question of its logical form.

Wittgenstein's quest to uncover the true logical form of the sentences of our language was motivated by more than the wish to demarcate clearly the line between what could and could not be said. In addition, he believed that the structure of reality mirrors the structure of propositions, so that to discover the form of language is to establish *a priori* the form of the world. For example, to take one clearly momentous would-be result, Wittgenstein holds that first-person sentences like 'I believe that P' (where P is some proposition) have the form ' "P" says that P'. The alleged subject – the believer *qua* Cartesian ego or mind – disappears in the analysis; reality thus contains no such entity as the self. By focusing on language the 'linguistic turn' in no way trivialized philosophy.

Many contemporary philosophers operate with some variant of the idea of logical form. Donald Davidson, for example, utilizes something like the classical Russellian idea of logical form. As Bernard Linsky points out in his essay on metaphysics in chapter 4, the aim of Davidson's work on the nature of events is to formulate ordinary event-statements in 'first-order logic'. As in the *Tractatus* the underlying motivation is to discover the true form of reality.

Other philosophers continue to seek a correct analysis, in the sense of finding the underlying form of philosophically significant propositions, but without assuming that this form is to be captured in the vocabulary of logic. *Such* concern with the hidden form of statements is found, for example, in Roderick Chisholm's treatment of the metaphysical question of the nature of appearances – those mysterious mental objects postulated by Descartes and so many subsequent thinkers, and which give rise to numerous puzzling questions.[5] Chisholm claims that a correct understanding of sentences about how things appear shows them to have an adverbial rather than a substantive core. If something that may or may not actually be red looks red to Jones, we might say that Jones is aware of a red appearance. Instead of this latter way of speaking, Chisholm holds that in truth what we should say is 'Jones is appeared to redly.' A surface grammatical substantive is to be replaced by a depth grammatical adverb. So in contradistinction to the message of surface grammar, reality does not contain such things as *red appearances*. It contains only agents, like Jones, who perceive in a certain way, described by the use of adverbs. Thus the old question about the nature of appearances (aka 'sense data') is rejected; the question, rather, is said to arise from a faulty understanding of the form of appearance-statements. While the search for logical form is one of the family-resemblance elements distinctive of Anglo-American philosophy, that inquiry itself can take on various guises, as just illustrated.

Another of the points at issue in the 'linguistic turn' is that of *meaninglessness*. (The topic is discussed in several places in the following essays, including William James DeAngelis's chapter on metaphysics.) The notion that certain seemingly important philosophical claims may be in fact hidden nonsense is an old one. There are versions of it in Hume and Kant, for example. In our century the early Wittgenstein's ideas were especially influential in bringing the idea of meaninglessness to centre stage. Every meaningful proposition, he held, has the form 'This is how things are,' where the proposition makes some empirical claim about the world; if it makes no empirical claim it is meaningless. This conception was developed by the *logical positivists*, whose empiricist criterion of meaning attempted to give a precise formulation to Wittgenstein's idea. For the positivists a meaningful sentence must either make some in principle verifiable statement about the world or else be 'tautological' like the statements of mathematics and logic. All other statements, despite their appearance of making sense, are to be judged nonsense. The following statement, for example, would fail their test: 'All the measuring rods in the universe, and anything capable of serving as such, are shrinking by one-half every second.' Since no evidence could possibly either confirm or deny the claim, and since it is no empty tautology like 'Either it is raining or it is not raining' the statement is judged senseless. Similarly for Russell's example: 'The universe came into existence five minutes ago, complete with all our memories, the fossil record, all signs of aging and decay pointing to a distant past, and so on.' These are merely illustrative instances; the positivists' test of meaningfulness had a more significant target. It was meant to exclude from the realm of the sensible such would-be questions as 'Does God exist?' – along with most of the other questions of traditional metaphysics. As Carnap wrote in 1950: 'Influenced by ideas of Ludwig Wittgenstein, the [Vienna] Circle [where logical positivism originated] rejected both the thesis of the reality of the external world and the thesis of its irreality as pseudo-statements; the same was the case for both the thesis of the reality of universals ... and the nominalistic thesis that they are not real.'[6]

While the verificationism associated with the positivists is not popular nowadays, and while therefore there is little corresponding talk of metaphysics as meaningless, nevertheless the influence of the positivist tradition lives on. For the positivists, when the hopelessly muddled questions or 'pseudo-statements' of traditional metaphysics are seen for what they are, the only job left philosophy is as an adjunct to science. Above all, then, the positivists were in the vanguard of the tradition some have called scientism, according to which philosophy becomes either subservient to or an ancillary of science, and in particular of the hard sciences, especially physics. A prediction made by Morton White at the midpoint of the century has certainly proven to hold, at least for a wide range of contemporary philosophers:

> Analytic philosophy will no longer be sharply separated from science, and an unbridgeable chasm will no longer divide those who see meanings or essences and those who collect facts.[7]

The idea of merging philosophy with science is certainly alive and well today, for instance in Carnap's pupil Quine. Again, writers like Jerry Fodor and Paul and Patricia Churchland, in such debates as that over so-called folk psychology, see themselves as doing science, though at a foundational or conceptually oriented level.[8] Correspondingly some social scientists employ ideas drawn from those philosophers in an attempt to establish hypotheses by observation – for instance they deploy field data in an attempt to say whether monkeys have a crude version of 'folk psychology' as Fodor and other philosophers understand that idea.

While concern with *meaninglessness* has certainly abated in our half of the century, concern with its opposite, *meaning*, still rides high. Concern with meaning has two facets: the theoretical problem of saying what meaningfulness or meaning consists in, and the applied problem of uncovering the meaning of particular philosophically important words or claims. Concerning the theoretical issue, perhaps the most influential contribution to it was Frege's distinction between *sense* and *reference*. The theoretical aspect of the problem of meaning is discussed by Professor Martinich; here I turn instead briefly to what I called the applied problem – finding the meaning of individual words.

Russell in his introduction to the *Tractatus* claimed that Wittgenstein was concerned with an ideal language rather than with language as it is. Frege, in his ground-breaking discussions, was explicitly concerned with developing a language that would serve the purposes of science, and thus was not concerned with language as it actually exists, in mufti. But that was not Wittgenstein's position. Wittgenstein thought that every ordinary-language statement was perfectly all right as it stands (*Tractatus*, 5.5563); it's just that we do not know its hidden form – something we can only come to through analysis, by finding the 'one and only complete analysis of the proposition' (*Tractatus*, 3.25).

Concern with an improved or ideal language and concern with the natural, unimproved language of ordinary life each take on various forms in the development of Anglo-American philosophy, and sometimes the one strain is dominant, sometimes the other. In the 1950s and 1960s 'ordinary-language philosophy' held a prominent place. Its paradigmatic practitioners were Gilbert Ryle and John Austin, though in fact the two are very different in their approaches. Wittgenstein's later philosophy is also, but I think wrongly, seen as belonging to the tradition of 'ordinary-language philosophy' associated with Austin and Ryle. Philosophers working roughly in that tradition sought to uncover the ordinary meaning of philosophically relevant words, for example the word 'ought' conspicuous in debates in ethics, or the word 'can' featured in discussions about freedom of the will. Would-be accounts of the meaning of such words – analyses of them – were tested against ordinary usage. In particular a would-be analysis could be refuted by 'counter-examples' – cases where 'what we would ordinarily say' is in conflict with a given account of what we would say. The guiding idea behind the enterprise of analysis was this: In talking about 'ought' (for instance) we use a word from our common vocabulary. Its meaning is already fixed by ordinary usage. To really know what we are saying when we use the word we must study it; we must analyse it. In attempting to provide such analyses philosophers would put forward alleged necessary and sufficient conditions for the application of a given word. Thus a much discussed analysis of 'knowledge' was as follows: Jones knows p *if and only if* (1) Jones believes p, (2) Jones has reliable evidence for p, and (3) p is true.

Alternative versions of analysis developed on the 'ideal-language' side. It was argued that one should not seek simply to uncover the ordinary meaning of philosophically significant words, for they might well be vague and perhaps even contradictory. Rather, as some held, one should seek 'rational reconstructions' of such terms, keeping their core meanings but sharpening up their boundaries and eliminating any inconsistencies. This move away from a standard form of 'ordinary-language philosophy' was to prove superior in survival value.

In subsequent decades 'analysis' took various forms. One was the search for so-called 'criteria'. For instance, the question 'What is

6

the criterion that governs our ascriptions of personal identity?' was (and still is) widely discussed. Here the term 'criterion' was drawn from Wittgenstein's later philosophy, but the procedure actually employed in discovering 'criteria' seems markedly similar to the old (non-Wittgensteinian) one of searching for an analysis, in the sense of searching for necessary and sufficient meaning-conditions. One surface difference is that now instead of appealing to what we would say, an appeal is made to our intuitions concerning various puzzle cases. What does our intuition tell us, for example, about Lockean examples of alleged change of bodies? If someone wakes up not only in the cobbler's bed, but occupying the body of the cobbler while retaining all the Prince's memories, desires, expectations, and so on, is the creature in the lowly cot the Prince?

One's answer reflects one's 'intuition'. Such intuitions fill roughly the role of perceptions in grounding scientific theory. Correspondingly, in recent times the search for analyses has been largely replaced by attempts to provide *theories*, so called. For instance philosophers may seek a theory of personal identity, or of proper names. In the latter instance the theory is supposed to tell us what relationship holds between a given name and its bearer. One such theory – Russell's – associates a set of definite descriptions with a given name, and holds that the object that meets or satisfies the definite descriptions is the thing the name names. On another theory the relationship between name and bearer is *causal*. These theories resemble analyses of the rational reconstruction type, in that one is allowed more leeway with regard to possible 'counter-examples'. In this connection, the point is sometimes made that old-style ordinary-language philosophy is conservative; it requires that the concepts we use in philosophy be restricted to those that exist in natural language. And, it is said, where would science be if it were so restricted? Like scientists, philosophers should be allowed their technical terms and their corresponding theories. Here the philosopher seeks to ally him or herself with science, the most prestigious twentieth-century institution.

One form of 'theory' was influenced by Chomsky's work in linguistics. Starting in the 1960s Jerrold J. Katz and Jerry Fodor attempted to extend Chomsky's ideas by postulating an empirical study of meaning, or 'semantics'.[9] This was a supposed supplement to Chomsky's theory of syntax. Katz argued that one could apply the empirical results of such a study to the direct solution of philosophical problems, offering a kind of scientific ordinary-language philosophy. The solutions would come about when we learned, through empirical work, the full-blown meaning in natural language of the terms involved in a given philosophical debate. On the other hand, meta-theoretical terms like 'analytic' could be given rational reconstructions in terms of the postu-

7

lated new science of meaning. Katz's methodological conjectures were one precursor of later undertakings by others to provide solutions to philosophical problems through scientific inquiry.

We have been examining some of the distinctive roots and paradigms of Anglo-American philosophy in this century. Modern logic first stimulated an interest in, and provided tools for, the study of language, but that study took on a life of its own, and an increased significance as the century progressed. The resulting Anglo-American tradition of inquiry was marked most significantly by the influence, in various ways, of Frege's account of propositions, Russell's paradigm of analysis, and Wittgenstein's *Tractatus*, an influence which is still felt strongly even in a time when it is 'theories' of various sorts that preoccupy analytic philosophers. As indicated, I believe the most valuable legacy of that triumvirate is a hard-headed search for clarity with regard to the basic problems of philosophy.

In keeping with the obvious historic importance of the linguistic turn the present collection begins with two essays on language. Subsequent articles on metaphysics, ethics and epistemology – those traditionally central areas of philosophy – document the significance of deliberations about language for twentieth-century Anglo-American philosophy, as does the chapter on the later philosophy of Wittgenstein. The remaining six chapters, on various *philosophies of*, vary in the importance they attach to the linguistic turn. Perhaps counter-intuitively, the essays on aesthetics and the philosophy of religion focus most on issues about language. At the other pole, philosophers' rejection of traditional analytic methodologies is evident in the essay on feminist philosophy and in the later sections of the chapter on political philosophy. The chapters on the philosophy of law and applied ethics fall between those two extremes.

As always, change is in the air. After a period of relative stability there are signs that major transformations are coming; the intellectual fashion seems due for a radical re-make. That outlying area the philosophy of education provides one indicator: it has almost wholly abandoned an until recently dominant analytic focus in favour of various post-modern and continental ideas. In mainstream philosophy the same sort of alteration is signalled by a relatively new concern on some people's part with the writings of Martin Heidegger – the same thinker that philosophers of my generation knew only as a target of Carnap's anti-metaphysical animus and consequently as the infamous author of the claim that 'The Nothing itself nothings.' On the other hand, there is certainly still a lot of vigorous life left in the sort of Anglo-American philosophy reported upon in these pages, which explicitly or implicitly pursues conceptual clarification. Pessimistic readers, foreseeing the sorts of changes indicated just above, and unwilling to forsake the quest for clarity, may find comfort in the fact that mainland Europe seems to be moving in the opposite direction, back towards the concerns and methods of analytic philosophy, in a belated recognition of the significance of Frege, Russell, Wittgenstein, Schlick, Carnap and other ground-breaking figures.

One of the most difficult of intellectual tasks is to survey a large and complex body of thought and present it in a clear, well-organized way. Each of my co-authors faced such a task, and I thank them for what they have completed so successfully.[10]

A final note: in recent philosophy science has, by and large, taken over the role once played by religion. Science is widely considered the ultimate source of truth, and as something the philosopher had best emulate or join. Given the importance of science for philosophy, I have reproduced here, from Stuart Shanker's volume IX in this series, and with his permission, a chronological table listing the major events in our century's development of science and technology.

❧ NOTES ❧

1 The presupposed geographic and linguistic contrast between Anglo-American and continental philosophy is a bit misleading. Several of those who formed the Anglo-American viewpoint were German or Austrian nationals, including the godfather of analytic philosophy, Gottlob Frege, the immensely influential figures Schlick and Carnap, and the immortal Wittgenstein. Frege's influence worked in part through Bertrand Russell and other Anglo-American figures, Wittgenstein's intellectual life had Cambridge, England, as its centre, and migrations out of Nazi Germany resulted in the impact of the logical positivism associated with Schlick and Carnap being most felt in Britain and North America. Again, the French writer Pierre Duhem deeply influenced that key contemporary American metaphysician Willard van Orman Quine. More significantly, neither the English-speaking nor the continental side is homogeneous; many markedly different ways of philosophizing fall under the one label and many still different ones under the other. Nevertheless the schools do diverge significantly.

2 'Philosophy', ed. Heikki Nyman, trans. C. G. Luckhardt and M. A. E. Aue, in *Ludwig Wittgenstein, Philosophical Occasions 1912–1951*, eds James Klagge and Alfred Nordmann (Indianapolis: Hackett, 1993): 183.

3 It is less well known that the American philosopher Charles Sanders Peirce independently made the same invention.

4 In fact the following account does not square perfectly with the actual text of 'On Denoting'; I give rather what has come to be commonly accepted in philosophy as the main lesson of that essay.

5 *Perceiving* (Ithaca, New York: Cornell University Press, 1957).

6 'Empiricism, Semantics and Ontology', reprinted in *Semantics and the Philosophy of Language*, ed. Leonard Linsky (Urbana: University of Illinois Press, 1952): 120, 121.

7 'The Analytic and the Synthetic: An Untenable Dualism', reprinted in *Semantics and the Philosophy of Language*, ed. Leonard Linsky (Urbana: University of Illinois Press, 1952): 286.

8 See for example essays in John D. Greenwood, ed., *The Future of Folk Psychology* (Cambridge: Cambridge University Press).

9 See for example Jerrold J. Katz and Jerry A. Fodor, 'The Structure of a Semantic Theory', *Language*, 39 (1963): 170–210.

10 In addition I want to thank Bernard Katz, Stewart Candlish, Robert Ennis, Hans Herzberger, John Hunter, Soruren Teghrarian, Lance Ashdown, York Gunther and Patrick Phillips for helpful suggestions.

CHAPTER 1

Philosophy of language
A. P. Martinich

◆━❈━◆

❧ LANGUAGE AND ITS USES ❧

Most philosophers of language[1] in the twentieth century distinguish between three aspects of language or its use: syntax, semantics and pragmatics.[2]

Syntax is the study of the ways that words and other elements of language can be strung together to form grammatical units, without taking the meaning of the sentence into consideration at all. The sentences, 'Smith are happy' and 'Smith happy is', are both syntactically incorrect. The sentence 'Smith is happy' is syntactically correct as is the sentence 'Green ideas sleep furiously'. The latter sentence may appear to be defective. If it is, it is because a literal meaning cannot be assigned to it. But meaning is a concept that belongs not to syntax but to semantics, which will be discussed shortly.

Human languages consist of an infinite number of sentences. It is easy to see how a new sentence can be built out of a simpler sentence indefinitely:

This is the house that Jack built.
This is the malt that lay in the house that Jack built.
This is the mouse that ate the malt that lay in the house
    that Jack built.
This is the cat that chased. . . .

Since human beings are limited in intelligence and they learn a language in a finite amount of time, its syntax must be finite. That is, a grammar for a human language must consist of a finite number of words and a finite number of rules from which the sentences are formed. Because most of the important work on syntax has been done by linguists and formal logicians, nothing further will be said here about this topic. (See chapter 2.)

11

Semantics is the study of the meaning of words and sentences. Meaning has generally been thought of as a relationship between words and the world. Reference and truth are the two principal concepts used in semantics. During the 1920s and 1930s, many philosophers thought that it was impossible to have a science of semantics, because semantics tries to use words to do something that words cannot do. Words can be used to talk only about things; but semantics is the attempt to talk about the relationship between words and things. That relationship cannot itself be a thing, because if it were, then one could ask what connects that relationship to those other things. If the answer is that there is some other relationship that connects them, then if that additional relationship itself is a thing, one can ask the very same question over again; and this would lead to an infinite regress. The problem that seems to undermine the possibility of semantics can be put in global terms. Language represents the world, but semantics exceeds the representational ability of language by trying to represent the *relationship* between language and the world.

In the 1930s, Alfred Tarski showed philosophers a way that semantics could be done without violating the expressive limits of language. Semantics then dominated the philosophy of language until the end of the 1950s. (See pp. 12–18 and 18–21.)

The study of pragmatics began to acquire importance in the early 1950s and flourished until the early 1980s. (See pp. 21–6.) Pragmatics is the study of how language is used. Speakers can use language to make statements, promises and bets; to ask questions; to issue commands; to express condolences; and so on. Pragmatics focuses on the interaction between speakers and hearers. The major idea that guides research in this area is that speaking is intentional behaviour and governed by rules. (For an alternative understanding of pragmatics, see chapter 2.)

Semantical studies were reinvigorated in the early 1970s and continue today. (See pp. 26–31.) But at the same time, some of the assumptions that made possible the distinction among syntax, semantics and pragmatics were challenged by other philosophers, and a very different conception of language has begun to emerge. (See pp. 31–5.)

❧ THE NAMING THEORY OF MEANING ❧

What originally motivated philosophers in the twentieth century to study the nature of language as intensively as they have is their traditional concern with the nature of truth and reality. An ordinary sentence or statement is true, it seems, when it corresponds with the facts. Truth then would seem to reside in language, and the nature of truth can be fully understood only when the nature of language is. Concerning reality, many philosophers at the beginning of the century were frustrated by the apparent failure of metaphysicians to discover the nature of reality by studying it directly. Thus arose the idea that perhaps reality could be studied indirectly by studying language. Since language reflects reality, discovering the structure of language would reveal the structure of reality. Here then were two reasons for philosophers to study language: to understand the nature of truth and to understand the structure of reality.

One aspect of language, namely referring, received a disproportionate amount of attention, because of its connection with truth. If truth requires correspondence between elements of language and entities in the world, and if language reflects the world, then language must attach to the world at certain points. The way that language attaches to the world is *reference*. Reference is usually thought of as a feature of proper names or subject expressions that denote individual objects, because individual objects existing in space and time seem to be the basic constituents of the world. Such considerations inspired the simplest and perhaps the most resilient semantic theory, the naming theory of meaning.

According to this theory, the meaning of a word is the object it names or refers to. Ludwig Wittgenstein presented a stark version of the theory in *Tractatus Logico-Philosophicus* (first published in German in 1921 and in English translation in 1922). He wrote, 'A name means [*bedeutet*] an object. The object is its meaning' (Proposition 3.203). Although names are the basic building blocks of sentences, names alone do not express a thought. Names are concatenated or strung together to form propositional signs (sentences). Since Wittgenstein defines a fact as an existing configuration of objects (2–2.011), propositional signs are themselves facts. Imagine a very simple language that expresses thoughts by the arrangement of its names. Then, the sentence

Adam Beth Carol

means that Beth is between Adam and Carol.

European languages are one-dimensional in the sense that the only significant aspect of the arrangement of a word in a sentence is its linear order. But nothing prevents two- or three-dimensional languages, in which information would be conveyed by other geometrical relations among the words. Thus, a two-dimensional language might use

Adam
Beth Carol

to express that Adam is above Beth and Beth is next to Carol. A three-dimensional language could use blocks as words and count three-dimensional placement of the blocks as semantically significant. Such possibilities inspire Wittgenstein to say that a sentence is a picture or model of reality (Proposition 4.021) and that hieroglyphic script indicates the 'essential nature of a proposition' (4.016). Consequently, what makes a proposition true is analogous to what makes a picture accurate: the meaningful elements of the proposition, that is, the names, must correlate with the objects in the (non-linguistic) fact it purports to describe; and the configuration of the names must be the same as the configuration of the objects in the represented fact. One-dimensional languages, such as English, tend to hide their true form (4.0031). Presumably, most human languages are one-dimensional because as a practical matter such sentences are easier to produce.[3]

Bertrand Russell developed a variation on Wittgenstein's naming theory. According to Russell, there are two kinds of names: proper names and common names. Proper names directly denote individual objects. For him, these individual objects are virtually always sense data, that is, sensations, in contrast with independently existing concrete objects such as tables, chairs, cats and dogs. Common names directly denote what philosophers have variously referred to as concepts, properties and universals. The difference between individuals and concepts can be explained with examples. In looking at a chalk board, a person sees a particular patch of black. This sensation is an individual. But this particular sensation of black is only one of many that can be seen either by the same person at different times or by many people at different times. These particular sensations of black have something in common; they are all instances of a certain general thing. That general thing is the concept, property or universal.

The distinction between individuals and universals gets reflected in language as the distinction between subjects and predicates. All and only proper names are subjects; all and only common names are predicates.[4] (The term 'common name' may be misleading because for Russell, adjectives and verbs are the paradigmatic cases of common names.) A sentence such as 'Socrates sits' is usually understood as having the subject 'Socrates' directly denote Socrates and as having 'sits' express the concept of sitting. The sentence is true just in case Socrates belongs under the concept of sitting.

Russell drew a sharp distinction between proper names and definite descriptions. Russell defined a definite description as any phrase of the form 'The Φ' (where Φ is any noun or noun phrase) such as 'The tallest person in China'. In doing so, he was directly opposing the great nineteenth-century logician Gottlob Frege, who had grouped proper names and definite descriptions together as 'singular terms'. Both kinds of expressions, it seemed to Frege, could occur as subject expressions of sentences and had the same function, namely, to refer to the object of which a property was to be predicated. Also, both denote objects through some sort of cognitive or conceptual element, which he called '*Sinn*' (sense or significance). For example, the phrases 'the third from the left' and 'the second from the right' have different senses, yet each refers to the same thing if four objects are placed in a row. In short, Frege had a two-tiered semantic system: a realm of senses (*Sinne*) and a realm of referents (*Bedeutungen*).

Russell had a one-tiered system. Since the meaning of a word is the object it directly denotes, names do not have any descriptive content (*Sinn*). The name 'Socrates' does not reveal anything about what Socrates is like. Even a seemingly descriptive name such as 'Sitting Bull' is not descriptive. Sitting Bull is not a bull and does not need ever to sit, so far as the naming function of 'Sitting Bull' is involved. In contrast, Russell thought that a description does not directly denote an object and hence has no meaning. It denotes its object, if at all, through the mediation of the concepts expressed by it. For example, 'the evening star' denotes Venus through the concept of being the first celestial body to appear in the evening sky. One consequence of the differences just mentioned is that proper names cannot fail to denote an object while descriptions can.

Another consequence is that descriptions are never subjects. This is initially implausible since 'the present king of France' appears to be the subject of the sentence 'The present king of France is wise.' On the other hand, there is a problem with holding that the description is the subject of the sentence: there is no king of France. How can the sentence be meaningful, as it is, and yet not be about anything?

There are three basic ways out of this problem. One is to designate an arbitrary object, say, the null set, to serve as the referent of any description that does not naturally denote an object. This was Frege's suggestion, and Russell rejected it as *ad hoc* and artificial. A second way is to maintain that there are non-existent beings that are actually denoted by such words and phrases as 'the present king of France', 'the golden mountain' and 'the largest natural number'. Russell himself had accepted something like this view in *Principles of Mathematics* (1903), but railed against anyone who should take such a position after he found a way around it. In *Introduction to Mathematical Philosophy* (1919), he writes: 'The sense of reality is vital in logic, and whoever juggles with it . . . is doing a disservice to thought. A robust sense of reality is very necessary in framing a correct analysis of propositions about unicorns, golden mountains, round squares, and other such pseudo-objects' ([1.28], 170).

The third way out of this problem is Russell's. He explains why 'the king of France' is not the subject of the sentence and further that, despite appearances, 'The present king of France is wise', is not a subject-predicate sentence. According to Russell, the sentence 'The present king of France is wise' is actually a complex existential sentence. That is, the sentence is correctly understood as saying something like the following: 'There exists an object x such that x is-male-and-monarchically-reigns-over-France;[5] nothing other than x is-male-and-monarchically-reigns-over-France; and x is wise.' Notice how the noun phrase 'king of France' has been eliminated altogether and its conceptual content has been transformed into a property, which is expressed by the principal verb phrase ('is-male-and-monarchically- . . .').

Russell presumably came up with this analysis of sentences in which definite descriptions occur by thinking about the conditions under which the sentence would be true. A sentence of the form 'The Φ is ψ' is true (roughly) if exactly one object has the property expressed by Φ and also the property expressed by ψ. Another way of saying that exactly one thing has a property is to say that at least one thing has it and at most one thing has it. The first two clauses of the analysans are supposed to capture this idea of exactly one object having a property.

One of the reasons that philosophers found Russell's theory of descriptions attractive was that it could be extended to handle problems that involved what seemed to be proper names. Consider this paradox:

The paradox of reference and existence
(1) Everything referred to must exist.
(2) 'Pegasus' refers to Pegasus.
(3) Pegasus does not exist.

Propositions (1)–(3) are paradoxical because they are jointly inconsistent and yet each seems to be true. Propositions (1) and (2) entail

~ (3) Pegasus exists.

Proposition (1) has been called 'The axiom of existence' because its truth seems axiomatic. Concerning (2), what could 'Pegasus' refer to except Pegasus? Concerning (3), the sense of reality that Russell urged philosophers to maintain forces one to affirm that Pegasus does not exist.

Russell's solution to the paradox is in effect to deny (2). 'Pegasus' does not refer to Pegasus, because 'Pegasus' is not a genuine or logically proper name. Indeed, no ordinary proper name is a genuine proper name. Proper names do not directly denote, even when they do fit an object. Rather, they are disguised or abbreviated descriptions. 'Pegasus', for example, is a disguised description for 'the flying horse'. A sentence such as 'Pegasus was captured' should then be understood, according to Russell, as meaning 'There exists an object x such that x is equine and flies, whatever is equine and flies is identical with x, and x was captured.' Since nothing is equine and flies, this sentence is false. According to Russell all of the sentences of mythology and fiction are false.

If ordinary proper names are not genuine names, what are? For some years after the publication of 'On Denoting' in 1905 Russell thought that 'this', 'that' and 'I' were proper names, because they seemed to directly denote some object that was 'ostensively' defined (pointed to). But eventually he came to think that 'this' was a disguised description for 'the object that is close to the speaker and being pointed to'; 'that' was a disguised description for 'the object that is remote from the speaker and is being pointed to'; and 'I' a disguised description for 'the one speaking'. Ironically, the initial contrast between proper names and definite descriptions, which justified his elaborate theory, collapses; and Russell concludes that nothing is a proper name.

Russell's theory is intuitively implausible, and the editor of *Mind* was reluctant to publish it. Nonetheless, within a short time, it came to be regarded as a brilliant piece of philosophical thinking because it offered precise solutions to the problems it addressed.

It was not until 1950, when P. F. Strawson published 'On Referring,' that the cogency of Russell's theory was seriously challenged. Strawson maintained that the sentence 'The present king of France is wise' is not only grammatically, but is logically a subject-predicate sentence, and that the sources of Russell's mistakes were fundamental confusions about language.

Strawson denies the basic claim of the naming theory of meaning. He says that the meaning of a word is never the object it is used to refer to. Sometimes the word 'mean' means 'refer'; for example, in the sentence, 'Jones meant George Eliot when he said that the greatest English novelist was a woman.' But in these cases, what is at issue is what the speaker meant and not what a word meant. If the meaning of a word were the object it referred to, then to take a handkerchief out of one's pocket would be to take the meaning of 'handkerchief' out of one's pocket. Also, to destroy a named object would be to destroy the meaning of a name. Each of these consequences is absurd.

As an alternative to the naming theory, Strawson adumbrates what is sometimes known as the use theory of meaning, which was extremely influential from the early 1950s until the early 1970s. He says, 'To give the meaning of an expression . . . is to give *general directions* for its use to refer to or mention particular objects; to give the meaning of a sentence is to give *general directions* for its use in making true or false assertions.'[6] (See chapter 8 in this volume for a further discussion of this idea.)

Strawson draws a sharp line between sentences and statements.

Sentences can be grammatical or meaningful, but they are neither true nor false. It is not the sentence but the statement or assertion that is made by using the sentence to represent the world that is true or false, according to Strawson. To think that the sentence 'The present king of France is wise' is either true or false simply because it is meaningful is absurd. Used in 1625, that sentence could have been used to make a statement about Louis XIII; used in 1650, it could have been used to make a statement about Louis XIV. But these are obviously two different statements, resulting from utterances of one and the same sentence. Used in the twentieth century, 'The present king of France is wise' cannot result in any statement at all even though it remains meaningful. Today a benighted speaker of the sentence could try to make a statement with that sentence but would fail. According to Strawson, it is not words that make statements or refer, but people. Consequently, the question, 'To what does the subject expression of the sentence "The present king of France is wise" refer?' should not arise.

Behind Strawson's objections is a view of language that is radically different from Russell's. For Russell, words and sentences are the fountains of meaning. For Strawson, people using words and sentences are. For Russell, semantics is the primary object of linguistic study. For Strawson, it is pragmatics, how people use words. Strawson's arguments in 'On Referring' were a harbinger of much work to be done between 1960 and 1980. Before discussing that work we need to look at further developments in semantics in the 1920s and 1930s.

❧ THE VERIFICATION THEORY OF ❧ MEANING

The naming theory of meaning takes names as the primary locus of meaning. A different view is held by the logical positivists. For them, the primary locus of meaning is the sentence.

Logical positivism flourished first in central Europe during the 1920s and early 1930s and then in England, the United States and Scandinavia from 1930 until the early 1950s. The original logical positivists were the philosophically oriented scientists and mathematicians who formed the Vienna Circle under the leadership of Moritz Schlick. Soon, most logical positivists were neither scientists nor mathematicians but were *scientistic* in the sense that they believed that only science discovers the truth about reality. They thought that metaphysics in contrast with science had hindered intellectual progress, and one of their goals was to discredit that once venerable area of philosophy.

With regard to the philosophy of language, logical positivists thought that meaningful sentences could be divided into two groups: those that were cognitively meaningful and those that were emotively meaningful. Although the cognitively meaningful sentences held pride of place, let's first deal with the others. Sentences that belong to ethics, aesthetics, politics and religion – in short, value-laden sentences – were thought to have what was called 'emotive' meaning. According to the logical positivists, such sentences were not intended to describe how the world is but to express or to induce some attitude or emotion. Thus, to say, 'Honesty is the best policy', 'That picture is beautiful', 'Democracy is the best form of government', or 'God is the creator of the universe', either is to express some positive attitude or emotion that the speaker holds or is intended to induce such in the audience. Sentences such as 'Lying is wrong' either express or are intended by their speakers to induce some negative attitude or emotion. There is undoubtedly some truth to this sort of account of value-laden language; but the account did not seem to present an adequate theory of such talk in general. Other philosophers tried to round out the picture by arguing that to say that something was good was to recommend or to commend it.

Although some of them thought seriously about value-laden language, most logical positivists had a dismissive attitude towards it. For them to distinguish such language was important in order to ensure that it was not confused with the only kind of language that was cognitively meaningful, namely, the language of science and logic.

Cognitively meaningful language consisted of two types of sentences: sentences of logic and empirical sentences. The sentences of logic were themselves of two kinds: tautologies and contradictions. Tautologies (sometimes known as analytic sentences) were sentences that had to be true, e.g. 'Either it is raining or it is not raining.' Contradictions, e.g. 'It is raining and it is not raining', were sentences that had to be false. Tautologies and contradictions have the truth-values that they do in virtue of the meanings of the words that compose them and independently of how the world is. Empirical sentences, in contrast, are true or false depending upon how the world is. The meaning of an empirical sentence determines what fact about the world makes it true (if it is true) and what fact or possible state of affairs makes it false (if it is false). For example, the meaning of 'The cat is on the mat' determines that the sentence is true if and only if it is a fact that the cat is on the mat.

It is not difficult to judge that 'The cat is on the mat' is an empirical sentence, that is, a sentence that purports to describe the physical world. Further, it may seem that it should not be difficult to characterize what an empirical sentence is. Nonetheless, the effort to characterize what an empirical sentence is was a total failure and led to the downfall of logical positivism.

The original motivating idea was that a sentence is meaningful[7] precisely when it is verifiable; that is, precisely when there is a method for determining whether it is true. This criterion of meaning inspired the slogan that the meaning of a sentence is its method of verification. The criterion also seemed to have the desired effect of excluding sentences of metaphysics from the realm of the meaningful ones. There is no way to verify the sentences, 'The Transcendental Ego is absolute', or 'Nothing nothings.' They are therefore adjudged meaningless by the verifiability criterion of meaningfulness. This result pleased the logical positivists, who thought of metaphysics as the antithesis of science.

Unfortunately for the logical positivists, the verifiability criterion is too strong because it rules out many sentences that they considered meaningful. For example, sentences that are formulated as universal propositions are not conclusively verifiable. Consider a straightforward sentence like 'All humans are mortal.' It is surely meaningful and everyone considers it true. All the individual instances of human beings who have died are empirical evidence for its truth. Nonetheless, there is no empirical guarantee that everyone now alive will die. Thus, the evidence of previous deaths does not conclusively establish the truth of the universal sentence.

Logical positivists responded to this and other challenges in various ways. All agreed that the original verifiability criterion did not work. One alternative to it was a falsifiabilty criterion; that is, a sentence is meaningful precisely when there is a method of determining when it is false. Affirmative universal sentences are meaningful on this criterion. But another kind of sentence is not, namely, universal negative sentences such as 'There are no unicorns.' Although there is no positive evidence for the existence of unicorns (and no sensible person thinks that unicorns exist), there is no evidence that could conclusively falsify that sentence. Even though no unicorn has ever been observed, it is conceivable that this is due to the fact that one lives in a remote region and moves too quickly to be seen.

A more popular way to circumvent the problems with the verifiability criterion was to revise it in ways that would avoid the counter-examples. For example, full verification was replaced with the idea of partial verification. None of these revisions worked. Many of them allowed metaphysical sentences to count as meaningful, contrary to the intentions of their authors. Another problem with the verifiability criterion is that it is self-refuting. By its own criterion, no statement of verifiability is itself meaningful. Such a statement cannot be a proposition of logic since it is supposed to be a substantive truth; and it cannot be an empirical proposition since it does not describe the world.

Indeed, the various statements of the verifiability criterion devised by logical positivists seemed to be metaphysical sentences. This realization led most philosophers not only to abandon the search for an empirical criterion of meaningfulness, but to abandon logical positivism.

～ UTTERER'S MEANING ～

Until the late 1950s, virtually all work done in the philosophy of language assumed or presupposed that the primary locus of meaning was in words or sentences. Philosophy of language was almost synonymous with semantics. Any connection that people had to language was thought to be within the purview of psychology. Much of Strawson's criticisms of Russell's theory of descriptions was grounded in a diametrically opposed view of language. For Strawson, the focus of the philosophical study of language was on people and what people do with language. However, Strawson did not present a well-developed alternative to the prevailing theory of meaning. The alternative was publicly presented in 1957 by Paul Grice, who had been Strawson's teacher and later his colleague at Oxford.

In 'Meaning' [1.14], Grice aims to explain what meaning is when meaning concerns communication. For example, he is interested in meaning as the concept that is expressed in the following sentences:

The ringing of the bell means that the bus is full.
By raising her hand, Mary meant that she knew the answer.
That remark, 'The coast is clear', means that the rebels have left.

Grice calls this 'nonnatural meaning.' This term is something of a misnomer since there is nothing unnatural about the kind of meaning he has in mind. It might better have been called 'communicative meaning', because Grice is interested in what is required for people to communicate with each other in a very broad sense. Linguistic meaning is a narrower concept that fits under the general category of non-natural or communicative meaning. Communicating through hand signals, flags and other non-linguistic gestures is obviously communication but not linguistic communication.

Grice's motivating insight is that for a person to mean$_{NN}$ (nonnaturally) something is for that person to engage in a complex kind of intentional behaviour that is directed towards another person. In short, he argues for the following analysis: a person means$_{NN}$ something by some thing or action if and only if the person intends to produce some effects in an audience by getting the audience to recognize through that thing or action that he intends that effect. Grice thinks that there are basically two kinds of effect that a person can induce in an audience:

a person can get an audience to believe something; and a person can get an audience to do something. In language, these two kinds of communication are reflected in the existence of the indicative mood ('Mary opens the door') and the imperative mood ('Mary, open the door'), respectively.

The crucial point in this analysis is the idea that the way in which the effect is achieved in the audience is by recognizing the intention of the speaker. An audience comes to the belief that the utterer is leaving simply by recognizing that the utterer, by waving his hand in the way that he does, intends him to believe this. In talking about intentions, Grice does not want to commit himself to a special kind of mysterious, unobservable entity. Intentional behaviour is a certain way of behaving; it is not behaviour plus some unseen mental object. Thus, he thinks that intentional behaviour is as open to empirical methods of investigation as any other.

❧ SPEECH ACTS AND CONVERSATION: ❧ A THEORY OF PRAGMATICS

Grice's theory of meaning is general enough to apply to any kind of communication, not only linguistic communication. J. L. Austin, a colleague of Grice at Oxford, developed a theory that in effect complements that of Grice by dealing with specifically linguistic aspects of communication. Austin first formed his theory in 1939, but it was not until 1955, when he presented his views at Harvard in the William James Lectures, that it became widely known. The lectures were later published as *How to Do Things with Words* (1962).

Austin's views originated as an elaborate attack on two related philosophical positions: that there is a difference between talking and acting; and that all talk aims at describing the world. The second position is characteristic of logical positivism in so far as it holds that every cognitively meaningful sentence must be empirically verifiable. Austin refutes this latter position by giving several counter-examples, each of which is a sentence containing only garden-variety words – that is, no evaluative, emotive or metaphysical terms: 'I name this ship the *Queen Elizabeth*'; 'I bequeath my watch to my brother'; 'I bet you five dollars that it will rain tomorrow.' These counter-examples direct attention back to the first philosophical position. What is characteristic of the counter-examples is that expressing them is equally talking and acting, or, to vary the formula: a saying and a doing. To put the point another way, there are many actions that are typically achieved by performing a speech act.

It may appear that although some talking is also acting, there is nonetheless an important distinction to be drawn between two kinds of talk: descriptive talk and non-descriptive talk. Statements and assertions have as their goal the correct description of reality; those that succeed are true, and those that fail are false. Austin calls such utterances 'constative'. In contrast, christening, bequeathing, betting, and the like do not have the goal of describing anything. They are neither true nor false. They have as their goal the performance of some action. Austin calls such utterances 'performative'.

The constative/performative distinction, founded as it is on the descriptive/non-descriptive distinction, would seem to be unshakeable. One of the features of Austin's genius is his dialectical destruction of this seemingly unexceptionable distinction. Attacking the idea of a constative, he shows that making a statement requires that certain conditions be satisfied that are strictly analogous to conditions for performative utterances. In order to make a statement, a speaker must have evidence for it; it must be relevant to the context of its utterance; and for many purported statements there must be an object of reference. Thus, there are many ways in which an attempt to make a statement can fail; and when there is a failure, the (attempted) statement fails to describe anything and is neither true nor false.

Focusing next on the idea of a performative, Austin shows that many performative utterances have a descriptive aspect. Consider, 'I bet that Cleveland will win the pennant', or 'I promise that Mary will be at the meeting.' The clauses, 'Cleveland will win the pennant' and 'Mary will be at the meeting', are fully descriptive and can be assigned truth-values, but they are an essential part of the performative utterance. Thus, the distinction between performative and constative is again undermined.

The complete breakdown of the constative/performative distinction is evident if one tries to categorize the sentence, 'I state that the cat is on the mat.' On the one hand, this sentence appears to be a paradigm case of a constative; it seems to say of itself that it is a statement. On the other hand, it has the very same structural form as paradigmatic cases of performative utterances ('I bet that p' and 'I promise that p'). Further, it appears that what is true or false is not what is expressed by the sentence as a whole ('I state . . .') but only what is expressed by the dependent clause, namely, that the cat is on the mat.

The breakdown of the constative/performative distinction leads Austin to develop a new theory of discourse or speech acts. He distinguishes between three different levels or aspects of speaking: the locutionary, the illocutionary and the perlocutionary. The locutionary act itself contains three component parts: linguistic entities can be thought of (1) as sounds (or typographical marks), (2) as words belonging to a language and (3) as having reference to things in the world and a meaning or significance. The illocutionary act consists of the *force* of the utterance, whether it be a bet, promise, statement, conjecture or something else. The perlocutionary act relates to the effect that is induced in the audience. Persuading, infuriating, calming or inspiring someone are perlocutionary acts. They can be intended or unintended, but what distinguishes perlocutionary from illocutionary acts, for Austin, is that while illocutionary acts always rely upon the existence of conventions, perlocutionary acts are natural or non-conventional.

Austin's work re-oriented the research of many philosophers and laid the groundwork for the standard theory of speech acts, which was developed by his student, John Searle. Searle first adumbrated his views in 'How to promise: a simple way' (1964) and then elaborated them in *Speech Acts* (1969).

Searle has shown that Austin's distinction between locutionary and illocutionary acts does not cut speech at a joint. He argues that paradigmatic cases of speech acts are illocutionary acts that express both a force and a content. Consider the sentences,

> I state that Mary will be at the meeting.
> I question whether Mary will be at the meeting.
> I bet that Mary will be at the meeting.
> I promise that Mary will be at the meeting.

Each of these sentences expresses the same content, namely, the proposition that Mary will be at the meeting. This proposition consists of a referent (Mary) and a predication (being at the future meeting). While Austin thought propositions, which he called 'the locutionary act', were complete entities, Searle shows that they are part of the illocutionary act. The other part of the illocutionary act is its force. The proposition (that Mary will be at the meeting) acquires a different force with the utterance of each sentence above. It is variously stated, questioned, bet or promised.

Searle noticed that there are different kinds of conditions that need to be fulfilled for different speech acts. For example, there are conditions on the kind of proposition that can be expressed in certain speech acts. Promises and commands require propositions about the future. Condolences presuppose a proposition about the past. Any condition that concerns the proposition or content of the speech act Searle calls 'a propositional content condition'. Virtually every speech act requires certain things to have preceded the speech act. For example, a promise requires that the speaker be able to do what he will promise to do; a request requires that the addressee be able to do the thing to be requested. Such conditions are called 'preparatory conditions'. Many speech acts require some kind of sincerity on the part of the speaker. Stating requires that the speaker believe what he is saying; promising requires that the speaker intend to do what he promises; requesting requires that the speaker want what he requests. Such conditions are called 'sincerity conditions'. Every speech act has an essential condition, which specifies what the point or purpose of the speech act is. The point of a statement is to describe the world; the point of a question is to get information; the point of a request and a command is to get the audience to do something.

The theory of speech acts tends to study the use of individual sentences. However, there are overarching principles that govern all conversation. The role that these principles play in conversation has been studied by H. P. Grice. Since communication is a co-operative enterprise in which the speaker tries to get the audience to understand what he or she has in mind and the audience does its part to understand the speaker, certain maxims standardly operate. Speakers are to say what they believe to be true and they should have evidence for what they say. They should say as much as is necessary and not more. What they say should be relevant to what has gone before. Finally, they should formulate what they have to say briefly, clearly, unambiguously and in an orderly way. Although these conversational maxims are the norm, they can go unfulfilled in a variety of ways. Sometimes people *violate* maxims; that is, they quietly and unostentatiously fail to fulfil one, not only when they lie, but when they make an honest mistake or misconstrue the direction of the conversation or presuppose more than they should. Sometimes people *opt out of* fulfilling a maxim. This is often required when two maxims clash in a particular situation. Someone who is asked to give a brief and clear explanation of Immanuel Kant's transcendental deduction of the categories may say, 'I can't give a brief explanation of it.' Sometimes people *flout* a maxim; that is, they openly and ostentatiously do not fulfil one. Figures of speech employ flouting. Meiosis flouts the maxim to say as much as necessary, for example, saying, 'There's some clean up to be done here', after a devastating hurricane. Ironic utterances such as, 'You're a fine friend', said after being betrayed by a friend, flout the maxim to say what one believes. Metaphor involves flouting the same maxim. To say metaphorically, 'My love is a red rose', is not to assert that one's lover is a certain kind of flowering plant. Thus conversational maxims can go unfulfilled in at least three ways: by being violated, opted out of or flouted.

The most important aspect of Grice's theory of conversation is his explanation of how the interaction of what a speaker says (or pretends to say), the conversational maxims and the context gives rise to 'conversational implicatures'. That is, speakers communicate much more to their audiences than what they say or what is logically implied by what they say. If a speaker says, 'There's a gas station around the corner', to a person whose automobile has run out of gas, then the speaker has implied that the gas station is open and has gas available even though he has not said as much. If a speaker says, 'Well, Smith tries very hard', and nothing more to a person who has asked about whether Smith is a good candidate for a job, then he is suggesting that Smith is not a good candidate.

Grice and other philosophers have shown that his simple observations about how language functions can be helpful in solving many traditional philosophical problems in epistemology, semantics and even ethics. To take a simple example (although Grice himself did not agree with this particular application), consider Moore's paradox. There is something odd about the sentence, 'It is raining and I do not believe that it is raining.' The sentence is not contradictory, and yet it is difficult or impossible to think of circumstances in which someone could seriously utter such a sentence. To assert such a sentence would usually be absurd, and yet, if it were asserted, it might say something true. A solution that appeals to Grice's theory explains that the sentence is odd because the assertion of the first clause conversationally implies 'I believe that it is raining' and that contradicts the second clause 'I do not believe that it is raining.' Thus, although the semantic content of Moore's sentence is not contradictory, what would normally seem to be communicated by the sentence is contradictory, and people communicate contradictions only in very special circumstances.

❦ THE CAUSAL THEORY OF NAMING ❦

Although the 1960s and 1970s were the heyday of pragmatics, Russell's theory of descriptions and his view that the semantic connection between genuine proper names and what they denote is direct (unmediated) received renewed support. We have already mentioned that Russell's theory of descriptions was the favoured way of dealing with problematic referring expressions until 1950. From 1950 until the middle 1960s, Strawson's treatment of referring had the upper hand. The publication of Keith Donnellan's article, 'Reference and Definite Descriptions', in 1966 introduced a new element into the theory of reference [1.12].

Donnellan thought that among the various uses of definite descriptions, there were two that were relevant to the dispute between Russell and Strawson: the attributive use and the referential use. The function of the referential use, on which Strawson had focused, is to get the hearer to pick out an individual that the speaker has in mind. If, intending to get the audience to think that Jones is insane, a speaker uses the sentence, 'Smith's murderer is insane',[8] then the definite description is being used referentially. The proposition expressed by the utterance can be represented as the ordered pair (Jones, being insane). This proposition would be true, according to Donnellan, just in case Jones is insane, whether or not Jones murdered Smith.

Donnellan's point can be illustrated by considering the following case. Suppose that Jones is on trial for the murder of Smith, a gentle and well-respected person, who was killed in a particularly brutal fashion. Further suppose that Jones in fact did not kill Smith but is insane. On the basis of Jones's bizarre behaviour in the courtroom, someone says, 'Smith's murderer is insane.' In such a situation, according to Donnellan, the speaker has successfully referred to Jones and has correctly said that he is insane even though the phrase used to refer to Jones does not fit him. The speaker successfully referred to Jones because of his intention to use the phrase to pick out Jones.

In contrast with the referential use, if a speaker uttered the very same sentence and did not intend the audience to pick out Jones or any other person that he has in mind but only intended to make a general comment about anyone who would murder as gentle a person as Smith, then the definite description would be used attributively. The proposition expressed by the utterance can be represented as the ordered pair (being the murderer of Smith, being insane). This proposition would be true just in case exactly one person murdered Smith and was insane. Obviously the truth-conditions are different. As the example about Smith and Jones illustrates, whether a description is being used attributively or referentially depends upon the speaker's intentions and context.

The upshot of Donnellan's distinction is that referring to an object does not require that the word or expression used has a descriptive content that fits the object referred to. Donnellan then applies this result to proper names. They do not have or in any way rely upon any descriptive content. In other words, ordinary proper names function the way that Russell claimed that logically proper names do. Thus, contrary to what Russell thought, ordinary proper names are logically proper names. Donnellan described his views as 'an historical account of referring'. He explained that a proper name refers to the object that it does because it is connected to that object through all the previous uses of that name to refer to that object. Since his explanation of referring uses the notion of referring, it should be clear that he did not intend to present a theory of what referring is, but an explanation of how a proper name refers to the object that it does, rather than to some other object.

Contemporaneously with Donnellan, Saul Kripke was developing a similar account of referring, which he called 'a causal account of referring' [1.17]. Like Donnellan, Kripke was interested in how the use of some name, such as 'Aristotle' picks out Aristotle rather than someone else. Much of Kripke's effort is devoted to attacking the description theory of proper names. According to that theory, proper names could not directly denote the object that they name, because there would be no way to connect a name to its object. Thus, according to this theory, each proper name must be associated with or connected to some more or less determinate cluster or disjunction of descriptions which is true of the named object and nothing else. Both the speaker and audience use the descriptive content of a name to pick out the object named. In short, to know the meaning of a proper name is to know what cluster of descriptions picks out a uniquely named object.

Kripke objects to the description theory on two main grounds. First, for very many names most people do not associate any uniquely identifying cluster of descriptions with the object named. For example, 'Cicero' for most people is *a* famous Roman orator, not *the* most famous Roman orator. Second, a person may know how to use a proper name even if the set of descriptions that he or she associates with the named object do not in fact correctly describe it. Suppose that the name 'Aristotle' is associated with this disjunctive cluster of descriptions: 'either the student of Plato, or the teacher of Alexander, or the author of *Metaphysics* and *De Anima*'. But further suppose that Aristotle was a fraud; that he did none of the things attributed to him but invented them through an elaborate ruse, which has never been detected by historians. Nonetheless, 'Aristotle' is the name of Aristotle, even though the descriptions associated with him are wholly false.

According to Kripke, the reason why 'Aristotle' picks out Aristotle is that there is a causal connection between the speaker's use of 'Aristotle' and Aristotle. At some point in the use of the term 'Aristotle', some speaker succeeded in referring to Aristotle by that name – Kripke suggests that this occurs in baptismal or analogous ceremonies – and that success has been passed on from speaker to speaker down to this very day. Obviously, this account of referring does not explain what referring itself is. It presupposes that referring has occurred in past uses of the name. What it purports to give is an account of how *the reference is fixed* of a name currently in use.

Various philosophers have pointed out that Kripke's account is flawed. There are many cases in which the causal chain of a name's use has gone awry. 'Madagascar', to mention one instance, originally was the name of part of the African mainland. The island acquired that name because Marco Polo mistook the reference. Native Americans received the name 'Indians' because Columbus mistakenly thought he had reached India. In short, the causal chain connecting a current use with the original use of a name does not alway determine the correct reference.

Kripke extends his views about proper names to common nouns that denote natural kinds, that is, to words like 'gold', 'dog' and 'tree': natural-kind terms denote their objects because of a causal, communicative tie between the word and the objects and not because of any descriptive content that the speaker may associate with it. Hilary Putnam developed a very similar view. Putnam's colourful way of putting this was to say that ' "meanings" just ain't in the head'.[9]

According to Putnam, common nouns have the reference or extension that they do because of a causal tie between the use of the word and the object referred to. 'Water' refers to water because in its paradigmatic uses people supposedly point to it and say, '*This* is water.' In other words, common nouns function in a way similar to proper names. Both are what Kripke calls 'rigid designators', that is, terms that pick out the same object in every possible world in which they exist.

Traditionally, common nouns were thought to denote or refer to objects indirectly, through a concept. Thus, a speaker who used the word 'gold' would expect his audience to know what object he was talking about because both the speaker and the hearer had a concept that was descriptive of gold and nothing else (for example, 'the yellowish, valuable metal, that dissolves in *aqua regia*') and by which a person is directed to gold. In Frege, this descriptive concept was called 'sense' (*Sinn*); in Locke, it was called 'an idea'. In scholastic terminology, the difference between the concept associated with a noun and its reference was the difference between intension and extension.

Putnam argues that there could be a planet (Twin Earth), which is just like Earth except that instead of water it contains a liquid that has the same gross properties of water – that is, the same taste, odour, smell, appearance and viscosity – but a completely different chemical composition. Because the gross properties of each liquid are the same, a person on Earth and a person on Twin Earth would seem to be in exactly the same mental state; yet they would be referring to different liquids. Consequently, a person's ideas or concepts of an object cannot determine what it is that he or she refers to.

One of the consequences that Putnam draws from his study of common nouns is that language use involves a division of labour. Water is all and only that which has the chemical composition of H_2O. Although virtually every speaker of English can use the word 'water' competently, some speakers of the language need to have the requisite technical knowledge to determine the genuine reference or extension

29

of 'water'. Thus, a further consequence is that using a language is much more of a co-operative enterprise than is usually thought.

❧ NAMES AND BELIEF ❧

In 1979, Kripke argued that neither the description theory of names nor his own causal account of names can solve the following problem about Pierre. Pierre is born and raised in France and initially knows how to speak only French. On the basis of what he is told about London, he forms the belief that London is pretty. Since he speaks only French he says or would think to himself 'Londres est jolie.' Not knowing English, Pierre does not and could not express his belief using the sentence

(1) London is pretty.

Later, Pierre leaves France and takes up residence in a squalid part of a city in another country. It is London. There he learns English as a native would, that is, with direct interaction with his local environment and without directly learning how to translate back and forth between English and French. In particular, he never learns that 'London' and 'Londres' name the same city. On the basis of his experience in London, he forms the belief that is expressed by

(2) London is not pretty.

The question is whether Pierre has contradictory beliefs. It would seem that he does since he would sincerely assert 'Londres est jolie', which means the same as (1) and would sincerely assert (2). But Kripke thinks it is impossible that Pierre has contradictory beliefs; for Pierre is a distinguished logician who 'would *never* let contradictory beliefs pass'.[10]

Most proposed solutions to this puzzle try to explain how it is that Pierre has contradictory beliefs and is not aware of them. What lies behind Kripke's denial that Pierre has contradictory beliefs is something like the following principle.

> **Nominal Transparency:** If (1) the semantic connection between a term and the object it denotes is direct (unmediated), (2) terms *x* and *y* denote the same object *o*, and (3) a person *p* is competent to use both *x* and *y*, then *p* must be aware of any contradictory beliefs that *p* has when *o* is represented by *x* and *y*.

Kripke thinks that his arguments in *'Naming and Necessity'* [1.14] proved clause (1); and he thinks clauses (2) and (3) are as a matter of fact satisfied by Pierre and his linguistic knowledge.

We can agree that all three clauses are correct and still deny that the consequent of nominal transparency is true. Kripke's mistake in part is, I believe, to think that a semantic connection is the only connection that is relevant to the ability to use a name. As a matter of fact, in order to be able to use a name, a person also needs to have some mental representation that connects the name with the object, but this representation is not a part of the meaning of the name. It cannot be part of the meaning of the name, because how people represent an object to themselves is not uniform, and individuals can change how they represent objects without any loss in their ability to refer to those objects. It need not interfere with their ability to communicate if one interlocutor thinks of Aristotle as the student of Plato and the other thinks of Aristotle as the teacher of Alexander. Similarly, it need not interfere with communication if a person thinks of Aristotle at one time as the student of Plato and at another time as the teacher of Alexander.

If people were aware of all the logical relations that held between the various ways that they mentally represent objects, then if two names named the same object, they would be aware of it. But many of these relations are opaque to the person who has them. The contents of (at least very many) beliefs are not immediately accessible to people, but only through their mental states or representations, which present the object from a perspective and not *in toto*. These limited perspectives often prevent people from recognizing all the consequences of their beliefs. It is the mental analogue of a person who sees an elephant from the front and later from behind and infers that he or she has seen two kinds of animal.

Perhaps behind Kripke's puzzle is an even more general misconception about language: the belief that language is self-contained and that purely linguistic knowledge is sufficient for using language. Both of these assumptions are under attack by the philosophers who will be discussed in the next section.

INTERPRETATION AND TRANSLATION

Most philosophers who have thought about language have focused on the utterer's role in communication. One might expect that looking at communication from the audience's point of view should not present a very different perspective if discovering what the utterer is doing is exactly what the audience does. As a matter of fact, these are very different perspectives. W. V. Quine is perhaps the first and certainly the most important Anglo-American philosopher to look at language from the audience's perspective.

In *Word and Object*, published in 1960, Quine explores the consequences of an uncompromisingly naturalistic view of language [1.20]. Only physical facts are relevant to understanding linguistic behaviour, and all the evidence humans have for thinking of something as language and for attributing significance to those utterances is purely empirical. This does not mean that the judgements that people make about linguistic behaviour are exclusively empirical. Judgements about linguistic behaviour are a mixture of empirical evidence and explanatory hypotheses. This latter point was the principal lesson of his classic article, 'Two Dogmas of Empiricism' [1.23]. Rather than as a pure empiricist, Quine thought of himself at this time as a kind of pragmatist. Later, he would think of his philosophy as empiricist, pragmatic and naturalistic.

Quine asks how an audience can come to understand what a speaker of an utterly foreign language means. The problem is to figure out how a person would correlate sentences of his or her own language with sentences of the speaker's language. Quine develops his answer picturesquely by describing 'a field linguist' coming upon 'a native'. He supposes that the native utters, 'Gavagai', as a rabbit runs by. The issue is, how does the linguist (the audience) understand what the native has said? Quine thinks that the linguist must ask the native questions. This of course implies that the linguist has formulated some hypothesis about what kind of behaviour corresponds to saying 'yes' in English and what kind corresponds to 'no'. These hypotheses are part of a complicated web of hypotheses that are devised with the goal of arriving at the most plausible understanding of the behaviour of the natives. Even if the native used the vocables 'yes' and 'no', the linguist could not simply assume that the native's 'yes' means the same as his or her own 'yes'. The native may mean just the opposite by these vocables. Nor could the linguist simply assume that the nod of the native's head means 'yes', or that shaking it means 'no'. Again, the native could mean just the opposite or something else. The native could have some completely different convention, such as exposing the right index finger for 'yes' and the left index finger for 'no'. So the actual process of hypothesis formation is quite complex.

The linguist has other difficulties. Suppose that the native often utters 'Gavagai' when a rabbit is present. The linguist may hypothesize that the proper translation of 'Gavagai' is 'Rabbit' (or 'There's a rabbit'). But how can the linguist be sure? Even if the linguist has settled on a hypothesis about how the native indicates 'yes' and 'no' the native's answer does not favour the linguist's proffered translation any more than it favours the translation 'More rabbit'; or 'There's an undetached rabbit part', or 'There's a temporal slice of a rabbit.' One way to determine whether 'Gavagai' refers to rabbits or undetached rabbit parts would be to point successively to two parts of the rabbit and ask the native whether the one *gavagai* is the same as the other *gavagai*. Of course, the whole thing must be said in the native's language. Suppose the linguist uses 'Gavagai plink gavagai' to express this. How can the linguist know whether 'plink' means 'is the same as' or 'is an undetached part of the same rabbit'? The linguist will get an affirmative response if 'plink' has either meaning. Quine claims that no matter how many checks the linguist may try to place on his or her translation by testing other sentences in other situations, there is no one correct translation of all the sentences. It is always possible that there are several incompatible ways of translating the sentences of the language, each translation of which fits the empirical data. In short, translation is indeterminate.

Whatever translation scheme is adopted, it will be the result of a system of hypotheses that takes into account not only what words and sentences of one language correlate with words and sentences of another, but under what conditions the observed sentences were uttered and what beliefs and intentions the speakers had at the time. That is, the translation scheme presupposes certain judgements about what the empirical evidence was, and the translation of any individual sentence will make sense only within the entire theory of translation and evidence. This view that linguistic meaning resides in the entire language and not in any sub-unit such as a word or sentence is known as linguistic holism.

Because Quine thinks of the audience's goal as the correlation of sentences of one language with sentences of another language that is completely unrelated in evolution to the first, he calls the linguist's project 'radical translation'. Although it may seem that Quine thinks of translation as a purely syntactic enterprise: utterances ('sequences') of one system are correlated with utterances of another system, that is not quite correct. The primary sentences of a language are those that are tied to observable things: 'Mama' uttered in the presence of a mother, 'Red' uttered in the presence of red or 'Rabbit' uttered in the presence of a rabbit. So some words and the rest of the world are related in this way. What Quine objects to is the notion that meanings are determinate, abstract entities, which attach individually to sentences.

Quine's insights about language have been revised and extended by his student, Donald Davidson. One of the important revisions is a tacit criticism. Davidson does not think that the search for a translation manual between languages is crucial. One might know that 'Es regnet' is the correct German translation for the Italian sentence 'Piove' without knowing what either sentence means. So merely knowing how to translate between sentences in this narrow sense does not constitute knowing a language. Knowing how to interpret a language does. Thus, Davidson explores the explicitly semantic idea of 'radical interpretation', which is the project of determining how a person figures out the conditions under which an utterance is true. In this regard, Davidson acknowledges his debt to Alfred Tarski, who made semantics philosophically respectable. Davidson claims that since to know the meaning of a sentence is to know its truth-conditions (the conditions under which it is true or false), to have a theory of truth is to have a theory of meaning. Davidson differs from Tarski in that Davidson takes truth as a basic notion that does not need to be defined and uses it to explain what an interpretation is, while Tarski assumed that there was no problem in coming up with translations of sentences and gave a definition of truth.[11]

In 'Belief and the Basis of Meaning', published in 1974, Davidson makes it clear that a basic difficulty in interpreting a speaker's words is that interpretation is not simply the task of assigning meanings to utterances [1.8]. Interpretation involves at least two interdependent activities. An audience must attribute both a certain belief to the speaker and a certain meaning to his utterance in order to come up with an interpretation. For example, suppose a speaker utters, 'The cat is on the mat', in the presence of a cat being on a mat. If the audience judges the speaker to *mean* that the cat is on the mat, the audience will also most likely judge the speaker to *believe* that the cat is on the mat. While this may appear trivial, the triviality disappears once we think about other cases. Suppose the speaker utters, 'The cat is on the mat', in the presence only of a dog on the mat. In such a situation, the audience has two likely – but in fact many more – options to choose between: (1) the speaker means that the cat is on the mat and has a false belief, or (2) the speaker means that the dog is on the mat and has a correct belief. Either interpretation is possible. Which interpretation makes the most sense depends upon various features of the context: for example, the age, intelligence, eyesight, integrity and native language of the speaker. Interpretation (1) may be more plausible if the speaker is very stupid or has poor eyesight. Interpretation (2) may be more plausible if the speaker is only 4 years old or is 40 years old but in the process of learning English. In the latter case, the speaker may think that 'cat' means 'dog' and thus use 'The cat is on the mat' to mean that the dog is on the mat.

In fact, the task of interpretation is even more complicated than Davidson has indicated. In addition to attributing beliefs to the speaker and a meaning to his or her utterance, the interpreter also needs to attribute a motive to the speaker, to determine the phonetic character to the utterance, and to judge his or her own cognitive capacities. For example, is the speaker intending to tell the truth, be deceptive, ironic, or humorous (motive)? Did the speaker utter the sentence 'She peaked in Stockholm' or 'She spoke in Stockton'? Did the audience really see a dog or was it a cat?

One upshot of the work of Quine and Davidson, is that it is a mistake to think of language as a complete and self-contained unit. Not only does speaking require other abilities, but in addition language itself is continuous with other intelligent behaviour. Linguistic behaviour is not a discrete segment of human behaviour. As Davidson says, 'we should realize that we have abandoned not only the ordinary notion of a language, but we have erased the boundary between knowing a language and knowing our way around in the world generally'.[12] One might speculate about the reason that people think of language as a well-defined entity. One suggestion is that when people are engaged in understanding what a speaker means, they often focus on the utterance itself and often think of the other aspects of the situation, such as the utterer's beliefs and intentions and the contextual facts, as merely background or collateral conditions. This is to say that utterances are salient; they jump out at the audience; nonetheless, the utterance itself is ultimately no more important to the interpretation than the other features just mentioned.

CONCLUSION

To study the philosophy of language is to see that there is progress in philosophy. The idea that the basic meaningful unit of language is the word was superseded by the idea that the basic unit is the sentence, and that was superseded by the twin ideas that the meaning of a sentence makes sense only as it relates to the language as a whole and that linguistic meaning ultimately rests upon people meaning things by their utterances. The idea that language is a discrete entity that can be understood independently of the non-linguistic context was superseded by the idea that language can be understood only in its context, and that idea was superseded by the idea that there is no sharp line to be drawn between linguistic behaviour and non-linguistic behaviour or between linguistic behaviour and the environment in which it occurs. Although there are no final answers, much has been learned in this century about the nature and uses of language, the primary locus of meaning, the nature of interpretation, the relation between language and empirical evidence, and the interrelation between meaning and the cognitive states of speakers.

ᕙ NOTES ᕗ

1 Hereafter, 'philosophers of language' refers to philosophers in the dominant tradition of Anglo-American philosophy in the twentieth century, unless otherwise indicated. An analogous remark holds for the term 'philosophy of language'.

2 A clear distinction between these three aspects of linguistic study was made at least as early as 1939 by Charles Morris [1.21], but we shall not follow his definitions exactly.

3 For another interpretation of Wittgenstein's view of picturing, see Canfield [1.6] and Wedin [1.30].

4 'Subject' and 'predicate' have been used in various ways by philosophers. In this article, the terms always refer to certain kinds of words or phrases. 'Subject' was sometimes used to refer to the topic of a sentence; that is, the thing referred to by the *subject* in my sense. 'Predicate' was sometimes used to refer to what a predicate in my sense expresses, that is, a property or concept. Bertrand Russell often used these terms in various senses.

5 The noun phrase, 'present king of France', needs to be replaced with a non-noun phrase, such as the complex verb phrase 'is-male-and-monarchically-reigns-over-France', in order to forestall the following line of argument: Since 'the present king of France' is a noun, it must name something. What does it name? If the noun phrase is replaced by a verb phrase 'is-male-and-monarchically-...', no question arises about any seeming king of France.

6 'On Referring', in Strawson [1.28], 9.

7 In the remainder of this section, 'meaningful' means 'cognitively meaningful', as understood by the logical positivists.

8 'Smith's murderer' needs to be understood as a variation on 'the murderer of Smith'.

9 'Meaning and Reference', in Martinich [1.17], 287.

10 'A Puzzle about Belief', in Salmon and Soames [1.24], 122.

11 'Radical Interpretation', in Davidson [1.7], 134.

12 'A Nice Derangement of Epitaphs', in Grandy and Warner [1.11], 173.

ᕙ BIBLIOGRAPHY ᕗ

1.1 Austin, J. L. [1962] *How to Do Things with Words*, 3rd edn, eds J. O. Urmson and G. J. Warnock, Cambridge, Mass.: Harvard University Press, 1990.

1.2 —— [1970] *Philosophical Papers*, 2nd edn, eds J. O. Urmson and G. J. Warnock, London: Oxford University Press, 1970.

1.3 Ayer, A. J. [1936] *Language, Truth, and Logic*, 2nd edn, London: Gollancz, 1946.

1.4 —— ed. *Logical Positivism*, New York: Free Press, 1959.

1.5 Burge, Tyler 'Philosophy of Language and Mind: 1950–1990', *Philosophical Review*, 101 (1992): 3–51.

1.6   Canfield, John 'A Model Tractatus Language', *Philosophical Forum*, 4 (1973): 199–217.
1.7   Davidson, Donald *Truth and Interpretation*, Oxford: Clarendon Press, 1984.
1.8   —— 'Belief and the Basis of Meaning', in Donald Davidson, *Truth and Interpretation*, Oxford: Clarendon Press, 1984: 141–54.
1.9   —— ed. *Words and Objections*, Dordrecht, D. Reidel, 1969.
1.10   —— and Gilbert Harman, eds *Semantics of Natural Language*, Dordrecht: Reidel, 1972.
1.11   Davis, Steven, ed *Pragmatics*, New York: Oxford University Press, 1990.
1.12   Donnellan, Keith S. 'Reference and Definite Descriptions', *The Philosophical Review*, 75 (1966): 281–304.
1.13   Grandy, Richard and Richard Warner, eds *Philosophical Grounds of Rationality*, Oxford: Clarendon Press, 1986.
1.14   Grice, H.P. 'Meaning', *The Philosophical Review*, 66 (1957): 377–88.
1.15   —— *Studies in the Way of Words*, Cambridge, Mass.: Harvard University Press, 1989.
1.16   Hahn, Lewis and Paul Arthur Schilpp, eds *The Philosophy of W. V. Quine*, La Salle, Ill: Open Court, 1986.
1.17   Kripke, Saul [1972] *Naming and Necessity*, Cambridge, Mass.: Harvard University Press, 1980.
1.18   Martinich, A. P. 'Austin, Strawson, and the Correspondence Theory of Language', *Critica*, 9 (1977): 39–62.
1.19   —— *Communication and Reference*, Berlin and New York: de Gruyter, 1984.
1.20   —— *The Philosophy of Language*, 3rd edn, New York: Oxford University Press, 1990.
1.21   Morris, Charles W. [1939] *Foundations of the Theory of Signs*, in *International Encyclopedia of Unified Science*, eds Otto Neurath, Rudolf Carnap and Charles Morris, Chicago: University of Chicago Press, 1955: 78–137.
1.22   Putnam, Hilary *Philosophical Papers: Mind, Language and Reality*, vol. 2, Cambridge: Cambridge University Press, 1975.
1.23   Quine, W. V. O. 'Two Dogmas of Empiricism', in W. V. O. Quine, *From a Logical Point of View*, Cambridge, Mass.: Harvard University Press, 1953: 20–46.
1.24   —— *Word and Object*, Cambridge, Mass.: MIT Press, 1960.
1.25   —— *From a Logical Point of View*, Cambridge, Mass.: Harvard University Press, 1961.
1.26   —— *Pursuit of Truth*, rev. edn, Cambridge, Mass.: Harvard University Press, 1992.
1.27   Russell, Bertrand *Principles of Mathematics*, New York: W. W. Norton, 1903.
1.28   —— *Introduction to Mathematical Philosophy*, London: George Allen & Unwin, 1919.
1.29   —— *Logic and Knowledge: Essays 1901–1950*, ed. Robert C. Marsh, London: George Allen & Unwin, 1956.
1.30   Salmon, Nathan and Scott Soames, eds *Propositions and Attitudes*, New York: Oxford University Press, 1988.
1.31   Searle, John *Speech Acts*, Cambridge: Cambridge University Press, 1969.
1.32   —— *Expression and Meaning*, Cambridge: Cambridge University Press, 1979.
1.33   —— *Intentionality*, Cambridge: Cambridge University Press, 1983.

1.34 Strawson, P. F. 'On Referring', *Mind*, 59 (1950): 320–44.
1.35 —— *Logico-Linguistic Papers*, London: Methuen, 1971.
1.36 Tarski, A. 'The Concept of Truth in Formalized Languages', in A. Tarski, *Logic, Semantics, Metamathematics*, Oxford: Clarendon Press, 1956: 152–268.
1.37 Urmson, J. L. *Philosophical Analysis: Its Development between the Two World Wars*, London: Oxford University Press, 1956.
1.38 Wedin, Michael 'Trouble in Paradise? On the Alleged Incoherence of the *Tractatus*', *Grazer Philosophische Studien*, 42 (1992): 23–55.
1.39 Wittgenstein, Ludwig [1921] *Tractatus Logico-Philosophicus*, trans. D. F. Pears and B. F. McGuinness, London: Routledge & Kegan Paul, 1961.
1.40 —— [1954] *Philosophical Investigations*, 2nd edn, trans. G. E. M. Anscombe, Oxford: Basil Blackwell, 1958.

CHAPTER 2

Formally oriented work in the philosophy of language
Nino B. Cocchiarella

One of the perennial issues in philosophy is the nature of the various relationships between language and reality, language and thought, and language and knowledge. Part of this issue is the question of the kind of methodology that is to be brought to bear on the study of these relationships. The methodology that we shall discuss here is based on a formally oriented approach to the philosophy of language, and specifically on the notion of a logically ideal language as the basis of a theory of meaning and a theory of knowledge.

THE NOTION OF A *CHARACTERISTICA UNIVERSALIS* AS A PHILOSOPHICAL LANGUAGE

The history of the formally oriented approach towards the philosophy of language goes back at least to René Descartes (1596–1650) and Gottfried Leibniz (1646–1716), and perhaps even further to the speculative grammarians of the twelfth century who believed that there was only one grammar underlying all of the natural languages of humanity (cp. Küng [2.28], 7). The speculative grammarians did not develop a formal methodology by which to study that grammar, however, because they believed that its structure was determined by the nature of things in the world and that the philosopher could discover that structure only by first considering the ontological nature of things. Descartes, the inventor/discoverer of analytic geometry and the idea of a *mathesis universalis*, also believed that underlying all speech there exists a *lingua universalis*, but what it represented was the form of human reason and not the nature of things in the world (cp. Cassirer [2.3], 1: 128). Descartes also did not attempt to construct or formalize such a

39

language, beyond insisting that it must contain a *mathesis universalis*, because he thought that its construction must await the analysis of all the contents of consciousness into the simple ideas that were their ultimate constituents.

Leibniz agreed with Descartes that there exists a *lingua universalis* underlying all speech and that such a language represented the form of human reason. Leibniz was more programmatic in his approach, however. He called the general framework of such a philosophical language a *characteristica universalis*, and he attempted to formulate some fragments of the system. For Leibniz, a *characteristica universalis* was to serve three main purposes. The first was that of an international auxiliary language that would enable the people of different countries to speak and communicate with one another. Apparently, because Latin was no longer a 'living' language and new trade routes were opening up to lands with many different local languages, the possibility of such an international auxiliary language was widely considered and discussed in the seventeenth and eighteenth centuries (cf. Cohen [2.4] and Knowlson [2.27]). There were in fact a number of proposals and partial constructions of such a language during that period, but none of them succeeded in being used by more than a handful of people. It was only towards the end of the nineteenth century when Esperanto was constructed that such a language came to be used by as many as eight million people. At present, however, the question of whether even Esperanto will succeed in fulfilling that purpose seems very much in doubt. Ido, another such language, which was constructed in 1907 by a committee of linguists, has not been used since about 1930 (cf. Van Themaat [2.46]).

The second and third purposes Leibniz set for his *characteristica universalis* are what distinguish it from its precursors and give his programme its formal or logistic methodology. The second purpose is that the universal character is to be based upon an *ars combinatoria*, i.e. an ideography or system of symbolization that would enable it to provide a logical analysis of all the actual and possible concepts that might arise in science. Such an *ars combinatoria* would contain both a theory of logical form, i.e. a theory of all the possible forms that a meaningful expression might have in such a language, and a theory of definitional forms, i.e. a theory of the operations whereby one could construct new concepts on the basis of already given concepts. The third purpose was that the universal character must contain a *calculus ratiocinator*, i.e. a complete system of deduction and valid argument forms, by which, through a study of the consequences, or implications, of what was already known, it could serve as an instrument of knowledge.

With a universal character that could serve these purposes, Leibniz thought that a unified encyclopedia of science could be developed throughout the world, and that, by its means, the universal character would then also amount to a *characteristica realis*, i.e. a representational system that would enable us to see into the inner nature of things and guide our reasoning about reality like an Ariadne's thread (cp. Cohen [2.4], 50). Thus, here in Leibniz's programme for a *characteristica universalis* we have an attempt to encompass the three relationships between language and reality, language and thought, and language and knowledge. In two fundamental parts of the programme, namely, the construction of an *ars combinatoria* and a *calculus ratiocinator*, we also have the critical components that are necessary for a formally oriented approach towards the philosophy of language.

❧ THE NOTION OF A LOGICALLY PERFECT ❧ LANGUAGE AS A REGULATING IDEAL

The idea of a grammar underlying all natural languages is really not the same as the idea of an international auxiliary language, and both are different from the idea of a formal, artificial language containing an *ars combinatoria* and a *calculus ratiocinator* as a unified language of science. In the nineteenth century, with the rise of the new science and the development of a more abstract, algebraic notation in mathematics, interest became focused on the prospect of constructing a *calculus ratiocinator* as a formal system of logic that could be applied in different domains of discourse and independently of the vagaries of natural language. The mathematician George Boole (1815–64), for example, maintained that algebraic formulas could be used to express logical relations between propositions, or between concepts or classes, no less so than they can be used to express numerical relations between numbers. He showed in particular that there are structural analogies between the operations of multiplication and addition as applied to numbers and the operations of conjunction and disjunction as applied to propositions or concepts, as well as the operations of intersection and union as applied to classes. The result of developing such analogies as an abstract calculus is known today as Boolean algebra, a mathematical system that has provided a foundation for the development of computers as well as an algebraic basis for much of the formally oriented work in the philosophy of language.

Although the algebraic operations of Boolean logic are quite different from the grammatical rules of the categorical subject-predicate propositions of traditional syllogistic logic, it is significant that the latter can be explained in terms of the former. A traditional subject-predicate proposition of the form 'All F are G', for example, can be analysed in terms of the subordination of the concept F to the concept G, or the inclusion of the class of things that are F in the class of things that are G (where inclusion is definable in terms of intersection as follows: $F \subseteq G =_{df} F \cap G = F$). A subject-predicate proposition of the form 'Some F are G' can also be analysed in terms of the intersection of the class of things that are F with the class of things that are G, namely, as that intersection not being identical with the empty class (i.e. as $F \cap G \neq o$, where 'o' represents the empty class). All categorical propositions and the entire system of traditional syllogistic logic can in this way be analysed and explained in terms of the algorithms of Boolean algebra. Boole himself believed that his calculus could be used 'to investigate the fundamental laws of those operations of the mind by which reasoning is performed' and that he could express those laws in the symbolic language of his calculus (Boole [2.2], chapter 1, section 1).

A different and more fundamental approach to the grammatical subject-predicate structure of natural language and to the idea of the laws of thought was taken by Gottlob Frege (1848–1925) in his book, *Concept-Script, A Formula Language for Pure Thought, Modeled upon that of Arithmetic*. What Frege did was utilize the newly developed function theory of arithmetic and mathematics to interpret a subject-predicate sentence of the form '*a* is *F*', where '*a*' stands for a singular term (e.g. a proper name or definite description), as the result of applying the concept *F*, now interpreted as a function (from objects to truth-values), to the argument *a*, i.e. as $F(a)$. A subject-predicate-object sentence of the form '*a R b*', where '*a*' and '*b*' stand for singular terms and '*R*' for a transitive verb (such as, for example, the verb 'love' in '*a* loves *b*') can then be interpreted as applying the relation *R*, now interpreted as a binary function (from objects to truth-values), to the arguments *a* and *b* (in that order), i.e. as $R(a,b)$. In this way, Frege was able to formally represent and explain a more fundamental aspect of predication than is represented in Boolean algebra, namely, that in which we can express the relation between an object and a concept under which it falls, as well as provide a framework for the logic of relations in general.

Frege applied his function-argument analysis not only to these basic subject-predicate forms, moreover, but to those of the categorical propositions of traditional syllogistic logic as well. It was this analysis that introduced a new, and brilliant, insight into the structure of quantifier phrases of natural language, i.e. phrases beginning with such words as 'all', 'every', 'some', 'there is (are)'. Providing an adequate analysis of such phrases had been a major problem for medieval grammarians and logicians, and it was only with Frege's theory that the beginnings of a real solution were finally attained.

A quantifier phrase, according to Frege, stands for a (variable-indexed) second-level concept within which first-level concepts fall, which, in terms of his function-argument terminology, amounts to a function from first-level concepts (i.e. those that predicate phrases stand for) to truth-values. Thus, a sentence of the form 'Everything is F' can be formally represented by '$\forall x F(x)$', where '$\forall x$' stands for the second-level concept that 'everything' stands for (as indexed by the variable 'x'). Similarly, 'Something is F' can be formally represented by '$\exists x F(x)$', where '$\exists x$' stands for the second-level concept that 'something' stands for (as indexed by the variable 'x'). A subject-predicate categorical proposition of the form 'All F are G' can then be equivalently interpreted as a sentence of the form 'Everything is such that if it is F, then it is G', which formally can be represented as '$\forall x[F(x) \rightarrow G(x)]$', where '$\rightarrow$' is the symbolic counterpart of the (truth-functional) 'if-then' conditional phrase. Similarly, a categorical proposition of the form, 'Some F are G' can be equivalently interpreted as 'Something is both F and G', which formally can be represented as '$\exists x[F(x) \& G(x)]$', where '$\&$' is the symbolic counterpart of the 'both-and' conjunctive phrase; and a proposition of the form 'No F are G' can be symbolized either as '$\sim\exists x[F(x) \& G(x)]$' or as '$\forall x[F(x) \rightarrow \sim G(x)]$', where '$\sim$' is the symbolic counterpart of the adverbial phrase 'it is not the case that'. Finally, and perhaps even more importantly, Frege's theory also accounts for quantifier phrases embedded within the scope of other quantifier phrases and explains the difference between, for example, 'Every man loves some woman', formally represented by '$\forall x[F(x) \rightarrow \exists y[G(y) \& R(x,y)]]$', and 'Some woman is loved by all men', formally represented by '$\exists y[G(y) \& \forall x[F(x) \rightarrow R(x,y)]]$', where '$F$' and '$G$' stand for the first-level concepts *being a man* and *being a woman*, respectively, and 'R' stands for the first-level relation *loving*.

What is especially important about these kinds of formal analyses of the sentences of natural language is that they amount to a perspicuous logical representation of the truth-conditions determined by the content of those sentences, and, in that respect, they are readily amenable to the application of inference rules and allow for a rigorous analysis of the notions of logical deduction and formal validity. It was these features that led Frege to maintain that his concept-script was 'not a mere *calculus ratiocinator*, but a *lingua characteristica* in the Leibnizian sense' (Frege [2.20], 90). That is, Frege's goal was to construct 'a logically perfect language', and not just an abstract calculus, that could be used as the general framework for a language of mathematics and science. It was not designed to serve the purposes of ordinary or natural language, as an international auxiliary language might be, but rather was intended as a tool for the analysis of concepts and the formal development of mathematical and scientific theories. In this regard

Frege maintained that the relation between his concept-script and ordinary or natural language was like that of the relation of the microscope to the eye. For even though the eye is superior to the microscope 'because of the range of its possible uses and the versatility with which it can adapt to the most diverse circumstances', nevertheless 'as soon as scientific goals demand great sharpness of resolution, the eye proves to be insufficient' (Frege [2.18], 6). That is, just as the microscope is a device 'perfectly suited' to the demand for great sharpness of visual resolution in science, so too Frege's concept-script is 'a device invented for certain scientific purposes, and one must not condemn it because it is not suited to others' (ibid.).

Another basic feature of Frege's function theory is the idea that the meaning of a complex expression is a function of the meanings of the component expressions that make it up, or what is generally called the compositionality law of meaning. Depending on what is meant by 'meaning', this law appears to be violated in natural language by contexts involving modal and intensional verbs, including in particular those used to ascribe knowledge, belief or desire (or what are generally called propositional attitudes) to someone. This led Frege to distinguish between the sense (*Sinn*) and denotation (*Bedeutung*) – or what others call the intension and extension – of an expression, where by the sense of an expression he meant the mode by which it presents its denotation. The senses, or intensions, of 'the morning star' and 'the evening star', for example, are different even though their denotation, or extension, is the same (namely, the planet Venus). Frege called the sense of a sentence a thought (*Gedanke*), by which he meant a proposition (as an abstract object) and not a mental episode of thinking. The denotation, or extension, of a sentence he took to be a truth-value, i.e. either the true or the false. As applied to denotations (extensions), the compositionality law then stipulates that the denotation (extension) of a sentence (i.e. its truth-value) is a function of the denotations (extensions) of the expressions that make it up; and as applied to senses (intensions) the law stipulates that the sense (intension) of a sentence, i.e. the thought (proposition) it expresses, is a function of the senses of those same component expressions. Thus because 'the morning star' and 'the evening star' have the same denotation (namely, the planet Venus) but different senses, the sentences 'The morning star is not the evening star' and 'The morning star is not the morning star' have the same truth-value (namely, the false) as their denotations but express different thoughts as their senses.

In applying his doubly aspected notion of meaning to indirect discourse – i.e. to the kinds of linguistic contexts in which a sentential phrase occurs as the grammatical object of an intensional verb for a propositional attitude – Frege maintained that the denotation of the embedded sentence is not the denotation it has in direct discourse but its sense instead. In this way we can consistently maintain the compositionality law for meaning, whether taken extensionally or intensionally, and also explain how we can ascribe to someone the (consistent) belief that the morning star is not the evening star without thereby also ascribing to that person the (inconsistent) belief that the morning star is not the morning star. For the truth-value (denotation) of a sentence such as 'Ronald believes that the morning star is not the evening star' is then a function not of the denotation of 'The morning star is not the evening star' – which, as noted, is the same as the denotation of 'The morning star is not the morning star' – but of its sense instead, which is different from the sense of 'The morning star is not the morning star.'

～ THE THEORY OF LOGICAL TYPES ～

Although Frege laid the foundation for a theory of meaning with his distinction between the sense and denotation of expressions, he did not formally represent the distinction in his own concept-script or theory of logical form. His primary interest in developing his concept-script was to provide a logical foundation for arithmetic, and for that purpose he thought he needed only an extensional language, i.e. one for which the compositionality law could be restricted to extensions without any regard at all for senses or intensions (or those aspects of natural language, such as indirect discourse, that call for an intensional analysis).

Frege's insight about arithmetic was that the natural numbers are first and foremost the numbers we use in counting things. He was the first to see in this regard that the natural numbers are based ultimately on our use of numerical quantifier phrases to state that a certain number of objects fall under a given first-level concept. Thus, for example, in stating that there are 12 Apostles, or that there is 1 moon (of the earth), or that there are 9 planets (of the solar system), etc., we are in effect stating that the concepts *being an Apostle*, or *being a moon*, or *being a planet*, etc., have 12, or 1, or 9, etc., instances, respectively. Numerical concepts, in other words, are the second-level concepts corresponding to such quantifier phrases as 'There are n many objects x such that . . . x . . .', where ' . . . x . . .' stands for a first-level concept.

The real philosophical problem about arithmetic, according to Frege, is to explain how conceptually we are able to move from numerical second-level concepts within which first-level concepts fall (i.e. from the concepts that numerical quantifier phrases stand for) to the natural numbers of arithmetic as denoted by numerals or other singular terms (i.e. to the natural numbers as objects that fall under first-level concepts), as represented in such statements as 'Two is a prime' and '$5 + 7 = 12$', as well as to such statements as 'The number of Apostles is 12', 'The number of moons is 1', and 'The number of planets is 9'.

It was for this purpose that Frege extended his concept-script to include a device for the representation of the extension of a concept (cf. Frege [2.19]). This device, which amounts to using the *spiritus lenis* (the comma sign over a letter) as a variable-binding abstraction operator, transforms an open sentential formula (i.e. a formula containing a free variable) into an abstract singular term that denotes the extension of the concept represented by that open formula. Thus, by applying the *spiritus lenis* to a symbolic formula '$F(x)$', we obtain the abstract singular term '$\acute{x}F(x)$', which is taken to denote the extension of the concept F, i.e. the class of things that are F. (A comparable device in set theory is the use of braces and a colon to transform a formula '$F(x)$' into a singular term '$\{x:F(x)\}$'.)

It is noteworthy that the application of this device, according to Frege, amounts to a formal counterpart of the process of nominalization in natural language, i.e. the process whereby a (simple or complex) predicate expression could be transformed into an abstract singular term – but which, in ordinary language, is usually taken to denote the content (or intension) of the concept that the predicate expression stands for and not the extension of that concept. Thus, for instance, the simple predicate 'wise' (or the phrase 'is wise'), as used, for example, in 'Socrates is wise', can be nominalized and transformed into the abstract singular term 'wisdom' (or the gerund, 'being wise'), as used in 'Wisdom is a virtue' (or 'Being wise is a virtue'). Similarly, 'triangular' and 'equals' can be nominalized into 'triangularity' and 'equality' (or into 'being triangular' and 'being equal', as well as into a singular term beginning with an appositional phrase, such as 'the concept (of) being triangular' and 'the concept (of) being equal', etc.). In general, the process of nominalization is effected in English through the use of gerunds and infinitive phrases, as well as the addition of such suffixes as '-ity' and '-ness'. This process, as we have said, transforms a predicate expression (which stands for a concept in the traditional sense of a universal as a predicable entity) into an abstract singular term, which in ordinary language is normally taken to denote the content (or intension) of the concept that the predicate otherwise stands for.

Frege's reason for interpreting a nominalized predicate as denoting the extension of the concept that the predicate otherwise stands for in its role as a predicate was primarily because he took his concept-script to be a strictly extensional language. Indeed, one of his basic laws of logic – namely (Vb), according to which the nominalizations of predicate expressions that stand for co-extensive concepts denote the same object – amounts to a principle of extensionality, which, formally, can be stated for monadic predicates as follows:

$$\forall x[F(x) \longleftrightarrow G(x)] \rightarrow \hat{x}\, F(x) = \hat{x}\, G(x).$$

Thus, because of his commitment to an extensional concept-script, there was no real point, according to Frege, to distinguish a predicate nominalization of the form 'the concept F' (i.e. as preceded by the appositional phrase 'the concept') from the somewhat longer abstract singular term of the form 'the extension of the concept F', the issue being one only of 'expediency' (cf. Frege [2.21], 106, and Cocchiarella [2.15], chapter 2).

It was by means of the nominalizing transformation of a predicate expression into an abstract singular term that Frege proposed to explain 'the miracle of number', i.e. the existence of numbers as objects, denoted by numerals and other singular terms, that are somehow derived from, or correlated with, the second-level concepts that numerical-quantifier phrases stand for. For in addition to correlating first-level concepts with their extensions as represented by such a transformation, Frege also correlated second-level concepts with first-level concepts, and, in effect, thereby correlated second-level concepts with the extensions of those first-level concepts – and it was these extensions as abstract objects that Frege took the natural numbers of arithmetic to be. In other words, by a double correlation of second-level concepts with first-level concepts and first-level concepts with their extensions, Frege showed how numbers as the second-level concepts that numerical-quantifier phrases stand for can be correlated with numbers as objects (cf. Cocchiarella [2.17], section 4).

Although we cannot go into the details of Frege's brilliant and insightful analysis of the natural numbers here, it is important to note how the notion of a hierarchy of concepts is implicit in that analysis – albeit a hierarchy that can be reflected downwards onto the level of objects through Frege's correlation of second-level concepts with first-level concepts and the latter with their extensions through a process corresponding to the nominalization of predicate phrases in natural language. It was this hierarchy, or reinterpretation of it, that became the basis of the theory of logical types that was developed later by Bertrand Russell (1872–1970) as a way to avoid Russell's famous paradox – a paradox that led to a contradiction in the extended version of Frege's concept-script.

Russell's paradox involves the very mechanism of nominalization that Frege represented in his concept-script by means of the smooth-breathing abstraction operator. For the paradox applies to an abstract singular term (such as 'the concept F') regardless whether that term is understood to denote the extension or the intension of a concept –

where, by the intension of a concept, Russell (who took concepts to be intensional entities) understood just the concept itself. That is why Russell's paradox may be formulated either in terms of the class of those classes that are not members of themselves, or in terms of the concept of being a concept that does not fall under itself. Thus in regard to the concept of being a concept that does not fall under itself, Russell argued that either this concept falls under itself or it does not fall under itself; but if it falls under itself, then, by definition of that very concept itself, it does not fall under itself; and if it does not fall under itself, then, again by definition, it does fall under itself, from which the contradiction that it both falls under itself and does not fall under itself follows.

Russell discovered his paradox some time around the turn of the century, and he then spent a number of years attempting a variety of solutions until he settled upon the doctrine of logical types. As described by Russell, this doctrine purports to set limits on what is meaningful or significant even in natural language, and for that reason, not without some justification, it has been strongly criticized. Nevertheless, in one form or another, the doctrine of logical types has been the mainstay of much of the formal work done in the philosophy of language – although today there are type-free alternatives, such as those developed by Cocchiarella (cf. Cocchiarella [2.15], chapter 2), that remain faithful to Frege's, and even Russell's, original insights.

As a source for insight into the logical structure of language, Russell's theory of logical types adds nothing new to what is already represented in Frege's concept-script. Both contain all the logical connectives for negation, conjunction, disjunction, etc., corresponding to the operations of Boolean algebra, and Russell adopted Frege's function theory for the elementary forms of predication – though, as noted, he did not interpret concepts extensionally as functions from objects to truth-values (the way Frege did) but rather intensionally as functions from objects to propositions, for which reason he also called concepts propositional functions. Russell also recognized the importance of Frege's development of the logic of quantifiers, which, following Frege, he allowed to reach into the positions of predicate expressions as well as into the positions for singular terms – i.e. Russell followed Frege in allowing quantifiers to apply to expressions for functions as well as to expressions for arguments. Finally, Russell also followed Frege in allowing predicate expressions to be nominalized and occur as abstract singular terms – though instead of using Frege's smooth-breathing abstraction operator as a formal device for transforming a function-expression into an abstract singular term, Russell used his cap-notation, '$^\wedge$', as a variable-binding operator that transforms a function-expression (or open formula) $\phi(x)$ to an argument-expression, i.e. a singular term,

$\phi(\hat{x})$. The main difference between them in this regard is that whereas for Frege such an abstract singular term denotes the extension of the concept represented by the open formula to which it is applied, Russell took it to denote the concept itself as a single entity. Accordingly, in respect to these factors – namely, (1) basic logical forms of predication (as represented by the function-argument notation), (2) propositional connectives (corresponding to the operations of Boolean algebra), (3) quantifiers that reach into predicate as well as subject (or argument) positions and (4) a device for nominalizing (complex or simple) predicate expressions and transforming them into abstract singular terms – Russell really did not add any new insights to the essentials of what constitutes a theory of logical form according to Frege.

What Russell did do, as a way to avoid his paradox, was divide the predicate expressions (and their corresponding abstract singular terms) of Frege's second-order logic with nominalized predicates as abstract singular terms into a hierarchy of different types, and then he imposed the grammatical constraint that nominalized predicates can occur as argument- or subject-expressions only of predicates of higher types – thereby ruling out as grammatically meaningless an expression of the form $\phi(\phi(\hat{x}))$, as well as its negation, $\sim \phi(\phi(\hat{x}))$, which purports to indicate that the concept denoted by $\phi(\hat{x})$ does not fall under itself, which is just the kind of expression needed to generate Russell's paradox. (Note: Russell's division of predicates actually involves two hierarchies, one a 'vertical' hierarchy corresponding to Frege's levels of concepts, and the other a 'horizontal' hierarchy corresponding to a ramification of all the concepts on a given level. The *simple* theory of types, which is all that is needed to avoid Russell's paradox, represents only the first hierarchy, whereas the *ramified* theory of types represents both.)

These grammatical constraints are undesirable, it should be emphasized, because they exclude as meaningless many expressions that are not only grammatically correct in natural language but also intuitively meaningful (and that sometimes even result in true sentences). Fortunately, it turns out, the logical insights behind these constraints can be retained without imposing the constraints as conditions of grammatical correctness. In fact, as shown by Cocchiarella, those logical insights can be retained – and Russell's paradox avoided – in a type-free second-order logic with nominalized predicates as abstract singular terms of essentially just the sort originally conceived by Frege (cp. Cocchiarella [2.15], chapter 2).

❧❧ RADICAL EMPIRICISM AND THE ❧❧ LOGICAL CONSTRUCTION OF THE WORLD

Russell took his theory of types to be the framework of 'a logically perfect language', by which he meant a language that would show at a glance the logical structure of the facts that are described by its means (cp. Russell [2.35]). Such a language, according to Russell, 'would be one in which everything that we might wish to say in the way of propositions that are intelligible to us, could be said, and in which, further, structure would always be made explicit' (Russell [2.36], 165). All that needs to be added to the theory of logical types to be such a language, Russell maintained, is a vocabulary of (non-logical) descriptive constants that correspond to the meaningful words and phrases of natural science and ordinary language (Russell [2.35], 58ff.). The constants of pure mathematics, unlike those of the natural sciences, do not need to be added to the framework because they, according to Russell, are all definable in purely logical terms within the framework itself. Knowledge of pure mathematics is explainable, in other words, as logical knowledge – a view known as logicism – and, in particular, as knowledge of the propositions that are provable in the theory of logical types independently of any vocabulary of descriptive constants.

Despite his logicism regarding mathematics, Russell was a radical empiricist as far as our knowledge of physical or concrete existence was concerned. All our empirical knowledge of the world, he maintained, must be reducible to our knowledge of what is given in experience, by which he meant that it must be constructible within the framework of the theory of logical types from the lowest level of objects, which he assumed to be events corresponding to our sensory experience. It was by means of logical constructions within this framework that Russell proposed to bridge the gulf between the world of physical science and the world of sense, and he was guided in this regard by 'the maxim which inspires all scientific philosophizing, namely "Ockham's razor": *Entities are not to be multiplied without necessity.* In other words, in dealing with any subject-matter, find out what entities are undeniably involved, and state everything in terms of these entities' (Russell [2.34], 112). Thus, because sense data are the entities that are 'undeniably involved' in all of our empirical knowledge according to Russell, 'the only justification possible' for such knowledge 'must be one which exhibits matter as a logical construction from sense-data' (ibid., 106).

Though Russell gave a number of examples of how such a construction might be given, it was Rudolf Carnap (1891–1970) who, using nothing more than the framework of the simple theory of logical types (and a certain amount of empirical science, such as gestalt psychology, about the structure of experience), gave the most detailed analysis indicating how we might reconstruct all our knowledge of the world in terms of what is given in experience (cp. Carnap [2.5]). This meant in particular that all the concepts of science could be analysed and reduced to certain basic concepts that apply to the content of what is given in experience. One of the important patterns for such an analysis is known today as *definition by abstraction*, whereby, relative to a given equivalence relation (i.e. a relation that is reflexive, symmetric and transitive), certain concepts are identified with (or represented by) the equivalence classes that are generated by that equivalence relation. This pattern was used by Frege and Russell in the analysis of the natural numbers (as based on the equivalence relation of equinumerosity, or one–one correspondence), and was then used again in the analysis of the negative and positive integers, the rational numbers, the real numbers and even the imaginary numbers. Carnap, who took definition by abstraction as indicative of the 'proper analysis' of a concept, generalized the pattern into a form that he called 'quasi analysis' (but which, he acknowledged, really amounted to a form of synthesis), which could be based on relations of partial similarity instead of full similarity, i.e. on relations that amount to something less than an equivalence relation. The concepts definable in terms of a quasi-analysis specify in what respect things (especially items of experience) that stand to one another in a relation of partial similarity agree, i.e. the respect in which they are in part, but not fully, similar (cp. Carnap [2.5], sections 71–4). In this way Carnap was able to define the various sense modalities (as classes of qualities that intuitively belong to the same sense modality, where concepts for sense qualities are definable in terms of a partial similarity between elementary experiences), including in particular the visual sense and colour concepts (as determined by the three-dimensional ordering relation of the colour solid).

Using the various sense modalities, Carnap went on to construct the four-dimensional space-time world of perceptual objects, which, with all its various sense qualities, 'has only provisional validity', and which, for that reason, 'must give way to the strictly unambiguous but completely quality-free world of physics' (Carnap [2.5], 207). We cannot go into the details of Carnap's 'constructional definitions' here, but we should note that all that Carnap meant by a logical analysis by means of such definitions was translatability into his constructional language – i.e. into an applied form of the simple theory of logical types as based on a primitive descriptive constant for a certain relation of partial similarity between elementary experiences. Such a translation need not, and in general did not, preserve synonymy, nor did it in any sense amount to an ontological reduction of ordinary physical objects to the sensory objects of experience. What it did preserve, according to

Carnap, was a material equivalence (i.e. an equivalence of truth-value) between the sentences of ordinary language, or of a scientific theory, and the sentences of the constructional language. (Note: the same claim is made in Goodman [2.22] for an alternative constructional language based on nominalist principles that are opposed to the predicate quantifiers of type theory.)

❧ THE LOGICAL EMPIRICIST THEORY OF ❧ MEANING

Carnap was a founding member of the Vienna Circle, a group of philosophers and scientists who, following Leibniz, sought to unify all the different sciences within a common linguistic framework based on modern symbolic logic (which, for them, meant the theory of logical types). The primary method of the Circle was logical analysis, which they took to involve the task of specifying the meaning of all scientific statements and concepts in a precise way and of thereby excluding as meaningless all the statements of traditional metaphysics. Metaphysical theories, they claimed, were too narrowly tied to ordinary, natural language, which uses the substantive not only for things, but for qualities, relations, processes, etc., as well, and thereby 'misleads one into a thing-like conception of functional concepts' (Hahn, Neurath and Carnap [2.24], 9). Curiously, they did not seem to realize (at least initially) that the theory of logical types itself formally incorporates a 'thing-like conception of functional concepts' through its incorporation of a device for nominalization (such as Russell's cap-operator), thereby allowing expressions for propositional functions to be nominalized and occur as argument- or subject-expressions of expressions for yet higher-order types of propositional functions. Indeed, the reduction of mathematics to logic, which was a central part of their view, is not possible without some such device corresponding to the process of nominalization of predicate expressions in natural language (cp. Cocchiarella [2.15], chapter 5).

Carnap and other members of the Vienna Circle adopted what is sometimes called *the linguistic doctrine of the a priori*, according to which a declarative sentence can be known to be true (or false) *a priori* if, and only if, the sentence is analytically true (or false, respectively). Here, by analytic truth (or falsehood) they meant truth (or falsehood) by linguistic convention, i.e. in virtue of the meanings of the words that make up the sentence. This doctrine amounts to a linguistic theory of the *a priori* and is intended as logical empiricism's answer to the Kantian question of how there can be *a priori* knowledge. Logic and mathematics are knowable *a priori,* according to such logical empiricists, because all logical and mathematical truths are analytic truths.

A basic principle of empiricism is that what is true, but not analytically true, is knowable only on the basis of experience. This led to a logical empiricist theory of meaning, according to which a (declarative) sentence is cognitively meaningful (in the sense that it can be said to be true or false) if, and only if, either it is analytically true or false, or its truth or falsity is capable of being tested by experiential evidence (cp. Hempel [2.25], [2.26]). Initially, the idea of being capable of being tested by experiential evidence was explained by early logical empiricists in terms of the notion of complete verification in principle, and for that reason their theory came to be called *the verifiability theory of meaning.* On this account, a declarative sentence is said to be empirically meaningful if, and only if, it is not analytic and follows logically from some finite, logically consistent class of observation sentences – where by an observation sentence is meant a sentence that asserts or denies that an object (or group of objects) has some particular observable characteristic. (The finitude of the class means that complete verification is possible after a finite number of observations.) This explanation fails for sentences of the form 'All F are G', however, even where 'F' and 'G' stand for observable characteristics – unless it is already empirically knowable that the number of things that are F's is finite. Such a sentence is completely falsifiable, however, by simply observing one thing that is F but not G, and, for that reason, one might consider redefining empirical meaning in terms of complete falsifiability in principle instead. But then, by the same argument, negations of sentences of the form 'All F are G' would not be empirically meaningful. Other attempts to explicate the idea of empirical meaning also failed for similar reasons. (Not everyone agrees that all these attempts have failed, however; for example, see Rynin [2.37].)

One of the more interesting proposals in this direction involves the notion of a logically correct empiricist language, by which, generally, was meant an applied form of the simple theory of types. The only (non-logical) descriptive constants of such a theory would be those that stand for observable characteristics of things, i.e. so-called observation predicates, where by an observable characteristic was meant an observable property of ordinary macro-physical objects and not the kind of characteristic that applies only to sense data. Such an empiricist language would involve only perspicuous logical forms by which the truth-conditions of any of its sentences could be determined in an exact way, and, in addition, it would embody the linguistic theory of the *a priori,* i.e. the doctrine that all and only analytically true (false) sentences can be known to be true (false) *a priori.* An additional constraint was that the language must be extensional (i.e. that Frege's compositionality principle must be valid when restricted to the extensions of expressions), which meant that the language could include no intensional operators (such as that for necessity) or counterparts of intensional verbs. A (declarative) sentence of natural language, or of a scientific theory, was then said to be cognitively meaningful if, and only if, it is translatable (preserving only material equivalence) into such a logically correct empiricist language.

The idea of such a proposal is that a logically correct empiricist language would give us control over vocabulary (by excluding nonsensical words) as well as over logical syntax, i.e. logical grammar and validity. In this regard the proposal is like Leibniz's programme for a *characteristica universalis*, except that Leibniz did not accept the empiricist principle that all concepts must be analysable in terms of the observable characteristics of things. Thus, on the proposal as initially formulated, a predicate expression of natural language will be empirically meaningful if, and only if, a formal, symbolic counterpart of it is definable in terms of the observation predicates of a logically correct empiricist language, and therefore, because both a sentence of the form 'All F are G' and its negation, where 'F' and 'G', are definable in the language in terms of observation predicates, are well formed in such a language, they will both be taken as empirically meaningful (thereby by-passing the problem of restricting ourselves to a finite number of observations).

The trouble with this proposal is that it is still too restrictive; for there are too many predicate expressions of both scientific and ordinary discourse that are clearly meaningful to us but that cannot be explicitly defined in terms of observation predicates. In particular, predicate expressions that stand for dispositions, or powers, or capacities, or tendencies, etc., cannot be defined in such a language unless we were to add to it, for instance, modal operators for causal necessity (or possibility) by which law-like counter-factual conditionals might be formulated. Such operators, however, generate non-extensional contexts and violate the restriction to an extensional language that logical empiricism demands. For this reason, Carnap suggested that the original proposal be modified so that dispositional predicates could be introduced into a logically correct empiricist language by a pattern of quasi-definitions (which he called *reduction sentences*) that get at some of the content of counter-factual conditionals but without requiring the introduction of intensional operators (cf. Carnap [2.7]). This way of extending a logically correct empiricist language vastly extends the range of significance it gives to the sentences of ordinary and scientific discourse, but, unfortunately, it still fails to account for most of the theoretical predicates of modern science that have to do with the micro-physical world – not to mention the intensional verbs of natural language that stand for the various propositional attitudes that are studied in cognitive science. Some attempts were made to overcome these problems (see Carnap [2.11] and [2.12] for his later analyses of theoretical predicates), but, at least in the case of the intensional verbs of natural language, they have not in general succeeded.

➤ SEMIOTIC AND THE TRINITY OF ➤ SYNTAX, SEMANTICS AND PRAGMATICS

In time Carnap did come to think that an explication of logical necessity could be given, but this involved a new kind of approach to language, namely, a semantical approach. Earlier, in Carnap [2.6], he had adapted certain metamathematical techniques and ideas of the mathematician David Hilbert (1862–1943) that he applied to the general analysis of the syntax of formal languages. In that work Carnap distinguished between the formal language whose logical syntax we want to study, which he called an *object-language*, and the language in which we carry out that study, which he called the *meta-language*. Originally, the latter was a *syntactical* metalanguage because it dealt only with the syntactical aspects of the object-language, such as its rules of formation (defining the well-formed expressions of the different logico-grammatical categories of the language) and its rules of transformation (defining the conditions under which sentences follow validly from other sentences of the language). On his later approach, however, Carnap extended the meta-language to include expressions that stand for semantical relations, such as the various *designation* relations that hold between the expressions of an object-language and the entities they stand for or designate. The primary goal of such a meta-language is to define the semantic notions of truth and falsehood – and the notions of logical truth and falsehood as well – as applied to the sentences of the object-language. The meaning of a sentence of such a language was then to be given in terms of its truth-conditions, i.e. the conditions under which the sentence can be said to be true or false, respectively (cp. Carnap [2.8], section 7).

The idea that the meaning of a sentence is its truth-conditions was emphasized earlier by Ludwig Wittgenstein (1889–1951) in his *Tractatus Logico-Philosophicus* ([2.47], 4.024, 4.46), which describes a metaphysical framework known as logical atomism. The elements of logical atomism are atomic states of affairs, each of which is logically independent of the rest, and the totality of which make up logical space. Different possible worlds, including the actual world, consist of all the atomic states of affairs that obtain in those worlds. It was essentially this framework that Carnap adopted in developing his semantics for logical necessity. For by associating an atomic sentence with each atomic state of affairs, the different possible worlds could be described in terms of certain classes of atomic sentences, or their negations, that Carnap called *state descriptions*. That is, a state description for the formal object-language is a class of atomic sentences, or their negations, such that for every atomic sentence of the language either it or its negation, but not both, is in the class. Truth in a possible world is then definable for all the sentences of the language in terms of the atomic sentences, or their negations, that are in the state description corresponding to that possible world; and logical truth is definable as truth in every logically possible world.

With the notion of a logically possible world at hand, Carnap realized, we are able to define the truth-conditions for sentences of the form 'It is (logically) necessary that...' (where '...' stands for a sentential clause) in terms of a strictly extensional meta-language. In this way, Carnap maintained, we may give up the thesis of extensionality for the object-language while retaining it for the meta-language, which is now the language that is of primary importance for philosophy. Thus, where $\Box$ is a sentential operator corresponding to the phrase 'it is (logically) necessary that', Carnap's criterion for the truth-conditions (and thereby the meaning) of an object-language sentence of the form $\Box\phi$ is that $\Box\phi$ is to be true (in a possible world) if, and only if, ϕ is logically true (i.e. if, and only if, ϕ is true in all logically possible worlds) (cf. Carnap [2.9]). (For a fuller discussion of how logical atomism provides a paradigmatic semantics for logical necessity, see Cocchiarella [2.15], chapters 6 and 7.)

The idea of an extensional semantical meta-language in which the notion of semantic truth (and falsehood) can be defined for the sentences of a formal object-language was also the goal, in the early 1930s, of a number of Polish logicians, including especially Alfred Tarski (1902–83). Tarski succeeded in defining such a notion in terms of what today is called *model theory*, where by a model is meant a set-theoretic construction that amounts to a counterpart to the notion of a possible world (cp. Tarski [2.43] and [2.42]). The language of set theory (which is an extensional language *par excellence*) has today become the principal framework within which most of the work of model theory and formal semantics is carried out, and different kinds of model-theoretic constructions have been used to give the truth-conditions for a variety of modal operators in addition to that for logical necessity, and even for some operators that stand for propositional attitudes as well. As a branch of set theory, in other words, model theory has been developed and applied not just to a number of extensional mathematical languages but to intensional fragments of natural language as well (cp. Addison, Henkin and Tarski [2.1]; Partee, ter Meulen and Wall [2.32]). It should be emphasized, however, that set theory, the general framework within which model theory has been developed, is primarily a mathematical framework, and in that regard the language of set theory is not a *lingua philosophica* in the sense originally intended by Leibniz, or as later developed by Frege, Russell, Carnap and others. (See Cocchiarella [2.16] for a more detailed discussion of this issue, and especially of the conceptual priority of a formal theory of predication over a formal theory of membership in a set or class.)

In addition to syntax (which studies the logico-grammatical rules of formation and transformation of an object-language) and semantics (which studies the different designation relations between the well-formed expressions of an object-language and the entities designated by those expressions, including especially the truth-conditions of the sentences of that object-language), there are also relations between the expressions of an object-language and the contexts in which those expressions are used, including especially the people who use the language in those contexts. The study of these kinds of relations is generally called *pragmatics*, and all three kinds of study together, i.e. syntax, semantics and pragmatics, is called *semiotic* (cp. Morris [2.30]). For Carnap, it should be noted, there can be only an empirical or descriptive pragmatics and not a pure (or analytic) pragmatics the way there can be a pure logical syntax and a pure logical semantics. This is because for Carnap the relation of designation in pragmatics is a psychological concept, and psychology is an empirical, descriptive science and not an analytic science. Thus, because the task for philosophy now is semiotical analysis (and not just syntactical or semantical analysis), the proper framework for philosophy, according to Carnap, is no longer pure, logical syntax (as Carnap had assumed it to be in 1936) – i.e. it is no longer a pure syntactical meta-language in which our goal is to study the logical syntax of different object languages – nor is it a pure logical semantics – that is, a pure, semantical meta-language by which we can study the notions of truth and logical truth and the relation of designation in general. Rather, the proper framework for philosophy now is one in which we can study 'the semiotical structure of the language of science, including the theoretical part of everyday language'. It is a framework in which we can engage not only in logical analysis (as part of pure semantics if meanings are involved, or as part of pure logical syntax if the analysis is purely formal) but also in the analysis of the problems of gaining and communicating knowledge, which, according to Carnap ([2.8], 250), properly belongs to pragmatics.

❧ PRAGMATICS FROM A LOGICAL POINT ❧ OF VIEW

The shift to pragmatics, i.e. to a study of the contexts of use of ordinary, natural language, was already made by some logical empiricists. Otto Neurath (1882–1945), for example, maintained that although the unification of scientific language is one of the goals of the movement, nevertheless 'one must test all theories by means of the language of daily life', and that, in particular, one must systematically analyse the 'correlations between the calculus of theories and the language of daily life' (Neurath [2.31], 19). Neurath, however, did not himself make any investigations of how 'the language of daily life' could be systematically correlated with the formal, ideal language of logical empiricism that would serve as a unified language for science. Indeed, instead of studying those correlations, a new generation of philosophers of language rejected the formal language approach altogether and insisted on studying only the functioning of ordinary language in daily life as an alternative to the formally oriented approach (cf. Wittgenstein [2.48]). It was argued, for example, that 'the concepts used in non-scientific kinds of discourse could not literally be *replaced* by scientific concepts serving just the same purposes; that the language of science could not in this way *supplant* the language of the drawing-room, the kitchen, the law courts and the novel' (Strawson [2.40], 505).

It is noteworthy that the response of the formally oriented philosophers of language to this sort of criticism was not to ignore ordinary language but to turn to a formal analysis of its various context-dependent features. One feature in particular that was taken as an object of study was the use of tenses to distinguish our references to events in the past, the present and the future in any given context of use of language. Arthur Prior (1914–69) suggested that this contextual feature of our speech acts could be formally represented by tense operators, such as '$\mathscr{P}$' and '$\mathscr{F}$', corresponding to the adverbial phrases 'it was the case that' and 'it will be the case that', respectively. (The simple present tense was assumed to be built into the form of an atomic formula, which could then be modified by the application of the past- and future-tense operators.) By means of these operators, formal counterparts for the adverbial phrases 'it always was the case that' and 'it always will be the case that' are definable as, '$\sim \mathscr{P} \sim$' and '$\sim \mathscr{F} \sim$', respectively (where '$\sim$', as already noted, is the negation sign and represents the adverbial phrase 'it is not the case that'). As is indicated in Prior [2.33], different tense logics, corresponding to our different conceptions of the structure of time, can be formulated in terms of these tense operators.

Some examples of laws of tense logic are ($\phi \rightarrow \sim \mathscr{P} \sim \mathscr{F}\phi$) and

($\phi \rightarrow \sim \mathscr{F} \sim \mathscr{P}\phi$), corresponding to the theses that if a sentence ϕ is (now) the case, then it always was the case that it was (then) going to be the case, and it always will be the case that it was the case (prior to then). Similarly, ($\mathscr{P}\mathscr{P}\phi \rightarrow \mathscr{P}\phi$) and ($\mathscr{F}\mathscr{F}\phi \rightarrow \mathscr{F}\phi$), with iterated applications of the same tense operators, represent the theses that what had been the case (prior to some time in the past) simply was the case, and what will be the case relative to some future time simply will be the case. (Note that '$\mathscr{P}\mathscr{P}$' represents the past-perfect tense of English and that '$\mathscr{F}\mathscr{P}$' represents the future-perfect tense.) The assumption that the structure of time in the past is dense (i.e. that between any two past moments there is another past moment) is represented by ($\mathscr{P}\phi \rightarrow \mathscr{P}\mathscr{P}\phi$); and that it is dense in the future as well is represented by ($\mathscr{F}\phi \rightarrow \mathscr{F}\mathscr{F}\phi$). The following two laws (where 'V' represents inclusive disjunction), defended by Cocchiarella in his tense logic but rejected by Prior (cf. Prior [2.33], chapter 3, section 6), assume that events in the past (or future, respectively) of the local time of any context are connected (i.e. that they either occurred at the same time or that one preceded the other):

$$\mathscr{P}\phi \ \& \ \mathscr{P}\psi \rightarrow \mathscr{P}(\phi \ \& \ \psi) \lor \mathscr{P}(\phi \ \& \ \mathscr{P}\psi) \lor \mathscr{P}(\psi \ \& \ \mathscr{P}\phi)$$
$$\mathscr{F}\phi \ \& \ \mathscr{F}\psi \rightarrow \mathscr{F}(\phi \ \& \ \psi) \lor \mathscr{F}(\phi \ \& \ \mathscr{F}\psi) \lor \mathscr{F}(\psi \ \& \ \mathscr{F}\phi).$$

Arthur Prior formulated a number of different tense logics, as we have said, corresponding to different conceptions of the structure of time. He applied those logics to different philosophical theses, including in particular J. M. E. McTaggart's argument against the reality of time (cf. Prior [2.33], chapter 1). Prior had no doubts about the reality of time in the present (with a past whose ontological status is now settled), but he did have his doubts about the reality of the future and the meaning of future contingent statements (as they occur, for instance, in Aristotle's famous sea-battle argument), and some of his logics make important formal contributions of different ways to represent the openness (or coming yet to be) of the future. Prior also showed how certain views of antiquity about the temporal nature of necessity – namely, Diodorus' view that what is possible is what is or will be the case, and Aristotle's view that what is necessary is what always has been, is and always will be the case – can be formally represented in tense logic.

In addition to doubts about the ontological status of the future, Prior also maintained that reference to past and future objects is meaningful only in so far as such reference (as it is represented by existential quantifier phrases, '∃x', '∃y', etc.) occurs within the context of the past and future tense operators. It should be emphasized that the issue here is not with the truth of statements about past or future objects but with the meaningfulness of those statements. The sentence 'There did exist someone before whom no one else existed', for example, is clearly meaningful and can be formally represented by '$\mathscr{P} \exists x[H(x) \ \& \sim \mathscr{P}$ $\exists y[y \neq x \ \& \ H(y)]]$', where the reference to a past person (with the predicate 'H' representing the verb phrase 'is a person') is within the scope of the past-tense operator. In this way an ontological commitment to a past person before whom no other person existed is said to be at best only indirect and weaker than a commitment in which an existential quantifier phrase applies to the time of the context of use and does not occur within the scope of a tense operator (where it would apply to a past or future time).

This solution does not work for sentences such as 'There did exist someone who is an ancestor of everyone now existing', however, which are also clearly meaningful (regardless whether or not they are also true). In this sentence the quantifier phrase 'everyone now existing', which refers only to people existing at the moment of speech, is within the scope of (or dominated by) the first quantifier phrase, 'there did exist someone', which refers to a past person who does not (or at least who may not) exist at the moment of speech. The formula '$\mathscr{P}$ $\exists x[H(x) \ \& \ \forall y[H(y) \rightarrow R(x, \ y)]]$', where '$R$' stands for the ancestor relation, will not do as an analysis because it represents the different English sentence, 'There did exist someone who was an ancestor of everyone *then* existing'; and the formula '$\forall y[H(y) \rightarrow \mathscr{P} \exists x[H(x) \ \&$ $R(x, \ y)]]$' will not do because it represents the different English sentence, 'Everyone now existing had an ancestor', with the order of dominance between the two quantifier phrases reversed. What this shows is that direct quantification over past objects (and over future objects as well), which is something that we commonly do in natural language, cannot be accounted for by indirect forms of quantification, i.e. by quantifier phrases occurring only within the scope of the past (or future) tense operator. Some other sort of formal device is needed – e.g. primitive quantifiers that refer directly to past (or future) objects, or a *now*-operator that semantically relates formulas occurring within the scope of a tense operator to the moment of speech (and perhaps a *then*-operator as well that relates embedded formulas to a past, or future, moment of reference) – in order to adequately represent these kinds of sentences of natural language (cp. Cocchiarella [2.14]). In that case, however, the nature of our ontological commitment to past (and future) objects cannot be as narrowly interpreted as Prior has maintained that it should be.

Tense logic was not the only subject in which pragmatics was formally studied. In the 1960s Richard M. Montague (1932–71) made important contributions and advances in this area. Montague showed, for example, how truth-conditions can be defined for pragmatic operators in general, including symbols for demonstrative and personal pronouns, once we replace the notion of a possible world (or model) by the notion of a context of use (or what Montague also called an *index* or *point of reference*). The set-theoretic representation of a context of use need not deal with all the complexities of a real context, but only with those aspects that are relevant to the linguistic expressions in question – such as, for example, the local time of the context (for the truth-conditions of the tense operators), who is speaking (as the referent the first-person pronouns), who is being spoken to (as the referent of the second-person personal pronouns), the objects that are indicated by the speaker (as the referents of demonstrative pronouns), etc.

Montague showed that even though the truth-value (or extension) of a sentence in a given context of use (or point of reference) is not in general a simple recursive function of the extensions of the component expressions of that sentence in that context (or at least not in the case of sentences containing pragmatic operators that shift the point of reference, as do the tense operators), nevertheless the intension of the sentence is a recursive function of the intensions of its parts. Thus, because the intension of an expression will determine its extension at a given point of reference, a recursive definition of truth for the formulas of a formal pragmatic language is available in terms of the intensions of those formulas and their parts. Following Carnap [2.10], Montague represented the intension of an expression of a given type as a function from the possible contexts of use (or indices, or points of reference) to the extensions that the expression has in those contexts (cp. Montague [2.29], chapters 3 and 4). Thus, for instance, the intension of an individual constant (as the formal counterpart of a proper name) is a function from the different possible contexts of use (i.e. the contexts in which that name might be used) to the objects (i.e. extensions, if any) denoted by that individual constant; and the intension of an n-place predicate constant is a function from the different possible contexts of use to the classes of n-tuples of objects that are the extensions of that predicate in those contexts. Montague called the first kind of intension an *individual concept* and the second an n-ary *relation-in-intension*, or, where $n = 1$, a *property*. The intension of a declarative sentence, which Montague called a *proposition*, was then represented as a function from possible contexts of use to truth-values (the Fregean extensions of sentences).

By means of this way of representing intensions, Montague was able to give a formal, set-theoretic definition of the semantic notion of truth in a context of use (or at an index or point of reference) of the sentences of a formal pragmatic language, and in terms of that notion he was then able to define the related semantic notions of *logical truth* and *logical consequence* in the sense of general pragmatics. In this way, the logic of general pragmatics became a part of pure, logical semantics.

❧ INTENSIONAL LOGIC ❧

Pragmatic operators, on Montague's approach, amount to higher-order properties and relations (in intension) of propositions, which means that pragmatic operators can be represented by the higher-order predicates of an intensionalized type theory – e.g. a type theory in which a modal operator for necessity has been added. Such a higher-order logic is generally what is meant by intensional logic, and it gives further justification for the claim that pragmatics is part of semantics. Montague himself formulated two such intensional logics, one corresponding to a Russellian perspective in which the intension–extension (or sense–denotation) distinction is not fundamental, and the other corresponding to a Fregean perspective in which it is. It is the latter that came to be of central importance in what is now called Montague grammar.

Montague applied his first intensional logic to a variety of philosophical puzzles, including in particular the analysis of such entities as pains, events, tasks and obligations (cf. Montague [2.29], chapter 5). Sentences in which we purport to speak of such entities 'play a conspicuous role in philosophy, perceptual psychology, and everyday discourse', Montague observed, and 'it therefore appears desirable to investigate the nature of the entities in question, construct an exact and convenient language in which to speak of them, and analyze the pertinent notion of logical consequence' (ibid., 148). Tasks, for example, are taken by Montague to be certain two-place relations-in-intension between persons and moments, so that by the performance of a task R by a person x at a moment t we are taken to mean that x stands in the relation R to t, i.e. $R(x,t)$. Pains, and experiences in general are then taken be of the same ontological sort as tasks. Thus, for instance, 'the experience of seeing a tree is the relation-in-intension born by x to t just in case x sees a tree at t' (ibid., 151), and therefore for x to have the experience R at t is for x to bear the relation-in-intension R to t, i.e. $R(x,t)$. Similarly, for a person x to discharge or fulfil an obligation R at a moment t is just for x to bear the relation-in-intension R to t.

The point of the reduction of such 'dubious ontological categories' as pains, tasks and obligations to relations-in-intension, according to Montague, is that it enables us to have 'an exact language capable of naturally accommodating discourse about the dubious entities' – namely, the language of intensional logic – and therefore a language for which we have 'an intuitively satisfactory notion of logical consequence' by which we can resolve a variety of philosophical puzzles or paradoxes purportedly regarding such entities (ibid., 154). One such puzzle, for example, concerns the analysis of a sentence such as 'Jones sees a unicorn having the same height as a table actually before him', which, because it involves a visual experience of a relation between something that does not exist and something that does, has been taken by some philosophers as implying the existence of sense data (some of which are indicative of an existent object and others of which are not). On Montague's analysis, the truth of the sentence does not imply either that a unicorn exists or that sense data purportedly indicative of a unicorn exist.

In his analysis of this sentence, Montague distinguished a veridical from a non-veridical sense of 'sees' and paraphrased the latter as 'seems to see', which he analysed in terms of a relation between a person and a property (such as the property of seeing a unicorn) that the person seems to (but might not really) have. Thus, for the non-veridical sense of 'sees', Montague paraphrased 'Jones sees a unicorn' as 'Jones seems to see a unicorn', which, in terms of the relation of seeming-to-have (a property), can be formally represented as 'Seems(Jones, to see a unicorn)'. Here, the property Jones seems to (but need not really) have is denoted by the infinitive phrase 'to see a unicorn', which is the result of nominalizing the complex predicate 'see(s) a unicorn'.

As nominalized predicates, infinitive phrases can be formally represented as abstract singular terms, which means that in the case of a complex predicate phrase (such as 'see(s) a unicorn') we need a formal, variable-binding device, such as Frege's or Russell's, whereby the predicate phrase can be nominalized and transformed into an abstract singular term. Montague did not use either Frege's or Russell's devices, however, but adopted instead (at least in his later work) Alonzo Church's λ-operator to represent complex predicates, which, by deleting the parentheses that are formally part of a predicate, he then also used to represent the abstract singular terms that result when those complex predicates are nominalized. Thus, whereas '[λy $\exists z$(Unicorn(z) & Sees(y,z))](   )', with the accompanying pair of parentheses for argument-expressions, represents the complex predicate phrase 'is a y such that y sees a unicorn' (where 'sees' is used in its veridical sense), the related expression '[λy $\exists z$(Unicorn(z) & Sees(y,z))]', without the accompanying pair of parentheses, is not a predicate but an abstract singular term that represents the infinitive phrase 'to be a y such that y sees a unicorn', or, more simply, the infinitive phrase 'to see a unicorn'.

The sentence 'Jones seems to see a unicorn' can now be formally represented as 'Seems(Jones, [λy $\exists z$(Unicorn(z) & Sees(y,z))])', which, as indicated above, implies the existence neither of a unicorn nor of sense data (veridical or otherwise) indicative of a unicorn. Similarly, the sentence 'Jones sees a unicorn having the same height as a table actually before him', with 'sees' taken in its non-veridical sense, can now be formally analysed as $\exists x$[Table(x) & Before(x,Jones) & Seems(Jones, [λy

$\exists z$(Unicorn(z) & Sees(y,z) & Has-the-same-Height-as(z,x))])], which also implies neither the existence of a unicorn nor of sense data (veridical or otherwise) indicative of a unicorn.

This kind of analysis, it should be emphasized, depends essentially on the use of circumlocution and paraphrase, which in the end Montague found unsatisfactory. This is especially so in the case of intensional verbs where, unlike the situation with a perception verb such as 'see', no distinction can be made between a veridical and a non-veridical sense of the verb. The verb 'seek', for example, is an intensional verb in that, unlike an extensional verb such as 'find', it generates a referentially opaque context. That is why the argument,

Jones seeks a unicorn; therefore, there is a unicorn

is invalid, whereas the argument,

Jones finds a unicorn; therefore there is a unicorn

is valid, even though the two otherwise appear to have the same logical form.

The difference between these two arguments can be explained in terms of Montague's first intensional logic by paraphrasing 'seeks' as 'tries to find', so that 'Jones seeks a unicorn' is analysed as 'Jones tries to find a unicorn', which, because of the infinitive phrase 'to find a unicorn', has a different logical form from 'Jones finds a unicorn'. Thus, whereas 'Jones finds a unicorn' is analysed as '$\exists x$[Unicorn(x) & Finds(Jones,x)]', which does imply the existence of a unicorn, 'Jones tries to find a unicorn' is analysed as 'Tries(Jones, [$\lambda y \, \exists x$(Unicorn(x) & Finds(y,x))])', which does not imply the existence of a unicorn but rather only relates Jones to the property (intension) of *being a y such that y finds a unicorn* as a property that Jones tries to, but need not really, have. Even though the above two arguments (about Jones finding a unicorn and Jones seeking a unicorn) appear to have the same logical form (in which case they would both be valid or both invalid), they are viewed on this analysis, where 'seeks' is paraphrased as 'tries to find', as really having different logical forms. In particular, whereas the second argument has the valid form,

$\exists x$ [Unicorn(x) & Finds(Jones, x)];
therefore, $\exists x$ Unicorn(x),

the first is assumed to have the different form,

Tries(Jones, [$\lambda y \, \exists x$(Unicorn(x) & Finds(y, x))]);
therefore, $\exists x$ Unicorn(x),

which is easily seen to be invalid.

The difficulty here is that although the above logical analysis explains the difference between 'Jones finds a unicorn' and 'Jones tries to find a unicorn', it still leaves unexplained the use of paraphrase in the analysis of 'Jones seeks a unicorn'. In English this sentence clearly has the same grammatical form as 'Jones finds a unicorn', and it seems reasonable to maintain that they have the same logical form as well – which leaves us with the original problem of explaining why what then appears to be the same argument form is valid with 'finds' but invalid with 'seeks'.

It was for this reason that Montague came to replace his first intensional logic, which, as indicated, corresponds to a Russellian view of higher-order logic in which the sense-denotation, or intension-extension, distinction is not fundamental, by his second intensional logic, which corresponds to a Fregean perspective in which that distinction is fundamental. Indeed, what Montague did was add an intension-forming operator '^' and an extension-forming operator '$^\vee$' to (Alonzo Church's formulation of) the simple theory of types (using Church's λ-operator), so that if ϕ is a meaningful (well-formed) expression of the new intensional logic, then both '$^\wedge \phi$' and '$^\vee \phi$' are also meaningful and stand for the intension (or sense) of ϕ and the extension (or denotation) of ϕ, respectively. Relative to this framework, Montague proposed that the direct object-expression (such as the quantifier phrase 'a unicorn') of any transitive verb (such as 'find' and 'seek') should be interpreted as standing not for what that expression would otherwise stand for in its occurrence as the grammatical subject of a sentence, but for the intension (or sense) of that expression instead. In the case of a quantifier phrase such as 'a unicorn', such an intension was represented by '$^\wedge[\lambda F\ \exists x(\text{Unicorn}(x)\ \&\ F(x))]$', which stands for the sense of *being a property that a unicorn has*, so that both 'Jones finds a unicorn' and 'Jones seeks a unicorn' are similarly analysed (ultimately) as 'Find(Jones, $^\wedge[\lambda F\ \exists x(\text{Unicorn}(x)\ \&\ F(x))])$' and 'Seek(Jones, $^\wedge[\lambda F\ \exists x(\text{Unicorn}(x)\ \&\ F(x))])$', which means that they have essentially the same logical form after all.

All transitive verbs, on this analysis, generate an intensional or referentially opaque context when they are applied to a direct-object expression, which means that 'find' is no different from 'seek' in this regard. Where they differ is not in their logical form, but in what additional conditions apply to those verbs as meaning postulates – such as, for example, a meaning postulate that allows the intensional context generated by 'find' to be transformed into an extensional context. (An intensional expression can be transformed into an extensional expression by applying the extension-operator; and, therefore, an intensional expression of the form $^\wedge\phi$ can be transformed into $^\vee {}^\wedge\phi$, which reduces simply to ϕ.) Thus, the reason why the existence of a unicorn follows from the truth of the one sentence but not from the truth of the other does not depend upon a difference in their logical form, but rather because whereas the one verb, 'find', is subject to a meaning postulate that allows for this inference, the other verb, 'seek', does not also have such a meaning postulate associated with it. (A related but different analysis in terms of active and de-activated referential concepts – where all referential concepts, including those based upon proper as well as common names, are represented by quantifier phrases – is given in Cocchiarella [2.17]. On this analysis, a de-activated referential expression, such as 'a unicorn' in both 'Jones finds a unicorn' and 'Jones seeks a unicorn', is represented by a nominalized predicate expression of the form '$[\lambda F\ \exists x(\text{Unicorn}(x)\ \&\ F(x))]$'. Unlike Montague's analysis, however, this analysis does not depend upon the intension- and extension-operators, but only on a conceptualist view of the difference in a type-free, second-order logic with nominalized predicates as abstract singular terms between the concepts that predicates stand for in their role as predicates and the intensional objects that their nominalizations denote as abstract singular terms.)

❧ UNIVERSAL MONTAGUE GRAMMAR ❧

In addition to the development of an intensional logic as a new theoretical framework for philosophy, Montague also constructed a framework within set theory that he called *universal grammar* (where 'universal' was taken only in the sense of utmost generality). Such a universal grammar was designed to contain a universal syntax and a universal semantics that could be applied to natural languages as well as to formal, artificial languages. The syntax and semantics of a natural language (or at least of a significant fragment thereof), according to Montague, could be given a description (within his universal grammar) that was no less mathematically precise than could be given for the artificial languages of mathematical logicians, so that (contrary to the claims of ordinary language philosophers) natural languages were no different in this regard from formal languages.

Montague's set-theoretic description of a language $\mathscr{L}$ (natural or otherwise) amounts to representing $\mathscr{L}$ by a system $\langle L, R \rangle$, where L is a syntactically disambiguated language (i.e. in effect, an artificial construct) and R is a two-place relation of syntactical analysis that relates expressions of $\mathscr{L}$ with expressions of L. (R will in general be a one–many relation because it will relate a syntactically ambiguous expression of $\mathscr{L}$ with several different disambiguated expressions of L as alternative analyses of that expression.) The disambiguated (artificial) language L consists in part of a free algebra (generated by a set of basic phrases), a set of structural operations on strings of expressions of L, a set of syntactical rules (specifying the type of expression that results when a structural operation is applied to a string of expressions of certain given types), and a specification of the syntactic categories of L, including in particular the category of the declarative sentences of L. The family of phrases of the different syntactic categories of L can then be defined inductively in terms of the basic phrases of L, and the closure conditions determined by the syntactical rules and structural operations of L (cf. Montague [2.29], chapter 7). By way of example, Montague specifies a set of syntactic categories, structural operations and syntactic rules for a fragment of English and shows how the various phrases of that fragment can be precisely characterized in terms of certain basic phrases of those categories. He also shows how his second intensional logic can be similarly specified in strictly formal terms.

Whereas the basic aim in syntax is to characterize the various syntactical categories of expressions of a language, including in particular the category of declarative sentences, the basic aim of semantics, according to Montague, is to characterize the notion of a true declarative sentence (under an interpretation) of that language and then, in terms of that notion, the relation of logical consequence between the declarative sentences of the language. By way of achieving this aim, Montague constructed a model theory based upon the theory of types of his second, Fregean intensional logic and showed how all the different types of intensions (or senses), as well as all the different types of extensions, can be given set-theoretic representations in his model theory. In this way, by correlating the different syntactic categories of a given language with the logical types of his intensional logic, Montague was able to characterize the semantic categories of a language (natural or otherwise), and he was then able to define the notions of truth and logical consequence between the declarative sentences of that language in terms of the model-theoretic structures (which he calls *Fregean interpretations*) associated with those semantic categories. (A Fregean interpretation includes not only a set of possible worlds, but also moments of time and contexts of use in those worlds.)

A third component of Montague's universal grammar, in addition to universal syntax and universal semantics, is a formally specified theory of translation. The theory involves correlating the syntactic categories of two languages $\mathscr{L}$ and $\mathscr{L}'$, where $\mathscr{L} = \langle L, R \rangle$ and $\mathscr{L}' = \langle L', R' \rangle$, in such a way as to generate a homomorphism (a certain type of mathematical function) from the free algebra underlying L to the free algebra underlying L'. Besides translating well-formed expressions of $\mathscr{L}$ into well-formed expressions of $\mathscr{L}'$, such a homomorphism also induces a Fregean interpretation (i.e. a certain model-theoretic structure) for $\mathscr{L}'$ in terms of a Fregean interpretation for $\mathscr{L}$. Thus, by constructing a translation function from a (fragment of a) natural language such as

English into his Fregean intensional logic, Montague is able to correlate the model-theoretic structures (Fregean interpretations) defined for the latter with model-theoretic structures for the former.

'The principal use of translations', according to Montague, 'is the semantical one of inducing interpretations' ([2.29], 232). Such an interpretation is really just a set-theoretic structure and does not provide the kind of perspicuous interpretation (by means of logical forms) that a translation into Montague's Fregean intensional logic does. Indeed, even Montague, who had at one time maintained that all philosophical analyses were to be carried out as definitional extensions of set theory (cf. [2.29], 154), did not remain satisfied with the idea of set theory as a *lingua philosophica*, and it was for that reason that he went on to construct his different intensional logics. Thus, according to Montague, 'philosophy is always capable of enlarging itself; that is, by metamathematical or model-theoretic means – means available within set theory – one can "justify" a language or theory that transcends set theory, and then proceed to transact a new branch of philosophy within the new language. It is now time to take such a step and to lay the foundations of intensional languages' (ibid., 155). In constructing and applying his Fregean intensional logic, Montague showed how – through a translation (which really amounts to a precise logical analysis) of English into an applied form of that intensional logic – a variety of constructions in English, including especially quantifier phrases and intensional verbs, can be given an intuitively satisfying and natural representation/interpretation in terms of that intensional language.

❧ SPEECH-ACT THEORY AND THE RETURN ❧ TO PRAGMATICS

The formal approach to the philosophy of language has been criticized, we have noted, by so-called ordinary–language philosophers. This criticism has been described in terms of a conflict between a speech-act (or communication-intention) theory of meaning and the formal truth-conditional theory of meaning, such as is given in Montague grammar (cf. Strawson [2.41], chapter 9). The meaning of a sentence is not in general the same as its truth-conditions, it is maintained, even when the latter is relativized to contexts of use; for, in addition to declarative sentences there are also imperatives, optatives, interrogatives, exclamatories, etc., which may have compliance- or fulfilment- conditions instead of, or in addition to, truth-conditions. The fundamental concept in the theory of meaning, on this view, is not the concept of truth but the concept of a speaker's meaning something by an audience-directed speech act (cp. Grice [2.23], chapter 5).

In performing a speech act (in a context of use), a speaker performs a number of distinguishable acts, including in particular what is called an illocutionary act, which in the simple case can be described as an act of the form $F(P)$ consisting of an *illocutionary force F* and of a propositional content P. The illocutionary force of a speech act determines how it is to be taken – e.g. as a statement, a question, a promise, an apology, an order, a declaration, an offer, a refusal, each of which is a different kind of illocutionary act (cp. Searle [2.38], chapter 1). Which illocutionary act is being performed in a context of use depends upon such illocutionary force-markers as verb mood, word order, punctuation signs and intonation. English and most other natural languages also have *performative verbs*, such as 'state', 'promise' 'ask', 'order', 'apologize', 'vow', that stand for different illocutionary forces. A performative sentence is a declarative sentence in which a performative verb occurs in such a way that a literal utterance of that sentence constitutes the performance by the speaker of the illocutionary act that the performative verb stands for.

Because performative sentences are in the indicative mood, some philosophers of language have thought that a semantic analysis of illocutionary acts could be given in terms of the truth-conditional semantics (relativized to contexts of use) of the performative sentences that could be correlated with those acts, and that, therefore, the logical forms of a Fregean intensional logic such as Montague's might suffice for the representation of such acts after all. Such an approach, however, gives no account of how non-declarative sentences are used to perform illocutionary acts, and in that regard it would fail to explain the relation of illocutionary entailment between performative and non-declarative sentences (such as between 'I ask if it is raining' and 'Is it raining?'). Indeed, in general, the attempt to reduce the meaning of all the different kinds of sentences that can be used in speech acts to an analysis based upon a logic only of sense and denotation (or intension and extension), or even just to a logic of extensions (as some philosophers of language insist), has failed to explain a variety of cases of truth-conditional and illocutionary entailments between sentences, and in that regard it has also failed to provide adequate identity criteria for the different kinds of speech acts that could be performed in a given context of use.

This does not mean that we must give up the project of an ideal language by which to perspicuously represent the logical forms of the different sentences that we can utter in a context of use, i.e. an ideal language by which we can represent and explain our linguistic competence in the use and understanding of language. Rather, what needs to be done is to develop intensional logic into a framework that contains an illocutionary logic as well, such as can be obtained by extending Montague's Fregean logic of sense and denotation by adding to it both new syncategorematic expressions to represent illocutionary forces and certain new values (e.g. a value of success and its failure, which can be called 'insuccess') to represent the successful performance or non-performance of speech acts in different possible contexts of use (cp. Vanderveken [2.44] and [2.45]). On this view, instead of identifying linguistic competence with the speaker's ability to understand the truth conditions of sentences, we should identify it with the speaker's ability to understand the illocutionary acts that can be performed by sentences taken literally in different contexts of use. That is, instead of representing the meaning of a sentence by a function from possible contexts of use to truth-values, the meaning is to be represented by a function from possible contexts of use to the illocutionary acts that can be performed by a literal utterance of that sentence in those contexts. Also, in addition to the syncategorematic signs for the logical constants (by which the truth-conditions of complex sentences are determined), the logical forms of the sentences in such an enlarged ideal language will now contain syncategorematic counterparts to those syntactic features of the sentences of natural language that determine which types of illocutionary acts can be performed by literal utterances of those sentences in different contexts of use.

One of the principles of such an enlarged framework is that an illocutionary act of the form $F(P)$, where F is an illocutionary act and P is a propositional content, has conditions of success as well as conditions of satisfaction. By the conditions of success of such an act is meant the conditions that must obtain in a context of use in order for the speaker to succeed in performing that act in that context, and by the conditions of satisfaction is meant the conditions that must obtain in the world of a context of use in order for that act to be satisfied in that context. This notion of satisfaction is broader than the notion of a truth condition. Thus, for example, although an assertion is satisfied if, and only if, it is *true*, an order is satisfied if, and only if, it is *obeyed*; and, similarly, a promise is satisfied if, and only if, it is *kept*, and a request is satisfied if, and only if, it is *granted* – and so on for each of the other illocutionary forces.

The conditions of success and satisfaction of an illocutionary act are determined, on this analysis, by certain components of the illocutionary force of that act – such as the *illocutionary point* of the force (which is the assertive point, the commissive point, the directive point, the declarative point or the expressive point), the *mode of achievement* (which determines how the point must be achieved), the *propositional content* (which determines the states of affairs that must obtain or come about for an act with that force to be successful), the *preparatory and sincerity conditions* (which determine the propositions presupposed by a speaker performing an act with that force, or which express the psychological states or modes of propositional attitudes of the speaker), and the degree of strength of the psychological states that enter into the sincerity conditions. These components of an illocutionary force are represented as parts of the logical form of that force, and the set of all possible illocutionary forces is recursively definable in terms of these components and five of the simplest types of illocutionary force that are taken as primitives of the framework (cp. Searle and Vanderveken [2.39]).

In addition to a recursive characterization of the class of illocutionary forces, the new expanded framework, which some call *general semantics*, allows for a variety of new semantic notions not realizable in intensional logic alone. In addition to *truth-conditional consistency*, for example, there is also the notion of a sentence being *illocutionarily consistent*, and, in addition to a sentence being *analytically satisfied* or *analytically unsatisfied* (such as 'I exist' and 'I do not exist', respectively), there is the notion of a sentence being *analytically successful* or *analytically unsuccessful* (such as 'I am speaking now' and 'I am not speaking now'). Also, at least eight different logical types of entailment between sentences can be characterized in the enlarged framework, such as truth-conditional and illocutionary entailments, truth-conditional entailments of success and satisfaction (cp. Vanderveken [2.45]). This enlarged framework is not at odds with Montague's intensional logic, it should be emphasized, but is really a conservative extension of the latter that simply adds a recursive theory of success and satisfaction to Montague's theory of truth. Of course, one important consequence of such an addition is that the primary units of meaning and communication are not isolated propositions but illocutionary acts of the form $F(P)$, which means that many illocutionary acts with strictly equivalent propositional contents have different conditions of success and therefore are not identical.

General semantics, on this interpretation, deals with the logical structure of all possible sentence and utterance meanings of all possible natural and scientific languages. The ideal language constructed in such a framework is intended to represent the *universals of language use*, i.e. both the formal and material universal features of both natural and scientific language. As governing the success conditions for the performance of illocutionary acts, the universal laws of this ideal language are viewed as reflecting *a priori* laws of thought, and as governing the satisfaction conditions of those acts, these same laws are viewed as reflecting *a priori* laws regarding the logical structure of the world (Vanderveken [2.44], 58 ff.). Clearly, such a view brings us back to something like the *characteristica universalis* originally envisaged by Leibniz.

General semantics includes pragmatics in that it contains the notion of a possible context of use of language as an essential part. But general semantics deals with speech acts taken only literally. That is, general semantics reduces speaker meaning to sentence meaning by assuming that a speaker who utters a sentence in a context of use means to perform the illocutionary act literally expressed by that sentence in that context – when that illocutionary act, taken literally, can be performed. A speaker may intend his speech act not to be taken literally, however, as in the case of metaphor, irony and certain indirect speech acts. Also, given a conversational background, a speaker may mean to perform a secondary non-literal illocutionary act in addition to his primary illocutionary act taken literally, but one that is not in fact entailed by the primary illocutionary act in any of the senses of entailment of general semantics. These kinds of secondary illocutionary acts are called *conversational implicatures* (cp. Grice [2.23], Part I). A professor, for example, in a context in which he is asked by a student what he thinks of the latter's outline for a proposed research project, does not literally imply his disapproval when he answers 'It is typed very nicely' – but such disapproval may be conversationally implied in the context in question. The analysis and interpretation of these kinds of 'implicatures', and the development of a general theory of speaker meaning capable of interpreting non-literal utterances, remains today a proper part of the task of pragmatics (cp. Vanderveken [2.44], 71).

Pragmatics, as the study of non-literal speaker meaning, remains then an essential part of semiotics, because 'the competence speakers have to perform and to understand non-literal illocutionary acts and conversational implicatures is part of their competence to use language and communicate' (ibid.). In this regard, pragmatics imposes an additional condition on the adequacy of a framework such as general semantics and requires a development of its own in terms, for example, of the notions of what Grice calls *conversational maxims* (or directives) and *conversational background*. Whether – and, if so, to what extent – pragmatics in the sense of the rules of conversation can be given a formal analysis and incorporated into an ideal language remains yet to be determined. In any case, the notion of a *lingua philosophica* as an ideal language containing both an intensional and illocutionary logic is no longer merely a programme but has already in many respects been realized.

❧ BIBLIOGRAPHY ❧

2.1 Addison, J. W. L., L. Henkin and A. Tarski *The Theory of Models*, Amsterdam: North-Holland, 1965.

2.2 Boole, G. *An Investigation of the Laws of Thought*, London: Walton & Maberly, 1853.

2.3 Cassirer, E. *The Philosophy of Symbolic Forms*, vol. 1: *Language*, New Haven: Yale University Press, 1955.

2.4 Cohen, J. 'On the Project of a Universal Character', *Mind*, 63 (1954): 49–63.

2.5 Carnap, R. [1928] *The Logical Structure of the World*, trans. R. George, Berkeley: University of California Press, 1967.

2.6 —— [1936] *The Logical Syntax of Language*, trans. A. Smeaton, London: Routledge & Kegan Paul, 1937, repr. 1951.

2.7 —— 'Testability and Meaning', Part I: *Philosophy of Science*, 4 (1936): 420–71; Part II: *Philosophy of Science*, 5 (1937): 2–40.

2.8 —— [1942] *Introduction to Semantics*, Cambridge, Mass.: Harvard University Press, 1959.

2.9 —— *Meaning and Necessity*, Chicago: University of Chicago Press, 1947.

2.10 —— [1955] 'Notes on Semantics', published posthumously in *Philosophia*, 2 (1972): 1–54.

2.11 —— 'The Methodological Character of Theoretical Concepts', in H. Feigl and M. Scriven, eds, *The Foundations of Science and the Concepts of Psychology and Psychoanalysis*, Minneapolis: University of Minnesota Press, 1956: 38–76.

2.12 —— 'On the use of Hilbert's ε-Operator in Scientific Theories', in Y. Bar-Hillel, ed., *Essays on the Foundations of Mathematics, Dedicated to A. A. Fraenkel*, Jerusalem: Magnes Press, 1961: 156–69.

2.13 Church, A. 'A Formulation of the Simple Theory of Types', *Journal of Symbolic Logic*, 5 (1940): 56–68.

2.14 Cocchiarella, N. 'Philosophical Perspectives on Quantification in Tense and Modal Logic', in D. Gabbay and F. Guenther, eds, *Handbook of Philosophical Logic*, vol. 2, Dordrecht: D. Reidel, 1984: 309–53.

2.15 —— *Logical Studies in Early Analytic Philosophy*, Columbus: Ohio State University Press, 1987.

2.16 —— 'Predication versus Membership in the Distinction between Logic as Language and Logic as Calculus', *Synthese*, 77 (1988): 37–72.

2.17 —— 'Conceptualism, Realism, and Intensional Logic', *Topoi*, 8(1989): 15–34.

2.18 Frege, G. [1879] 'Begriffsschrift: A Formula Language, Modeled upon that of Arithmetic, for Pure Thought', in J. van Heijenoort, ed., *From Frege to Goedel*, Cambridge, Mass.: Harvard University Press, 1967.

2.19 —— [1893] *The Basic Laws of Arithmetic*, trans. and with an introduction by M. Furth, Berkeley: University of California Press, 1964.

2.20 —— *Conceptual Notation and Related Articles*, ed. and trans. T. W. Bynum, Oxford: Oxford University Press, 1972.

2.21 —— *Posthumous Writings*, ed. H. Hermes, F. Kambartel and F. Kaulbach, Chicago: University of Chicago Press, 1979.

2.22 Goodman, N. *The Structure of Appearance*, Cambridge, Mass.: Harvard University Press, 1951.

2.23 Grice, P. *Studies in the Way of Words*, Cambridge, Mass.: Harvard University Press, 1989.

2.24 Hahn, H., O. Neurath and R. Carnap [1929] *The Scientific Conception of the World: The Vienna Circle*, Dordrecht: D. Reidel, 1973.

2.25 Hempel, C. 'Problems and Changes in the Empiricist Criterion of Meaning', *Revue Internationale de Philosophie*, 11 (1950): 41–63.

2.26 —— 'The Concept of Cognitive Significance: A Reconsideration', *Proceedings of the American Academy of Arts and Sciences*, 80 (1951): 61–75.

2.27 Knowlson, J. *Universal Language Schemes in England and France, 1600–1800*, Toronto: University of Toronto Press, 1975.

2.28 Küng, G. *Ontology and the Logistic Analysis of Language*, Dordrecht: D. Reidel, 1967.

2.29 Montague, R. M. *Formal Philosophy*, ed. and with an introduction by R. Thomason, New Haven, Conn.: Yale University Press, 1974.

2.30 Morris, C. W. [1938] 'Foundations of the Theory of Signs', in *International Encyclopedia of Unified Science*, vol. 1, Chicago: University of Chicago Press, 1955: 78–137.

2.31 Neurath, O. [1938] 'Unified Science as Encyclopedic Integration', in *International Encyclopedia of Unified Science*, vol. 1, Chicago: University of Chicago Press, repr. 1955: 1–27.

2.32 Partee, B., A. ter Meulen and R. Wall *Mathematical Methods in Linguistics*, Dordrecht: Kluwer Academic, 1990.

2.33 Prior, A. *Past, Present and Future*, Oxford: Oxford University Press, 1967.

2.34 Russell, B. [1914] *Our Knowledge of the External World*, London: George Allen & Unwin, 1952.

2.35 —— [1918] *The Philosophy of Logical Atomism*, ed. and with an introduction by D. Pears, La Salle, Ill.: Open Court, 1985.

2.36 —— *My Philosophical Development*, London: George Allen & Unwin, 1959.

2.37 Rynin, D. 'Vindication of L*G*C*L P*S*T*VSM', *Proceedings and Addresses of the American Philosophical Association* (1957): 46–66.

2.38 Searle, J. *Expression and Meaning*, Cambridge: Cambridge University Press, 1979.

2.39 —— and D. Vanderveken *Foundations of Illocutionary Logic*, Cambridge: Cambridge University Press, 1985.

2.40 Strawson, P. F. 'Carnap's Views on Constructed Systems versus Natural Languages in Analytic Philosophy', in P. A. Schilpp, ed., *The Philosophy of Rudolf Carnap*, La Salle, Ill.: Open Court, 1963: 503–18.

2.41 —— *Logico-Linguistic Papers*, London: Methuen, 1971.

2.42 Tarski, A. 'The Semantic Conception of Truth', *Philosophy and Phenomenological Research*, 4 (1944): 341–75.

2.43 —— *Logic, Semantics, Metamathematics*, Oxford: Oxford University Press, 1956.

2.44 Vanderveken, D. *Meaning and Speech Acts*, vols 1 & 2, Cambridge: Cambridge University Press, 1990.

2.45 —— 'On the Unification of Speech Act Theory and Formal Semantics', in

P. R. Cohen and M. E. Pollack, eds, *Intentions and Communications*, Cambridge, Mass.: MIT Press, 1990: 195–220.

2.46 Van Themaat, P. 'Formalized and Artificial Languages', *Synthese*, 14 (1962): 320–6.

2.47 Wittgenstein, L. [1921] *Tractatus Logico-Philosophicus*, trans. D. Pears and B. F. McGuiness, London: Routledge & Kegan Paul, 1971.

2.48 —— *Philosophical Investigations*, trans. G. E. M. Anscombe, New York: Macmillan, 1953.

CHAPTER 3

Metaphysics I (1900–45)
William James DeAngelis

❧❖❧

❧ INTRODUCTORY REMARKS ❧

The first half of the twentieth century marks a change in philosophical attitudes towards metaphysics which is as sharp and dramatic as any in the history of philosophy in the English-speaking world. For the preceding three centuries, metaphysics had been a central concern of European philosophers. The central assumption of these metaphysical philosophers – that the human intellect is capable of uncovering important aspects of the nature of reality which the sciences and common sense cannot – was widespread from the time of Descartes until the present century. The bolder metaphysical systems associated with continental rationalism held that many of the most important truths about reality are of this type. Further, it cannot be denied that the work of their leading British counterparts – even those associated with the more cautious empiricist tradition – included striking metaphysical claims and rested upon deep metaphysical assumptions.

To be sure, Hume and Kant, the acknowledged philosophical giants of the late eighteenth century, offered explicit warnings about the central assumptions and the doctrines of these metaphysical philosophers. These, however, were neither heeded nor, it seems, well understood by philosophers of their own or closely subsequent generations. Later, in the nineteenth century, currents of principled anti-metaphysical thought became more common and influential in Europe and the United States. Even so, metaphysical philosophy continued to flourish on the European continent, and, in Britain and the United States, it is fair to say that it flourished as never before. As the twentieth century neared, traditional metaphysics, in its most ambitious and systematic form, was alive and well in the English-speaking world.

All this was about to change dramatically and, it would certainly now appear, irrevocably. To be sure, many prominent English-speaking philosophers of the early twentieth century and even beyond continued to engage in philosophical activities that were more or less continuous with traditional metaphysics. Nonetheless, far more powerful philosophical movements developed during this period which were destined both to threaten the very existence of metaphysics and to change its nature profoundly. These dominant tendencies of thought, when not avowedly anti-metaphysical, sought – at the very least – to place strict limitations upon both the methods and the domain of metaphysics. This essay concerns itself with these philosophical movements, their principled opposition to traditional metaphysics, and their dramatic effects on the conception, the scope, and the practice of metaphysics in Britain and the United States during this century. As such, it reflects its author's conviction that these movements are of such surpassing importance, that they alone constitute the proper focus of this effort.

❧ ABSOLUTE IDEALISM: NEO-HEGELIANISM ❧ IN BRITAIN AND THE UNITED STATES

At the beginning of the twentieth century, neo-Hegelian philosophy was well represented by important philosophical figures in England and the United States. Doctrines inspired by Hegel were a major, if not *the* major, focus of philosophical interest and discussion. This was especially true in metaphysics. In the late nineteenth century and in the early years of the twentieth, F. H. Bradley (1846–1924) and Bernard Bosanquet (1848–1923) of Oxford, J. E. McTaggart (1866–1925) of Cambridge, and Josiah Royce (1855–1916) at Harvard were among the most prominent English-speaking philosophers. All of them held Hegelian metaphysical views. While their philosophical motives and styles varied, and they certainly differed on matters of substance, their most basic metaphysical beliefs were remarkably similar. Speaking generally it can be said that each represented, in his own way, a school of thought which was still in its ascendancy at this time and shortly thereafter. This ambitiously metaphysical school of thought came to be known as absolute idealism.

The views of this school were remarkable in many respects. For one thing they included metaphysical doctrines that were strikingly at odds with fundamental beliefs of common sense and – perhaps historically and culturally even more significant – with those of modern science. Its methods and conclusions were dramatically contrary to the traditional – and more cautious – empiricist tradition in British philosophy. This latter feature was one which its British advocates saw in a most positive light as a long overdue development. It was felt that Bradley, who was regarded as the leading figure of this movement, had

77

brought British philosophy at last into the mainstream of European thought. For a decade or two, it even seemed that this development would prove to be permanent.

It was true enough that absolute idealism had almost nothing in common with the empirical doctrines and methods of Locke, Berkeley, Hume and Mill – arguably the most influential British philosophers of the preceding centuries. Its influence, however, was not to prove permanent in the English-speaking world. As we shall see, its prominence constituted only a brief break with long-standing traditions in British philosophy. Indeed, the most noteworthy early twentieth-century metaphysical thought in Britain can be seen to have been, in both its motives and content, a self-conscious and energetic reaction against absolute idealism, its doctrines, methods and spirit. This is most notably true of the early work of G. E. Moore and Bertrand Russell, who would prove to play a major role in discrediting the movement. Once they had rejected neo-Hegelian metaphysics, neither of the two ever wavered in his fierce opposition to it. Indeed each spent a good part of his philosophical career, in effect, constructing what he hoped would be a successful alternative. Significantly, these alternatives fell very clearly within the longer-standing traditions of British philosophy with which Bradley and the others had broken. It has been observed that Hume and Berkeley would have been sadly puzzled by the pages of Bradley or Hegel, but that either might have conversed quite naturally with Moore, and even with Russell in his less technical moments.

The work of Ludwig Wittgenstein, who, as a young philosopher, was himself influenced by Russell and, to a lesser degree, by Moore, deserves mention in this context too. While Wittgenstein never concerned himself specifically with Hegel, Bradley or their followers, his philosophical work consistently emphasized that writings like theirs amounted quite literally to *nonsense*. His remarkable statement of this view in *Tractatus Logico-Philosophicus* indeed helped inspire a prominent school of philosophy, logical positivism, which sought, as we shall see, to undermine *all* metaphysics.

The influence of Moore, Russell, Wittgenstein and the logical positivists was scarcely less dramatic in the United States than in Britain. In addition, the powerfully influential American pragmatists, notably C. S. Peirce, William James and John Dewey, were also dissatisfied with neo-Hegelian thought and sought to construct a philosophy which went right where they believed it had gone wrong. More generally, the philosophical perspective of these influential pragmatists was openly hostile to metaphysics in its traditional forms. While Peirce and James, like Russell, held some hope that metaphysics, through great effort and radical change, could be reformed, the notion that metaphysics was a species of nonsense came to have as much currency in the United States as it did in Britain, with similar long-term results.

Certainly, absolute idealism has ceased to be taken seriously in Britain and the United States. The school, so influential at the turn of the century, when it was defended by philosophers who were highly regarded and – in some cases – very much in their prime, is barely mentioned less than one century later. Still, it is important to get some sense of what Bradley and the others believed in order to understand the vehement reaction against it which galvanized much early twentieth-century thought in England and America.

For one thing, absolute idealism was an ambitiously metaphysical school of thought. It sought to establish unassailable truths about the universe taken as a whole. This metaphysical concern with the *whole* of reality was especially insisted upon. It was contrasted with the approaches of non-philosophical disciplines which, it was believed, were necessarily partial and fragmentary. The absolute idealists insisted too, that the truths that they had uncovered were of a different sort from those established in other disciplines: they were presumed to be absolutely necessary, ultimate and essential to the very nature of reality.

Perhaps most important, Bradley insisted that reality constituted an *indissoluble unity*. To explain this, consider that we all believe as a natural matter of course that the universe contains a very large number and variety of objects that are often independent of one another, having various different properties and interrelations. Galaxies, stars, planets, people, rocking chairs, pumpkins and earthworms exist, have very different properties and can arrange themselves in different ways with respect to one another. Seemingly nothing could be more commonplace. Yet this is exactly what absolute idealism denied. Against this common mode of thought, it was urged that the universe was intrinsically an unsegmented and undifferentiable whole. The sciences and common sense, which deal with this or that *object*, with this or that *portion* of reality, were thought to involve a necessary element of distortion or falsification. Reality was essentially one – any intimation that it consisted of independent parts was condemned as necessarily false.

Hegel's British disciples never merely assumed this. Bradley set the philosophical tone by arguing for this view in a remarkable book, published in 1893, called *Appearance and Reality* [3.6]. He believed that the universe, reality or, to use his own term, 'the Absolute', did not consist of parts and that any notion that it did was, in the final analysis, incoherent. His arguments for this perhaps owed more to Zeno than to Hegel. One of his most basic premises became a subject of controversy and a special target for criticism. The view, which he regarded as a necessary truth, is known as the doctrine of internal relations.

According to it, any relational fact about an object – for example, that it is below another object – is really a fact about the intrinsic nature of the object in question. In effect, Bradley refused to take relations as ultimate and unreducible: they are not real and are better thought of as intrinsic properties of objects. The unreality of relations – itself a striking view – had, for Bradley, even more remarkable consequences. He thought it follows from this principle that whenever two things are related, each can be said to 'enter into the nature of the other'. When x is below y, then being below y is part of the nature of x and being above x is part of the nature of y, so that y is part of the nature of x and x is part of the nature of y. Now since everything presumably bears some relation to everything else, it follows that everything else enters into the nature of any given thing. Using some auxiliary principles, Bradley arrived at the remarkable conclusion that there is no 'other thing' relative to any given thing – and this, in turn, meant that the only thing that exists is one all-consuming entity. This line of thought was characteristic of Bradley who often directed *reductio ad absurdum* arguments against common modes of thought that divide reality into independent objects with relations. His intent was to show that this mode collapses, and leaves his own metaphysical view of reality as the only viable alternative. The doctrine of internal relations, which holds that relations between presumably different objects are unreal and reduced to intrinsic properties, is a crucial step in his central argument.

It is helpful to draw some of the further consequences of this striking metaphysical claim. Since Bradley believed that reality does not consist of parts and is not (to use his own phrase of contempt) 'a bare conjunction' of objects, he boldly drew the conclusion that it was not physical. If reality were physical, then it would be segmentable and this is just what he insisted was not the case. So reality was claimed to be spiritual. Bradley was an idealist and, so, a monist too. Unlike Berkeley – British philosophy's other great idealist – who embraced idealism in part because he believed it was the only metaphysical view compatible with common sense, Bradley endorsed it for very different reasons. He saw in it the *benefit* of being antithetical to common sense, which he completely rejected.

Bradley's rejection of any segmentation in reality is connected to his remarkable conclusion that space and time – conceptually segmentable themselves – are also unreal. McTaggart attempted to supplement Bradley's case with ingenious *reductio ad absurdum* arguments designed to show that the concepts of space and time are incoherent. Far from soft-pedalling these nearly incredible claims, Bradley and McTaggart insisted on them explicitly. Far from being vexed by *any* of his surprising conclusions, Bradley and virtually all his followers were very much *attracted* to them. Their striking rejection of common sense and their recognition of only a unitary spiritual reality, jibed well with their shared sense – one that could fairly be characterized as religious or mystical – that the apparent defects of the world are somehow unreal and that, in some ultimate sense, everything is all right.

All this invites a number of very basic questions. How could the beliefs of science and common life which are so basic and which, after all, seem to serve us all pretty well, be false? Bradley acknowledged this question and insisted that such beliefs concern only *appearances*, whereas his metaphysical concept of the absolute was the only correct accounting of the reality which contrasts with those appearances. Bradley's metaphysics of the absolute was, he believed, the real truth about reality – a truth the magnitude of which only philosophy could establish.

❧ C. S. PEIRCE: EARLY ANTI-METAPHYSICAL ❧ STIRRINGS

Charles Sanders Peirce (1839–1914) is now acknowledged as the originator of the pragmatic school of philosophy in the United States and often as its most profound practitioner. His work and thought – some of which was published as early as the 1870s – was largely unnoticed during his lifetime. While he inspired and greatly influenced the early leaders of the pragmatist school in personal discussions, his own writings remained almost entirely unpublished and did not themselves have much influence until they were compiled and published posthumously, beginning in 1931, as *The Collected Writings of Charles Sanders Peirce* [3.18]. The son of a Harvard University mathematician, he was given a rigorous home education. He had a great talent for logic, mathematics and the sciences, and he took an undergraduate degree in chemistry. Eventually he turned to philosophy. He lectured on philosophy briefly at Harvard, and then again at Johns Hopkins; he was not, however, well suited to the life of a university professor. He was a frighteningly perceptive intellectual critic who did not spare his own thoughts. He was rarely, if ever, satisfied with his own written work. His only long-term professional position was as a surveyor for the US Coast and Geodetic Service.

Peirce, like many other twentieth-century philosophers with mathematical and scientific training, was convinced that the state of philosophy could only be improved by instilling in philosophers the discipline and rigour characteristic of those enterprises. He believed that much of philosophy-as-practised failed to meet such standards. Quite early in his intellectual development, he came to the conclusion that metaphysical thought was especially lacking in this respect; so much so, he characterized the arguments of metaphysicians as 'moonshine' – American slang for illegally home-distilled whisky. Less colourfully, he used the term 'nonsense' to characterize metaphysical doctrines. While he did not use the latter term in nearly so technical a manner as Wittgenstein and the logical positivists would decades later, there is no doubt that there are important connections between Peirce's early view of metaphysics and their far more formally developed views. In addition, it should be noted that Peirce explicitly credited his reading of Kant's *Critique of Pure Reason* not only as an early source of his dissatisfaction with traditional metaphysics, but as an inspiration for some of his own thoughts on the subject. It is to these ideas that we now turn.

Two of Peirce's earliest writings are, 'The Fixation of Belief' and 'How to Make Our Ideas Clear', which appeared in *Popular Science Monthly* in 1877 and 1878 respectively. Although he continued for decades to develop the ideas expressed in them, they have come to stand as classic statements of his views. In them, he spelled out, albeit informally, ideas which anticipated some of the important pragmatic and positivist criticisms of metaphysical thought. His main concern was to offer a full-blown theory of inquiry. While he took an anthropological interest in actual modes of human inquiry, he was far more concerned to develop *normative* or *prescriptive* canons of inquiry. Towards this end, one of his chief concerns was the 'clarification' of theoretical terms. His main contention on this subject was elegant in its simplicity: we cannot be clear about the meaning of a theoretical term unless we are clear in advance on the practical *consequences* that are to be encountered under specifiable circumstances in virtue of which the term can be said to apply. In effect, Peirce was insisting on *practical criteria* for the application of a theoretical term. To take his own example; for the term 'hard' to have a clear meaning, we should be able to say with clarity just what we should expect – in practical terms – under specifiable conditions from an object to which the term applies. His actual suggestion, in this case, is that a hard object should scratch most other objects and should not be scratched by many other objects. His implicit claim is that a term for which there are no such practical, condition-related consequences connected to its proper application, would be a term with no meaning at all.

By extension, Peirce came to similar conclusions about propositions. He insisted that we cannot be clear about the meaning of a proposition unless we can be clear in advance about what practical consequences are, in given situations, to count in favour of its truth; if there is no clear accounting of such consequences, the proposition in question is so unclear as to have no meaning at all. It is extremely important to notice that Peirce's insistence on *practical* consequences in these contexts virtually rules out the sorts of claims made by traditional metaphysicians. Indeed, from the point of view of a metaphysician like Bradley, Peirce's practicality requirement might seem question-begging, since it insists that the meaning of every metaphysical term be linked to what Bradley believed to be mere appearances. Peirce's rejoinder, in effect, was that what Bradley called 'appearances' are better thought of as 'reality'; that if there are to be *any* criteria for the use of theoretical terms, or the truth of theoretical propositions, they can only reside within the realm of the practical. Pure metaphysics is so far removed from practical human life as to be meaningless. He stated explicitly that the propositions of ontological metaphysics, reaching no practical terminus, were 'theoretically meaningless' – amounting to nothing more than 'gibberish' (which is presumably no better than 'moonshine').

Interestingly, Peirce did believe that something deserving the name 'metaphysics' might be fruitfully pursued. Indeed, Peirce thought that some form of metaphysics might be practically testable and, at least to that extent, continuous with the sciences. It was never exactly clear what he had in mind. Although he made some modest attempts at proper metaphysical research, none of these have received much attention and they appear to be tangents to his major line of philosophical inquiry. While it is clear that he thought that metaphysics must be testable and confirmable, he noted too that its confirming experiences would involve the most common, pervasive facts of experience rather than the specialized sorts of observations that are characteristic of the exact sciences. It is also significant that Peirce insisted that legitimate metaphysics must, by its nature, be a co-operative or social inquiry made by many investigators.

What is most important here, however, is what Peirce *rejects* and why. There are powerful principles at work: science is the paradigm for intellectual inquiry; theoretical concepts have meaning only when there are practical tests for their proper application; theoretical propositions have meaning only when there are practical tests for their truth or falsity; purported concepts and propositions for which no such practical tests exist are meaningless; finally, philosophical researches must somehow meet standards of practical testability to be legitimate. These are ideas which the American pragmatic philosophers took seriously and developed in characteristic ways throughout the twentieth century. There is much in Peirce, as we shall see, that anticipates the doctrines of the logical positivists as well. Finally, his sense that traditional metaphysics had gone wrong by completely isolating itself from practical life, while deriving from elements in Kant's thought, resonates interestingly with the philosophical perspective of G. E. Moore – to whom we now turn.

❧ G. E. MOORE: AN APOSTLE OF COMMON ❧ SENSE

Against the philosophical background of absolute idealism, G. E. Moore (1873–1958) came to Cambridge University to study classics. As a matter of course he read philosophy and, after very briefly acquiescing to the doctrines of absolute idealism (to some degree, as expounded in his discussions with McTaggart), he rebelled against them. In so doing, he became increasingly absorbed in philosophy. He excelled in philosophical discussion and made a great impression at Cambridge. Gradually his initial intention to become a classicist weakened. By degrees, and somewhat to his surprise, he became a philosopher. It was not long before he dedicated himself almost completely to combating the influence of absolute idealism. Years later he doubted whether the world or the sciences would ever have suggested to him any philosophical problems. Rather, he believed, philosophical problems had engaged him only as a result of his hearing and reading the strange things that other philosophers espoused. Moore's early philosophical motives were so tied up with undermining the strange metaphysical claims of absolute idealism, he would probably never have become a philosopher had he not encountered them.

Moore was a unique thinker. He had a vivid and forceful personality which his philosophical peers could not help but take seriously. There was nothing flamboyant about Moore. To the contrary, his strength lay in his directness, his uncompromising honesty, and his firm independence of mind. Moore was neither quick-witted, nor particularly imaginative, but his clarity of thought and relentless commitment to truth were truly remarkable. He was never a systematic philosopher, but his approach to philosophy was fresh and original. He displayed both a strong determination and a rare ability to achieve *clarity* on philosophical problems. For him, this meant posing them, as well as expressing his views on them, with exact precision, making all necessary distinctions, leaving nothing out and leaving nothing obscure or vague. In this, he succeeded, perhaps better than anyone of his time.

Moore's most influential work pertaining to metaphysics can be divided into two categories. First, he wrote some early essays critical of the claims of, and arguments for, idealism. This work was influential and demonstrates both Moore's characteristic insistence upon clarity and his talent for making fine distinctions. Moore's early essay, 'The Refutation of Idealism' (1903), is concerned chiefly to undermine the arguments that idealist philosophers have offered in support of their position [in 3.14]. Moore tried to show that idealist thought is a web of confusions, incomplete thoughts and unjustified claims. Acknowledging that idealism (which he first, quite characteristically, took great pains to clarify with sufficient precision) might be true, he concludes that there is no good reason to believe that it is. He takes special pains to refute Berkeley's *esse es percipi* principle. In 'External and Internal Relations', an earlier, less influential piece, he criticizes Bradley's principle of internal relations, attempting to show that the doctrine involves a major confusion [in 3.14]. These essays are essentially critical.

It was, however, much later work of Moore in which he boldly defended what he called 'the Common Sense View of the World' and rejected any metaphysical view incompatible with it, for which he is justifiably best known. That work represents thoughts that are dramatically characteristic of its author. The 'Defence of Common Sense' (1925), perhaps Moore's best-known essay, is a remarkable work which employs a strategy that is both elegant and deceptively simple [3.16]. He begins by offering a list of propositions which he calls 'truisms'. He divides these into three categories. First he asserts some commonplace propositions such as that he has a body, that he was born a number of years ago, that he has lived his whole life on or near the surface of the earth, which itself has existed for many years prior to his birth, and upon which many other human beings have lived and do live. A second category of propositions concerns experiences. Moore states that he has often perceived his own body and other things in its environment including other human bodies, and that he has often observed facts about these things. He gives some examples of these facts. They include quite particular and familiar observations about his immediate environment, recollections about the past, and facts about his own present and past beliefs, feelings and expectations. The third and final category consists of a single proposition which states that with regard to many other human beings who resemble Moore, that each of them frequently knows propositions which correspond to those Moore listed for himself in the first two categories. He insists that all of these propositions are wholly true and that he knows with certainty that each is true. He goes on to say that the meaning of each proposition is clear. Moore refers to the propositions he enumerates collectively as 'the Common Sense View of the World'.

One might wonder why Moore bothered to state all this – much less strive to state it with his characteristic clarity, completeness and care. The answer, as he insists in the article, is that many philosophers have asserted things that conflict with these very basic truths of common sense. He thought it immensely important to point out this idiosyncratic feature of such assertions. Bradley and McTaggart, for example, actually held that material objects are unreal, and that space and time are unreal. But, of course, if they really knew that they had bodies, that their bodies were near the Earth, and that their bodies had existed for many years, then that would mean that they knew things incompatible with their philosophical pronouncements. In effect, Moore was responding to such philosophers in this work as he had so many times in discussion. To the claim that time is unreal, Moore might say, 'You mean I ought not believe that I had my breakfast today *before* I had my lunch? But I know with certainty that I did!' The power of Moore's article (and of such a direct argumentative ploy) is that it places extremely plausible constraints upon metaphysical claims. It urges that everyone, including philosophers, forbear from saying things that are clearly in conflict with what he or she knows with certainty to be true. Moore thought it important to note just how far afield many metaphysical philosophers had strayed.

This strategy was bold in its conception. Whereas Moore's earlier work sought to show mistakes in the reasonings of idealist metaphysicians, the 'Defence of Common Sense' by-passed such efforts. His stance had changed dramatically, implying, as it did, that no satisfactory argument could possibly establish conclusions contrary to what each of us knows with certainty to be true. In effect, Moore was saying, 'I don't care what your argument is, if your conclusion is inconsistent with common sense, then your argument is certainly faulty because its conclusion is certainly false!'

Moore's 'Proof of an External World' is similarly bold. First given as a lecture to the British Academy in 1939 and later published posthumously in his *Philosophical Papers* [3.16], it begins with a detailing of some of Kant's thoughts about scepticism with respect to 'things outside us'. There is a characteristically detailed discussion of the latter expression, and a detailing of what sorts of things it might refer to. He suggests dogs, planets, stars, shadows and hands as clear exemplars. The climax of Moore's presentation came when he, gesturing appropriately with his right hand, said, 'Here is one hand', and then, gesturing with his left, 'Here is another.' Thus, he concluded that there certainly *are* things outside us, adding that his premises are certainly true and that his conclusion certainly follows from those premises. So, once again, Moore rejected any notion which runs counter to what is straightforwardly and non-problematically known to all of us.

It is worth noting here that Moore never used a derisive or disrespectful tone in any of these works. He never suggested that any of the philosophers he criticized for holding views incompatible with common sense were stupid or ridiculous for doing so, although he certainly thought they were wrong. His feeling, rather, was that they had lost their way – that they had somehow lost sight of the simple but elusive fact that philosophical work has *a standing in real life* and that when its content conflicts with the most evident features of real life, then it has gone wrong.

This leaves open an important question. If Moore is correct that the beliefs of common sense are unassailable and that no philosophical views that conflict with them are acceptable, what, if anything, is left for metaphysical philosophers to do? Moore's absolute refusal to contradict the common sense view of the world, or to accept the views of other philosophers which do, might seem like a final resting place. Remembering especially that Moore's initial motive for philosophizing was to combat the strange metaphysical views of the absolute idealists, it might seem as if he had at last found a response to such views that he could accept as definitive, enduring and final. In fact, he pretty much had. Nonetheless, he did not think that his defence of common sense was the end of all such matters.

Drawing the interesting and proper distinction between understanding the meaning of a proposition and explicating or analysing that meaning, Moore insisted that it is a legitimate, even necessary, philosophical function to analyse some of his common sense propositions. As this programme developed, Moore became convinced that there was much philosophical work still to do in this area. All this work, he thought, fell under the category of analysing propositions which are known with certainty to be wholly true. Thus philosophical analysis, so conceived, would offer no major surprises and could only elaborate upon – never undermine – common sense.

What exactly did Moore mean by 'analysis'? For one thing, he recognized that it was perfectly possible to understand the meaning of a proposition without being able to state or explain its meaning. This latter endeavour required analysis. Beyond this, it is fair to say that he never developed a satisfactory general account of what an analysis of a proposition is. He admitted as much, and this may well have been his greatest philosophical frustration. One may gain some understanding of what he intended by taking a concrete example. As mentioned, Moore argued for the existence of things outside us in part by holding up a hand and saying, 'This is a hand' – a proposition he considered to be wholly true, in no way doubtful, and perfectly clear. He believed however that the proposition could be analysed, and he undertook to do so. In 'A Defence of Common Sense', he stated that such a proposition, upon analysis, is ultimately about some *sense datum* – some object of immediate awareness which is the subject of the fully analysed proposition or judgement. Beyond this, he was not clear. For one thing, he did not think that the proposition, 'This is a hand', ultimately attributed to a sense datum the property of being a hand. This leaves open the question of just what else the relationship between the sense datum and the hand in question might be. While Moore thought that the proper analysis of the proposition in question would illuminate that relationship, he never felt that he had succeeded in arriving at the proper analysis. One of the most creative approaches to this problem was formulated by Bertrand Russell.

❧ BERTRAND RUSSELL ❧

Old metaphysics and the new logic

Russell was a very different intellectual type from Moore. He was an accomplished mathematician who, as is well known, did much work of historical importance in logic and in the foundations of mathematics. The publication, between 1910 and 1913, of the three volumes that comprised *Principia Mathematica* – which Russell co-authored with A. N. Whitehead – was an important event in the history of ideas. As we shall see, that work influenced his metaphysical views. Russell was an astonishingly clever man, imaginative, quick-witted and articulate. He was also a man of wide-ranging interests who was intellectually ambitious. No doubt greatly emboldened by his successes in logic, he was, for quite some time, optimistic about the prospects for employing some of the strategies which served him so well there with similar success in other areas of philosophy.

Russell always had a philosophical temperament. A contemporary of Moore at Cambridge, he too was first intrigued with, and later rebelled against, the neo-Hegelian metaphysics of the absolute idealists. His assessment of, and opposition to, absolute idealism was disposition-ally different from Moore's. For one thing, Russell thought in more sweeping and systematic terms than Moore; for another, he was far less shy about impugning what he took to be the motives of the neo-Hegelians.

Some of Russell's initial opposition to absolute idealism stemmed from the suspicions he held regarding the philosophical motives of its proponents. At times he felt that their motives were not entirely rational, and, perhaps, even dishonest. This should not be under-estimated. The proponents of absolute idealism were the objects of some of his most scornful criticism. He came to regard Hegel, Bradley and many of their followers as 'paradox peddlers' who, he believed, were less motivated to understand the world than they were to convict it of unreality in the interests of a supra-sensible absolute.

Russell made his objections of substance clear as well. Signifi-cantly, they were quite different in focus from Moore's. Whereas Moore's criticisms were quite specifically aimed at this or that propo-sition or argument, Russell's focus was far more systematic. More or less independently of his dislike of the metaphysical conclusions of Hegel and Bradley, he came to think (in fairness, with justification) that their thoughts about logic, which played an important role in their metaphysics, were unsophisticated and antiquated.

This came out in a number of ways. Russell, in his work in logic and the foundations of mathematics, was determined – though this was by no means his only concern – to revolutionize and systematize the discipline of logic. If his ambitions were high, so were the standards of rigour he employed. Not only did his work bring together many dramatic innovations – both his own and those of other important thinkers – into the discipline, but it also helped direct public attention to these improvements. In the end, his work played a major role in building a new consensus among philosophers and mathematicians of the twentieth century concerning logic. Needless to say, philosophers rarely achieve such successes.

When Russell first read Hegel and Bradley, his work in logic was only beginning. Yet, he detected, even then, elements in their thought which, he felt, were utterly at odds with a correct sense of what logic should be. He wrote of these misgivings, expressing in a tone of undisguised scorn, his assessment of Hegel's *Greater Logic*, as 'muddle-headed nonsense'. Later on, he gained greater clarity about these matters. In the preface to *Principia Mathematica*, written quite a few years after Russell's dramatic break with monistic, idealist metaphysics, he explains

> The logic, which I shall advocate is atomistic, as opposed to the monistic logic of the people who more or less follow Hegel. When I say that my logic is atomistic, I mean that I share the common-sense belief that there are many separate things; I do not regard the apparent multiplicity of the world as consisting merely in phases and unreal division of a single indivisible reality.
>
> [3.22, I: vii]

This almost makes it look as if Russell built his metaphysical presumptions into his logic, but the impression is misleading. As it turned out, Russell's reasons for advocating an 'atomistic' logic were, to a great extent, unrelated to his metaphysical predispositions. He, and other logicians on the cutting edge – many of whom were not at all interested in metaphysics – were mostly concerned with the development of a logic with strong deductive and expressive power. Those were the main criteria for judging success. It was by such standards, and not quirks of metaphysical temperament, that an atomistic logic developed.

How did absolute idealism conflict with what have come to be accepted as correct logical procedures in the twentieth century? It is possible to give a synoptic view of some of the connections. For one thing, Bradley's doctrine of internal relations conflicted with a very basic feature of modern logic as developed in *Principia Mathematica*. That doctrine, as we have seen, held that what we think of as relations between supposedly separate objects are actually illusory. Connected with this, it held that relational terms can be dispensed with and replaced by terms designating properties of individuals. This not only conflicted with Russell's intuitions, but he soon was able to show on logical grounds that some relational terms – most notably those associated with asymmetric properties such as 'north of', 'older than', 'higher than', and 'below' – cannot plausibly be reduced to individual predicates in this way. For these and other technical considerations, modern logic allows relational statements as basic and irreducible, and presumes that they are capable of being true. To this extent, it can be said that twentieth-century logic has repudiated, if it has not refuted, late nineteenth-century neo-Hegelian metaphysics.

Logical constructionism

Russell's own metaphysical views changed considerably during his life. After rejecting idealism, he embraced an extreme form of realism which he was soon to abandon as hopelessly confused. In *The Problems of Philosophy*, published in 1912, he embraced a version of the causal-representative theory of perception of Locke and Descartes. Shortly thereafter, Russell's metaphysical thinking changed dramatically. He conceived, employed and, for quite some time, remained committed to a genuinely innovative approach to metaphysical problems. It was connected to a strategy which he had used successfully in his work on the logical foundations of mathematics. He called it 'logical constructionism'. When employing it in the context of metaphysics he stated it in this way: 'Wherever possible, logical constructions are to be substituted for inferred entities' [3.24, 155].

What did this mean and how did this apply to metaphysics? For centuries after the time of Descartes, modern philosophers have tended to believe that physical objects are not directly perceived. The view, while no longer pervasive, persists to this day. To this is added the conviction that what we are directly aware of in perception is something accessible only to the individual perceiver which is caused by, but not identical to the object of perception. This element of direct awareness can be thought of as an inner experience which is an end point in the process of sensation and which represents the physical object being perceived. The experience of an object represents and is caused by the object; they are not the same. So, on this view it is theoretically possible to have qualitatively exactly the experiences that would normally result from perceiving, say, a pumpkin without their being caused by a pumpkin – and such things do seem to occur in dreams and hallucinations. Even worse, if all one ever experiences directly are inner experiences or immediate sense data, then how could one ever know that these represent independent physical objects? On the view in question, there could, in principle, be no direct check of this: since experiences are all one can ultimately examine, one could never confirm whether they are caused by extra-experiential objects. In short, if such a view of perception were true, then one could not know it. The problem here is, in large measure epistemological: How could one know on the basis of inner sense data that there are physical objects? Russell took this problem seriously. His response to it was to employ logical constructionism. Its ramifications were significant for metaphysics as well as epistemology.

His strategy was to analyse troublesome entities in terms of more familiar or less troublesome ones. For example, the problem at hand is how to justify a belief in physical objects given that we are directly aware only of sense data. There seems, in the final analysis, to be no way of *inferring* the objects from the immediate sense data. Russell's innovative alternative was this: treat the physical object not as a distinct entity to be inferred from sense data, but as what he would call *a logical construction out of sense data*. What does this mean? Russell's suggestion was, in effect, to treat physical objects not as *independent of* sense data but rather as *analysable in terms of* sense data. This meant, in effect, treating physical objects as metaphysically non-basic and sense data as the more fundamental category of being.

This suggestion was to be carried out by showing that all propositions about physical objects can be, in principle, analysed in terms of propositions about sense data. If successful, this procedure would, Russell thought, solve the philosophical problem about physical objects which proceeds on the assumption that propositions about sense data and propositions about physical objects are logically independent. He explored this possibility in *Our Knowledge of the External World* which was published in 1914 [3.19]. Two papers, 'The Relations of Sense-Data to Physics' and 'The Ultimate Constituents of Matter', which were published in 1914 and 1915 respectively (and reprinted in his *Mysticism and Logic and other Essays* in 1917 [3.20]), employed the same strategy. Russell adapted the technique of logical constructionism to mental phenomena in *The Analysis of Mind*, published in 1921 [3.21]. Only in *The Analysis of Matter*, published in 1927 [3.23], did Russell begin to abandon this strategy, but, by then, it had already exerted a powerful influence upon a generation of philosophers.

Logical atomism

It is important to recognize that this creative metaphysical strategy was ultimately viewed by Russell as one feature of a larger, more ambitious and systematic philosophical programme. This was explained in 'The Philosophy of Logical Atomism', a remarkable work published in two instalments in 1918 and 1919, which established – in overall terms, if not in final detail – what was to be Russell's more global approach to metaphysics for much of the period during which he did his most respected work in the area [3.25]. His implementation of the programme led to different results at different times. He never was able to satisfy himself that he had employed it so as to achieve a final or definitive result. It seems clear, however, that during his most productive years, he did not seriously doubt the underlying assumptions of the programme itself.

Russell wanted to use the new logic to establish something enduring in philosophy. The philosophical system he envisaged was certainly metaphysical in nature. His idea proceeded from his assumption, often stated in many of his writings, that the new logic of *Principia Mathematica* represented the formal structure or syntax of a 'logically perfect language'. What it lacked, of course, was a vocabulary. Russell's metaphysical programme was, in effect, to decide upon that vocabulary which, when added to the syntax provided by the new logic, would complete the search for a logically perfect language.

Russell felt that common language tended often to confound the search for truth. For one thing, as he showed wonderfully well in his work on logic (especially in his landmark essay, 'On Denoting', 1905), the surface forms of a natural language like English often obscure the logical form of a proposition or of an argument [3.25]. One of the most striking successes of modern logic is that it provides a language carefully constructed to lay bare the logical structure of propositions and arguments. In a similar way, Russell thought, the logically perfect language he sought would not only lay bare the logical structure of its propositions, but would – when the details of its application to the world were clarified – also lay bare the logical structure of reality. Satisfied that he had gone a long way towards laying bare the *syntactics* of a logically perfect language, he proceeded to set his sights on *semantics*.

How did Russell think he could arrive at a vocabulary for such a language? Here, he made a number of assumptions he regarded as unassailable. First, he held that all the propositions in such a language would either be basic – 'atomic' propositions he called them – or else analysable into basic propositions. He held that the non-basic or 'molecular' propositions would be truth-functions of the atomic propositions – that is, the truth or falsity of any molecular proposition would be a function of the truth or falsity of the atomic propositions out of which it is constructed. Second, he believed that atomic propositions served to state facts – the basic or atomic *facts* in the world. The atomic propositions of a logically perfect language were said to be *logical* atoms and the facts which they corresponded to were taken to be *metaphysical* atoms. His programme, then, amounted in large measure to arriving at a satisfactory account of what an atomic fact is and what its constituent elements are.

This issue fascinated and vexed Russell, but he was never able to resolve it. He had two powerful philosophical intuitions regarding the matter. First, he was strongly inclined to believe that atomic propositions were about *particulars* to which they referred. Atomic facts, he thought, should have particular constituents. Second, he was greatly attracted to the view that these particulars are *objects of immediate awareness*. For some time he wanted to identify the constituents of atomic facts with sense data – an assumption which perfectly jibed with his logical constructionist programme. Indeed, it constituted his purest empiricist intuition – amounting, as it did, to the opinion that all meaningful propositions ultimately refer to immediate experiences. Though he struggled to do so, Russell could never fully accommodate a fully articulated account of atomic facts with either of these two assumptions, and he found difficulties, too, with reconciling the assumptions with one another.

These difficulties notwithstanding, Russell never completely abandoned the hope that metaphysical clarity might be achieved. Ironically the metaphysical thoughts of his logical constructionist/logical atomist period were to stimulate his friend and collaborator Ludwig Wittgenstein to thoughts of his own, which would soon inspire him to write one of the most influential, vivid, and radically *anti*-metaphysical philosophical works of the twentieth century.

WILLIAM JAMES: PRAGMATISM, METAPHYSICS AND NEUTRAL MONISM

William James was the first great public exponent of pragmatism. Like so many of the figures discussed here, he was trained in science and approached philosophy with the attitude of a reformer. Specializing in medicine and psychology, he taught at the Harvard Medical School for some years before he joined its philosophy faculty. Inspired by Peirce, James sought to expand pragmatic principles and apply them to the major problems of philosophy. He was confident that pragmatism was essentially correct and destined to have a revolutionary effect upon philosophical thought. Of the philosophers treated here he was certainly the least careful about details. While his ideas were novel and sweeping in their consequences and his written expressions of them were remarkably vivid and engaging, his most powerful thoughts were frequently not completed. Nonetheless his writings had a great influence in both the United States and Britain. There was, in James, a strongly empiricistic element of thought. Indeed, he described himself as a 'radical empiricist'. To that extent, he was a principled opponent of traditional metaphysics in general, and absolute idealism in particular. There was also, in James, a great respect for religion. He strove, in much of his work, to justify religion on pragmatic grounds, without compromising the empiricistic, pro-science, underpinnings of his thought. Whether he ultimately succeeded in this is an interesting, and very much open, question. It is, however, beyond the scope of this essay which will not address James's views on religion, but, rather, concentrate on the underpinnings of his thought.

James explicitly acknowledged a great philosophical indebtedness to Peirce. He was greatly impressed with Peirce's insistence that theoretical propositions should directly connect with practical consequences and shared Peirce's conviction that the propositions of traditional metaphysics characteristically failed to so connect. As such, James expressed a similar hostility to most metaphysics. His development of Peirce's main contentions placed special importance on the failure of metaphysical propositions to have *experiential* consequences. In his last work, the posthumously published *Some Problems of Philosophy*, he wrote:

> The pragmatic rule is that the meaning of a concept may always be found, if not in some particular which it directly designates, then in some particular difference in the course of human experience which its being true will make.
>
> ([3.9], 60)

James believed that many familiar metaphysical doctrines were not meaningful, precisely because they imply nothing relating to the course of human experience; more specifically, such views are consistent with *any experiences whatsoever*. James regarded this as a fatal defect in any purported view. A colourful writer, James often expressed the point metaphorically by writing that such metaphysical views have no 'cash value'.

Nonetheless, James, like Peirce and Russell, did not want to end metaphysics altogether; rather, he wished to make it intellectually respectable. He believed that meaningful metaphysical discourse is possible, going so far as to suggest that metaphysical philosophers occasionally make valuable suggestions – legitimate observations with genuine 'cash value'. For example, in *Pragmatism*, published in 1907, James distinguished between two forms of materialism [3.10]. The first is the traditional doctrine of material substrate which postulates unperceivable entities in which the perceivable qualities of objects inhere. This view, of course, he regarded as empty or meaningless, since it had no 'cash-value' link to any experiential consequences. Significantly, he commends Berkeley, at least, for pointing out this defect in the view, describing Berkeley's objections as 'absolutely pragmatistic'.

Against this empty version of materialism, James urged what he thought was a legitimate form. He suggested that one might deny material substrate as vehemently as Berkeley did and still be a materialist 'in the wider sense, of explaining higher phenomena by . . . laws of physical nature' ([3.10], 93). This meaningful version of materialism holds that the various phenomena in the world that we naturally judge to involve intelligence, purpose, consciousness or intent can all, in principle, be accounted for in terms of the laws of physical science. While not specifically advocating this view, he took it to be, at least, meaningful. His thought would seem to have been that the view does have links to possible, observable consequences: roughly, it will stand or fall according to whether or not certain kinds of explanations for certain kinds of phenomena are discovered. This is no matter of *simple* observations, but it would appear at least to meet James's rough pragmatic requirement that a conception have some implications that make a difference relative to the course of human experience. Here, then, is meaningful metaphysics. It is testable and continuous with science.

James made a similar distinction with respect to the notion of personal identity. He regarded Descartes's analysis of the notion as pragmatically meaningless. Locke's account, on the other hand, he took seriously as a worthy contribution to philosophy. Briefly, Descartes believed that the sensations, thoughts, affections, memories, dreams and fantasies of a given individual belong to that individual in virtue of being contents or modes of the same underlying spiritual substance or soul. Descartes explicitly distinguished this spiritual substance itself from its contents, and acknowledged that it is never itself experienced; still, he urged that the unity of a person consists in the unity of this underlying mental substance. James offered a spirited pragmatic criticism of this view. This conception of mental substance, he argued, is entirely empty, since its purported existence cannot in any way register in real experience. There would be no way, in experience, to distinguish its presumed presence from its absence – and no way to detect a situation where one enduring unchanging mental substance is suddenly replaced by another. These would be, in James's parlance, 'distinctions without a difference'.

Against this, he commended Locke's quite similar criticism of spiritual substance as well as Locke's alternative analysis of personal identity which he praised for reducing this notion to its pragmatic value in terms of experience – namely, the fact that at one moment in life we remember other moments, and feel them all as parts of one and the same personal history. James never explicated Locke's view with care nor did he explain exactly why he so approved of it. He evidently thought that by citing consciousness as the locus of a person, and memory as (in some way) its principle of unity or identity, Locke had succeeded at least in reducing personal identity to the right sorts of terms – namely features of experience. A continuing person is a continuing stream of consciousness; and what unifies individual experiences into a continuing stream has to do with the possibility of certain kinds of memory interrelations among these experiences.

These remarks anticipated and, in part, influenced some of Russell's metaphysics. There is a deep suspicion of most old-style metaphysics, a hopeful sense that metaphysics can be reformed, and a strong conviction that a correct metaphysics would have to use terms and propositions whose ultimate content is experiential. Like Russell, James was an empiricist-minded metaphysical reformer. It is worth noting that his overall view of metaphysics inspired one of Russell's most radical strategies – a subject to which we now turn.

James was drawn to phenomenalism, the view – of which Russell's logical constructionism was an instance – that physical objects can somehow be identified or reduced to experiences. There was nothing terribly radical in phenomenalism *per se*, and James, characteristically, did not try to work out the details of such a view with nearly the same care as did Russell. He did conceive however, of a quite innovative extension of this view from physical objects to minds or consciousness. James first explained this conception in an essay published in 1903, 'Does Consciousness Exist?' [3.12]. Believing that physical objects can be identified as suitably interrelated sets of experiences, he further suggested – perhaps following Locke's hint – that minds or streams of consciousness could be analysed using the same general strategy. Such a view, he reasoned, was not only plausible, but involved a wonderful sort of conceptual economy: specifically, only one ultimate category of existence – namely experience – needed to be postulated. In effect, he was suggesting a new form of monism in which the ultimate 'stuff' of the universe was neither mind nor matter, but pure experience.

James very much liked an interesting consequence of this view: namely, that one and the same experience can be part of a set of experiences that constitutes a physical object *and also* part of a set of experiences that constitutes a stream of consciousness or a conscious mind. This observation was, he thought, liberating in that it undermined deep Cartesian assumptions about the radical separateness of mind and body from which flowed seemingly endless metaphysical puzzles. This non-idealist, non-materialist form of monism became known as neutral monism.

Russell, influenced by James, embraced neutral monism for some time. His book, *The Analysis of Mind*, published in 1921, constitutes a remarkable attempt to develop a metaphysics along neutral monist lines [3.21]. As it turned out, the view was not to prove influential. In the long term, subsequent generations of philosophers were to uncover deep problems with phenomenalism, an essential component of the view. More immediately, the viability of metaphysics of any sort was about to come under the severest scrutiny.

❧❧ LUDWIG WITTGENSTEIN: METAPHYSICS ❧❧ OVERTHROWN

It is not entirely clear whether or not Ludwig Wittgenstein (1889–1951) should be included in an essay restricted to English and American philosophers. He was born and raised in Vienna. He wrote philosophy in German, his first language. Dispositionally, he was, in many ways, Viennese. Yet, his professional career in philosophy was pursued entirely at Cambridge and he eventually became a citizen of the United Kingdom. Many of his closest friends and most of the relatively few individuals with whom he had serious philosophical discussions were British. His influence in the English-speaking world is extensive. Finally, there is a great deal of precedent for treating Wittgenstein's views in works on British philosophy.

Wittgenstein was a difficult, enigmatic individual and his writings are extremely daunting. Regarding their ultimate value, it is significant that many contemporary philosophers – including quite a few who do not share his conclusions – regard him as a philosopher of the highest historical importance. He wrote only two books for publication. One, *Tractatus Logico-Philosophicus* (1921), is said to represent 'the early Wittgenstein'; the other, *Philosophical Investigations* (1953), 'the late Wittgenstein'. It is the early work and thought of Wittgenstein and its influence that was to impact upon the first half of this century.

Wittgenstein was trained as an engineer, became interested in problems in the foundations of mathematics and went to Cambridge to study with Russell, who quickly came to regard him as a philosophical equal. Wittgenstein took a keen interest in Russell's philosophical work and, although the two never co-authored a work in philosophy, it is proper to say that they were collaborators for an extended period of time before World War I. In 'The Philosophy of Logical Atomism' Russell explicitly cites Wittgenstein's major role in shaping his ideas. Wittgenstein, in the *Tractatus*, cites Russell's ideas as an important stimulus. The two works share many central themes – but their differences are significant too.

Perhaps the most striking feature of the *Tractatus* is its explicit rejection of metaphysical philosophy. This rejection was of the most radical sort. Wittgenstein did not claim, as Moore did, that metaphysical propositions are often *false*. He did not hold, with Russell or Peirce, that metaphysical philosophy as traditionally practised was logically sloppy and needed to employ rigorous new techniques in order to become a worthy subject of study. Instead, he stressed that metaphysical philosophy by its very nature was *meaningless*. The writings of traditional metaphysicians, he insisted, fail even to present propositions that are capable of being either true or false. They quite simply fail to make sense at all.

The *Tractatus* is a difficult book. It is a very short, but extremely concentrated work. Its style is oracular. It consists of short entries that are systematically numbered. Most are terse or aphoristic. They concern language, logic, thought, the world and, most important, the interrelations among them. Its views about these subjects are strikingly original, but certainly not commonsensical. The reader is offered almost nothing in the way of guidance. Many difficult points are never clarified. Central contentions are barely supported. The author says nothing in the main text about the development and evolution of his philosophical conclusions. For decades the book was not well understood – and there is still much disagreement about many points of its interpretation.

Wittgenstein explains in a short preface that the *Tractatus* seeks to show that there is a limit upon 'what can be said' – by which he means, of course, on what can be said *meaningfully*. Employing the metaphor of a limit, he writes, 'on the other side of the limit will be simply nonsense'. In outline, at least, his overall strategy emerges fairly clearly: in showing the limits upon what can be meaningfully expressed in language, it will become clear that metaphysics (as well as ethics, aesthetics and religion) lies on 'the other side' – in the realm of 'simply nonsense'. Wittgenstein intended nothing less than to show that philosophers who tried to write metaphysical, ethical, aesthetic or religious works necessarily succeeded in producing only nonsense. In Wittgenstein's view, they quite straightforwardly had nothing to say because *there was* nothing to say. Unsurprisingly, this idea proved to be provocative in the extreme. While it inspired a prominent and vigorous school of philosophy – the logical positivism advocated by members of the Vienna Circle and their followers – it also elicited passionate criticism. Wittgenstein characteristically wanted almost nothing to do with either his self-professed followers or his critics. Believing he had definitively answered the most important questions of philosophy, he behaved with admirable consistency and gave the subject up entirely. He trained as a schoolteacher, taught in rural Austrian elementary schools, worked as a gardener, designed and built a house for his sister – but for about a decade after completing the *Tractatus*, Wittgenstein did no work in philosophy. Only when he began to doubt his Tractarian views did he return.

Wittgenstein's rejection of metaphysics in the *Tractatus* was a consequence of that work's novel view of language. Unlike Russell, who thought of a logically perfect language as an ideal alternative to ordinary language, the early Wittgenstein believed that such an ideal lay hidden beneath the surface forms of ordinary language. Indeed, he appears to have thought that something like Russell's ideal had to underlie common language in order for it to work at all. He believed that ordinary language required, and possessed, an elaborate logical understructure. That difference aside, borrowing from Russell, he believed that all meaningful propositions are truth-functions of atomic propositions. To this, he added a strikingly new idea: atomic propositions were *pictures* of atomic facts. The details of this claim are intricate and difficult, but he was explicitly clear on one consequence of it: the truth or falsity of an atomic proposition can never be established *a priori*. Each is a picture, and so, its truth or falsity is a matter of whether it correctly or incorrectly pictures the world. Ascertaining the truth or falsity of an atomic proposition requires comparing the proposition with the world. Its truth or falsity, then, is evidently an empirical matter. An atomic proposition is true if and only if the world contains the fact pictured in the proposition.

Wittgenstein believed that all propositions are either atomic or else truth-functions of atomic propositions, which he, following Russell, called 'molecular'. He took great care to explicate the notion of a *tautology* – that is, a molecular proposition which is true no matter what the truth or falsity of its components. For example, suppose *P* is an atomic proposition and consider the proposition 'Either *P* or not-*P*'. This very simple molecular proposition will be true whether its single atomic component, *P*, is true or false. It is a *logical* truth. Its truth is a matter of its logical structure and is compatible with any factual situation in the world. It is certainly true, but it is an empty or trivial truth which really gives us no direct factual information about the world. He recognized, of course, that there are logical falsehoods ('Both *P* and not-*P*' might serve as an example) which are false in virtue of their logical form alone, which – like tautologies – convey no factual content.

Wittgenstein made the powerful claim that tautologies constitute the only species of *necessary*, or *a priori* truth. All other truths depend upon the factual nature of the world. First, atomic propositions either correctly picture the world or they don't. Their truth depends upon nothing more than what the world is like. Those molecular propositions which are not tautologies (and not logical falsehoods) will turn out to be true only on *some* patterns of truth or falsity among their atomic components. So their truth or falsity will always depend on which of their atomic components are true and which false, which, in turn, is inevitably a mere matter of fact.

In overview, Wittgenstein held that there are just two sorts of truths. Tautologies are *a priori*, necessary truths – but they are devoid of factual content. All other truths require, in effect, that the world be a certain way – which is a contingent and *a posteriori* matter. He was clear and explicit that this left no room for metaphysical truths, which purport to be both necessary and also to transcend mere facts in their significance. For him all necessary truths are empty and all truths of substance are merely factual. There can be no significant truths which go beyond empirical facts, while traditional metaphysics claimed to establish such trans-empirical truths. Wittgenstein's scheme, then, leaves no room for traditional metaphysics. It was these details of Wittgenstein's rejection of metaphysics that so appealed to the logical positivists and shaped their opposition to metaphysics.

WITTGENSTEIN AND THE LOGICAL POSITIVISTS

Shared beliefs

During the 1920s, a remarkable group of like-minded philosophers formed in the city of Vienna. The group, known as the Vienna Circle, came together under the leadership of Moritz Schlick (1882–1936). They were philosophers who were, as a group, remarkably well schooled in mathematics and the sciences as well as in philosophy. Its leading members included Otto Neurath, Freidrich Waismann, Hans Hahn, Rudolf Carnap, Gustav Bergmann, Herbert Feigl and Olga Hahn-Neurath. Karl Popper was more loosely associated with the Circle. They were to exert a profound impact on philosophical thought in this century.

As with Wittgenstein, it is not easy to decide whether to include these thinkers in an account of philosophy in Britain and America. None of them was born in either country. None was a native speaker of English. However, some of them would emigrate to English-speaking countries in the 1930s or 1940s. Carnap and Feigl were to establish themselves in the community of philosophers in the United States during their later years. Their views were as influential in the English-speaking world as anywhere. They were themselves influenced by the early work of Russell and Wittgenstein – indeed, Schlick explicitly stated that the *Tractatus* had brought modern philosophy to a 'decisive turning point'. At his urging, a number of the Circle's members engaged in a collective, systematic reading of the *Tractatus*. They admired the work, found much in it to agree with and were inspired by it. Schlick prevailed upon Wittgenstein to hold discussions with some members of the Circle when the latter returned to Vienna during the late 1920s. Later, two younger philosophers – W. V. Quine, an American, and A. J. Ayer, an Engishman – were to establish contacts with the Circle. The former became one of the most brilliant and important American philosophers of this century; the latter, the leading exponent of the Circle's views in the English-speaking world and a master of clear, lively philosophical prose. While it is not credible to think of the original formation of the Circle as an event in the history of British or American philosophy, the group as a whole certainly exerted an influence in those histories – nowhere more than with respect to metaphysics. A brief account of their overall view of the subject – especially as it relates to that of Wittgenstein – is certainly appropriate.

The members of the Vienna Circle self-consciously thought of themselves as exponents of a philosophical movement. In many respects they behaved like members of a political movement. They held congresses, published philosophical journals for the dissemination of their views and even issued a joint manifesto, 'The Scientific World-View: The Vienna Circle' (1929). For more than a decade they were a major force in European philosophy and, as mentioned, their ideas had a dramatic impact in the English-speaking world. While they disagreed on some important points of philosophical substance, they were in remarkable agreement in their overall view of many philosophical matters. Their shared view was called 'logical positivism' or 'logical empiricism'. While their interests included the philosophy of science, the foundations of mathematics, epistemology, the philosophy of language and ethics – it was, perhaps, their view of metaphysics that inspired the most interest and controversy.

In this respect, at least, the views of the positivists were virtually identical to those expressed by Wittgenstein in the *Tractatus*. They accepted the view of Wittgenstein (indeed, Schlick appears to have arrived at much the same view independently) that all meaningful propositions are either tautologies or else factual and *a posteriori* in nature. They sympathized with Russell and Wittgenstein's notion that every meaningful factual proposition is a truth-function of basic propositions. As such, they agreed that each such factual proposition has a specific set of truth-conditions, and that the question of whether or not those conditions obtain is empirical. Although they did not accept

Wittgenstein's picture theory of meaning, they took his insistence that the basic propositions of language must be compared with the world to establish their truth or falsity to be a clear signal that he had *verification by observation* in mind. Attributing even greater importance to the notion of verification by observation than Wittgenstein had, they linked it to a shared principle around which they rallied. This they called the verification principle.

The rough idea behind this principle (the members of the Circle never settled upon a *precise* definition) was this: it is a mark of a meaningful non-tautological proposition that there be, in principle, a method of verifying it empirically. Conversely, if there is, in principle, no way to verify a purported non-logical proposition, then it is not a meaningful proposition – it is what the positivists called a 'pseudo-proposition'. They believed all the supposed 'propositions' of traditional metaphysicians to be pseudo-propositions which wrongly presumed to describe a transcendent reality necessarily outside the realm of any possible observational verification. Thus, while its underpinnings were slightly different for the positivists, they shared with Wittgenstein the view that the writings of traditional metaphysicians are factually and theoretically meaningless.

Shared problems

If Wittgenstein and the positivists shared basic beliefs about language and the impossibility of metaphysics, they also came to see a number of difficulties with their view of these matters. First, there was a problem with their overall views on language and metaphysics which was both fundamental and almost embarrassingly ironic. Upon examination, it appeared that their shared view of language – which ruled out metaphysics as meaningless – had exactly the same effect when applied to itself; that is, by the tenets of their position, the position was itself meaningless! This, of course, suggested that there was something fundamentally wrong with their shared position.

The problem is perhaps easiest to explain with respect to the verification principle of the positivists. That principle, in effect, allows that, tautologies aside, only verifiable, empirical propositions can count as meaningful truths. But what of the principle itself? It certainly did not appear to be an empty tautology – indeed, the positivists trumpeted it as if it had the same sort of significance as did the law of gravity. They certainly were disinclined to view it as empty. However, the principle itself did not appear to be empirically verifiable either – after all, the positivists' acceptance of it was not the result of any scientific observations or experiments, nor did it seem that any such observations could serve to confirm it. This problem vexed some members of the Vienna Circle for some time and they were never to agree upon a resolution. Thus, the Circle – which endorsed the verification principle by consensus – not only could not agree upon a proper formulation of it, they were also at pains to show how it could be rescued from itself.

This problem was no isolated paradox. The positivists, by restricting meaningful truths to tautologies and empirical propositions, were similarly at pains to show how any of their philosophical pronouncements could count as meaningful. After all, the members of the Circle wrote books on philosophy which were certainly works neither in science nor in logic, however much they admired those disciplines. How, then, could their own words count as meaningful? Further, this seemed to lead to a dilemma: with this problem still unresolved, the positivists could not condemn metaphysics without condemning their own condemnation of it; and, if they opted to ignore this and continue writing their books, it was hard to see how they could, with consistency, condemn metaphysicians who did the same.

Similar difficulties were even more dramatically interwoven into the fabric of Wittgenstein's *Tractatus*. Its author, ever reflective, was explicitly well aware of them. Specifically, he recognized that the sentences of that book were neither tautologies nor empirical propositions and so, on Tractarian grounds, must be counted as nonsense. Far from trying to avoid this conclusion, Wittgenstein embraced it – and did so in a spirit that approached triumph. Towards the end of the *Tractatus*, Wittgenstein wrote the following:

> 6.54 My propositions serve as elucidations in the following way: anyone who understands me eventually recognizes them as nonsensical, when he has used them – as steps – to climb up beyond them. (He must, so to speak, throw away the ladder after he has climbed up it.)
>
> He must transcend these propositions, and then he will see the world aright.

Wittgenstein, then, flatly admitted that the sentences of the *Tractatus* amounted to nonsense – but, he urged, it was helpful nonsense that showed or pointed to or elucidated something important that cannot, strictly, be said. Granting this, however, it might be asked whether a metaphysician might make the same, or similar, plea on behalf of his or her own 'transcendent' views. Presumably, Wittgenstein would have resisted such a plea on behalf of metaphysics, somehow insisting on a difference between the 'elucidary' nonsense of the *Tractatus* and the misleading nonsense of metaphysics.

For Wittgenstein, there was another parodoxical aspect to his rejection of metaphysics. The *Tractatus*, for all its anti-metaphysical conviction, itself contains sentences that look for all the world to be as traditionally metaphysical as any pronouncement of, say, Plato, Leibniz or Bradley. Readers of the *Tractatus* – including most members of the Vienna Circle – did not pay much attention to the very earliest or the very latest passages of that book. This is hardly surprising. Those passages contain extremely difficult paragraphs that seem jarringly discontinuous with the rest of the book which, relatively speaking, and, at least in outline, is easier to understand. In the opening passages, for example, Wittgenstein engages the same subject that had so troubled Russell – namely the nature of atomic propositions, atomic facts, and their constituents. While Wittgenstein never gives an example of an atomic proposition and appears to have thought that they lay deeply obscured beneath the surface phenomena of language, he does offer a number of remarks on the subject. He holds that atomic propositions are concatenations of elemental names; that the propositions picture atomic facts; and that the names refer to the basic constituents of those facts which he calls 'simple objects'. These simple objects are, in the Tractarian scheme of things, nothing less than the ultimate referents of language, and so the ultimate furniture, so to speak, of the world.

His characterizations of these simples are most remarkable. He insists upon their absolute simplicity, indivisibility, indestructibility and timelessness; indeed, his words suggest entities no less remarkable and extraordinary than Platonic forms, Leibnizian monads or perhaps even Bradley's absolute. Further, while allowing that these simples are capable of relating to one another in various ways, he states that the set of possible variations – of possible facts – is fixed as a matter of *necessity*, that it is timeless and unchangeable, established, as it were, once and for all. Taking him at his word, it would appear that this necessity is nothing less than a *metaphysical* necessity, which determines the possibilities for the world independent of language or thought. He uses the expression 'the form of the world' to elucidate this set of possible arrangements of the simples into facts – a set which, he adds, determines and fixes the set of possible propositions about the world. This would appear to be traditional metaphysics with a vengeance. And it points to another paradox in the *Tractatus*. Not only do its sentences condemn themselves to meaninglessness; its radically anti-metaphysical doctrines rest on a view of language which evidently has deeply metaphysical underpinnings.

While none of this concerned Wittgenstein much when he wrote the *Tractatus*, his later thoughts – largely products of work done in the 1930s and 1940s after his return to philosophy – explicitly reject these features of his early work. Specifically, his definitive later work, the *Philosophical Investigations*, takes care to show that its remarks on language, far from undermining themselves, apply straightforwardly to its own sentences. It exposes the metaphysical underpinnings of the *Tractatus* and rejects them as pathology of thought. While still insisting that metaphysics is senseless, the *Investigations* takes a somewhat more sympathetic view. It denies that metaphysical pronouncements, which seem to capture deep features of reality itself, actually succeed in doing so; but it allows that such statements, stripped of such pretensions, and seen in the right light, can succeed in calling attention to important features *of language*. Wittgenstein believed that the metaphysician was deceived by language itself and confused truths about words – 'grammatical truths' in his terminology – with truths about the world. Wittgenstein devotes a great deal of effort to making these claims.

It is interesting that Carnap, perhaps the Vienna Circle's most enduring figure, working independently of Wittgenstein, developed a similar view of metaphysics in his more mature work. He argues, in *Logical Syntax of Language* published in 1937, that a major source of metaphysical pseudo-statements concerns a tendency to express syntactical distinctions in what he called 'the material mode of speech' rather than the more appropriate 'formal mode' [3.7]. Where for Wittgenstein, metaphysics was misconstrued 'grammar'; for Carnap, it was misconstrued syntax. The two views are closely aligned. Both philosophers emphasized that truths about words were confused with truths about the world and both tried to identify the source of such confusion in language. Their views, while sharing continuities with those of the *Tractatus* and the early positivist tracts, show greater sophistication. They are expressed in works that are more attentive to the origins of metaphysics in details of linguistic confusion, more willing to grant to metaphysicians a measure of insight, albeit confused, more self-reflectively constrained and more attuned to connections among logic, meaning and context. It might be said that the work of some leading philosophers of the second half of the century who have allowed themselves to discuss issues relating to ontology, modality, realism and essentialism – Quine, Ayer, Goodman, Strawson, Kripke, Dummett, Putnam and others – is carried out in a recognizably similar spirit.

As such, metaphysics has re-emerged in some measure, but in a form that recognizes, as a matter of course, constraints that would have been anathema to Hegel, Bradley or McTaggart. These constraints can be viewed as the legacy of the great philosophical figures discussed in this essay. The most notable of these connects with a new philosophical consensus concerning the relationship between philosophy and science. The absolute idealists, less than one hundred years ago, were willing to express metaphysical views clearly incompatible with the most basic views of modern science. Those philosophers of today still willing to engage in metaphysics, do so, almost unanimously, while rejecting any notion that it can produce substantive results that can add to – much less supersede – those of the sciences. This attitude, perhaps, reflects a more global cultural shift: one in which the approved methods for finding substantive truths about the world, its structure and its components simply are those of the sciences. Metaphysics, on such an assumption, can add nothing to this; it must be satisfied with a meaningful but secondary role of interpretation, clarification or proper conceptualization.

❧ BIBLIOGRAPHY ❧

3.1 Ayer, A. J. *Language, Truth, and Logic,* 2nd edn, London: Gollancz, 1946.

3.2 —— ed. *Logical Positivism,* Glencoe, Ill.: The Free Press, 1959.

3.3 —— *The Origins of Pragmatism: Studies in the Philosophy of Charles Sanders Peirce and William James,* San Francisco: W. H. Freeman, 1968.

3.4 —— *Philosophy in the Twentieth Century,* New York: Random House, 1982.

3.5 —— *Russell and Moore: The Analytical Heritage,* London: Macmillan, 1971.

3.6 Bradley, F. H. *Appearance and Reality,* London: Oxford University Press, 1893.

3.7 Carnap, Rudolf *The Logical Syntax of Language,* New York: Harcourt Brace Jovanovich, 1937.

3.8 James, William *The Meaning of Truth: A Sequel To 'Pragmatism',* New York: Longman, 1909.

3.9 —— *Some Problems of Philosophy,* New York: Longmans, Green, 1911.

3.10 —— *Pragmatism: A New Name for Some Old Ways of Thinking,* New York: Longman, 1925.

3.11 —— *The Will to Believe and Other Essays in Popular Philosophy,* New York: Longman, 1897.

3.12 —— 'Does Consciousness Exist?', reprinted in *The Writings of William James,* ed. John J. McDermott, New York: Random House, 1967.

3.13 Malcolm, Norman *Nothing is Hidden,* Oxford: Oxford University Press, 1986.

3.14 Moore, G. E. *Philosophical Studies,* London: Kegan Paul, Trench & Trubner, 1922.

3.15 —— *Some Main Problems of Philosophy,* London: Allen & Unwin, 1953.

3.16 —— *Philosophical Papers,* London: Allen & Unwin, 1959.

3.17 Munitz, Milton K. *Contemporary Analytic Philosophy,* New York: Macmillan, 1981.

3.18 Peirce, Charles Sanders *The Collected Papers of Charles Sanders Peirce,* 8 vols, vols 1–6 ed. C. Hartshorne and P. Weiss, vols 7–8 ed. A. W. Burks, Cambridge, Mass.: Harvard University Press, 1931–58.

3.19 Russell, Bertrand *Our Knowledge of the External World,* La Salle, Ill.: Open Court, 1914.

3.20 —— *Mysticism and Logic and Other Essays,* London: Allen & Unwin, 1917.

3.21 —— *The Analysis of Mind*, London: Allen & Unwin, 1921.
3.22 —— *Principia Mathematica*, 3 vols, 2nd edn, written with A. N. Whitehead, Cambridge: Cambridge University Press, 1925.
3.23 —— *The Analysis of Matter*, London: Kegan Paul, Trench & Trubner, 1927.
3.24 —— *The Problems of Philosophy*, New York: Oxford University Press, 1967.
3.25 —— *Logic and Knowledge*, ed. R. C. Marsh, London: Allen & Unwin, 1956.
3.26 Schilpp, P. A. ed. *The Philosophy of G. E. Moore*, Library of Living Philosophers, vol. 4, Evanston, Ill.: Northwestern University Press, 1942.
3.27 Thayer, H. S. *Meaning and Action: A Study of American Pragmatism*, Indianapolis: Bobbs-Merrill, 1973.
3.28 Urmson, J. O. *Philosophical Analysis: Its Development between the Two World Wars*, Oxford: Oxford University Press, 1956.
3.29 Warnock, G. J. *English Philosophy since 1900*, London: Oxford University Press, 1966.
3.30 Wittgenstein, Ludwig *Tractatus Logico-Philosophicus*, trans. D. F. Pears and B. F. McGuiness, London: Kegan Paul, Trench & Trubner, 1961.

CHAPTER 4

Metaphysics II (1945 to the present)

Bernard Linsky

❧❦❧

❧ THE REDISCOVERY OF METAPHYSICS ❧

Metaphysics in the analytic tradition since 1945 has been a sustained reaction to the anti-metaphysical position of logical positivism. In his *Logical Syntax of Language* (1937), Rudolf Carnap lists a number of philosophical problems and notions that arise from mistaking puzzling features of language for substantive questions about reality. The traditional theories of truth, realism, universals, essential properties, time, causation, and so on, the subject matter of metaphysics since Aristotle, are, he charges, all due to confusion of language in its ordinary use, in the 'material mode' and language that really is about language, the 'formal mode' of speech. They confuse trivial, or meaningless assertions about language with substantive claims about the world. Though positivism denied the meaningfulness of most traditional issues, in the very linguistic approach of that denial one can see a somewhat traditional nominalist position emerging. What followed in the 1930s and 1940s were developments in logic and the philosophy of science that vindicated some aspects of the traditional problems of truth and the nature of necessity, causality, space and time. Since 1945 there has been a steady process by which problems have come to be seen as meaningful (although perhaps primarily logical or empirical in nature) and then become subject to many of the sorts of theories that had been presented at various other times in the history of metaphysics. The story, then, is of the re-emergence of metaphysics, primarily a certain Aristotelian tradition in metaphysics. The role of modal notions of necessity and essence clearly indicate that origin. For the most part there has also been a relative lack of interest in the metaphysical questions of the Kantian tradition. Discussions of free will versus determinism, the nature and place of the self and of God in the natural world, have not been central. Rather, the emphasis has been on questions of ontology and the most general features of the natural world, time, space and matter. One Kantian issue that has come to the centre of discussion again is the problem of realism versus idealism, now formulated as realism versus 'anti-realism'.

This survey traces what seems to have been the main line of development of metaphysics in the English-speaking world, namely the mainstream of the analytic tradition. Metaphysics, more so than other fields of philosophy in this century, has been a field in which schools of thought have clearly distinguished themselves from that main stream. Pursuing metaphysics as an independent subject has been a rallying point for those opposed to analytic philosophy, seeing it as the heir to the anti-metaphysical stance of logical positivism. Inevitably, then, this survey will miss what many may well see as the centre of the real metaphysics done in this period. Peripheral or not, all these groups maintained their version of the classical issues in metaphysics and, during this period since 1945, have, to varying extents, contributed to the rediscovery of metaphysics.

Thomism, the philosophy of Saint Thomas Aquinas, has been a persisting and central part of philosophy as taught in Catholic institutions of higher education throughout the English-speaking world. The *Review of Metaphysics*, edited at the Catholic University of America (founded in 1947), has served to maintain what might be seen as the broader tradition in metaphysics, publishing essays in the Thomistic tradition, as well as papers on topics from the whole history of metaphysics, discussions of metaphysics in the continental tradition, as well as several classics of analytic metaphysics. The position of maintaining a minority tradition in metaphysics is also that of the students of 'process philosophy' following Charles Hartshorne and Paul Weiss in his inspiration by the later work of Alfred North Whitehead. Closer to the mainstream, but still a self-identified minority position has been that of Gustav Bergmann's students, who have maintained discussions of metaphysics in the realist tradition of Bertrand Russell's logical atomism from before World War I. They maintained an interest in classical issues of realism about universals and the nature of particulars which re-entered the centre of discussion with the revival of interest in universals in the late 1970s. Bergmann insisted that logical positivism had not destroyed metaphysics as a subject, but had rather contributed a method for the study of traditional issues. And, he claimed, it had come to traditional positions, nominalism, materialism or phenomenalism in different hands. These views are becoming the accepted view. Accompanying the re-emergence of metaphysics has been a growing self-conciousness, an awareness that many apparently 'semantic' issues in logic and philosophy of language had import for metaphysics and embodied traditional metaphysical positions.

❧ NOMINALISM ❧

Nelson Goodman's *The Structure of Appearance* appeared in 1951 although the Harvard doctoral thesis on which it is based was completed in 1940. It was essentially an analysis of and improvement on Carnap's *The Logical Structure of the World*. The project was to 'construct' the world of space, time and material objects from the basic experiences or *qualia* presented in sense. The underlying ontology is that of phenomenalism. Material objects are just collections of appearances. The subject matter of the theory is experience, conceived as composed of individual items with sensory qualities, units of perception of colour and sound, etc. For Goodman the goal of a constructionist project is only to produce a reconstruction of a notion which is *extensionally isomorphic* to the pre-theoretic original. Isomorphism requires only the sameness of structure as represented in extensional logic, objects and relations which mimic the original. These constructions were to be effected with only the apparatus of *mereology* the 'calculus of individuals' originally developed by the Polish logician Lesniewski in the 1920s. That calculus is axiomatized by Goodman using only the one primitive first-order relation of 'overlap'. The *mereological sum* of individuals is another individual, importantly of the same logical type as its parts. For Goodman the characterizing feature of nominalism is that it does not involve commitment to any abstract objects such as sets or intensional entities, just objects and their sums. Logical type is the test of ontological category for Goodman.

While metaphysicians in this period have been reluctant to accept other categories of objects, in particular resisting any abstract entities other than sets, a generous ontology of particulars (assumed to be material, or at least physical) has been a general starting point. Every collection of objects and parts of objects forms a sum which has as its parts precisely those objects. Thus there is an object consisting of my hand, that book and the city of London. It has been seen as a problem to be solved, just what it is that distinguishes what we think of ordinarily as objects. Are they just those mereological sums that are of importance or interest to us? The problem of how and why we 'individuate' objects as we do, immediately comes to the fore, not as in earlier times as an epistemological question of our identifying and perhaps synthesizing objects from a stream of experience, but rather a question of explaining which of the many existing mereological sums are in fact those that are important to us. The 'construction' of the

Carnap–Goodman project does not create objects, rather it reconstructs our conceptual scheme and those objects that are important to us from a few primitive psychological notions, such as perceived similarity, thus explaining what it is that we select for our interests from the huge pre-existing ontology of the 'external' world of phenomena. The division of the world into objects and those in turn into kinds based on shared properties is all seen as in some way arbitrary, not 'real'. This form of nominalism, is, then, allied to anti-realism.

Goodman's account of qualities, or universals, illustrates the central role which mereology plays in his constructive project. Carnap had followed the nominalist strategy of constructing qualities as classes of individuals similar in the right way to each other. Roughly, a quality like blue is just a class of things similar to each other, the class of all blue things. Membership is determined not by possession of the same universal colour, but rather by greater similarity with other members of the class than with things outside the class. The class is the only general object, the one having many members as its 'instances'. This led, however, to the problem of 'imperfect community'. It is not possible to define a property as a class of objects more similar to each other than to anything outside the class as, for example, a red rubber ball, a blue wooden ball and a red wooden cube might resemble each other more closely than other objects such as some other red or wooden things, or balls, without sharing any real property in common. Goodman's solution is this: by treating mereological sums as individuals, they become possible candidates for the similarity relation. It is the mereological sum of individuals, not the individuals separately, which another must resemble to have the quality they share. Thus while taken pairwise the objects in the group may resemble each other strongly, the mereological sum of the group does not have the uniformity necessary to be similar to other objects whether red, wooden or balls.

Another feature of Goodman's nominalism which became more important in his later thought is the emphasis on predicates as the only general or universal entities. Thus 'green' is as good a predicate, and hence as good a property as his famous invented predicate, 'grue' (being observed before 2000 AD and green, otherwise blue). This leads to problems in epistemology when it is asked why inductions on actual emeralds, all of which are both green and grue, can lead to opposite predictions about emeralds inspected after the year 2000? Still later this nominalism leads to Goodman's version of anti-realism. To use his example, if predicates such as 'stereo system' are human contrivances, carving up the world according to our human interests and so mind-dependent, then so is 'star', and hence stars are every bit as much mind-dependent.

Goodman's nominalism influenced both his senior colleague

Quine and the whole generation of metaphysicians trained at Harvard University, even if it was principally by contrast with the austere ontology of their teacher that positions were defined.

❧ IDENTITY AND INDIVIDUATION ❧

The 'ordinary-language philosophy' centred at Oxford and flourishing after 1945 and through the 1950s, tried to find in the study of ordinary language the resolution of traditional philosophical problems by diagnosing and eliminating some confusion underlying them. In practice it continued the hostility of logical positivism towards metaphysics. Thus David Pears' article, 'Universals' (1951), proposed an almost psychoanalytic account of the search for universals to underpin or explain the use of predicates [4.16]. Universals are shadows of predicates and the search is for an explanation where none is to be found. What do all red things have in common? Well, they are red. What more could be needed or provided as an explanation? We can explain what particular things have in common in different ways, but not what is common to all cases of similar objects. The problem of universals is not to give an account of some sort of entity which performs a certain theoretical function, but rather to provide a cure for the desire to find such entities. While Renford Bambrough's 'Universals and Family Resemblances' (1960) ostensibly grants that there is a problem of universals, it finds the solution to the problem in Wittgenstein's notion of family resemblance, a solution that in effect denies the assumption of the problem that there is some one thing in common to the instances of a general term for which we need an account.

Not all discussions of metaphysical topics were so dismissive of the purported problems. Max Black's article 'The Identity of Indiscernibles' (1952) presented the thesis that no two objects could have all the same properties as quite clearly meaningful, but just as clearly false [4.5]. He suggested that one could easily imagine a universe consisting of two metal indiscernible metal spheres, and nothing else. Black introduced the approach of the ordinary-language school in analysing attempts to argue against his counter-example. Repeatedly it appears that we cannot insist that certain words have meaning, that we can, for example, succeed in referring to one sphere rather than another, just by having certain thoughts. We must show that such thoughts are not just pictures that lead us astray. We must remember the public and objective nature of the referring process in language by which things get their names. For example, we cannot name the spheres in the story, since, by hypothesis, no one exists in the universe to give them names. Black's article raised issues of the connection between the particularity of objects and of the preconditions for identifying and naming objects that was central to the metaphysical discussions of the next years, including in the work of Strawson.

Peter F. Strawson, with *Individuals; An Essay in Descriptive Metaphysics* (1959), moved away from the the anti-metaphysical tradition of the logical positivists as it had been continued by the ordinary-language movement [4.23]. Strawson called his project 'descriptive metaphysics'. His goal was to unearth the metaphysical scheme of our ordinary, non-scientific view of the world, to be found embedded in our ordinary language. Thus moving from the basic speech acts of referring and describing which correspond with the subject-predicate structure of our language, Strawson attributed a basic conceptual scheme composed of objects located in space and time with their qualities. The ability to use names requires 'identifying' and then 're-identifying' their referents at another time and thus the presupposition of a framework of enduring spatial objects within which such identification could proceed. Questions of ontological dependence are replaced by issues of conceptual priority. We do not ask whether space is absolute, or whether spatial relations depend on objects. Rather the question becomes whether a spatial framework is necessary for re-identifying objects. That may be so, if indeed we can only re-identify objects by tracing them through space from one time to another. Strawson devotes a chapter to investigating the intelligibility of a 'sound world' in which we only perceive sounds of different pitches in a temporal sequence.

Strawson's view of universals is a combination of conceptualist and nominalist elements. The concept of universal or property results from considering predication to 'introduce' an entity much as reference does. The entity is identified by the concept which we associate with the predicate. Strawson's interest was not with the ontological status of what is introduced by predicates as much as in the asymmetry between referring and predicating. He was concerned with the difference in category between objects and predicates. Objects can only be introduced by referring expressions, whereas predicated entities can also be referred to. Strawson argued that the asymmetry of logical role is not due to a difference in kinds of entities involved, but rather our talk of kinds of entities is a reflection of the prior differences in logical role. The difference between particulars and universals reflects the difference between referring and predicating. Strawson was also concerned with the conceptual relations between general qualities and particulars. What is the process of 'individuation' by which talk of a property being instantiated is replaced by talk of individuals? Here Strawson disagreed with Quine who considers the very same problem. Strawson argued that a language that merely 'places' features at various locations, saying that there is snow or water in such and such a place, can only be an artificial one, and must depend on a prior conceptual scheme in which places are identified by objects that occupy them and features are the properties of those objects. Our ordinary scheme of objects with their properties located in space and time is conceptually prior to others that might be proposed as scientific or less ontologically laden.

In addition to material particulars, Strawson presented persons as an equally fundamental ontological category. The traditional problem of relating the mind to the body is resolved by seeing persons as a fundamental conceptual and hence ontological category, to which we attribute both mental and physical predicates. It is the person which both thinks and has material properties. This view has come to be known as 'property' dualism, as it avoids the familiar dualism of substance and is a forerunner of contemporary functionalism in the philosophy of mind.

Strawson's influence continued with David Wiggins who introduced versions of Aristotelian notions of natural kind and essential property using the Strawsonian framework of notions of identification and conceptual dependence. Those properties that we rely on to make sense of claims of identity through time, to 're-identify' the same object later, are candidates for essential properties, those properties an object could not but have had. This leads to a conceptualist account of modal notions. Properties are essential to objects because they underlie our conceptual framework. We could not have useful concepts for certain objects unless we attribute to them, that is, see them as having, certain essential properties. This move to attributing ontological significance to the preconditions of reference or use of language had led to a dispute over the notion of 'relative identity'. It has been argued that we only make sense of claims that one thing is the same as another relative to a category; something is the same statue or the same lump of bronze, not merely the same 'thing'. The view that we can always supply a 'sortal' term to supplement identity claims and that they seem incomplete otherwise has led some to the thesis that the relation of identity itself is relativized to such sortals. This in turn has led to an investigation of the nature of personal identity, those conditions under which we would say that one is the same person as someone before.

Contemporary treatment of the problem of identity started with examples from Locke of the same soul animating different bodies over time and went on to discuss science fiction scenarios involving such things as brain duplication and matter transfer. Work on these puzzles led to a widespread interest in the self and an awakening to the importance of the concept of personal identity. If one argues that the present self is not strictly identical with the later one, what is the rationality of self-interested actions now when the later person will benefit? What happens to the notion of moral responsibility as well? The topic of 'personal identity' has also led to discussion of the seemingly perspectival nature of certain concepts. The very notions of self-interest, or self-knowledge, require that there is a difference between objects that from a third person, or detached point of view are the same. Aside from the fact that so-and-so has certain properties, what more is added to the belief or knowledge that *I* am so-and-so? It is by this route that metaphysical problems of the self and our place in the world have emerged out of the original interest in the simple relation of identity.

Willard van Orman Quine has developed a metaphysical theory as a part of his coherent philosophy of language and science, replacing Strawson's 'ordinary' conceptual scheme with the metaphysics of science. Like Strawson, his approach to metaphysics is to investigate the metaphysical view imputed by a certain conceptual or linguistic scheme, only in this case the scheme is that of science broadly construed, rather than that of ordinary language. At the beginning of his *Word and Object* we find: 'Entification begins at arm's length; the points of condensation in the primordial conceptual scheme are things glimpsed, not glimpses' ([4.20], 1). Objects are the result of 'entification', as much our doing as really there. Quine openly sees ontology as something that is imputed by a theory which can at the same time be seen as chosen for various seemingly subjective reasons. We select the simplest theory, the one which requires minimum revision to our previous theory, and so on, fully realizing that this may not be leading us to how things 'really are'. That he sees as a remnant of the 'transcendental' metaphysics that logical positivism overthrew.

Quine assumes the ontology of science, which he sees as that of a single, four-dimensional distribution of matter across points of space-time, and the language of science, the language of first-order logic enriched with predicates for both theoretical and observational terms. Quine's commitment to the language of first-order logic as a starting point in metaphysics has various consequences. One is Quine's test for the ontological commitment of a theory. A theory is committed to those objects that are quantified over in its statements. In his influential article 'On What There Is' [4.19], Quine criticizes Meinong's theory of objects which holds that even Pegasus must have some sort of being in order to be an object of thought. Quine responds that this is a mistake, based on that fallacious assumption that names must refer to something in order to be meaningful. The meaning of names, like that of definite descriptions, such as 'the tallest mountain', are given by expressions of logic that do not depend for their meaning on having a referent. One can meaningfully deny 'The winged horse exists' without there having to be a winged horse. That is because the sentence only involves predicates and quantifiers. It says, roughly, that there is some winged horse (and at most one winged horse). That sentence is simply false. True sentences with names or descriptions in them only commit one to the objects that the resulting quantifiers and their variables range over. Statements such as 'Some quarks have up spin', when regimented as 'There exists an x such that x is a quark and x has up spin', is seen clearly to commit us to quarks. This results from the view that variables are the genuinely referring devices in a language, names being eliminable in terms of definite descriptions and those in turn eliminable via Russell's theory of descriptions. Bound variables, such as the x above are said to 'range over' certain objects, and the commitment of the theory to them is determined by that quantification alone. Quine's slogan is: 'To be is to be the value of a bound variable'.

There are several immediate consequences of this simple doctrine. Any such notion as Meinong's distinction between entities with being as objects of thought, and those that exist, is ruled out. 'Everything exists' is a simple theorem of logic when read as 'Everything is identical with something', yet it has ontological consequences. There is no realm of non-existent or merely possible beings. Second, no other part of language besides bound variables will produce any ontological commitment. Quantification is the only way a theory commits one to objects. The use of predicates does not commit one to the existence of universals. Quine is quite openly nominalistic about predication. A predicate is simply 'true of' its many instances. They do not have to have any *thing* in common, any universal. To be a man, Quine says, is just to be such that one's name with the predicate 'is a man' produces a true sentence. It is that which all men have in common. As the thesis that what is general is only a general term, this is a classic statement of nominalism. Quine himself followed Goodman's slightly different definition by which any acceptance of abstract entities, even particulars such as sets, is a move away from nominalism and towards Platonism. The seemingly unavoidable use of mathematics, and thus of the set theory to which it is reduced, within science led Quine to take the variables of set theory at face value as ranging over sets, objects differing from the individuals of Goodman's mereology.

Quine's criterion for deciding to make an ontological commitment is the pragmatic test of the needs of 'science' for the proposed entities. Does the simplest, most comprehensive theory of the phenomena quantify over entities? If so, then adopt the theory and accept the accompanying ontological commitment. Simplicity and fruitfulness are pragmatic criteria. It is easy to see why one might make use of such theories, but it is not obvious, to a realist, why they make a theory more likely to be true. Quine's philosophy is thus following in the Harvard pragmatist tradition of James and Peirce. Truth is to be explained, or at least judged on pragmatic grounds. For making an ontological commitment Quine defers to science, but in practice he argued against certain entities on more *a priori* grounds. Science, and common sense, require that theoretical entities be well defined. Quine's primary test for recognizing entities, came to be the easy statement of 'identity conditions'. The model answers are provided for material objects, which are the same if they occupy the same spatio-temporal locations, and sets; sets x and y are the same if and only if the members of x are exactly the members of y. This condition does not define identity for the objects in question, since it takes the notion of identity as primitive, nor does it describe how to 'identify' entities, as in Strawson's notion. It is simply a thesis of the theory of sets, one which gives necessary and sufficient conditions for the identity of sets. The lack of such identity conditions was used by Quine as a complaint about universals and other 'intensional' entities such as propositions and possible objects. 'No entity without identity' is the slogan for this aspect of Quine's metaphysics. Between the quantifiers and identity we have all of the conceptual apparatus that Quine needs. Where Strawson was concerned about the dependency of our notion of object on a framework of space and time, Quine speculates about the emergence of the notion of individual when mass terms such as 'water' get supplemented with the use of identity to produce individuals. Thus at some point a child's notion of 'mama around' is replaced by the notion of a persisting object, her mother, that is distinct from others. Time is not a framework in which objects are identified and re-identified, but rather a dimension along which the temporal parts of objects can be located. For an object to be red at one time and green (thus not red) at another, requires that the object have distinct parts, one of which is located 'at' the first time and is red, and the other of which is 'at' the second and which is green. The relation between the two is not identity, rather they are parts of a particular mereological sum which is identified as an object.

That the language of science is the guide to ontology has consequences when Quine considers that the truth-conditions for sentences and the range of quantifiers are only stated in a background metalanguage. This leads to the doctrine of ontological relativity: the thesis that one can only specify the ontological commitment of a theory in the terminology of another theory and that different such accounts can be equally justified. Indeed very distinct background theories and assignments can agree on the truth of all sentences in the object theory. Quine gives this example: an account of a language which interprets the term *gavagai* as true of rabbits which is as empirically adequate as one that interprets the term as true of undetached rabbit parts. There is thus a slack that can be taken up in different ways, producing incompatible accounts of ontological commitment, and giving an ineliminable relativity to claims about ontology. There is not a fact of the matter about our ontological commitment, except as it is revealed by a particular choice of meta-language and theory. When we are studying our own ontology this meta-language is an extension of our own object language. While 'There are quarks with up spin' commits us to quarks, there is no theory-neutral way to explain what that commitment amounts to. Quine presents this as an aspect of the pragmatist element in his thinking. We work inside a conceptual scheme, or theory, trying to improve it as we go, but, in the image he takes from Otto Neurath, like sailors in a ship who must rebuild at sea. We make the best of the theory we have and do not strive for some external, God's-eye view from which to assess our knowledge. This doctrine of ontological relativity and the accompanying view of our attitude towards our own ontology was later taken up by anti-realists.

Donald Davidson proposed the study of the ontological commitments of a meta-language as a method for metaphysics. Davidson argued that a theory of truth, in the form proposed by Tarski, is not only an approach to an account of meaning for a language, but also a guide to its ontology. Following Quine, he agreed that the ontological commitment of a theory is determined by the range of its quantifiers, but then went on to suggest that quantification could be found in contexts where it is not on the surface. Thus Davidson argued for the recognition of *events* in our ontology on the grounds that a proper account of inferences of certain sentences about actions requires them to be treated as quantifying over events. A theory of truth must account for logical inferences in a language and so one may go from knowledge of inferences to a theory of truth that would justify them and that may reveal hidden ontological commitments. Thus, one may infer from 'Jones buttered the toast in the bathroom with a knife at midnight' that 'Jones buttered the toast in the bathroom with a knife', 'Jones buttered the toast in the bathroom', 'Jones buttered the toast', and more. The ordinary formulation of such sentences in first-order logic, using a relational expression 'x buttered y in z with w at t', will not permit such inferences. Only a formulation with explicit quantification over events will capture those inferences, he argued. One must treat the original as of the form 'There is an event e and e is a buttering and e is of the toast and e is by Jones and e is in the bathroom and e is at midnight' which permits the inference to the other sentences, easily, once they are seen to be of the forms 'there is an event e and is a buttering and e is of the toast' for example. Putting sentences into a logical form in first-order logic, because it is necessary for giving a theory of truth for a language, becomes in turn a method in metaphysics, the 'method of truth in metaphysics'.

Quine had identified events simply as classes of points in space-time, thus seeing ordinary objects as simply enduring events (those oriented along the time axis in space-time). Davidson felt required to postulate them as *sui generis* entities, since it appears that two distinct events can occupy the same space at the same time. He suggested the example of a sphere slowly rotating and growing warm at the same time. It seems that there are two events occurring together, the rotating of the sphere and its warming. If not spatio-temporal location, then what are the identity conditions for events? Several rival accounts have been proposed, usually involving reducing events further to some other category, usually to combinations of objects and properties. Perhaps the two events are distinguished by the different properties they involve, growing warm and moving around an axis. Davidson, with the same nominalist inclinations as Quine, would have none of that. Rather, he suggested, events are to be identified by their causes and effects, same causes and effects, same event, to mimic Quine's criterion for sets, same members same set. The criterion has struck most as quite different from Quine's and not as successful. The ensuing discussion of events was most fruitful for the theory of action, as well as reviving interest in events and related notions such as that of facts which had been absent from metaphysical discussions since the time of logical atomism.

Davidson's discussion of events was driven by the need to formulate event sentences in first-order logic. His and Quine's philosophy is deeply committed to the validity of first-order logic and its extensional nature as the proper language of science. Quine's purely technical objections to the logic of necessity (quantified modal logic) were accompanied, however, by the conviction that making sense of that logic would lead to unsavoury metaphysical involvements, the 'jungle of Aristotelian essentialism'. His opposition to modal logic was met as a challenge, by some of his own students, and so was perhaps the leading cause of a revival of the very Aristotelian metaphysics that he dreaded.

MODAL METAPHYSICS

Saul Kripke introduced a new era of metaphysical theorizing with his possible-world semantics in the early 1960s and particularly his lectures 'Naming and Necessity' given in 1970 at Princeton University. As part of his qualms about intensional notions, Quine had charged that quantifiers could not always be intelligibly combined with sentence operators such as 'It is necessary that'. Quine held that one might try to make sense of 'It is necessary that there exists some x such that x is F', what is called *de dicto* necessity, as some disguised claim about the sentence 'There exists an x such that x is F', perhaps one which claims it is an analytic truth or an axiom. This account is true to the etymology of 'dictum' as 'what is said'. The other combination, or relative scope for the quantifier and operator, as in 'There is an x such that it is necessary that x is F', leads to an assertion of *de re* necessity (necessity in the thing, *res*). Here it is at least one thing x which is claimed to have a necessary property. This cannot be easily interpreted as an attribution of necessity to something that is said. Quine thought that interpreting such sentences would require a forced and arbitrary distinction between the properties of an object, those it has merely in virtue of how it is described and those it has of necessity, or essentially. To use the example which Quine favoured, a bicycling mathematician seems to be essentially two-legged when described as bicycling, and rational when described as a mathematician, but does not have one property more essentially than the other. Discriminating properties on such a subjective basis leads, Quine feared, to the hopeless confusions, or 'jungle' of Aristotelian essentialism, the logical positivist's equivalent of the early modern philosopher's horror of scholasticism.

Kripke's possible-world semantics provided a way of modelling such distinctions. A sentence is to be interpreted in terms of a class of possible worlds in addition to a distinguished *actual* world. For a sentence asserting necessarily p to be (simply) true (that is, true at the actual world), p must be true at all possible worlds. *De re* necessity is represented by seeing the worlds as each having a domains consisting of the objects existing at that world, domains which can overlap in membership. An object x is essentially F if it is F at every world in which it exists. The *de dicto* assertion above is taken as true if there is some object or other in each world which is F. For example (to modify one of Quine's famous examples) the *de dicto* claim 'Necessarily there is a shortest spy' is true because in each world some spy is shorter than all others. For the *de re* assertion to be true there must be one object that is F at all worlds in which it exists. Thus the clearly false *de re* claim 'Some spy is necessarily the shortest spy' requires that there be some one individual spy who is shorter than all other spies in all the worlds in which that spy exists. Much of recent modal metaphysics can be seen as an attempt to explore the metaphysical commitments and assumptions of this possible-world semantics.

With a way of making sense of *de re* necessity in hand, Kripke went on to make several claims about particular examples of *de re* necessary truths. One which has had a great impact in the philosophy of language has been the claim of the necessity of identity. One consequence of Kripke semantics is that for any x and y, if $x = y$ then necessarily $x = y$. This is compatible with the failure of substitutivity in modal contexts, the intensionality which is a defining characteristic of this logic. It may be that both a *de dicto* truth that:

It is not necessary that nine = the number of the planets

and a *de re* truth that:

Of the number of the planets (i.e. nine) and nine, it is necessarily the case that the former = the latter.

While definite descriptions do not pick out the same object in each world, and hence lead to apparently contingent identity claims, 'rigid designators' which do pick out the same object across worlds will appear in necessary identity statements. Thus, claimed Kripke, if 'Hesperus' and 'Phosphorus' are both names (for Venus) and hence rigid designators, then 'Hesperus = Phosphorus' is a necessary truth. Kripke presented this as an example of a necessary truth which is knowable only *a posteriori*, which runs against the traditional identification of the necessary with the *a priori*. While this abandonment of the traditional epistemology of necessity had a liberating effect on metaphysical speculation it has not been replaced by an agreed-upon alternative epistemological account.

Kripke's extension of his notion of rigid designator to natural-kind terms produced another class of candidate *de re* necessary truths. If general terms such as 'water', 'tiger' and 'H_2O' pick out natural kinds rigidly, i.e. across possible worlds, then such claims as 'Water = H_2O' and 'Tigers are animals' may express necessary truths of the new class, *a posteriori*, *de re* necessities. A large debate has developed surrounding the essential properties of natural kinds and whether, in fact, such considerations from the philosophy of language about designation can have such substantive metaphysical consequences.

A second kind of *de re* necessity which Kripke explored was the essentiality of origin. He asserted that it is essential to an object to have the particular origin that it does. Origin is essential for artifacts as well as natural objects, thus a particular wooden lectern was necessarily originally composed of the particular wood from which it was in fact made, although it might later come to be made of different wood over time. (A modal version of the ship of Theseus was soon presented as a challenge to this. Suppose a material object could have been made of slightly different material from that which actually makes it up, say that a wooden ship could have had three or four planks different from those in actuality. But if that differently composed ship would still be the same ship then that different collection of planks could have varied even more, and so on, until, it seems, the ship could have been made of any collection of planks. As with identity through time, identifying objects 'across' worlds seems to be subject to puzzles.) Kripke's thesis also holds for natural objects, in particular people. If so, then a human being, such as Queen Elizabeth, essentially came from the particular egg and sperm from which she did arise. Other offspring of the same person would not have been Elizabeth, and a person even atom for atom like Elizabeth now, but having arisen from a different origin, would not have been the same person.

These theses about the essential properties of individuals and natural kinds have produced much contemporary debate as well as inspiring investigation of those figures in the history of philosophy who investigated modal notions, in particular the Aristotelian tradition. An immediate consequence was various attempts to apply Kripke's notion of natural kinds and essential properties to one prominent example of natural kinds, biological species. The 'species problem' in the philosophy of biology entered the mainstream of metaphysics and soon led to the rival thesis more in keeping with current evolutionary thinking that species are just classes of objects related to each by ancestry, or even best seen as single individuals, mereological sums of the ordinary organisms that belong to them.

Another consequence of Kripke's semantics has been a resurgence of interest in the ontological argument, and other theological issues such as the problem of divine foreknowledge. Alvin Plantinga has defended a modal version of the ontological argument. It is a simple axiom or theorem of modal logic that what is possibly necessary is in fact true. If it is part of God's nature to exist necessarily, from the mere possibility of God's existence we can infer His actual existence. This in turn has led him and many others to look at the epistemological status of modal claims of necessity and possibility, as they do appear as premises of many traditional arguments. Plantinga is one of a number of prominent modal metaphysicians who are also believers. Long thought by its religious detractors to be a part of the atheistic world-view of twentieth-century science, analytic metaphysics has now emerged as a tool for traditional theological speculation and philosophers have moved from the main technical questions of metaphysics to investigations of their own faith with relative ease. Traditional theological notions such as omnipotence, omniscience, atemporal existence, and predestination are all readily explained in modal terms with possible world semantics.

The interpretation of possibility and necessity using possible worlds has also led to a revival of interest in the notions of freedom and determinism. The model of the world as having a fixed, single past, but a branching structure of possible futures has liberated many from the seemingly deterministic metaphysics of natural science with its single space-time extending from past to future. This natural model of an indeterministic world has revived interest in the problem of free will, trying to reconcile the assumption of our freedom to act with the deeply entrenched belief that the world is governed by natural laws that have some sort of modal force. While the Quinean scientific world-view that dominated post-1945 analytic metaphysics gave no special ontological status to natural laws, laws just being universal generalizations arrived at in the right way and with the appropriate epistemological status, it was still felt that being subject to laws was an appropriate analysis of the notion of determinism. To the extent that determinism had content, it was felt to be true. The introduction of possible-world semantics for talk of necessity changed that attitude. The problem of free will has re-emerged in full force.

Developing out of his alternative to Kripke's version of possible-world semantics, David Lewis has developed a complete metaphysical scheme culminating in his *On the Plurality of Worlds* [4.14]. Kripke's semantics makes sense of *de re* necessity by saying that an object x has a property F necessarily, just in case x has F at every possible world w at which x exists. Lewis's alternative counterpart theory holds that each object exists in only one world. When we say that x has F necessarily we mean that in each world w, the *counterpart* of x at w has the property F. Lewis has a surprisingly Quinean view about the reality of counterparts and the possible worlds that contain them. For Lewis possible worlds are spatio-temporally extended objects containing their members as mereological parts. The actual world is just 'me and my surroundings', the universe. Other possible worlds are just like this world, composed of material objects that exist every bit as much as the objects in the actual world. They are separated from this world only by lacking any spatial or temporal relations to objects in this world. Lewis's possible worlds look very much like the world on Quine's view, except there are many of them. Thus it is possible for him to identify properties with sets of objects, although objects drawn from many possible worlds. The property of redness, then, is the set of all red objects, including both the actual and all possible red objects. Using only Quine's physical objects and sets, Lewis is able to distinguish entities that Quine must identify. Lewis also shares Quine's view of the world as composed of objects extended in four dimensions, thus as with Quine, change is explained by different temporal parts of objects having different properties.

The seemingly small addition of what look like many additional versions of Quine's universe of course has far-ranging consequences. Many of the modal notions banned from Quine's ontology are re-introduced by this simple expedient. In addition to the background notion of metaphysical necessity explained as truth at all possible worlds, Lewis is also able to account for more relative or restricted notions of necessity as in causal laws and counter-factual claims about what would have happened under certain circumstances. The basic notion underlying these analyses is Lewis's account of counter-factual conditionals. To say that 'if the match had been struck, it would have lighted' is to say that while the match may not have been struck in the actual world, in those worlds sufficiently similar to this world, but differing by having the match struck, the match also lights. The notion of similarity of possible worlds is taken by Lewis as a primitive for the analysis of a range of other notions. With an account of counterfactual conditionals in hand Lewis then analyses particular causal statements, as in 'the striking of the match caused it to light' in counterfactual terms. The match was struck and lighted, and if it had not been struck, it would not have lighted. Causal laws are then generalizations over actual and possible causal connections. With these analyses in hand, Lewis has ventured into some of the topics not common to recent metaphysics. Thus he can give an account of the traditional 'compatibilist' account of freedom of the will. It is possible for Lewis to give some detail to the account by which actions can be simultaneously caused and subject to natural law, and free in so far as they are caused by our desires and will. An action, however law-governed, is free in so far as had we chosen otherwise, we would have done otherwise. These analyses have also allowed Lewis to speculate more meaningfully about the notion of time-travel with its accompanying puzzles about causation and determination.

What of Quine's criterion of ontological commitment and his rejection of the Meinongian notion of objects that do not exist, but merely have being? Lewis fully accepts Quine's criterion of ontological commitment; all objects one quantifies over in a theory are commitments of the theory. Thus Lewis allows that talk of 'all donkeys' ranges over not only the actual donkeys, but also the possible talking donkeys we are committed to by saying that possibly (i.e. in some possible world) there are talking donkeys. Unlike a Meinongian object, possible entities (*possibilia*) do not have a special status such as being which is distinct from, and somehow inferior to, existence. They exist every bit as much as real entities. But surely, it will be said, then Lewis believes that talking donkeys exist, but donkeys don't talk! Here Lewis replies that there are indeed talking donkeys, but no *actual* talking donkeys. That, however, does not mark a distinction of ontological category, for, according to Lewis, the term 'actual' is an indexical term like 'I' or 'here', meaning something like 'in the same world as the speaker' and so does not mark out a special category of thing any more than other indexicals do.

Lewis's counterpart theory, in particular the view that *every object exists in only one world*, is essential for this 'indexical' theory of actuality, and to his view that every world is just as real as the actual world: what has been dubbed his (extreme) modal realism. Worlds could not be Quinean universes if they contained ordinary objects having properties they do not actually have. Lewis argues for his counterpart theory, indeed, by finding it incoherent for an object to have different properties at different worlds. He formulates this as the 'problem of accidental intrinsics'. Consider, he says, some internal or non-relational property of an object which is not essential to it. It is hence accidental and intrinsic. Thus a person Hubert, who actually has five fingers on his hand, might have had six. Suppose we analyse this by saying that while Hubert has five fingers at the actual world w^* he, Hubert, has six fingers at some other world w'. But having a certain number of fingers is intrinsic to Hubert. What object has six fingers at w'? Hubert, who has five fingers. How can something which has five fingers have six? The reply that the notion of having a property at one world and not at another is primitive to modal metaphysics does not move Lewis. He finds that primitive notion incoherent. Lewis's view is in the minority. The more common view is that objects can exist in different possible worlds. One version of this is sometimes called *haecceitism* (echoing medieval discussions) to indicate that objects have a haecceity or 'thisness' which is independent of any properties they may have, and thus makes sense of existing in a world independent of the properties that are had at the world. Haecceitism is not the only view that supports cross-world entities. An alternative view is that objects can only exist across worlds in virtue of an 'individual essence' (echoing the older 'quiddity' or 'suchness') which provides their identity despite differing (perhaps intrinsic) properties in different worlds.

Both Lewis's notion of actuality and the debate over counterpart theory have led to a growing interest in medieval views of notions of existence, identity and individual essences among modal metaphysicians.

❧ MEINONGIANISM ❧

Consideration of the notions of actuality and of the status of *possibilia* has led to new interest in the object theory of Alexius Meinong and his students which was so intertwined with Russell's theory of descriptions and the rise of analytic philosophy. Although developed originally as a logical theory making sense of non-referring names like 'Pegasus' and the contradictions surrounding postulating 'round squares', some developments of Meinongianism are more explicitly metaphysical. All accept the distinction between being and existence. There is a wide domain of entities with being, such as round squares and golden mountains, only some of which have the property of existence. Terence Parsons in *Nonexistent Objects* [4.15] distinguishes ordinary nuclear properties such as colour and physical properties from special extra-nuclear properties such as existence and other categorical properties such as being an object, and so on. This distinction allows him to reconcile the Meinongian drive to postulate as many entities with being as possible, without engendering contradiction. We cannot define into existence the 'existent golden mountain' because existence is extra-nuclear. Still, 'the golden mountain' will have being. Parsons' Meinongian metaphysics is directed primarily at providing an ontology for the semantics of natural languages, where reference to the non-existent is ubiquitous. Parsons counts fictional objects, characters in fiction such as Sherlock Holmes and Hamlet among his non-existent entities. They are typical incomplete Meinongian objects; while Sherlock Holmes had an address and a famous costume, he neither had nor lacked a mole on the heel of his left foot. Fictional characters only have the properties attributed to them in the story, or which follow closely from those attributed. Parsons' work, and related work on what is known as the 'logic of fiction' has drawn considerable interest within literary theory, and is a point at which the disciplinary isolation of much of recent analytic philosophy is breaking down.

Edward Zalta's *Abstract Objects* [4.26] is more explicitly metaphysical, developing a theory of objects in which other metaphysical notions of possible world, monad, universal and more can be modelled. His basic notion, derived from Ernst Mally, a student of Meinong, is to distinguish two modes of predications, inherence and encoding. While ordinary properties inhere in concrete objects, abstract objects, both more traditional ones such as sets and universals, and the new Meinongian round squares, rather encode those properties. While explicitly metaphysical in nature, Zalta's system lends itself to formalization and promises what he terms 'axiomatic metaphysics', allowing the derivations of theories of objects such as possible worlds and intentional objects from a small list of basic axioms. As with the modal metaphysics of Kripke and Lewis, Meinongianism began as a theory of interest to logic and formal semantics, but is taking on a life of its own as a metaphysical programme.

❧ NATURALISM ❧

The orientation of logical positivism towards natural science, and in particular physics as the model of a science, combined with the positivist doctrine of the 'unity of the sciences', has led to a strong tradition of naturalism in recent metaphysics. In the work of Quine, for example, it is clear that the methods and theories of science are continuous with respect to those of common sense, but refined and self-conscious, and therefore to be given a privileged status. The doctrine of the unity of the sciences and the principle of the reducibility of all sciences ultimately to physics give the ontology of physics a privileged position for Quine. That ontology is composed of points of space-time bearing familiar physical, material, properties of mass and energy states, and so on. For Quine, the needs and current theories of physics are the arbiters of ontological commitment. Hartry Field and others have found Quine's commitment to sets as out of keeping with the physicalism of the ontology of science and thus see as a fundamental project that of clearing science of any apparent commitment to such abstract objects.

David M. Armstrong, and a school of Australian philosophers influenced by him, have found that a commitment to universals is compatible with that overriding physicalism. Armstrong's *Universals and Scientific Realism* (1978) has led to a wide-ranging discussion of realism about universals in connection with natural laws, induction and causation within the philosophy of science, as well as in metaphysics. He characterizes his own 'world-hypothesis' with the following three theses '(1) The world contains nothing but particulars having properties and related to one another (2) The world is nothing but a single spatio-temporal system and (3) The world is completely described in terms of (completed) physics' ([4.1], 126) He argues that universals are not to be postulated to explain the appearances of language, in particular the nature of predication, but rather to be introduced on the purely scientific basis of being theoretical entities required to explain the observed phenomena. In the case of universals the phenomenon is exact similarity. This is best explained as the result of an identity. The very same universal is present in the various exactly similar instances. Armstrong's realism avoids what he sees as the major non-physicalist feature of Platonic realism by arguing that universals are spatio-temporally located in their instances and not in some Platonic realm. This 'immanent' realism which Armstrong cites as Aristotelian in tradition rather than Platonic, has the result that universals can exist only when instantiated. By individuating universals via their connection with causal powers, Armstrong also has reason to question the existence of higher-order universals, properties of properties. Only objects subject to causal influences can possess the properties that explain that causation.

Universals are central to Armstrong's account of natural laws. Breaking with the long-standing empiricist tradition of holding a regularity theory of laws, Armstrong holds that laws are due to relations between universals. While there may be all sorts of constant regularities in the world, what makes most 'accidental' is that they are not due to a relation between the universals involved, rather just their co-extensiveness. It is this primitive relation of necessitating that is what is added to that mere coincidence when one really has a law. This marks a quite dramatic change from all the metaphysicians of this period. Quine certainly subscribes to a regularity theory of law, finding what distinguishes laws from mere accidental regularities in the special role of statements of law in our theories. Even Lewis reduces necessity, causal or otherwise, to a regularity over all possible, or all physically possible worlds.

Causal relations play a central role in other parts of Armstrong's systematic philosophy, including his accounts of epistemological notions such as perception and knowledge. Armstrong defends an 'externalist' account of epistemic justification by which the evidential properties of sensory experience, for example, derive from their being reliably related to certain external evidence via systematic causal relations. Armstrong's physicalism has also been influential in the philosophy of mind via his *A Materialist Theory of Mind* (1968) which advocated what has come to be known as 'reductive materialism' [4.2]. That position holds that mental states such as pain, belief, self-consciousness are all identical with certain states of the brain or central nervous system. Just as science has identified lightning with the discharge of electricity, or water with H_2O, it is the chore of science to find the right physical states with which to identify mental states. The model of ontological commitment for Armstrong, as for all physicalists, has been the reductions and identifications provided by the natural sciences.

Wilfred Sellars' distinction between the *manifest* and *scientific images,* the world of macroscopic, continuous, coloured, etc., objects, and the world of sub-atomic particles and no secondary qualities, has inspired a range of attitudes towards naturalism in response. The eliminative materialism of the philosophy of mind, which dismisses the manifest image as 'folk psychology' on a par with talk of phlogiston and witches, advocates revising our ordinary notions and adopting the scientific image of the world as our ordinary conception. Those notions that do not fit in well with naturalism, then, those that resist reduction, are simply to be abandoned. This extreme naturalism is charged with being an overvaluing of science, a scientism. It also leads to certain forms of anti-realism.

ANTI-REALISM

The various forms of naturalism and physicalism discussed above all shared in reaction to classical logical positivism a realism about the theoretical objects of science. That realism was extended to a general realism by Hilary Putnam in conjunction with the theory of natural-kind terms developing with the causal theory of reference. The idea was that all terms, including theoretical terms that were once to be given operationalist or empirical meanings, in fact get their reference by causal connection with an object or kind or property in the world.

In two addresses in 1976 and 1977, Putnam quite dramatically announced his abandonment of realism, soon to be followed by a number of other prominent philosophers. The 'anti-realism' that is to replace realism takes different forms, but uniting them all is an abandonment of the simple picture of reference and of realism about theoretical terms that went with it. Putnam relied originally on semantic arguments, familiar facts from logic about the possibility of many alternative models or interpretations of a given theory. Realism, Putnam charged, relies on there being one distinguished interpretation which stands out from the others. But any theory of what that relationship is is just that, 'more theory' itself subject to radically different interpretations. That one may well have a notion of reference 'within' a theory, as a causal, or other ordinary relation between words and things in the world, Putnam allows, as long as this is an 'internal' realism. Thus, for example, the realism of science towards its own entities may be seen as a legitimate scientific hypothesis and understandable as an internal, or theory-dependent sort of realism. But if one tries to assert that science as a whole, or our language as a whole, is true because of correspondence with an independent reality, then one has entered into the incoherent 'metaphysical' realism that his arguments attack. This realism is thus not a view about the existence of particular entities, but rather a global view about the nature of truth. Putnam characterizes metaphysical realism by the view that truth is radically non-epistemic, that all our justified beliefs could turn out to be false. He has introduced the vivid 'brain in a vat' hypothesis (to echo Descartes's 'evil genius') to make this position clear. Might we just be brains kept alive in a vat of nutrient solution by a mad scientist? Thus all our ordinary beliefs about ourselves and our bodies would be false, however well justified by the carefully designed sensory input we are given. No, Putnam says, the very notions of belief and reference do not allow for such a possibility. We cannot so separate out the content of our beliefs and their objects. Nor can we make sense of a notion of truth so divorced from our beliefs. Instead, Putnam has advocated a more pragmatic notion of truth, one tied more to our epistemological practices and standards. He has argued that abandoning the realist picture allows a reconciliation of the dichotomies of fact and value, natural and interpretive social science, that have plagued western culture.

Michael Dummett had argued since the 1950s for the application of notions from intuitionistic mathematics more generally in philosophy, in particular the intuitionist notion of truth as similar to the notion of proof or of what has been verified. That attitude, which makes it possible for statements to be neither true (verified) nor false (shown false), and the consequent truth-value gaps, he termed 'anti-realism'. This version of anti-realism can be seen as coming close to a return to the sort of verificationism with which positivism began. As with Putnam, Dummett's anti-realism centres on the notion of truth. Dummett's emphasis, however, is on the theory of meaning that might allow for a realist theory of truth. Basing his arguments on the views of Wittgenstein about the public nature of meaning, Dummett has argued that meaning must be such that grasping of meaning can be publicly demonstrated and verified. But how, he asks, could anyone demonstrate a grasp of truth-conditions if these are independent of verification? We can either grasp the meanings of terms directly in terms of the conditions for verifying sentences in which they occur, or indirectly via their connections with terms that can be so understood. There is no way to give meaning to terms that run beyond possible verification. As a result, claims about domains which are 'verification-transcendent' are neither true nor false. Intuitionists argue that while many elementary claims about numbers can be verified, others, including many that involve quantification over all numbers, are not verifiable. The famous intuitionist example is the claim that there is a series of seven consecutive sevens in the decimal expansion of π. The assertion that such a statement nevertheless has a definite truth-value presupposes a 'God's-eye view' of the infinite series of digits in the expansion, something that runs beyond any human capacity and hence is not true or false. Dummett extends these notions throughout our language by comparing the class of decidable sentences about numbers with those verifiable claims about objects about which we are 'realists' in contrast with those realms where verification is impossible and about which we must be 'anti-realist'. The telltale logical distinction is that we accept the law of the excluded middle for statements about ordinary physical objects and others about which we are realists, but are not entitled to that when we go outside that realm, talking of the past which is no longer accessible to verification, or to use another example, when we speak of dispositional character traits, such as bravery, of those who are gone, and no longer able to manifest such traits. This anti-realism could be limited to certain realms and aspects of our discourse or of the world it is taken to describe, although recently followers of Dummett have argued for a more global anti-realism, arguing that no class of statements is conclusively decidable. Dummett's emphasis on the theory of meaning and his reliance on Wittgensteinian arguments to ground his anti-realism has meant that fewer connections have been drawn between it and traditional issues in metaphysics, in particular the traditions of German idealism and American pragmatism.

Other sorts of anti-realism are less verificationist. Bas van Fraassen in his *The Scientific Image* (1980) advocates an anti-realist view in science that allows full meaningfulness to statements about theoretical entities that range beyond what is established by the empirical evidence [4.24]. While fully meaningful, van Fraassen claims, the truth of such statements is simply not a concern of science. Science aims at empirical adequacy, theories aim only at being able to predict observations correctly, and that they can do even if it is only as if they were true. (Van Fraassen consciously echoes Vaihinger's 'philosophy of as if', in contrast with the positivism of the late nineteenth century when presenting his views.) Science can be agnostic about the truth of sentences about theoretical entities while granting that those assertions do have a truth-value. This is a much less global anti-realism than those of Putnam and Dummett. In fact, some identify it as a 'scientific' anti-realism, or identify it by van Fraassen's term 'constructive empiricism' and see it as independent of the issue of 'metaphysical' realism. It does, for example, contrast the status of theoretical entities such as electrons with that of the instruments and apparatus with which they are studied. In addition, the classical correspondence notion of truth (explained in terms of logicians' 'models') is held to make sense, but just not to be the object or goal of science. While van Fraassen is primarily considered a philosopher of science, it is unclear, however, why his view should not be taken as a stand on the nature of 'metaphysical' realism, much as Vaihinger's philosophy was. It is in the nineteenth-century positivist tradition that verifiable human knowledge (in science, but what other sort is there for heirs of logical positivism?) must be limited to the phenomena. Like Vaihinger, van Fraassen holds that statements of 'metaphysics', which go beyond the phenomena are meaningful, and can be accepted on other grounds, such as revelation or faith. The echoes here are of the Kantian distinction between the phenomenal and noumenal realms and it certainly seems to be an approach to the 'metaphysical' problem of realism.

Richard Rorty [4.22] challenges the metaphor of the mind as a mirror of nature which underlies these concerns about the truth of theoretical statements in contrast to the evidence that we have for them. This characterization of realism identifies it closely with the correspondence theory of truth, as earlier idealist critics of realism had also done. The 'problem of truth' has returned from the field of semantics to metaphysics where it was discussed in the nineteenth century. Rorty claims that the problem of realism will dissolve when we see that it is based on a faulty metaphor of the mind as a medium which reflects a world to which it does not belong. Only with this image in place are we able to ask questions about what represents the world and what is represented and whether there is a 'real' world 'behind' those representations. While rejecting the very notion of a world going beyond the evidence which is adopted by other anti-realists, he still finds his position to be more akin to the anti-realists than the realists. As with Putnam he argues that practices of justification are all that can be studied and that the further question of whether they lead to truth, must be abandoned. This, therefore, undermines the attempt to ground epistemological practices or to place philosophy in the role of an adjudicator of genuine knowledge. Instead of placing itself beyond other epistemological traditions philosophy is to mediate instead in a 'conversation' between distinct traditions. Unlike Putnam, who sees his anti-realism as a step forward, at least for the analytic philosophers who had abandoned the continental tradition in metaphysics, Rorty sees his anti-realism as part of an 'end' of philosophy. The metaphysical picture of realism, and with it the epistemological project that accompanies it, and which has defined modern philosophy, must give way to a post-modern abandonment of that traditional project.

Anti-realism thus takes various forms, though generally adopting a semantic thesis concerning the meaning of terms that go beyond experience. There is also an epistemological aspect to anti-realism in the common denial of a great gap between justified belief and truth, of the world as 'found' and as somehow 'constructed' by humans. Many anti-realists, as well, are finding a renewed interest in post-Kantian German philosophy as a way of articulating their views. Anti-realism as a philosophical phenomenon invites speculation about the course of analytic philosophy as beginning with the rejection of idealism by Moore and Russell, and ending with a return to it. Anti-realism is also often associated with the more general cultural phenomenon of 'post-modernism' and is seen not as a return to an earlier idealism but rather as marking the 'end of philosophy'.

❧ BIBLIOGRAPHY ❧

4.1   Armstrong, D. *Universals and Scientific Realism*, Cambridge: Cambridge University Press, 1978.

4.2   —— *A Materialist Theory of the Mind*, London: Routledge & Kegan Paul, 1968.

4.3   Bambrough, R. 'Universals and Family Resemblances', *Proceedings of the Aristotelian Society*, 41 (1960–1): 207–22.

4.4   Bergmann, G. *The Metaphysics of Logical Positivism*, Madison: University of Wisconsin Press, 1954.

4.5   Black, M. 'The Identity of Indiscernibles', *Mind*, 61 (1952): 153–64.

4.6   Carnap, R. *Logical Syntax of Language*, London: Routledge & Kegan Paul, 1937.

4.7   —— *The Logical Structure of the World and Pseudoproblems in Philosophy*, trans. R. George, Berkeley: University of California Press, 1967.

4.8 Davidson, D. 'The Logical Form of Action Sentences', in D. Davidson and G. Harman, eds, *The Logic of Grammar*, Encino: Dickenson, 1975: 235–45.

4.9 Dummett, D. *Truth and Other Enigmas*, London: Duckworth, 1978.

4.10 Field, H. *Science Without Numbers; A Defence of Nominalism*, Princeton, NJ: Princeton University Press, 1980.

4.11 Goodman, N. *The Structure of Appearance*, Cambridge, Mass.: Harvard University Press, 1951.

4.12 Kripke, S. *Naming and Necessity*, Cambridge, Mass.: Harvard University Press, 1980.

4.13 Leonard, H. and N. Goodman 'The Calculus of Individuals and its Uses', *Journal of Symbolic Logic*, 5(2) (1940): 45–55.

4.14 Lewis, D. *On the Plurality of Worlds*, Oxford: Basil Blackwell, 1986.

4.15 Parsons, Terence *Nonexistent Objects*, New Haven, Conn.: Yale University Press, 1980.

4.16 Pears, D. 'Universals', *Philosophical Quarterly*, 1 (1951): 218–27.

4.17 Plantinga, A. *The Nature of Necessity*, Oxford: Oxford University Press, 1974.

4.18 Putnam, H. *Meaning and the Moral Sciences*, London: Routledge & Kegan Paul, 1978.

4.19 Quine, W. 'On What There Is', *Review of Metaphysics*, 2 (1948): 21–38.

4.20 —— *Word and Object*, Cambridge, Mass.: MIT Press, 1960.

4.21 —— *Philosophy of Logic*, Englewood Cliffs, NJ: Prentice Hall, 1970.

4.22 Rorty, R. *Philosophy and the Mirror of Nature*, Oxford: Blackwell, 1980.

4.23 Strawson, P. *Individuals; An Essay in Descriptive Metaphysics*, London: Methuen, 1959.

4.24 van Fraassen, B. *The Scientific Image*, Oxford: Oxford University Press, 1980.

4.25 Wiggins, D. *Sameness and Substance*, Oxford: Basil Blackwell, 1980.

4.26 Zalta, E. *Abstract Objects: An Introduction to Axiomatic Metaphysics*, Dordrecht: D. Reidel, 1983.

CHAPTER 5
Ethics I (1900–45)
Michael Stingl

◆◆❖◆◆

Early twentieth-century philosophy was largely, in Ian Hacking's neat phrase, the heyday of meanings. This is not to say, as Hacking stresses in his book *Why does Language matter to Philosophy?* [5.22], that the point of the philosophy of this period was to study meaning: the point of studying meaning was to do better philosophy. The general focus of the period was on the words or phrases used in asking or attempting to answer the questions of traditional concern to philosophy, and in particular, how, or even if, these terms were meaningful. Its philosophical conceit was that once meaning was clarified, philosophical truths could easily be distinguished from philosophical confusions. But by the end of the period even this had become unclear; by then, the central question of philosophy was whether there were, in fact, any truths of the kind that philosophers had traditionally supposed themselves to be after. The worry was that once their meaning was clarified, traditional philosophical questions would show themselves to be literally meaningless.

The focus of the moral philosophy of the period was on metaethics, and more specifically, the question of whether, once the meaning of terms like 'good' and 'right' had been clarified, a science of ethics might be possible. For while science, and in particular physics, seemed to be logging in one stunning success after another, ethics seemed no closer at the beginning of the twentieth century to anything that might count as moral knowledge than it had been at the time of the early Greeks. Or so things seemed to G. E. Moore, who set out in 1903 to clarify once and for all the meaning of 'good', and in so doing clear the way for a genuine science of ethics, one which might justifiably pretend to give us definitive knowledge of right and wrong.

MOORE'S *PRINCIPIA ETHICA*

My 1971 paperback copy of *Principia Ethica* bears this advertisement:

What is GOOD?
To answer this question, G. E. Moore
wrote one of the most influential books
of this century – *Principia Ethica*
[5.44]

Cover advertisements being what they are, it is not surprising to find this one standing distinctly at odds with what might be called the received view of Moore's book among philosophers more contemporary with the particular edition it adorns. A representative example of this view is furnished by Alasdair MacIntyre's *A Short History of Ethics*:

> [Moore] says that if we consider *good* and, let us say, *pleasant*,
> or any other notion with which we might be tempted to
> confuse *good*, we can see that we 'have two different notions
> before our minds'. This technique of holding one's concepts
> up to the light, as it were, is reinforced by Moore's method of
> calm assertion. More unwarranted and unwarrantable assertions
> are perhaps made in *Principia Ethica* than in any other single
> book of moral philosophy, but they are made with such well-
> mannered, although slightly browbeating certitude, that it seems
> almost gross to disagree. But what, then, *is* Moore's case?
> ([5.35], 250)

Not much, MacIntyre goes on to suggest. And generally speaking, this is the received view of Moore's book among philosophers in the second half of the century: a Pandora's box filled to overflowing with singularly unpersuasive arguments, many of them directed at wildly mistaken readings of the earlier moral philosophers against whom Moore took himself to be providing definitive criticism.

One of Moore's main targets was John Stuart Mill. Like Moore, Mill was a utilitarian. And like all utilitarians, Mill advanced two linked moral theories, a theory of the good and a theory of the right. The general idea behind the utilitarian combination of these two sorts of theories is that one can't really say what kinds of actions are right until one is able to say what sorts of outcomes are good. Simply put, right actions are those which produce good consequences. What one needs, then, at the very foundation of any moral theory is an account of what kinds of things are intrinsically valuable: things worth pursuing not merely as means to some other thing, but in and of themselves. Some utilitarians, Mill arguably among them, offer a purely subjective theory of the good, one that takes particular states of consciousness, such as pleasure or happiness, as being the only things that are intrinsically valuable, good in and of themselves. Other utilitarians, like Moore, offer a more objective theory of the good: some things are intrinsically valuable, such as knowledge or friendship, whether they happen to make human beings happy or not.

Moore's chief criticism of Mill was not so much that he had proposed a mistaken theory of the good, but that he had made a deeper, meta-ethical mistake, one which had then led him to misidentify the sorts of things that might properly be said to be good.

To understand the point of this criticism, we need to start with the passages in Mill's *Utilitarianism* against which it is targeted. In his first chapter, Mill claims that

> [q]uestions of ultimate ends are not amenable to direct proof. Whatever can be proved to be good must be so by being shown to be a means to something admitted to be good without proof.
>
> ([5.37], 4)

Later, in chapter IV, entitled 'Of What Sort of Proof the Principle of Utility is Susceptible', Mill repeats his assertion that questions of ultimate ends, questions, that is, about what things are good in and of themselves, do not admit of strict proof. He goes on to say the following:

> Questions about ends are, in other words, questions [about] what things are desirable. The utilitarian doctrine is that happiness is desirable, as an end; all other things being only desirable as means to that end.
>
> The only proof capable of being given that an object is seen is that people actually see it. The only proof that a sound is audible is that people hear it; and so of the other sources of our experience. In like manner, I apprehend, the sole evidence it is possible to produce that anything is desirable is that people do actually desire it.
>
> ([5.37], 34)

That these last two passages have become as well known as they have is due, in no small part, to their almost equally well-known rejoinder in *Principia Ethica*:

> There, that is enough. That is my first point. Mill has made as naive and artless a use of the naturalistic fallacy as anybody could desire. 'Good', he tells us, means 'desirable', and you can only find out what is desirable by seeking to find out what actually is desired.
>
> The important step for ethics is . . . the step which pretends

to prove that 'good' means 'desired'. . . . Well, the fallacy in this step is so obvious, it is quite wonderful how Mill failed to see it.

([5.44], 66–7)

His discovery of the 'naturalistic fallacy' was for Moore the centrepiece of *Principia Ethica*. On the one hand, it turned out to be ubiquitous, 'to be met with in almost every book on Ethics'. On the other hand, the failure to understand it for what it was blocked all progress in ethics, for to commit the fallacy was to misunderstand the very nature of goodness. If we don't understand what goodness is, we are hardly in any position to say what sorts of things are good, much less what kinds of actions are right. So what then was this alleged fallacy, the discovery of which was so propitious? According to Moore, it was simply the most prevalent form of what we might call, following the subsequent discussion of William Frankena's 'The Naturalistic Fallacy' [5.20], the definist fallacy: the fallacy of supposing that the property of goodness can be defined in terms of some other property or set of properties.

In the naturalistic version of the fallacy, the other property in terms of which goodness is defined is a natural one. In Mill's case, for example, 'good' is said to be defined as 'desired'. Now whether or not a desire exists is a question of human, or perhaps animal, psychology; in any case, it is a question that can be answered by empirical investigation. It is a question, that is, about some state of the natural world, in this case the actual psychological state of some creature or another. On this view, then, to see what's good in and of itself, we simply check to see what, in point of actual fact, people desire in and of itself. And here Mill's answer would seem to be short and to the point: happiness.

Against Mill, Moore thought that any move to define goodness in terms of some other property, natural or not, could be conclusively shown to be fallacious by an appeal to what has come to be called the open question argument. An open question is one whose answer is not immediately obvious, but instead requires further thought or investigation. Moore's point is that for any proposed definition of goodness, we can raise an open question of the form 'but is this good?' Regarding Mill's view, for example, we can raise the question, 'but is happiness good?' That this question is an open one proves that goodness can't be defined as happiness, for then we should only be asking 'but is happiness happiness', a question which certainly isn't open. Because it can be applied to any proposed definition of goodness, the open question argument appears to be a powerful one: if it works, it shows that goodness is undefinable.

This, in fact, was Moore's conclusion: the property of goodness is a simple, undefinable, non-natural object of thought. Like 'yellow', there may be some other property that all good things possess; but 'good', like 'yellow', denotes something else, a property that we know by direct acquaintance. With regard to yellow, we know it when we see it. Now it may of course be that all things that are yellow turn out to reflect light in a particular sort of way, but to be able to meaningfully claim that this is so, we cannot mean the same thing by 'yellow' and 'reflects light in such and such a way'. Rather, we know what yellow is by direct perceptual acquaintance with yellow things, and we go on to find out what physical property all yellow things possess by studying the reflective properties of light. Similarly, we know what goodness is by some sort of direct cognitive acquaintance with it when we contemplate good things, and it is then up to the science of ethics to tell us whether there is some other property, or set of properties, that can be linked to goodness.

It is in this sense that Moore can be called an intuitionist, although he himself rejected the label. There is a property of goodness of which we can be directly cognitively aware, but since this awareness is obviously not perceptual, it must be of some other, purely intellectual kind, perhaps something like our awareness of mathematical objects. In any event, since we are not aware of goodness perceptually, and it is not definable in terms of other perceptual properties, it follows that it must be a non-natural property.

This raises three important philosophical problems. First, there is the metaphysical question of just what sort of property this 'non-natural' property might be. Second, there is the related epistemological question of how knowledge of it would actually be possible. Lastly and perhaps most importantly for ethics, there is the question of how goodness so understood might be connected to the human motivational system. How could knowledge of a non-natural property of the world be motivationally effective? How could it, that is, give us a reason, much less an obligation, to act?

These were not problems that Moore concerned himself with in *Principia Ethica*; the point of the book was simply to clarify the meaning of 'good', and then to begin pursuing what Moore took to be the chief task of the science of ethics, attempting to identify the class of things that actually did possess the simple, non-natural property of goodness. The good, as something distinct from goodness, was thus something that Moore thought it might be possible to define, and indeed, this is precisely what he thought ethics should try to do: define precisely that class of things that were, in fact, good. His fundamental point was that the question about the good was parasitic on the logically prior question about the definition of goodness; ethics couldn't begin to address the former without an answer to the latter. This, in short, was Mill's mistake. Having confused the two questions, he had turned a plausible but incorrect answer to the question of what sorts of things might be good into an utterly fallacious answer to the question of what goodness itself might be.

As indicated earlier, history has not been kind to Moore. Ironically, later philosophers have been as abrupt with him as he was with Mill. In 'The "Proof" of Utility in Bentham and Mill', Evert Hall argues that Mill is guilty of no fallacy. He begins his vindication of Mill with this critical barb:

> I can only account for this flagrant reading into Mill of the definist fallacy by supposing that Moore could not grasp any other sense to Mill's argument and so thought that Mill *must* have committed this fallacy. But *there is* another and obvious sense to any interpreter not debauched with verbal casuistry.
>
> ([5.23], 150)

This other, obvious interpretation calls attention to the fact that Mill begins the passage that is the focus of Moore's attack with the caveat that no proof of his theory of the good is possible. His point is that even if strict proof is impossible, there may still be other, less rigorous tests to which proposed theories of the good might be held accountable. According to Hall, then, what Mill is doing in the passage in question is suggesting just such a test: whatever a theory says is good had better be the sort of thing that actually motivates people to act. So in arguing that people actually desire happiness, Mill is not offering a definition of goodness, but attempting to show that his proposed theory of the good passes an important empirical test, a test of motivational efficacy. According to the doctrine of psychological hedonism, people are ultimately motivated, in fact, by what they think will make them happy. Hall's point is that, although this psychological doctrine is deeply problematic, Mill's appeal to it in the context of trying to justify his theory of the good commits no logical mistake.

Moore undoubtedly got Mill wrong. Yet *Principia Ethica* was influential, and its influence was not inconsiderable. To see why, we must place the book and its arguments in their original context. We must ask why Moore would have been so absolutely convinced that whatever Mill himself might have thought that he was doing, part of what he was doing, if he was doing anything at all, was offering a definition of goodness. In particular, we must ask why Moore would have found the open-question argument such a thoroughly damning criticism against any attempt to define goodness.

Moore's is a case where language very clearly mattered to philosophy. Unless his concern with ethics as a science is placed in the context of the referential theory of meaning which he and Bertrand

Russell were beginning to develop in the early decades of the century, the main moral arguments of *Principia Ethica* can only appear as they have to many of Moore's critics: as pompous as they are misguided.

On the referential theory of meaning, powerfully developed by Russell in 'On Denoting', *The Principles of Mathematics, Principia Mathematica* and *The Problems of Philosophy*, and less powerfully developed by Moore himself in the opening pages of *Principia Ethica*, the meaning of a term was just what it referred to. According to the earliest versions of this theory, some terms, like 'Socrates', referred to particular individuals; others, like 'yellow', to universals, in this case the property universally shared by all yellow things. To know what a sentence meant, one needed to know the meanings, or referents, of its terms. So to say what sorts of things were good, at least in a philosophically informative sort of way, Mill would have had to have been clear about what it was that 'good' referred to. And on this point, it would seem, Mill does not disappoint: he seems to say quite clearly that 'good' is what people desire, and what people desire is happiness. But in the context of Moore's referential theory of meaning, this is just as clearly absurd; as the open question argument conclusively shows, whatever 'good' refers to, it cannot refer to happiness. Thus the point of the Bishop Butler quote which prefaces *Principia Ethica*: everything is what it is, and not another thing. Whatever goodness is, it is not happiness.

Now someone who held the referential theory of meaning to be true might try to defend Mill by saying that what he was trying to do in the contested passage was to argue, in an admittedly misguided way, that 'good' and 'desired', like 'yellow' and 'reflects light in such-and-such a way', are extensionally equivalent: all and only all those objects are good which are also desired. Mill didn't, then, suppose that 'good' referred to what people desire, happiness, but he did think that the properties of intrinsic goodness and happiness were shared by exactly the same class of objects. Moore's second line of defence, however, would once again be tied to his own understanding of the referential theory of meaning: if Mill had had any understanding at all that 'good' referred to goodness itself and nothing else, he would not have gone on to propose the obviously mistaken doctrine that happiness was the sole good. Moore thought it obvious, that is, that once anyone grasped the idea of goodness as an independent object of thought, he or she would see that goodness attached itself to things like friendship and knowledge, as well as happiness. To reach the conclusion that he did, Mill must have been, to some significant degree, confusing goodness with happiness.

But if locating *Principia Ethica* within the context of a particular theory of language and meaning displays the true mettle of its arguments, it also makes clear their ultimate infirmity: they are only as good as the theory of meaning they presuppose. And while the referential theory of meaning was only to reach its final flourish in the 1921 publication of Ludwig Wittgenstein's *Tractatus*, the quickness of its subsequent demise was surpassed only by the finality of its eventual rejection. Still, not unlike certain of the doctrines of the *Tractatus* which continue to fascinate the philosophical mind long after it has categorically rejected them, the arguments of *Principia Ethica* have continued to haunt philosophical thinking about ethics. Moore showed that language could not be ignored when doing ethics, and that unless moral philosophers could give some indication of what words like 'right' and 'good' meant, no progress in the purely philosophical pursuit of ethics was possible. Moreover, the philosophical problems posed by Moore's objective theory of the good have become important puzzles to be solved by any successful approach to ethics: whatever moral value turns out to be, how is knowledge of it possible, and how does it function to motivate human beings to act? Attempts to answer these questions are at the heart of the naturalism of Perry and Dewey, the emotivism of Ayer and Stevenson, and the contractarian moral and political philosophy of the current day.

➤ INTUITIONISM ➤

They are also at the heart of intuitionism, although its answer to them is ultimately no more cogent than Moore's.

The impetus for intuitionism was H. A. Pritchard's 1912 *Mind* article, 'Does Moral Philosophy Rest on a Mistake?' [5.49]. The question, as one might suppose, was rhetorical. According to Pritchard, the problem with all earlier moral philosophy was that it failed to give a convincing account of moral obligation: it failed to give a satisfying answer to the question of why one *ought* to do the right thing. The mistake behind all such failures was to suppose that this question could be answered by some sort of proof. Once one saw that it could not, one was free to see that no proof is in fact necessary: that one ought to do the right thing is part of one's direct apprehension of the act in question as being right.

One might, like Moore, attempt to ground the obligatoriness of right acts in the fact that they lead to good outcomes. But this, as Pritchard says, 'presuppose[s] . . . that what is good ought to be', which is false. Certain states of the world, such as an end to human suffering, may indeed be very good things; but the fact that an end to human suffering is good does not entail, by itself, that I or anyone else possesses an obligation to bring it about. Nor does the alternative of supposing that right acts are themselves good fare any better, for good acts, according to Pritchard, are simply right acts done for the right reasons. That an act is a good one, that is, has completely to do with its motive, which for Pritchard has nothing to do with its rightness; doing *what* we ought to do, says Pritchard, is completely divorced from doing it *as* we ought. The underlying idea here is that if rightness cannot be derived from goodness, then neither can moral obligation.

Towards the end of his paper Pritchard briefly develops a more general argument that our obligation to do the right thing admits of no philosophical proof. To prove that we know anything, Descartes thought that we had to prove that we know that we know it. But this, says Pritchard, is impossible: it leads epistemology into an infinite regress. The parallel with ethics is this. Just as in the face of past mistaken beliefs we are led to wonder how we know what we think we know, in the face of conflicting inclinations we are led to wonder why we ought to do what we think is right. But if we suppose that to answer the question of why we ought to do what we think is right we must find some sort of proof that we are so obliged, we make the task of ethics impossible. In looking for such a proof, we would be looking for something that would oblige us to be obliged to act in a certain way; something, in other words, which would threaten the same sort of regress that makes the Cartesian epistemological project an imposs-ible one. If I can only be obliged to do the right thing by being obliged to be so obliged, it is not clear why this same problem about obligation doesn't simply reassert itself one level down.

Pritchard's rejection of the task of traditional epistemology is an interesting precursor to the current rejection of the philosophical search for necessary and sufficient conditions for '*s* knows that *p*' in favour of the empirical study of the cognitive processes that actually produce what we would otherwise be willing to think of as knowledge. But strangely enough, despite his insight that the question of why we ought to do what we ought expresses a similarly misconceived demand for absolute certainty, Pritchard's own account of moral obligation is quix-otically Cartesian: we know it when we see it. If someone doesn't feel obliged to perform a right act, he or she has merely failed to concentrate fully enough on what it is that makes the act right. To apprehend the act as right is to apprehend it as obligatory.

This, then, is the leading idea of intuitionism: the question of what it is right to do is wholly independent of any arguments regarding what is good, and indeed, what it is right to do is not something for which *any* argument can be given, whether it appeals to the good or not. That an act is right is something that must be directly apprehended.

This idea of direct apprehension is to some extent further developed by W. D. Ross in *The Right and The Good* [5.52] and

Foundations of Ethics [5.53], and by E. F. Carritt in *The Theory of Morals* [5.7]. According to Ross, what we apprehend in apprehending rightness is something about *types* of acts. It is because we see, for example, that an act is the keeping of a promise, that we are able to intuit that it is right. The recognition that certain types of acts, such as keeping promises, telling the truth, and repaying one's benefactors, are right is for Ross the basis of his theory of *prima facie* duties: types of acts that are *prima facie* right. Duties so understood are *prima facie* right rather than actually right, since in certain situations they may come into conflict with one another; in such situations, only one *prima facie* duty can be one's actual duty. As we shall see below when we examine this theory in more detail under the heading of 'Substantive Ethics', what our actual duty is is not something that we can directly intuit.

This point is explicitly denied by Carritt, who is in many ways a precursor of what is today called situational ethics. On Carritt's view moral intuition applies itself directly to particular situations, in their full particularity. What we intuit is that *this* act, in *this* situation, is right. We may later realize that our intuitions fall into certain general types, perhaps according to Ross's list of *prima facie* duties; but these types are not a part of what we directly intuit. In a deep sense, no theory of ethics is possible. Thus Carritt:

> You cannot prove to a man that he has duties, or should do his duty, or that justice is a duty, or that this act is just. All you can do is give him fuller information of the consequences and antecedents of what he is doing and then ask him to agree with you that it is right or wrong. If he knows the situation and consequences as well as you do and still differs, one of you must be wrong. All you can do is get him to imagine the situation again and repeat the act of moral thinking with greater attention.
>
> ([5.7], 72)

A modest view of ethics, perhaps, but in the end one which is no less extravagant than Moore's account of goodness. To say that we know 'by intuition' what things are right does nothing to tell us how we are epistemologically connected to the moral value at issue, much less what that connection might have to do with the actual structure of the human motivational system. It is a curious feature of the human intellect that explaining something mysterious by appealing to something even more mysterious has the attraction that it does. Still, the deeper mystery can remain intellectually satisfying only as long as there are no other explanations on the field which possess what it does not, some real explanatory power. This is why it has proved historically necessary, where the deeper mystery has been emotionally and politically satisfying, to have at one's disposal the stake, along with the various other unpleasant instruments of non-rational persuasion: instruments unavailable to the intuitionists, as the despairing quote from Carritt makes only too clear. If some poor soul cannot see that what is plainly right is plainly right, we must attempt to open his or her eyes, over and over again, until one of us tires and gives in or up.

❧ NATURALISM ❧

By defining moral values primarily in terms of human interests, the naturalists were able to offer what the intuitionists were not: a straightforward answer to the question of how moral knowledge was possible, as well as to the deeper question of how such knowledge could be motivationally effective.

For both Moore and the other British intuitionists, morality was objective in the sense that moral values, like goodness, were to be found among the qualities of objects as these existed independently of any and all subjective experience. For the naturalists, this idea of moral objectivity was absurd. In *The Winds of Doctrine*, the American philosopher George Santayana offered the following argument:

> For the human system whisky is truly more intoxicating than
> coffee, and the contrary opinion would be an error; but what
> a strange way of vindicating this real, though relative, distinction,
> to insist that whisky is more intoxicating in itself, without
> reference to any animal; that it is pervaded, as it were, by an
> inherent intoxication, and stands dead drunk in its bottle!
>
> ([5.60], 267)

According to Santayana, that whisky is intoxicating is a relational fact about the world, a fact, that is, which involves not only the chemical properties of alcohol, but the physiological properties of the human constitution. So too for moral facts: that something is morally good is a relational fact involving creatures with certain interests and capacities for purposeful action, and an environment in which it is possible for them to act so that more rather than fewer of their interests are satisfied.

The idea of an ethics thus naturalized was further developed by two other American philosophers, Ralph Barton Perry and John Dewey, both of whom tried to give more exact definitions of what moral goodness might amount to on such an approach.

In his *General Theory of Value* [5.47] and its sequel, *Realms of Value* [5.48], Perry suggested that we should say that something possessed value if and only if it was the object of an interest, and that it was morally good if and only if it was the object of an interest which was itself a member of a set of interests harmoniously arranged. By the term 'interest' Perry meant to include any attitude of a subject towards an object which was favourable or disfavourable; his examples of such attitudes are liking and disliking, hoping and fearing, and desiring and avoiding. In so far as animals could feel dislike or aversion, they too had interests, and although they themselves could not be active participants in the harmonious arranging of interests, their negative interests, at least, had to be taken into account under any such arrangement. On the naturalistic view developed by Perry, this was because unsatisfied interests were, objectively speaking, bad.

By 'interests harmoniously arranged', Perry seemed to have in mind something similar to an idea developed more recently by John Rawls in his *A Theory of Justice* [5.50], the ideal of a well-ordered society. And while this idea is also to be found in John Dewey's *Theory of the Moral Life* [5.15], neither he nor Perry ever developed it fully. At its most general, the idea is this: interests cruelly conflict; some interests are more significant than others; human beings flourish only in social environments; the best set of interests, both within and across lives, is therefore a set of interests which are mutually reinforcing. Our lives are best structured, then, when the satisfaction of my interests is part of the satisfaction of yours, and vice versa. It is in this sense, in a well-ordered society, that the interests of each become the interests of all.

All this, of course, claims to be doing exactly what Moore said could not be done: providing a definition of moral goodness. In partial agreement with Moore, Perry did think it impossible to replace the concept of goodness, or more generally, value, with some alternative set of concepts which would mean the same thing, but express that meaning in a more readily comprehensible fashion. Perry did, however, think it entirely possible to replace our actual concept of value, the contours of which were at best vague and at worst ambiguous and confusing, with a more precise alternative, the merit of which was to be assessed in terms of how well it enabled us to carry out our reflections about value, moral or otherwise. Given the nature of this sort of reforming definition, the significance of the open question argument for Perry was simply to voice the demand that for any reform proposed, acceptance should be conditional on its proving to be more interesting and fruitful than its rivals; then and only then could that sort of thing, whatever it turned out to be, be said to be good by 'definition'.

Like Santayana, Perry was not a moral objectivist in the sense intended by Moore. He was greatly concerned, however, to establish a distinction between having an interest in something and making a judgement about that interest, so that a thing's value would not, in the end, consist in the mere fact that it was judged to possess value. That things are valuable only because they are judged to be so is the characteristic mark of moral subjectivism, a view vigorously disavowed by the naturalists.

Dewey's effort to avoid subjectivism was in some respects more subtle than Perry's, in others less. Instead of trying to finesse his way around the great metaphysical divide of subject and object assumed by Moore's notion of moral objectivity by arguing for some sort of secondary epistemological divide, such as that between interest and judgement, Dewey argued that the widely shared metaphysical assumption was itself a mistake. The upshot of his argument is compactly stated in chapter VIII of *The Quest for Certainty*:

> If we see that knowing is not the act of an outside spectator but of a participator inside the natural and social scene, then the true object of knowledge resides in the consequences of directed action.

([5.14], 196)

If an experimental interaction between us and the world yields the result we expected, to that extent we have gained objective knowledge of the world. The experiment may be one of physics or it may be one of morality: in either case the general method is the same, and what it tells or fails to tell us is no more objective in the one instance than the other.

In short, moral knowledge is generated, according to Dewey, through the general scientific method of hypothesis and experiment. In contrast to Moore's idea of what a science of ethics might look like, this sharing of a single methodology was, for Dewey, the only way in which ethics might be genuinely scientific. To take an example from the first edition of Dewey's and James Tuft's *Ethics* (1908), the moral ideal of individualism that served to legitimate the excesses of the robber-barons of early twentieth-century North America was a hypothesis that was in the process of being shown to be dramatically mistaken. The moral expectation in which the hypothesis was grounded was that a social order so inspired and arranged would be more stable and productive than one based, say, on principles of a more socialist bent. The social upheaval of the times made it clear, according to Dewey and Tufts, that this was not so. The failed experiment of unrestrained capitalism showed that a purely individualistic moral ideal was incapable of producing a set of social interests harmoniously arranged.

In addition to offering a coherent account of moral knowledge, Dewey's naturalism offered a coherent account of moral motivation. If the experimental method promised to show us how our interests might be best arranged into complex social wholes, education promised to produce individuals with the right sorts of interests. That we should restructure the basic institutions of our society to produce such individuals was first to be grasped by intelligence, and second, to be pursued out of self-interest and sympathy. Once our intelligence showed us that our own particular good was essentially tied to the good of those around us, self-interest and sympathy would push us to pursue the greater good of interests harmoniously arranged. The most direct way of doing this, of course, was to start with individuals whose interests were not yet formed, and educate them in such a way that the interests they did form were of the appropriate sort.

Whatever other worries it might raise, this quick sketch of Dewey's account of the human motivational system leads us to the deepest meta-ethical objection that later philosophers have had to ethical naturalism, the objection that while human motivation is one thing, moral obligation would seem to be quite another. Put another way, how does what naturally *is* get us to conclusions about what morally *ought to be*? This worry, sometimes called the is/ought dilemma, has been taken by at least some later philosophers to be the real point of the open question argument, whether Moore realized it or not. On this view, the naturalistic fallacy is the unadorned move from the claim that something is naturally good for us, perhaps because of the kind of creatures we are, to the further claim that this natural fact gives us an obligation to pursue that thing. Interests harmoniously arranged might, as a point of natural fact, be good for us; but how does this create an obligation, on anyone's part, to pursue such an arrangement?

In his *Theory of the Moral Life* [5.15] and *Human Nature and Conduct* [5.13], Dewey offers a response to such worries. At its briefest, his argument is that the moral obligation to arrange our interests harmoniously is derived from the human necessity of a social existence:

> social pressure is involved in our . . . lives, as much so as the air we breathe and the ground we walk on. If we had desires, judgements, plans, in short a mind, apart from social connections, then the latter would be external and their action might be regarded as a nonmoral force. But we live mentally and physically only *in* and *because* of our environment. Social pressure is but a name for the interactions that are always going on and in which we participate, living so far as we partake and dying so far as we do not.
>
> ([5.13], 327)

Beyond the bare desire to lead a human life, there is for Dewey no deeper answer possible to the question of why we ought to do what it is good for us to do.

✦ LOGICAL POSITIVISM ✦

Whatever their philosophical merits or shortcomings might have been, ethical naturalism and moral intuitionism were both swept away by the rising tide of logical positivism.

Logical positivism was a general approach to problems of language and meaning. As a movement, its genesis and early growth was within the Vienna Circle, a group of scientists and philosophers who met, in Vienna, from the early 1920s to the mid-1930s. Two of the more important figures in the Circle were Moritz Schlick and Rudolf Carnap, and although Ludwig Wittgenstein was never actually part of it, his *Tractatus Logico-Philosophicus* and some of his subsequent ideas greatly influenced the Circle's discussions and views. Among English-speaking philosophers, A. J. Ayer was briefly associated with the Circle; in 1936, he published its chief polemical text, *Language, Truth, and Logic*. At the centre of this book was the principle of verification:

> We say that a sentence is factually significant to any given person, if, and only if, he knows how to verify the proposition it purports to express – that is, if he knows what observations would lead him, under certain conditions, to accept the proposition as being true, or reject it as being false.

([5.2], 35)

According to the positivists, sentences expressing scientific propositions obeyed this principle. Because they could be observationally tested, they were meaningful. According to all the positivists except Schlick, the sentences of ethics did not; because moral claims could not be observationally tested, they were literally meaningless. On this view of science and ethics, then, no science of ethics was possible.

Three qualifications are important here. First, there is the problem of naturalism; if Dewey, for example, was right in his claim that moral judgements were best understood as hypotheses about how interests might be best arranged, then it would seem that moral claims could be tested by observation. Against this, Ayer sided with Pritchard's point that claims about the good could not tell us anything about moral obligation. This point has been echoed by a number of philosophers in the positivist tradition, starting with Wittgenstein's remark (6.41) in the *Tractatus* that if values were part of the world, they would be in an important sense 'accidental'. The general idea was that although goodness naturally defined might tell us important psychological or social truths about human beings, truths that were contingent on the way the world turned out to be structured, it could not tell us any truths about what ought to be. In Ayer's terminology, naturalistic accounts of moral language missed the point of the normative use of terms like 'good' and 'right', which was to goad us into action.

This point leads us to a second qualification: to say that moral claims were literally meaningless was not to say that they had no meaning at all. Some claims, like those of science, were only meaningful in so far as they described, truly or falsely, the world disclosed to us by observation. Other claims, however, might be meaningful because of the ways in which they allowed us to express our feelings. Such a view of moral claims, embraced by all the positivists except Schlick, who was an ethical naturalist, came to be known as emotivism. In the English-speaking world, an emotivist account of the meaning of moral terms was first articulated in 1923 by C. K. Ogden and I. A. Richards in *The Meaning of Meaning*:

> 'good' is alleged to stand for a unique, unanalysable concept. This concept, it is said, is the subject-matter of Ethics. This peculiar ethical use of 'good' is, we suggest, a purely emotive use. When so used, the word stands for nothing whatever ... it serves only as an emotive sign expressing our attitude ... and perhaps evoking similar attitudes in other persons, or inciting them to actions of one kind or another.
>
> ([5.46], 125)

In discussing this view in 'Is "Goodness" the Name of a Simple, Non-natural Quality?' [5.5], C. D. Broad aptly characterized it as the 'Hurrah-Boo' theory of moral language. For according to emotivism, when I say, for example, that stealing is wrong, all that I really mean is, 'Boo on stealing!' This makes it hard, of course, to see how such a theory might ever begin to make sense of moral argumentation, a worry raised by G. E. Moore in 'The Nature of Moral Philosophy'. If I say 'Boo' to something to which you say 'Hurrah', there is no claim to the truth of which we disagree about; I merely express my feelings about the thing, and you yours.

Ayer's response to this worry was to meet it head on, and to deny that moral disputes were, in fact, possible. Ayer claimed that in a 'moral' disagreement with someone we might argue over facts relevant to the case, or even over questions of whether those facts fell within the purview of this moral principle or that; what we could not argue over was why someone should accept one moral principle as opposed to another. That we are able to get along as well as we are, as often as we are, was for Ayer a simple artifact of our having been brought up within particular societies, defined by certain shared values.

But this view of moral disputes hardly begins to do justice to the ways in which we actually argue about ethical issues. In a series of important articles, culminating in 1944 with his *Ethics and Language*,

Charles Stevenson tried to extend the emotivist account of moral argumentation. He agreed with Ayer that at least some putatively moral
disputes were really nothing more than disputes regarding the facts of
the matter at issue. For Stevenson, however, there could be genuine
moral disagreements:

> We must distinguish between 'disagreement in belief' (typical of
> the sciences) and 'disagreement in interest.' . . . Disagreement
> in interest occurs when A has a favourable interest in X, when
> B has an unfavourable one in it, and when neither is content
> to let the other's interest remain unchanged.
>
> ([5.66], 426)

In the course of such disagreements, each of A and B will attempt to
influence the other to drop or otherwise modify his or her original
interest in X. The most important way of doing this is to use what
Stevenson calls the persuasive method, which

> depends on the sheer, direct emotional impact of words – on
> emotive meaning, cadence, apt metaphor, stentorian,
> stimulating, or pleading tones of voice, dramatic gestures, care
> in establishing *rapport* with the hearer or audience, and so on.
>
> ([5.69], 139)

Something of an advance, to be sure, over the method of moral persuasion advocated by Carritt.

Yet whatever its inadequacies as a descriptive theory of moral
argumentation, emotivism does offer a coherent story about moral
motivation. Unlike naturalism, however, emotivism regards the problem
of moral knowledge as moot, a point which leads us to the third
important qualification of its claim that moral judgements are literally
meaningless.

Emotive meaning is not descriptive meaning. Moral judgements,
that is, are in the end no more about the subjective realm of human
feelings and interests than they are about the objective realm of natural
or non-natural goodness. While moral judgements express feelings, they
do not, except perhaps incidentally, serve to describe those feelings.
Emotivists, like the naturalists, emphatically disavowed subjectivism,
but only because they believed that moral judgements, in their purely
normative use, had no propositional content. Another way of putting
this point is to say that moral claims do not express cognitive judgements about the way the world is, subjectively, objectively or even
relationally. For this reason, emotivism and its descendants are often
referred to as non-cognitivist theories of ethics.

Narrowly construed, logical positivism gradually sank under the
weight of its own assumptions. As might be remarked from Ayer's

preface to the second edition of *Language, Truth, and Logic*, it turned out to be extremely difficult to state the verification principle in a coherent fashion. As a distinct school of thought, logical positivism has since given way to more generally empiricist approaches to language, meaning and knowledge. Regarding ethics, however, the situation is more confused; by 1945, emotivism had swamped its chief rivals, intuitionism and naturalism. But since then emotivism has itself been swamped by a widely disparate variety of alternatives, some of them non-cognitive, some of them not, each about as plausible as the next. Still, as the twentieth century draws to a close, it would not be unfair to say that the influence of positivism in general, and emotivism in particular, has been much more pervasive than that of either intuitionism or naturalism.

More lasting as enigma than influence has been the ethical doctrine of Wittgenstein's *Tractatus*. The central logical claim of the book, that the limits of what can be meaningfully said extend no further than empirical propositions about the world of the natural sciences, was eagerly embraced by the early positivists. For Wittgenstein, however, this logical point was itself of the utmost moral importance. In showing the limits of what could be said, Wittgenstein took himself to be showing the limits of the world, in its entirety. What he took to be of deep moral importance was that in showing the limits of the world, he showed that he himself could not be part of it. As a psychologically or physically describable subject of desires, experiences or actions he certainly was a part of the empirical world; but as the metaphysical subject who saw what logic showed about its limits he certainly was not.

Since the metaphysical subject was not part of the world, nothing that happened in the world could affect it for good or ill; goodness or badness must lie wholly within the metaphysical subject itself, quite apart from the actual events of the empirical world. What this meant for Wittgenstein was that the good person, the happy self, was the self who completely identified with the world as a whole: the self who accepted whatever happened without trying to alter the course of events to satisfy the desires of the particular empirical subject with whom it might otherwise and unhappily be tempted to identify itself. Wittgenstein's own ethics, with its roots in the decidedly un-English intellectual tradition of Vienna and the late Habsburg empire, was thus entirely out of step with the approaches to moral philosophy being developed in either England or the United States in the first half of the twentieth century. It is unlikely that either Russell or Moore, for example, Wittgenstein's examiners when he submitted the *Tractatus* for a degree at Cambridge and two of the English philosophers who knew him best, ever really understood the main unstated claim of the book which according to Wittgenstein was more important for what it didn't say than what it did: the stark moral command found in his *Notebooks 1914–1916* to 'Live happily!'

❧ SUBSTANTIVE ETHICS ❧

As remarked at the outset, the main focus of the moral philosophy of the first half of the century was on meta-ethical questions pertaining to the meaning of moral terms. Questions of substantive ethics – questions, that is, about what sorts of things might actually be good or bad, right or wrong – took what seemed to be a legitimate second place to questions about what one might mean in applying these terms to one thing or another. Nevertheless, in so far as at least several of its participants thought themselves to have successfully settled such questions of meaning, the period also included two significant developments with respect to questions of ethics proper.

The first development, already mentioned, was Ross's theory of *prima facie* duties. This theory is deontological, since it takes questions of rightness, or duty, as the basic questions of ethics, rather than questions about goodness. For Ross, the foundations of morality were to be found in our intuitions about right and wrong, intuitions which disclosed to us moral truths about certain types of actions: telling the truth, lying, keeping or violating promises, respecting or failing to respect human life or property. While our intuitions told us that keeping promises, for example, was *prima facie* right, they also told us that violating promises was *prima facie* wrong. But what of rightness and wrongness themselves? To take first the simple case, actions which instantiated but one of these types were, in fact, right or wrong, depending on the type of action of which they were an instance. For actions which were instances of more than one type, however, the possibility existed that while on the one hand they might be *prima facie* right, on the other they might be *prima facie* wrong; how were we to know, in such cases, whether the action was right or wrong? According to Ross, this was not something that could be determined by intuition. If, for example, we were confronted with an action that was at once both the keeping of a promise and a lie, the best we could do would be to try and assess the relative weight of the two conflicting *prima facie* considerations in this particular situation, and then choose accordingly.

This has generally been held to be the chief failure of the theory of *prima facie* duties: it is simply not a theory of right and wrong. The point of this criticism is that we typically look to moral theory because we are baffled by the question of what it would be right to do in a particular case. We suppose that if we were able to determine, in general, what it is that makes right acts right, then we would also be able to see what we ought to do in the particular case at hand. In failing to tell us what rightness might amount to in cases that are morally puzzling, Ross's theory fails to deliver what a moral theory must, if it is to be interesting or useful.

Two other problems with this theory are well put by Dewey in his *Theory of the Moral Life*. His first point is that our moral intuitions are only as good as their source in the actual process of our moral education:

> If the conditions of their origin were intelligent, that is, if parents and friends who took part in their creation, were morally wise, they are likely to be intelligent. But arbitrary and irrelevant circumstances often enter in, and leave their impress. . .
>
> ([5.15], 125–6)

A second, deeper problem has to do with moral change. To base one's moral theory on intuitions is to make it inherently conservative:

> Men become attached to their judgements as they cling to other possessions which familiarity has made dear. Especially in times like the present, when industrial, political, and scientific transformations are rapidly in process, a revision of old appraisals is especially needed.
>
> ([5.15], 127)

Dewey's 'present' is, of course, in certain respects no longer ours; but his point is not without its current relevance. In our own time of rapid change, John Rawls, for example, bases his theory of justice on what he calls our considered moral judgements in reflective equilibrium. But as feminists and others have pointed out, our considered moral judgements, even in reflective equilibrium, may be deeply divided by differences of race, gender and class. One way of understanding this fairly widespread complaint against *A Theory of Justice* is to see it as a direct response to the conservativism inherent in Rawls' method of reflective equilibrium.

This raises a significant question for the period under study. Where, for example, are the women? They are not, by and large, at the universities, professionally developing theories of ethics. But they are at the centre of a number of important early twentieth-century social movements, directed towards such things as temperance, suffrage, birth control, pacifism and general social reform. In their participation in these various movements, prominent women thinkers wrote books, articles, speeches and letters, all of which must stand as a rich, untapped resource of ideas about right and wrong, good and bad. To reconstruct ethical theories out of these ideas would be a large and challenging task; we can only begin to wonder about its ramifications for a more thorough understanding of early twentieth-century ethics. Would an extra section or two need to be added to a history of the period such as this, to take into account the moral thinking of women and other marginalized groups, or would the whole thing need to be recast? If recent work in feminist ethics provides any measure of the depth of such omissions in the moral philosophy of the latter half of the century, the second, more radical alternative is not at all implausible (Kittay and Meyers [5.34]; Hanen and Nielsen [5.24]).

Given the current unsettled state of philosophical thinking regarding such issues, these questions must remain speculative. This is not to say that they can be fruitfully ignored. For a reliable line on substantive ethics, the considered moral judgements of those in the margins of society are, *prima facie*, a much more important starting point for theory than the considered judgements of those who represent, by and large, the interests of those who wield social power. This is not to say that those in the margins are entirely innocent of prejudice, but only that social evils are more readily apparent to those suffering them than those profiting from them.

With this thought in mind, let us turn to the second significant theoretical development of the period as it is currently understood, Moore's ideal utilitarianism. Moore believed that once we knew what goodness was – a simple and unanalysable non-natural property – we could then go on to address the question of what sorts of things actually possessed this property. In addition to pleasure, Moore thought it immediately apparent that personal affection and the contemplation of beauty were in and of themselves, quite apart from any pleasure that might be connected to them, good. A little more thought, Moore thought, would suffice to show that knowledge, too, was objectively good. Against Mill's hedonistic utilitarianism, which declared there to be only one intrinsic good, that of pleasure, Moore's ideal utilitarianism thus seemed to provide a broader, pluralistic alternative. The assumption here is that Mill really did believe that pleasure was the sole intrinsic good, a point over which there is currently some debate (Anderson [5.1]); however this debate resolves itself, it is clear that Mill's theory of the good was much more subtle than Moore supposed it to be.

Theories of the good to one side, the basic utilitarian theory of the right is straightforward. If something is good, more of it must be better. Right actions, then, are actions which maximize the good. Depending on the comparative goodness or badness of their consequences, some actions are right, others are wrong, and still others are morally indifferent. Because on such views the rightness of actions depends on the goodness of their consequences, this class of moral theories is often referred to as consequentialist.

Now one might suppose that a consequentialist theory, as opposed to a deontological one, would be a more likely tool of social reform than conservativism. Not so for Moore. Because of the great difficulty attendant upon assessing the overall goodness of any proposal for social change, Moore thought it unlikely that any such change could be shown to be a good thing. His advice, then, was simply to follow certain of what he referred to as the rules of common sense: respect human life and property, keep your promises, and be industrious and temperate. This does not mean, as is often supposed, that in Moore's view we are simply to give ourselves over to all of the many demands of conventional morality; as Tom Regan makes persistently clear in *Bloomsbury's Prophet* [5.51], Moore's point is exactly the opposite. The *only* rules of common sense to which we ought to be obedient are those which have shown themselves beyond all reasonable doubt to provide the social and personal stability required for the free, individual pursuit of good things. This pursuit, rather than the dictates of conventional morality, ought to define our personal lives.

But whatever relevance Moore's views on this point might have had to the liberal principles of tolerance and individual freedom, and however liberating they might have seemed to the upper-class membership of the Bloomsbury Group, the fact remains that he was simply not the sort of social reformer that Mill was. The author of *Principia Ethica* may have been able to endorse the general principles of *On Liberty*, but he would certainly not have been able to endorse the sweeping calls for social change contained in *The Subjection of Women*. Regarding Moore's appeal to common sense, then, the most apposite response from a contemporary moral philosopher is once again Dewey's, from *The Quest for Certainty*:

> It is not for a moment suggested that we can get away from customs and established institutions. A mere break would doubtless result simply in chaos. But there is no danger of such a break. Mankind is too inertly conservative both by constitution and by education to give the idea of this danger actuality. What there is genuine danger of is that the force of new conditions will produce disruption externally and mechanically: this is an ever present danger. The prospect is increased, not mitigated, by that conservativism that insists upon the adequacy of old standards to meet new conditions.
>
> ([5.14], 272–3)

For Dewey, the search for moral knowledge is not something we can so easily choose to abandon. Moreover, the pursuit of such knowledge requires, *contra* Moore, our active moral participation in the world of social and technological change. Because of their probable consequences, participation is morally better than passivity.

Writing in 1929, Dewey could not have foreseen the shattering and abrupt technological disruption of human moral thinking that was to take place in the New Mexican desert on 16 July 1945, at 5:30 in the morning. Among those most directly responsible for the nearly instantaneous release of nuclear energy that took place that day, some physicists, like Niels Bohr and Leo Szilard, vainly attempted to influence the government of the United States not to put this terrible new weapon of indiscriminate mass destruction to actual military use. Others, like J. Robert Oppenheimer, took an active hand in planning on which cities to drop the first bomb. But after a brief flurry of organized, political effort following the war's end, most physicists had, by 1947, turned from politics back to science. Albert Einstein located the cause of his own discouragement in the apathetic response of the American people: 'The public, having been warned of the horrible nature of atomic warfare, has done nothing about it and to a large extent has dismissed the warning from its consciousness' (Jungk [5.33], 249).

Having mentioned Einstein, it is appropriate here to return to another important intellectual figure of the period, one who has until now been mentioned only in passing. However great his contributions to the development of analytic philosophy in the twentieth century, or to its intellectual life in general, Bertrand Russell's place within the history of early twentieth-century ethics remains problematic. As Bart Schultz notes in 'Bertrand Russell in Ethics and Politics' [5.64], Russell's writings on ethics, in particular, are no less remarkable than they are elliptical. Moreover, as intertwined as his views are with the main threads of the period's history, to that same extent is it difficult to weave them into any reasonably straightforward delineation of anything that might count as its warp or woof. Beginning as a Moorean objectivist in the early decades of the century, Russell soon sets off on his own emotivist tack, anticipating in a number of significant respects the later and more fully articulated views of not only Ayer, but Stevenson as well (Schultz [5.64], 597–9). But by at least 1952, Russell has already developed views that go off in another new direction, one which combines elements of emotivism and naturalism on the one hand, and utilitarianism and a social ideal of interests harmoniously arranged on the other (Russell [5.57]; Schultz [5.64], 603–4 and 613–14).

What is more interesting in the present context, however, is the breadth of Russell's own politically engaged life. In his voluminous writings addressed to a popular audience rather than to other professional philosophers, he wrestles with the dangers a well-developed set of sciences poses for society, and in particular, the ways in which technology may be effectively used to prevent people from thinking for themselves. Refusing himself to follow public opinion, which according to Russell could all too easily be manufactured to conform to the interests of those with social power, Russell was twice imprisoned: first for protesting Britain's involvement in World War I, and then again in 1961 for protesting British involvement in the nuclear arms race.

For those engaged in moral reflection at the close of the twentieth century, Russell's example is important in more ways than one. Technology and mass communication have, if anything, tightened their grip on free, democratic thought. And while the Cold War has at least temporarily abated, the threat of nuclear holocaust has hardly vanished: while the number of countries with nuclear capability continues to grow, the world itself continues to become increasingly more politically unstable. Third, and perhaps most important, we are now at a scientific and technological brink of our own. Just as few moral philosophers before 1945 could really have contemplated the possible annihilation of life as we know it, few contemporary moral philosophers are really able to contemplate the enormity of the potential for changing the basic structures of life raised by the possibility of genetic engineering.

At mid-century, the basic structure of the atom was suddenly laid bare to science and technology. At the century's end, the basic structure of DNA promises to be similarly disclosed to human understanding and manipulation. As we prepare to enter the twenty-first century, it is hard to tell which of these events will have deeper and more far-reaching ramifications for moral thought and action.

⟞ LOOKING BACK ⟝

If early twentieth-century moral philosophy began with Moore's confident assertion that the good was a simple, non-natural quality of certain intellectually evident objects of moral knowledge, it most certainly ended with the emotivist claim that moral judgements did nothing more than express subjective feelings about right and wrong. In between, the world was witness to two major wars, the Nazi holocaust, and the United States' atomic annihilation of the Japanese cities of Nagasaki and Hiroshima. Yet it would be too simple to say that by 1945 science and ethics had finally and unequivocally parted ways. As one of the patients in the insane asylum of Friedrich Dürrenmatt's play *The Physicists* [5.17] points out, any one of us who passively flicks on an electric light without knowing the physics of what he or she is doing is guilty of abusing not only science, but humanity. As long as such passivity is our social norm, none of us is safe, not even, it turns out, a physicist who believes himself to have escaped from the insanity of a world in which atomic bombs are dropped on cities to the relative calm of a madhouse.

More poignant is Bertolt Brecht's *Galileo* [5.4]. This play's central moment of dramatic tension occurs when Galileo, under threat of torture, recants his rationally founded belief in the Copernican theory. According to his followers, Galileo has, as the great physicist of his day, failed both science and humanity. In publicly abandoning the scientific method, he has violated the onerous responsibility that attaches itself to the social role he finds himself, like it or not, thrust into; in publicly recanting, he has plunged humanity back into the darkness of ideology and the unbalanced social order which it enshrouds. As his main disciple shouts after him, 'Unhappy is the land that breeds no hero'. So too have many accused the physicists who produced the bomb of moral cowardice. To them we might recommend Galileo's own response, which is underscored by the counterpoint of the play's final scene: 'Unhappy is the land that needs a hero' (115). In its stubborn refusal to think for itself, it is humanity itself which has failed.

In this same connection, and in direct response to the is/ought dilemma, it is worth considering a point to which Dewey often returned: when ethics is banished to a separate, ethereal realm above and beyond science, hypothesis and action, the real world in which we must actually conduct our lives is left to the mercy of uncontrolled commercial and military interests. As he puts the point in *The Quest for Certainty*,

> [t]he narrow scope which moralists often give to morals, their isolation of some conduct as virtuous and vicious from other large ranges of conduct . . . is perpetuated by this habit of exclusion of the subject-matter of natural science from a role in the formation of moral standards and ideals. The same attitude operates in the other direction to keep natural science a technical specialty, and works unconsciously to encourage its use exclusively in regions where it can be turned to personal and class advantage, as in war and trade.　　　　　　　　([5.14], 274)

In contrast, Dewey's naturalistic moral philosophy was closely conn-ected to his concern over the social conditions produced by the capitalism of early twentieth-century North America. These included the exploitation of child labour, the creation and maintenance of utterly inhumane living and working standards in cities and factories, and the coercive threat of unemployment that made such conditions inevitable and inescapable for large numbers of people.

Social unrest, socialist ferment, the progressive movement of which Dewey and other intellectuals were a part, trade unionism and subsequent government regulation all played a role in ameliorating such conditions, at least enough so that the growing threat of national chaos and social revolution could be nipped in the bud. But while nationally bounded capitalist concerns may thus have proved themselves to be controllable, it has become increasingly clear as the century has wound down that there is no controlling capitalism's Promethean capacity for escaping such bounds. In the face of national regulation of its concerns, capitalism has simply gone transnational with its conditions, relocating its child labour, starvation wages, unsafe working standards and shows of military force to the Third World. Moreover, as the standard of living consequently continues to fall in Canada, the United States and the United Kingdom, it is also becoming clear that if capitalism is indeed a great leveller of social differences, its natural grade favours Third World conditions over First.

In terms of ultimate influence, then, the work of Dewey and the other naturalists may turn out to be of the most lasting importance. In any social network where the many starve so that the few may overconsume, we may suppose, that is, that interests will not have been harmoniously arranged. As the early twenty-first century shapes up to be a transnational replay of the early twentieth-century conditions of Dewey's United States, we might thus allow ourselves the hope that a concern for ethics, rather than meta-ethics, will mark the dawn of the new century. Dewey's question, of course, would be what we, now, might do in pursuit of that hope.

❧ BIBLIOGRAPHY ❧

5.1 Anderson, Elizabeth S. 'John Stuart Mill and Experiments in Living', *Ethics*, 102(1) (1991): 4–26.

5.2 Ayer, A. J. [1936] *Language, Truth, and Logic*, 2nd edn, New York: Dover, 1946. Ch. VI, 'Critique of Ethics and Theology', excerpted in W. Sellars and J. Hospers, eds, *Readings in Ethical Theory*, New York: Appleton-Century-Crofts, 1952.

5.3 Bernstein, Richard J. *John Dewey*, New York: Washington Square Press, 1966.

5.4 Brecht, Bertolt *Galileo*, trans. Charles Laughton, ed. Eric Bently, New York: Grove Press, 1966. First US productions in Hollywood and New York, 1947.

5.5 Broad, C. D. 'Is "Goodness" the Name of a Simple Non-natural Quality?', *Proceedings of the Aristotelian Society*, 34 (1933–4): 249–68.

5.6 Cahn, Steven M. *New Studies in the Philosophy of John Dewey*, Hanover, NH: University Press of New England, 1977.

5.7   Carritt, E. F. *The Theory of Morals: An Introduction to Ethical Philosophy*, London: Oxford University Press, 1928.

5.8   Chomsky, Noam 'On Changing the World', in *Problems of Knowledge and Freedom: The Russell Lectures*, London: Barrie & Jenkins, 1972.

5.9   —— *Necessary Illusions: Thought Control in Democratic Societies*, Toronto: CBC Enterprises, 1989.

5.10 Darwall, Stephen, Alan Gibbard and Peter Railton 'Toward *fin de siècle* Ethics: some trends', *Philosophical Review*, 101(1) (1992): 115–89.

5.11 Dewey, John *Theory of Valuation*, Chicago: University of Chicago Press, 1939.

5.12 —— [1920] *Reconstruction in Philosophy*, Boston: Beacon Press, 1957.

5.13 —— [1922] *Human Nature and Conduct: An Introduction to Social Psychology*, New York: Modern Library, 1957.

5.14 —— [1929] *The Quest for Certainty: A Study of the Relation of Knowledge and Action*, New York: G. P. Putnam's Sons, 1960. Ch. X, 'The Construction of the Good', reprinted in W. Sellars and J. Hospers, eds, *Readings in Ethical Theory*, New York: Appleton-Century-Crofts, 1952.

5.15 —— *Theory of the Moral Life*, New York: Holt, Rinehart & Winston, 1960. Reprint of J. Dewey and J. H. Tufts, *Ethics*, 2nd edn, New York: Henry Holt, 1932, Part II.

5.16 —— and James H. Tufts *Ethics*, New York: Henry Holt, 1908.

5.17 Dürrenmatt, Friedrich *The Physicists*, trans. James Kirkup, New York: Grove Press, 1964. *Die Physiker* was first performed in Zurich in 1962.

5.18 Edwards, James C. *Ethics without Philosophy: Wittgenstein and the Moral Life*, Tampa: University Presses of Florida, 1982.

5.19 Edwards, Paul *The Logic of Moral Discourse*, Glencoe, Ill.: Free Press, 1955.

5.20 Frankena, William [1939] 'The Naturalistic Fallacy', in W. Sellars and J. Hospers, eds, *Readings in Ethical Theory*, New York: Appleton-Century-Crofts, 1952.

5.21 Gibbard, Allan *Wise Choices, Apt Feelings: A Theory of Normative Judgement*, Cambridge, Mass.: Harvard University Press, 1990.

5.22 Hacking, Ian *Why does Language matter to Philosophy?*, Cambridge: Cambridge University Press, 1975.

5.23 Hall, Evert 'The "Proof" of Utility in Bentham and Mill', in J. B. Schneewind, ed., *Mill*, New York: Anchor, 1968.

5.24 Hanen, Marsha and Kai Nielsen, eds *Science, Morality, and Feminist Theory*, Calgary, Alta.: University of Calgary Press, 1987.

5.25 Hanfling, Oswald *Logical Positivism*, N.Y.: Columbia University Press, 1981.

5.26 Harman, Gilbert *The Nature of Morality: An Introduction to Ethics*, New York: Oxford University Press, 1977.

5.27 Heims, Steve J. *John von Neumann and Norbert Wiener: From Mathematics to the Technologies of Life and Death*, Cambridge, Mass.: MIT Press, 1981.

5.28 Heldke, Lisa 'John Dewey and Evelyn Fox Keller: A Shared Epistemological Tradition', in Nancy Tuana, ed., *Feminism and Science*, Bloomington: Indiana University Press, 1989.

5.29 Hersey, John [1946] *Hiroshima*, New York: Alfred A. Knopf, 1985.

5.30 Hudson, W. D., ed. *The Is/Ought Question: A Collection of Papers on the Central Problem in Moral Philosophy*, London: Macmillan, 1969.

5.31 —— *Modern Moral Philosophy*, London: Macmillan, 1970.

5.32 Janik, Allan and Stephen Toulmin *Wittgenstein's Vienna*, New York: Simon & Schuster, 1973.

5.33 Jungk, Robert *Brighter than a Thousand Suns: A Personal History of the Atomic Scientists*, trans. James Cleugh, New York: Harcourt, Brace, 1958.

5.34 Kittay, Eva Feder and Diana T. Meyers, eds *Women and Moral Theory*, Totowa, NJ: Rowman & Littlefield, 1987.

5.35 MacIntrye, Alasdair *A Short History of Ethics*, New York: Macmillan, 1966.

5.36 Mill, John Stuart [1859] *On Liberty*, ed. Elizabeth Rapaport, Indianapolis: Hackett, 1978.

5.37 —— [1861] *Utilitarianism*, ed. George Sher, Indianapolis: Hackett, 1979.

5.38 —— and Harriet Taylor *Essays on Sex Equality*, ed. Alice Rossi, Chicago: University of Chicago Press, 1970.

5.39 Minear, Richard, ed. and trans. *Hiroshima: Three Witnesses*, Princeton, NJ: Princeton University Press, 1990.

5.40 Monk, Ray *Ludwig Wittgenstein: The Duty of Genius*, New York: Free Press, 1990.

5.41 Morgenbesser, Sidney, ed. *Dewey and His Critics: Essays from the Journal of Philosophy*, New York: The Journal of Philosophy, 1977.

5.42 Moore, G. E. *Ethics*, Oxford: Oxford University Press, 1912.

5.43 —— 'The Nature of Moral Philosophy', in *Philosophical Studies*, London: Kegan Paul, Trench & Trubner, 1922.

5.44 —— [1903] *Principia Ethica*, Cambridge: Cambridge University Press, 1971.

5.45 Novack, George (1975) *Pragmatism versus Marxism: An Appraisal of John Dewey's Philosophy*, New York: Pathfinder Press, 1975.

5.46 Ogden, C. K. and I. A. Richards [1923] *The Meaning of Meaning*, 8th edn, New York: Harcourt, Brace, 1946.

5.47 Perry, Ralph Barton, *General Theory of Value: Its Meaning and Basic Principles construed in Terms of Interest*, Cambridge, Mass.: Harvard University Press, 1926. Excerpts from Ch. V, 'Value as Any Object of Any Interest', reprinted in W. Sellars and J. Hospers, eds, *Readings in Ethical Theory*, New York: Appleton-Century-Crofts, 1952.

5.48 —— *Realms of Value: A Critique of Human Civilization*, Cambridge, Mass.: Harvard University Press, 1954.

5.49 Pritchard, H. A. [1912] 'Does Moral Philosophy Rest on a Mistake?', in W. Sellars and J. Hospers, eds, *Readings in Ethical Theory*, New York: Appleton-Century-Crofts, 1952.

5.50 Rawls, John, *A Theory of Justice*, Cambridge, Mass.: Harvard University Press, 1971.

5.51 Regan, Tom, *Bloomsbury's Prophet: G. E. Moore and the Development of his Moral Philosophy*, Philadelphia: Temple University Press, 1986.

5.52 Ross, W. D. *The Right and the Good*, Oxford: Oxford University Press, 1930.

5.53 —— *Foundations of Ethics*, Oxford: Oxford University Press, 1939.

5.54 Russell, Bertrand [1903] *The Principles of Mathematics*, New York: Norton, 1938.

5.55 —— *Principia Mathematica*, Cambridge: Cambridge University Press, 1910.

5.56 —— *The Problems of Philosophy*, London: Williams & Norgate, 1912.

5.57 —— [1952] *Human Society in Ethics and Politics*, New York: Simon & Schuster, 1955.

5.58 —— [1905] 'On Denoting', in Robert C. Marsh, ed., *Logic and Knowledge*, London: Allen & Unwin, 1956.

5.59 Ryan, Alan *Bertrand Russell: A Political Life*, New York: Hill & Wang, 1988.

5.60 Santayana, George 'Hypostatic Ethics', in W. Sellars and J. Hospers, eds, *Readings in Ethical Theory*, New York: Appleton-Century-Crofts, 1952. Excerpted from *The Winds of Doctrine*, New York: Scribner's, 1913.

5.61 Schilpp, Paul Arthur, ed. *The Philosophy of John Dewey*, Chicago: Northwestern University Press, 1939.

5.62 —— *The Philosophy of G. E. Moore*, London: Cambridge University Press, 1942.

5.63 Schlick, Moritz [1939] *Problems of Ethics*, trans. David Rynin, 2nd edn, New York: Dover, 1962.

5.64 Schultz, Bart 'Bertrand Russell in Ethics and Politics', *Ethics*, 102(3) (1992): 594–634.

5.65 Sellars, Wilfrid and John Hospers, eds *Readings in Ethical Theory*, New York: Appleton-Century-Crofts, 1952.

5.66 Stevenson, Charles L. 'The Emotive Meaning of Ethical Terms', *Mind*, 46 (1937): 14–31. Reprinted in C. L. Stevenson, *Facts and Values: Studies in Ethical Analysis*, New Haven, Conn.: Yale University Press, 1963, and in W. Sellars and J. Hospers, eds, *Readings in Ethical Theory*, New York: Appleton-Century-Crofts, 1952.

5.67 —— 'Ethical Judgements and Avoidability', *Mind*, 47 (1938): 45–57. Reprinted in C. L. Stevenson, *Facts and Values: Studies in Ethical Analysis*, New Haven, Conn.: Yale University Press, 1963.

5.68 —— 'Persuasive Definitions', *Mind*, 47 (1938): 331–50. Reprinted in C. L. Stevenson, *Facts and Values: Studies in Ethical Analysis*, New Haven, Conn.: Yale University Press, 1963.

5.69 —— *Ethics and Language*, New Haven, Conn.: Yale University Press, 1944.

5.70 —— *Facts and Values: Studies in Ethical Analysis*, New Haven, Conn.: Yale University Press, 1963.

5.71 Strickland, Donald A. *Scientists in Politics: The Atomic Scientists Movement, 1945–46*, Indiana: Purdue University Studies, 1968.

5.72 Urmson, J. O. *The Emotive Theory of Ethics*, London: Hutchinson University Library, 1968.

5.73 Warnock, G. J. *Contemporary Moral Philosophy*, London: Macmillan, 1967.

5.74 Warnock, Mary *Ethics since 1900*, New York: Oxford University Press, 1960.

5.75 Weiner, David Avraham *Genius and Talent: Schopenhauer's Influence on Wittgenstein's Early Philosophy*, Toronto: Associated University Presses, 1992.

5.76 Wittgenstein, Ludwig 'A Lecture on Ethics', *Philosophical Review*, 74(1) (1965): 3–12.

5.77 —— [1921] *Tractatus Logico-Philosophicus*, trans. D. F. Pears and B. F. McGuiness, New York: Routledge & Kegan Paul, 1974.

5.78 —— *Notebooks 1914–1916*, Chicago: University of Chicago Press, 1979.

CHAPTER 6

Ethics II (1945 to the present)
Robert L. Arrington

❧

In the years immediately following World War II, the field of ethics was dominated by discussion of the meta-ethical theory known as emotivism. This theory maintained that moral judgements are expressions of emotions and attitudes and not statements of fact about objective reality. As a set of claims about the meaning and the epistemological status of moral judgements, emotivism represented a new, meta-ethical conception of ethics. Earlier in the century G. E. Moore had inquired about the meaning of the word 'good', and hence he and his fellow British intuitionists might be said to have initiated the meta-ethical approach. But it was the emotivists who first restricted ethical inquiry to meta-ethical investigations. Rather than making normative judgements about what is right and wrong or good and evil, they saw the role of philosophy as one of elucidating the linguistic character of normative judgements. Questions of meaning and justification were central to the emotivists' conception of meta-ethics as a second-order enterprise of linguistic analysis. According to this conception, no first-order, normative conclusions follow from meta-ethical analyses. Understood in this sense, meta-ethics became the preferred way of doing ethics for the following two decades.

The theory of emotivism was first proposed by several philosophers identified with logical positivism, the influential philosophy of the 1920s and 1930s whose main thrust was to articulate a criterion of meaningful speech and, in accordance with this criterion, to limit meaningful discourse to statements that are empirically verifiable. The positivists' verifiability criterion of meaningfulness in effect restricted meaningful discourse to scientific statements, from which domain the class of moral and ethical statements (as well as aesthetic and religious ones) was excluded. But if moral utterances are not meaningful statements about the world, about human beings and their actions, what are they? Rudolf Carnap suggested that they are not statements at all

163

but rather commands: to say, for example, that stealing is wrong is just a way of ordering someone not to steal. In a similar vein, A. J. Ayer maintained that the real function of moral and ethical remarks is to give vent to the feelings and emotions of the person making the remarks – hence 'stealing is wrong' is another way of saying 'Stealing, ugh!' Clearly, commands and exclamations are not factual statements at all, and they cannot be thought of as true or false (although an expression of emotion can be insincere). Hence they do not convey any form of knowledge. Moral judgements, according to this way of thinking, are non-cognitive. Instead of imparting information and knowledge about human nature and human action, moral utterances are emotive in function, aimed at expressing affective states or influencing attitudes and actions. Hence the appropriateness of referring to this view as the emotive theory of ethics.

Charles L. Stevenson's *Ethics and Language*, published in 1944, is undoubtedly the most sophisticated and elaborate development of emotivism. Stevenson was interested in explaining why there is so much moral disagreement and why this disagreement is often so difficult to overcome. If, as naturalistic moral philosophers maintained, moral terms refer to natural properties detectable by the use of scientific method, the moral judgements containing them should be subject to empirical verification or falsification. If naturalism were true, the processes of scientific inquiry should be adequate to establish the truth of moral propositions to the satisfaction of all rational minds. Likewise, if moral judgements make reference to non-natural qualities detectable by a special sense of moral intuition (as the intuitionists had claimed earlier), the exercise of this allegedly cognitive capacity should lead to the resolution of moral disagreements. Or, finally, if philosophers like Kant were correct and there is some rational, quasi-logical decision procedure that is to be applied to moral decision-making, then rational human beings should be able to come to agreement over moral truth. But disagreement is rampant and unceasing. Why is this so? Have our scientific, intuitive or rational decision procedures not been properly applied? Or is moral disagreement perhaps not something that is always amenable to cognitive resolution?

Stevenson was impressed by the fact that moral disagreements and arguments are highly dynamic affairs – the parties to the disputes are trying, it appears, not just to get their opponents to believe something different, but to *feel* and *act* differently. The language used in the debates is emotively charged: the words 'good' and 'bad', 'right' and 'wrong' appear to express positive and negative feelings and attitudes on the part of the speakers, and these and other emotionally potent words also seem to serve as instruments which the disputants use to influence one another and to goad one another into action.

Stevenson shows how, to his mind, these attitudes and activities are built into the very meanings of moral terms and judgements. The latter, he maintains, have both emotive and descriptive meaning – they serve to express and evince or evoke attitudes as well as to make descriptive claims. The word 'good', for instance, is often used by a person to describe herself as approving of some object or action, but at the same time it is used dynamically to *express* the speaker's pro-attitude to the object. Finally, it is also used to call on the person spoken to to approve of the object or action as well. Hence, according to Stevenson, '*x* is good' often means something like 'I approve of *x*, do so as well.' 'Good' at one and the same time describes the speaker as approving of the object (just as she might describe herself as five feet tall), expresses the speaker's approval (much in the way in which 'Ouch!' expresses pain and 'Ugh!' expresses disgust) and urges others to approve of it (just as she might command someone to close a door).

Stevenson provides us with a sophisticated causal and dispositional analysis of the notion of meaning. In the first place, meaning is to be understood in terms of the conditions that give rise to an utterance, and also in terms of the conditions that are brought about as a result of this utterance. Frequently certain beliefs and attitudes will causally lead a person to use certain words, and the use of these words in turn often causes other people who hear or read them to come to have the same beliefs and attitudes. If I believe it is about to rain, this may cause me to say that it is about to rain, and my doing so in turn may lead others to believe this. If I disapprove of something my daughter has done, I may be led to say that what she did was wrong, and as a result of my saying so others (including, I hope, my daughter) will also come to disapprove of it. The meaning of what I say relates to the beliefs and attitudes that give rise to my utterances and are in turn caused by them.

The meaning of a word, however, is not just the set of ideas or attitudes that causes a person on a particular occasion to utter the word (or that on a particular occasion is produced in others by the utterance of the word). Such causes and effects are too variable to constitute meaning. But over an extended period of time, words, as a result of their use, develop a tendency to cause specific beliefs and attitudes in those who hear them, just as they develop a tendency to cause a person to say certain things. These tendencies may be referred to as dispositions, and these dispositions have a constancy which allows them to figure into an account of meaning. Thus Stevenson is led to think of the meaning of a word as its disposition to evoke a specific set of ideas and attitudes and its disposition to be used by a person who has these beliefs and attitudes.

Consequently, the meaning of a word like 'good' can be defined in terms of its dispositions vis-à-vis a specific set of attitudes and beliefs. One meaning it may have is its disposition to cause others to approve of an object and to believe that the speaker approves of it, together with its disposition to be used by a speaker when that speaker approves of the object. We may say that in such cases its *descriptive meaning* is its disposition to cause others to believe that the speaker approves of the object, while its *emotive meaning* is its disposition to express and evoke approval of the object. (Stevenson allows for a richer descriptive meaning as well, but the analysis just given captures the essential thrust of his theory.)

Given that moral judgements (and value judgements more generally) are functions of both beliefs and attitudes, understanding disagreements in the moral sphere requires grasping how these two components can come into conflict and how they can interact with one another. Two or more individuals may have a straightforward disagreement in belief: one believes that Clinton will win the 1996 presidential election and the other believes that Dole will do so. Or they may have a disagreement in attitude: one approves of Dole and the other heartily disapproves of him. More often than not, the disagreement in belief can be conclusively resolved: either Clinton or Dole will win the election and one party to the dispute will be correct and the other wrong. It is slightly more complicated in the case of disagreement in attitude. Many, perhaps most, disagreements in attitude are the result of disagreements in belief. Two potential voters may have different attitudes about Clinton because they have different opinions about what his policies would be if he were elected president. They may debate the issue of what his policies would be, and one of them may succeed in changing the other's mind. And this may lead the other person to develop a new attitude towards Clinton: agreement in belief would lead to agreement in attitude. But such a functional relationship need not always hold. Two individuals may agree in belief to the effect that Dole favours a widespread cut in the capital gains tax and Clinton does not. One of the individuals, however, approves of Clinton because of his position on this issue; the other disapproves of him for the very same reason. Here we would have a disagreement in attitude that, at least on the surface, is not based on a disagreement in belief and cannot be resolved by bringing about agreement in belief (it is possible, of course, that the two parties to the dispute have *other* disagreements in belief – perhaps about the general nature of society and the economy – which are ultimately responsible for their conflicting attitudes towards the capital gains tax). Hence it is conceivable that there may be disagreements in attitude which are independent of disagreements in belief. If so, they would not be resolvable by attaining agreement in belief.

The dual – emotive and descriptive – meaning of value judgements together with the different possibilities for agreement and disagreement in attitude and belief lead Stevenson to conclude that there is a limit to the effectiveness of rational debate in the moral sphere. To the extent that moral disagreements reflect disagreements in attitude that are based on disagreements in belief, these moral disagreements are potentially resolvable by rational means, namely those empirical and logical techniques used to bring about agreement in belief. But to the extent that moral disagreements reflect attitudinal differences not based on differences of belief, rational means alone cannot guarantee agreement. In such cases, the use of reason, scientific method, and the like may bring all parties to agreement on the facts, but their differing, belief-independent attitudes would remain in spite of this. Theoretically, then, there is a limit to what we can expect from the use of reason in the moral sphere.

Another important implication follows from Stevenson's emotive analysis of moral judgements. This analysis implies that the notion of validity does not apply in the case of many moral arguments. If the judgement 'Tom is a good person' means, as Stevenson suggests, 'I approve of Tom, do so as well', someone disagreeing with this judgement may be taken to say 'I disapprove of Tom, do so as well.' Finding themselves in disagreement, the two individuals, A and B, may proceed to argue with one another, and this argument would involve an attempt on the part of each person to bring forth information about Tom which would hopefully change the other's beliefs and hence her attitudes towards Tom. Let us assume that one of the parties to the dispute, A, is successful in this way in winning over the other person, B, to the view that Tom is a good person. What would be the relationship between all the reasons A gives in favour of 'Tom is a good person' and this normative conclusion itself? Is it possible that A's reasons have proved that Tom is a good person? Do we have here an argument in which the reasons constitute premises from which one might validly derive the conclusion that Tom is a good person?

Stevenson's answer is negative. The reasons given by A should not be seen as evidence in favour of A's assertion that Tom is a good person. After all, this assertion amounts simply to A's saying that she, A, approves of Tom together with her admonition that B do so as well. We may reasonably expect B to agree with the statement that A approves of Tom – that is not what is at issue, and hence not what A is trying to convince B of when she argues with her. The reasons provided by A are not, then, intended to prove A's statement that Tom is a good person; rather, they are intended to change B's beliefs about Tom and hence her attitudes towards him. They are either effective in doing so or not, and hence the only question that can be raised about these 'reasons' is whether they are causally effective in changing someone else's moral judgement, not whether they are rationally effective in proving the speaker's moral judgement. The notion of validity has no central place in moral debate (although, of course, it has a subsidiary role in determining whether the beliefs involved in the debate have been rationally defended).

The consequences of Stevenson's emotivism are shocking, at least to those who believe that reason has a central role to play in moral debate and that if it were used by all parties, rational agreement would in the end occur. Validity, the central component of the concept of rationality, turns out to have only a limited role to play in moral argumentation, and the threat of disagreements in attitude that are not rooted in disagreements in beliefs calls into question any general faith in the rational resolution of moral disagreements. Moreover, emotivism gives us a picture of moral discourse quite different from what we are commonsensically accustomed to. It pictures this discourse as a set of strategies for influencing, persuading, and on occasion goading people to develop desired sets of attitudes, not as a dispassionate search for truth. In this context, truth and validity count for little: agreement in attitude, by whatever means, seems the ultimate goal. When the guns of World War II grew silent, philosophical debate over the nature of morality began with a bang!

Although emotivism has a deep and wide sceptical appeal, many philosophers soon began to view this scepticism as based, as scepticism so often is, on a misunderstanding of the actual shape or form of our language, in this instance moral language. Some critics argued that the emotivists failed to make a necessary distinction between guiding a person's attitudes and actions and goading a person into feeling and acting in certain ways. Others expressed doubt over Stevenson's causal theory of meaning and insisted that we define the meanings of moral terms by reference to the linguistic rules governing ordinary discourse. Perhaps the greatest concern with emotivism was its derogation of reason in the moral sphere, its claim that the concept of validity has no central application in moral argumentation. This claim seems to fly in the face of our frequent criticisms of the moral arguments of others and our own efforts to make our moral convictions as well grounded as possible. Thus began a revolt against emotivism, the first major critics being advocates of the meta-ethical theory of prescriptivism.

The philosopher primarily associated with prescriptivism is R. M. Hare. His book *The Language of Morals*, published in 1952, is a landmark in twentieth-century moral theory. It puts forth a position that continues to be held today by many philosophers. Although critical of emotivism, Hare's prescriptivism remains a non-cognitivist theory. It shows, however, a greater sensitivity to the actual use of moral language.

Hare was one of those thinkers concerned that emotivism gave too little acknowledgement to the role of reason and logic in moral argumentation. Once we grasp the structure of such an argument, he thinks, we will see that it often has the form of a syllogism. Consequently the rules of valid reasoning can be strictly applied to it. Consider this example of a moral argument:

A: It was wrong of Mary to have an abortion.
B: Why?
A: Because it involved the taking of a human life.
B: Why does that make it wrong?
A: Because it is always wrong to take a human life.

This argument can be turned around to reveal the following syllogism:

1 It is always wrong to take a human life.
2 In having an abortion, Mary was taking a human life.
3 It was wrong of Mary to have an abortion.

This is a perfectly valid argument and hence proves its point as forcefully as possible. But, as with all valid arguments, one is required logically to accept the conclusion only if one accepts the premises. Hence a debate may break out over whether it *is* always wrong to take a human life. In this debate, a defender of premise (1) may construct another syllogistic argument which looks like this:

4 It is always wrong to disobey the commandments of God (which include the commandment not to kill).
5 Taking a human life is disobeying one of the commandments of God.
6 It is always wrong to take a human life.

Whatever else one may say about it, this extended argument has logically impeccable credentials. If there are reasons to be sceptical about moral argumentation, *reason itself* cannot be faulted. The concept of validity, according to Hare, applies in morality as much as in other spheres.

The examples just considered suggest that moral justification ultimately leads to basic or fundamental moral principles which are not themselves susceptible of the type of proof they help generate for less basic principles and particular moral judgements. Consider premise (4): it is always wrong to disobey the commandments of God. In the minds of many believers, this principle is ultimate – there are no other principles from which it itself is deductively derived. What if another person does not accept this principle? Perhaps that person does not even believe in the existence of God, in which case she surely will not agree that one ought to obey God's commandments. If moral arguments have the deductive structure that Hare describes, and if in the course of an argument we arrive at an ultimate principle, in the nature of the case no further deductive justification can be given for the ultimate principle. Thus there is no way to prove this principle to someone who does not accept it.

Hence we must say that while Hare shows us that reason has an important and central role to play in moral disputation, his analysis suggests that there is a limit to the ability of reason to bring about rational moral agreement. In defending our particular moral judgements and most of our principles, we must abide by the canons of logic. But reason and logic will bring about agreement on moral matters among people only if they accept the same ultimate principles. It may not always be clear whether or not people do accept the same ones, but the possibility of irreconcilable disagreement over such principles seems an inescapable sceptical implication of Hare's analysis. It leads us to question whether reason can be said to prove any of our moral judgements (if all of them finally rest on unproved ultimate premises), and thus it leads us to doubt whether we can really claim knowledge of our moral convictions.

The non-cognitivism inherent in Hare's meta-ethics becomes even more apparent as we attend to his analysis of the role or function of moral judgements. Moral judgements, according to Hare, are prescriptive, quasi-imperative in nature. Prescriptions cannot be true or false, and it makes little sense to talk of knowing them. Although I may know that someone commanded me to close the door, it is senseless to say I know the truth of the command 'Close the door'. The prescriptive status of moral judgements precludes the possibility of moral knowledge, in spite of the fact that, according to Hare, reason requires that we be consistent in our use of moral prescriptions.

Taking the word 'good' as the focus of his prescriptive analysis of moral language, Hare reminds us that it is a word of commendation. As such, it is used to commend things in situations of choice. If I say that the new Honda is a good car, I am recommending that someone, perhaps I myself, buy one. I am guiding someone's choice of a car. If I say that Gandhi was a good person, I am commending the kind of life he led and recommending that others emulate this life. The function of commendation in these examples can be characterized in prescriptive terms – I am prescribing the choice of the new Honda, or the way of life exemplified by Gandhi. I am answering the questions: What shall I choose? What shall I do? Contrary to emotivism, Hare claims, the function of a value judgement is not to get someone (causally) to do something or have a certain attitude but rather to tell her to do it. In telling someone this, I use prescriptive language.

I am not, however, just arbitrarily prescribing choices. In saying that something is a good car or life, etc., I imply, according to Hare, that there are good reasons for choosing this kind of car or life. I imply that the objects commended have certain properties that make them good and in virtue of which I commend them. These properties Hare calls the good-making properties of the class of objects into which the one I am commending falls, e.g. the good-making properties of cars, or of human lives. It is always appropriate, Hare insists, to demand of someone commending a certain object, person or action that she provide reasons for this commendation, and these reasons should refer to the good-making properties of the object.

In articulating the good-making properties of a class of objects into which the commended entity falls, I am in effect appealing to a universal standard or principle, e.g. 'Good cars have properties *a*, *b* and *c*' or 'Good lives have properties *f* and *g*.' My particular value judgement always implies a universal value judgement. This universal standard or principle, together with a statement to the effect that the entity I am commending in fact *has* the appropriate good-making characteristics, yields the value judgement that I initially made. Hence:

7 Good cars have properties *a*, *b* and *c*.
8 This new Honda has *a*, *b* and *c*.
9 This new Honda is a good car.

How are we to characterize the universal standard or principle that serves as the major premise in arguments of this sort? It too, Hare thinks, must be seen as prescriptive. Just as in saying the new Honda is a good car I was prescribing its choice, so in saying that cars with properties *a*, *b* and *c* are good cars I am commending, and prescribing for choice, cars having these properties. General principles are no less prescriptive than the particular moral judgements falling under them.

Hare's thesis concerning the commendatory, prescriptive nature of value terms and judgements and his claim about good-making properties allow him to maintain that moral terms and judgements have both evaluative and descriptive meaning. The commendatory function or prescriptive role can be called the evaluative meaning of a moral term or judgement; the implied statement about the good-making properties of the object commended can be referred to as its descriptive meaning. Normally, moral terms and judgements have both evaluative and descriptive meaning. The evaluative meaning, however, is primary. It remains constant regardless of the class of object commended, while the descriptive meaning varies with this class. The primacy of the evaluative over the descriptive meaning also comes out in this way: unless I am willing to commend a certain set of properties for choice, I will not take them to be the good-making characteristics of the class of object in question.

Hare's claim that value judgements are prescriptive allows him to demonstrate the close connection between evaluation and action, a task which, he maintains, cannot be accomplished by those who interpret value judgements simply as descriptions. In accepting a value judgement, I am in fact assenting to the prescription to choose the object or perform the action in question. The criterion of assent to a prescription is that, other things being equal, I in fact do what the prescription tells me to do (in other words, I have not assented to the prescription unless, other things being equal, I perform the prescribed action). Of course, other things may not be equal: I may change my mind about assenting to the prescription, or find I cannot do what I am told to do, or forget what I was to do, etc. But if one or another of these conditions does not exist, assent to a prescription entails that I obey the prescription. Contrariwise, assent to a *description* never entails that I will perform a certain action; indeed, it never entails that I will do anything whatsoever. Hence Hare's analysis of practical discourse indicates why it is *practical*, why it issues in action. (One should note that the intimate relationship between prescriptions and actions also poses a major problem for Hare, the problem of weakness of the will. It certainly appears that I may assent to a prescription without any of the *ceteris paribus* conditions mentioned above holding and still fail to act – my will may be weak. Explaining this weakness of the will is a major problem for a prescriptivist.)

The commendatory function of 'good' and other value terms has an important logical consequence. Commending, we have seen, involves the prescription of choices. Prescriptions are logically distinct from descriptions and incapable of being logically derived from them alone. No matter what properties I describe a car as having, in describing it I have not taken the step of recommending that it be chosen: I have not said 'Choose this one.' Hence no prescriptive value judgement follows from premises that contain only true/false descriptions. We have seen that evaluative arguments contain not only a descriptive minor premise but also a prescriptive universal standard or principle as the major premise. We now can observe that this is the structure that a valid evaluative argument *must* have. A prescriptive conclusion follows from an appropriate prescriptive major premise and an appropriate descriptive minor premise, but not from the latter alone. And no matter how many factual, descriptive statements are added to the argument, the evaluative conclusion will not follow from them until such time as an appropriate prescriptive judgement is entered as a premise as well.

Important consequences for the issue of moral agreement follow from these logical observations. Agreement on facts will not by itself ensure agreement on a disputed moral judgement. Two or more people may operate with different moral standards or principles, in which case they may agree on all the properties of the object, person or action they are evaluating and still disagree on its moral or evaluative character. If they bring the same standards or principles to the discussion, agreement on the facts is to lead to agreement regarding the evaluative conclusion, but if they do not do so, they may find themselves in irresolvable disagreement. Of course, as noted above, they may attempt to obtain agreement on the standards or principles by arguing for them. But this argument must have, as we have seen, another standard or principle of greater generality as its major premise, and unless two or more people can agree on such a major premise of higher generality, they will not obtain agreement on standards or principles of lesser generality. In so far as no evaluative judgement can be deduced from factual statements alone, ultimate principles must be seen as based on fundamental commitments or decisions of those who hold them. If people have made commitments to different standards or principles of highest generality, there will be no way in which one of them can be compelled logically or rationally to adopt a different basic principle.

Hare seems willing to accept these consequences, but he thinks they imply no basic arbitrariness in the area of moral discourse. Moral discourse is such that moral judgements conceptually require that reasons be given to support them. In tracing out the series of factual claims and standards or principles supporting a moral judgement, in pointing to the consequences of following these standards or principles and showing how doing so satisfies even higher, more ultimate principles, one is in effect revealing a way of life. To be able to articulate this way of life in defending a moral claim is to be a fully rational creature. To ask for more, to demand that we be able to justify the way of life by deducing it from some set of factual propositions, is to ignore the fact that morality is a matter, not ultimately of the world being a certain way, but of our choosing to live a certain kind of life.

Hare's prescriptivism dominated discussion in moral philosophy during the 1950s and 1960s, and it quickly became the paradigm of non-cognitivist approaches to moral discourse. But reaction against prescriptivism began in the late 1950s and picked up steam in the 1960s. Although no competing theory gained the position of dominance attained by Hare's prescriptivism, a number of powerful technical arguments were directed against it. Slowly, as a result of this attack, the pendulum began to swing back in the direction of cognitivism. To this day, however, no cognitivist position has attained the level of consensus that Hare's views previously attained.

A leader in the attack on prescriptivism was the Oxford philosopher Philippa Foot. In two pioneering articles, 'Moral Arguments' [6.8] and 'Moral Beliefs' [6.9], published in 1958 and 1959, she set out a form of moral philosophy that has been called neonaturalism, the central idea of which is that moral claims relate intrinsically or conceptually to the notion of human well-being. Consequently, these claims can be evaluated for their truth or falsity, and we can achieve an understanding of what really is right and wrong by understanding how our actions impact on human well-being. Our attention here will be directed primarily at Foot's reasons for opposing prescriptivism, for these reasons in the end have been more influential than her own constructive theory.

Foot objects to the idea that we can create criteria for the goodness of objects or the rightness of actions simply by approving of or deciding to commend a set of properties possessed by these things. Hare's view, she claims, would allow us to identify the class of good men as those with red hair, simply by virtue of our approving of and commending red hair. We could think it right to be cruel, just by deciding to prescribe the choice of cruel actions. To claim that good men are those with red hair, and right actions those that are cruel, is not, however, merely to make false claims. Such statements are absurd; they are conceptual nonsense. The proper use of words is defined by the rules of language, and the rules governing 'good' and 'right' do not allow us to apply them, respectively, to red-headed persons exclusively and to cruel actions. These rules prohibit us from using moral terms as we please. Hare made the descriptive meaning of moral terms dependent on their evaluative meaning: the good-making properties of a certain class of objects are the set of properties we decide to commend for choice. Such a view would allow the descriptive meaning to vary widely from one person to another. Foot thinks such a view implies conceptual anarchy, and she rejects this anarchy as inconsistent with the rule-guided nature of moral terminology. When we look to see what these rules are, we will find, she thinks, that moral terms are conceptually linked to certain sets of properties related to well-being. We cannot, without talking nonsense, use these terms in ways that do not acknowledge these conceptual links.

Another leader in the assault on non-cognitivism was Peter Geach. In 'Good and Evil', Geach argues that in phrases such as 'good person' or 'good auto' the term 'good' is being used attributively, not predicatively [6.12]. If its use were predicative, it would have a sense that could be understood independently of the senses of the terms with which it is combined in these phrases, just as 'red' can be understood independently of 'cat' when it occurs in the phrase 'red cat'. A red cat is something that is red and that is also a cat. Hare's claim that the evaluative meaning of 'good' is independent of its criteria of application or descriptive meaning, and his assertion that the evaluative meaning is primary because it is constant across classes of objects having different criteria, requires that 'good' in 'good person' or 'good car' be taken as predicative. Geach argues that, on the contrary, its use in phrases of this sort is attributive. Take the case, he urges, of 'a good burglar' – this is not a person who is good and who is also a burglar. Understanding 'good burglar' requires understanding the meaning of the phrase as a whole – we do not know what 'good' means in this context unless we know what a burglar is. Hence we cannot postulate in this and similar cases an evaluative meaning of 'good' that is independent of the descriptive meaning of the term to which the normative term is attached.

In another influential essay, 'Assertion', Geach tries to show that the meaning of 'good' cannot be understood in terms of its commendatory use [6.11]. He points to numerous sentential contexts in which the use of this word cannot be taken to commend anything, e.g. 'If the child is good, she should be allowed to go out to play.' In saying, 'If the child is good . . .' one is certainly not commending the child. The meaning of 'good' in this context cannot, then, be explained in terms of its commendatory function or force. But, Geach goes on to argue, the term must have the same meaning in this context as it does in others if we are to preserve the validity of arguments in which it occurs. Take, for instance, the following argument:

> If the child is good, she may go out to play.
> The child is good.
> Therefore the child may go out to play.

If the meaning of 'good' in the first premise were different from its meaning in the second premise, this argument would be invalid; it would commit the fallacy of equivocation. The argument, however, is valid. It follows that, in so far as 'good' in the first premise does not have a meaning connected to the role of commendation, neither does it have this kind of meaning in the second premise. Geach grants that terms like 'good' may on occasion be used to commend – this fact, however, does not preclude it from having a primary descriptive meaning which it contributes to the propositions in which it occurs, in *whatever* context these propositions occur.

Another influential attack on meta-ethical views similar to Hare's came from John Searle in his article 'How to derive "Ought" from "Is" ' [6.16]. Searle argues that, contrary to a long tradition of thinking descending from Hume and captured in Hare's prescriptivism, it *is* possible to derive an evaluative judgement (about what one *ought* to do) from a purely descriptive one (about what *is* the case). Take the following descriptive remark: 'John uttered the words "I hereby promise to pay you, Smith, five dollars."' From this, Searle claims, we can derive the evaluative conclusion 'John ought to pay Smith five dollars.' Admittedly there are some intermediary steps that have to be filled in between the premise and the conclusion, but Searle maintains that none of them contains any evaluative statements or principles. The ought-statement, therefore, follows from the is-statements or descriptive premises alone. Searle's argument is controversial, but it has an initial plausibility that forced many philosophers to rethink the 'is/ought' controversy. It led them to reconsider whether, as Hare alleged, prescriptions cannot be derived solely from descriptive premises, or even more fundamentally, whether ought-judgements and other evaluative claims really are non-descriptive (at least in any important sense).

Still other criticisms can be levelled at Hare and the non-cognitivist approach that his views exemplified. An important part of Hare's meta-ethical theory is the assumption that moral justification proceeds by deducing particular moral judgements from universal standards or principles together with statements of fact that serve to subsume the particular judgements under the universal principles. We are not justified in accepting a particular judgement unless it is capable of being subsumed in this measure under one of our universal moral commitments. But why, some philosophers such as Renford Bambrough [6.7] and Jerome Schneewind [6.15] ask, do general principles have this justificatory priority? In fact, do they always have it in our everyday moral practices? It can be argued that we often feel far more certain that a particular act is wrong than we do about the general principle it instantiates. For example, it would certainly be wrong of me to break my promise to repay Jones five dollars in most ordinary circumstances, but would it always be wrong to break such a promise? We can think of many instances in which it might not be. Surely I should break a promise in order to save a life, and sometimes breaking a promise to promote a higher good seems perfectly permissible. Promise-keeping in some individual cases may have overriding weight, but in others it may not. Epistemically, we are far more certain of the duty to break a particular promise in special circumstances than we are of the principle that universally prescribes promise-keeping.

In fact, it could be argued that we actually arrive at many of our general moral principles by something like induction – because doing x was the right thing to do in so many particular circumstances, we generalize to the effect that doing x is always right. Such a generalization should be seen more as a guideline than as an absolute principle and should be held with considerable caution. As an absolute principle, it would be subject to refutation in a particular instance if we had a confident sense (some might say intuition) that it was wrong to do x on this occasion.

A sophisticated development of this latter mode of thinking has been developed by John Rawls. In fact, Rawls's proposed method of *reflective equilibrium* has become an attractive approach to the issue of moral reasoning for many philosophers today. Any attempt to arrive at a set of general principles (Rawls's own search is for principles of justice) must initially be tested by comparing, on the one hand, what a set of proposed general principles suggests we do, with, on the other, our own particular judgements or intuitions about what to do in specific circumstances, especially those judgements in which we have a high degree of confidence. The applications of the principles need to match up with these intuitions. Of course, we are not always so confident about what, in particular circumstances, we ought to do – and we can continue to put the proposed principles to the test by seeing if they can give us guidelines that we find we can accept in these problematic circumstances. Indeed, once we come to have considered confidence in our proposed principles – because of the way they match the deliverances of intuition and the way they provide acceptable guidelines in problematic situations – we may extend their use and actually use them to *correct* the deliverances of intuition. That is to say, after considerable testing, general principles may be used to overturn particular judgements we are inclined to make when these judgements are unguided by general principles. In this way, our principles can come to correct our particular beliefs just as our particular beliefs can function to correct our principles. The end result of this process of mutual adjustment is that we bring our principles and particular judgements into a state of reflective equilibrium. Such a state bestows on both the considered principles and the considered judgements a level of epistemic warrant that is superior to the warrant either of these possessed at earlier stages in the process.

The method of reflective equilibrium appears to resemble in some important ways the method used in science to arrive at warranted beliefs. The development of general scientific theory is driven in part by particular observations, and concurrence with these observations is the test that general theoretical statements or statements of laws must pass. But once we have in hand a theory with some warrant, we can begin to use it to predict new observations, and we can even use it to reject observations that appear aberrant in light of the theory. In science, then, we seek reflective equilibrium between particular observations and general theory. If Rawls is correct, this is what we do in moral inquiry as well. Hence it is not difficult to think of moral inquiry as much closer in nature to scientific thought than the emotivists or prescriptivists believed. The parallels we have noted appear to bestow on moral thought a degree of cognitivity and credibility that was denied it by the non-cognitivists. Rather than constituting a distinct mode of discourse that fundamentally expresses non-cognitive states of mind, moral judgements may reflect something like scientific method applied to a distinctive area of human experience. Again, the pendulum begins to swing from non-cognitivism to cognitivism.

Questions about the conceptual constraints on moral judgements and arguments about the nature of moral inquiry and methodology were part of a more general interest in the notion of morality itself. What is this area of experience and discourse we call morality? If we obtain a clear picture of it, we may see that morality deals with very distinctive concerns and questions which limit the kinds of considerations and reasons that can properly occur in a moral argument. Further, the very concept of morality may set limits on what kinds of actions can be judged right and what kind of people good. Rather than being matters of individual choice or attitude, as the non-cognitivists maintained, they may be identified fairly precisely by the requirements imposed by the concept of morality.

But what is built into the concept of morality? What distinctive concerns are moral ones? What dimensions of action and the world are morally relevant? A lengthy debate ensued over these issues, one party claiming that the concept of morality makes certain kinds of factual issues relevant and decisive for moral debate, the other party denying that the concept of morality imposes any material conditions of this type. The latter group of thinkers granted that the term 'morality' has a distinctive meaning, but for them this meaning reflects the distinctive *form* of moral judgements, e.g. their prescriptive nature and their universal or universalizable character. While the first group proposed *material* conceptions of morality which identify a distinctive moral subject matter, the second group argued that the concept of morality imposes only *formal* conditions on what can be a moral judgement.

One of the most influential advocates of a material definition of 'morality' was William K. Frankena. In 'The Concept of Morality,' Frankena first puts forward for purposes of argument a formal definition of the term which he thinks captures the conceptions of his philosophical opponents [6.17]. This definition tells us that a person has a morality if and only if she accepts certain judgements and principles (a) that are prescriptive, (b) that she universalizes as being binding on all persons and (c) that she regards as definitive, overriding or supremely important. Frankena then offers as an alternative a material definition which states that a person has a morality only if she accepts judgements and principles that take into account the effects of her actions on others from the point of view of the other people themselves rather than from the point of view of her own self-interest.

The formalist definition would allow there to be conflicting moral principles, one of which supports a purely egoistic way of life while the other recommends actions that take the interests of others into account. The material definition would restrict moral principles to those that take the interests of others into account. If one accepts the material definition, then considerations about how an action affects the lives of others are *necessarily* relevant to deciding what one morally ought to do. But if one accepts the formal definition, one cannot determine from the meaning of 'morality' alone whether these considerations are relevant.

Frankena argues for the material conception of morality by (1) suggesting that it accords best with the way we actually use the term 'morality' and (2) rebutting the arguments of those who prefer the formalist definition. He is particularly concerned with R. M. Hare's claim that if we build social constraints into the meaning of 'morality', we win the argument against the egoist by linguistic fiat. Any judgement about what 'morality' means, according to Hare, must leave open the substantive issues that separate the egoist from someone who promotes the interests of others. Frankena agrees that the substantive issues remain even if we adopt the material conception. We do not dispose of the egoist's claim that we should always pursue self-interest simply by pointing out that this position is not a moral one; in arguing with the egoist we confront the issue of why we should prefer the moral perspective to the non-moral one. Thus one can grant that a disagreement remains, without giving up one's idea that the notion of morality itself requires consideration of the interests of others. If the egoist insists that his position *is* a moral one, then the only appropriate response is to see if his arguments in favour of this claim are acceptable. The egoist may suggest that it is not contradictory to say that an action involving an utter disregard for other people is not wrong on moral grounds. Is this correct? Frankena thinks not.

Many philosophers have been concerned that a material definition might serve to make something like utilitarianism true by definition – a consequence perhaps acceptable to utilitarianism but not to the many thinkers who reject it and still consider themselves to be moralists. Frankena's material conception of morality, however, is sufficiently broad to include deontological theories that emphasize duties to others as well as those theories committed to a policy of maximizing the pleasure or happiness of the greatest number. It excludes from morality only such principles as those of pure egoism.

The debate over the proper conception of morality came to no definitive conclusion. Some agreed in principle with the formalist conception but rejected the requirement expressed in the third component of Frankena's rendition of it – the requirement that moral considerations be considered supremely authoritative. They claimed that religious, even personal, considerations may take priority over moral ones in the minds of some people without these people having made any conceptual errors. Other attempts were undertaken to shore up both the material and the formal conceptions so as to provide necessary and sufficient conditions for the proper use of the term 'morality'. But necessary and sufficient conditions for the use of almost any term are hard to come by, as the case in point amply demonstrates.

A development in moral philosophy parallel and related to the search for a definition of morality was the good-reasons approach to moral discourse. This approach was initially articulated by S. Toulmin in his *The Place of Reason in Ethics* [6.21] and by Kurt Baier in his *The Moral Point of View* [6.20]. Toulmin and Baier urge us to attend more to the kinds of reasons that are submitted in defence of a moral position or judgement than to the logical character or content of moral judgements themselves. If we do so, they assure us, we will note that some considerations are particularly relevant to moral discourse and debate. Reasons appealing to accepted rules that define duties are perfectly appropriate considerations in most instances. But these rules may conflict with one another, in which case we may need to appeal to the very function of morality, which is to co-ordinate our attitudes and actions in ways that maximize the possibilities for everyone's aims and desires being fulfilled. Good reasons, therefore, ultimately are those that speak to the manner in which an action promotes the goal of fulfilling everyone's desires and aims. (It is not difficult to see how a philosopher like Hare might detect here an attempt to introduce utilitarianism into morality by linguistic fiat.) Clearly there is a fact of the matter about the impact of actions on this end state, and hence appeal to good reasons may allow us to achieve moral truth and knowledge.

Kurt Baier attempted to strengthen the notion of good reasons by showing that certain considerations or reasons are such that it would be irrational not to take them into account. In an early essay, he argued that the fact that an action will bring pain to oneself is a relevant consideration and one that normally counts against engaging in the action. Of course, there may be other reasons favouring an action that brings pain to oneself, e.g. the action may be in the best interests of one's family, and these reasons may show that an action is right even though it brings pain to the agent. But if there are no such overriding reasons, the fact that an action brings pain to oneself is a conclusive reason not to do it. If a person engages in an action only on the grounds that it would bring pain to him, we would consider this person irrational. Hence, everything else being equal, the production of pain is an objectively good reason *not* to perform the action in question.

Having established to his satisfaction that there are such things as objectively good reasons for or against an action, Baier turns his attention to moral reasoning. His argument here involves showing that there is a distinctive moral point of view such that assuming this point of view amounts to seeing certain kinds of reasons as relevant to the determination of what is morally right or wrong. A person acts from the moral point of view when he acts on general principles and does not make exceptions for himself even when following these principles frustrates his own interests. Hence moral rules or principles are universal – binding on everyone, including the speaker. Furthermore, moral principles or rules must be meant to promote the good of everyone alike, i.e. to take into account and further the interests of all.

Baier goes on to argue that it is more rational to promote moral aims than to pursue aims that conflict with morality, e.g. selfish aims. Our very purpose in reasoning, he tells us, is to increase our satisfactions and decrease our frustrations as much as possible. From this it follows that if I enjoy doing something, and my doing so does not hurt anyone else, then I have a good reason to do it. My enjoying doing x is objectively a good reason for doing x in these cases because not to think of it as being a good reason would be perverse or mad. But if my doing x would harm someone else, the situation changes. Our moral rules forbid us to harm others, even if doing so is enjoyable to us. Moral rules override those of self-interest. But the fact that moral rules have priority over rules of self-interest is also rational. As Thomas Hobbes observed, if everyone followed the rules of self-interest, this would lead to a state of nature in which life for everyone is nasty, brutish and short. Such a situation is contrary to self-interest, and promoting it is contrary to reason. We are more rational to accept rules which override self-interest in those instances in which pursuing this self-interest would be harmful to others. Those moral rules which are for the good of all are therefore in the interest of everyone alike. It follows that, within a society in which we can expect others for the most part to follow the moral rules, the moral rules are recommended by reason. The moral point of view is thus the rational point of view.

This argument can certainly be criticized. For one thing, it is possible to develop sophisticated forms of egoism which appear to be as rational as morality, perhaps even more so. We will not, however, pursue the argument at this point, although some theories we consider later will take up the case in favour of morality. Suffice it to say that the good-reasons approach to ethics made the notion of rational action (and the very concept of rationality) a central one in much of the moral philosophy that followed. Many philosophers approach the subject matter of ethics by inquiring whether our notion of rationality will allow us to construct an objective defence of morality.

Before discussing some of these 'rationality' approaches to moral objectivity, let us consider another question that arises out of the attempts to define morality and the moral point of view. Assume that we have done so adequately – the question then presents itself: why should I be moral? Baier, as we have seen, thinks the answer is: because being moral is in accord with reason – because it is in everyone's interest to do so. Other philosophers disagree with this type of answer – not because they are egoists, but because they think it is the wrong *kind* of answer to the question. Whether morality is in anyone's interest or not, they would say, is irrelevant. One ought to be moral simply because it is the right thing to do. The alternative – acting in preference for one's own interest when doing so brings harm to others – is simply wrong and vicious. Once we know what we ought to do morally, doing anything that conflicts with this is forbidden by morality.

But, another philosopher might observe, to answer the question 'Why be moral?' in this way begs the question; it adduces moral reasons in favour of being moral. The question posed is not whether there are moral reasons for acting in a certain way, but whether there are reasons to choose the moral point of view over other points of view, particularly the self-interested point of view.

A defender of morality might reply: what you are asking is whether there is an egoistic reason for preferring morality to egoism. And given that morality, with its emphasis on the good for all, often requires sacrifices of us, the answer will probably be negative. But what does this show other than that morality and self-interest are often opposed, as we knew before the argument began. If by chance we ascertained that it *would* be in our self-interest to be moral, this is not a justification of morality that a moral person is likely to accept. A person should be moral because she recognizes the superiority of moral reasons over self-interested, egoistic ones. One isn't really acting morally if one does so for selfish reasons.

We have here what appears to be a standoff. We cannot justify being moral by appeal to moral reasons or by appeal to egoistic ones. Perhaps we cannot justify being moral at all. Perhaps our decision to throw in our lot with the moral way of life is arbitrary. Baier himself does not think so. He thinks that moral reasons are superior to selfish ones because they are more rational. Others have argued that morality is at least not unreasonable. It is time to examine some of the recent theories that focus on morality from the standpoint of rational choice.

The first such theory to be considered is that of John Rawls. And it must be said at the outset that the brief description offered of this theory can in no way convey the enormous impact it has had in contemporary ethics. Rawls is one of the major figures in post-World-War-II ethics, and his normative system has had considerable influence outside ethics: in social and political philosophy and indeed in the political sphere itself. We will view Rawls's attempt to define and defend a set of principles of justice simply as one attempt to show how the notion of rational choice can generate an ethical position.

Rawls's position first came to the attention of a large philosophical audience through his early essay, 'Justice as Fairness' [6.29]. Other articles followed, and then in 1971 there appeared the monumental *A Theory of Justice* [6.28]. In 'Justice as Fairness', Rawls suggested that we begin our inquiry into the principles of justice by asking ourselves what principles a group of people (ourselves) would accept if they were in a position of having to identify the ways in which their future lives together would be organized and regulated. What principles would they agree on? Each person might initially prefer principles that would benefit him or herself, even at the expense of others, but would on reflection recognize that such principles would not be accepted by others. What is needed is a technique for determining what principles would be accepted by all. This technique would have to ensure that the principles for organizing society would be viewed by each person as being to his or her advantage, for only then would each person agree to them. The technique offered by Rawls involves identifying an 'original position of equality' which we might take up, a position in which we are all equal with respect to selecting principles that would be to our advantage, and hence a position in which we can have some assurance that everyone would agree to the principles proposed.

Getting into this original position, for Rawls, requires placing ourselves behind a 'veil of ignorance' from which vantage point we do not know what our individual interests or talents are or what our position in society is or would be. Not knowing such details about ourselves, we would be unable to propose principles that are uniquely designed to benefit us, to serve our interests and position and to capitalize on our talents. If we assume only general knowledge about the basic goods for human beings and basic facts about human nature and society, the principles we select could only further our common interests, those resulting from our general nature and condition. Not knowing who we are or would be in the future, and hence how certain policies might uniquely benefit us as distinctive individuals, we would select principles that would benefit us regardless of who we turn out to be. We would not, for instance, select principles authorizing slavery, since we might turn out to be slaves; we would not select principles that benefit the wealthy, since we might turn out to be poor. We would, on the contrary, select principles that would benefit everyone, and certainly would benefit the worst off among us, for we might very well fall into that group. The principles selected in this way behind a veil of ignorance are principles that could be accepted by all parties to the deliberations. It would be reasonable for everyone to agree to the principles that suggest themselves to those in the original position.

In defining the principles of justice – the principles for organizing and governing our lives – as those that people would agree to accept behind the veil of ignorance, Rawls is not saying that this type of pact was ever in fact entered into. The agreement he is talking about is a hypothetical one: what we *would* accept were we to put ourselves behind a veil of ignorance. We are not, therefore, committed to the implementation of some social contract into which we have entered earlier. But in so far as the hypothetical agreement is one we can envisage in thought, and in so far as the conditions imposed on the thought experiment guarantee that the results would benefit us regardless of who we are, then it would be reasonable for us to accept the principles identified and to implement them in our actual lives.

What principles would we accept behind the veil of ignorance? Rawls identifies two principles. The first requires that each person have the maximum liberty compatible with equal liberty for others. The liberties Rawls has in mind are political liberty, freedom of speech and assembly, liberty of conscience and freedom of thought, freedom of the person, and freedom from arbitrary arrest and seizure. The second principle deals with the distribution of the goods of nature and society and requires that these goods be equally distributed among all people, except in those circumstances in which an unequal distribution would be in the interest of everyone, including those who are the worst off with respect to material resources and powers. The second principle also requires equal opportunity or access with respect to positions of authority in society. If the two principles conflict with one another, the first is to have priority over the second. In arguing for these two principles, Rawls uses the method we have identified earlier as the strategy of seeking reflective equilibrium among our intuitions about what would be right and fair in particular instances and the general principles we propose. In defending two normative principles, Rawls also began the process of turning ethics away from its concentration on meta-ethical issues of meaning and justification and pointing it in the direction of its more traditional task of seeking the principles that define for us what really is right and good. His theory of justice is not just a major contribution to normative ethics; it is also responsible for making the project of normative ethics a legitimate and respectable one once again. In this latter role it promoted the development of numerous other normative theories and also supported the developing interest in practical or applied ethics, which began to seek normative answers to specific ethical problems that we face in society today.

Many philosophers have followed the lead of Rawls in defining the basic issues of ethics in terms of the question of what reason would say regarding the best way to satisfy our preferences and maximize our chances for well-being. Some have made even stronger claims about the verdict of reason. David Gauthier [6.26], for instance, has argued that opting for unfettered self-interest as opposed to a set of rules impartially acknowledging the interests of others would be irrational. Gauthier sees morality as a part of the theory of rational choice. Using the techniques of decision theory (which defines principles of rational choice under conditions of risk or uncertainty) and game theory (which considers choices made on the basis of expectations about how other agents will choose), he believes it can be demonstrated that one rationally ought to agree to those moral rules of impartiality which would require an occasional sacrifice of our own interests in order to promote impartially the interests of all concerned. Application of the theory of rational choice would show that constraining the pursuit of our own interests by the principles of impartiality is actually in our own interest, and, indeed, that we would be irrational not to agree to constrain our actions in such a way. Gauthier's work is clearly an extension of the perspective of Kurt Baier, which we discussed earlier.

Perhaps the most ambitious use of reason in recent ethics is found in the rationalist ethics of Alan Gewirth. Gewirth [6.27] believes that it is possible to prove a fundamental moral principle in the optimally strong sense of showing that anyone attempting to deny the principle would contradict herself. This fundamental principle, called by Gewirth the principle of generic consistency, requires that one act in accord with the generic rights of others as well as oneself, these generic rights being those to freedom and well-being. Gewirth gives a highly complex (and controversial) proof of the principle of generic consistency. The proof begins by showing that each of us, as an agent who acts with purposes and goals, must favour our own freedom and well-being, these being the conditions required for us to attain any of our particular goals or realize any of our purposes. Consequently, our freedom and well-being are *necessary goods* for each of us. Having established that we must acknowledge that our freedom and well-being are required in all of our actions, Gewirth further argues that we must assert our *rights* to freedom and well-being – otherwise, they would not be goods we *must* have. But if each of us is committed to our own rights to freedom and well-being, based on the fact that they are necessary conditions for the realization of the specific purposes and goals to which we are committed, we must grant that others, for whom freedom and well-being are also necessary goods, must also demand their freedom and well-being. If each of us demand our rights on such grounds, each of us must admit that all other persons are equally justified in demanding their rights on the same grounds. To deny that everyone has the rights to the generic goods would put us in the irrational position of allowing that we have these rights on these grounds but that others do not. This denial would amount, Gewirth argues, to an inescapable inconsistency. Thus we cannot, without contradicting ourselves, deny the truth of the principle of generic consistency. Here we have one of the strongest advocacies in the history of philosophy of the power of reason to prove the truth of a moral principle.

The good-reasons approach to ethics established early on by Toulmin and Baier leads, then, to contemporary views of the role of reason in ethics that attributes to reason the ability to offer objective proofs of moral truths. As we have seen, there are a variety of such views (and we have examined only a small representative sample), but all of them put the notion of rationality at the heart of ethical thinking. Such views, although immensely popular today, by no means exhaust contemporary approaches to ethics. We will now turn our attention to some contemporary perspectives that see 'rationalism' as a misguided form of moral philosophy.

An increasingly influential movement in contemporary ethics is that of moral realism. There are two different forms of this theory, one that is basically intuitionistic (and British) in nature, and one that emerges from the scientific realism that is very popular these days, especially in America. The two strands have in common the fact that their advocates believe in the reality of objective moral properties – properties of obligation, goodness, and so on – which attach to actions, people, and circumstances independently of human belief or desire. They also believe in our ability to grasp these properties and thereby attain objective moral knowledge. Their primary difference relates to their understanding of the cognitive ability yielding this knowledge. The intuitionists stress our perception-like ability to directly confront the fact that actions and agents have certain moral properties. The scientific realists maintain that a form of inquiry similar to scientific theorizing often results in knowledge of the moral character of actions and agents.

The intuitionistic realists suggest that we are not well served by pursuing ethical inquiry primarily with respect to such abstract notions as the right and the good. Rather, they think, we should look at very specific moral notions such as kindness and courage. We have no difficulty in ascertaining that a person is kind or courageous, and in so doing we are detecting moral characteristics. It makes perfect sense to say that we *see* that a person is kind or courageous. To be sure, our 'perception' of these qualities is always based on a perception of other qualities of the person or her actions: we see that a person is kind because she did x or y, or courageous because she reacted to situation s in manner r. But the moral characteristic cannot be *reduced* to these other characteristics. Nevertheless, the latter constitute the ground or basis for the moral property. We directly confront the fact that a person is kind, although we may refer to her other characteristics (which may be non-moral) in giving our reasons for the moral claim. The moral property is said by the realists to supervene on the base property or properties. This relation of supervenience captures the notion that moral properties are not inferred from non-moral characteristics and must be directly confronted in moral awareness; it also stresses, however, the fact that moral characteristics are not independent of the specific detail of character and circumstance in which they are embedded. The intuitionistic realists emphasize the need to pay close attention to the specific detail and circumstances of each action, so that we may detect the moral character directly and also the base properties which give rise to it and afford us reasons for asserting its existence.

Many of the intuitionistic realists approach the issue of moral reality from a perspective they think reflects the philosophy of the later Wittgenstein. Rejecting any form of scientism that would attempt to reduce all discourse to scientific propositions, they claim that our ordinary language incorporates concepts of moral properties and moral knowledge. In coming to master this language (play the 'language-game' of morality), we develop an ability to apply moral terms on the basis of perceptual criteria. If we do so correctly on a particular occasion, we can be said to state a moral truth and to achieve moral knowledge. No mystery attaches to the perception of moral reality – the appearance of oddness disappears once we realize that moral concepts shape and inform perception no less than do scientific concepts. We learn to apply scientific concepts, and when we do so correctly we have scientific knowledge; we learn to apply moral concepts, and when we do so correctly we have moral knowledge. Our moral language-game contains conceptual articulations and rules which we appeal to in actually playing the game. Theories that deny us moral knowledge, or that equate it with naturalistic, scientific knowledge, have failed to grasp the true nature of moral language. And the rationalists and others who put rules at the centre of morality have likewise failed to see that the moral language-game is one of directly seeing, confronting or detecting the moral character of particular actions and individuals, not one of deducing moral truths from general rules.

Scientific moral realism is in many ways a thousand philosophical miles away from the intuitionistic version. Its advocates do stress, along with the intuitionists, that in ordinary language we often speak of the moral properties of actions and agents as real and objective. They also note that in this ordinary discourse we have no hesitation in claiming that these moral properties are causally responsible for what happens in the world: we say, for example, that an army's defeat was caused by the general's cowardice, or that a dictator's cruelty led to his downfall. Taking their license for talking this way from ordinary discourse, the scientific realists propose that we attempt to construct theories of individual behaviour and societal change that take into account the causal efficacy of moral properties. Such theories will posit moral properties as part of their explanatory apparatus. These theories can be tested in terms of their ability to explain the course of human behaviour and societal change. The reality of the moral properties posited in these theories is no more suspect than the reality of sub-atomic particles. We accept both because of the ability of the resultant theories to explain what would otherwise be puzzling aspects of the world. We are justified in affirming the reality of an objective moral domain because of the explanatory utility of moral concepts.

The appeal to reason or rational choice, to intuition, or to scientific theorizing are three contemporary ways in which philosophers attempt to demonstrate the nature and reality of objective moral knowledge. The prevalence of such theories shows how far ethics has come from the scepticism inherent in emotivism and prescriptivism. But not all philosophers have accepted the claim to objective moral knowledge. To be sure, most ethical thinkers today have given up non-cognitivism for some form of cognitivism – the view that we do have moral knowledge. But being a cognitivist does not require that one think moral truth is objective, something independent of human attitudes and customs and available for inspection or demonstration by any normal human being. An option that remains, and that offers an attractive face to those who still feel the pull of moral scepticism, is relativism. Relativism has been with us since the earliest days of western philosophy, and it is still a viable option today. Relativism of some form or another seemed to be implied by the non-cognitivist positions of emotivism and prescriptivism. Even if these positions are rejected, as by and large they are today, there is still room for relativism in the current cognitivist environment. The theory has recently been given outstanding articulation and defence by two American philosophers, Gilbert Harman and David Wong.

In approaching any discussion of relativism, a basic distinction needs to be made between cultural and ethical relativism. Cultural relativism is the thesis that different cultures or societies have different moral codes; it is the denial that there are any moral values universally accepted by all people. As such, it is an empirical, scientific thesis (one often asserted by anthropologists) and not a philosophical one. Ethical relativism is a philosophical thesis: it claims that none of the numerous moral codes found in history can be validated as the true or correct code. This form of relativism is a repudiation of ethical absolutism, the claim that there are actions that are right or wrong for everyone, regardless of what beliefs they hold. Hence, according to the ethical relativist, what is right is only what is right *for you* in your society. Your moral code is valid for you, just as the moral codes of others are valid for them. None of them is valid or true for everyone.

Ethical relativists are often criticized for basing their philosophical, epistemological claim on the empirical thesis of cultural relativism. It does not, of course, follow from the fact that people have different moral beliefs that no one of these beliefs is superior to the others or that there are no universally valid, absolute moral principles. So, the critic argues, ethical relativism is based on a logical fallacy.

But it is not necessary to assert one's ethical relativism on the grounds that moral codes vary from society to society. The denial that there are moral codes valid for everyone can be asserted on different grounds, and an excellent example of such a theory is found in the work of Gilbert Harman. Harman [6.40] denies that it makes sense for us to affirm general principles identifying what it is morally right for all people to do. To tell someone that she morally ought to engage in some action is to presuppose that she accepts a principle enjoining this kind of action. If she does not accept such a principle, she has no reason to engage in the action, and if she has no reason to engage in it, then it is inappropriate for us to suggest that she ought to do so. It makes no sense, Harman tells us, for us to say that cannibals morally ought not to eat their victims, because, having no moral principle prohibiting this, they have no reason to abstain from the practice. Likewise, it is logically absurd for us to say that Hitler was morally wrong to attempt the extermination of the Jewish people. Not subscribing to a principle that proscribed genocide – being as he was beyond the moral pale – Hitler had no reason not to do so, and it is therefore empty for us to say that he morally ought not to have done so.

In general, when one makes an 'inner judgement' about what a person morally ought to do, one is making a judgement about the relationship between that person's principles and her actions. If these principles vary from person to person, as Harman thinks they obviously do, it follows that inner judgements are inappropriate when the person addressed does not subscribe to the principle justifying the judgement. Hence the nature of these inner judgements about what one morally ought to do prevents us from making the absolutist claim that all human beings morally ought to behave in certain ways.

David Wong's brand of relativism is of a more traditional nature [6.43]. He grants that there are true and false moral judgements but denies that any of them are true for all persons. To claim that a particular moral judgement is true, he maintains, is to say that the act it enjoins accords with the ideal standards or principles of one's group. If these standards vary from one group to another, then what moral judgements are true for one group may not be true for another – the actions judged to be in accord with the standards of one society may not accord with the standards of another.

Wong is sensitive to the charge that relativism would allow any action whatsoever to be judged right or wrong, a charge often levelled by absolutists. But, as we have seen, for an action to be right, in Wong's relativism, it must accord with the *ideal* standards or principles of a group. These ideal standards are those that are held in light of relevant factual information and that cohere with the other standards of the group. Hence constraints are placed on what accepted standards can generate true moral judgements. A sensitivity to relevant factual information and to logical considerations would rule out some standards. Finally, acceptable standards must perform the job that moral standards in all societies are designed to accomplish: they must help to resolve personal and interpersonal conflicts. Not all standards will succeed in this task, and those that fail are excluded from the set of ideal standards. So, Wong argues, not just anything goes. Moral truth requires an acceptable set of moral standards or an acceptable moral system.

Still in all, Wong claims, there are multiple moral codes that equally meet the criteria of acceptability set out above. He gives us as examples the virtue-oriented morality of eastern cultures and the rights-oriented morality of western Europe. The moral codes of these two moral systems will generate conflicting true moral judgements, so that for an easterner it is right to do *x* and for a westerner it is wrong to do *x*. For example, given the virtue-oriented morality's emphasis on the common good and the rights-centred morality's emphasis on individual liberties, the two moralities might conflict with regard to whether a person should contribute to the common good or pursue her own interests. Given the equal acceptability of the two moral codes, we are left with an ineradicable relativity of moral truth.

No account of the field of ethics since 1945 would be complete without an acknowledgement of the re-emergence of interest in two traditional ethical theories: utilitarianism and virtue ethics. Contemporary utilitarianism is an attempt to expand upon, refine and, according to some, radically alter the utilitarian views that were prevalent in the eighteenth, nineteenth and early twentieth centuries, particularly those of Jeremy Bentham and John Stuart Mill. Virtue ethics has a more ancient heritage: the philosophy of Aristotle. We shall conclude this chapter with a brief discussion of these two resurrected theories.

Utilitarianism, as articulated in the classical accounts of Bentham and Mill, is a theory which defines right actions as those that are productive of the overall greatest good. Such a theory is often characterized as teleological in nature: it defines right action in terms of the consequences of the action. Theorists may differ as to what constitutes good consequences – some say pleasure, others the avoidance of pain, still others happiness, and some few identify a plurality of ideals which right actions may produce. But all agree that what we ought to do is to engage in the action that produces more good than any other alternative action would produce. To produce the greater good is to have what is called utility. Right actions are those possessing utility.

Contemporary interest in utilitarianism has largely focused on the question whether the rightness of actions is a function of the consequences of the individual action itself or of the class of actions – the general kind of action – to which the individual instance belongs. Those who opt for the first form of the theory adopt what is called act utilitarianism, while those opting for the second form accept what is referred to as rule utilitarianism. To illustrate the difference in terms of an example, take the case of keeping a promise. For an act utilitarian, I should keep a promise I have made on a particular occasion only if in doing so I would thereby bring about better consequences – more happiness, say – than I would if I failed to keep the promise. It is perfectly conceivable that keeping the promise might *not* bring about more good than failing to keep it, in which case the act utilitarian would say that in those circumstances I should not keep it. This possibility disturbs some utilitarians and has led them to opt for rule utilitarianism. The rule utilitarian will say that I should keep the particular promise I made because it is enjoined by a general rule of promise keeping ('one should always keep one's promises'), and adherence to this rule brings about better consequences than making exceptions to it or abandoning it altogether. The rule utilitarian might agree that on a particular occasion my breaking my promise might produce better consequences than keeping it, but she will still insist on the rule's being followed because it is more desirable to have and follow the rule than not to do so. The act utilitarian thinks that such allegiance to rules, even those that have proved in general to be productive of good consequences, is irrational. If, on a particular occasion, I know that breaking my promise will bring about more happiness than keeping it, reason demands that I break it.

The debate that we see beginning to emerge between rule and act utilitarians has been one of the central features of contemporary discussions of utilitarianism. Another central feature relates to the conception of rules themselves. As a result of John Rawls's classic essay 'Two Concepts of Rules' [6.45], philosophers today distinguish between a summary and a practice or constitutive conception of rules. The summary conception is a statistical one: to say that promise-keeping as a rule has utility (produces better consequences than the alternatives) is to say that more often than not keeping promises turns out to be beneficial. The possibility of an exception is built into the summary conception, according to which a rule or principle should be put forward only as a guideline, to be followed more often than not. The practice conception pictures a rule, not as a statistical frequency but as a way of defining a certain kind of activity or organization. Chess rules afford us an example here. To say that the king cannot be captured is not to say that the king has not, as a matter of fact, ever been captured or that the king almost always escapes capture. The king, by definition, cannot be captured – such status is in part what makes the piece a king. The rule of chess that disallows capture of the king is a constitutive rule, not just a summary one. Likewise, in our society we find many rules that define certain forms of activity – what we might call practices. The practice of punishment is an example. The rules of punishment, for instance the rule that we are not to punish the innocent, are not summary rules but constitutive ones. They define for us what a practice like punishment is. Within a society that has a constitutive rule prohibiting punishment of the innocent, we do not examine individual instances of actions that would violate this rule to see if they might possibly have utility. To be engaged in punishment at all requires following this rule – otherwise what we are engaged in is simply not punishment. But the practice of punishment, with its constitutive rules prohibiting the punishment of the innocent and so on, might itself be examined to see if it has utility. If it does, it can be pronounced justified. The actions falling under the constitutive rules then are justified not because they themselves have utility but because the practice containing the constitutive rules does. Hence by construing rules as constitutive, many rule utilitarians are able to give additional substance to their form of utilitarianism. And they are able to save utilitarianism from the frequent charge that it would permit such morally heinous acts as punishing an innocent person on a particular occasion because doing so has utility.

As we noted, the current interest in virtue ethics amounts to a revival of something like Aristotle's conception of ethics. Instead of concentrating on general rules of duty, obligation and right action, Aristotle thought of ethics as an attempt to identify the features of character that are essential for achieving the good life for humankind. These excellencies of character he called virtues, and he set out to define them and show the manner in which they produce the good life. Of particular importance to Aristotle were those virtues that relate to our activities as citizens. The good life can be found only within society, and developing the civic virtues is essential for full and rewarding participation in the social sphere. Aristotle was suspicious of absolute, hard-bound rules. Frequently they require actions that are inconsistent with a proper, virtuous response to our loved ones and fellow citizens. In implementing the life of the virtues we are not so much to follow rules as pay close attention to specific cases. Frequently, becoming a good person is best achieved by emulating the example of a good person.

All these themes have found favour with some contemporary philosophers who are frustrated by the unresolved debates in meta-ethics and, more recently, dissatisfied with the current attention so often given to rules and their justification. The leader in the renewal of virtue ethics is Alasdair MacIntyre, whose book *After Virtue* [6.4] is one of the most discussed works in ethics in recent times. MacIntyre believes that contemporary moral philosophy has not overcome the nihilism and scepticism of Nietzsche, which he sees embodied in such contemporary views as emotivism. Unfortunately, however, those who eschew emotivism and talk about human rights and duties and obligations have no clear conceptual understanding of these notions – they lack the theological background needed to give significance to talk about rights and other moral characteristics. And in fact rights-talk often degenerates into the rhetoric of rampant individualism, attempts on the part of an individual to get her way in the midst of conflicting egos (much as the emotivists construed moral talk). For MacIntyre, our only hope is to rethink ethics and reinstate the Aristotelian conception of virtue. He recognizes that to do this we cannot appeal to the form of teleological biology that Aristotle used to ground his theory – such a metaphysical view is simply unacceptable to the contemporary mind. But if we recognize the role of practices in our lives, we will find the logical space to reintroduce talk of virtues. Our practices are co-operative forms of human activity aimed at realizing goods that can only be achieved by participating in these activities. There are family practices, political practices, economic practices, religious practices, and many others. Within such practices, the participants have roles – as husbands or wives, children or parents, citizens or politicians, workers or businessmen, church-goers or civic leaders – and these roles require certain modes of behaviour, and hence excellencies of character, in order to contribute to the attainment of the goods inherent in the practices. Without our distinctive roles, and the practices incorporating them, we would not be who we are. So in developing the virtues inherent in the roles we play in these practices, we are realizing ourselves – and helping to achieve the common good. Practices also must be understood in terms of their traditions, which link human beings with their forbears and their contemporaries, and hence with a human community within which the individual must realize herself. MacIntyre admits that all this may sound strange to contemporary readers accustomed to a different way of thinking about morality, but, as so many philosophers have done before, he suggests that we must reject the prevailing views of the day if we are at last to see the truth, in this case the truth about ethics.

This brings us to the end of a tumultuous half-century of ethical theory. The beginning of this period witnessed a radical departure from the traditional forms of ethical thought, but before the period ends we find a return to some of these very traditions. Between the beginning and end points a plethora of theories and issues have emerged. Although perhaps confusing to the novice because of the variety of positions and the shifts of focus contained in it, this period in the history of ethics is, perhaps for the very same reasons, notable for its vigour and the intellectual excitement it generates. As the end of the century approaches, ethics is alive and well, waiting for its next major controversy and its next major theory.

❧ BIBLIOGRAPHY ❧

Emotivism

6.1 Ayer, A. J. *Language, Truth, and Logic*, New York: Dover, 1946.
6.2 Carnap, Rudolf *Philosophy and Logical Syntax*. London: Kegan Paul, Trench & Trubner, 1935.
6.3 Falk, W. D. 'Goading and Guiding', *Mind*, 67 (1953): 145–69.
6.4 Kerner, George C. *The Revolution in Ethical Theory*. New York and Oxford: Oxford University Press, 1966.
6.5 Stevenson, Charles L. *Ethics and Language*, New Haven, Conn.: Yale University Press, 1944.
6.6 Urmson, J. O. *The Emotive Theory of Ethics*, London: Hutchinson University Library; New York: Oxford University Press, 1968.

Prescriptivism

6.7 Bambrough, R. *Moral Scepticism and Moral Knowledge*, London: Routledge & Kegan Paul, 1979.
6.8 Foot, Philippa 'Moral Arguments', *Mind*, 67 (1958): 502–13.
6.9 —— 'Moral Beliefs', *Proceedings of the Aristotelian Society*, 59 (1958–9): 83–104.
6.10 —— *Virtues and Vices*, Berkeley: University of California Press, 1978.
6.11 Geach, Peter 'Assertion', *Philosophical Review*, 74(1965): 449–65.
6.12 —— 'Good and Evil', *Analysis*, 17 (1956): 33–42.
6.13 Hare, R. M. *The Language of Morals*, Oxford: Clarendon Press, 1952.
6.14 —— *Freedom and Reason*, Oxford: Oxford University Press, 1963.
6.15 Schneewind, J. 'Moral Knowledge and Moral Principles', *Knowledge and Necessity*, Royal Institute of Philosophy Lectures, 3 (1968–9): 249–62.
6.16 Searle, John 'How to derive "Ought" from "Is"', *Philosophical Review*, 73 (1964): 43–58.

The definition of morality

6.17 Frankena, William K. 'The Concept of Morality', *Series in Philosophy*, 3 (1967), University of Colorado Studies; reprinted in G. Wallace and A. D. M. Walker, eds, *The Definition of Morality*, London: Methuen, 1970.

6.18 Wallace, G. and A. D. M. Walker, eds *The Definition of Morality*, London: Methuen, 1970.

The good-reasons approach

6.19 Baier, K. 'Good Reasons', *Philosophical Studies*, 4 (1953): 1–15.

6.20 —— *The Moral Point of View*, Ithaca, NY: Cornell University Press, 1958.

6.21 Toulmin, S. *An Examination of the Place of Reason in Ethics*, Cambridge: Cambridge University Press, 1950.

Why should I be moral?

6.22 Gauthier, D., ed. *Morality and Self Interest*, Englewood Cliffs, NJ: Prentice Hall, 1970.

6.23 —— 'Morality and Advantage', *Philosophical Review*, 76 (1967): 460–75.

6.24 Nielsen, K. 'Why should I be Moral?', *Methodos*, 15 (1963): 275–306.

Rational – choice theories

6.25 Daniels, N., ed. *Reading Rawls*, New York: Basic Books, 1975.

6.26 Gauthier, D. *Morals By Agreement*, Oxford: Oxford University Press, 1986.

6.27 Gewirth, Alan *Reason and Morality*, Chicago: University of Chicago Press, 1978.

6.28 Rawls, John *A Theory of Justice*, Cambridge, Mass.: Harvard University Press, 1971.

6.29 —— 'Justice as Fairness', *Philosophical Review*, 67 (1958): 164–94.

Moral realism

6.30 Sayre-McCord, G., ed. *Essays on Moral Realism*, Ithaca, NY: Cornell University Press, 1988.

Intuitionistic

6.31 Lovibond, Sabina *Realism and Imagination in Ethics*, Oxford: Basil Blackwell, 1983.

6.32 McDowell, John 'Virtue and Reason', *The Monist*, 62 (1979): 331–50.

6.33 Platts, Mark *Ways of Meaning*, London: Routledge & Kegan Paul, 1979.
6.34 Wittgenstein, L. *Philosophical Investigations*, 3rd edn, ed. G. E. M. Anscombe and R. Rhees, trans. G. E. M. Anscombe, New York: Macmillan, 1969.

Scientific

6.35 Boyd, R. 'How to be a Moral Realist', in G. Sayre-McCord, *Essays on Moral Realism*, Ithaca, NY: Cornell University Press, 1988.
6.36 Post, J. *The Faces of Existence*, Ithaca, NY: Cornell University Press, 1986.
6.37 Railton, P. 'Moral Realism', *Philosophical Review*, 95 (1986): 163–207.
6.38 Sturgeon, N. 'Moral Explanations', in D. Copp and D. Zimmerman, *Morality Reason and Truth*, Totowa, N.J.: Rowman and Allenheld; and in G. Sayre-McCord, *Essays on Moral Realism*, Ithaca, NY: Cornell University Press, 1988.
6.39 Werner, R. 'Ethical Realism', *Ethics*, 93 (1983): 653–79.

Ethical relativism

6.40 Harman, Gilbert *The Nature of Morality*, Oxford and New York: Oxford University Press, 1977.
6.41 —— 'Moral Relativism Defended', *Philosophical Review*, 84 (1975): 3–22.
6.42 Krausz, M. and J. W. Meiland, eds *Relativism: Cognitive and Moral*, Notre Dame, Ind.: University of Notre Dame Press, 1982.
6.43 Wong, David *Moral Relativity*, Berkeley: University of California Press, 1984.

Utilitarianism

6.44 Bayles, Michael D., ed. *Contemporary Utilitarianism*, New York: Anchor Books, 1968.
6.45 Rawls, J. 'Two Concepts of Rules', *Philosophical Review* 64 (1955): 3–32.
6.46 Smart, J. J. C. and B. Williams *Utilitarianism: For and Against*, Cambridge: Cambridge University Press, 1973.

Virtue ethics

6.47 MacIntyre, Alasdair *After Virtue*, Notre Dame, Ind.: University of Notre Dame Press, 1981.

Surveys

6.48 Arrington, R. L. *Rationalism, Realism, and Relativism: Perspectives in Contemporary Moral Epistemology*, Ithaca, NY: Cornell University Press, 1989.
6.49 Hudson, W. D. *Modern Moral Philosophy*, Garden City, NY: Doubleday, 1970.

CHAPTER 7

Epistemology

Paul K. Moser

Epistemology is the theory of knowledge, the philosophical study of the nature, origin and scope of knowledge. During the twentieth century, accordingly, epistemologists have debated (1) what knowledge consists in (e.g. justified true belief), (2) what knowledge is based on (e.g. sensory experience) and (3) what the extent of our knowledge is (e.g. objective, conceiver-independent facts as well as subjective, conceiver-dependent facts). Debates over (1)–(3) have occupied epistemologists since the time of Plato. Twentieth-century epistemologists have not put an end to such debates, but they have made some distinctive contributions. This chapter will identify some of these contributions, giving special attention to the fundamental issue whether we have genuinely objective knowledge: knowledge of conceiver-independent facts.

EMPIRICISM REVIVED

Common sense empiricists: Moore and Russell

Twentieth-century Anglo-American epistemology begins with the rebellion of Bertrand Russell (1872–1970) and G. E. Moore (1873–1958) against Kantian and Hegelian idealism at Oxford and Cambridge. F. H. Bradley (1846–1924) and John McTaggart (1866–1925) were two leading proponents of the British idealism challenged by Russell and Moore. Russell reports:

> It was towards the end of 1898 that Moore and I rebelled against both Kant and Hegel. Moore led the way, but I followed closely in his footsteps. I think that the first published account of the new philosophy was Moore's article in *Mind* [1899] on 'The Nature of Judgement'. Although neither he nor I would

now adhere to all the doctrines in this article, I, and I think
he, would still agree with its negative part – i.e., with the doctrine
that fact is in general independent of experience.

([7.92], 42)

Russell, following Moore, opposed any kind of idealism entailing
that 'there can be nothing which is not experienced or experience'
(ibid., 107). The view of Russell and Moore that 'fact is in general
independent of experience [and other mental activity]' entails *realism*
about facts. Realism about a fact, *F*, is just the view that *F* exists but
does not depend for its existence on a conceiver's experiencing or
conceiving of *F*.

Moore contrasted his realism with Kantian and Hegelian idealism
as follows:

> [My] theory . . . differs ['from Kant's theory of perception']
> chiefly in substituting for sensations, as the data of knowledge,
> concepts; and in refusing to regard the relations in which they
> stand as, in some obscure sense, the work of the mind. It rejects
> the attempt to explain 'the possibility of knowledge,' accepting
> the cognitive relation as an ultimate *datum*. . . . It thus
> renounces the supposed unity of conception guaranteed by
> Idealism even in the Kantian form, and still more the boasted
> reduction of all differences to the harmony of 'Absolute Spirit,'
> which marks the Hegelian development.

([7.53], 183)

Moore claimed that a 'concept is not a mental fact, nor any part of a
mental fact' (ibid., 179). Concepts, he held, are the only objects of
knowledge, and existing things are simply concepts or complexes
thereof. Russell's talk above of facts 'independent of experience' evidently refers to Moore's non-mental concepts. (The following
discussion of realism about external objects does not depend, however,
on the view that objects are concepts.)

Ontological claims concern what exists. *Epistemological* claims
concern what is, or can be, known – or at least justifiably believed.
Russell and Moore opposed idealism not only with the ontological
claim that there are mind-independent facts, but also with the epistemological claim that they *know* that there are such facts. What was the
ground for the latter epistemological claim? Russell explains:

> Bradley argued that everything common sense believes in is mere
> appearance; we [Moore and Russell] reverted to the opposite
> extreme, and thought that *everything* is real that common sense,
> uninfluenced by philosophy or theology, supposes real. With a
> sense of escaping from prison, we allowed ourselves to think

that grass is green, that the sun and stars would exist if no one was aware of them, and also that there is a pluralistic timeless world of Platonic ideas.

([7.89], 12)

The ground, according to Russell, is 'common sense, uninfluenced by philosophy or theology'. What exactly is common sense? Surprisingly, Russell and Moore do not say in any detail. A plausible, if rough, interpretation is that common sense for a group of people consists of beliefs common to a wide range of people within that group. Neither Russell nor Moore, however, appeals just to common sense of that sort. Neither argues, for instance, that since most people believe that God exists, we know that God exists.

Russell speaks of common sense *uninfluenced by philosophy or theology*. Why should we regard such common sense as a philosophically adequate ground for challenging idealism and supporting realism? In particular, why should we regard such common sense as a reliable source of *correct* belief regarding idealism and realism? Russell does exclude common sense influenced by philosophy or theology. This raises two issues.

First, are common sense beliefs ever altogether uninfluenced by philosophy, given a familiar broad sense of 'philosophy'? Don't common sense beliefs, in other words, typically involve broadly theoretical assumptions that are 'philosophical'? Common sense empirical beliefs about household physical objects, for example, typically rest on subjunctive conditionals: if I were to drop this mirror, it would shatter. Such conditionals are theoretical in that they go beyond simple description of what is currently present in one's perceptual experience. Russell does not say whether theoretical beliefs of that sort are 'philosophical'. It is difficult, however, to assess Russell's view without a clear statement of what he means by 'philosophy'.

Second, why should we think that common-sense beliefs uninfluenced by philosophy or theology are reliable, or are any more reliable than other common-sense beliefs? Common-sense beliefs influenced by certain kinds of sociology, psychology, politics or astronomy, for example, can be just as unreliable as common-sense beliefs influenced by certain kinds of philosophy or theology. A widely held belief uninfluenced by philosophy or theology could still be highly unreliable owing to influence from other sources: for example, prejudicial political tactics. Perhaps, then, Russell would appeal to common-sense beliefs uninfluenced by *any* other beliefs. This would avoid the problem at hand, but only by making it questionable whether there are any common-sense beliefs of the relevant sort. It is unclear that any common-sense beliefs are influenced by *no* other beliefs. If there are such common-sense beliefs, they are very rare indeed.

In 'A Defence of Common Sense' (1925), Moore contends that 'the "Common Sense view of the world" is, in certain fundamental features, *wholly* true' ([7.54], 44). He claims, too, that he knows the relevant common sense propositions 'with certainty'. These propositions include the following:

(a) There now exists a living human that is my body.
(b) Before now many human bodies other than mine have lived on earth.
(c) The earth had existed for many years before my body was born.
(d) I have often perceived my own body and other things that form part of its environment, including other bodies.

([7.54], 33)

Moore also holds that each of us has frequently known, with respect to oneself, the propositions in question. Moore does not specify what feature common to such propositions makes them 'common-sense' propositions. He does hold, however, that we know such propositions *with certainty.*

Moore claims that the common-sense propositions in question find support from a simple consideration. If, according to certain philosophers, no such common-sense proposition is true, then 'no philosopher has ever existed, and therefore none can ever have held with regard to any such class [of common-sense propositions], that no proposition belonging to it is true' (ibid., 40). One's denial of the truth of every such common-sense proposition, according to Moore, entails that one must be wrong in denying this. In short, such a denial lands one in self-refutation.

In reply, one might make two points. First, Moore assumes that if one denies that the common-sense propositions in question are true, then one exists as a living human body. Such denial, according to Moore, requires one's actually being a living human body. What, however, supports this assumption? Conceivably, we are really disembodied thinking things who do not depend on physical substances for our intellectual lives. Descartes, in the seventeenth century, suggested this possibility in questioning presumed certainty regarding common-sense beliefs. Moore owes us evidence for his key assumption that only living human bodies could deny his common sense propositions.

Second, Moore assumes that we know his common-sense propositions *with certainty.* One can contest this assumption without denying that Moore's common-sense propositions are true. One can deny simply that we know those propositions with certainty, regardless of whether those propositions are true. Whether a proposition is true or false is one issue; whether we know that proposition with certainty, another. I can deny, for example, that I know with certainty that pandas eat peas in China. This denial does not require that I deny that it is true that pandas eat peas in China. My denial might be only a disclaimer of supporting evidence for the proposition in question. Moore owes us evidence in support of his assumption that we know his common sense propositions with certainty.

Moore did hold that he could give a proof of various common-sense propositions in question. In 1939 Moore published his 'Proof of an External World', relying on the following claims:

> I can now give a large number of different proofs ['of the existence of things outside of us'], each of which is a perfectly rigorous proof.... I can prove now, for instance, that two human hands exist. How? By holding up my two hands, and saying, as I make a certain gesture with the right hand, 'Here is one hand', and adding, as I make a certain gesture with the left, 'and here is another'.
>
> ([7.55], 145-6)

Moore claims that his 'proof' is 'perfectly rigorous', and that it would be 'absurd' to suggest that he did not actually know – but merely believed – that there were two hands in the places indicated by his gestures. Such, then, is Moore's 'proof' of the existence of external physical objects.

Moore claimed to prove, in addition, that there have been external objects in the past. Thus: 'I held up two hands above this desk not very long ago; therefore two hands existed not very long ago; therefore at least two external objects have existed at some time in the past' (ibid., 148). Moore insists that he does know that he held up two hands in the past, and thus that he has given a 'perfectly conclusive proof that external objects have existed in the past'.

Moore must face an objection. His 'proofs' do not give us dis-proofs of either the claim that he is simply *dreaming* that he is holding up two hands or the claim that he is simply *misremembering* that he held up two hands. Moore's reply is that he cannot prove his claim that here is one hand and there another, but that this is no real problem (ibid., 149). He finds it adequate that he has 'conclusive evidence' for the previous claim, and for the claim that he is not now dreaming or misremembering. We can have, on Moore's view, conclusive evidence for, and certain knowledge of, claims we cannot prove. Moore thus claims to have conclusive evidence that he is not dreaming, even though he cannot tell us what all that evidence is.

In his 1941 paper, 'Certainty', Moore considers objections to his claim to certainty that he is not now dreaming. He proposes that 'the conjunction of my memories of the immediate past with [present] sensory experiences *may* be sufficient to enable me to know that I am not dreaming' ([7.56], 250). The objector's reply will, of course, be that it *is* logically possible that Moore has all his present sensory experiences and memories – qualitatively characterized – but still is dreaming. Moore counters that 'the conjunction of the proposition that I have these sense experiences and memories with the proposition that I am dreaming does seem to me to be very likely self-contradictory' (ibid., 251). This reply, however, fails to convince. Moore gives no reason whatever to suppose it contradictory or inconceivable that he is dreaming while having his present experiences and memories. We have no reason to think that Moore cannot be dreaming while having his present experiences and memories. On the contrary, Moore's dreaming seems perfectly compatible with those experiences and memories. Moore's case for certainty about his common sense propositions is thus unconvincing.

One might reply that Moore's standards for certainty and conclusiveness fit with our ordinary, non-philosophical talk of certainty and conclusiveness. Even if there is a merely logical possibility that our bodies do not exist, we typically regard ourselves as knowing with certainty – with conclusive evidence – that our bodies exist. The only *relevant* standards, on this view, are those we typically employ in ordinary, common sense talk. Since we ordinarily regard our sensory experiences of our bodies as providing conclusive evidence that we have bodies, we may claim certainty that we have bodies. Two troublesome questions arise now: How can such an appeal to ordinary standards even begin to engage familiar philosophical questions about the reliability of sensory experience? Can we plausibly ignore those philosophical questions on the ground that they are simply 'irrelevant'? We shall return to questions about reliability in the section below on scepticism (pp. 232–41).

A key component of the common sense theories of Moore and Russell is *empiricism*: the view that the empirical evidence of the senses – e.g. visual, auditory, tactile or gustatory experiences – is a sort of evidence appropriate to genuine knowledge. Russell's empiricism is more explicit, and perhaps more extreme, than Moore's. Russell claims:

> Nothing can be known to *exist* except by the help of experience. That is to say, if we wish to prove that something of which we have no direct experience exists, we must have among our premises the existence of one or more things of which we have direct experience. Our belief that the Emperor of China exists, for example, rests upon testimony, and testimony consists, in

the last analysis of sense-data seen or heard in reading or being spoken to.

([7.84], 74–5; cf. [7.92], 97–8)

Russell here sides with such empiricists as Locke, Berkeley and Hume, against the rationalist view that *a priori* knowledge – knowledge independent of specific experience – can provide knowledge of what actually exists. Russell sides with such rationalists as Descartes and Leibniz, however, on the point that logical principles – whether deductive or inductive – are not known on the basis of support from experience. All support from experience, Russell claims, *pre*supposes logical principles. Russell does allow, though, that our knowledge of logical principles is elicited or caused by experience. He thus permits a distinction between the *warrant* and the *cause* of a belief. In sum, Russell holds that 'all knowledge which asserts existence is empirical, and the only *a priori* knowledge concerning existence is hypothetical, giving connexions among things that exist or may exist, but not giving actual existence' ([7.84], 75). Russell's empiricism is thus moderate, allowing for some *a priori* knowledge.

Russell's talk of 'sense-data' signifies whatever in sense experience 'might be singled out by attention: particular patches of colour, particular noises, and so on' ([7.85], 142). Prior to 1918, Russell's empiricism regarded sense data as 'the epistemological basis of all our knowledge of external particulars', and as something known by 'acquaintance'. Russell ([7.83]; [7.84], chapter 5) distinguished between knowledge *by acquaintance* and knowledge *by description*, and between knowledge of things and knowledge of true propositions. Knowledge of things can be either knowledge of things by acquaintance or knowledge of things by description. Knowledge by description requires knowledge of a true proposition: knowledge *that* something is the case. Knowledge by acquaintance, in contrast, consists of direct non-propositional awareness of something, not of knowledge of truths. Russell holds that 'to say that *S* has acquaintance with *O* is essentially the same thing as to say that *O* is presented to *S*' ([7.83], 202–3). Russell would say that you are acquainted with the colour of these printed words as you read them.

After 1918 Russell abandoned sense data as the objects of cognition, and sensations as a special kind of cognition.[1] He came to reject the view that in visual colour experience, for example, there is a *subject* related via awareness to a patch of colour. Russell claimed that the subject is a 'logical fiction', much like mathematical points and instants. Having rejected the subject as an actually existing thing, Russell also rejected a distinction between sensations and sense data. The sensation of a patch of colour is, on this view, no different from the patch of colour. Such sensation thus does not qualify as a kind of knowledge. Much of Russell's epistemological work after 1918 seeks an explanation of awareness, acquaintance and empirical evidence without appeal to sense data – and often with help from John Watson's behaviourism about psychological phenomena.

Russell's epistemology, unlike Moore's, attributes definite epistemological significance to the natural sciences – a significance that gives the sciences an epistemological priority over common sense. (This is especially true of Russell's epistemological views after 1918.) Russell acknowledges that the sciences begin with common sense notions and judgements: e.g. notions of causation, space, time and things. The sciences, however, often need to revise or to eliminate such common notions to achieve their explanatory purposes. Russell observes that we typically start our theorizing from 'naive realism', the view that things are as they seem. We initially think that the objects we perceive really are as they appear: that snow is white, that fire is hot, that feathers are soft. The natural sciences, however, provide a strikingly different view of the objects we perceive – a view entailing that the features ascribed to external objects by naive realism do not really inhere in the external objects themselves. Russell thus remarks that 'naive realism leads to physics, and physics, if true, shows that naive realism is false' ([7.88], 15).

Philosophy, according to Russell, serves an important purpose here: it identifies how fundamental common sense notions might be reconstructed to benefit the explanatory aims of the sciences. Russell denies, however, that philosophy offers a kind of knowledge ultimately different from scientific knowledge. He holds that 'philosophy involves a criticism of scientific knowledge, not from a point of view ultimately different from that of science, but from a point of view less concerned with details and more concerned with the harmony of the whole body of special sciences' ([7.87], 2).

Why, however, should we take science as our ultimate epistemological authority? This question will be especially pressing for those inclined towards scepticism about the reliability of science. Russell offers little by way of reply:

> For my part, I assume that science is broadly speaking true....
> But against the thoroughgoing sceptic I can advance no
> argument except that I do not believe him to be sincere.
>
> ([7.91], 382)

This reply will probably convince nobody. Russell understands the *truth* of statements as their describing *facts* that may be objective in that they transcend experience ([7.90], 149, 151; [7.88], chapters 16–17). He gives no reason, however, for thinking that everyone doubtful of science's providing such truth is insincere. Epistemologists have long debated whether perception, memory, and the procedures of the natural sciences deliver objective truths. We cannot cogently settle this debate by assuming that beliefs based on perception, memory or the sciences are broadly true, and that people doubting this assumption are insincere. The use of the latter assumption aims to secure by theft what will be secured, if at all, only by extensive philosophical toil.

Let us turn now to some leading logical positivists, to see if they avoid the epistemological problems facing Moore and Russell.

Logical positivism

The science-oriented empiricism of Russell was taken to an extreme by various logical positivists, originally represented in the early 1920s by the group of philosophers, logicians, mathematicians and scientists who called themselves the Vienna Circle. Moritz Schlick (1882–1935) started the Circle at the University of Vienna, and attracted such participants as Rudolf Carnap (1891–1970), Otto Neurath (1882–1945), Herbert Feigl (1902–88), Friedrich Waismann (1896–1959), Kurt Gödel (1906–78) and Hans Hahn (1879–1934). While disagreeing on a number of substantive epistemological issues, the members of the Circle shared an interest in certain philosophical and scientific problems, and favoured an approach to these problems that was analytical, scientific and anti-metaphysical.

In 1929, Neurath, Carnap and Hahn published a manifesto for the Circle, entitled 'The Scientific Conception of the World: The Vienna Circle'.[2] They identified David Hume, the leading eighteenth-century empiricist, as one of their main philosophical forerunners. In his *Inquiry concerning Human Understanding* (1748), Hume had reached the following positivist, anti-metaphysical conclusion:

> If we take in our hand any volume, of divinity or school metaphysics, for instance, let us ask, *Does it contain any abstract reasoning concerning quantity or number*? No. *Does it contain any experimental reasoning concerning matter of fact and existence*? No. Commit it then to the flames: for it can contain nothing but sophistry and illusion.
>
> (section VII, part III).

The Vienna Circle (with the possible exception of Gödel) shared Hume's antipathy to metaphysics. They aimed to use modern logic (deriving from Frege and Russell) and various analytical techniques to restrict philosophical pursuits to the advancement of 'scientific' knowledge, thereby banishing metaphysical concerns from philosophy.

Hume's extreme empiricism had questioned the meaningfulness of concepts lacking a basis in experience. The Vienna Circle, too, doubted the cognitive meaningfulness of experience-transcendent, metaphysical notions and theses.

Ludwig Wittgenstein (1889–1951) had a decisive influence on the philosophical views of the Vienna Circle. In his *Tractatus Logico-Philosophicus* (1921), Wittgenstein enunciated the following doctrines attractive to the anti-metaphysical members of the Circle:

> 4.11 The totality of true propositions is the whole of natural sciences (or the whole corpus of the natural sciences).
> 4.112 Philosophy aims at the logical clarification of thoughts. Philosophy is not a body of doctrine but an activity. . . .
> Philosophy does not result in 'philosophical propositions', but rather in the clarification of propositions.
> 6.53 The correct method in philosophy would really be the following: to say nothing except what can be said, i.e., propositions of natural science – i.e., something that has nothing to do with philosophy – and then, whenever someone else wanted to say something metaphysical, to demonstrate to him that he had failed to give a meaning to certain signs in his propositions.
>
> ([7.108])

The members of the Circle focused – typically with favour – on such anti-metaphysical theses of the *Tractatus*, rather than on its avowed mysticism: '6.522 There are, indeed, things that cannot be put into words. They *make themselves manifest*. They are what is mystical.' The Circle also welcomed Wittgenstein's view that knowledge of logical propositions is not a special kind of metaphysical knowledge about the world. Wittgenstein proposed the following: 'The propositions of logic are tautologies. . . . Therefore the propositions of logic say nothing. (They are the analytic propositions.)' (6.1–6.11).

The hallmark of logical positivism is a principle of verification regarding meaning and understanding – a principle not found in the *Tractatus* itself. The *Tractatus* had enunciated the following view of understanding: '4.024 To understand a proposition means to know what is the case if it is true. (One can understand it, therefore, without knowing whether it is true.)' By the late 1920s, however, Wittgenstein was endorsing a verification principle regarding meaning and understanding. In late 1929, Wittgenstein claimed:

> if I can never verify the sense of a proposition completely, then I cannot have meant anything by the proposition either. Then the proposition signifies nothing whatever. In order to

determine the sense of a proposition, I should have to know a very specific procedure for when to count the proposition as verified.

([7.112], 47)

A characterization of meaning and understanding in terms of verification and justification surfaces in some of Wittgenstein's works in the late 1920s and early 1930s. In his *Philosophical Remarks* (c. 1930), Wittgenstein states that 'to understand the sense of a proposition means to know how the issue of its truth or falsity is to be decided' ([7.110], 77).[3] In his *Philosophical Grammar* (c. 1933), Wittgenstein remarks that 'it is what is regarded as the justification of an assertion that constitutes the sense of the assertion' ([7.111], I §40). In the early 1930s a number of logical positivists endorsed a principle of verification regarding meaning. Noting Wittgenstein's influence, Waismann published one of the first endorsements: 'If there is no way of telling when a proposition is true, then the proposition has no sense whatever; for the sense of a proposition is its method of verification' ([7.107], 5). We can thus put *the verification principle* succinctly: the meaning of a proposition is its method of verification.

If metaphysical claims about gods, souls, essences, values and the like lack a method of verification, we can use the verification principle to dispense with them as meaningless. The Vienna Circle did indeed dispense with them as meaningless, not just as unknowable. They construed the needed method of verification as a method of justification, or confirmation, in terms of *observable* events or situations. They thus held that every meaningful claim could be expressed in terms of observational claims: i.e. claims susceptible to confirmation or disconfirmation on the basis of observation. Schlick [7.94] specified that the meaning of a claim depends not on its actual verification, but only on the *possibility* of its verification on the basis of experience.

The members of the Circle divided over the nature of the fundamental observational claims – so-called 'protocol statements' – that set the standard for confirmation and meaningfulness.[4] One key issue was whether these observational claims are solely about what is given in subjective, private experience or can include intersubjectively testable claims about physical states of affairs. In his *The Logical Structure of the World* (1928), Carnap aimed to show in detail how all meaningful concepts could be reduced to 'the "given", i.e., ... experiences themselves in their totality and undivided unity' ([7.14], 108). In particular, Carnap sought to define a range of observationally relevant concepts (e.g. colour concepts, visual-spatial concepts) on the basis of the single fundamental concept of 'recollection of similarity' between elementary experiences. By the early 1930s, however, Carnap had moved to

Neurath's view that protocol statements can be formulated in intersubjectively shared language about physical situations.

The main problems facing logical positivism concern not the conditions for protocol statements, but rather the status of the verification principle itself. One problem is that some meaningful claims seem not to admit of a 'method of verification'. Consider, for example, the claim that an omnipotent being exists: a being sufficiently powerful to accomplish anything that can be coherently described. Presumably, I understand this claim, but I have no method of confirmation or disconfirmation for it. I seemingly understand what, in general, it would be for that claim to be true or false; at least our ordinary notions of meaning and understanding allow for this. I lack, however, any means – including any observational means – of confirming or disconfirming that claim. Indeed, there seems not to be even a possible means available to me for confirming or disconfirming that claim. I lack a *method* of verification, but the claim in question still seems meaningful – at least by ordinary standards. If we weaken conditions for verification, to allow for the desired method, we shall disable the principle of verification from excluding metaphysical claims as meaningless.

What about the principle of verification itself? Does it itself admit of a method of verification resting on observational evidence? This seems doubtful. Our observational evidence, deriving from sensory and perceptual experience, fails to provide a straightforward method of verification for the verification principle itself. Perhaps, then, the verification principle is meaningless by its own standard for meaningfulness. A. J. Ayer (1910–89), who attended meetings of the Vienna Circle by 1933, treats this self-referential difficulty as follows:

> The Vienna Circle tended to ignore this difficulty: but it seems to me fairly clear that what they were in fact doing was to adopt the verification principle as a convention. They were propounding a definition of meaning which accorded with common usage in the sense that it set out the conditions that are in fact satisfied by statements which are regarded as empirically informative. Their treatment of *a priori* statements was also intended to provide an account of the way in which statements actually function. To this extent their work was descriptive; it became prescriptive with the suggestion that only statements of these two kinds should be regarded as either true or false, and that only statements which were capable of being either true or false should be regarded as literally meaningful.
>
> ([7.9], 15)

Carnap [7.15] had also suggested that the verification principle was a 'convention' resting on a choice about how to use certain language.

The claim that an omnipotent being exists raises problems for the descriptive and the prescriptive use of the verification principle. We seemingly have no method for the possible verification of that claim; nonetheless, common usage of 'meaningful' allows us to regard that claim as meaningful. The descriptive use of the verification principle thus runs afoul of common usage of 'meaningful'. As for the prescriptive use of that principle, we need a good reason for regarding as meaningless such a claim as that an omnipotent being exists. Even if we can clearly distinguish what is empirically verifiable from what is empirically unverifiable, we need a specific reason to regard the unverifiable as the meaningless. Given our ordinary understanding of meaningfulness, the claim that an omnipotent being exists is not gibberish. That claim makes sense even if it is unverifiable. It is doubtful that we have a compelling reason to give up this ordinary approach to meaningfulness.

The role of convention in the epistemology of the Vienna Circle led to a kind of pragmatism – an emphasis on purpose-relative, practical considerations in epistemology. This is understandable because questions about which linguistic conventions to adopt are naturally understood as questions about which conventions best serve one's linguistic and theoretical purposes. Carnap identified one practical consideration as follows:

> Suppose a sentence S is given, some test-observations for it have been made, and S is confirmed by them in a certain degree. Then it is a matter of practical decision whether we will consider that degree as high enough for our acceptance of S. . . . Although our decision is based upon the observations made so far, nevertheless it is not uniquely determined by them. There is no general rule to determine our decision. Thus the acceptance and the rejection of a (synthetic) sentence always contains a *conventional component*.
>
> ([7.16], 49)

This view entails only that our decisions about rational acceptance have an ineliminable conventional component, not that they are wholly conventional.

By 1950 Carnap's pragmatism was explicit. Realists about the external world typically affirm that there really are observable spatiotemporal things and events. Subjective idealists question the reality of the thing world itself. The controversy between realists and idealists has persisted since the beginning of philosophy. Carnap gives the controversy a pragmatic spin:

> Those who raise the question of the reality of the thing world

itself have perhaps in mind not a theoretical question . . ., but rather a practical question, a matter of practical decision concerning the structure of our language. We have to make the choice whether or not to accept and use the forms of expression in the [linguistic] framework in question.

([7.17], 207)

Carnap acknowledges that 'the thing language' efficiently serves many purposes of everyday life, and that it is advisable to accept the thing language on this pragmatic basis. He rejects, however, any suggestion that such a pragmatic basis can provide confirming evidence for 'the reality' of the thing world. A statement of the reality of the total system of certain entities (e.g. spatio-temporal things), according to Carnap (ibid., 214), is a 'pseudo-statement without cognitive content'. Questions about the total system of certain entities – what Carnap called 'external questions' – make sense, on this view, only as *practical* questions about whether to adopt certain ways of using language.

Agreeing with Carnap, Herbert Feigl emphasized the role of pragmatic considerations in epistemology. He noted that if we try to justify the rules of deductive logic in terms of *what follows from* what we mean by certain terms – e.g. 'correct reasoning', we then rely on the very rules we seek to justify. Such circularity, according to Feigl [7.31], indicates that we have reached the limits of justification. Feigl notes, however, that we can still pursue *pragmatic vindication* in such a case; for we can recommend adoption of the rules relative to achieving certain ends: e.g. avoidance of the perplexities of ambiguity and inconsistency. Regarding our familiar talk of mind-independent things, Feigl takes a similarly pragmatic approach: 'The only sort of justification we can give . . . consists in showing the indispensability and the adequacy of the language required for the purpose of such sciences as physics, psychology, or history' (ibid., 132–3). Such pragmatic justification involves something's serving as a means to an end, or a purpose, we have. Barring circularity, ultimate justification, on Feigl's account, is instrumental and pragmatic: relative to certain purposes an inquirer has.

By the 1950s the logical positivists of the 1920s had moved towards pragmatism in epistemology. In doing so, they were reviving themes from an American movement that antedated the Vienna Circle. We turn now to some themes from classical American pragmatism.

Classical American pragmatism

C. S. Peirce (1839–1914), the founder of American pragmatism, offered his pragmatism originally as a view about meaning: 'there is no distinction of meaning so fine as to consist in anything but a possible difference of practice' ([7.71], 30). The general idea is that for any conception we have, we can understand the meaning of that conception solely in terms of the experiential and practical effects of its object. Peirce thus suggests that if Protestants and Catholics agree about all the possible experiential effects of the object of the notion of Communion (involving wafer and diluted wine), they actually agree on the meaning of 'Communion'. This view may surprise Protestant and Catholic theologians (who take themselves to disagree), but Peirce offers it as a way to avoid both 'deception' and empty controversy from metaphysics.

We saw in the previous section that the verification principle of logical positivism conflicts with what many of us understand as meaningfulness. That principle rigidly ties meaningfulness to a method of empirical verification. Peirce's principle ties meaning instead to the possible experiential effects of the object of a notion. One problem is that some notions – e.g. mathematical, logical and certain fictional notions – lack objects with possible experiential effects, but nonetheless seem meaningful. Another problem is that the meaningfulness of some notions seems to derive simply from *what we imagine would be the case* if that notion were realized (or, had an instance). What we imagine would then be the case, however, is not necessarily the same as *what we would (possibly) experience* as being the case. The Catholic notion of transubstantiation and the Protestant notion of Communion require (for their satisfaction) different things to *be* the case – regardless of whether we (possibly) *experience* different things as being the case. (The Catholic notion requires for its satisfaction a transformation of the bread and wine; the Protestant notion does not.) In so far as the Catholic and Protestant notions require different things for their satisfaction, we can plausibly regard those notions as meaning different things. This may leave us with some difficult, perhaps even undecidable questions about what actually exists or occurs. It seems implausible, however, to try to avoid such questions by stipulating a notion of meaning that entails their meaninglessness.

William James (1842–1910) expounded pragmatism in considerable detail, for non-philosophers as well as philosophers. He offered his pragmatic account of truth as capturing 'the meaning' of 'truth'. In a chapter of *Pragmatism* entitled 'Pragmatism's Conception of Truth', James writes:

> True ideas are those that we can assimilate, validate, corroborate, and verify. . . . That is the practical difference it makes to us to have true ideas; that, therefore, is the meaning of truth, for it is all that truth is known as.
>
> ([7.44], 97; cf. [7.45], 3–4)

Some philosophers have objected that James simply confuses what it is for a claim to be *true* and what it is for a claim to be *verified*.[5] These philosophers typically cite cases where a claim is true but not verifiable. Consider, for example, the status of the claim that the Earth is round before this could be verified.

James is unmoved. In disputes with critics – including those offering the view that truth does not depend on anything like verification – James invokes his 'pragmatic method':

> When a dispute arises, that [pragmatic] method consists in auguring what practical consequences would be different if one side rather than the other were true. If no difference can be thought of, the dispute is a quarrel over words. What then would the self-transcendency [of true ideas] affirmed to exist in advance of all experiential mediation or termination, be *known as*? What would it practically result in for *us*, were it true?
>
> ([7.43], 39–40)

Given this pragmatic method, James infers that a dispute over the nature of truth (e.g. whether truth is independent of verification) is an empty verbal matter if unaccompanied by a difference in practical consequences.

James ([7.45], 61–9) holds that his pragmatic method enables a non-mysterious account of what it is for a knower to have a perceptual object 'in mind'. James characterizes one's having an object in mind as one's having a certain sequence of experiences. He understands something's being a perceptual *representation* of a sensory object as that thing's being a *substitute* for that sensory object. James uses his pragmatic method to clarify what it is to be such a substitute: an idea is a substitute if it has certain 'practical consequences' relative to a knower's purposes, viz. the same practical consequences as the object for which it is a substitute. Representation, on James's account, is thus a matter of two things fulfilling the same function: sameness of practical consequences of what represents and what is represented.

It is difficult to assess James's view in the absence of a straightforward account of what count as 'practical consequences'. It helps only a little to say that a practical consequence is whatever 'makes a difference to experience'. This just shifts the task to giving a straightforward account of 'making a difference to experience'. We saw above, in connection with Peirce's approach to meaning, that meaningfulness is not obviously fully determined by consequences for experience. James's pragmatism, like Peirce's, rests on a questionably restrictive approach to meaning.

John Dewey (1859–1952) and C. I. Lewis (1883–1965) shared the view of James that knowledge has an ineliminable pragmatic component.

This pragmatic component is an element of 'active interpretation' that supposedly resides in all knowledge. In sensory, empirical knowledge, we use interpretation via concepts to organize and characterize input from sensation. The American pragmatists offered a distinctive account of when an interpretation of sensory input is 'correct.' The key idea is that an interpretation is correct to the extent that it 'usefully leads' from one experience to another, where useful leading depends on practical results relative to one's purposes in explaining and ordering one's experiences. The pragmatists' emphasis on practical results and useful leading aims to provide an alternative to an older empiricist view that the correctness of an interpretation depends on 'correspondence' to the facts of experience. James and other pragmatists faulted that older approach for failing to provide an intelligible or verifiable account of when an interpretation actually corresponds to the facts of experience.

In *The Quest for Certainty* (1929), Dewey offered an 'experimental theory of knowing' that aimed to improve on empiricism, rationalism and the influential hybrid epistemology of Immanuel Kant (1724–1804). According to Dewey, 'the method of physical inquiry is to introduce some change [in experience] in order to see what other change ensues; the correlation between these changes, when measured by a series of operations, constitutes the definite and desired object of knowledge' ([7.29], 84). Dewey's experimental theory implies that an object of knowledge arises from controlled experimental operations, and does not exist in advance of an act of knowing. Dewey's stress on the role of control in knowledge emerges from his following remarks:

> [I]f we frame our conception of knowledge on the experimental model, we find that it is a way of operating upon and with the things of ordinary experience so that we can frame our ideas of them in terms of their interactions with one another, instead of in terms of the qualities they directly present, and that thereby our control of them, our ability to change them and direct their changes as we desire, is indefinitely increased. Knowing is itself a mode of practical action and is *the* way of interaction by which other natural interactions become subject to direction.
>
> ([7.29], 106–7)

Dewey thus puts *doing* at the heart of knowing, stressing that a knower is an *active* participant in a knowing situation, and not a mere spectator. Dewey finds active participation even in connection with the so-called 'data' of sensation. He characterizes knowers as *selecting*, and not merely being *given*, such data. Dewey countenances, nonetheless, the importance of both sensation and reason in knowledge. Ideas of reason, in his view, are important for relating experiences and making predictions, and experience is important as a basis for the testing of ideas, including predictions.

Lewis concurs with Dewey's stress on the active role of knowers. Indeed, Lewis regards the distinguishing feature of pragmatism as its emphasis on a knower's act of interpretation relative to the data of sensation. Truths about experience, on Lewis's pragmatism, are always expressed by, and thus depend on, a conceptual system chosen on pragmatic grounds. Lewis explains:

> [T]he point of the pragmatic theory is . . . the responsiveness of truth to human bent or need, and the fact that in some sense it is made by mind. . . . [T]he interpretation of experience must always be in terms of categories and concepts which the mind itself determines. There may be alternative conceptual systems, giving rise to alternative descriptions of experience, which are equally objective and equally valid, if there be not some purely logical defect in these categorial conceptions. When this is so, choice will be determined, consciously or unconsciously, on pragmatic grounds. . . . [T]he pragmatic element in knowledge concerns the choice in application of conceptual modes of interpretation.
>
> ([7.49], 271–2; cf. p. 257)

Lewis holds that all interpretation includes an experience-independent, *a priori* element, and that this interpretive element receives support not from experience, but from pragmatic factors: e.g. 'some demand or purpose of the mind itself' (ibid., 267).

Lewis argues that empirical knowledge consists of three elements: the immediate data of sensation, the concept or category under which those data are subsumed, and the mental act that interprets the data by means of the concept. Both Lewis and James hold that apart from an act of interpretation, one's experience would be the 'buzzing, blooming confusion of the infant'. An act of interpretation, in their view, enables such confusion to become an ordered world of experience. Lewis takes pains to defend the independence of a purely sensory, 'given' element in experience; but as a pragmatist, he stresses the pragmatic basis for the application of concepts to the data given in experience.[6] Concepts, on his view, are 'instruments of interpretation'. Lewis sums up his view thus: 'wherever such criteria as comprehensiveness and simplicity, or serviceability for the control of nature, or conformity to human bent and human ways of acting play their part in the determination of such conceptual instruments, there is a pragmatic element in knowledge' ([7.48], 211).

James, Dewey and Lewis agree, then, that knowledge requires active interpretation, and that the rationale for a particular mode of interpretation is pragmatic, deriving from one's interpretive purposes. Often we do seek a pragmatic rationale for a manner of interpretation. We then wonder about the practical consequences of wielding certain concepts (or, ways of classifying), relative to our explanatory purposes. Such a pragmatic rationale concerns the instrumental effectiveness of certain concepts in achieving our theoretical purposes, whatever those purposes happen to be.

Can there be a rationale for concepts that is not pragmatic? Has Lewis, for example, overlooked a cognitive basis for choosing concepts that is not merely pragmatic? *Perhaps* we can assess concepts relative to something more objective and less variable, viz. relative to the reliability of their portrayal of the objective, conceiver-independent world. Some philosophers hold that the latter kind of assessment, in terms of objective reliability, is distinctively 'epistemological', and that a merely pragmatic rationale can be (and often is) irrelevant to such epistemological assessment. The underlying assumption is that epistemological assessment is centrally concerned with objective, purpose-independent truth and reliable indications of such truth. Pragmatic success can sometimes get by with beliefs that are unreliable and even false – such as when it is convenient for our purposes to maintain an unreliable, false view on something.

If we can make sense of talk of objective, purpose-independent correctness, we can distinguish epistemological from pragmatic assessment. A notion of purpose-independent correctness can allow that what set of concepts we wield in theorizing often depends on our purposes in theorizing. The key issue now is, however, whether it makes sense to talk of the purpose-independent correctness of concepts. The rough idea from the critic of pragmatism is this: the external world is featured in certain mind-independent ways (e.g. many of its objects have 'natural' boundaries), and our classificatory concepts can be more or less accurate, or reliable, in how they 'fit' the mind-independent features of the external world. If we can make sense of such talk of accurate fitting, we can acknowledge a distinctively epistemological concern: do our concepts accurately fit the external world? Here we have an issue of crucial importance in epistemology. We shall return to questions about reliability in the section below on scepticism (pp. 232–41), after considering some further developments in epistemology.

❧ PROBLEMS FOR EMPIRICISM ❧

Prominent twentieth-century empiricists before 1950 typically accepted an analytic-synthetic distinction: roughly, a distinction between propositions true just in virtue of meaning (or, definition) and propositions true in virtue of considerations other than meaning. Corresponding to this distinction, empiricists typically drew a distinction between empirical (*a posteriori*) knowledge and non-empirical (*a priori*) knowledge. A common view among empiricists was that all *a priori* knowledge is knowledge of analytic truths, that there can be no *a priori* knowledge of synthetic truths. Ayer, for example, had argued for a linguistic conception of the *a priori* implying that the truths of logic and mathematic are *a priori* in that we cannot deny them without violating the rules governing our use of language ([7.7], chapter 4). Ayer argued that the analyticity of the truths of logic and mathematics is the only good explanation of their being knowable *a priori*, and that we can have no *a priori* knowledge of empirical reality or of synthetic truths.

Quine on analyticity

In 1951, W. V. Quine published 'Two Dogmas of Empiricism' [7.74], challenging the following so-called dogmas of modern empiricism: belief in a dichotomy between analytic and synthetic truths, and belief in reductionism according to which every meaningful sentence is equivalent to some sentence whose terms refer to immediate sensory experience. In the aftermath of Quine's essay, philosophers have generally regarded talk of analyticity as suspect at best, and mythical at worst. A common view among epistemologists is that talk of analyticity has no genuine explanatory value in epistemology.

Quine [7.74] argues that any suitable appeal to analyticity in epistemology presupposes a notion of *cognitive synonymy* that is no more intelligible than talk of analyticity itself. One class of analytic statements – so-called *logically true* statements – does not attract this objection from Quine. Such statements, represented by 'No unmarried man is married', remain true under all reinterpretations of their non-logical components. A second class of statements, represented by 'No bachelor is married', does invite Quine's objection. Some philosophers hold that the members of the latter class reduce to logical truths by substituting synonyms for synonyms: e.g. 'unmarried man' for 'bachelor'. Other philosophers have talked instead of reducing the second class of analytic statements to the first *by definition*. They rely on the proposal that we *define* 'bachelor' as 'unmarried man'. Quine objects to such talk of definition, claiming that it typically rests on an inadequately explained notion of synonymy concerning what is defined and certain antecedent linguistic usage. The presumed notion of *synonymy*, according to Quine, needs clarification no less than does the notion of analyticity.

Quine has related objections to the view that synonymy consists in interchangeability of linguistic forms *salva veritate* – without change of truth-value. In a language free of such modal adverbs as 'necessarily', interchangeability *salva veritate* will not guarantee synonymy. It will provide only such statements as: 'All and only bachelors are unmarried men.' Proponents of synonymy hold that truths of that sort depend only on considerations of *meaning*, not on coincidental factual matters. We might, accordingly, introduce the adverb 'necessarily' to preserve a contrast between considerations of meaning and considerations of contingent matters. Quine objects, however, that such use of 'necessarily' is intelligible only if the notion of analyticity is already understandable – and it is not. We still need, then, an account of analyticity.

Quine anticipates an effort to explain analyticity via a verification theory of meaning. An analytic truth, in this view, is a statement confirmed 'no matter what', i.e. 'come what may'. Quine endorses *epistemic holism* instead: the view that statements are confirmed or disconfirmed not individually on the basis of experience, but only as a 'field'. Given Quine's holism, any statement can be accepted come what may, so long as we revise – perhaps drastically – other parts of our field of accepted statements. Holism entails also that no statement is in principle beyond revisability. Quine thus concludes that the verification approach to analyticity relies on an implausibly atomistic approach to confirmation and disconfirmation. In 'Two Dogmas,' Quine allows only for analyticity by conventional abbreviation:

> There does ... remain still an extreme sort of definition which does not hark back to prior synonymies at all: namely, the explicitly conventional introduction of novel notations for purposes of sheer abbreviation. ... Here we have a really transparent case of synonymy created by definition; would that all species of synonymy were as intelligible. For the rest, definition rests on synonymy rather than explaining it.
>
> ([7.74], 26)

Quine says no more about such conventional definition as a basis for analyticity. He does not consider the possibility that a philosophically important notion of analyticity emerges from such definition. Quine now contends that holism removes any epistemological need for analyticity:

> I now perceive that the philosophically important question about analyticity and the linguistic doctrine of logical truth is *not* how to explicate them; it is the question rather of their relevance to epistemology. The second dogma of empiricism, to the effect

that each empirically meaningful sentence has an empirical content of its own, was cited in 'Two Dogmas' merely as encouraging false confidence in the notion of analyticity; but now I would say further that the second dogma creates a need for analyticity as a key notion of epistemology, and that the need lapses when we heed Duhem and set the second dogma aside.

([7.76], 207)

Quine's (qualified) holism about meaning implies that we do not need analyticity to account for the meaningfulness of logical and mathematical truths. Their meaningfulness can be regarded as deriving from their figuring in the natural sciences for the implication of various observationally testable statements. Logical and mathematical truths, on this view, are not divorced from empirical content; they rather participate, if indirectly, in the empirical content of various observational statements. Similarly, we do not need analyticity to explain the *necessity* of logical and mathematical truths. According to Quine: 'Holism accounts for it by freedom of selection and the maxim of minimum mutilation' ([7.78], 56). Necessity, on this view, is just a matter of our current unwillingness to dispense with certain statements at the centre of our web of belief.

In sum, Quine's objection to analyticity is twofold: first, 'for all its *a priori* reasonableness, a boundary between analytic and synthetic statements simply has not been drawn' ([7.74], 37); and second, the epistemological need for analyticity lapses once we accept holism of a certain sort. Some philosophers oppose Quine's objection on the ground that the viability of a notion of analyticity does not really depend on an account of analyticity of the sort demanded: namely, an account independent of the aforementioned notions deemed insufficiently clear by Quine. The issue here is whether Quine's standards for adequate clarity in an account of analyticity are simply too rigid. (On this matter, see Grice and Strawson [7.49].)

Carnap on analyticity

In reply to Quine, Carnap proposes that a statement is analytic if and only if it is a logical consequence of 'meaning postulates' that specify meaning relations holding among certain terms ([7.18]; [7.19], 918). (We can use stipulative definitions as a familiar kind of meaning postulates.) Quine objects that we do not gain real understanding by talking of 'meaning postulates', since we lack clear understanding of talk of 'meaning'. Quine's objection seems plausible on this point: we do need a standard of some sort to clarify talk of meaning and analyticity. Quine himself demands an empirical behavioural criterion, for this reason: 'There is nothing in linguistic meaning beyond what is to be gleaned from overt behavior in observable circumstances' ([7.78], 38).

Quine's reason will be uncompelling from the perspective of various *non*-behaviourist conceptions of meaning: conceptions allowing that meaning can arise from psychological processes or events that need not be identifiable in overt behaviour. These conceptions allow that psychological behaviour can be covert yet constitutive of meaning. Since Quine does not undercut such conceptions, he must restrict the kind of meaning he anchors in overt behaviour. His requirement that meaning be 'gleaned from overt behavior in observable circumstances' must be restricted to *socially learned*, public linguistic meaning – the kind of meaning in shared natural languages. Given that restriction, we can allow for Quine's behavioural criterion; for social linguistic meaning does depend on public behavioural evidence.

Carnap has tried to meet Quine's demand for a public behavioural criterion for analyticity. Consider a case of two linguists disagreeing over whether the following sentence is analytically true for you in your language: 'All ravens are black.' These linguists test their competing hypotheses by asking you whether you would withdraw your assertion of 'All ravens are black' if someone showed you a white raven. You could reply in either of two ways: (1) I would withdraw my assertion if presented with adequate evidence for the existence of a white raven; (2) I would not withdraw my assertion, since I do not call white birds 'ravens'; there cannot be white ravens, given my use of the term 'raven'. Carnap holds that response (2) supports the hypothesis that 'All ravens are black' is analytic for you, whereas response (1) supports the hypothesis that it is not. He concludes that ascriptions of analyticity can be tested by observation of public linguistic behaviour ([7.19], 920).

We can put Carnap's point as follows: whenever you reject all falsifiers of an assertion, by invoking only considerations about your usage of that assertion's constituent terms, we may regard that assertion as analytically true for you. This provides a behavioural criterion for analyticity, but not an infallible criterion. You might reject all falsifiers, when asked, simply because of an aim to deceive us about what is analytic for you, or simply because of confusion over what your usage of the relevant terms actually is. A rejection of all falsifiers thus does not guarantee analyticity in any familiar sense.

An improved criterion for analyticity is: a sentence, S, is analytically true for you if and only if you would reject all falsifiers of S owing just to your actual usage of S's constituents. This criterion restricts the basis of one's rejection of all falsifiers to one's actual usage of S's constituent terms; it disallows rejection due to linguistic confusion or an aim to deceive. Carnap would have us understand actual usage in terms of one's 'intentions' regarding ways of using terms. He claims that theorists are 'free to choose their [meaning] postulates, guided not by their beliefs concerning facts of the world but by their intentions with respect to the meanings, i.e., the ways of use of the descriptive constants' ([7.18], 225). The analytic truths of one's linguistic system, on Carnap's view, result from intentions, or 'postulates', concerning 'the ways of use' of terms.

Carnap denies that his approach identifies analytic truths with truths that 'hold come what may' ([7.19], 921). He distinguishes two kinds of change in accepted statements: a change in the language one uses, and a change in a truth-value ascribed to a statement whose truth-value is not fixed just by the rules of one's language. Analytic statements, by definition, do not undergo changes of the second sort. One can change one's language, however, by adopting different meaning postulates. Some truth-values, on Carnap's view, are fixed just by the rules of language; others are not. This is a key assumption of Carnap's approach to analyticity. We must recognize the person-relativity of analyticity on Carnap's view. What is analytic, on this view, can vary from person to person, owing to variability of intentions regarding use of terms. Quine does not give adequate attention to such person-relativity of analyticity.

Let us turn now to the question whether Quine's epistemology can really make do without any notion of analyticity.

Analyticity in epistemology

An adequate epistemology relies on *epistemic principles* that specify what conditions epistemic warrant (or, justification) consists in. These principles yield an intelligible notion of warrant. Even Quine's epistemology relies on epistemic principles. One of Quine's main epistemic principles is his 'maxim of minimum mutilation': a principle of conservatism implying that it is good not to alter our antecedent theory more than necessary ([7.78], 15, 56). Quine does hold that another epistemic principle – concerning the maximization of the 'simplicity' of theory – can prevail over his principle of conservatism; but this will not affect the point to be made. We shall consider only cases where the two principles do not conflict.

The key question now is: in virtue of what is Quine's epistemic principle of conservatism true, or correct? In virtue of what is it true – or actually the case – that warranted theory revision conforms to the maxim of minimum mutilation? What, in other words, makes Quine's epistemic principle true rather than false? These questions will highlight the importance of analyticity for epistemology. They are not questions seeking a causal explanation of why certain people use Quine's epistemic principles. They rather seek an explanation why Quine's principles are true rather than false. What answer might Quine give?

One cannot answer by simply saying that the principle of conservatism requires that warranted theory revision be constrained by the principle of conservatism. It is not informative now to say that given the principle of conservatism, the principle of conservatism is true. The question above asks what *makes it the case* that *warranted* theory revision is constrained by the principle of conservatism. It is highly plausible to assume that it is just part of Quine's usage of the term 'epistemic warrant' that the principle of conservatism constrains epistemic warrant. Given this assumption, we may say that it is analytically true for Quine that the principle of conservatism constrains epistemic warrant.

Quine suggests that his epistemic principles of conservatism and simplicity find support in actual scientific practice. He claims that these principles 'are maxims by which science strives for vindication in future predictions' ([7.78], 15). This suggests the view that Quine's epistemic principles are *justified* by their role in actual scientific practice. One might propose further that Quine's principle of conservatism is *true* in virtue of its role in actual scientific practice. We can grant this proposal now, if only for the sake of argument, and then ask: In virtue of what is it true – or the case – that actual scientific practice constrains epistemically warranted theory revision? The most plausible answer is that it is just part of Quine's usage of 'epistemic warrant' that actual scientific practice constrains epistemic warrant. It is analytically true for Quine that scientific practice constrains epistemic warrant. Appeal to scientific practice thus does not free one from the importance of analyticity. Barring analyticity, we would have difficulty answering questions of the sort just raised. This may explain why Quine remains silent on such questions.

Appeals to holism take nothing away from the importance of analyticity. The epistemic holist uses the term 'epistemic warrant' in such a way that considerations of coherence determine warrant. A question of the sort just raised can thus reveal the importance of analyticity even for the epistemic holist, Quine included. Since Carnap's aforementioned characterization of analyticity is not a characterization of justification or evidence, it is not an alternative to epistemic holism – the sort of holism Quine uses to criticize analyticity ([7.74], 41). As for *semantic* holism – holism about meaning rather than evidence, Quine's commitment is explicitly qualified, given his view that some observation statements do have their empirical content individually ([7.77], 426). Holism about warrant, in any case, does not require holism about meaning. Considerations about holism thus do not threaten the foregoing remarks about analyticity.

Quine might seek refuge in the view that we can simply forego talk of epistemic warrant and all such normative talk. This, however, would be an implausibly extreme move, a move inconsistent with Quine's own linguistic practices. Such a move would remove all evaluative talk from epistemology and philosophy in general. Instead of evaluating statements relative to epistemic standards, we could, on this view, only describe statements relative to how entrenched, or firmly held, they are. Quine himself does not settle for mere descriptions of how entrenched statements are. He is, in fact, well known for his view that 'the lack of a standard of identity for attributes and propositions can be viewed . . . as a case of defectiveness on the part of "attribute" and "proposition" ' ([7.75], 244). Such talk of *defectiveness* is not the language of someone shunning normative, or evaluative, talk. In 'Two Dogmas' and elsewhere, Quine uses his views of actual scientific theory revision to set *evaluative* epistemic standards – standards involving holistic coherence, simplicity and minimum mutilation. Since Quine does have evaluative epistemic standards, he must face the questions about correctness raised above. Those questions reveal the philosophical importance of analyticity.

We should observe a distinction neglected by Quine, especially in 'Two Dogmas': the distinction between *what is true* in virtue of a certain policy of linguistic usage and *what justifies* such a policy. This is the distinction between what a policy of usage involves or entails and what supports such a policy. Confusion over this distinction apparently underlies Quine's opposition to analyticity. A statement can be analytically *true* just in virtue of a usage policy, even if that usage policy is supported, or *justified*, only by certain alterable explanatory purposes a language-user has. The alterability of the supporting purposes does not discredit the analyticity arising from a policy of usage. The category of the analytic is not the epistemic category of the *a priori*; nor does it entail unrevisability. Usage policies can and do change – often as a result of changing explanatory purposes. Change in a usage policy is a change in language. The category of the analytic characterizes a kind of *truth* resulting just from a policy of usage. It is not an epistemic category that connotes a special kind of warrant or evidence. Still, the category of analyticity can contribute to epistemology: it enables answers to the questions above about correctness of epistemic principles.

❧ EPISTEMIC JUSTIFICATION ❧

We noted above (p. 217) that Quine endorses epistemic holism: roughly, the view that the epistemic warrant, or justification, of a statement depends on the warrant of other statements. According to the so-called 'traditional analysis' of knowledge, suggested in Plato's *Theaetetus*, you know that *P* if and only if you have a *justified* true belief that *P*. You might believe a true groundless conjecture, but would not thereby *know* that this conjecture is true. Standardly construed, knowledge requires not only that a belief-condition and a truth-condition be satisfied, but also that the satisfaction of the belief-condition be *appropriately related* to the satisfaction of the truth-condition. The latter requirement leads to a justification-condition for knowledge, a condition that excludes such coincidental phenomena as lucky guesses.

Twentieth-century epistemologists have given special attention to the conditions for epistemic justification, the kind of justification appropriate to knowledge. They typically have allowed for justified false beliefs, and this allowance is called *fallibilism* about justification. Fallibilism allows, for example, that the Ptolemaic astronomers before Copernicus were justified in holding their geocentric model of the universe – even though it was a false model. Justification for a proposition, according to most twentieth-century epistemologists, need not logically entail the proposition justified: it need not be such that necessarily if the justifying proposition is true, then the justified proposition is true too. When justification does logically entail what it justifies, we have *deductive* justification. *Inductive* justification, in contrast, does not logically entail what it justifies; it rather is such that if the justifying proposition is true, then the justified proposition is, to some extent, *probably* true. Twentieth-century epistemologists do not share a single account of the sort of probability appropriate to inductive justification. Most recent epistemologists do agree, however, that epistemic justification is *defeasible*, that a justifying proposition can cease to be justifying for a person when that person acquires additional justification. For instance, your justification for thinking that there is a pool of water on the road ahead can be overridden by new evidence acquired upon approaching the relevant spot on the road.

A major topic of controversy in twentieth-century epistemology concerns the kind of justification we have for our beliefs about the external world, including the belief that conceiver-independent physical objects exist. Most twentieth-century epistemologists agree that such beliefs are justified only inductively, in terms of justification that does not logically entail the beliefs justified. Some sceptics, doubting that we have epistemic justification for the belief that external objects exist, have required deductive support for that belief; others have questioned whether we can even have inductive, probabilistic justification here (see below, pp. 232–41).

Some sceptics have used a *regress argument* to contend that we are not justified in believing anything about the external, conceiver-independent world (cf. Oakley [7.69]). This argument stems from the question whether, and if so how, we are justified in holding any belief about the external world on the basis of other beliefs, i.e. on the basis of so-called *inferential* justification. A sceptic's use of the regress argument aims to show that each of the available accounts of inferential justification fails, and thus that such justification is not to be had. The initial sceptical worry is: if one's belief that external objects exist is supposedly justified on the basis of another belief, how is the latter, allegedly justifying belief itself justified? Is it supposedly justified by a further belief? If so, how is the latter belief itself justified? We seem to be threatened by an endless regress of required justifying beliefs – a regress that seems too complex to employ in our actual everyday reasoning. Our options, according to many epistemologists, are straightforward: (1) explain how an endless regress of required justifying beliefs is not actually troublesome, or (2) show how we can terminate the threatening regress or (3) accept the sceptical conclusion that inferential justification is impossible.

A concrete example illustrates the problem of inferential justification. While walking along Lake Michigan, we decide that a swim today would be pleasant, but that the current dangers of swimming outdoors are too great. Our belief that swimming outdoors is dangerous today is supported by other beliefs we have. We believe, for example, that (1) local meteorologists have predicted lightning storms today in our area, (2) there are foreboding cumulonimbus clouds overhead and (3) the meteorologists' reports and the presence of the cumulonimbus clouds are reliable indicators of impending lightning. Our belief that swimming outdoors is dangerous today receives support from our belief that (1), (2) and (3) are true. What, however, supports (1), (2) and (3) for us? Other beliefs we have will naturally contribute support here, and thus the chain of inferential justification will continue. Part of our support for (1) might be our belief that (4) we heard radio reports today from some local meteorologists; and part of our support for (2) might be our belief that (5) we see dark thunderclouds overhead. Our support for (4) and (5) might be similarly inferential, thus extending the chain of inferential justification even further.

Non-sceptical epistemologists have offered four noteworthy replies to the regress problem concerning inferential justification. The first reply, which we may call *epistemic infinitism*, proposes that regresses of inferential justification are indeed infinite, but that this consideration does not preclude genuine justification. Our belief that swimming outdoors is dangerous today, on this reply, would be justified by belief (1) above, belief (1) would be justified by belief (4) above, belief (4) would be justified by a further belief, and so on endlessly. Such infinitism, while attracting very few proponents, was supported by Charles Peirce ([7.70], 36–8), the founder of American pragmatism. Infinitism evidently requires that one must have an infinity of justifying beliefs to have an inferentially justified belief.

Sceptics will argue that infinite chains of supposedly inferential justification cannot provide genuine justification. They will note that no matter how far back we go in an infinite regress of inferential justification, we find only beliefs that are *conditionally* justified: justified *if*, and *only if*, their supporting beliefs are justified. The problem is that the supporting beliefs themselves are at most conditionally justified too: justified if, and only if, *their* supporting beliefs are justified. At every point in the never-ending chain we find a belief that is merely conditionally justified, and not actually justified. Another problem is that one's having an infinity of supporting beliefs seemingly requires an infinite amount of time, on the assumption that belief-formation for each of the supporting beliefs takes a certain amount of time. We humans, of course, do not have an infinite amount of time, and thus it is doubtful that our actual justification includes infinite regresses of justifying beliefs. Even if these considerations are not decisive, they indicate that the proponent of infinitism has some important explaining to do.

A second non-sceptical reply to the regress problem is *epistemic coherentism*: the view that all justification is inferential and systematic in virtue of 'coherence relations' among beliefs. Justification for any belief, according to epistemic coherentism, terminates in a system or network of beliefs with which the justified belief coheres. This view denies that justification is linear in the manner suggested by infinitism. We should not confuse a coherence theory of *justification* – epistemic coherentism – with a coherence theory of *truth*. A coherence theory of truth, of the sort endorsed by Brand Blanshard ([7.11], 268; [7.12], 590), aims to specify the meaning of 'truth', or the essential nature of truth; a coherence theory of justification aims to explain the nature not of truth, but of the kind of justification appropriate to knowledge. Recent proponents of epistemic coherentism, of one version or another, include: Wilfrid Sellars ([7.95]; [7.96]; [7.97]), Nicholas Rescher ([7.79]; [7.80]), Gilbert Harman ([7.40]; [7.41]), Keith Lehrer ([7.46]; [7.47]) and Laurence BonJour ([7.13]).

Proponents of epistemic coherentism have tried to answer two pressing questions: first, what kind of coherence relation is crucial to justified belief? Second, what kind of belief-system must a justified belief cohere with? Regarding the first question, many proponents of epistemic coherentism acknowledge logical entailment and explanation as coherence relations among beliefs. Explanatory coherence relations obtain when some of one's beliefs effectively explain why some other of one's beliefs are true. For example, my belief that it is raining outside might effectively explain the truth of my belief that my office windows are wet. Regarding the second question, not just any belief-system will serve the purpose of epistemic coherentism. Some belief-systems, such as those consisting of science-fiction propositions, seem obviously erroneous, and thus seem unable to provide a basis for epistemically justified belief. However one answers the previous two questions, epistemic coherentism implies that the justification of any belief depends on that belief's coherence relations to other beliefs. Such coherentism is thus systematic, stressing the role of interconnectedness of beliefs in epistemic justification.

Sceptics will ask why we should regard coherence among one's beliefs as a reliable indication of empirical truth, of how things actually are in the empirical world. (See the section below on scepticism, pp. 232–41, for more on this matter.) Consider, in addition, the following so-called *isolation objection* to epistemic coherentism: epistemic coherentism entails that one can be epistemically justified in accepting a contingent empirical proposition that is incompatible with, or at least improbable given, one's total empirical evidence (Moser [7.59], 84–103; [7.61]; [7.62], 176–82). A proponent of this objection does not restrict empirical evidence to empirical propositions believed or accepted by a person.

The isolation objection becomes universally applicable to coherence theories of justification once we expand the scope of empirical evidence beyond the propositions (or, judgements) believed or accepted by a person. Suppose, for example, that one's empirical evidence includes the subjective non-propositional contents (e.g. visual images) of one's *non*-belief perceptual and sensory awareness states, such as one's seeming to perceive something or one's feeling a pain. If there are such contents, then they, being non-propositional, are not among what one believes or accepts. One might, of course, accept that one is having a particular visual image, but this does not mean that the image itself is a proposition one accepts. If we include the non-propositional contents of non-belief perceptual and sensory states in one's empirical evidence, the isolation objection will bear directly on coherence theories of justification. Coherence theories, by definition, make epistemic justification depend just on coherence relations among propositions one believes or accepts. They thus neglect, as a matter of principle, the evidential significance of the non-propositional contents of non-belief perceptual and sensory states. Proponents of epistemic coherentism have not yet achieved a uniform resolution of the problem raised by the isolation objection.

A third non-sceptical reply to the regress problem is *epistemic foundationalism*. Put generally, foundationalism about epistemic justification states that such justification has a two-tier structure: some instances of justification are non-inferential, or foundational; and all other instances of justification are inferential, or non-foundational, in that they derive ultimately from foundational justification. This structural view was proposed in Aristotle's *Posterior Analytics* (as a view about knowledge), received an extreme formulation in Descartes's *Meditations* and is represented, in one form or another, in the twentieth-century epistemological works of Bertrand Russell [7.88], C. I. Lewis [7.49]; [7.50], and Roderick Chisholm [7.22]; [7.23]; [7.25], among many others.[7]

Versions of foundationalism about justification differ on two matters: the explanation of non-inferential, foundational justification, and the explanation of how justification can be transmitted from foundational beliefs to non-foundational beliefs. Some philosophers, following Descartes, have assumed that foundational beliefs must be *certain* (e.g. indubitable or infallible). Such an assumption underlies *radical* foundationalism, a view requiring not only that foundational beliefs be certain, but also that such beliefs guarantee the certainty of the non-foundational beliefs they support. Two considerations explain why radical foundationalism attracts very few epistemologists. First, very few, if any, of our perceptual beliefs are certain;[8] and, second, the beliefs that might be candidates for certainty (e.g. the belief that I am thinking) are insufficiently informative to guarantee the certainty of our highly specific inferential beliefs concerning the external world (e.g. beliefs about physics, chemistry and biology).

Most contemporary foundationalists accept *modest* foundationalism, the view that foundational beliefs need not possess or provide certainty, and need not deductively support justified non-foundational beliefs. Foundationalists typically characterize a *non-inferentially justified, foundational* belief as a belief whose epistemic *justification* does not derive from other beliefs; but they leave open whether the *causal* basis of foundational beliefs includes other beliefs. Further, they typically hold that foundationalism is an account of a belief's (or a proposition's) *having* justification for a person, not of one's *showing* that a belief has justification or is true.

Modest foundationalists can choose from three influential approaches to non-inferential, foundational justification: (1) self-justification, (2) justification by non-belief, non-propositional experiences and (3) justification by a reliable non-belief origin of a belief. Recent proponents of self-justification have included Roderick Chisholm [7.22] and C. J. Ducasse [7.30]. They contend that a foundational belief can justify itself, apart from any evidential support from something else. In contrast, proponents of foundational justification by non-belief experiences shun literal self-justification. They hold, following C. I. Lewis ([7.49]; [7.50]), that foundational perceptual beliefs can be justified by non-belief sensory or perceptual experiences (e.g. my non-belief experience involving seeming to see a keyboard) that either make true, are best explained by or otherwise support those foundational beliefs (e.g. the belief that there is, or at least appears to be, a keyboard here). Proponents of foundational justification by reliable origins hold that non-inferential justification depends on non-belief belief-forming processes (e.g. perception, memory, introspection) that are truth-conducive to some extent, in virtue of tending to produce true rather than false beliefs. The latter view invokes the reliability of a belief's non-belief origin,[9] whereas the previous view invokes the particular sensory or perceptual experiences that underlie a foundational belief. Despite the disagreement here, proponents of modest foundationalism typically agree that non-inferential justification, at least in most cases, can be defeated upon expansion of one's justified beliefs. The justification for your belief that there is a red flower in the vase, for example, might be overridden by the introduction of new evidence that there is a red light shining on the flower.

Wilfrid Sellars [7.96] and Laurence BonJour [7.13] have offered an influential argument against claims to non-inferential justification. They contend that one cannot be non-inferentially epistemically justified in holding any beliefs, since one is epistemically justified in holding a belief only if one has good reason to think that the belief is true. This, they claim, entails that the justification of an alleged foundational belief will actually depend on an argument of the following form:

(1) My foundational belief that P has feature F.
(2) Beliefs having feature F are likely to be true.
(3) Hence, my foundational belief that P is likely to be true.

If the justification of one's foundational beliefs depends on such an argument, those beliefs will not be foundational after all; for their justification will then depend on the justification of further beliefs: the beliefs represented by the premises of the argument (1)–(3).

It seems too demanding to hold that the justification of one's belief that P requires one's being *justified in believing* premises (1) and (2). Given that requirement, you will be justified in believing that P only if you are justified in believing that your belief that P has feature F. Further, given those requirements, you will be justified in believing that (1) your belief that P has F only if you are justified in believing an additional proposition: that (2) your belief that (1) has F. Given the requirements in question, we have no non-arbitrary way to avoid the troublesome implication that similar requirements apply not only to this latter proposition – viz. (2) – but also to each of the ensuing infinity of required justified beliefs. The problem is that we seem not to have the required infinity of increasingly complex justified beliefs.

An apparent lesson here is that if justificational support for a belief must be accessible to the believer, that accessibility should not itself be regarded as requiring further justified belief. Current debates over *internalism* and *externalism* regarding epistemic justification concern what sort of access, if any, one must have to the support for one's justified beliefs. Internalism incorporates an accessibility requirement, of some sort, on what provides justification, whereas externalism does not. Debates over internalism and externalism are currently unresolved in contemporary epistemology.[10]

Foundationalists must explain not only the conditions for non-inferential justification, but also how justification transmits from foundational beliefs to inferentially justified, non-foundational beliefs. Modest foundationalists, unlike radical foundationalists, allow for non-deductive, merely probabilistic connections that transfer justification. They have not, however, reached agreement on the exact nature of such connections. Some modest foundationalists hold that some kind of 'inference to a best explanation' can account for transmission of justification in many cases. For example, the belief that there is a computer before me can, in certain circumstances, provide a best explanation of various foundational beliefs about my perceptual inputs. This, however, is a controversial matter among epistemologists.

A special problem troubles versions of foundationalism that restrict non-inferential justification to subjective beliefs about what one *seems* to see, hear, feel, smell and taste. Those versions must explain how such subjective beliefs can provide justification for beliefs about conceiver-independent physical objects. Clearly, such subjective beliefs do not logically entail beliefs about physical objects. Since extensive hallucination is always possible, it is always possible that one's subjective beliefs are true while the relevant beliefs about physical objects are false. This consideration challenges foundationalists endorsing *linguistic phenomenalism*, the view that statements about physical objects can be translated without loss of meaning into logically equivalent statements solely about subjective states characterized by subjective beliefs.[11] Perhaps a foundationalist, following Chisholm [7.23] and Cornman [7.27], can invoke a set of non-deductive relations to explain how subjective beliefs can justify beliefs about physical objects. This remains, however, as a challenge, since no set of such relations has attracted widespread acceptance from foundationalists. We should note, though, that some versions of foundationalism allow for the non-inferential justification of beliefs about physical objects, and thus avoid the problem at hand.

A fourth non-sceptical reply to the regress problem is *epistemic contextualism*, a view suggested by Wittgenstein [7.109] and formulated explicitly by Annis [7.3]. Wittgenstein set forth a central tenet of contextualism with his claim that 'at the foundation of well-founded belief lies belief that is not founded' [7.109], §253). If we construe Wittgenstein's claim as stating that at the foundation of justified beliefs lie beliefs that are unjustified, we have an alternative to infinitism, coherentism and foundationalism.[12] In any context of inquiry, according to contextualism, people simply assume (the acceptability of) some propositions as starting points for inquiry; and these 'contextually basic' propositions, while themselves lacking evidential support, can support other propositions. Contextualists emphasize that contextually basic propositions can vary from social group to social group, and from context to context – e.g. from theological inquiry to physical inquiry. Thus, what functions as an unjustified justifier in one context need not in another.

The main problem for contextualism comes from the view that unjustified beliefs can provide epistemic justification for other beliefs. If we grant that view, we need to avoid the implausible view that *any* unjustified belief, however obviously false or contradictory, can provide justification in certain contexts. If any unjustified proposition can serve as a justifier, we shall, it seems, be able to justify anything we want. Even if we do typically take certain things for granted in certain contexts of discussion, this does not support the view that there are unjustified justifiers. Perhaps the things typically taken for granted are actually supportable by good reasons; and if they are not, we need some way to distinguish them from unjustified beliefs that cannot transmit justification to other beliefs. The contextualist must explain, then, how an unjustified belief – but not just any unjustified belief – can provide inferential justification for other beliefs. Contextualists have not reached agreement on the needed explanation.

In sum, then, the regress problem for inferential justification has a troublesome resilience about it. Infinitism, coherentism, foundationalism or contextualism may provide a viable solution to the problem, but only after a resolution of the problems noted above. Let us turn briefly now to some complications facing the analysis of knowledge.

❧ CONDITIONS FOR KNOWLEDGE ❧

Some recent epistemologists have proposed that we give up the traditional justification-condition for knowledge. They recommend, following Alvin Goldman [7.37], that we construe the justification-condition as a *causal* condition. Roughly, the idea is that you know that P if (1) you believe that P, (2) P is true and (3) your believing that P is causally produced and sustained by the fact that makes P true. This is the basis of a *causal theory of knowing*, a theory that admits of various manifestations.

A causal theory of knowing faces apparently serious problems from knowledge of universal propositions. Perhaps we know, for instance, that all computers are produced by humans; but our believing that this is so seems not to be causally supported by the fact that all computers are humanly produced. It is not clear that the latter fact causally produces *any* beliefs. At a minimum, we need an explanation of how a causal theory can account for knowledge of such universal propositions.

The analysis of knowledge as justified true belief, however elaborated, faces a challenge that initially gave rise to causal theories of knowledge: *the Gettier problem*. In 1963 Edmund Gettier published an influential challenge to the view that if you have a justified true belief that P, then you know that P. Here is one of Gettier's [7.35] counter-examples to this view: Smith is justified in believing the false proposition that (i) Jones owns a Ford. On the basis of (i), Smith infers, and thus is justified in believing, that (ii) either Jones owns a Ford or Brown is in Barcelona. As it happens, Brown is in Barcelona, and so (ii) is true. Thus, although Smith is justified in believing the true proposition (ii), Smith does not know (ii).

Gettier-style counter-examples are cases where a person has justified true belief that P but lacks knowledge that P. The Gettier problem is the problem of finding a modification of, or an alternative to, the standard, justified-true-belief analysis that avoids difficulties from Gettier-style counter-examples. The controversy over the Gettier problem is highly complex and still unsettled. Many epistemologists take the lesson of Gettier-style counter-examples to be that propositional knowledge requires a *fourth* condition, beyond the justification-, truth- and belief-conditions. No specific fourth condition has received overwhelming acceptance by epistemologists, but some proposals have become prominent. The so-called 'defeasibility condition', for example, requires that the justification appropriate to knowledge be 'undefeated' in the general sense that some appropriate subjunctive conditional concerning defeaters of justification be true of that justification. For instance, one simple defeasibility fourth condition requires of Smith's knowing that P that there be no true proposition, Q, such that if Q became justified for Smith, P would no longer be justified for Smith. So if Smith knows, on the basis of his visual perception, that Bubba removed books from the library, then Smith's coming to believe the true proposition that Bubba's identical twin removed books from the library would not undermine the justification for Smith's belief concerning Bubba himself. A different approach shuns subjunctive conditionals of that sort, and claims that propositional knowledge requires justified true belief that is sustained by the collective totality of actual truths. This approach requires a detailed account of when justification is undermined and restored.[13]

The Gettier problem, according to many epistemologists, is epistemologically important. One branch of epistemology seeks a precise understanding of the nature – i.e. the essential components – of propositional knowledge. Our having a precise understanding of propositional knowledge requires our having a Gettier-proof analysis of such knowledge. Epistemologists thus need a defensible solution to the Gettier problem, however complex that solution is. This conclusion is compatible with the view that various epistemologists employ different notions of knowledge at any level of specificity.

❧ SCEPTICISM ❧

Epistemologists have long debated the limits, or scope, of knowledge. The more restricted we take the scope of knowledge to be, the more sceptical we are. Two influential types of scepticism are *knowledge*-scepticism and *justification*-scepticism. Unrestricted knowledge-scepticism implies that no one knows anything. Unrestricted justification-scepticism implies the more extreme view that no one is even justified in believing anything. Some forms of scepticism are stronger than others. Knowledge-scepticism in its strongest form implies that it is *impossible* for anyone to know anything. A weaker form would deny the *actuality* of our having knowledge, but leave open its possibility. Many sceptics have restricted their scepticism to a particular domain of supposed knowledge: e.g. knowledge of the external world, knowledge of other minds, knowledge of the past or the future or knowledge of unperceived items. Limited scepticism is more common than unrestricted scepticism in the history of epistemology.

Arguments supporting scepticism come in many forms. One of the most difficult is *the problem of the criterion*, a version of which comes from the sixteenth-century sceptic Michel de Montaigne:

> To adjudicate [between the true and the false] among the appearances of things, we need to have a distinguishing method; to validate this method, we need to have a justifying argument; but to validate this justifying argument, we need the very method at issue. And there we are, going round on the wheel.[14]

This line of sceptical argument originated in ancient Greece, with epistemology itself. (See Sextus Empiricus, *Outlines of Pyrrhonism*, Book II.)[15] It forces us to face this question: how can we specify *what* we know without having specified *how* we know, and how can we specify *how* we know without having specified *what* we know? Is there any reasonable way out of this threatening circle? This is one of the most difficult epistemological problems, and a cogent epistemology must provide a defensible solution to it. Contemporary epistemology still lacks a widely accepted reply to this urgent problem. One influential reply from Roderick Chisholm [7.24] rules out scepticism from the start, with the assumption that we do know some specific propositions about the external world. Chisholm endorses a *particularist* reply that begins with an answer to the question of what we know. Such a reply seems, however, to beg a key question against the sceptic. A *methodist* reply to the problem of the criterion begins with an answer to the question of how we know. Such a reply risks divorcing knowledge from our considered judgements about particular cases of knowledge. It also must avoid begging key questions raised by sceptics.

Let us consider another sceptical argument (developed in detail in Moser ([7.63] and [7.64]). Suppose that you are a realist claiming knowledge that external, mind-independent objects exist, and that you take such knowledge to entail that it is objectively the case that external objects exist. Suppose also that you regard yourself as having a cogently sound argument for your claim to knowledge that external objects exist.

Your argument, let us suppose, takes the following general form:

1 If one's belief that *P* has feature *F*, then one knows that *P*.
2 My belief that external objects exist has *F*.
3 Hence, I know that external objects exist.

Even critics of realism may grant premise (1) – if only for the sake of argument. That premise may be just a straightforward implication of what a realist *means* by 'knows that *P*'.

Feature *F* can incorporate any of a number of familiar well-foundedness properties: (a) suitable doxastic coherence (cf. Lehrer [7.47], chapter 7), (b) maximal explanatory efficacy (cf. Lycan [7.51], chapter 7), (c) undefeated self-evidentness (cf. Foley [7.33], chapter 2), (d) consistent predictive success (cf. Almeder [7.1], chapter 4), (e) uncontested communal acceptance (cf. Annis [7.3]), (f) causal sustenance by such a belief-forming process as perception, memory, introspection, or testimony (cf. Goldman [7.38], chapter 5), (g) adequate theoretical elegance in terms of such virtuous characteristics as simplicity and comprehensiveness (cf. Thagard [7.105], chapter 5), (h) survival value in the evolutionary scheme of things (cf. Carruthers [7.20], chapter 12), or (i) some combination of (a)-(h) (cf. Cornman [7.27]). Such well-foundedness properties cannot conceptually exhaust F; for by hypothesis one's knowing that P (unlike those well-foundedness properties) *entails* its objectively being the case that P.

If knowledge involves more than objectively true belief, as it does on standard conceptions since the time of Plato's *Theaetetus* (cf. 202b), then F will be a complex property – involving the property of being objectively true plus some additional property. The additional property, on standard conceptions of knowledge, incorporates a well-foundedness feature of some sort (and sometimes a no-defeaters restriction on that feature to handle the aforementioned Gettier problem). Let us call this *the well-foundedness component of F*. A well-foundedness feature serves typically to distinguish knowledge from true belief due simply to such coincidental phenomena as lucky guesses. In this respect, such a feature may be regarded as making a belief 'likely to be true' to some extent. As suggested in the section above on epistemic justification (pp. 228-9), an *internalist* well-foundedness feature is accessible – directly or indirectly – to the knower for whom it yields likelihood of truth; an *externalist* well-foundedness feature is not. (Cf. Alston [7.2], chapters 8, 9.)

If, as standardly assumed, knowledge that P entails that it is objectively the case – or objectively true – that P, the relevant kind of likelihood of *truth* must entail likelihood of what is objectively true, or objectively the case. So, whether internalist or externalist, a well-foundedness feature must yield likelihood of what is objectively the case. It must, in other words, indicate with some degree of likelihood what is the case conceiver-independently. A well-foundedness component of F violating this requirement will fail to distinguish knowledge from true belief due simply to such coincidental phenomena as lucky guesses.

Premise (2) generates a problem motivating scepticism about realism concerning external objects. It affirms (a) that your belief that external objects exist is objectively true, and (if you hold that knowledge has a well-foundedness component) (b) that a well-foundedness feature indicates with some degree of likelihood that external objects exist. A sceptic can plausibly raise this question:

Q1. What non-question-begging reason, if any, have we to affirm that your belief that external objects exist is objectively true?

If you are a typical realist, committed to a well-foundedness component of knowledge, you will appeal to your preferred well-foundedness component of F to try to answer Q1. In particular, you will answer that the satisfaction of the conditions for that well-foundedness component provides the needed reason to affirm that your belief is true. This answer to $Q1$ is not surprising, given the aforementioned assumption that a well-foundedness component yields likelihood of truth.

For any well-foundedness component a realist offers, a sceptic can raise the following challenge:

> $Q2$. What non-question-begging reason, if any, have we to affirm that the satisfaction of the conditions for *that* well-foundedness component of F is actually indicative, to any extent, of what is objectively the case?

Realists might reply that it is true in virtue of what they *mean* by 'indicative of what is objectively the case' that their preferred well-foundedness component is indicative of what is objectively the case. (Cf. Pollock [7.73], chapter 5.) This move uses definitional (or, conceptual) fiat to try to disarm sceptics, but actually fails to answer their main concern.

We can put the main concern more exactly:

> $Q3$. What non-question-begging reason, if any, have we to affirm that the satisfaction of the conditions for a preferred well-foundedness component of F – including the satisfaction of conditions definitive of what a realist means by 'indicative of what is objectively the case' – is ever a genuinely reliable means of representational access to what is objectively the case?

Equivalently, what non-question-begging reason, if any, have we to affirm that some claim satisfying the conditions for a preferred well-foundedness component (e.g. the claim that external objects exist) is actually objectively true? We can grant realists their preferred definition of 'indicative of what is the case', but then follow up with $Q3$. A sceptic may begin with $Q1$, but will move to $Q3$ once a realist appeals to a well-foundedness component of F. It would be a shallow sceptic indeed who failed to regard $Q3$ as just as troublesome for realism as $Q1$ is.

Clearly, your invoking your preferred well-foundedness component to defend realism against $Q3$ would be question-begging. The reliability of your preferred well-foundedness component is precisely what is under question now; and begging this question offers no cogent support for realism. If, for instance, you hold that coherent belief is indicative of objective truth, you cannot now simply presume that coherent belief is indicative of objective truth; the issue now is whether coherent belief (or any similar well-foundedness component) is actually indicative of objective truth. Perhaps *given* your preferred well-foundedness component, that well-foundedness component is itself well-founded. This consideration, however, does nothing to answer $Q3$. $Q3$ asks what *non-question-begging* reason, if any, we have to regard your preferred well-foundedness component as ever being a reliable means to objective truth. In effect: *apart from* appeal to (the reliability of) your preferred well-foundedness component, what reason have we to regard that component as ever being a reliable means to objective truth – e.g. objective truth regarding your belief that external objects exist?

A sceptic's use of $Q3$ allows for fallibilism about well-foundedness: the view that a well-founded belief can be false. In addition, a sceptic's use of $Q3$ need not assume that evidence on which a claim is well-founded must logically entail (or, deductively support) that claim; nor does it require that we take a controversial stand on purely conceptual disputes over the exact conditions for epistemic justification. These are some virtues of a sceptic's use of $Q3$ to challenge realism.

Suppose then that you are a realist wielding argument (1)–(3), along with the standard view that F has a well-foundedness component (say, coherent belief). You will then hold that your belief that external objects exist illustrates a case where a belief's meeting the conditions for your preferred well-foundedness component (such as coherent belief) is an objectively true belief. You will then hold, given premise (2), that your belief that external objects exist is objectively true, and that your preferred well-foundedness component of F (namely, coherent belief) is satisfied by an objectively true belief in this case. You will, however, still owe the sceptic a non-question-begging reason for thinking that your preferred well-foundedness component of F (namely, coherent belief) is, in this case, a genuinely reliable means to objectively true belief.

Realists might aim to silence the sceptic by claiming, following Pollock [7.73], that our concept of an external object is actually constituted, or wholly determined, by certain well-foundedness conditions involving one or more of the well-foundedness properties noted above. The claim here is that certain conditions for well-founded ascription of our concept of an external object *fully* determine that concept. This claim entails a kind of verificationism about our notion of an external object, and is not equivalent to the previous view that appealed to considerations of meaning regarding 'indication of what is objectively true'.

It seems, in reply, that our notion of an external object logically outstrips various standard well-foundedness conditions for that notion. Our concept of an external object seemingly involves, for instance, the condition that any object falling under it does not perish whenever one looks away from it, but would exist even when unperceived. The condition that an external object would exist even when unperceived seems not to be logically entailed by various standard well-foundedness conditions for our notion of an external object. For example, maximally effective explanation of (the origin of) our common perceptual experiences does not *logically* require that there be objects that exist when unperceived. Further, even if well-foundedness conditions fully determined our notion of an external object, it would still be an open question whether one's having our notion of an external object involves one's *actually satisfying* those well-foundedness conditions with one's belief that external objects exist. If those conditions entail the subjunctive condition just noted, a sceptic will demand a non-question-begging reason to think it is ever actually satisfied; and then the now familiar worries motivating scepticism will resurface. Realists, in any case, are not typically verificationists about our notion of an external object.

We may return, then, to the sceptic's main challenge, in Q_3, for the realist to deliver a non-question-begging reason. Such a reason will not simply *presume* a realism-favouring answer to a sceptic's familiar questions about reliability. Some of these familiar questions concern the reliability, in any actual case, of our belief-forming processes (e.g. perception, introspection, judgement, memory, testimony) that sometimes produce belief in the existence of external objects. Some other familiar questions concern the reliability, in any actual case, of suitably coherent, explanatorily efficacious, or predictively successful belief regarding the existence of external objects. Each of the well-foundedness properties noted above will attract such a question about reliability from a sceptic. A sceptic will thus be unmoved by observations concerning the simplicity and comprehensiveness provided by realism about external objects. The application of Q_3 will ask for a non-question-begging reason to affirm that the simplicity and comprehensiveness provided by such realism is ever a reliable means to objectively true belief. Any higher-order use of a well-foundedness component – to support a well-foundedness component – meets the same fate as first-order use; for Q_3 applies equally to any higher-order use. Lacking answers to the sceptic's questions, we cannot cogently infer that realism about external objects has been substantiated.

A sceptic is not guilty of this empty challenge: give me a cogent argument, but do not use any premises. The challenge is rather: give me a cogent, non-question-begging reason to hold that your belief that external objects exist is a case where a belief satisfying your preferred well-foundedness component is an objectively true belief. The demand is not that realists forego the use of premises; it rather is just that the realist forego the use of *question-begging* premises – premises that beg relevant questions about reliability motivating scepticism. Q_1–Q_3 illustrate some standard sceptical questions. A question-begging argument from a realist will not even begin to approach cogency for a sceptic. Mere soundness of argument, then, is not at issue; *cogent* non-question-begging soundness is.

One familiar consideration – perhaps employed only for the sake of argument by a sceptic – indicates that a sceptic wielding Q_3 will *not* be successfully answered by a realist. Cognitively relevant access to *anything* by us humans depends on such belief-forming processes as perception, introspection, judgement, memory, testimony, intuition and common sense. Such processes are subject to question via Q_3, and cannot themselves deliver non-question-begging support for their own reliability. Put bluntly, we cannot assume a position independent of our own cognitively relevant processes to deliver a non-question-begging indication of the reliability of those processes. This, for better or worse, seems to be the human cognitive predicament; and no realist has yet shown how we can escape it. This, too, is a straightforward consider-ation favouring the conclusion that we must take scepticism quite seriously. Until we have the needed non-question-begging reason, scep-ticism seems more defensible, epistemically, than realism. Our inability to provide the needed non-question-begging reason does nothing to undercut the sceptic's challenge; it rather undercuts claims to cogent support for realism.

A non-question-begging reason favouring realism would be a reason that provides *effective* discernment of conceiver-independent truth. We cannot, it seems, effectively rely on *our* eyesight, for example, to test the objective reliability of our own eyesight. The familiar Snellen test for vision thus cannot effectively measure objectively reliable vision. I shall briefly develop this point to illustrate, by way of a concrete example, how effective discernment of conceiver-independent truth is typically unavailable.

The familiar Snellen chart tests the function of the fovea, the most sensitive part of the retina. Clinical use of this chart assumes that the component letters, 'E', 'F', 'P', 'T', etc. – which subtend an angle of 5 minutes of arc at the eye's nodal point – can be identified 'appropriately' by the 'normal eye'. (Incidentally, many people can resolve letters subtending a smaller visual angle; accordingly, the letters on some Snellen charts are designed to subtend an angle of only 4 minutes.) Tests are typically given at a distance of 6 metres, or 20 feet. At this distance, the light rays from the chart's letters are roughly parallel, and the perceiver does not – or at least should not – have to strive to focus. If a perceiver seated 6 metres from the chart reads the line of letters subtending a visual angle of 5 minutes at 6 metres, we say that her vision is 6/6, or (in the foot-oriented United States 20/20). The numerator of the fraction indicates the distance at which the test is given. The denominator denotes the distance at which the smallest letters read subtend a visual angle of 5 minutes.

We cannot plausibly hold that 6/6 vision, by the standard of the Snellen test, qualifies as objectively reliable vision – vision conducive to objectively true visual beliefs. Testing for visual acuity relies on a standard of 'normal vision' determined by reference to how the 'typical human eye' actually operates in resolving the Snellen letters. The standard set by the subtending of a visual angle of 5 minutes arises from what is, liberally speaking, visually typical among the community of human visual perceivers. The 'typical' human perceiver, loosely speaking, clearly sees – without blurring, fuzziness or duplication – three bars of an inverted 'E' when she is standing 6 metres from the Snellen chart. Such visual experience, according to the Snellen test, is the standard for 'normal vision'.

Vision that is normal by the Snellen standard does not obviously qualify as objectively reliable or truth-conducive in a way pertinent to scepticism about realism. Normal vision by the Snellen standard is based loosely on an assumed statistical average concerning human visual perceivers, not on considerations purporting to indicate objective reliability of vision. A sceptic, in accord with Q3, will naturally question whether that statistical average is ever a reliable means to conceiver-independent reality. It is doubtful that we have any non-question-begging reason to hold that it is thus reliable. We cannot presume the reliability of our vision to provide non-question-begging reasons in favour of the reliability of our vision.

More generally, we cannot effectively rely on the deliverances of our belief-forming processes (e.g. perception, introspection, judgement, memory, testimony, intuition and common sense) to test the reliability of those processes regarding their accessing conceiver-independent facts. Appeal to the deliverances of those processes would beg the key question against an inquirer doubtful of the reliability of those deliverances and processes. The belief-forming processes in question need testing, with respect to their reliability, in order to provide non-question-begging support for the realist's claim to objective truth. The realist claims to know conceiver-independent facts about external objects. A doubtful inquirer will naturally demand an effective, non-question-begging reason for the realist's claim. A question-begging reason will settle nothing in this philosophical dispute.

A sceptic's use of Q1–Q3 bears on a wide range of positions commonly called 'realism'. This range includes each of the following species of realism: *weak* realism (i.e. something objectively exists independently of conceivers); *common sense* realism (i.e. tokens of most current observable common sense, and scientific, physical types objectively exist independently of conceivers); and *scientific* realism (i.e. tokens of most current unobservable scientific physical types objectively exist independently of conceivers). Michael Devitt has claimed that weak realism is 'so weak as to be uninteresting' ([7.28], p. 22). Even if it is, this is just so much coincidental biography. It does not excuse the realist from providing non-question-begging reasons in support of weak realism. The realist cannot plausibly follow Devitt in appealing just to our current science to settle epistemological debates about realism. The realist must, to defend against the sceptic, explain how our current science gives us the needed effective reason in favour of realism. It settles no philosophical questions simply to say, with Devitt, that 'scepticism [regarding knowledge of conceiver-independent facts] is simply uninteresting: it throws the baby out with the bath water' ([7.28], 63). One pressing question is whether the realist actually has a real baby – i.e. effectively supportable knowledge – to throw out. We cannot simply beg this question, if we wish to make genuine philosophical progress.

Questions under dispute in a philosophical context cannot attract non-question-begging answers from mere *presumption* of the correctness of a disputed answer. If we allow such question-begging in general, we can support *any* disputed position we prefer: simply beg the key question in any dispute regarding the preferred position. Given that strategy, argument becomes superfluous in the way circular argument is typically pointless. Question-begging strategies promote an undesirable arbitrariness in philosophical debate. They are thus rationally inconclusive relative to the questions under dispute. What is question-begging is always relative to a context of disputed issues, a context that is not necessarily universally shared. (For doubts about any purely formal criterion of vicious circularity in argument, see Sorensen [7.100].)

A pragmatic defence of realism, in terms of a belief's overall utility, fares no better than the well-foundedness properties noted above. A variation on *Q3* applies straightforwardly: what non-question-begging reason, if any, have we to affirm that a belief's overall pragmatic utility is ever a genuinely reliable means of access to what is objectively the case? Clearly, it does no good here to note that it is pragmatically useful to regard pragmatic utility as a reliable means to objective truth. A sceptic, once again, seeks non-question-begging reasons. Given the aforementioned human cognitive predicament, we can offer little hope for the needed non-question-begging support on pragmatic grounds. Pragmatic support for realism is one thing; non-question-begging support, another. A sceptic demands, but despairs of achieving, the latter.

Even if realism has certain theoretical advantages over various species of idealism, it still must face a sceptic's worries about the absence of non-question-begging supporting reasons. Sceptics doubtful of the correctness of realism need not be idealists holding that an individual's mental activity creates all objects. They rather can plausibly hold that we lack non-question-begging reasons to endorse – to any degree – idealism as well as realism. Scepticism shuns *any* position that does not enjoy non-question-begging reasons; for question-begging support is really no support at all. The burden of cogent argument is now squarely on the realist's shoulders. The future of epistemology will reveal whether that burden is ultimately discharged.[16]

❧ NOTES ❧

1 The first published statement of Russell's abandonment of sense data is [7.86], 305–6. Cf. Russell ([7.92], 100).

2 See Neurath [7.68], 299–318. For a more detailed statement of some of the anti-metaphysical views of the Vienna Circle, see Ayer [7.7].

3 Cf. [7.110], 200: 'The verification is not *one* token of the truth, it is *the* sense of the proposition.'

4 For some of the controversy, see Neurath [7.67], Schlick [7.93] and Ayer [7.5].

5 See, for example, Russell [7.82]. For James's reply see his paper 'Two English Critics' ([7.45], 146–53). For discussion of whether James's approach to truth includes a correspondence condition, see Moser [7.58].

6 For an exposition of Lewis's views on the given element in experience, see Firth [7.32] and Moser [7.60].

7 For a bibliography of works on foundationalism, see Moser ([7.65], 273–6) and Triplett ([7.106], 112–16). For some recent attempts to defend epistemic foundationalism of one sort or another, see Pollock [7.72], [7.73]; Cornman [7.27]; Swain [7.104]; Moser [7.59], [7.62]; Foley [7.33]; Audi [7.4]; Alan Goldman [7.36]; and Alston [7.2].

8 For a survey and assessment of some prominent views about the certainty of subjective beliefs about sensations, see Meyers ([7.52], chapter 3) and Alan Goldman ([7.36], chapter 7). Cf. Alston ([7.2], chapters 10, 11).

9 The view that reliable belief-forming processes confer epistemic justification has come to be known is *reliabilism*. Reliabilism of one sort or another has been defended by Swain [7.104], Alvin Goldman [7.37], Alston [7.2] and Sosa [7.101].

10 For some indication of these debates, see BonJour ([7.13], chapter 3); Alston ([7.2], chapters 8, 9); and Moser ([7.59], chapter 4; [7.62], chapter 2).

11 For discussion of this and other versions of phenomenalism, see Ayer [7.6], [7.8]; Chisholm ([7.21], 189–97); Cornman [7.26]; and Fumerton [7.34].

12 It is noteworthy that the interpretation of Wittgenstein's *On Certainty* is a matter of controversy among philosophers. For efforts at interpretation, see Shiner [7.98] and Morawetz [7.57]. Another influential proponent of contextualism is Rorty [7.81]. For discussion of Rorty's version of contextualism, see Moser ([7.62], chapter 4) and Sosa ([7.101], chapter 6).

13 For some details on this general approach, see Pollock ([7.73], 180–93) and Moser ([7.62], chapter 6). On the history of the Gettier problem, prior to 1982, see Shope [7.99].

14 Michel Montaigne, 'An Apologie of Raymond Sebond', in *The Essays of Montaigne* (New York, Modern Library, 1933), p. 544.

15 For relevant historical discussion, see Striker [7.102] and [7.103] and Barnes [7.10].

16 A chapter of this size cannot deal with all the movements and issues characterizing twentieth-century epistemology. For some other surveys, touching on some different movements and issues, see Chisholm [7.22] and Hill [7.42].
   I thank John Canfield for his comments on a draft of this chapter.

❧ BIBLIOGRAPHY ❧

7.1 Almeder, Robert *Blind Realism*, Lanham, Md.: Rowman & Littlefield, 1992.

7.2 Alston, William *Epistemic Justification*, Ithaca, NY: Cornell University Press, 1989.

7.3 Annis, David 'A Contextualist Theory of Epistemic Justification', *American Philosophical Quarterly*, 15 (1978): 213–19.

7.4 Audi, Robert *Belief, Justification, and Knowledge*, Belmont, Cal.: Wadsworth, 1988.

7.5 Ayer, A. J. [1936] 'Verification and Experience', in A. J. Ayer, ed., *Logical Positivism*, New York: Free Press, 1959: 228–43.

7.6 —— *The Foundations of Empirical Knowledge*, London: Macmillan, 1940.

7.7 —— *Language, Truth, and Logic*, 2nd edn, New York: Dover, 1946.

7.8 —— [1947] 'Phenomenalism', in A. J. Ayer, *Philosophical Essays*, London: Macmillan, 1954.

7.9 —— 'Editor's Introduction', in A. J. Ayer, ed., *Logical Positivism*, New York: Free Press, 1959: 3–28.

7.10 Barnes, Jonathan *The Toils of Scepticism*, Cambridge: Cambridge University Press, 1990.

7.11 Blanshard, Brand *The Nature of Thought*, Vol. 2, London: Allen & Unwin, 1939.

7.12 —— 'Reply to Nicholas Rescher', in P. A. Schilpp, ed., *The Philosophy of Brand Blanshard*, La Salle, Ill.: Open Court, 1980: 589–600.

7.13 BonJour, Laurence *The Structure of Empirical Knowledge*, Cambridge, Mass.: Harvard University Press, 1985.

7.14 Carnap, Rudolf *The Logical Structure of the World*, trans. R. A. George, Berkeley: University of California Press, 1967.

7.15 —— 'On the Character of Philosophical Problems', *Philosophy of Science*, 1 (1934): 5–19.

7.16 —— [1936] 'Testability and Meaning'. in Herbert Feigl and May Brodbeck, eds, *Readings in the Philosophy of Science*, New York: Appleton-Century-Crofts, 1953: 47–92.

7.17 —— 'Empiricism, Semantics, and Ontology', in R. Carnap, *Meaning and Necessity*, 2nd edn, Chicago: University of Chicago Press, 1956: 205–21.

7.18 —— 'Meaning Postulates', in R. Carnap, *Meaning and Necessity*, 2nd edn, Chicago: University of Chicago Press, 1956: 222–9.

7.19 —— 'W. V. Quine on Logical Truth', in P. A. Schilpp, ed., *The Philosophy of Rudolf Carnap*, La Salle, Ill.: Open Court, 1963: 915–22.

7.20   Carruthers, Peter *Human Knowledge and Human Nature*, New York: Oxford University Press, 1992.

7.21   Chisholm, Roderick *Perceiving: A Philosophical Study*, Ithaca, NY: Cornell University Press, 1957.

7.22   —— [1964] 'Theory of Knowledge in America', in R. Chisholm, *The Foundations of Knowing*, Minneapolis: University of Minnesota Press, 1982: 109–93.

7.23   —— *Theory of Knowledge*, 2nd edn, Englewood Cliffs, NJ: Prentice Hall, 1977.

7.24   —— 'The Problem of the Criterion', in R. Chisholm, *The Foundations of Knowing*, Minneapolis: University of Minnesota Press, 1982: 61–75.

7.25   —— *Theory of Knowledge*, 3rd edn, Englewood Cliffs, NJ: Prentice Hall, 1989.

7.26   Cornman, James *Perception, Common Sense, and Science*, New Haven, Conn.: Yale University Press, 1975.

7.27   —— *Skepticism, Justification, and Explanation*, Dordrecht: D. Reidel, 1980.

7.28   Devitt, Michael *Realism and Truth*, Oxford: Basil Blackwell, 1984.

7.29   Dewey, John *The Quest for Certainty*, New York: Putnam, 1929.

7.30   Ducasse, C. J. 'Propositions, Truth, and the Ultimate Criterion of Truth', in C. J. Ducasse, *Truth, Knowledge, and Causation*, London: Routledge & Kegan Paul, 1968.

7.31   Feigl, Herbert 'De Principiis Non-Disputandum...?', in Max Black, ed., *Philosophical Analysis*, Ithaca, NY: Cornell University Press, 1950: 113–47.

7.32   Firth, Roderick 'Lewis on the Given', in P. A. Schilpp, ed., *The Philosophy of C. I. Lewis*, La Salle, Ill.: Open Court, 1969: 329–50.

7.33   Foley, Richard *The Theory of Epistemic Rationality*, Cambridge, Mass.: Harvard University Press, 1987.

7.34   Fumerton, Richard *Metaphysical and Epistemological Problems of Perception*, Lincoln: University of Nebraska Press, 1985.

7.35   Gettier, Edmund 'Is Justified True Belief Knowledge?', *Analysis*, 23 (1963): 121–3. Reprinted in Paul Moser and Arnold vander Nat, eds, *Human Knowledge: Classical and Contemporary Approaches*, New York: Oxford University Press, 1987.

7.36   Goldman, Alan *Empirical Knowledge*, Berkeley: University of California Press, 1988.

7.37   Goldman, Alvin 'A Causal Theory of Knowing', *Journal of Philosophy*, 64 (1976): 357–72.

7.38   —— *Epistemology and Cognition*, Cambridge, Mass.: Harvard University Press, 1986.

7.39   Grice, H. P. and P. F. Strawson 'In Defense of a Dogma', *Philosophical Review*, 65 (1956): 141–51.

7.40   Harman, Gilbert *Thought*, Princeton, NJ: Princeton University Press, 1973.

7.41   —— *Change in View*, Cambridge, Mass.: MIT Press, 1986.

7.42   Hill, Thomas *Contemporary Theories of Knowledge*, New York: Ronald, 1961.

7.43   James, William [1904] 'A World of Pure Experience', in W. James, *Essays in Radical Empiricism and a Pluralistic Universe*, New York: Dutton, 1971: 23–48.

7.44   —— [1907] *Pragmatism*, Cambridge, Mass.: Harvard University Press, 1975.
7.45   —— [1909] *The Meaning of Truth*, Cambridge, Mass.: Harvard University Press, 1975.
7.46   Lehrer, Keith *Knowledge*, Oxford: Clarendon Press, 1974.
7.47   —— *Theory of Knowledge*, Boulder, Col.: Westview, 1990.
7.48   Lewis, C. I. [1926] 'The Pragmatic Element in Knowledge', in P. K. Moser and A. vander Nat, eds, *Human Knowledge*, New York: Oxford University Press, 1986: 201–11.
7.49   —— *Mind and the World-Order*, New York: Scribner, 1929.
7.50   —— *An Analysis of Knowledge and Valuation*, La Salle, Ill.: Open Court, 1946.
7.51   Lycan, William *Judgement and Justification*, Cambridge: Cambridge University Press, 1988.
7.52   Meyers, Robert *The Likelihood of Knowledge*, Dordrecht: D. Reidel, 1988.
7.53   Moore, G. E. 'The Nature of Judgement', *Mind*, n.s., 8 (1899): 176–93. Reprinted in G. E. Moore, *The Early Essays*, ed. Tom Regan, Philadelphia: Temple University Press, 1986.
7.54   —— 'A Defence of Common Sense', in J. H. Muirhead, ed., *Contemporary British Philosophy*, 2nd series, London: Allen & Unwin, 1925: 193–223. Reprinted in G. E. Moore, *Philosophical Papers*, London: Allen & Unwin, 1959: 32–59. Reference is to this reprint.
7.55   —— 'Proof of an External World', *Proceedings of the British Academy*, 25 (1939): 273–300. Reprinted in G. E. Moore, *Philosophical Papers*, London: Allen & Unwin, 1959: 127–50. Reference is to this reprint.
7.56   —— [1941] 'Certainty', in G. E. Moore, *Philosophical Papers*, London: Allen & Unwin, 1959: 227–51.
7.57   Morawetz, Thomas *Wittgenstein and Knowledge*, Amherst: University of Massachusetts Press, 1978..
7.58   Moser, Paul 'William James's Theory of Truth', *Topoi*, 2 (1983): 217–22.
7.59   —— *Empirical Justification*, Dordrecht: D. Reidel, 1985.
7.60   —— 'Foundationalism, the Given, and C. I. Lewis', *History of Philosophy Quarterly*, 5 (1988): 189–204.
7.61   —— 'Lehrer's Coherentism and the Isolation Objection', in J. W. Bender, ed., *The Current State of the Coherence Theory*, Dordrecht: D. Reidel, 1989: 29–37.
7.62   —— *Knowledge and Evidence*, Cambridge: Cambridge University Press, 1989.
7.63   —— 'Realism and Agnosticism', *American Philosophical Quarterly*, 29 (1992): 1–17.
7.64   —— *Philosophy after Objectivity*, New York: Oxford University Press, 1993.
7.65   —— ed. *Empirical Knowledge: Readings in Contemporary Epistemology*, Totowa, NJ: Rowman & Littlefield, 1986.
7.66   —— and Arnold vander Nat, eds *Human Knowledge: Classical and Contemporary Approaches*, New York: Oxford University Press, 1987.
7.67   Neurath, Otto [1932] 'Protocol Sentences', in A. J. Ayer, ed., *Logical Positivism*, New York: Free Press, 1959: 199–208.
7.68   —— *Empiricism and Sociology*, ed. Marie Neurath and R. S. Cohen, Dordrecht: D. Reidel, 1973.

7.69 Oakley, I. T. 'An Argument for Scepticism Concerning Justified Belief', *American Philosophical Quarterly*, 13 (1976): 221–8.

7.70 Peirce, C. S. [1868] 'Questions concerning Certain Faculties claimed for Man', in Philip Wiener, ed., *Charles S. Peirce: Selected Writings*, New York: Dover, 1966: 15–38.

7.71 —— [1878] 'How to make Our Ideas Clear', in Justus Buchler, ed., *Philosophical Writings of Peirce*, New York: Dover, 1955: 23–41.

7.72 Pollock, John *Knowledge and Justification*, Princeton, NJ: Princeton University Press, 1974.

7.73 —— *Contemporary Theories of Knowledge*, Totowa, NJ: Rowman & Littlefield, 1986.

7.74 Quine, W. V. [1951] 'Two Dogmas of Empiricism', in W. V. Quine, *From a Logical Point of View*, 2nd edn, New York: Harper & Row, 1963: 20–46.

7.75 —— *Word and Object*, Cambridge, Mass.: MIT Press, 1960.

7.76 —— 'Reply to Geoffrey Hellman', in L. E. Hahn and P. A. Schilpp, eds, *The Philosophy of W. V. Quine*, La Salle, Ill.: Open Court, 1986: 206–8.

7.77 —— 'Reply to Hilary Putnam', in L. E. Hahn and P. A. Schilpp, eds, *The Philosophy of W. V. Quine*, La Salle, Ill.: Open Court, 1986: 427–31.

7.78 —— *Pursuit of Truth*, Cambridge, Mass.: Harvard University Press, 1990.

7.79 Rescher, Nicholas *The Coherence Theory of Truth*, Oxford: Clarendon Press, 1973.

7.80 —— *Cognitive Systematization*, Oxford: Basil Blackwell, 1979.

7.81 Rorty, Richard *Philosophy and the Mirror of Nature*, Princeton, NJ: Princeton University Press, 1979.

7.82 Russell, Bertrand [1908] 'William James's Conception of Truth', in B. Russell, *Philosophical Essays*, London: Allen & Unwin, 1966: 112–30.

7.83 —— [1911] 'Knowledge by Acquaintance and Knowledge by Description', in B. Russell, *Mysticism and Logic*, Garden City, NY: Doubleday, 1957: 202–24.

7.84 —— *The Problems of Philosophy*, London: Oxford University Press, 1912.

7.85 —— [1914] 'The Relation of Sense-Data to Physics', in B. Russell, *Mysticism and Logic*, Garden City, NY: Doubleday, 1957: 140–73.

7.86 —— [1919] 'On Propositions: What They are and How They mean', in B. Russell, *Logic and Knowledge*, ed. R. C. Marsh, London: Allen & Unwin, 1956: 285–320.

7.87 —— *Philosophy*, London: Norton, 1927.

7.88 —— *An Inquiry into Meaning and Truth*, London: Allen & Unwin, 1940.

7.89 —— 'My Mental Development', in P. A. Schilpp, ed., *The Philosophy of Bertrand Russell*, Evanston, Ill.: Northwestern University Press, 1944: 3–20.

7.90 —— *Human Knowledge: Its Scope and Limits*, New York: Simon & Schuster, 1948.

7.91 —— [1950] 'Logical Positivism', in B. Russell, *Logic and Knowledge*, ed. R. C. Marsh, London: Allen & Unwin, 1956: 367–82.

7.92 —— *My Philosophical Development*, London: Allen & Unwin, 1959.

7.93 Schlick, Moritz [1934] 'The Foundation of Knowledge', in A. J. Ayer, ed., *Logical Positivism*, New York: Free Press, 1959: 209–27.

7.94 —— 'Meaning and Verification', *Philosophical Review*, 45 (1936): 339–69.

7.95 Sellars, Wilfrid [1956] 'Empiricism and the Philosophy of Mind', in W. Sellars, *Science, Perception, and Reality*, London: Routledge & Kegan Paul, 1963.

7.96 —— 'Epistemic Principles', in H.-N. Castañeda, ed., *Action, Knowledge, and Reality*, Indianapolis: Bobbs-Merrill, 1975: 332–48.

7.97 —— 'More on Givenness and Explanatory Coherence', in G. S. Pappas, ed., *Justification and Knowledge*, Dordrecht: D. Reidel, 1979: 169–81.

7.98 Shiner, Roger 'Wittgenstein and the Foundations of Knowledge', *Proceedings of the Aristotelian Society*, 78 (1977): 102–24.

7.99 Shope, Robert *The Analysis of Knowing*, Princeton, NJ: Princeton University Press, 1983.

7.100 Sorensen, Roy ' "*P*, Therefore, *P*" without Circularity', *Journal of Philosophy*, 88 (1991): 245–66.

7.101 Sosa, Ernest *Knowledge in Perspective*, Cambridge: Cambridge University Press, 1991.

7.102 Striker, Gisela 'Sceptical Strategies', in Malcolm Schofield, Myles Burnyeat and Jonathan Barnes, eds, *Doubt and Dogmatism*, Oxford: Clarendon Press, 1980: 54–83.

7.103 —— 'The Problem of the Criterion', in Stephen Everson, ed., *Epistemology*, Cambridge: Cambridge University Press, 1990: 143–60.

7.104 Swain, Marshall *Reasons and Knowledge*, Ithaca, NY: Cornell University Press, 1981.

7.105 Thagard, Paul *Computational Philosophy of Science*, Cambridge, Mass.: MIT Press, 1988.

7.106 Triplett, Timm 'Recent Work on Foundationalism', *American Philosophical Quarterly*, 27 (1990): 93–116.

7.107 Waismann, Friedrich [1930] 'A Logical Analysis of the Concept of Probability', in F. Waismann, *Philosophical Papers*, ed. B. F. McGuinness, Dordrecht: D. Reidel, 1977: 4–21.

7.108 Wittgenstein, Ludwig [1921] *Tractatus Logico-Philosophicus*, trans. D. F. Pears and B. F. McGuinness, London: Routledge & Kegan Paul, 1961.

7.109 —— *On Certainty*, ed. G. E. M. Anscombe and G. H. von Wright, trans. Denis Paul and G. E. M. Anscombe, New York: Harper & Row, 1969.

7.110 —— *Philosophical Remarks*, ed. Rush Rhees, trans. R. Hargreaves and R. White, Oxford: Basil Blackwell, 1975.

7.111 —— *Philosophical Grammar*, ed. Rush Rhees, trans. Anthony Kenny, Oxford: Basic Blackwell, 1974.

7.112 —— *Wittgenstein and the Vienna Circle* (conversations recorded by Friedrich Waismann), ed. B. F. McGuinness, trans. J. Schulte and B. F. McGuinness, Oxford: Basil Blackwell, 1979.

CHAPTER 8

Wittgenstein's later philosophy

John V. Canfield

> *In thinking be simple.* (Tao te Ching)

The early philosophy of Ludwig Wittgenstein (1889–1951) was inspired by the writings of Gottlob Frege and Bertrand Russell. The work of this trio of thinkers forms the stem from which twentieth-century analytic philosophy derives. Wittgenstein's particular influence first showed itself in Russell's 1918 lectures 'The Philosophy of Logical Atomism,' which were, Russell said, 'very largely concerned with explaining certain ideas which I learnt from my friend and former pupil Ludwig Wittgenstein'. Those ideas received their mature form in Wittgenstein's *Tractatus Logico-Philosophicus* (1921). The Vienna Circle philosophers studied this work closely and adopted some of its leading motifs. Rudolf Carnap has been perhaps the most influential of those who initially came under the book's spell. His writings in turn helped shape the position of W. V. Quine, the pivotal American philosopher of the second half of the century.

While elements of the *Tractatus* survive in Wittgenstein's later thought, the two systems differ fundamentally. The later philosophy had its beginnings in Vienna. Wittgenstein, after ventures as a primary-school teacher and monk–gardener, was engaged as an architect when his return to intellectual work was prompted by the Austrian philosopher Moritz Schlick. Starting in 1927, Wittgenstein met occasionally to discuss philosophy with Schlick and others. In 1929 Wittgenstein returned to Cambridge and took up full-time work in philosophy. It was there that his later views grew to completion. Although Wittgenstein never published material from his later thought during his lifetime, his ideas gained currency through his classes, dictated and privately circulated notes (now published as the *Blue and Brown Books*), rumour and various printed reports by others. Those who, through talking or studying with him, were marked by his vision of philosophy, include: Frederick Waismann, Alice Ambrose, Norman Malcolm, G. E. M. Anscombe, Rush Rhees and G. H. von Wright.

The *Philosophical Investigations*, the definitive expression of Wittgenstein's later thought, was published posthumously in 1953. Given Wittgenstein's reputation this book was bound to make an impact on the philosophical community. It was studied closely and mined for insight. It became a major focus of philosophical discussion, and some of its ideas and terms – the terms more than the ideas – became common coin in philosophical discussion. Nonetheless, in the following decades critical response to the book's ideas within the Anglo-American community tended to the negative. Evidently a philosophical world so strongly influenced by the early Wittgenstein left little room for the acceptance of the later philosophy's diametrically opposed position. Thus in the 1950s and 1960s a good deal of Wittgenstein's substantive impact was to provide an adversary view. Throughout this period critics often preferred to deal with the Wittgenstein they found in the secondary literature, thus letting themselves off the difficult job of engaging the primary text itself. An essay by Kripke on rule-following, which appeared in 1981, inaugurated a more recent period of involvement with Wittgenstein's thought. Again the impact on contemporary discussion came largely through the secondary literature.

I believe the cycle has come round: we are entering a period of sustained concern with Wittgenstein's actual words. This return to the texts is long overdue; they contain riches as yet barely touched. For instance Wittgenstein's insightful *Remarks on Philosophical Psychology* is little studied by philosophers working in that area.

On the other hand, that for several decades now Anglo-American philosophers have tended to ignore Wittgenstein's *Nachlass* as a source of substantive insight is not surprising. Above all there is the difficulty of comprehending him. The challenge will be evident to anyone who looks through the *Remarks* just referred to, for example. It is hard, very hard, to see what Wittgenstein is about. The major obstacle is that he writes always from deep within his unique system of thought. Unless we have some sense of the main contours of that system we will find his prose strangely unintelligible. Each sentence taken by itself may be clear; what is hard to grasp is what the sentences are in aid of. What is Wittgenstein up to?

This essay is an attempt to make clear some of the fundamental ideas and assumptions of the *Philosophical Investigations*. I focus on the 'anthropological' element I find in the *Investigations* and on the book's appeal to the simple.

❧ THE MOVE TO THE LATER PHILOSOPHY ❧

Overall aim

In his early thought Wittgenstein took the goal of philosophy to be 'the logical clarification of thoughts' (*Tractatus*, 4.112). Consequently, 'The result of philosophy is not a number of "philosophical propositions", but to make propositions clear' (ibid.). And again:

> The right method of philosophy would be this. To say nothing except what can be said, *i.e.* the propositions of natural science, *i.e.* something that has nothing to do with philosophy: and then always, when someone else wished to say something metaphysical, to demonstrate to him that he had given no meaning to certain signs in his propositions.
>
> (*Tractatus*, 6.53)

The *Tractatus*, then, is anti-philosophical in intent; metaphysics is hidden nonsense. The *Investigations* also sees metaphysics as resulting from a misreading of language. The philosopher has been fooled by certain surface features of language. Wittgenstein's position is an extremely radical one. He saw himself as the last philosopher, remarking that in philosophy the one who comes in last wins the race ([8.12], 34). Last, because he viewed his work as destroying philosophy, at least in its classical metaphysical form. The cure for philosophical delusion remains the same as in the *Tractatus*: a direct confrontation with the actual facts of language. 'What we do', he says in the *Philosophical Investigations*, 'is to bring words back from their metaphysical to their everyday use' ([8.9], §116). The difference is in the nature of such confrontation. I shall begin by looking briefly at both sides of this contrast, illness and cure.

Grammatical fictions; metaphysical pictures

In the *Tractatus* all sensible propositions are pictures; they portray the way things are. In the later philosophy, in contrast, 'pictures' are the bad guys. They are what lead the philosopher into error: 'A picture held us captive. And we could not get outside it, for it lay in our language and language seemed to repeat it to us inexorably' ([8.9], §115). In the later philosophy, the analogue to the metaphysician is not the truth-seeking scientist or austere logician, but rather that hopelessly muddled person, the King in *Through the Looking Glass*, who thinks the Messenger's report that he passed nobody on the road is about a person named 'Nobody'. The King is in the grip of a 'metaphysical picture', his

Nobody an example of a 'grammatical fiction'. Because 'Nobody' in the Messenger's report has the look and surface-grammatical position of a name, the King misreads its depth grammar, taking it to be a singular referring expression; that is to say, he thinks 'nobody' refers to some particular person. His resultant, innocently insulting remark to the Messenger, 'So of course Nobody walks slower than you', is in reality not false but senseless. He speaks a word we understand, but uses it in a manner contrary to its nature, and thereby talks nonsense.

Actual metaphysical pictures are of the same type: a mistaken projection of the surface grammar of an expression. Our understanding is befuddled by a false analogy. For instance, one takes talk about one's intention to be talk about a certain mental something or other. The mistake is virtually forced on us by our language. We say things like: 'I intend to go to the store', or 'My intention is to go to the store', or even, 'I have the intention of going to the store.' When, as philosophers, we wonder about the nature of intention, we recall such examples. In reflecting upon them we already unthinkingly assume that if one has an intention, then surely one has *something*. What could that something be? It isn't anything physical, obviously. I couldn't put my intention in a box, or show it to someone. So it must be something mental. Perhaps a thought of my goal, or perhaps a decision – a mental act – to seek that goal. In 'I have lost my watch, but I have the intention of getting a new one', both 'intention' and 'watch' appear to refer to something. That simple false analogy provides the root strength behind the philosopher's subsequent discussions of intention – discussions that get very sophisticated and convoluted, while never transcending their origin in the absurd.

Again, the word 'I' in 'I think . . .', 'I intend . . .', and so on, has every appearance of being a referring expression. It is a basic question for metaphysics to settle the nature of that referred-to entity. For reasons I shall touch on below, Wittgenstein denies that those uses of 'I' refer. If he is right, the self of philosophy, the alleged or assumed referent in 'I think . . .' is a grammatical fiction; the 'I' of the metaphysician is pictured, not conceived.

There are two plausible objections to the points just made. The first is that in the last two examples the alleged nonsense-producing philosophical pictures are in fact correct. Intentions *qua* mental entities and Cartesian selves are real, not grammatical fictions. The second objection is that since no one will willingly give up philosophy, Wittgenstein's contrary attitude is preposterous.

With regard to the first objection, the strength of one's conviction that intentions are inner and that the I is real are acknowledged and indeed insisted upon by Wittgenstein. There would be no point in combating those views if they did not have such a powerful appeal.

The theses that Wittgenstein fights against are ones that have a strong hold on anyone who begins to think about such matters. More than that, Wittgenstein's real target is not the elaborations of such ideas that one finds in the history of philosophy or in contemporary writings, but rather the root sources of those ideas: the compelling, deeply held intuitions that, for example, intentions must be inner, and that the I – this thing I talk about when I speak in the first person – is real. Such intuitions or strongly held, basic philosophical or proto-philosophical beliefs are the targets of Wittgenstein's critical examinations.

The general methodological objection, that Wittgenstein must be wrong in attacking philosophy *per se*, is initially persuasive. In one form the objection holds that since Wittgenstein grants the existence of various 'language-games' (see below) he must grant philosophy a role, since it too can be considered a language-game. But before making up one's mind on this point it would be well to comprehend fully the position one is rejecting. An essential part of doing that in the present case is to understand what philosophical 'pictures' are being contrasted with. Perhaps the greatest impediment to understanding Wittgenstein is the difficulty of grasping his positive account of the nature of language – his view of meaning as use.

Use

The major change marking Wittgenstein's later philosophy is a movement from his earlier mentalistic to a social view of meaning. The change becomes apparent if we look at a term central to both the *Tractatus* and the *Investigations* – the word 'use' ('*Gebrauch*'). If we took the following proposition from the *Tractatus* out of context it would fit right into the *Investigations*:

> §6.211. In philosophy the question, 'What do we actually use this word or this proposition for?' repeatedly leads to valuable insights.

This thesis, for example, seems congruent with the famous claim of the *Investigations* that, 'For a *large* class of cases . . . the meaning of a word is its use in the language' ([8.9], 43).

But 'use' has undergone a sea change in the transition from the one book to the other, and the agreement here is only on the surface. It is true that in both books *use* is the magical point at which mere signs – mundane things in the world – take on significance, become truly part of language. In the *Tractatus*, *use* is the mental projection of a propositional sign onto its sense by means of a thought. The view is broadly Fregean, and one finds something similar in such contemporary mentalists as Jerry Fodor [8.62]. In the *Investigations*, *use* has nothing to do with the mental; rather, it refers to something social. Wittgenstein takes his cue from the obvious fact that language is something exchanged between people. Words pass back and forth, and change the way we interact. For example, a request is made and complied with. Wittgenstein gives this notion of use *qua* exchange a special interpretation. He holds that the symbol-token is used when it is put in play, when it is uttered in the *language-game*.

The notion of a language-game is perhaps the central term of art of the later philosophy. To understand Wittgenstein one must be able to see language as he did, namely as a collection of language-games. Thus one must understand what a language-game is. But one must also understand how to understand what a language-game is.

A language-game is a custom, a socially constrained pattern of interaction. The word 'game' here emphasizes the fact that word usage is inextricably meshed with human interactions. A word is analogous to a game marker of some sort, a chess knight or an ace of hearts. These objects, themselves inert, take on their usual significance when they are in play. Particular patterns of interaction provide an atmosphere within which the objects live and function. Similarly the child's 'Juice!' functions as a demand only within a certain human context, a custom-regulated pattern of interaction where requests are acknowledged and sometimes complied with. But an explanation of 'language-game' in terms like 'pattern of interaction' doesn't take us very far; and the more general issue arises, of how to explicate any of the concepts we come upon in doing philosophy. We are led to questions of method.

But first let me tie together the ideas of 'picture' and 'use' discussed above, in order to state more clearly Wittgenstein's goal in his later philosophy. Higher-level concepts like intention are essentially linked to lower-level practices; for example, one states what one is up to without using the corresponding high-level word 'intention'. We can approach the understanding of a given such concept either from the top or from the bottom. Here are two series of related utterances ordered from top to bottom. (1) 'I have the intention of going upstairs.' 'I intend to go upstairs.' 'I am going upstairs.' 'Upstairs!' (A child's one-word intention-utterance.) (2) 'I have the belief that the book is heavy.' 'I believe the book is heavy.' 'The book is heavy.' 'Heavy!' (A child's one-word belief-utterance.) Top-down elucidations try to explain or define one high-level concept in terms of others. For instance, 'intention' might be explained by means of 'propositional attitude', or 'language' in terms, in part, of 'mental representations'. We end up giving elucidations in terms of concepts that themselves need elucidation. But as the child's holophrastic utterances exemplify, we learn to use words to state intentions or beliefs, and so on, before we learn meta-level concepts like that of intention and belief. Fruitful efforts at elucidation, the later Wittgenstein believes, follow that bottom-up order of learning.

We all display a perfect mastery of the ground-level linguistic practices. But we have no reflective knowledge of such usages. We haven't stood back and observed them. Instead, we turn our attention to a word like 'intend' or 'language' and try to think what such a thing could be. In this, Wittgenstein said in the *Philosophical Investigations*, we are like primitive men who form the strangest ideas of their own practices ([8.9], §194). The way out is to turn ourselves into own-culture anthropologists, and actually examine our practices. Examining the basic, lower-level word-uses is the proper way to a reflective under-standing of the corresponding higher-level logical words. The result of that examination is to dispel the false picture we form by wrongly projecting words like 'intention', 'belief' or 'I' onto their supposed referent. In general then, confronting the pictures that lie at the roots of metaphysics with a survey of how the related pieces of language actually function is supposed to reveal the fact that our philosophical positions are at their base nonsensical. Thus Wittgenstein [8.9] writes:

§464. My aim is: to teach you to pass from a piece of disguised nonsense to something that is patent nonsense.

The main exegetical strategy of the present essay is to show that nonsense-revealing method at work, primarily in the example of 'inten-tion' and 'I'.

The reversal

The *Tractatus* was top-down in that it deduced its findings from the most general features of language, as in its famous proof of 'simple objects' (2.0211, 2.0212). It was top-down also in that it stated its results in abstract terms. The *Tractatus*'s concern with the simple was thus rather misleading. The simplest proposition, the elementary one, is not known directly, in terms of examples; the latter do not interest the pure logician the author of the *Tractatus* conceived himself to be. One knows only that there are elementary propositions, and that they are made up of a concatenation of simple names that name simple, unanalysable objects. The core of this description is an assumed distinc-tion between naming and saying. But the concepts both of naming and saying, in this special sense, are not given through instances; rather, one presupposes an abstract grasp of the concepts. The later Witt-genstein would say that we have only a misleading picture of such saying and naming, and no real understanding of them.

The reversal of that top-down approach is an essential feature of his later thought. The inversion is announced in this passage from the *Philosophical Investigations*:

§108. . . . The [Tractarian logician's] *preconceived idea* of crystalline purity can only be removed by turning our whole examination round. (One might say: the axis of reference of our examination must be rotated, but about the fixed point of our real need.)

The real need is to understand the nature of language – where this is now seen as something that lacks an essence – and to understand those concepts that are central to philosophy. The reversal, I suggest, is the 180-degree turn from top-down to bottom-up. Instead of looking at the concrete and simple from the vantage-point of the abstract, examine and come to understand the abstract in terms of the simple and concrete. And specifically, in terms of *examples* of simple language-use.

The centrality of examples was announced in the *Blue Book*:

The idea that in order to get clear about the meaning of a general term one had to find the common element in all its applications, has shackled philosophical investigation; for it has not only led to no result, but also made the philosopher dismiss as irrelevant the concrete cases, which alone could have helped him to understand the usage of the general term.

([8.6], 19)

Wittgenstein claims here that the only thing that will enable us to understand the concepts we are interested in are relevant 'concrete cases'. His emphasis on *simple* examples is evident at many places; it is seen in his practice of philosophy when he turns again and again to simple imagined examples, and when he urges us, at numerous points, to consider how a child might learn a given concept. For example his discussion of *belief* in the *Investigations* ([8.9], 190) opens with the question, 'How did we ever come to use such an expression as "I believe?"' What the child first learns will presumably be simple.

To make Wittgenstein's 180-degree reversal is to adopt a genealogical framework, where sophisticated uses of language are to be understood by comparing them to developmentally related simple ones. The reversal also involves focusing one's concern with language at the level of actual use. This is the basic level where one human engages with another in face-to-face interactions in the flow of daily life.

'Logic' in the Philosophical Investigations

In a way reminiscent of the *Tractatus*, the logician's goal is insight into the nature of language in general, and individual, philosophically important concepts in specific. One major difference is the surrender of the idea of the homogeneity of language, and the allied assumption that language has an essence. We can already see Wittgenstein approaching this result in his transitional 'Some Remarks on Logical Form'. There he abandoned the stance that the logician need not sully himself with actual examples, and tried to look in detail at possible analyses of colour propositions. As a result he had to abandon the idea that the logical rules governing language hold universally, across the board. The rule that if a point in visual space is one colour it cannot be another is now conceived, not as a hidden, truth-functional tautology (not, that is, as an instance of a general logical truth) but as a special rule holding of colour words. But such 'special' rules are still thought of as 'logical'.

The idea of Wittgenstein's transitional writing, as given in the manuscripts published in *Philosophical Remarks*, that words belonged to families, and that language is thus analysable into distinct calculi, with their own rules, developed in his later thought into the idea of embodied calculi, as it were, where words are employed in language-games. Language thus comes to be conceived of as a collection of language-games. There is nothing in common among these 'games'; nothing that makes them part of language. They have no shared essence. Rather essence becomes scattered. Each language-game has its own logic, its own unique rules and offices.

Logic remains, as in the *Tractatus*, the deepest part of philosophy. But the business of the logician has changed. It is no longer to investigate the universal presuppositions of propositions – general features of 'logical space' – but to investigate one by one the distinctive properties of the multifarious language-games. There is no longer *a* logical space; each language-game has its own unique logical space. The idea of coming in contact with the simplest case – the atomic proposition – only through abstract and very general characterizations is replaced by the idea of looking at, in the sense of actually observing, various simple examples of words in use. Wittgenstein's changed conception of logic is a natural consequence of his changed views on language. It should perhaps be emphasized that that view of logic is radically opposed to the standard one found in elementary logic courses.

For Wittgenstein the subject matter of logic is broadened enormously. Traditionally logic deals, for the most part, with propositions or truth-claims. From the point of view of someone impressed by the power of mathematics and science such a study would cover what matters in language. In contrast Wittgenstein points to a multiplicity of word uses beyond the scope of traditional logic. The list he gives in the *Investigations* provides only a limited idea of that diversity, but it is a starting point:

> Giving orders and obeying them.... Describing the appearance of an object, or giving its measurements.... Constructing an object from a description (a drawing).... Reporting an event.... Speculating about an event.... Forming and testing a hypothesis.... Making up a story; and reading it.... Play-acting.... Singing catches.... Guessing riddles.... Making a joke; telling it.... Asking, thanking, cursing, greeting, praying.
>
> ([8.9], §23)

A Wittgensteinian logic takes language in all its variety, and with its full involvement with human life, as its subject. 'Logic' no longer deals with presuppositions common to all our contentful utterances, but with assumptions common to a type of utterance – where the types are counted in terms of language-games. To state the 'logical' presumptions of a given utterance is to describe the 'logic' or 'depth grammar' of the language-game it is uttered in. In one such language-game, for example, we make first-person intention-utterances, and one 'logical feature' of such utterances is that they are governed by a criterion of truthfulness, a point I shall discuss below.

What is the simple, that we might examine it?

The new 'logician,' unlike the old, scorns analysis of the sort that tries to explicate a given concept in terms of its supposed meaning-elements. What then corresponds to the simple in the later philosophy, since Wittgenstein no longer believes in that product of analysis, the atomic proposition? What corresponds to elementary propositions, I believe, are what he sometimes calls 'signals'. These are utterances, often of one word, that play a role in a simple language-game, as in the example of the child's request 'Juice!' Instead of atomic propositions, words uttered in simple language-games.

There are two sources for such simple language-games. One is to make them up. The well-known example of the builders ([8.9], §2) supposes that in the only piece of language a tribe has, a builder cries out the names of various materials, such as 'Slab!' or 'Beam!' whereupon helpers respond by bringing the objects named. Such language-games allow Wittgenstein to discuss difficult problems in a sharply focused way. But his imaginary examples may strike the reader as too schematic; it is hard to connect those simple games with our actual language.

I believe the examples work effectively only when considered along with another type of simple example. Wittgenstein alludes to such examples in his frequent admonitions to examine how a child might learn a given piece of language. (In addition to the example cited earlier, see: [8.9], 200; [8.11], I: §§163, 309, 346, 375.) If we carry out those suggested examinations in detail we can come to see his own made-up examples in the right light and we can gain an understanding of his many 'logical' remarks.

I suggest we drop the 'might' from the question about the child, and replace it with a 'does' – how in fact do children master speech? Observing them doing so can lead to a clear view of the simple language-games that form what is perhaps Wittgenstein's primary paradigm. There the conceptual link between learning and thing learned that Wittgenstein stressed (for example in *Remarks on the Philosophy of Psychology* [8.11], II: 337) becomes plain: observing children coming to a mastery of speech allows us to perceive the details of the language-games they master. Such examples are to be our tutors. They will lead us to an understanding of two things: the puzzling terms of art Wittgenstein employs, including 'language-game' and 'use,' and second, the concepts of central interest to philosophy, such as *intention, reference* or *self*. That appeal to the simple is a Wittgensteinian, bottom-up approach to understanding Wittgenstein. This line of interpretation develops suggestions by Norman Malcolm ([8.34], 133–53) concerning Wittgenstein's claim that language is an extension of action.

It might be argued, however, that there is an element in Wittgenstein's thought inconsistent with a genetic approach. He sometimes makes the point that our present way of speaking and acting could conceivably be what it is independently of what we were taught as children ([8.6], 12). If so, then the connection between the child's early language and the language of the adult would be broken; learning about the former would not teach us about the latter. But here and in similar passages Wittgenstein is talking about a causal connection; he is making the point that one can conceive, for instance, of someone just inheriting a capacity to speak without his having been educated or trained in language. The focus of my concern with tracing paths from the child's language-games to the adult's is not causal; the causes of the adult's speech behaviour are not in question. What is in question is the nature or character – the shape and function – of that behaviour. The hypothesis I attribute to Wittgenstein is that getting clear about the character of the child's language-games tells us something about the adult's. The patterns may be similar, whether or not there is a causal connection between the two. Finding the simple pattern in the more complex, or seeing the more complex as a variation of the simple, provides insight of a sort into the complex. Analogously, examining a primitive internal-combustion machine may help us understand the workings of a later, more complex version even if the later one sprang independently of any prototypes from the mind of its inventor, so that there exists no causal connection between the two variants.

❧ THE ROOTS OF LANGUAGE ❧

Action

I have been underscoring Wittgenstein's primitivism. The present section enlarges upon his appeal to the primitive, in part by introducing a threefold typology of 'proto-type,' 'gestural stage' and 'primitive language-game'. This categorization is implicit in Wittgenstein, and stating it helps us understand him. Some readers may object that the subsequent discussions of language-learning and primate behaviour have no place in an introductory presentation of Wittgenstein, and certainly the discussions will sound strange in comparison to standard accounts. My justification is that the following remarks emphasize two crucial, interconnected elements of Wittgenstein's later thought that are often overlooked or underplayed. One is his bottom-up approach, the other is his assumption that language is an extension of action.

'Instinctive' behaviour

I have already introduced the first point, and shall start here with the second, in particular with some quotations establishing the interpretive thesis that for Wittgenstein language is an extension of action patterns underlying early speech. The following passage from On Certainty [8.13] shows the 'logician' explicitly concerned with the primitive:

> §475. I want to regard man here as an animal; as a primitive being to which one grants instinct but not ratiocination. As a creature in a primitive state. Any logic good enough for a primitive means of communication needs no apology from us. Language did not emerge from some kind of ratiocination.

The essay 'Cause and Effect: Intuitive Awareness' is central for understanding Wittgenstein on the primitive. He writes there, for instance:

> The origin and the primitive form of the language-game is a reaction: only from this can more complicated forms develop.

> Language – I want to say – is a refinement, 'im Anfang war die Tat' [In the beginning was the deed.]
>
> ([8.8], 420)

Instead of 'primitive form' he later speaks of the 'proto-type' of the language-game (ibid., 421). He speaks of 'instinctive' behaviour, as when a person 'instinctively' (or perhaps better, *naturally*) looks from the effect to the cause, for example looking to see what has just stung him (ibid., 410). He also refers to the 'biological function' of these 'primitive forms' of behaviour:

> The [language-]game doesn't begin with doubting whether someone has a toothache, because that doesn't ... fit the game's biological function in our life. In its most primitive form it is a reaction to somebody's cries and gestures, a reaction of sympathy or something of the sort.
>
> (ibid., 414)

Wittgenstein believes we can gain insights into our concepts by examining their roots in primitive or natural forms of interactive behaviour:

> Believing that someone else is in pain, doubting whether he is, are so many natural kinds of behaviour towards other human beings; and our language is but an auxiliary to and extension of this behaviour. I mean: our language is an extension of the more primitive behaviour. (For our *language-game* is a piece of behaviour).
>
> ([8.11], I: §151)

The child naturally comes to participate in the primitive behaviour patterns basic to language. Thus consider the acts and responses connected with request words. At the earliest stage the child simply cries when hungry, or cold, or wet, and so on. Then the mother responds, say by bringing it to her breast, whereupon the child does its part by suckling. Similarly, there is the interaction pattern of the child's reaching towards something, and the mother's response of handing it to the child.

Such interactions arise naturally, without any drill or explicit instruction, between child and caretaker. They support the development of language, which could not arise without them. I shall call the basic stage of interaction just discussed the language-game's proto-type. The proto-typical behaviour occurs at a stage preceding even the simplest symbol use, as it precedes the simplest use of what I shall call natural gestures.

Intention

In the interaction underlying the child's mastery of intention-language the mother responds to what she sees the child is up to. She might react by calling out a warning, and the child in turn might respond to her fear-laden voice by stopping in its tracks. We might speak here of the child's *projects* – its being engaged in doing something, for example, feeding itself with a spoon, putting small stones one by one into a can or buttoning its shirt. Such actions are paradigmatically voluntary ones ([8.11], II: §270). In the language-game proto-type in question, then, the child is engaged upon some project; the mother observes or antici-pates the child's project and reacts appropriately, and the child in turn may respond to that response. This action pattern is rooted in our animal nature, in particular in our ability to anticipate one another's actions and our propensity to respond appropriately. The same antici-pation and similar responses are found among apes.

The gestural stage

Natural gestures arise in the context of, and are inseparable from, such proto-type behaviours. An underlying action pattern is modified, emphasized or added to, in a way that brings it to the other's attention, and thus it becomes a natural gesture. For example one might turn an action into a gesture by performing it in the absence of the interactive behaviours normally preceding it.

The biologically based nature of such primitive gestures can be seen in examples from primate studies:

> In order to groom [the chimpanzee infant's] side and armpits, [the mother] takes his arm and pulls it upwards. [Later] the infant ... adopt[s] this posture unaided while his mother grooms him.... At the age of 11 months an infant ... came up to his mother, sat down in front of her and adopted this posture.... Almost predictably, his mother groomed him.
>
> (Plooij [8.75], 117)

Similarly Plooij speaks of, 'The development by human infants of an arm-raising gesture which at first appears in the infant's repertoire as a passive response to being picked up and later becomes an active request to be picked up' (ibid.).

Here is an example of a natural gesture of intention. A pre-verbal child, moving towards the steps and obviously aiming to climb them, stops, turns its head and makes eye contact with its mother. In doing so the child calls attention to its crawling towards the stairs, using a natural gesture indicative of what it is up to; its look, in that context, signals its intention to climb the stairs. The mother may respond by walking up the stairs behind the child, allowing it to hone its developmental skills while ensuring its safety.

The gesture cannot live outside the context distinctive of the corresponding proto-behaviour. That is, it cannot be *that* gesture outside that particular context. For two reasons. One is that context disambiguates a gesture; the same motion can be a request- or an intention-gesture, depending upon the context. A second, more radical reason, is that a social group cannot employ, say, a gesture to initiate grooming if they are not creatures that groom one another. Nor give an intention-gesture if they are not creatures who do anticipate and respond to one another's projects.

The simple language-game

The natural gesture seems to say this: take up the usual interaction pattern at this point. There is the interaction pattern of the infant chimp climbing onto the mother to be transported. The gesturing mother is saying in effect, take up the climbing-aboard routine now. Or, in the instance of the baby's stopping to make eye contact: take up the routine of your responding to my crawling to the stairs and climbing them. The gestures are a stylized overlay upon the prior naturally existing interaction pattern.

A further and crucial stylization is made within the same proto-forms: one-word language-games develop from within the proto-type or its gestural embellishment. The word is no mere simple embellishment or stylization of the foundational, proto-behaviour. The word *qua* symbol-token is so stylized that its connection with the job it performs is purely conventional, and in that sense arbitrary. Any other short and readily pronounceable or readily perceived token-type would have served the same purpose equally well. This arbitrary thing, the word, or other symbol, replaces the gesture and takes over its function. In moving spontaneously to a use of one of its culture's words the child steps into language.

In the simple language-game the symbol *qua* signal takes over the role of the gesture, which in turn took over the role played by the mother's observation of the child within the proto-typical behaviour pattern. The word stands in for the gesture and does the same job. For instance, the child might say 'up' instead of gesturing with a look; the word, like the gesture, tells the mother what the child is about. Language is thus an extension of an underlying action pattern; and we see the point of Wittgenstein's quoting Goethe's 'In the beginning was the deed.' The symbol is the symbol-token employed in the corresponding language-game. To have a concept – to know the symbol – is to be able to use the symbol-token in the language-game. Grasping a concept is a matter of having a certain skill, not a matter of connecting some idea, 'sense' or referent to a symbol-token.

In being able to speak its intention the child manifests two linked abilities. The first is one shared with any number of animals – it is to evince the behaviour we call acting with an aim. It is to pursue a project. The second ability is, it seems, unique to humans, at least if we confine the contrast to animals in the wild. It is to speak a word or otherwise provide a symbol-token that indicates the end point of the project the person is in fact engaged upon.

While this later ability is (with the earlier qualification) unique, it is but a small embellishment of a capability which is not unique – the talent of indicating one's project by a natural gesture. The passage to speech does not cross some great ontological divide; there is no fundamental difference between us and other animals. In fact, captive chimpanzees can learn to 'express their intentions' in symbols. Here Wittgenstein, as opposed say to Chomsky, is a Darwinian [8.57].

From the primitive to the sophisticated

The child's one-word uses look back to more primitive stages, and forward to sophisticated adult uses. Developments that lead towards our complex everyday talk of intentions include the use of intention-utterances of two or more words such as 'Climbing chair'. The end point of a project is now indicated by several words, one betokening an action and the other the object to be acted on. The function of the intention-utterance – to betoken the project's end point – remains unchanged.

Ordered intention-utterances, such as 'Jump first, then shirt', are another development from the holophrastic phase, as are a child's later conditional intention-utterances, such as: 'When I get to Daniel's I'll have a drink of juice.' Eventually, with the learning of clock and calendar time, the child will come to amalgamate temporal references and intention-utterances to produce statements like 'I'm going upstairs at seven o'clock.'

Simple intention-utterances stand at the base of one of the major branches of our language. Promising, making assignations, exhorting someone, deliberating all presuppose or in some way incorporate the early simple language-game of intention-utterance. In general simple language-customs grow out of proto-typical interaction patterns; in turn the simple customs change, grow and combine into the multitude of complex ones we participate in daily. At the far end of that evolution are language-games of extreme complexity such as theoretical physics, but even these retain their roots in the primitive.

For Wittgenstein a perspicuous way of viewing adult intention-utterances is to compare them with the core interaction pattern present in the language-game proto-type. A statement like 'I'm going out to get a paper' has a clear similarity to the child's 'I'm going upstairs' gesture. Both reflect that earlier pattern of anticipation and response.

The child learns its language by mastering an increasingly complex set of interaction patterns – customs – in which words, like tools, serve various ends, have various functions. This transition to increased complexity and variety nowhere requires a passage from word use to mentally resident concept. The players learn more language-games and more complicated ones; but that never requires any inward, mental playing.

Third-person intention-statements; syntax

The one-word intention-utterances I have described are first-person uses. The child also masters third-person uses attributing intentions to others. The distinction between the two types of use is critical and I shall discuss it later in the section on *Äusserungen* (pp. 269–71). Here I shall confine myself to a few observations about 'I'.

To master the third-person uses the child must learn to deploy two distinct criteria. One governs whether or not the person referred to has the intention in question. Here the child will rely upon what it observes, including what the described person may say. The second criterion concerns the identity of the described person. The child must be able to pick out the person named 'Daddy' or referred to as 'you', and so on. Neither of these criteria operate in the first-person case. The child does not base its intention-utterance on self-observation, or, of course, upon hearing its own utterance. Nor does it deploy some criterion to establish that it is the person whose intention is being stated. As Wittgenstein put it, the speaker here does not choose the mouth through which it speaks ([8.6], 68). Similarly, when the child indicates what it wants by a gesture, it does not choose the arm with which it points. It simply points, and in the other case, it simply says 'Upstairs'.

Consider the syntax of first- and third-person intention-statements. The regimentation of syntax operates upon symbol-token uses. In the simplest third-person intention case two functional elements are regimented, one betokening the end point of the person's project, the other indicating whose project it is. In 'Daddy upstairs', both functional places are filled. 'Daddy is going to go upstairs' is a correctly regimented, or grammatical, version.

In the first-person case the regimentation of grammar requires that a word occur where there is no corresponding function. Here the child initially does not betoken itself; and as far as function goes there is not and need never be a need for such a betokening. The child employs no criterion of identity to pick itself out; and the hearer, being in the presence of the child, and observing that it is the child who speaks, needs no word to tell it who is speaking. The child's 'Upstairs' matches functionally the role the utterance plays. But grammar requires regimentation into subject and predicate, and so the child learns to embellish its 'Upstairs' and to say instead something along the lines of 'I am going upstairs.' These reflections lay the ground work for understanding Wittgenstein's rejection of the idea that 'I' is a referring expression.

❧ TERMS OF ART ❧

I shall now show how the examples discussed above shed light on some of the later Wittgenstein's ideas.

Use; language-game

To use a word is to utter it in a language-game. But what is a language-game? A folk-philosophical criticism of Wittgenstein is that he fails to answer that question, in that he supplies no 'criterion of identity' for 'language-game'. What he fails to supply, presumably, is some top-down account of when something counts as a given language-game. By his own lights, however, Wittgenstein does not owe us a top-down elucidation of 'language-game'. Defining his technical terms by means of one another is bootless; defining them in a non-circular way in ordinary speech or in someone else's system is impossible. What one really needs to learn is how to use the term; and one can. The proper answer to 'What is a language-game?' is: this is one, and this, and this, and so on. Presented thus the answer may seem lame, but it is another matter if the this's refer to detailed and closely examined examples, for instance of the sort indicated in the previous section. The answer to the objection then is to reject the possibility of a useful top-down definition or analysis of 'language-game'. The concept is to be communicated rather by means of examples and remarks about them.

In introducing the term 'language-game' in the *Investigations*,

Wittgenstein appeals to examples from a child's mastery of language. He writes:

§7. We can also think of the whole process of using words in (2) [the slab-beam language] as one of those games by means of which children learn their native language. I will call these games 'language-games' and will sometimes speak of a primitive language as a language-game.

When Wittgenstein says, 'I call these games "language-games"', the reference class is 'games by means of which children learn their native language'. But the latter phrase is misleading. Wittgenstein does not mean merely that the 'games' in question have the heuristic function of getting the child to learn some further piece of language. Rather, what the child learns in those cases *is* language – primitive, simple, but *bona fide* language.

In the *Blue Book* Wittgenstein introduces 'language-game' as follows:

Language-games are the forms of language with which a child begins to make use of words. The study of language-games is the study of primitive forms of language or primitive languages.

([8.6], 17)

Here it is less obvious, but nonetheless true, that the explanation is in terms of examples; on the other hand the passage says more clearly than does the *Investigations* §7 that the paradigmatic instances are children's simple language-games. His reason for introducing the idea of a language-game, and thus turning our attention to the phenomena in question, is also made clear in the *Blue Book*:

When we look at such simple forms of language the mental mist which seems to enshroud our ordinary use of language disappears. We see activities, reactions, which are clear-cut and transparent. On the other hand we recognize in these simple processes forms of language not separated by a break from our more complicated ones.

([8.6], 17).

I have mentioned only a few such 'simple forms of language'. A more complete answer to the question 'What is a language-game?' would consider numerous others. A fundamental tenet of Wittgenstein's is that language-games are widely diverse.

Wittgenstein's use of 'use' is also to be learned through examples, and indeed the same ones as before, 'use' and 'language-game' being linked terms. Certain words *qua* sounds take on 'meaning' by being used, that is by being proffered within a language-game. Wittgenstein's use of 'use' is peculiar to him, being parasitical on his unique conception of a language-game.

Function

This word is used originally with regard to artifacts and machines. Biologists apply it, by analogical extension, to animals and plants. Wittgenstein further extends its use to the case of words that play a role in language-games (see, for example, [8.9], §555).

In its original use 'function' is applied at three different locations. Parts of an artifact have functions in so far as they contribute to the functioning of the whole. The artifact itself has a function. We also speak of the function of a function: of the role an artifact with a particular job plays in the life of the people who employ it. This stone-age tool drills holes in rock, but what did the people who made it want such holes for?

Different words, like the various parts of an artifact, function differently in a given utterance. One word in a sentence may indicate when something will be done, and another what that something is. Or compare the various jobs of the words in Wittgenstein's example of the request 'Five red apples' ([8.9], §1). The various language-games themselves have functions – for instance to state intentions, or requests. And that a language-game has such a function may be useful for a people in various ways.

Some characterizations of Wittgenstein on 'usefulness' collapse that threefold distinction of function of part, function of whole and function of function (for example Kripke [8.68], 294).

Family resemblance

As noted, the later Wittgenstein rejects his earlier search for the essence of language, in the sense of some feature or group of features necessary and sufficient for something to count as speech. He compares the concept of language to that of a game. What do all and only games have in common? One will be unable to give a non-circular answer. Examining various games will reveal the same sort of thing one might find in examining a family portrait. Granddad and Junior may have the same-shaped nose, Junior and Sally may have quite different noses but closely similar eyes, and so on. In the case of games this means that something is admitted to the family not because it has the common and defining features of a game; there are none. It is admitted rather because it has some of the properties of standard examples of games.

Wittgenstein is not saying we cannot distinguish games from other things. Warfare is no game, nor is ordering pizza, and so on. We distinguish games from non-games but not on the basis of necessary and sufficient properties. When all the features of some newly invented activity are plainly visible and noticed, to call the thing a game is not to make a hypothesis, but rather to make an implicit decision to count this in the class of games. Wittgenstein thinks that in addition to 'language' and 'game' many ordinary concepts are of the family-resemblance type. 'Rule' and 'expectation', for example.

Criteria

As ordinarily used a 'criterion' may be evidence or it may be something stronger. In the *Blue Book* Wittgenstein says he shall use 'criterion' in that second way. Thus he distinguishes symptoms of angina from phenomena that establish the presence of angina in virtue of rule of language. Suppose that angina is defined by medical science as 'an inflammation caused by a particular bacillus' ([8.6], 25). Then:

> I call 'symptom' a phenomenon of which experience has taught us that it coincided . . . with the phenomenon which is our defining criterion. Then to say 'A man has angina if this bacillus is found in him' is a tautology or it is a loose way of stating the definition of 'angina'. But to say, 'A man has angina whenever he has an inflamed throat' is to make a hypothesis.
>
> (ibid).

The many discussions of criteria in the secondary literature sought to establish more clearly what Wittgenstein's conception is. In doing so they concentrated on the example of pain, which does not fit too well with the symptom-definition distinction just presented. Wittgenstein was widely believed to have accepted two claims: (1) the criteria for a person's being in pain are behavioural, but (2) the behaviour in question may be present even though the person is not in pain (it might be a case of pretence, for instance). How, in the face of the phenomenon of pretence, could it be a 'tautology' that someone's behaving in the way normally indicative of pain really is in pain? To surmount the difficulty it became common to say that Wittgenstein accepted behavioural criteria for psychological predicates, but held some fancy view about the nature of the connection between criterion and inner state. He was said by some, for example Gordon Baker [8.53], to have discovered a new logical relationship, halfway, as it were, between empirical support and entailment. Some called the relationship that of 'necessary evidence': that such and such behaviour is *evidence* for saying a person is in pain is itself a necessary or conceptual truth (Hacker [8.25]). Again, the alleged virtue of the 'necessary-evidence' interpretation of criteria is that it saves us from a wrong commitment to definitional criteria in cases like pain-allegation.

Wittgenstein, however, gives a different account of the phenomenon of pain-attribution, one that reflects the developmental or genealogical aspect of his thought. He writes, for example:

> If pretending were not a complicated pattern, it would be imaginable that a newborn child pretends.
>
> Therefore I want to say that there is an original genuine expression of pain; that the expression of pain therefore is not equally connected to the pain and to the pretence.

([8.15], 56)

The language-game allowing judgements of pain comes before – is logically prior to – one allowing judgements of pretence. When Wittgenstein says that the behavioural expression is not equally connected to the pain and to the pretence, he means that the fundamental connection is to pain; the behaviour can only be counted as pretence against a further complicated background of conditions that block the normal move to an ascription of pain.

The person who applies a criterion does so while situated in certain life circumstances, as a fly-fisher casts a line while standing in a stream. The person need not be able to describe the circumstances; need not even be aware of them as such. They are the place he operates from. For a criterion to be met those circumstances – of everyday normal life – may be required. The mother who judges her child to be in pain does so against a background of such normal circumstances. She makes the judgement without first establishing that those circumstances obtain. It is a rule of language – a truth of implicit definition – that in those circumstances that behaviour establishes that the child is in pain. There is no need here to appeal to a special relationship of 'necessary evidence'. This is so even though we can imagine a case where what appears to be identical behaviour is present and the pain absent (Martians secretly substitute an android for the baby, and so on). In other, more complex cases, indecisiveness is built into the rule governing the application of psychological predicates. In some such cases the rule dictates there is no telling – say about whether a person is sincere or pretending ([8.15], 59).

Questions of circumstance enter into philosophical discussions of criteria in another way. Philosophers' debates over 'personal identity' often deal with questions like this: if Jones enters a matter-transportation booth, disappears, and an identical person appears in the receiving station, is it Jones? If two identical people appear in two receiving stations, is either Jones? Are both Jones? Here the philosopher appeals to our intuition to make judgements about such cases; the philosopher then tries to discover criteria of personal identity that capture those intuitions. If as Wittgenstein believes ([8.9], §80) criterial rules govern judgements only within normal circumstances of application, such appeals to intuition are bogus; in making judgements about those outré cases one is, by implicit stipulation, extending the rule to cover those cases. Before such extension the questions have no right or wrong answer, because our concepts are geared to work in the world as it is and do not come complete with a decision procedure for every possible case. So the interesting question is not what our intuitions are, in such cases, but rather what stipulative extensions of the normal concept those intuitions presuppose.

Äusserungen

This is one of the later philosophy's most significant technical terms; it is used in contrast with certain closely related *descriptions*. Writers have discussed *Äusserungen* under the rubric 'avowals'. I find that term misleading and since I can discover no suitable single English rendition, I shall use the German. As an approximation (but see the caveat below) *Äusserungen* may be defined as first-person present-tense psychological assertions. 'I am in pain' and 'I intend to go' are *Äusserungen*; 'I was in pain', 'He is in pain', 'I intended to go,' and 'She intends to go' are descriptions. The distinction between *Äusserungen* and descriptions is at the core of Wittgenstein's philosophy of psychology.

Whether something is an *Äusserung* is not solely a function of syntax. A sentence such as 'I am afraid' may sometimes express an *Äusserung* and sometimes not. If my words are as it were a groan of fear, they are an *Äusserung*; if, in contrast, they report the results of my reflecting on how I have been behaving during the day, they constitute a description ([8.11], I:§832; II:§156). In the latter case my words are a description since they are based on my observations or remembrances of how I have been acting.

In its primitive, one-word form an *Äusserung* replaces a gesture inside some language-game proto-type. An exaggerated or deliberately prolonged groan of fear might be replaced, in a later case, by a word like 'Afraid!' Or the looking gesture I have discussed by the word 'Upstairs!' The word in each case is no more a description than is the gesture it replaces. The first gesture says in effect, 'Take up the responding-to-my-expression-of-fear behaviour', and that is no description of an inner state. Similarly for the other case. If 'I am afraid' serves the same function as 'Afraid!' in the above example, then it too is an

Äusserung. Assertions of third-person psychological predicates function differently; for one thing, they are subject to distinctive truth-criteria. Thus my judgement that *she* intends to go upstairs will normally be made on the basis of observation of her behaviour. Perhaps she told me where she is going, or I saw her get up and move towards the stairs, obviously intending to climb them. My first-person intention-utterance – at least in the standard case reminiscent of the child's one-word intention-utterances – is not based on observation. 'I intend to go upstairs' is not said on the basis of my seeing how I behave, nor on the basis of looking within and becoming aware of some inner intention-state.

One reason for thinking that utterances like 'I intend to go!' do nevertheless describe the inner is that the one who makes them is certain they are true; whereas with regard to third-person remarks like 'She intends to go' there is uncertainty: perhaps for all I know she does not really intend that. The alleged explanation for this asymmetry is that the speaker is directly aware of his inner state of intention, while he cannot be aware of the inner states of another person. Wittgenstein's concept of an *Äusserung* yields an alternative account of the asymmetry. The idea is that the certainty in the first-person case is a feature of the language-game in which the utterance is made. In particular, *Äusserungen* are governed by what he calls a criterion of truthfulness: unless the speaker is lying or otherwise fooling around, what he says is true ([8.9], 222). The language-game itself allows no room for an honest mistake. This feature carries over from a stage in the unfolding of language that precedes doubt and uncertainty. This is an early phase, encountered in simple language-games of children where questions of uncertainty or doubt simply have no place. The question 'Does it really want that?' makes no sense in reference to the child from an earlier example who is making a grasping gesture directed at a toy. When the child has learned to ask by name for things, doubt and uncertainty are still precluded. In context the child's request 'Ball!' allows no uncertainty about what it seeks. That early pattern of request and response can be altered later into one where doubt is in order. A psychoanalyst may doubt the truth of a patient's desire-report, while granting its sincerity. But now a new twist has been added to the language-game; new criteria introduced. The primitive stage – the original language-game – is not outgrown. The earlier use of request words survives and is honoured throughout the speaker's life; it is the main branch from which the psychoanalytic pattern is an offshoot. Similarly, at any stage we may revert to a language of gestures in order to communicate, as we might have done as children, what we want from another. The language-game of a bygone time may once more be in play, just as the simple language-game, with its criterion of sincerity, is often in play between adult speakers. When the child has mastered the relevant piece of language there is no room for doubting whether it really is afraid when it sincerely says it is – on the assumption that its 'I am afraid' can be seen as a replacement for the earlier, primitive, *Äusserung* 'Afraid!' Whereas in the *description* 'I am afraid', based on self-observation and memory, a sincere mistake is possible.

Äusserungen do not describe the inner. That feature was noted in my previous discussion of intention-utterances. That intention-*Äusserungen* do not function to point to something internal to the speaker is shown by the fact that the hearer has no interest whatever, here, in the inner life of the speaker. Be that as it may, the important point for the hearer is what the speaker is up to. *That* is what the speaker wishes to communicate, and what the hearer responds to by some appropriate act. We can observe the feature in question quite clearly when we consider simple language-games of the kind discussed earlier. Wittgenstein puts the point graphically:

> Does something happen when I . . . intend this or that? – Does nothing happen? – That is not the point; but rather: why should what happens within you interest me? (His soul may boil or freeze, turn red or blue: what do I care?)
>
> ([8.11], I: §215)

The distinctiveness of first-person psychological utterances is important for Wittgenstein because the mistaken idea that *Äusserungen* are descriptions leads to philosophical confusion. If for example 'I am in pain' describes something, it must obviously be something inner; and thus is born the idea of pain as an inner object. And so too for the range of psychological terms of interest to philosophy, including intention and belief. In short the 'logical' observation that intention-utterances and the like are not descriptions helps destroy the false picture of those utterances that underlies the metaphysical hypostatization of mind.

The bedrock of language

Section 201 of the *Philosophical Investigations* reads in part:

> There is a way of grasping a rule which is *not* an *interpretation*, but which is exhibited in what we call 'obeying the rule' and 'going against it' in actual cases.
>
> Hence there is an inclination to say: every action according to the rule is an interpretation. But we ought to restrict the term 'interpretation' to the substitution of one expression of the rule for another.

271

Wittgenstein's point is that the instances in which we interpret some-thing – whether a rule, or a remark – are underwritten by cases in which we simply act according to a rule, or simply respond to a remark.

In a normal case the mother does not interpret her child's reaching and pointing gesture; she simply responds, perhaps by giving the child the object it wants. She reacts similarly to the child's one-word request-utterance. The language-game is one of verbal act and response: com-plying, refusing, pointedly ignoring, suggesting an alternative, and so on. One pitches, the other catches. It is like a baboon troop-leader's gestural offering to carry one of its females past a dangerous point; a matter of gesture and, immediately, response.

A rule of the simple language-game is that the mother's response centres on the object the child has named; *that* is what she gives the child, or what she refuses it, and so on. Once the language-game has been established, the mother's behaviour constitutes a 'way of grasping a rule which is not an interpretation but which is exhibited in what we call "obeying the rule"'.

The bedrock of language is such patterns of action and response comprising the simple language-games and their more elaborate forms. Questions of whether a word should be interpreted this way or that, or of whether a certain action is in accordance with a given rule, presuppose those earlier forms, where questions of interpretation have no place.

Those basic interaction forms count as customs:

> To obey a rule, to make a report, to give an order, to play a
> game of chess, are *customs* (uses, institutions).

([8.9], §199)

If we add 'to make a request', and 'to state an intention' we can see more clearly the truth of that remark. Simple language-games are customs, in that they are elaborations of naturally existing interaction patterns. In these elaborations certain arbitrary elements – words – play a role. That these words function as they do is not solely a matter of some natural or instinctive bit of behaviour being implemented. Rather it is in part a question of what the customary usage is; a matter determined by the culture. Another tribe will employ another word. But the language-game proto-type in which the various alternative words function is common to the different tribes:

> The common behaviour of mankind is the system of reference
> by means of which we interpret an unknown language.

([8.9], §205)

To interpolate some inner activity of meaning assessment that suppos-edly mediates between, say, the hearing of a request and the response to it is to add a head to the head we already have (to borrow an expression). This sort of interpolative fallacy is plain in the following example. To explain a baby's smiling at the appearance of its mother one might suppose – some social scientists have indeed hypothesized – that the baby inwardly consults a series of stored images of those it favours, compares the images to its present visual perceptions and smiles when it gets a match (Sroufe and Waters [8.80]). But then how does it recognize a match between perception and image? Does it do so by interpolating a series of images of matches between face-images and face-perceptions? That way lies an infinite regress. But if one supposes the baby just does recognize the match between image and perception, why not suppose that it just does recognize its mother? That the baby responds in that way to its mother, to the one who has fed and protected it since its birth, appears a basic feature of human biology. The inner machinery alleged to explain that response does no real work. The natural, just plain recognition of its mother, its just plain smiling in that situation, *sans* benefit of any supposed inner intermediaries, is a model for language response, in Wittgenstein's view. For example our ability, when raised in some normal social context, to signal where we are going by uttering a certain sound is one of our natural talents; we do it, just as we, or for that matter any number of other animals, just often do anticipate, in the basis of what we see, where another is headed. And here don't think of anticipation as something mental, something inner.

Private language

The most famous sequence of passages in the *Investigations* – roughly sections 243 to 315 – opposes the possibility of a private language. The topic has raised a huge exegetical literature. In considering the subject the first question to be asked is: what does the private-language argument repudiate? Intuitively the idea is this. We naturally suppose that pains, thoughts, emotions, and the like, are inner things of some sort. As such they are private in a special way. Someone might have a pain exactly like this one of mine, but cannot possibly have *it*. I might let some made-up word or mark stand for that private object. The word says in effect 'There is *this*!' Now while the *this* lies forever beyond anyone else's grasp it is certainly within mine. My word for it would belong to a private language of the sort Wittgenstein sets himself against. The topic is important because the possibility of such a private language is a natural consequence of an assumption that Wittgenstein again and again rejects – the postulation of the existence of a realm of special, mental entities.

Where I spoke above of an intuition Wittgenstein would speak of a 'picture'. Our ordinary day-to-day speech, where we issue both ground- and meta-level statements, stands in contrast to metaphysical parlance where we employ everyday words but understand them in terms of some misleading picture and thus in a manner contrary to their actual depth grammar. A 'private language' is above all something we picture.

In the following well-known passage in the *Investigations* the distinction between ordinary speech and metaphysical picture is crucial:

§256.... What about the language which describes my inner experiences and which only I myself can understand? *How* do I use words to stand for my sensations? – As we ordinarily do? Then are my words for sensations tied up with my natural expressions of sensation? In that case my language is not a 'private' one. Someone else might understand it as well as I. – But suppose I didn't have any natural expression for the sensation, but only had the sensation? And now I simply *associate* names with sensations and use these names in descriptions.

If we use 'pain' or 'fear' as we ordinarily do, then the manner of its use can be studied in simple language-games. Natural expressions of pain are responded to, as are such natural gestures as a deliberately emphasized grimace. The child learns to replace natural expressions or gestures with words from the common vocabulary. The private-language argument does not deny such pain-claims. Indeed, how could it? Everyone will understand the child's 'It hurts' just 'as well as' the child does, and all will grant its truth: a move made in one of our common and important language-games occasions one of the usual responses. This is not to say that Wittgenstein offers or requires a behaviouristic account of pain-utterances. If the latter were used to express some behavioural facts, then the person's 'It hurts!' would mean something like: 'I am behaving in the is-in-pain way.' But the speaker is talking about his pain, not his behaviour: '§244.... The verbal expression of pain replaces crying and does not describe it'.

What about the meta-level case? Hearing Joe say 'I have a pain in my finger', I remark that he referred to something inner and private. If that gloss has its ordinary use, then, naturally, Wittgenstein would not deny it. For example, my remark might be addressed to someone who is learning our language; it tells him Joe's words were categorically different from a statement like 'I have a splinter in my finger': they were not about anything discernible in space and time. To call pain an inner private state will be to say in effect 'Don't ask anyone to show you their pain or make it available for observation.' Here the objection comes immediately: 'You have it backwards! One cannot make one's pain available for observation because it is inner!' That at least is one's intuition, one's strong conviction. But convictions can be wrong. Perhaps the matter is as Wittgenstein says:

§248. The proposition 'Sensations are private' is comparable to: 'One plays patience by oneself.'

That one plays patience (or solitaire) by oneself is true in virtue of the rules of that game. Analogously, 'Sensations are private' only describes a feature of our language-game with sensation words; it does not express a deep metaphysical truth, despite our strong temptation to think it does. It is a meta-linguistic or grammatical remark, not a philosophical one.

In §256 the possibility is posed of a piece of language that refers to pain while yet being independent of the natural expression of pain. It is precisely when we grant that possible independence that we enter the realm of metaphysics. That we must grant the possibility seems obvious. Given the metaphysical picture of the private object, it should be possible to introduce words that refer to such objects, regardless of whether I give natural expression to them. Here the metaphysical picture understands 'pain' on the analogy of 'splinter'; it takes it to refer, but of course not to anything public.

The aim of the private-language argument, then, is not to deny that people have pains and the like, nor to insist on a behaviouristic rendition of such mundane facts. Nor does Wittgenstein reject the claim, in natural speech, that sensations like pain are inner or private. Wittgenstein's job rather is to make hidden nonsense plain.

The difficulty of the task is directly proportional to the strength of one's conviction that, for example, *this* – the headache I now contemplate – is something I directly experience, something directly before the mind's eye, as it were. What could be more plausible than that assumption of direct acquaintance? The 'private-language argument' has its work cut out for it.

Section 258 gives what has been taken to be the central formulation of the private-language argument. There Wittgenstein considers the assumption that the ordinary use of mental words is abrogated while yet one succeeds in referring to the mental, by means of privately set-up ostensive definitions. He says, in the voice of his alter ego:

– But still I can give myself a kind of ostensive definition. . . .

Granted one cannot point to the sensation in the ordinary way, but rather, alter-ego goes on:

I speak, or write the sign down, and at the same time I

concentrate my attention on the sensation – and so as it were point to it inwardly.

In his own voice Wittgenstein now observes that the foregoing process seems merely an empty ceremony. What is it supposed to accomplish? Alter-ego's reply is that the inner pointing 'serves to establish the meaning of the sign' (that is, in Wittgenstein's example, the sign or mark 'S' which allegedly demarcates the inner sensation in question). The inner pointing achieves that because by its means 'I impress on myself the connection between the sign and the sensation.' And now comes the famous *reductio* that has been taken as expressing the core of the 'private-language argument' and that has been the subject of so much exegetical controversy:

> §258. . . . – But 'I impress it on myself' can only mean: this process brings it about that I remember the connection *right* in the future. But in the present case I have no criterion of correctness. One would like to say: whatever is going to seem right to me is right. And that only means that here we can't talk about 'right'.

On one way of reading these remarks they express a verificationist argument. I can't verify that I am correct in calling this present sensation 'S' since the sensation used to define 'S' is *ex hypothesi* no longer present. What I can't verify is meaningless; therefore the idea of a private language is meaningless. Judith Jarvis Thompson [8.81] attributed such a verificationist reading of Wittgenstein to Malcolm, and repudiated it on the grounds that the presupposed verificationist test of meaningfulness is unacceptable.

In a famous paper Saul Kripke offered an alternative, non-epistemic account of the inner workings of the private-language argument. Kripke tried to displace the exegetical focus of the private-language discussions by holding that the real argument gets expressed already in §202:

> What is really denied [by Wittgenstein in §202] is what might be called the 'private model' of rule following, that the notion of a person following a given rule is to be analyzed simply in terms of facts about the rule follower and the rule follower alone, without reference to his membership in a wider community.
>
> (Kripke [8.68], 206)

Thus Kripke reads the private-language argument as a straightforward inference from the idea of rule-following: the concept of a private language is inconsistent, because using language entails following rules, and following rules entails being a member of a community. This line of interpretation has prompted a discussion in the secondary literature over the so-called 'community view'. The issue under debate is, roughly, 'Did Wittgenstein believe that the idea of a forever solitary rule follower is a conceptual impossibility?' The issue, like the broader one of the exact nature of the private-language argument, remains unresolved.

Both the verificationist and the no-solitary-rule-follower interpretations present arguments of a kind I think are antithetical to Wittgenstein's general approach to philosophy, which seeks not quick knock-down refutations but slow cures of philosophical perplexity. On a more promising interpretation offered by Anthony Kenny [8.67] Wittgenstein is said to deny that the would-be private diarist has succeeded in attaching meaning to his sign 'S'. The problem is not the verificationist one, that the original sensation used to define 'S' is irretrievably lost in the past. Put it this way: even if God could look inside the diarist's mind, and even if God, unlike the diarist could directly access the now past sensation used in the alleged ostensive definition of 'S', still God would not know whether to call the present sensation 'S', for the term has not been properly defined – has not been given a meaning.

But what would be Wittgenstein's reasons for denying the success of the alleged private ostensive definition? One has to do with the *Investigations'* discussion of ostensive definition, as Kenny points out. Wittgenstein's idea is that for an ostensive definition to succeed there must already be in place some language-game within which the defined term plays a role. As Wittgenstein once put it: 'Ostensive definition explains the use of a word only when it makes one last determination, removes one last indeterminacy' ([8.7], 447, 448). One last indeterminacy, that is, within some presupposed language-game where the term being defined will have a use. For example one might know everything about playing chess up to this last point: what shape piece is called the 'king'? The next step then would be to justify Wittgenstein's rejection of the idea of a 'private' language-game. The nub of this suggestive approach is to get clearer on Wittgenstein's view of the nature of *public* language. The denial of private language would then entail pointing out differences between the public and private cases that justify withholding the application of the term 'language' to the latter.

❧ METHOD AND SCOPE ❧

'The right method of philosophy'

I shall rehearse the general methodological points made at the beginning of this essay; after the previous discussions they may appear more credible. A metaphysical problem arises as the result of our viewing some part of our language in the light of a false analogy. The result of that misreading is a metaphysical picture; the entity called into being through that picture is a grammatical fiction. If the picture is seen for what it is, the metaphysical problem will vanish. That one is in the grip of a metaphysical picture, or that correspondingly one is engrossed by a grammatical fiction, will become apparent upon a close look at the language that has misled one. So the right method in philosophy is to confront those 'pictures' with an examination – along Wittgenstein's lines – of the use of the underlying, puzzle-generating words ([8.9], §116). In this therapeutic enterprise the logician who examines language and the metaphysician who is confused by it are one and the same. The *Philosophical Investigations* is a 'dialogue' between the author and his alter ego. 'Nearly all my writings', Wittgenstein said, 'are private conversations with myself. Things that I say to myself *tête-à-tête*' ([8.12], 77). The metaphysical temptations Wittgenstein deals with are ones he has succumbed to or has felt the strong pull of. The 'therapy' he advocates is to be applied by the reader to himself or herself, on the assumption that the same linguistic pitfalls lie in wait for everyone. The first step is to feel the full force of the metaphysical picture. The strength or psychological force of the picture gives the therapy its significance.

Wittgenstein and academic philosophy

Wittgenstein seldom speaks directly to the problems and issues that occupy academic philosophers. Those have been raised to levels of sophistication that would not immediately concern him. He thinks there is more to be learned in the valley of stupidity than on 'the barren heights of cleverness' ([8.12], 80). His work is nevertheless relevant to professional philosophers, if their sophisticated issues have their roots in naive misreadings of language.

In one present-day controversy it is alleged that the ordinary person, in speaking of his beliefs, desires, intentions, reasons, and so on, is deploying a rudimentary psychological theory, so called *folk psychology* (Fodor [8.63]). Another way of putting this is that the folk psychologist – Everyman – deploys a naive 'theory of mind'. That is, in saying what someone believes, and so on, people utilize a theory that attributes to the speaker or to others certain mental states, where these are taken as *causes*. Thus if I say I'm going to be at the airport at 3.00 p.m. you take me to be describing an inner state of affairs, an intention *qua* mental state that will cause me to show up at the airport at 3. One controversy in the literature is over whether folk psychology, so understood, is substantially true or not.

Wittgenstein's work undercuts the discussion pro and con folk psychology, by showing that everyday claims about intentions, and so on, are not claims about the causal connections holding between mental entities. They cannot be, for they are not claims about mental entities. The philosopher, in the grip of a metaphysical picture, is wildly mistaken in his reading of the ordinary person's claims. And it doesn't help that the ordinary person, if the question were posed to him, would say, like the philosopher, that in speaking out his intention he is describing an inner cause. That he would is taken by the philosopher as one of those 'intuitions' that support his interpretation. It would be taken by Wittgenstein not as data but as the expression of a picture; it would show only that the picture has deep roots in our language, and a strong appeal for anyone who begins to reflect philosophically upon such things as intentions and beliefs.

Science-minded philosophers who speak of the mind and its objects – thereby employing the vocabulary of seventeenth-century metaphysics in the alleged context of philosophy-*qua*-science – avoid being thought unscientific by holding out the possibility that someday talk about minds may be replaced by talk about brains. But if Wittgenstein is right the route they take to the brain goes by way of a grammatical fiction. Intentions, for example, are misread as mental entities, and those mental things are projected, in turn, onto the brain. The brain-equivalent of an intention *qua* mental state is a grammatical fiction once removed.

The scope of Wittgenstein's critique

Not only philosophers philosophize. Science and especially social science contains conceptual claims and presuppositions that are philosophical at heart. For example neurobiologists explicitly address 'the mind-body problem,' and attempt to find explanations for 'consciousness' (Horgan [8.66]). Again, scientists attempt to discover if vervet monkeys have a 'theory of mind' – a notion derived directly from that of a 'folk psychology' (Cheney and Seyfarth [8.60], 205).

One might speculate that a full generalization of the intention case I have discussed at length will stand up: beliefs, desires and reasons, understood as mental something or others, will turn out to be, on examination, grammatical fictions. Then a well-known remark of Wittgenstein's would be borne out:

> In psychology there are experimental methods and *conceptual* confusion.

([8.9], 232)

And the same sort of radical conclusion would hold for examples from neurobiology and animal studies. Experiments or empirical observation on the one hand, hidden nonsense on the other. But speculation here is of little value. What is needed, rather, is to test our deeply felt metaphysical 'intuitions' about such things as reasons, wants, intentions, consciousness and mind against a sustained examination of the use of the relevant words. This is not to champion a mere dealing in words. For, as I have been at pains to illustrate, our uses of language are grounded in action. 'The essence of the language-game is a practical method (a way of acting) – not speculation, not chatter' ([8.8], 421). To examine use is not to do 1950s-style ordinary-language philosophy but something better described as philosophical anthropology. Out of that study there might arise in turn a new branch of inquiry, an empirical but purely descriptive cultural anthropology of language-customs, one developmental or genealogical in approach but purged of mentalistic assumptions. Wittgenstein seems to grant the possibility of such a study when he writes: 'What we are supplying are really remarks on the natural history of human beings; we are not contributing curiosities however, but observations which no one has doubted, but which have escaped remark only because they are always before our eyes' ([8.9], §415).

BIBLIOGRAPHY

For a bibliography of works by and concerning Wittgenstein consult Virgina A. and Stuart S. Shanker, *A Wittgenstein Bibliography*, London: Croom Helm, 1981.

Works by Wittgenstein (in order of composition)

8.1 —— *Notebooks, 1914–16*, ed. G. H. Von Wright and G. E. M. Anscombe, trans. G. E. M. Anscombe, Oxford: Blackwell, 1961.

8.2 —— *Tractatus Logico-Philosophicus*, trans. C. K. Ogden, London: Kegan Paul, 1922.

8.3 —— 'Some Remarks on Logical Form', *Proceedings of the Aristotelian Society*, suppl. vol. 9 (1929): 162–71.

8.4 —— *Philosophical Remarks*, ed. Rush Rhees, trans. Raymond Hargreaves and Roger White, Oxford: Blackwell, 1975.

8.5 —— *Philosophical Grammar*, ed. Rush Rhees, trans. Anthony Kenny, Oxford: Blackwell, 1974.

8.6 —— *The Blue and Brown Books*, New York: Harper, 1958.

8.7 —— 'Notes for the Philosophical Lecture', in *Philosophical Occasions 1912–51*, ed. James Klagge and Alfred Nordmann, Indianapolis: Hackett, 1993.

8.8 —— 'Cause and Effect: Intuitive Awareness', ed. Rush Rhees, trans. Peter Winch, *Philosophia* (Israel) 6 (1976): 409–25.

8.9 —— *Philosophical Investigations*, trans. G. E. M. Anscombe, Oxford: Blackwell, 1958.

8.10 —— *Remarks on the Foundations of Mathematics*, ed. G. H. von Wright, R. Rhees and G. E. M. Anscombe, trans. G. E. M. Anscombe, Cambridge, Mass.: MIT Press, 1978.

8.11 —— *Remarks on the Philosophy of Psychology*, vol. I, ed. G. E. M. Anscombe and G. H. von Wright, trans. G. E. M. Anscombe; vol. II, ed. G. H. von Wright and Heikki Nyman, trans. C. G. Luckhardt and M. A. E. Aue, Chicago: University of Chicago Press, 1980.

8.12 —— *Culture and Value*, ed. G. H. von Wright, trans. Peter Winch, Oxford: Blackwell, 1980.

8.13 —— *On Certainty*, ed. G. E. M. Anscombe and G. H. von Wright, trans. Denis Paul and G. E. M. Anscombe, Oxford: Blackwell, 1969.

8.14 —— *Last Writings on the Philosophy of Psychology*, vol. I, ed. G. H. von Wright and Heikki Nyman, trans. C. G. Luckhardt and M. A. E. Aue, Oxford: Blackwell, 1982.

8.15 —— *Last Writings on the Philosophy of Psychology*, vol. II, ed. G. H. von Wright and Heikki Nyman, trans. C. G. Luckhardt and M. A. E. Aue, Oxford: Blackwell, 1992.

Biographies of Wittgenstein

8.16 McGuinness, Brian *Wittgenstein: A Life*, Berkeley: University of California Press, 1988.

8.17 Malcolm, Norman *Ludwig Wittgenstein: A Memoir*, Oxford: Oxford University Press, 1984.

8.18 Monk, Ray *Ludwig Wittgenstein: The Duty of Genius*, London: Vintage, 1990.

Books on Wittgenstein

8.19 Anscombe, G. E. M. *Metaphysics and the Philosophy of Mind*, Oxford: Blackwell, 1981.

8.20 Baker, G. P. and P. M. S. Hacker *Wittgenstein: Meaning and Understanding*, Oxford: Blackwell, 1983.

8.21 —— *Wittgenstein: Rules, Grammar and Necessity*, Oxford: Blackwell, 1985.

8.22 Canfield, John V. *Wittgenstein: Language and World*, Amherst: University of Massachusetts Press, 1981.

8.23 —— *The Looking-Glass Self*, New York: Praeger, 1990.

8.24 Diamond, Cora *The Realistic Spirit*, Cambridge: University of Massachusetts Press, 1995.

8.25 Hacker, P. M. S. *Insight and Illusion*, Oxford: Clarendon Press, 1972.

8.26 —— *Wittgenstein: Meaning and Mind*, Oxford: Blackwell, 1990.

8.27 Hilmy, S. Stephen *The Later Wittgenstein: The Emergence of a New Philosophical Method*, Oxford: Blackwell, 1987.

8.28 Hunter, J. F. M. *Essays After Wittgenstein*, Toronto: University of Toronto Press, 1973.

8.29 —— *Understanding Wittgenstein*, Edinburgh: Edinburgh University Press, 1985.

8.30 Kenny, Anthony *Wittgenstein*, London: Penguin, 1973.

8.31 Malcolm, Norman *Dreaming*, London: Routledge & Kegan Paul, 1959.

8.32 —— *Knowledge and Certainty*, Ithaca, NY: Cornell University Press, 1963.

8.33 —— *Memory and Mind*, Ithaca, NY: Cornell University Press, 1977.

8.34 —— *Wittgenstein: Nothing is Hidden*, Oxford: Blackwell, 1986.

8.35 —— *Wittgenstein: A Religious Point of View?* Ithaca, NY: Cornell University Press, 1994.

8.36 —— and D. M. Armstrong *Consciousness and Causality*, Oxford: Blackwell, 1984.

8.37 Pears, David *The False Prison*, Oxford: Clarendon Press, 1990.

8.38 Rhees, Rush *Without Answers*, London: Routledge & Kegan Paul, 1969.

8.39 —— *Discussions of Wittgenstein*, London: Routledge & Kegan Paul, 1970.

8.40 Schulte, Joachim *Wittgenstein: An Introduction*, trans. William H. Brenner and John F. Holley, Albany: State University of New York Press, 1992.

8.41 Stroll, Avrum *Moore and Wittgenstein on Certainty*, Oxford: Oxford University Press, 1994.

8.42 Wright, G. H. von *Wittgenstein*, Oxford: Blackwell, 1982.

Collections of essays on Wittgenstein

8.43 Arrington, Robert L. and Hans-Johann Glock, eds *Wittgenstein's Philosophical Investigations: Text and Context*, London: Routledge, 1991.

8.44 Block, Irving *Perspectives on the Philosophy of Wittgenstein*, Oxford: Blackwell, 1981.

8.45 Canfield, John V., ed. *The Philosophy of Wittgenstein*, vols I–XV, New York: Garland, 1986.

8.46 —— and Stuart Shanker, eds *Wittgenstein's Intentions*, New York: Garland, 1993.

8.47 Pitcher, George *Wittgenstein: The Philosophical Investigations*, New York: Anchor Books, 1966.

8.48 Shanker, Stuart *Ludwig Wittgenstein: Critical Assessment*, vols I–IV, London: Croom Helm, 1986.

8.49 Teghrarian, Souren *Wittgenstein and Contemporary Philosophy*, Bristol, England: Thoemmes Press, 1994.

Additional essays and books relevant to Wittgenstein's later thought

8.50 Albritton, Rogers 'On Wittgenstein's Use of the Term "Criterion" ', *Journal of Philosophy*, 56 (1959): 845–57.
8.51 Anderson, A. R. 'Mathematics and the Language-Game', *Review of Metaphysics*, 11 (1958): 446–58.
8.52 Austin, J. L. *Philosophical Papers*, ed. J. O. Urmson and G. J. Warnock, Oxford: Oxford University Press, 1961.
8.53 Baker, Gordon 'Criteria: A New Foundation for Semantics', *Ratio*, 16 (1974): 156–89.
8.54 Candlish, Stewart 'The Real Private Language Argument', *Philosophy* 55 (1980): 85–94.
8.55 ——'*Das Wollen ist auch eine Erfahrung*', in Robert L. Arrington and Hans-Johann Glock, eds, *Wittgenstein's Philosophical Investigations: Text and Context*, London: Routledge, 1991: 203–26.
8.56 Canfield, John V. 'The Living Language: Wittgenstein and the Empirical Study of Communication', *Language Sciences*, 15 (3) (1993): 165–93.
8.57 —— 'The Concept of Function in Biology', *Philosophical Topics*, 18 (1990): 29–54.
8.58 —— 'The Rudiments of Language', *Language and Communication*, 15 (1995): 195–211.
8.59 —— 'The Passage into Language: Wittgenstein and Quine', in Robert Arrington and Hans-Johann Glock, eds, *Wittgenstein and Quine*, London: Routledge, 1996.
8.60 Cheney, Dorothy L. and Robert M. Seyfarth *How Monkeys see the World*, Chicago: University of Chicago Press, 1990.
8.61 Davidson, Donald, 'Actions, Reasons, and Causes', in Davidson, *Essays on Actions and Events*, Oxford: Clarendon Press, 1985: 3–20.
8.62 Fodor, Jerry A. *The Language of Thought*, Cambridge, Mass.: Harvard University Press, 1979.
8.63 —— *Psychosemantics*, Cambridge, Mass.: MIT Press, 1988.
8.64 Grice, Paul 'The Causal Theory of Perception', *Aristotelian Society, suppl. vol.* 70 (1961): 121–34.
8.65 Hacking, Ian *Why does Language matter to Philosophy?* Cambridge: Cambridge University Press, 1975.
8.66 Horgan, John 'Can Science explain Consciousness?' *Scientific American*, 271 (1) (1994): 88–94.
8.67 Kenny, Anthony 'The Verification Principle and the Private Language Argument', in O. R. Jones, ed., *The Private Language Argument*, London: Macmillan, 1971: 204–28.
8.68 Kripke, Saul 'Wittgenstein on Rules and Private Language', in Irving Block, *Perspectives on the Philosophy of Wittgenstein*, Oxford: Blackwell, 1981: 238–312.

8.69 Malcolm, Norman 'Anselm's Ontological Arguments', in Malcolm, *Knowledge and Uncertainty*, Ithaca, NY: Cornell University Press, 1963: 141–62.
8.70 —— 'The Groundlessness of Belief', in Malcolm, *Thought and Knowledge*, Ithaca, NY: Cornell University Press, 1977: 199–216.
8.71 —— 'Wittgenstein's *Philosophical Investigations*', *Philosophical Review*, 62 (1954): 530–59.
8.72 Nielson, Kai *Contemporary Critiques of Religion*, London: Macmillan, 1971.
8.73 Phillips, D. Z. *The Concept of Prayer*, London: Routledge & Kegan Paul, 1965.
8.74 —— ed. *Religion and Understanding*, Oxford: Blackwell, 1967.
8.75 Plooij, Frans 'Some Basic Traits in Wild Chimpanzees', in Andrew Lock, ed., *Action, Gesture and Symbol*, London: Academic Press, 1978.
8.76 Ryle, Gilbert *The Concept of Mind*, London: Hutchinson's University Library, 1949.
8.77 Savigny, Eike von 'Common Behaviour of Many a Kind: *Philosophical Investigations* §206', in Robert L. Arrington and Hans-Johann Glock, eds, *Wittgenstein's Philosophical Investigations: Text and Context*, London: Routledge, 1991.
8.78 Searle, John 'Proper Names', *Mind*, 67 (1958): 166–73.
8.79 Shoemaker, Sydney S. *Self Knowledge and Self Identity*, Ithaca, NY: Cornell University Press, 1963.
8.80 Sroufe, L. Alan and Everett Waters 'The Ontogenesis of Smiling and Laughter', *Psychological Review*, 83 (3) (1976): 173–89.
8.81 Thompson, Judith Jarvis 'Private Languages', *American Philosophical Quarterly*, 1 (1964): 20–31.

CHAPTER 9

Political philosophy
Arthur Ripstein

For the first half of the twentieth century, political philosophy was shaped by trends in other areas of philosophy. Conceptual analysis and clarification were central, and the philosopher's task was to clarify substantive political argument rather than participate in it. Several other features are worth mentioning: the widespread acceptance of utilitarianism as an adequate account of political morality; the interpretation of and reaction to its rivals, and the rise of pragmatism as an alternative view of philosophy in general and politics in particular. The second half of the century was marked by the rebirth of political philosophy. Justice emerged as the central issue, and debates continue about both its nature and its centrality to political life.

META-ETHICS AND CONCEPTUAL ANALYSIS

The rise of philosophy of language and conceptual analysis set the tone for philosophical inquiry more generally. One consequence of this was that moral and political philosophy focused on meta-ethical issues, such as the nature of moral truth, rather than on substantive questions of political morality. The two dominant positions in meta-ethics made substantive inquiry seem even less promising. Intuitonists insisted that moral truths are as evident as those of mathematics or the deliverances of the senses, and evident to any right-thinking person. Those with persistent perceptual deficits (Prichard used the analogy of colour-blindness) were beyond the reach of rational argumentation. Thus there was little for political philosophy to discuss. At the other extreme, emotivists suggested that moral and political discourse was non-cognitive – the expression of feelings and preferences, and the attempt to get others to share them – and thus incapable of rational adjudication (Ayer

[9.3]). On either view, such topics as justice or equality were not the sort of things about which respectable philosophers were expected to have theories.

❧ UTILITARIANISM ❧

Despite official philosophical distance from political issues, the dominant outlook in political culture more generally was tied to various versions of utilitarianism, the view that social institutions are to be assessed on the basis of their consequences for promoting human happiness. Utilitarianism was developed in the nineteenth century by Jeremy Bentham (1821 [9.6]) and John Stuart Mill (1864 [9.35]). Its appeal stems from the combination of three ideas: first, that in the end, the only thing that could really matter to political questions was how well or badly people's lives went; second, that in political morality, each person's interests should be counted equally; and third, that diffi-cult moral and political questions admit of rational resolution provided that sufficient information is available. Utilitarianism combines these ideas to evaluate social institutions on the basis of their consequences for human happiness. Everything from the judiciary and penal insti-tutions, through representative democracy, to trade and tax policy can and should be arranged to provide a framework within which indi-viduals, looking largely to their own advantage, could bring about the best results overall. At least as important as its emphasis on conse-quences is utilitarianism's unwillingness to allow the appeal to such notions as natural rights.

L. T. Hobhouse's *Liberalism* (1911 [9.24]) exemplified this pattern of political argument. Reforms advocated by Hobhouse that at the time seemed radical have since been adopted in the industrialized world: an active role for the state in education and health, welfare provisions, and redistribution of wealth through progressive income taxes and taxes on inheritance and speculation. Hobhouse's tone is at once confident and tentative. All his policy proposals are offered as experiments about how best to achieve the common good. Although he acknowledges the difficulties of weighing goods against each other (for example, the con-science of a few as opposed to the convenience of the many) Hobhouse sees the only burden of argument to be to establish the empirical claim that the policies he advocates do promote the overall social good. Any other appeal – to abstract rights, especially property rights – he sees as unhelpful obscurantism, unworthy of serious response.

In the 1920s debates about the feasibility of planned economies as opposed to markets also took a utilitarian form. Even Friedrich Hayek (1941 [9.21]), perhaps the most vocal and influential critic of economic and social planning of the time, appealed primarily to the consequences of planning. Hayek argued that large-scale social planning was doomed to failure. Any increase in social planning was sure to hinder individuals carrying out their own plans. Thus he doubted that the state could have any role other than setting up the broad legal framework within which individuals could go about their business. Despite its apparent anti-utilitarian orientation, Hayek's argument actually appealed to the idea that each individual is better situated both to know and to achieve his own welfare than any other agency. Thus, he suggested, the overall consequences of social planning are counter-productive.

MARXISM

The economic downturn and resulting political turmoil of the 1930s created widespread popular interest in Marxism. Like utilitarianism, Marxism developed in the nineteenth century. From the 1840s until his death in 1883, Marx both advocated and predicted worldwide socialist revolution. He saw it as the only solution to the recurrent economic crises that plagued capitalist economies, and as the end to the domination of man by man that he saw throughout human history. Like ancient slavery and feudalism before it, capitalism must give way to a more advanced mode of production. Marx held his socialism to be 'scientific', because it accounted for the development of forms of ownership on the basis of the independent development of human abilities to appropriate nature. Socialism was seen as the inevitable outcome of the tremendous development of productive forces that capitalism had unleashed; an end to material scarcity would bring about collective control of human affairs.

As Marxism gained in popular interest, it drew philosophical attention as well. Many philosophers were sympathetic to Marxism's broad political goals. But the overall thrust of philosophical reflection on Marxism in the 1930s remained deeply critical. Most treatments focused on epistemological issues, particularly the idea of the historical inevitability of socialism. That idea was attacked for being unscientific, for denying the role of human choice in history, and for conceptual confusions about the relation between individual and society. For example, Karl Popper argued that there can be no historical laws, on the grounds that individuals can choose to act contrary to them (Popper [9.43]; Acton [9.1]). Others argued that Marxism's idea of equality was indefensible; still others that Marxism was self-refuting, because it sought to explain ideas in terms of material conditions of production, thus undermining its own claim to truth.

❧ PRAGMATISM ❧

At the same time, across the Atlantic in the United States, pragmatism was gaining popularity as an account of both philosophy and politics. Pragmatism was part of a broader movement against formalism in American thought. In such diverse areas as law (Llewellyn [9.30]; Cardozo [9.8]) and architecture, themes of experimentation and practice were dominant; ideas of method were down-played. As part of this movement, pragmatist philosophy was deeply suspicious of the sort of conceptual puzzles with which British philosophy was largely occupied.

John Dewey [9.13] was the leader of the pragmatic movement in social and political philosophy. Rather than investigating general relationships among such concepts as the individual, state, property and family, Dewey thought the role of social philosophy must be to 'help men solve concrete problems by supplying them hypotheses to be used and tested in projects of reform' [9.14]. To fix on abstract conceptions, as traditional political philosophy had done, is to help 'clever politicians' to 'cover their designs and make the worse seem the better cause'. Instead, institutions should be 'viewed in their educative effect: – with reference to the type of individuals they foster'.

Dewey also called for the increased democratization of American life. The equalization of wealth and elimination of privilege were offered as goals all Americans could embrace, and the task of philosophy was seen as clearing away inherited philosophical obstacles to the sharing of those goals. What Dewey characterized as 'dualisms' between mind and body, fact and value, and subject and object were to be removed in the hope of making room for a social experiment in which all could flourish. In place of both tradition and any attempt at developing a scientific method, Dewey advocated 'the application of intelligence to solving problems', by which he meant free and open discussion involving as many participants as possible. For Dewey, the only justification democracy needed was showing that it was the most effective way of broadening the pool of intelligence to apply to social problems. Anything less deprives society of the full contribution of all its members. It is central to Dewey's view that there is no general answer to the problems of social life, only particular solutions that are appropriate in response to particular problems as they arise. No general theory about happiness, freedom or justice will help – only democratic discussion of particulars is possible.

Perhaps the most striking feature of political philosophy through the first half of the century was the extent to which it supposed that political argument is not itself a philosophical task. Whether philosophy was seen as confined to conceptual questions, or charged with clearing away obstacles to democratic discussion, few supposed that it had anything to contribute directly to politics. Deep divisions ran through political life, but these were seen as either the results of conceptual confusion or simply false belief. One result was that philosophy was all but silent on what now seem the fundamental questions of politics.

By the 1950s political philosophy looked as though it had lost its subject matter. In the social sciences, the 'end of ideology' was proclaimed (Waxman [9.54]). Piecemeal social engineering in the service of goals that were supposed to be widely shared was to replace impassioned debate over the fundamental terms of social life.

❧ THE SIXTIES ❧

All that changed in the 1960s. The mood of philosophy began to shift, and scruples about addressing large normative topics began to wane. Conceptual analysis lost much of its grip on philosophy, and interest in meta-ethics began to waver. Equally important, were a variety of social changes. The intended audience for academic philosophy grew enormously with the growth of state universities in the United States and 'red-brick' universities in Britain. At the same time, that audience's diversity increased. In 1954, the US Supreme Court ruled that segregation was unconstitutional. In the years that followed, the civil-rights movement demanded that abstract constitutional provision be put into practice. In so doing, it put an end to the idea that only the details of social life needed to be worked out. At the same time, the threat of nuclear war led to increased distrust of governments around the world. The Vietnam War brought both of these issues to a head. Disproportionately many blacks were drafted, and many viewed the war as an imperialist exercise.

One response was another wave of interest in Marxism. Marx's early writings were translated into English in 1960. Rather than historical necessity and economic crises, their central theme was the profound alienation endemic to capitalist society. In addition, Marxist thought had continued to develop in Europe throughout the twentieth century, and came to have an increasing influence. The 'critical theory of society', developed in Germany in the 1920s (Adorno [9.2]; Jay [9.26]) provided much of the vocabulary of student radicals in the 1960s (Marcuse [9.33]). Still, these remained very much marginal positions in the academy.

Many of the dissatisfactions of the period took the form of attacks on liberalism. The criticisms varied, but two were prominent. One charge was that liberalism emphasized individual liberty at an unacceptable cost in equality. The other was that it lacked a coherent political morality, and was little more than the result of a series of shifting political coalitions and compromises. The liberal commitment to the welfare state was seen as nothing more than a reaction to changing political demands.

Utilitarianism was subject to parallel attacks. It was suggested, for example, that the wanton destruction of the Vietnam War had its theoretical basis in the idea that all values are commensurable. If all values can be reduced to a single common scale, then policy-planners could rationally decide to commit atrocities for the sake of their supposed long-term benefits. This argument, popular among both peace activists and scholars, cut deeply against utilitarianism's claim to be a viable philosophy for public justification (Griffin [9.19]; Williams [9.56]; Berlin [9.7]).

❧ RAWLS ❧

It was in this setting that John Rawls's *A Theory of Justice* [9.44] brought new vigour to liberalism, and with it, political philosophy. Rawls seeks to provide an alternative to utilitarianism that will reconcile freedom and equality. The book begins with a bold claim: 'Justice is the first virtue of social institutions', and spells out a conception of justice as fairness. Rawls draws on the social-contract tradition of Locke, Rousseau and Kant to describe a powerful thought experiment. The intuitive idea is simple: suppose you had to choose the basic structure governing your society. To choose, it would help to have information about a variety of things – economics, and human psychology, for example. Now suppose that choice were to be made from behind what Rawls calls 'a veil of ignorance' – you had all the general factual information you could want, but you didn't know who you were, nor what mattered most to you in life. In such circumstances, it would be rational to choose cautiously, so that no matter how badly things went, you would do at least passably well. So, for example, you would never agree to a system that allowed some people to own slaves, for fear that when the veil was lifted, you would turn out to be one of the slaves. Nor would you agree to a state religion, for fear that you turned out to be a member of a persecuted minority. Nor, for that matter, would you ever adopt utilitarian principles of social organization, for fear that your own most important interests might be sacrificed for the sake of less significant, but more numerous interests of others. Even if some practice, such as slavery, were to have the best consequences overall, no rational person would agree to it if it carried with it the risk of being a slave.

Rawls argues that this sort of reasoning leads to two highly specific principles of justice. The first generalizes freedom of religion, and demands the maximum liberty compatible with the same liberty for others. The second, which Rawls dubs 'the difference principle', calls for the equal distribution of material resources and powers, except when an unequal distribution will benefit those who receive less than an equal share. The first principle is supposed to take priority over the second: liberty can never be sacrificed for material gain.

Rawls deploys the two principles of justice to address a number of further issues including justice between generations, civil disobedience, conscientious objection and moral education. In each case the general thrust is the same: society is to be viewed as what Rawls calls 'a co-operative venture for mutual advantage', in which all share a common fate which is articulated and adjudicated in terms of publicly accepted principles of justice.

In order to get such a determinate result out of such a simple thought experiment, Rawls assumes that the parties in the original position desire certain 'primary goods' – goods that are likely to be useful in pursuit of whatever conception of the good they might have. These include liberty, material resources and what Rawls calls 'the social bases of self respect'. These are the sorts of goods that it is the business of the liberal state to oversee the distribution of. Rawls's point is not that everybody necessarily wants these things, but that by thinking of them as the goods to be distributed, we are able to embrace the idea that individuals are responsible for their ends (hence the importance of liberty) without supposing them to be responsible for their material circumstances (hence the importance of material wealth).

Critics of liberalism had long supposed freedom and equality to sit in an uneasy balance, with no principled relation between them. Rawlsian liberalism offers the two principles of justice in order to interpret the importance of each in terms of the other. Equality gives each an equal claim on primary goods; freedom is important so that each person can use his or her fair share of resources to carry out his or her own life plan. Without equality, though, individual freedom loses its claim. Legitimate shares of material resources set the limits of freedom, because they ensure that one's pursuit of some conception of the good is not imposing unreasonable costs on others.

If Rawls reinvigorates liberalism, it is a liberalism with a difference. Individual political and personal liberties are still central to it. But the emphasis on property and market freedoms characteristic of the traditional liberalism of Locke (or the US Constitution) is gone. For Rawls, property rights are no longer central to the liberal political vision. At best, forms of ownership are to be understood as subservient to equality and personal liberty.

Of course, Rawlsian liberalism leaves many important questions unanswered. How much material inequality is to the advantage of the worst off? How are liberties to be balanced against one another? But if Rawls does not answer these questions, he at least provides a vocabulary in which liberals could address them systematically. The power of that vocabulary is revealed by the extent to which divisive issues have been fruitfully debated in its terms. By making equality central to justice, Rawls provides a way of avoiding fruitless disputes about the relation between freedom and equality, or between fairness and desirable consequences. On Rawls's view, each can only be understood in relation to the others. For example, debates about the legitimacy of affirmative-action programmes (reserving employment or educational opportunities for members of groups that have historically been discriminated against) typically played themselves out as battles between fairness and desirable consequences. Drawing on Rawls's work, Ronald Dworkin showed how ideas of fairness and merit are always tied up with ideas of social purposes (Dworkin [9.15]).

❧ RAWLS'S CRITICS ❧

Rawls's arguments drew criticism from a wide variety of perspectives. In so doing, they provided the background against which political philosophers could raise their disagreements. Four directions of criticism are particularly noteworthy. One took Rawls to task for failing to consider seriously the distinctness of persons and the importance of property. Another criticized Rawls for not going far enough in the service of equality. A third held that Rawlsian liberalism, with its emphasis on justice, left no room for the moral community that is fundamental to political life. The fourth may well turn out to be most significant in the long run. Drawing on developing feminist scholarship, it points to the way that liberalism fails to take seriously the politics of private life.

Libertarianism

Where Rawls had drawn on the tradition of Rousseau and Kant, Robert Nozick's *Anarchy, State and Utopia* [9.38] sought to reinvigorate the ideas of ownership and individual liberty that were prominent in Locke's political thought. Deeply suspicious of ideas of distributive justice, Nozick argued that 'income tax is on a par with forced labor'. He suggested that the idea of equality is simply a reflection of the envy of those who have less, whether through laziness, stupidity or simple bad luck. In place of concerns about how to create and distribute resources as fairly and effectively as possible, Nozick insists that the important questions about the distribution of goods must all be looked at as questions of entitlement. Entitlements can arise through the acquisition of something initially unowned, through voluntary exchange or gift or as compensation for wrongs suffered. They cannot be acquired in any other way – particularly not on the basis of need or one's comparative share in relation to others.

The root idea of Nozick's view is that liberty must be given priority over any distributive goal. He offers little by way of argument for this claim, apart from some general musings about how each person's life is his or her own to develop or waste, and the suggestion that any alternative to libertarianism would violate the Kantian prohibition on treating others as mere means to ends they do not share. Nozick's development of his position depends much more on the intuitive force of a series of examples.

For example, Nozick invites us to suppose that income was distributed on the basis of whatever distributive principle we think is best. Each person must be entitled to spend their legitimate share however they see fit. Now suppose that one million of these people are each willing to pay a premium of 25 cents to watch their favourite basketball player, Wilt Chamberlain, play. By refusing to play without this premium, Chamberlain thus puts himself in a position to gain an additional quarter-million dollars. This would upset the original distributive pattern. Yet surely each person can dispose of his or her holdings as he or she sees fit. Nozick insists that the example generalizes: liberty would always disrupt any distributive pattern.

Again, in response to the claim that property rights must give way to each person's claim to have a say over those things that effect him or her, Nozick suggests we consider whether the same principles would apply to a woman's choice of suitor – should a rejected suitor get a say in this matter, which plainly affects him deeply? Again, if I am nice enough to lend you something, do you thereby acquire a say over the uses to which I will put it in the future? Nozick suggests not.

Nozick's dependence on intuitive examples lead many to doubt whether much depth lay beneath the book's witty veneer. Thomas Nagel [9.36] describes it as 'libertarianism without foundations'. The difficulty is that the book's theoretical apparatus is so thin that it is very difficult to know what to make of the examples. For example, it is hard to think of a distributive scheme that is 'patterned' in Nozick's sense. Rawls's difference principle, for example (presumably Nozick's target), specifies the structure within which people can acquire and dispose of goods, rather than a pattern that would require constant interference every time a transfer took place. Thus the example doesn't seem to cut any ice against any position anyone ever actually held. Nozick's other arguments about interference are comparably ambiguous: we might think that a woman's sovereignty over which suitor she accepts is tied to the importance of controlling one's own emotional life, rather than any more general principle that excludes workers from exercising any sort of control over their working conditions.

Nozick's project gains much of its impetus from the idea that people should be able to decide what to do with their lives and with whatever abilities and assets they find themselves with. On the face of it, this is an attractive, even inspiring idea. Yet Nozick is surely confused here. For we cannot take seriously the idea that politics could be a matter of letting people do what they want, *simpliciter*. Indeed, the political philosopher's activity of trying to formulate principled grounds for competing social arrangements gets its point from the need for an articulate account of why some wants count and others do not. In this respect, prohibitions of violence are on a par with limits on election-campaign contributions – all stop people from doing what they might otherwise do. No appeal to freedom, understood as letting people do what they want, can settle these questions. Nor can Nozick claim that people should be left to do as they please so long as they don't harm anyone else. To give content to that claim, he would need some ways of identifying which harms count – something like Rawls's catalogue of primary goods. Otherwise he cannot rule out any state functions, for those seeking state action would be able to argue that they are harmed by not getting their way (Leiberman [9.29]). At bottom, though, Nozick has little to offer to resolve these issues.

Other libertarian projects also sought to pose a challenge to Rawls. Most prominent among these are more radical interpretations of his contractarian apparatus. By modifying the conditions under which the contract might be reached, some sought to derive principles of justice that put more emphasis on property and less on equality. Where Rawls looks to Kant and Nozick to Locke for historical antecedents, Hobbes provides the inspiration for radical contractarianism. In *Morals by Agreement* [9.17], David Gauthier provides the most sophisticated version of this position. Gauthier begins by pointing to the difficulties in appealing to intuitive plausibility in political argument. Intuitions too often reflect past socialization, and they are too easily shifted to do duty in place of arguments. Concerned in part about the problems that plagued Nozick's view, Gauthier seeks instead to ground libertarianism in the theory of rational choice as developed in economics and game theory. The emphasis on rational choice is rooted in the view, widely accepted in both academic and popular culture, that values and standards of evaluation are at bottom rooted in individual preferences. Thus no utilitarian theory of the good, or Rawlsian index of primary goods, can provide a firm basis for justification. Instead, we must look to a well-defined problem of choice: what principles would fully informed rational agents, concerned only to advance their own ends, agree to, *regardless of what those ends turned out to be*? The broad outlines of the story are clear enough. Each would agree to such limits as would protect his or her own choices, and leave him or her free of any obligations to aid others. Various bundles of specific property rights, and methods of dividing the benefits of co-operation have also been suggested (Gauthier [9.17]; Narveson [9.37]).

Radical contractarians have doubtless produced some of the most elegant contributions to political philosophy. Yet their mathematical accounts tend to be so idealized that it is very difficult to see how they are supposed to make contact with actual people pursuing their own diverse ends. Worse, many of the simplifying assumptions required to make their formal apparatus yield determinate conclusions seem to beg important political questions. If the model of rational choice is supp-osed to describe actual human behaviour, then it seems to be compatible with the wide variety of different institutional arrangements that have resulted from human interaction. For they too are the product of individuals pursuing their diverse ends. To get the highly specific results of Gauthier's contract, and a unique solution to the problem of rational agreement, the agents making the agreement must be idealized. But if they are, it becomes difficult to see how the radical contractarian project is any less dependent upon intuitive plausibility than are competing views. (Ripstein [9.45])

Analytical Marxism

Perhaps the most interesting criticisms of libertarianism come from a group that describes itself as 'analytical Marxists'. Where libertarians argue that liberalism sacrifices liberty for the sake of equality, analytical Marxists suggest that liberalism pays insufficient heed to equality. As a group, they are highly selective of what they take from Marx's thought (Elster [9.16]; Roemer [9.47]). Their work is of interest here because of its use of the same conceptual tools and vocabulary as liberal and even libertarian thought. Where an earlier generation of Marxists was suspicious of such tools as 'bourgeois', today they are embraced as neutral and effective. This has helped to make it clear that technical tools cannot decide between political ideals; at best they can make the presuppositions and commitments of competing views more nearly explicit (Roemer [9.46]; Cohen [9.10], [9.9]).

Communitarianism

A third line of criticism of Rawlsian liberalism also takes aim at libertarianism. Both are charged with a destructive obsession with individual rights, and an indifference to the importance of community both to making political life fulfilling, and to providing the context within which normative claims could be made and discussed.

The communitarian argument has taken a variety of forms. In *Liberalism and the Limits of Justice* [9.49], Michael Sandel focused on Rawls's view, and argued that both Rawls's argument and the politics of liberalism more generally reflect a number of indefensible metaphysical assumptions. Each of the parties behind Rawls's veil of ignorance chooses without knowing his or her own conception of the good. Sandel suggests that this hardly qualifies as a choice at all. First of all, the parties are given a sharply defined problem of choice and an algorithm for its rational solution; their agreement is more like the agreement of a number of students on the solution to a mathematical problem than an agreement between a number of people about how to regulate their affairs. But for Sandel, there is a deeper problem lurking here as well. By choosing in the absence of any shared conception of the good, Rawls's contractors are making shallow choices, devoid of moral significance. Only choices made in light of one's view about what is most important in life will fully engage one's moral capacities. Yet Sandel maintains that a liberal society cannot allow such choices to inform political life. Because of its official neutrality on questions of the good life, a liberal society can at best appeal to neutral procedures all can accept, rather than speak with a common voice that all can recognize as their own. As a result, it has trouble asking for the sort of sacrifices that political life requires. Instead, any sacrifice it demands will be seen as made for someone else's good. For example, Rawls's second principle of justice requires those with marketable abilities to accept less than they might for the sake of those with less. They may make the requisite sacrifices, but they do so out of compromise rather than principle. Sandel insists that this is the fate of contemporary liberal democracies: interest groups compete to control the apparatus of government with no common vision of the good life to limit their pursuit of their interests.

In *After Virtue: A Study in Moral Theory* [9.31], Alasdair MacIntyre sets his sights wider, arguing that the liberalisms of both Rawls and Nozick are nothing more than the dying gasps of a moral culture in decline. MacIntyre suggests that the vocabulary of rights on which both rely lacks the only sort of background against which it could have a coherent use. Nozick's difficulties in explaining the rights he focuses on is merely a special case of a more general cultural trend, in which talk about rights becomes nothing more than an emphatic way of insisting on some claim. MacIntyre fears that, however inadequate as an account of the meaning of moral language the emotivist meta-ethics of the first part of the century might have been, it is very close to the truth about the use of moral language in the latter part. Without strong ties of community and tradition, moral language becomes just another species of rhetoric, influencing behaviour rather than providing reasons.

MacIntyre sees the failure of liberalism as a special case of a more general failure of the enlightenment project of providing a universalistic grounding for morality and politics. The theme is not a new one. In the 1940s, Michael Oakeshott had attacked what he characterized as 'rationalism in politics', the view that human reason has the power to solve all social problems (Oakshott [9.39]). MacIntyre focuses on the related, though distinct idea of universality. He argues that the idea of universality misses the significance of particular commitments in making us the people we are. The enlightenment project of providing a universal standpoint, able to evaluate particular cultures and practices from outside, was a failure. It missed the way in which an on-going way of life provides the cultural space within which people can regard their particular social roles as appropriate. So long as we demand a justification from outside our practices, we are bound to end in disappointment.

For MacIntyre, tradition is important to giving sense to moral discussion because it gives concrete content to the idea of sharing a common fate. Moral thinking and discussion is essentially interpretive. Traditions provide the raw material for interpretation, without which political argument deteriorates into nothing more than veiled bargaining.

While Sandel is silent about what specific conception of the good would be appropriate to any contemporary society, MacIntyre is more specific on this score. He suggests that the appropriate ethical outlook is to be found in the traditions of Christianity, especially Roman Catholicism. The final chapter of *After Virtue* suggests that the only two moral options left open to us are the piety of St Benedict and the nihilism of Nietzsche.

Other communitarians have made parallel points. In *Habits of the Heart* a group of social scientists sought to document the debasement of the moral vocabulary that MacIntyre pointed to; they found that the subjects they interviewed often felt alienated from society and their moral relationships (Bellah *et al.* [9.5]). They also found that they had difficulty in articulating the moral standpoint that they spoke from.

The communitarian criticisms of liberalism are difficult to assess, in part because the criticisms are posed at so many different levels. For example, Sandel argues that Rawls ends up with a shallow view of politics because he begins with bad metaphysics. And so he misses 'The good we can know in common that we cannot know alone'. But Sandel doesn't tell us what that good is. And it is difficult to see how he could: because he focuses on metaphysical issues, it is not clear whether or how his arguments are supposed to issue in any particular politics. At another level, he is clear about the need for community, rather than a mere association of isolated individuals. But, as Will Kymlicka has pointed out, he never explains why the state should be the proper place in which that sense of community is to be fostered. Why not in secondary associations, like churches, unions, clubs and neighbourhoods? If these are the *loci* of community, the state may need to change in ways that nurture those communities. But that is very different from acting as a primary community itself (Kymlicka [9.27]; Guttman [9.20]).

Still, communitarians are sensitive to something important that is missing from liberalism. Liberalism sees no need for the state to be a community, except in the thinnest sense of something to identify with, and a common forum of justification. But there is a lingering question of whether a liberal state can provide even this much. For the emphasis on private pursuit of the good life (even where this includes secondary associations) may not foster the commitment to the state required in order to make the sacrifices it demands. Often those sacrifices benefit those to whom one is related only as a fellow citizen. Charles Taylor argues that the liberal state cannot make any plausible claims about mutual advantage, because each individual's contribution makes little difference to the long-term survival of the state. So it seems to rely instead on moral high-mindedness, and the claims of justice. It is not clear that this is enough to call forth sacrifices from citizens (Taylor [9.52]). Still, if Taylor is right in his diagnosis of the problem, it is difficult to see how a communitarian state that emphasizes its common traditions and way of life can do any better at sustaining itself in a world in which individuals have lives of their own. All the communitarians' favoured examples of successful communities – democratic Athens, eighteenth-century Geneva – excluded large portions of their populaces from political participation, and identified political participation with the good life (Herzog [9.23]). MacIntyre gives slightly different examples, but they involve groups that share a conception of the good for religious reasons. Yet their treatment of dissenters was unacceptable, and it is hard to imagine how such a model could be generalized to a society that is religiously divided. Unless some way is found to include everyone in political life, so that it is the most central of each person's identity-conferring life project, the same problem will just recur. Most people will be unwilling to make sacrifices, unless they take them to be demanded by justice.

❧ FEMINISM ❧

Liberalism, libertarianism, Marxism and communitarianism have all been questioned in recent feminist criticism. Liberalism and libertarianism have been attacked because of the way they have focused on voluntary relations between adults of roughly equal power without antecedent ties, at the expense of the more pervasive relations of dependence and domination that characterize relations between parents and children, or women and men. While communitarians have focused more on relationships involving antecedent ties, they have attached too much weight to the founding of communities and their traditions. As a result, they have failed to acknowledge the ways in which virtually all communities have oppressed women and excluded them from public life. Marxists, in turn, have been criticized for focusing on production and ignoring reproduction (Pateman and Shanley [9.42]; Sunstein [9.51]; Jaggar [9.25]).

At one level, feminists can be thought of as occupying various positions along the previous political spectrum. There are conservative feminists, liberal feminists and socialist feminists. Which has the legitimate claim to the name 'feminist' is itself a contested question within feminism. But to focus on those differences is to miss the originality and intellectual power of feminism as a philosophical position.

Feminism is a comparatively new social movement. Where Rawls and Nozick can carry on a debate by developing positions already articulated by Kant or Locke, many feminists are uneasy about helping themselves too readily to the arguments and outlooks of philosophers who, whatever other disagreements they may have had, verged on unanimity in their relegation of women to second-class status. From Plato through the middle ages, women were thought of as imperfect realizations of the ideal male form; from the seventeenth through the nineteenth centuries, they were seen as a different kind of thing, subject to feeling rather than reason, and incapable of participating in public life. One strategy for working within the traditional mould is to simply ignore its overt sexism, and look instead to the universal roles that particular thinkers have described, and try to find a way to enable women to participate more fully in those social roles. Susan Moller Okin has dubbed this strategy 'add women and stir' and many feminists join her in rejecting it, on the grounds that it takes for granted that the position of men within sexist societies is the appropriate goal for women to aspire to (Okin [9.40]; [9.41]).

Feminist research has drawn attention to a variety of ways in which traditional debates about politics have overlooked important power relations and injustices. Of particular significance are the division between public and private life and the assumption that the family is a realm beyond justice. Feminists have also been critical of the assumption that male experience provides the appropriate lens though which social relations in general, and the status of women in particular, ought to be viewed.

Public and private

Modern political thinkers have drawn a division between a public sphere in which decisions are made and carried out, and the private sphere within which individuals pursue their own private ends. For Nozick (to use an extreme example) the public is exhausted by its role of mutual protection and enforcement of property rights; everything else is private, the domain of individual contract and consent, in which the public has no say or legitimate interest. In Rawls, the public enjoys a more expansive role, ensuring fair shares of resources and guaranteeing equality of opportunity. Communitarians draw the line between public and private differently, supposing that its contours depend on the shared practices of an on-going way of life. They also tend to attach more significance to the public; where liberals and libertarians see the private as the realm of freedom, communitarians suppose freedom has its proper place in participation in collective control over public life. But they share the emphasis on that division.

Feminists have recently challenged these divisions. The reasons for the challenge become clear if we focus on the place of family in relation to the distinction. Is the family private or public? Traditionally, both in political philosophy and in legal decisions, the answer has seemed obvious: it is private. Important constitutional decisions in the United States have been made on the basis of the family's right to privacy. Rawls seeks to determine the appropriate rate of savings in a just society by asking us to suppose that the contractors in the original position are 'heads of households'. None of the prominent political philosophers we've looked at even considers questions of social responsibility for the rearing of children. And despite the obvious inequalities of status and power that are to be found within the traditional family, these too seem to fall outside the scope of justice, and to be viewed instead as private arrangements between individuals.

Feminists note two striking features of these omissions. One is that political philosophy, which aspires to study 'the first virtue of social institutions', is silent on so many aspects of social life. The other is that the very features about which it is silent are those traditionally involving women.

One response has been to suppose that the distinction between public and private must simply be eliminated, since it has plainly been both unreflectively drawn and harmful. Another approach has sought to keep the distinction while re-drawing its boundaries. Preserving a private sphere, free from state interference is important, especially for those who find themselves outside the mainstream of public culture, such as lesbians and gay men. Feminist arguments in favour of reproductive rights also draw on the legitimacy of a private sphere. But if a private sphere remains, it cannot be organized around the prior boundaries of the domestic sphere. Inequalities within the family, whether in household tasks, access to resources or the threat of physical violence, all admit of assessment in terms of justice. Pornography, long considered a private matter by liberals, can be viewed instead as a matter of creating and reinforcing the conditions of the oppression of women.

Feminist critiques of pornography provide a clear example of questioning the division between public and private. The argument has two components; the first is the claim that pornography is harmful to women, and so ought not to be thought of as protected expression. The second, deeper strand, questions the traditional liberal understanding of the role and nature of political expression. In *On Liberty*, John Stuart Mill [9.34] defended free expression on the grounds that it is necessary to encourage the search for truth and to make room for a responsible, because informed, citizenry. Recent feminist scholarship has suggested that this view misunderstands the nature of expression in general, and pornography in particular. Pornography does not make claims to truth that might be examined on the basis of their merits; instead, it constructs social roles in which individuals have no choice but to live. Catherine MacKinnon [9.32] points out that nobody would take pornography's implicit claims about the role and availability of women seriously if they were made explicit. But that is not how pornography works.

The critique of traditional divisions between public and private enters again here: where liberal thought views pornography as something that is enjoyed in private, feminists look at it as an essentially public activity, because of its role in shaping social roles. The suggestion is that one does not view pornography (or live in a society in which pornography is widely consumed) without coming to think of women in a very specific way.

This emphasis on the political nature of the split between the public and the private also explains feminism's characteristic attitude towards traditional philosophy's claim to universality. By identifying what it is to be truly human with participation in the public life of markets and politics, and interaction with equals, traditional philosophy relegated many of the activities women have been involved into a secondary status. The past several decades have seen increasing numbers of women entering the workforce. Yet incomes and opportunities for advancement have been structured in ways that disadvantage women. They have typically been tied to the model of a breadwinner who has a wife at home capable of taking care of his needs, and of preparing him to work another day, both through feeding him and by providing an emotional respite from the pressures of the working world. These practical issues have a philosophical dimension, because such concepts as procedural fairness, merit, freedom and equality of opportunity have been understood in terms of unexamined assumptions about private life.

Other strands in feminism pose different challenges to traditional political philosophy. The primacy of justice has been challenged, on the grounds that relationships involving dependence, such as the care of children or the elderly, cannot be assimilated to questions of justice. But rather than supposing that these fall outside the scope of political philosophy, or can be treated as simply different, some feminists have argued that relations of care and nurture should be thought of as primary, and relations of justice derivative. This emphasis on non-contractual relationships has led to proposals for a radical re-thinking of such concepts as autonomy (Baier [9.4]; Gilligan [9.18]; Held [9.22]; Ruddick [9.48]). Still other feminist scholarship has urged the re-thinking of the political implications of such concepts as embodiment and power, in directions very different from those pursued by the mainstream of English-speaking political philosophy (Scott [9.50]).

One other recent development in political philosophy deserves mention: the renewed interest in radical democracy. Dewey's influence dwindled for decades, but many of the themes he emphasized are again the focus of debate. Part of the reason is continuous with feminist concerns about illusory models of universality and the need to hear voices that had been excluded. Representative democracy made many of the same promises of universality as did classical liberal theory; both arguably failed to take seriously the claims of those who did not readily fit into their models of normal life. The institutions of representative democracies have been organized around assumptions about typical needs and demands. As the electoral franchise has been extended this century, increasing numbers of people have acquired the legal right to vote, yet many have no further concern with politics than voting in periodic elections. Ordinary citizens – especially, but by no means exclusively, women and members of minorities – have been excluded from having an effective political voice in the democracies. The project of radical democracy is to re-think democratic institutions in a way that makes room for full participation by all. Like Dewey, radical democrats emphasize participation both for its benefits to those involved and for its promise of solving problems.

Much of the impetus for democratic theory has come from outside the English-speaking world, but its influence continues to grow. One major force has been the Brazilian social theorist Roberto Unger. Unger first came to prominence as a communitarian critic of liberalism; his *Knowledge and Politics* [9.53] argued that liberalism rested on an indefensible metaphysics and psychology, and on moral scepticism. His more recent work has abandoned communitarianism in favour of what he calls 'superliberalism', the idea that 'the basic terms of social life' should be permanently up for grabs, all institutions subject to subversion from below.

The politics of radical democracy are represented by the 'Rainbow coalition' in American politics. Made up of women's groups, members of more traditional leftist movements, people of colour, environmentalists and parts of the peace movement, it has been defined (so far) more by a sense of making common cause in the face of perceived exclusion than by concrete political proposals. Philosophically, it shares with the Deweyan pragmatism of the 1930s a commitment to eliminating privilege and an insistence that making institutions more open and participatory will thereby also make them more effective (Laclau and Mouffe [9.28]; Cohen and Rogers [9.11]; Cunningham [9.12]; Young [9.57]). Radical democracy also shares Dewey's suspicions of such philosophical buttresses of traditional politics as the dualisms of reason and imagination, or reason and passion. The vocabulary in which the rejections are phrased has changed, but their upshot has not. Abandoning such dualisms carries with it some risks. Allowing every social context to be overturned may strike many liberals as a recipe for disaster. Pragmatist or radical democrat, the response to this worry is the same: no amount of philosophy will keep the barbarians from the gate – only an involved and reflective public can. In the end, their deepest commitment is to replacing philosophy with politics.

❧ BIBLIOGRAPHY ❧

9.1   Acton, H. B. *The Illusion of the Epoch: Marxism as a Philosophical Creed*, London: Cohen & West, 1955.

9.2   Adorno, Theodor W. *Minima Moralia: Reflections from Damaged Life*, trans. E. F. N. Jephcott, London: NLB Verso, 1978.

9.3   Ayer, A. J. *Language, Truth, and Logic*, New York: Dover, 1936.

9.4   Baier, Annette C. 'The Need for More than Justice', in Kain Nielsen and Marsha Hanen, eds, *Science, Morality, and Feminist Theory*, Calgary: Canadian Journal of Philosophy, 1987 (suppl. vol.).

9.5   Bellah, Robert N., Richard Madsen, William M. Sullivan, Ann Swidler and

Steven M. Tipton *Habits of the Heart: Individualism and Commitment in American Life*, New York: Harper & Row, 1985.

9.6 Bentham, Jeremy *Principles of Morals and Legislation*, London, 1815.

9.7 Berlin, Isaiah, *Fathers and Children*, The Romanes Lecture, Oxford: Clarendon Press, 1972.

9.8 Cardozo, Benjamin R. *The Nature of the Judicial Process*, Storrs Lectures at Yale Law School, New Haven, Conn.: Yale University Press, 1949.

9.9 Cohen, G. A. *History, Labour, and Freedom*, Oxford: Clarendon Press, 1988.

9.10 —— *Karl Marx's Theory of History: A Defence*, Oxford: Clarendon Press, 1978.

9.11 Cohen, Joshua and Joel Rogers *On Democracy*, Harmondsworth: Penguin, 1984.

9.12 Cunningham, Frank *Democratic Theory and Socialism*, Cambridge: Cambridge University Press, 1987.

9.13 Dewey, John [1922] *Human Nature and Conduct: An Introduction to Social Psychology*, New York: Modern Library, 1930.

9.14 —— [1948] *Reconstruction in Philosophy*, enlarged edn, Boston: Beacon Press, 1957.

9.15 Dworkin, Ronald 'Why Bakke has No Case', *New York Review of Books*, 10 Nov. 1977: 11–15.

9.16 Elster, Jon *Making Sense of Marx*, Studies in Marxism and Social Theory, Cambridge: Cambridge University Press, 1985.

9.17 Gauthier, David P. *Morals by Agreement*, Oxford: Clarendon Press, 1986.

9.18 Gilligan, Carol *In a Different Voice*, Cambridge, Mass.: Harvard University Press, 1982.

9.19 Griffin, James 'Are There Incommensurable Values?', *Philosophy and Public Affairs*, 7 (1977): 39–59.

9.20 Guttman, Amy 'Communitarian Critics of Liberalism', *Philosophy and Public Affairs*, 14 (1985): 308–22.

9.21 Hayek, Friedrich, *The Road to Serfdom*, Chicago: University of Chicago Press, 1941.

9.22 Held, Virginia 'Non-Contractual Society', In Kain Nielsen and Marsha Hanen, eds, *Science, Morality, and Feminist Theory*, Calgary: Canadian Journal of Philosophy, 1987 (suppl. vol.).

9.23 Herzog, Don 'Some Questions for Republicans', *Political Theory*, 14:3 (1986): 473–94.

9.24 Hobhouse, L. T. *Liberalism*, London: Oxford University Press, 1964.

9.25 Jaggar, Allison *Feminist Politics and Human Nature*, Totowa, NJ: Rowman & Allenheld, 1983.

9.26 Jay, Martin *The Dialectical Imagination: A History of the Frankfurt School and the Institute of Social Research 1923–1950*, Boston: Little, Brown, 1973.

9.27 Kymlicka, Will *Liberalism, Community, and Culture*, Oxford: Clarendon Press, 1989.

9.28 Laclau, Ernesto and Chantal Mouffe *Hegemony and Socialist Strategy*, London: Verso, 1985.

9.29 Leiberman, Jethro 'The Relativity of Injury', *Philosophy and Public Affairs*, 2 (1977): 60–3.

9.30 Llewellyn, Karl [1932] *The Bramble Bush*, Chicago: University of Chicago Press, 1951.

9.31 MacIntyre, Alasdair *After Virtue: A Study in Moral Theory*, Notre Dame, Ind.: University of Notre Dame Press, 1981.

9.32 MacKinnon, Catherine *Feminism Unmodified: Discourses on Life and Law*, Cambridge, Mass.: Harvard University Press, 1987.

9.33 Marcuse, Herbert *Studies in Critical Philosophy*, trans. Joris de Bres, Boston: Beacon Press, 1972.

9.34 Mill, John Stuart *On Liberty*, London: Longmans, Green, 1865.

9.35 —— [1864] *Utilitarianism*, Indianapolis: Hackett, 1979.

9.36 Nagel, Thomas 'Libertarianism without Foundations', *University of Pennsylvania Law Review*, 25 (1975): 325–60.

9.37 Narveson, Jan, *The Libertarian Idea*, Philadelphia: Temple University Press, 1989.

9.38 Nozick, Robert *Anarchy, State, and Utopia*, New York: Basic Books, 1974.

9.39 Oakeshott, Michael *Rationalism in Politics*, London: Methuen, 1962.

9.40 Okin, Susan Moller *Women in Western Political Thought*, Princeton, NJ: Princeton University Press, 1979.

9.41 —— *Justice, Gender and the Family*, New York: Basic Books, 1989.

9.42 Pateman, Carole and Mary Lyndon Shanley, *Feminist Interpretations and Political Theory*, University Park: Pennsylvania State University Press, 1990.

9.43 Popper, K[arl] R. *The High Tide of Prophecy: Hegel, Marx, and the Aftermath*, vol. 2 of *The Open Society and Its Enemies*, New York: Harper & Row, Harper Torchbooks/The Academy Library, 1963.

9.44 Rawls, John *A Theory of Justice*, Cambridge, Mass.: Harvard University Press, 1971.

9.45 Ripstein, Arthur 'Foundationalism in Political Theory', *Philosophy and Public Affairs*, 16 (1987) 115–37.

9.46 Roemer, John *Free to Lose*, Cambridge, Mass.: Harvard University Press, 1989.

9.47 Roemer, John, ed *Analytical Marxism*, Cambridge: Cambridge University Press, 1987.

9.48 Ruddick, Sara 'Maternal Thinking', in J. Treblicot, ed., *Mothering: Essays in Feminist Theory*, Totowa, NJ: Rowman & Allenheld, 1984.

9.49 Sandel, Michael *Liberalism and the Limits of Justice*, Cambridge: Cambridge University Press, 1982.

9.50 Scott, Joan W., ed. *Feminists theorize the Political*, London: Routledge, 1992.

9.51 Sunstein, Cass, ed. *Feminism and Political Theory*, Chicago: University of Chicago Press, 1990.

9.52 Taylor, Charles 'Cross Purposes: The Liberal Communitarian Debate', in N. Rosenblum, ed., *Liberalism and the Moral Life*, Cambridge, Mass.: Harvard University Press, 1990: 159–82.

9.53 Unger, Roberto *Knowledge and Politics*, London: Macmillan, 1975.

9.54 Waxman, Chaim, ed. *The End of Ideology Debate*, New York: Simon & Schuster, 1968.

9.55 Weldon, T. D. *The Vocabulary of Politics*, Harmondsworth: Penguin, 1963.

9.56 Williams, Bernard 'Morality and Pessimism', The Leslie Steven Lecture, Cambridge: Cambridge University Press, 1972.
9.57 Young, Iris M. *Justice and the Politics of Difference*, Princeton, NJ: Princeton University Press, 1991.

CHAPTER 10

Feminist philosophy[1]
Sarah Lucia Hoagland and Marilyn Frye

Feminism re-emerged in the turmoil of the 1960s in anger and resistance, committed to revolution, to change. Heralding this wave and
following nineteenth-century themes, Simone de Beauvoir wrote in
1947: 'One is not born, but rather becomes, a woman.' There is a
difference between being anatomically female and becoming what
society recognizes as a woman: while there are facts, they take on
meanings only within a social context. What we are as women we
become, formed by oppression, being defined in relation to men as
Other, different.

The women's liberation movement went on to name western
society, whether in Europe, Scandinavia, Australia/New Zealand, Great
Britain or America – South, Central and North, as male-dominated:
men define and legislate women's place in society. The stereotypical
concept of women as helpmates or temptresses (of man) and as feminine
(passive, emotional, dependent, not-masculine) defines woman only in
relation to man. This man-made concept of woman, falsely presented
as women's nature by theories of biological or psychological difference,
both legitimizes and conceals individual and institutional violence of
men against women, and locks out any positive conception of female
power, collective or individual female resistance, or female bonding.
Feminists protest the violence, the erasure and the imposition of
definition.

Unlike most other systems of oppression and exploitation, the
oppression of women is hard to perceive because its mechanisms include
extensive mind-binding discourse – a multi-layered and inconsistent
mythology which women internalize in the process of learning their
native language, being schooled, being inducted into religious practice
and community, and being on the receiving end of marketing, advertising, commerce and entertainment. Much about the circumstances of
women in male-dominated societies promotes confusion, befuddlement

and false consciousness: for example, the mythology of love, the sexual double standard, the division of life into public and private (Firestone; Atkinson; in R. Morgan; in Gornick and Moran; in Koedt; Daly). Consigning women to realms of privacy, intimacy and mundane processes of maintenance, and to mind-numbing personal service, as well as clerical and factory work, encourages a microscopic apolitical mode of experience – close-up, fragmented, non-systematic perceptions and interpretations of our worlds.

Feminists began promoting consciousness-raising groups in which women talked with each other about their personal lives. Discussing subjects such as sex, work, marriage, motherhood, childhood experiences, sex roles and health led to recognizing how women's lives are laced with sexism. (In R. Morgan; in Gornick and Moran; in Koedt.) Consciousness-raising (CR) is a means of appropriating our experience, previously suffered as apolitical dailiness, and reading off it and through it the patterns of social power. CR is a strategy for people whose first critical task of liberation is to clearly perceive the problem. (Hartsock.)

Patterns of social power are made difficult to perceive in a variety of ways. Global patterns are played out differently in different women's lives. For example, the masculine myth of women as dangerous may be etched in different ethnic and racial communities on one woman's life as 'temptress', on another's as 'castrator'. And the pattern of male access to women's bodies is played out on some women through required exposure of their bodies, on others through required concealment, veiling. The practical contradictions of double binds make it difficult to perceive the political meanings of our actions. For example, a woman may brilliantly defend women's rights, but her engagement in the debate aligns her with the *status quo* sexist value that makes women's but not men's rights debatable. Patterns of power are also obscured by semantic voids and historical erasure, and by our being censored or manipulated into silence. Middle-class white women, finding their seamless lives intolerable, faced a 'problem with no name' and began defining it (Friedan). Black women, addressing their erasure as women and as blacks, recovered their herstory of agency and resistance (Shange; Parker; Wallace; in Hull; Lorde). Lesbians, realizing the censoring of our lives, proclaimed our love for women (Wittig; in Birkby; Johnston; in Myron and Bunch; in Penelope and Wolfe; in Beck; in Ramos). And progressive white men, finding their place at centre stage threatened, guilt-tripped white women by claiming that addressing women's issues was racist because it diverted attention from the struggle against racism ... a claim often welcomed by black men who had been challenged by black women for making them 'the slave of a slave' (in Cade).

As feminists overcome these barriers to perception, we find connections between apparently disparate and contradictory phenomena. For example some US politicians attacking abortion favour forced sterilization of poor women and women of colour; and while professing concern with the fetus in the womb they do not support the child outside. Feminists began realizing that the consistent pattern suffusing these contrary manifestations was one of institutional control of women's bodies and control of women's biologically and socially reproductive (socializing, care-taking) labour. Patterns of systematically related barriers functioning in the dominant group's interest serve to maintain male domination, police class divisions and ensure white supremacy (Frye).

Feminist theory is a collective process that appeals to, is based in and is mediated by experiences which variously situated women name and appropriate in CR as authoritative grounds for action and thought. All this work involves a fascinating and intricate dance between experience and theory: while experience remains the checkpoint, analyses affect the meanings of our experiences and enlarge their scope. The process engages us in struggles both among feminists and with others which, though sometimes painful, fan the flames of our imaginations.

Feminists expanded the concept of politics to include sexual politics – power relations between men and women as individuals but especially as classes (Millett). Following themes of suffrage, some feminists took up the call for equal rights in order to bring the republic into conformity with its ideology as a democratic society. They argue that sex differences do not justify civil discrimination and insist on women getting equal opportunity, benefits and protection under the law. This liberal-feminist demand has exposed the subordination of women as necessary to the social contract among privileged men. While the patriarchal state may have ended in Europe for men with the overthrow of the monarchies, it did not end for women: the social contract between men includes the division of society into public and private spheres, establishing men's political right over women and their access to and use of women's bodies and labour in the private sphere. (Pateman.)

Other feminists point out that demanding equality with men paradoxically endorses men's status as the norm or paradigm of humanity and citizenship. Furthermore it actually cedes this status not just to any men or all men, but to privileged men (middle to or upper-class, able-bodied, heterosexual, Christian, white), and thus validates the structures and stratifications of western liberal industrial capitalism. This system grew on colonialism, genocide and slavery; it works by extraction of 'surplus value' from the labour of workers. Worker exploitation is facilitated by assigning women to lower status and pay and maintaining an unacknowledged substratum of women's unpaid labour in the 'private' sphere of home, subsistence production and child-care. This requires the subordination in various ways of women of all races and places; even women of aristocratic and owning classes often play a role in domestic and social management of acknowledged economic value to privileged men. The system also requires that privileged males control the reproduction of a population of suitable workers and consumers, which they do in part by regulating women's sexuality, fertility and child-rearing. (Eisenstein; Hartsock; Ferguson.) Capitalism is a system of stratification, inequality, exploitation, oppression. It is neither structurally possible, nor morally defensible, for all women to have the rights and privileges such a system gives those at the top. For the oppression of women to end, there must be entirely different structures.

Many feminists have noted that male violence against women transcends the material or economic requirements of capitalism; it appears to maintain male dominance as an end in itself. They argue that there is a declared war on women manifest in assault and murder, rape, child sexual abuse, sexual harassment, medical abuse, etc. Some feminists argue that rape is a terrorist institution (Card), benefiting all men because it keeps women believing they need men for protection (Griffin; Brownmiller). Others focus on the misogyny that suffuses men's entertainment, and argue that pornography eroticizes rape and abuse, solidifying the connection between sex and violence characteristic of masculinist life (MacKinnon). Others note that pornographic sons hold the same contempt for the body as church fathers against whom they rebelled (Griffin). Expressing this contempt, pornography is necrophilic and emphasizes sensations without feelings, promotes the mind/body split, and robs women of erotic desire as a source of knowledge and a kind of power (Lorde). Resisting woman-hating agendas that divide women against ourselves, some feminists reach for the dis-covery/creation of woman's Self capable of sisterhood and integrity (Daly; Dworkin; R. Morgan).

Many feminists see female heterosexuality not as a biological given but as a social construct made to seem natural. Central to the systematic oppression of women, the institution of heterosexuality supports dualistic, hierarchical conceptions of difference which underlie other structures such as racism (Daly; Frye; Wittig). Feminists have argued that the institution of female heterosexuality is necessary to the traffic in women which constitutes patriarchal kinship and mediates men's personal and economic relations (Rubin in Reiter; Sedgwick). Some argue that it secures individual women's unpaid services to individual men essential to the structures of domination (capitalism, colonialism, etc.). Some say the institution is grounded in men's very definition of 'woman': 'woman' is defined as what turns men on, as (hetero)sexual availability on men's terms (MacKinnon), as 'appropriated by man'. By these definitions lesbians are not women: not 'women' to men sexually, but also economically, politically and socially (Wittig). Others note that female heterosexuality works politically to separate women from each other, inhibiting our solidarity and our bonding in resistance. Instituted female heterosexuality, presented as natural, renders lesbian experience invisible, or if visible, aberrant and abhorrent. Some note the erasure of lesbian existence even in the women's movement and academic feminist scholarship (Rich). Suggesting a lesbian continuum (Rich; in B. Smith; Card), some have emphasized the wide range of woman-bonding (in marriage-resistance, nunneries, lesbian connection, etc.) and look to female friendship as a model both of ethics and resistance (Raymond). Some argue that it is only friendship, intimate connection, and not mere commitment to political principles, that adequately supports women's solidarity across barriers of race and class (Lugones and Spelman in Pearsall; Anzaldúa; Hoagland).

Focusing on still another material reality of women's situation, racism, women of colour have continuously challenged white feminists. Arguing that black feminism has distinct origins, theorists articulate the interrelatedness and simultaneity of oppressions (in B. Smith; Moraga). Naming a different history of economic participation, domination by white women, and 'freedom' from the dubious privileges of femininity, feminists argue that black women face distinct problems in resisting capitalist male domination, and have distinct cultural sources of resistance (in B. Smith; A. Davis; Lorde; Kingston). Feminists decry finding themselves in someone else's discourse or story, trapped either in a picture that distorts their lives because of hidden cultural assumptions, or in silence because they have ceased to try to fit into the dominant context (Lugones and Spelman in Pearsall). Noting the relation of ignorance to acts of ignoring (Frye), feminists began articulating privileges that some women enjoy in patriarchy which permit them to distort, co-opt and exclude the concerns of other, less privileged women. Arguing that race and class differences must not be simply tolerated, feminists show they provide the 'fund of necessary polarities between which our creativity can spark like a dialectic' (Lorde). Thus feminists analyse the importance of theories of women of colour moving from margin to centre (hooks).

Some feminists focus on separating from men and from masculine discourse as a way of undermining heterosexual patterns and male parasitism, of becoming woman-identified (Radicalesbians in R. Morgan). Total power is unconditional access, and the first act of shifting power involves taking control of male access to women (Frye). Further, some say that when white feminists argue that women must work with men, they in effect align themselves with white men, their connections with women of colour being at best distant and lacking the revolutionary intimacy of friendship. Thus their analyses are too simple, failing to acknowledge both the differences in the situations of women of colour and the possible fruits of alliance (Lee in Hoagland and Penelope). In not reaching towards women of colour, they acquiesce for example in black men's assuming the right to define black culture. Others argue that separatism is a lens through which we perceive the world and is the prism for many of our ethical choices, focusing our attention on matters central to lesbians and other women (Anderson in *Signs*, 19.2). As such, separatism is a form of engagement. Actually most feminists engage in separating in one way or another from patriarchal values – humanism, masculine notions of rationality, gender roles, individualism, for example – in the effort to free up feminist imagination from defensive focus on men's agendas and to construct new values in new frameworks.

As feminist philosophy moves on, each achievement of clarity reveals more complexity. One early problem and all its variations has yielded a central contribution of feminist philosophy: explorations of how women are agents while neither fully in control of our situation nor total victims – how we are both subjects (agents) and subjected (de Lauretis). Actually the related questions of agency and subjectivity inform, explicitly or implicitly, most feminist philosophy.

A good portion of feminist theory starts from understanding ourselves as victims and therefore as unlike the free-willed, self-defined Man of dominant western philosophy. Prior to feminist activism, rape, wife-beating, incest and sexual harassment were all regarded as private and personal matters, a woman's fault and, contradictorily, a matter of boys being boys. Much feminist work involves articulating ways men victimize and then blame women. However, by the mid 1970s, feminists noted that we must avoid both blaming the victim *and* victimism – the perception of a woman as only a victim and not also a resister. (Barry.) In fact, perceiving women only as victims fails to acknowledge that women *act* in patriarchy. There are many ways both of resisting male domination and of collaborating, and this must be acknowledged to fully understand women's situations and agency. Even direct coercion standardly involves arranging circumstances and options and then depending upon the victim to choose the least bad option available. We are agents, but not free agents, when we choose intercourse over life-threatening bodily harm. (Frye.) We collaborate when we hold men to lower standards as colleagues, friends and lovers than we hold women to. On the other hand, many feminine stereotypes, as is true of slave stereotypes, obscure resistance to domination, for example acts of sabotage are interpreted as incompetence or insanity (Hoagland).

Perceiving women only as victims also keeps us from realizing how women participate in other oppressive structures, for example ways white women in feminist organizations ignore African-American or Latina women, ways middle-class women use middle-class standards against working-class women, ways heterosexual women silence lesbians, ways able-bodied lesbians ignore disabled women's needs, ways Christian-cultured women (white, black or Latina) foster Christian values uncongenial to Jewish and Native American women, ways middle-aged women champion ageist values when perceiving old women and discount the young. (In Moraga and Anzaldúa; in Anzaldúa; in B. Smith; Macdonald in Macdonald and Rich; in Bunch and Myron.)

An historic example shows how tricky this gets. In one of the early US works dealing cross-culturally with disciplinary inscriptions of power on the body, Mary Daly investigated forms of men's torture of women: European witch-burning, Chinese foot-binding, Indian suttee, African genital mutilation and American gynaecology. By researching men's agendas she shows, for example, that the history of gynaecology is a continuation of the history of the contest over women's bodies. Audre Lorde, however, points out that Daly explored all these atrocities but provided only European images of resistance, and thus does disservice to women of other cultures by erasure of the fact that they have constructed means of resistance within their own traditions. How would Chinese women, for example, be recognized beyond the victim status (Chow in Mohanty)? Even active engagement in resistance does not ensure that we are not also participating in oppression.

Women's agency, ability to act, is compromised overtly by men's violence and imposed barriers to movement, and covertly by masculinist conceptions of female virtue and the self. Early feminist work on morality involves naming the immorality of masculine political agendas and demanding rights, such as the right to control our bodies. Other work challenges socially prescribed feminine virtues such as nurturance and volunteerism, and argues that the standards of womanhood involve self-sacrifice to a degree that is immoral. (In R. Morgan; in Gornick and Moran.)

Some have noted that in masculine discourse the traits defining women's goodness mark them as morally deficient, and have undertaken to revalue stereotypical feminine traits. For example women's 'weak ego boundaries' actually indicate the capacity of empathy, women's 'deference' is actually sensitivity to the needs of others. (Gilligan.) Others question the revaluing of feminine 'virtues'. Nurturing has not cured the violence in women's lives; a woman's misplaced gratitude towards men for taking less than full advantage may be mistaken for care, and misplaced gratitude is a form of moral damage. Women have developed these skills and capacities to survive under patriarchal domination; it does not mean they are timeless virtues. (Card.)

Nevertheless, responding to the fractured view of ethical relations produced by a focus on rights and justice and duty, many feminists reach for an ethics of care (Held; Noddings; Manning; Tronto). Such an ethics more accurately addresses relationships among people than does the fiction of the masculine ethical agent, one who is autonomous, aggressive and competitive (i.e. socially inept), for example the contractual man of liberal utilitarian theory. This model is inadequate to the majority of social arrangements. For example the mother/child relationship is neither voluntary nor contractual. An ethics that uses the model of a mother acknowledges dependency and sharing in relationships. (Held.) Further an ethics that involves not a stance of impartiality (ignoring institutionalized social oppressions) but a stance of partiality (within which one can empathize with the individuals involved) reveals a ground from which different sorts of solutions to moral problems become apparent (Friedman).

All thought arises out of social practice, and maternal practice is governed by concern for the preservation, growth and acceptability of children. It arises out of practices oppressive to women and children and can involve inauthenticity, so it needs a feminist analysis. Nevertheless, maternal practices can give rise to distinctive ways of conceptualizing, ordering and valuing which can found a feminist peace politics capable of exposing flaws in masculinist militaristic thinking and masculine conceptions of peace (Ruddick). Other feminists question the ideology of heterosexual virtue by which women are held to be better than men because allegedly nurturant and non-violent. Noting this ideology ignores the material history of nurturance (women give freely, expect nothing in return, and are responsible for righting the destruction of men's actions without appropriate power and resources), they argue this framework obliterates women who reject these values and women who actively resist men's appropriation of women's labour (Allen).

Other feminists note that dominant western conceptions of womanhood have excluded black women from the definition of woman and femininity (A. Davis; Cannon; Carby). Some argue that many women do not have the relationship to motherhood that is romanticized in patriarchal images. The cult of womanhood as applied to the southern plantation mistress glorified a wifehood and motherhood and was denied to black women slaves: white men's control over white women yielded heirs and citizens, their control over black women yielded property and capital. (Carby) Consequently some concepts that apply to white women don't apply to black women. For example, self-sacrifice is not a *moral* imperative for those consigned to sacrifice in a state of slavery (Cannon). Others argue distinctive values emerge from women of colour's motherwork, namely survival, identity and empowerment. Simply contrasting an ethics of care with an ethics of justice may by-pass survival values as in effect pre-moral. Questions of survival are central and cannot be taken for granted; black mothers resist oppressive ideology both in terms of their own capacity to mother and their children's ability to develop a meaningful racial identity. (Collins.)

Some question the rejection of a justice ethic. An ethics that leaves starving strangers outside the realm of moral consideration, as a care ethic seems to do, is inadequate, especially when we have had a hand in creating those conditions and/or benefit from them (Card). Others note the care ethic's inadequacy in addressing those outside the caregiver's circle, and they question the opposition between justice and care (Friedman; Okin; Young). In developing a feminist concept of justice, they continue challenging the impartial masculine moralist, arguing for a body politic that articulates rather than homogenizes difference (Young).

Significantly, resistance often emerges from neither the care nor the justice frameworks (in Anzaldúa). On the one hand, if we were to focus on women's choices in resisting rape, we might find values emerging that are different than those associated with the care ethic (Moody-Adams in Card). On the other hand, some address questions of survival and resistance, arguing that the moral sphere of black women is survival against tyrannical systems of oppression. Moral agency, thus, involves developing virtues under these circumstances. The virtue of feistiness allows black people to resist white agendas. Unctuousness, acting sincere with the insincere, can help women create possibilities where none existed before. While drawing on notions of care, theorists nevertheless contextualize it with an ethics of survival and resistance that derives from the lives of black women during 250 years of slavery and 100 years of segregation. The emerging moral wisdom involves not only how to survive but how to prevail with integrity. (Cannon)

Central to moral agency under oppression is realizing one is neither in total control nor a total victim: it is not because we are free and moral agents that we are able to make moral choices; rather, by making choices, acting within limits, we declare ourselves to be moral beings. Some suggest the function of lesbian ethics is the development of lesbian integrity, agency and community, and that rather than value autonomy and regard ourselves as related to others antagonistically as occurs under patriarchal ethics whose function is social control, we value autokoenony – self in community. Thus we regard ourselves as one among many, realizing our possibilities emerge only in community and across communities. (Hoagland.)

Revolutionary interacting across communities involves playful world-travel. This is not men's idea of play: to conquer and kill, to colonize and demoralize; one must not play with conquerors. World-travel instead involves flexibility, playfulness and epistemic uncertainty. (Lugones) Here we encounter the trickster who unsettles our solidity, seriousness, our ignorance, our arrogance (Cameron). The trickster and play (which can be life-threatening, but then ignorance is life-threatening) become ethical options to disciplinarian notions of duty and justice, dismantling the dismissing power of privilege and erasing the dominant power of ignorance. Here also we become each others' resources, learning about ourselves and each other by travelling to each others' worlds. World-travel offers passage from the constraints of any one culture's ethical construction and is essential to realizing the liberatory potential of feminist thought. (Lugones.)

The theme of women-as-agents transposes, in the realm of epistemology and philosophy of science, to the theme of women-as-knowers. Feminists have consistently attended to the matter of who the scientist or knower is; they have not accepted the abstraction of knowledge from the knowers. They indict the 'impartial' knower much as they do the 'impartial' moralist.

Current feminist challenges to science, following nineteenth-century feminist criticisms, began by exposing the sexist bias of (male) scientists. For example, at a time when scientists thought the frontal lobe was the centre of thought, men did studies 'proving' women's frontal lobes were slightly smaller than men's. When upper- and middle-class women were wearing torturous corsets, their tendencies to fainting were cited by men as 'proof' of their frailty. Some feminists argue that the construction of the masculine *rational* and *orderly* stands on the grave of the feminine *passionate* and *unruly*, and they challenge the whole endeavour for its fractured construction (Griffin). Related feminist queries challenge the laboratory construction of knowledge which extracts pieces from nature, and wonder at the knowledge thereby lost (Merchant; Keller). Still others question the research methods meant to obtain objectivity, questioning the sort of knowledge that is thereby constructed (in Tuana).

Contrasting the earlier nature-as-organism metaphor with the nature-as-mechanism metaphor underlying modern science, feminists argue that the rise of science as an ideology of (male) control over (female) nature results in wilful disregard for and exploitation of the planet and thereby in ecological disasters. Exposing sexual and sexist metaphors scientists use, they argue that sexual politics structures the nature of the scientific empirical method which pretends to be free of cultural and political assumptions. Scientists also inject values into their descriptions of the facts to be investigated. Sexism is intrinsic to scientific discourse. (Merchant; Keller; Irigaray in Tuana) Many feminists explore the use of scientific authority and ideology to keep women 'in their place' – economically dependent and intellectually deprived.

Others focus on the elitism and classism of the professional endeavour – the gate-keeping that ensures that science is a preserve of privileged men. They trace the theft of knowledge/practice from women and the suppression of knowledgeable women, for example the out-lawing of midwives during the rise of gynaecology. They demand the reclamation of science, both of empirical, common-sense knowledge (knowledge, for example possessed by European witches about herbs) and of sophisticated technologies, for the service and benefit of the people who are not to be the passive consumers of the mysteries of the elite. And they argue that the professionalization of science, together with the ideology of progress, develops knowledge which primarily benefits only certain classes. (Ehrenreich and English.)

Feminists have exposed some spectacularly bad science which promotes sexism and sexist agendas (Bleier). Arguing about whether the practice of science is intrinsically sexist and racist or whether sexism and racism distort a science which is intrinsically a sound practice, they agree nonetheless that science is not value-neutral (Harding). Some think feminism can bring science more in line with its own goals, exposing the wilful ignorances of a self-selected group of male thinkers. Others argue that the goals themselves are hopelessly mired in the depths of masculine imagination. A collage of contributions to the understanding of science emerge out of these critical discussions. Many feminists set about recovering women's contributions to science, women whose work has been used by men who receive awards. Others con-tinue to expose the sexist and racist underpinnings of scientific work. Others develop feminist methodology and epistemology or theory of knowledge.

The science upheld as paradigm and most prestigious and, not accidentally, the science most male-identified and 'hardest', is physics. Feminists challenge the assumption that physics is paradigm on the grounds that (1) the subject matter of physics is not complex; (2) physics provides descriptive formulas which are not explanations, and explanations which are vague metaphors, e.g. 'Big Bang' and 'Black hole'; (3) it excludes intentional, learned and 'irrational' behaviour. Reality is complex; science should explain; and the phenomena of intelligent animals have as much right to a high place on the agenda as sub-atomic particles. (Harding.) Standard conceptions of science take the visual knowing of an inanimate object as the paradigm of knowing. Developing a theme of interdependency, some feminists suggest, instead, knowing a person as the paradigm (Code). The latter involves knowing something massively complex; in knowing persons we constantly provide ourselves with explanations; and such knowledge is interactive. Conceiving the knower or researcher as non-interactive enables 'him' to remain transparent. The ideal of scientist as a neutral, objective, irrelative observer allows particular political agendas (*status quo*) to go unquestioned (as is the case with the impartial moralist), promotes knowledge as an instrument of domination and silences his objects of study, his subjects. Acknowledging and inviting interaction between knower and known casts the knower as an interactive agent in the world.

Pursuing the question of bias in science and knowledge, some feminists have articulated various versions of a 'standpoint' theory (Hartsock; Frye; Gilligan; Collins; Harding). The core theme of 'standpoint theories' is that knowers differently located in history and social structures have access to different knowledge of both the social and non-social worlds. For example, men's studies of lions, invoking king-of-the-jungle mythology, portray males as dominant. Actually, however, lions are socially expendable, unable to join together in mutual co-operation and protection; 'lion' prides centre on the activities of adult lionesses (Reed). In this and other studies of animal behaviour women observers have discovered very different things than are recorded by men observers (Haraway). In situations where immediate observations are unlikely to differ so dramatically, research agendas and design are affected by the locations and interests of the inquirers. At the very least this means a complete science would require contributions from many locations. Furthermore different lives may also generate quite different, even non-communicating, conceptual frames, values and meanings, so the different knowledges may not be readily assimilable into a collective unified knowledge of a unitary world.

Many feminists also suggest there are different concepts of rationality. Masculine rationality is constructed by excluding attributes and experiences of women and the underclasses. Some pursue the observation that a rational (coercive) unity that appeals to 'truth' doesn't necessarily move people to action; there is no evidence that appeals to reason, knowledge or truth are uniquely effective. Political action and change involve many capacities besides reason including capacities for empathy, anger and disgust. (Flax.)

Feminist rethinking of the knower has also led to the suggestion that individuals' knowing is derivative of community knowing. In a sense the primary knower is a community: what counts as evidence is communal, and construction and acquisition of knowledge are communal processes (Nelson).

Some feminists have questioned the feminist preoccupation with epistemology understood as matters of relations among knowledge, knowers and truth. The interesting relations include those among knowledge, desire, fantasy, passion and various kinds of power (Daly; Flax; Jaggar). The claim that feminist revisions will increase the objectivity and truth of science may be an attempt to make feminism innocent when what we want is power. When we don't pay attention to desire and fantasy and power, we more easily make epistemology a site of retreat from the conflicts and complexities of interpersonal and political issues (Flax). For example, when privileged white feminists' own projects of knowledge are criticized by other women, women of colour and/or less privileged, as harmful to them, the response often has been not to attend to the women who are being harmed but to attend to theoretical questions about knowledge and theory (Lugones).

Partly as a result of these sorts of considerations, feminists began to realize that the concept of standpoint is not sufficiently complex. It tends to be about fixed locations in a reified 'world'; in the background is an image of two people standing on opposite sides of a statue seeing different things, where one observer is the Husband and the other is the Wife. A much more complex concept was developed, 'situated knowledges' (Haraway). It adds to that background picture, acknowledging differences in allegiances among observers (for example, they may be members of cultures which are in conflict), and places the observers in three-way conversations with the statue which is now animate and talks back. Some ecofeminists have perhaps been most insistent on some version of the world as an active subject (Griffin; Adams; in Gaard; in *Hypatia*, 6.1; in Warren) and on making room for the world's independent sense of humour (Bigwood). We can acknowledge the trickster, 'give up mastery but search for fidelity, knowing all the while we will be hoodwinked' (Haraway).

One reason for a feminist emphasis on epistemology in relation to the project of exploring women's agency has been to rescue women from men's 'knowledge'/construction of women. Feminists focusing on psychology note how it constructs the female (Weisstein in R. Morgan). For example, mental health for a woman is defined by psychiatrists as her being feminine, heterosexual and sexually accessible to therapists (Chesler), and the adult standard replicates the male standard while the female standard is quite different. Early challenges to psychology note the circularity of psychoanalysis: women who deny being phallically oriented in fantasy or reality merely 'prove' that orientation by their denials, women who report incest merely 'affirm' theories of rape fantasy, etc. Feminists expose the theory that women fantasize rape as a male professional cover-up for the sins of the fathers (Rush).

Others challenge concepts such as hysteria and frigidity, while also suggesting one investigate instances of testeria (the ability to calmly, efficiently and maturely carry out assaults, torture and genocide, and planetary disaster such as war, capitalism, totalitarianism) (in R. Morgan; in Gornick and Moran; Loesch in Kramarae and Treichler). Feminists note the types of behaviour for which one is most often hospitalized are disturbingly correlated with race, caste and sex (in Gornick and Moran; in R. Morgan). Others note that psychology, including some feminist psychology, interprets political phenomena as personal problems and pathologies, reversing the feminist-activist discovery that the personal is political (Kitzinger and Perkins). One feminist 'take' on psychoanalysis interprets it as an unwittingly revealing description of patriarchal society and the damage done to individuals as they are inducted into it (Mitchell; Rubin in Reiter).

Focusing on men's relationship to power and the effect material life has on consciousness, some argue that because of the way women are responsible for rearing children in nuclear families in western industrial societies, the infant's first intimacy is solely with a person who is female and socially subordinate. The process of identity formation, thus, is different for boys and girls. This suggests that in such societies men's propensity towards separation and aggression and women's propensity for connection and community result from the sexual division of labour in child-rearing. The social organizing of parenting produces women more capable of non-hostile relations but it also perpetuates patriarchy through the reproduction of mothers. (Chodorow; Hartsock)

In the western patriarchal tradition 'the knower' is unitary, that is, all knowers are in principle the same – the rational man. Feminists introduced plurality and complexity, recognizing many knowers with different knowledges, first with the revolutionary addition of women as knowers and the exploration of differences between women and men as knowers and agents. But the concept of the self, male or female, as having unity and stability is also challenged. A feminist picture emerges of the partial autonomy of a world of desire and fantasy, suggesting that the subject is a shifting and always changing intersection of complex, contradictory and unfinished processes (Flax). The unitary self exists only through the practice of domination, and can sustain its unity only by repressing other parts of its own and others' subjectivity (Flax; Lugones). Particularly in the work of women of colour, we find that plural subjectivities are fluid rather than solid, and contextual rather than universal (Lugones; Anzaldúa).

Challenging the phallic appropriation of meaning and knowledge, refusing to enter the male symbolic by leaving females' sex as negative or unnamed, some feminists undertake to construct a positive female difference that is elusive, fluid and ambiguous (Irigaray), wild, chaotic and disorderly (Daly). By giving voice to that which has been repressed in the canon of philosophy, feminists force canon-mongers to abandon their pretence of neutrality and reveal themselves as gendered, indeed sexed.

Far from being neutral, the ideally rational moralist, scientist and citizen of the liberal state constructs and unifies himself by splitting off aspects of the self he associates with the lives of the disenfranchised, and he thereby commits himself to the logic of paranoia (Scheman). He is threatened by the always already impending accusations from abused women (Nye). The resulting problems of modern philosophy (mind/body, reference and truth, other minds, scepticism) are the neuroses of privilege and are unsolvable so long as the subject's identity is constituted by those estrangements (Scheman; Bordo). Post-modern masculine renditions of the mind/body split are no less abstract, metaphysical, psychotic, misogynistic (Brodribb).

White identity is similarly dependent on marginalization of difference (Spellman): only by defining women and the East as peripheral can western man/humanism present itself as central (Spivak). Much of the theory of oppression in the earlier phases of feminist philosophy concerned oppression by the most privileged people, whose locations of oppression were the most simple (namely privileged white males). Feminist theories of the nature and mechanism of oppression have been made more complex and nuanced since attention has shifted to the ways oppression is enacted by people in mixed positions, like for instance that of white women in western societies or class-privileged women in other societies, and how oppression is experienced by other women who might desire sisterhood and alliance with them.

When western feminists write about Third World women, making assumptions about women's oppression which are rooted in western experience, western feminists become the only true subjects of the counter-history. This contributes to the colonization or erasure of Third World women, robbing them of their history and political agency. (Mohanty; Chow in Mohanty.) When white feminists construct the category of woman as unitary and universal, they replicate patriarchal pseudo-neutrality – this time a cultural or racial neutrality. They achieve the unity by infusing the notion of woman with their own cultural experience and meanings, splitting off and marginalizing women of other cultures. This ethno-centring enables white western women to write about Third World women in ways that impose white western women's meanings and agendas and which erase Third World women's history, agency *and* perceptions of white western women. Western feminists can learn from Third World women they study that the latters' access to the political and sexual scene is autonomous and authoritative. There must be simultaneous questions: 'Who is the other woman? How am I naming her? How does she name me?' (Spivak.) Who am I to her?

Feminist projects involve progressive revisions of our understanding of ourselves as we dialogue with each other, discover problems in earlier theory, and explore new ways of appropriating our experiences and enlarging their scopes through consciousness-raising, playful world-travelling and theory-making. We focus on divergent aspects of our subjectivity emerging from our experiences as variously situated selves, and in the process offer and find varied contributions to creating/ dis-covering feminist resistance and revolutionary constructions of female agency.

Simone de Beauvoir argued that women must come to full con-sciousness by antagonistically opposing men as men have opposed women and each other, making Others of men. Many feminists have rejected both de Beauvoir's individualism and this vision of liberation, but it does provide a picture of the fate that befalls you if you decide resistance is enough: you end up in the masculine world of selves busily trying to annihilate each other. Feminists have emphasized the urgency of creating for women (and other oppressed folk) alternatives to a life or self defined only by resistance to and assimilation to male orders of law and language. More significantly, many argue that enduring alterna-tives cannot be created, like camp-sites for campers, by some women for all women. They have to be continuously created through the creation of selves in community – identities independent of the oppressors and their agendas that do not await validation or legitimation by dominating individuals or institutions (Daly; hooks).

Though much of de Beauvoir has been rejected, many of her themes endure: the theme that selves are continuously created; the idea that making of selves is mortally risky and requires existential courage; the recognition that if you fail to create yourself you will collapse into someone else's creation; the idea that in creating one's self (selves) one is creating value. Feminists variously characterize such selves as wild, radical, creative, feisty, plural, lesbian, self-critical, fiery. The continuous creation and instability of the female selves is also emphasized by many theorists (Daly; Anzaldúa; Lugones). Consciousness is never fixed because discourses change, because historical and material conditions change, because the relationships with others through which identity which is negotiated change; because we are alive. Subjectivity, thus, is not a fixed point of departure or arrival but an on-going construction. (de Lauretis.) The difficulty of women's self-construction leads some feminists to focus on rehabilitating genuine passions such as anger and lust (Daly; Lorde; Parker), some to focus on respect (Addelson; Card), and some to focus on the prerequisites of the integrity necessary to resist coercion, manipulation and de-moralization (Cannon; Hoagland).

The idea that making female selves is mortally risky and requires great courage is perhaps most vividly expressed in the work of some mestiza women (women who cross borders, women of mixed race)

(Anzaldúa; Lugones). Leaving behind the familiar, predictable, boundaries and frames within which female and racialized selves have been constructed, giving up the hope of integrity in a prefabricated identity, there is the possibility of being nothing – going someplace unimaginable and not finding yourself upon arrival. Removing masks: the possibility that there is no one at the core (in Anzaldúa). It is a creative project of freedom to recognize one's varied selves in different contexts, to recognize one's self deprived of agency but retaining imagination, to recognize the self oppressed as another face of the self resisting, to grasp that an intention formed by the self you are in one place cannot be carried out by the self in another, and still recognize yourself (Lugones; Anzaldúa).

Mestiza plurality/multiplicity is distinct from the multiplicity of those who develop multiple personalities as a creative survival technique in the face of severe childhood trauma and/or abuse. Mestiza plurality is often characterized as plural modes of being which are available and evolving in plural or ambiguous external situations. While there is no uniform experience of multiple personality, its multiple modes flow in relation to present external situations, as well as according to logics of past situations no longer externally real, and logics internal to the structure of multiple selves. These experiences wreak havoc with the whole constellation of concepts related to *self*: unified self, core personality, choice, authenticity/inauthenticity, conscious/unconscious, memory, epistemic community, co-operation, consensus, difference, community, 'I'. (Leighton.)

The human possibility of multiple personality, as distinct from the plurality of a sort exemplified by the mestiza, reveals that there is more to self and subjectivity and their formation by violence and domination than feminists have yet understood. What can become a problem for people with multiple personalities is not multiplicity but amnesia and sabotage and what is required is not sterile singularity but memory, hobnobbing and solidarity – which suggests that multiple personality may be the useful analogue of communities created under oppression. (Card; Cuomo in Card; Leighton.) Having unavoidable and intimate acquaintance with simultaneous multiple perspectives, some multiples can verify most decisively that there are different ways of simultaneously thinking and feeling with integrity about one and the same thing – something feminists resisting patriarchal science, ethics and politics may need verified repeatedly (Leighton).

Mestiza consciousness also provides for new understanding. It models a tolerance for ambiguity, a transgression of rigid boundaries, of borders set up by dominant groups to distinguish 'us' from 'them'. (Anzaldúa.) It is a consciousness that lives on the borders – lives in neither place and both. Mestiza consciousness raises questions and suggests new thinking about locatedness and its relation to identity.

Mestiza consciousness, unlike a unitary patriarchal consciousness that preserves itself by insisting on seriousness and a unitary world, can show to all feminists the possibility of playful world-travelling which undermines the seriousness fertilizing tyranny and indicates how liberatory possibilities only emerge in community with others. When we travel to another's world, we see what it is to be them in their world. And we see ourselves as we are constructed in their world. (Lugones.) By travelling to each other's worlds, we gain knowledge we need to change, we begin to unravel some of the mind-binding of professional masculine authority, and we thereby begin to dismantle dominant ideology. We are each other's sources of knowledge.

World-travellers engage in conversations, moving the centre around. If they never did before, they begin to speak for themselves, they recognize in others what was hidden in themselves, they speak to their sisters, resisting the gaze of conquerors. If they ever did before, they cease trying to speak for the other, cease trying to exercise an imperialist moral gaze, cease trying to be in charge; instead they listen in a way that finds the other speaking back to challenge not only their understanding of her but their understanding of themselves. They see and are seen in her life. And they locate themselves in the histories of women.

Feminist philosophers generally reject any biological determinism according to which the oppression of women might be explained or justified as a natural consequence of anatomical configurations and functions of male and female human bodies (de Beauvoir; Daly; Wittig; Butler). Perhaps as a result of the desire to avoid any hint of such biological determinism, a good deal of feminist philosophy neglects the female 'sexedness' of our bodies, leaving it unremarked and not integrated in the theories, except in connection with critiquing or revaluing motherhood. But some feminists are very concerned with female bodies, sensual pleasures, physical eroticism and sexuality, independently of their connection with reproduction (Irigaray; Frye; Wittig; J. Allen; Spivak; Zita; Bartky). It is suggested that a fundamental process of the oppression of women is the suppression, indeed annihilation of autonomous female sexuality – eroticism intrinsically related neither to male/men/masculinity, nor to reproduction, and this is connected by many feminists with the erasure of autonomous female selves or subjectivities and with the enormity and riskiness of the projects of self-construction (Irigaray; Cixous; Daly; J. Allen; Spivak).

The suppression of autonomous female eroticism is vividly enacted in the erasure of the lesbian alternative, or its co-optation in pornography, and many feminists have argued that making lesbian eroticism a real and practical option for all women is an essential part of liberation strategy (Hoagland; Frye; Card; J. Allen; Trebilcott; Wittig; Wittig and Zeig).

Some claim that the feminist focus on reproductive freedom or the patriarchal appropriation of the womb – especially the tendency to make this the defining issue of feminism – is a mistake and mistakenly buys into the image of woman as mother. Prior to coupling and maternity, cross-culturally and transhistorically, is physical, symbolic and/or psychological clitoridectomy. The suppression of the clitoris is presupposed by patriarchy and family. It may well be that the patriarchal suppression and feminist reinstatement of clitoral (independent of men and non-reproductive) sexuality constitutes an intersection of cultures and simultaneously an intersection of body and identity at which the immense variety of women and our needs, perceptions, creations and theories can communicate and be articulated. (Spivak.)

Each feminist effort gives us yet another aspect of our possibilities. There is truth in all of them. The political discussion and the process of constructing female selves and agency is multivocal (Lugones). Many feminists argue that only plural subjects can invent ways to struggle against domination that will not merely recreate it, and that subjectivities can be imagined whose desires for plurality impel them towards liberatory action (Lugones; Flax).

Wild Women (Daly). Willful Virgins (Frye). Womanists (A. Walker). Lesbians. Amazons. Home girls (in B. Smith). Witches. Spinsters. Las Mestizas (Anzaldúa). Crones (Macdonald in Macdonald and Rich; B. Walker). Lovhers (Brossard). Sorceresses. Woman warriors (Kingston). *Les guérillères*:

> There was a time when you were not a slave, remember that.
> You walked alone, full of laughter, you bathed bare-bellied.
> You say you have lost all recollection of it, remember.... You
> say there are not words to describe this time, you say it does
> not exist. But remember. Make an effort to remember. Or, failing
> that, invent.
>
> (Monique Wittig)

❧ NOTE ❧

1 In feminist philosophy there is such a rich ferment of ideas and so many women tumbling over each other in discussing them, that it is formidable, if not impossible, to attribute origination of these ideas to any individual. Key ideas have often emerged nearly simultaneously in several authors' work, and ideas

expressed most influentially in a particular text may have originated elsewhere, in particular, among feminist activists and artists engaged in political activity and struggle. Further, it is misleading to attribute a view to a person which she held five years ago, but not now, thereby encapsulating her thought and denying the incredible vitality of the field. The movement of these ideas is not a history of individuals. Thus we avoid forms which attribute ideas to one person while nevertheless naming some who were there and in whose work you can find this material. Further, we are not trying to be textually faithful to particular writings in characterizing positions; we are blending the accounts of several feminists in the ideas we explore. Our work exhibits a North American slant, particularly in the forms disputes over difference have taken, because that is our location of feminist activism and philosophizing. Finally, virtually no claim here ascribed to 'feminists' or 'some feminists' should be assumed to be shared by all feminists; none should be taken to serve as the criterial test of who or what counts as 'feminist'.

A note on reference style: authors referred to are named in the Bibliography and cited in parentheses in the text (inside the sentence punctuation when the scope of the reference is just one sentence, and outside the sentence punctuation when the scope is more than one sentence). If just a name is given, the reference is to that author's book(s). If a name is preceeded by 'in', the reference is to an anthology edited by that woman. If a reference has the form 'Smith in Jones', the reference is to one or more articles by Smith in an anthology edited by Jones.

❦ BIBLIOGRAPHY ❦

Books

Adams, Carol *The Sexual Politics of Meat*, New York: Continuum, 1990.

Addelson, Kathryn Pyne *Impure Thoughts*, Philadelphia: Temple, 1991.

Albrecht, Lisa and Rose Brewer *Bridges of Power: Women's Multicultural Alliances*, Philadelphia: New Society, 1990.

Alcoff, Linda and Elizabeth Potter *Feminist Epistemologies*, New York: Routledge, 1993.

al-Hibri, Azizah and Margaret Simmons, eds *Hypatia Reborn*, Bloomington: Indiana University Press, 1990.

Allen, Jeffner *Lesbian Philosophy*, Chicago: Institute of Lesbian Studies, 1986.

—— *Reverberations: Across the Shimmering*, Albany: State University of New York Press, 1994.

—— ed. *Lesbian Philosophies and Cultures*, Albany: State University of New York Press, 1990.

—— and Iris Young, eds *The Thinking Muse: Feminism and Modern French Philosophy*, Bloomington: Indiana University Press, 1989.

Allen, Paula Gunn *The Sacred Hoop: Recovering the Feminine in American Indian Traditions*, Boston: Beacon Press, 1986.

Altbach, Edith Hoshino *et al.*, eds *German Feminism*, Albany: State University of New York Press, 1984.

Anderson, Margaret and Patricia Hill Collins, eds *Race, Class, and Gender*, Belmont, Cal.: Wadsworth, 1991.

Andolsen, Barbara Hilkert *et al.*, eds *Women's Consciousness, Women's Conscience*, New York: Winston, 1985.

Anthias, Floya and Nira Yuval-Davis *Racialized Boundaries: Race, Nation, Gender, Colour and Class and the Anti-Racist Struggle*, New York: Routledge, 1992.

Anthony, Louise and Charlotte Witt *A Mind of One's Own*, San Francisco: Westview, 1993.

Anzaldúa, Gloria *Borderlands/La Frontera*, San Francisco: Spinsters/Aunt Lute, 1987.

—— ed. *Making Face, Making Soul: Haciendo Caras: Creative and Critical Perspectives of Women of Color*, San Francisco: Aunt Lute Foundation Books, 1990.

Aptheker, Bettina *Tapestries of Life*, Amherst: University of Massachusetts Press, 1989.

Arditi, Rita *et al.*, eds *Science and Liberation*, Boston: South End, 1980.

Asian Women United of California, eds *Making Waves: An Anthology of Writings by and about Asian American Women*, Boston: Beacon Press, 1989.

Atkinson, Ti-Grace *Amazon Odyssey*, New York: Link Books, 1984.

Bar On, Bat-Ami, ed. *Engendering Origins: Critical Feminist Readings in Plato and Aristotle*, Albany: State University of New York Press, 1994.

—— ed. *Modern Engendering: Critical Feminist Readings in Modern Western Philosophy*, Albany: State University of New York Press, 1994.

Barrett, Michèle *The Politics of Truth: From Marx to Foucault*, London: Polity Press, 1992.

Barry, Kathleen *Female Sexual Slavery*, Englewood Cliffs, NJ: Prentice Hall.

Bartky, Sandra *Femininity and Domination: Studies in the Phenomenology of Oppression*, New York: Routledge, 1990.

Battersby, Christine *Gender and Genius: Towards a Feminist Aesthetics*, Bloomington: Indiana University Press, 1989.

Beck, Evelyn Torton, ed. *Nice Jewish Girls: A Lesbian Anthology*, Boston: Beacon Press, 1989.

Belenky, Mary *et al.*, *Women's Ways of Knowing*, New York: Basic Books, 1986.

Bell, Linda *Rethinking Ethics in the Midst of Violence*, Lanham, Md.: Rowman & Littlefield, 1993.

Bell, Rosann *et al.*, eds *Sturdy Black Bridges*, New York: Anchor, 1979.

Benhabib, Seyla *Situating the Self: Gender, Community and Postmodernism in Contemporary Ethics*, New York: Routledge, 1992.

—— and Drucilla Cornell, eds *Feminism as Critique*, Minneapolis: University of Minnesota Press, 1987.

Bigwood, Carol *Earth Muse*, Philadelphia: Temple, 1993.

Birkby, Phyllis *et al.*, eds *Amazon Expedition: A Lesbianfeminist Anthology*, New York: Times Change, 1973.

Bishop, Sharon and Marjorie Weinzweig, eds *Philosophy and Women*, Belmont, Cal.: Wadsworth, 1979.

Blackbridge, Persimmon and Sheila Gihooly, eds *Still Sane*, Vancouver: Press Gang, 1985.

Bleier, Ruth *Science and Gender*, New York: Pergamon, 1984.
—— ed. *Feminist Approaches to Science*, New York: Pergamon, 1986.
Bono, Paola and Sandra Kemp, eds *Italian Feminist Thought*, Cambridge: Blackwell, 1991.
Bordo, Susan *The Flight to Objectivity: Essays on Cartesianism and Culture*, Albany: State University of New York Press, 1987.
—— *Unbearable Weight: Feminism, Western Culture, and the Body*, Berkeley: University of California Press, 1993.
Boston Women's Health Collective *The New Our Bodies Ourselves*, New York: Simon & Schuster, 1984.
Braidotti, Rosi *Patterns of Dissonance*, Cambridge: Polity Press, 1991.
Brant, Beth, ed. *A Gathering of Spirit: North American Indian Women's Issues*, Amherst, Mass.: Sinister Wisdom, 1983.
Brennan, Teresa *Between Feminism and Psychoanalysis*, New York: Routledge, 1989.
Brighton Women and Science Group *Alice Through the Microscope*, London: Virago, 1980.
Brodribb, Somer *Nothing Mat(t)ers: A Feminist Critique of Postmodernism*, Melbourne, Australia: Spinaflex, 1992.
Brossard, Nicole *Lovhers*, Montréal, Quebec: Guernica Editions, 1986.
—— *The Ariel Letter*, Toronto: Women's Press, 1988.
—— *Picture Theory*, New York: Roof Books, 1990.
Browne, Susan *et al.*, eds *With the Power of Each Breath: A Disabled Women's Anthology*, Pittsburgh: Cleis, 1985.
Brownmiller, Susan *Against Our Will: Men, Women, and Rape*, New York: Simon & Schuster, 1975.
Bulkin, Elly *et al.*, eds *Yours in Struggle: Three Feminist Perspectives on Anti-Semitism and Racism*, Ithaca, NY: Firebrand, 1984.
Bunch, Charlotte *Passionate Politics*, New York: St Martin's Press, 1987.
—— and Nancy Myron, eds *Class and Feminism*, Baltimore: Diana, 1974.
Butler, Judith *Gender Trouble*, New York: Routledge, 1989.
—— *Bodies that Matter: On the Discursive Limits of 'Sex'*, New York: Routledge, 1993.
—— and Joan Scott, eds *Feminists theorize the Political*, New York: Routledge, 1992.
Cade, Toni, ed. *The Black Woman*, New York: New American Library, 1970.
Caldecott, Leonie and Stephanie Leland *Reclaim the Earth*, London: Women's Press, 1983.
Cameron, Anne *Daughters of Copper Woman*, Vancouver: Press Gang, 1981.
Cannon, Katie *Black Womanist Ethics*, Atlanta: Scholars, 1988.
Caputi, Jane *The Age of the Sex Crime*, Ohio: Bowling Green State University Popular Press, 1987.
—— *Gossips, Gorgons & Crones*, NM: Bear Books, 1994.
Carby, Hazel *Reconstructing Womanhood: The Emergence of the Afro-American Woman Novelist*, New York: Oxford University Press, 1987.
Card, Claudia *Feminist Ethics*, Lawrence: University Press of Kansas, 1991.
—— *Lesbian Choices*, New York: Columbia University Press, 1994.

—— ed. *Adventures in Lesbian Philosophy*, Bloomington: Indiana University Press, 1994.

Castle, Terry *The Apparitional Lesbian*, New York: Columbia University Press, 1993.

Chamberlin, Judy *On Our Own*, London: MIND Publications, 1977.

Chaudhuri, Nupur and Margaret Strobel, eds *Western Women and Imperialism*, Bloomington: Indiana University Press, 1992.

Chesler, Phyllis *Women and Madness*, New York: Vintage, 1972.

Christian, Barbara *Black Feminist Criticism*, New York: Pergamon, 1985.

Chodorow, Nancy *The Reproduction of Mothering*, Berkeley: University of California Press, 1978.

Chrystos *Not Vanishing*, Vancouver: Press Gang, 1988.

—— *Dream On*, Vancouver: Press Gang, 1991.

—— *In Her I Am*, Vancouver: Press Gang, 1993.

Cixous, Hélène *Newly Born Woman*, Minneapolis: University of Minnesota Press, 1986.

Code, Lorraine *What can She know*, Ithaca, NY: Cornell University Press, 1991.

Cole, Eve Browning *Philosophy and Feminist Criticism*, New York: Paragon House, 1993.

—— and Susan Coultrap-McQuin, eds *Explorations in Feminist Ethics*, Bloomington: Indiana University Press, 1992.

Collard, Andrée and Joyce Contrucci *Rape of the Wild*, Bloomington: Indiana University Press, 1989.

Collins, Patricia Hill *Black Feminist Thought*, London: HarperCollins, 1990.

Copper, Baba *Over the Hill: Reflections on Ageism between Women*, Freedom, Cal.: Crossing, 1988.

Corea, Gena *The Hidden Malpractice*, New York: William Morrow, 1977.

Cornell, Drucilla *Beyond Accommodation*, New York: Routledge, 1991.

—— *Transformations*, New York: Routledge, 1993.

Covina, Gina and Laurel Galana, eds *The Lesbian Reader*, Oakland, Cal.: Amazon, 1975.

Daly, Mary *Beyond God the Father*, Boston: Beacon Press, 1973.

—— *Gyn/Ecology*, Boston: Beacon Press, 1978.

—— *Pure Lust*, Boston: Beacon Press, 1984.

—— *Websters' First New Intergalactic Wickedary of the English Language*, Boston: Beacon Press, 1987.

—— *Outercourse*, San Francisco: HarperCollins, 1992.

Davis, Angela *Women, Race, and Class*, London: Women's Press, 1982.

—— *Women, Culture and Politics*, London: Women's Press, 1984.

Davis, Elizabeth Gould *The First Sex*, New York: Putnam's Sons, 1971.

de Beauvoir, Simone *The Second Sex*, New York: Bantam, 1970.

—— *The Ethics of Ambiguity*, New York: Citadel, 1948.

de Lauretis, Teresa *Alice Doesn't: Feminism, Semiotics, Cinema*, Bloomington: Indiana University Press, 1984.

—— ed. *Feminist Studies/Critical Studies*, Bloomington: Indiana University Press, 1986.

—— *The Technologies of Gender*, Bloomington: Indiana University Press, 1987.

Delphy, Christine *Close to Home: A Materialist Analysis of Women's Oppression*, Amherst: University of Massachusetts Press, 1984.

Demming, Barbara *We are All Part of One Another: A Barbara Demming Reader*, ed. Jane Meyerding, Philadelphia: New Society Educational Foundation, 1984.

Diamond, Irene and Lee Quinby, eds *Feminism and Foucault*, Boston: Northeastern University Press, 1988.

Dinnerstein, Dorothy *The Mermaid and the Minotaur*, New York: Harper & Row, 1977.

Di Stefano, Christine *Configurations of Masculinity*, Ithaca, NY: Cornell University Press, 1991.

Dreifus, Claudia, ed. *Seizing Our Bodies: The Politics of Women's Health Care*, New York: Vintage, 1978.

duBois, Page *Sowing the Body: Psychoanalysis and Ancient Representations of Women*, Chicago: University of Chicago Press, 1988.

Duchen, Claire *Feminism in France: From May '68 to Mitterrand*, New York: Routledge, 1986.

—— ed. *French Connections*, Amherst: University of Massachusetts Press, 1987.

Duran, Jane *Toward a Feminist Epistemology*, Savage, Md.: Rowman & Littlefield, 1991.

Dworkin, Andrea *Woman Hating*, New York: E. P. Dutton, 1974.

—— *Pornography*, London: Women's Press, 1981.

—— *Right Wing Women*, London: Women's Press, 1983.

—— and Catherine MacKinnon *Pornography and Civil Rights*, Minneapolis: Organizing Against Pornography, 1988.

Ecker, Gisela, ed. *Feminist Aesthetics*, Boston: Beacon Press, 1985.

Ehrenreich, Barbara and Deirdre English *Witches, Midwives, and Nurses*, Old Westbury, NY: Feminist Press, 1973.

—— *Complaints and Disorders*, Old Westbury, NY: Feminist Press, 1974.

—— *For Her Own Good*, Garden City, NY: Anchor, 1979.

Eisenstein, Zillah *Capitalist Patriarchy and the Case for Socialist Feminism*, New York: Monthly Review Press, 1979.

—— *The Radical Future of Liberal Feminism*, New York: Longman, 1981.

Eisler, Riane *The Chalice and the Blade*, New York: Harper & Row, 1987.

el Saadawi, Nawal *The Hidden Face of Eve: Women in the Arab World*, Boston: Beacon Press, 1980.

—— *Woman at Point Zero*, London: Zed Books, 1983.

Elshtain, Jean Bethke *Public Man, Private Woman*, Princeton, NJ: Princeton University Press, 1981.

—— *The Family in Political Thought*, Amherst: University of Massachusetts Press, 1982.

English, Jane, ed. *Sex Equality*, Englewood Cliffs, NJ: Prentice Hall, 1977.

Ezorsky, Gertrude *Racism and Justice*, Ithaca, NY: Cornell University Press, 1991.

Fausto-Sterling, Anne *Myths of Gender*, New York: Basic Books, 1985.

Ferguson, Ann *Blood at the Root: Motherhood, Sexuality and Male Domination*, London: Pandora, 1989.

—— *Sexual Democracy*, Boulder, Col.: Westview, 1991.

Figes, Eva *Patriarchal Attitudes*, London: Panther Books, 1972.

Firestone, Shulamith *The Dialectic of Sex*, London: Women's Press, 1979.

Fisher, Elizabeth *Woman's Creation: Sexual Evolution and the Shaping of Society*, New York: McGraw-Hill, 1979.

Flax, Jane *Thinking Fragments: Psychoanalysis, Feminism, and Postmodernism in the Contemporary West*, Berkeley: University of California Press, 1990.

—— *Disputed Subjects: Essays on Psychoanalysis, Politics and Philosophy*, New York: Routledge, 1991.

Forman, Frieda Johles and Caoron Swoton, eds *Taking Our Time: Feminist Perspectives on Temporality*, New York: Pergamon, 1989.

Fraser, Nancy *Unruly Practices*, Minneapolis: University of Minnesota Press, 1989.

—— and Sandra Bartky, eds *Revaluing French Feminism*, Bloomington: Indiana University Press, 1992.

Frazer, Elizabeth *et al.*, eds *Ethics: A Feminist Reader*, Cambridge: Blackwell, 1992.

French, Marilyn *Beyond Power*, New York: Ballantine, 1985.

—— *The War against Women*, New York: Summit Books, 1992.

Friedan, Betty *The Feminine Mystique*, Harmondsworth: Penguin, 1963.

Friedman, Marilyn *What are Friends For?*, Ithaca, NY: Cornell University Press, 1993.

Frye, Marilyn *The Politics of Reality*, Freedom, Cal.: Crossing, 1983.

—— *Willful Virgin*, Freedom, Cal.: Crossing, 1992.

Funk, Nanette and Magda Mueller, eds *Gender Politics and Post-Communism: Reflections from Eastern Europe and the Former Soviet Union*, New York: Routledge, 1993.

Fuss, Diana *Essentially Speaking: Feminism, Nature and Difference*, New York: Routledge, 1989.

Gaard, Greta *Ecofeminism*, Philadelphia: Temple, 1993.

Gallop, Jane *The Daughter's Seduction: Feminism and Psychoanalysis*, New York: Macmillian, 1982.

—— *Thinking through the Body*, New York: Columbia University Press, 1988.

Garry, Anne and Marilyn Pearsall, eds *Women, Knowledge, and Reality*, Boston: Unwin Hyman, 1989.

Gatens, Moira *Feminism and Philosophy*, Bloomington: Indiana University Press, 1991.

Genova, Judith *Power, Gender, Value*, Edmonton: Academic Printing and Publication, 1987.

Giddings, Paula *When and Where I enter: The Impact of Black Women on Race and Sex in America*, Toronto: Bantam, 1985.

Gilligan, Carol *In a Different Voice: Psychological Theory and Women's Development*, Cambridge, Mass.: Harvard University Press, 1982.

Golden, Catherine, ed. *The Captive Imagination: A Casebook on 'The Yellow Wallpaper'*, New York: Feminist Press, 1992.

Gordon, Linda *Woman's Body, Woman's Right: A Social History of Birth Control in America*, New York: Viking, 1976.

Gornick, Vivian and Barbara Moran *Woman in Sexist Society*, New York: New American Library, 1971.

Gould, Carol, ed. *Beyond Domination*, Totowa, NJ: Rowman & Allanheld, 1984.

—— and Max Wartofsky *Women and Philosophy*, New York: Putnam's Sons, 1976.

Grahn, Judy *Another Mother Tongue*, Boston: Beacon Press, 1984.

Grant, Judith *Fundamental Feminism: Contesting the Core*, New York: Routledge, 1994.

Greer, Germaine *The Female Eunuch*, London: Paladin, 1971.

Griffin, Susan *Women and Nature*, New York: Macmillan, 1978.

—— *Rape: The Power of Consciousness*, San Francisco: Harper & Row, 1979.

—— *Pornography and Silence*, New York: Harper & Row, 1981.

Griffiths, Morwenna and Margaret Whitford, eds *Feminist Perspectives in Philosophy*, Bloomington: Indiana University Press, 1988.

Grimshaw, Jean *Philosophy and Feminist Thinking*, Minneapolis: University of Minnesota Press, 1986.

Grosz, Elizabeth *Crossing Boundaries*, Boston: Allen & Unwin, 1987.

—— *Sexual Subversions: Three French Feminists*, Sydney: Allen & Unwin, 1989.

—— *Jacques Lacan: A Feminist Introduction*, New York: Routledge, 1990.

Gunew, Sneja, ed. *Feminist Knowledge: Critique and Construct*, New York: Routledge, 1990.

—— ed. *A Reader in Feminist Knowledge*, New York: Routledge, 1991.

Hall, Kim *Writing with a Woman in Mind*, Albany: State University of New York Press, 1994.

Hanen, Marsha and Kai Nielson, eds *Science, Morality, and Feminist Theory*, Calgary, Alberta: University of Calgary Press, 1987.

Haraway, Donna *Primate Visions: Gender, Race and Nature in the World of Modern Science*, New York: Routledge, 1989.

—— *Simians, Cyborgs, and Women*, New York: Routledge, 1991.

Harding, Sandra *The Science Question in Feminism*, Ithaca, NY: Cornell University Press, 1986.

—— ed. *Feminism and Methodology*, Bloomington: Indiana University Press, 1987.

—— *Whose Science, Whose Knowledge?*, Ithaca, NY: Cornell University Press, 1991.

—— and Hintikka Merrill, eds *Discovering Reality*, Dordrecht: D. Reidel, 1983.

—— and Jean O'Barr *Sex and Scientific Inquiry*, Chicago: University of Chicago Press, 1975.

Harley, Sharon and Rosalyn Terborg-Penn *The Afro-American Woman*, New York: Kennikat, 1978.

Harth, Erica *Cartesian Women*, Ithaca, NY: Cornell University Press, 1992.

Hartman, Joan and Ellen Messer-Davidow, eds *(En) Gendering Knowledge*, Knoxville: University of Tennessee Press, 1991.

Hartsock, Nancy *Money, Sex, and Power: Toward a Feminist Materialism*, Boston: Northeastern University Press, 1985.

Haug, Frigga, ed. *Female Sexualization*, London: Verso, 1987.

Hawksworth, Mary *Beyond Oppression*, New York: Continuum, 1990.

Heckman, Susan *Gender and Knowledge: Elements of a Postmodern Feminism*, Boston: Northeastern University Press, 1990.

Hein, Hilde and Carolyn Korsmeyer, eds *Aesthetics in Feminist Perspective*, Bloomington: Indiana University Press, 1993.

Held, Virginia *Feminist Morality*, Chicago: University of Chicago Press, 1993.

Hennessy, Rosemary *Materialist Feminism and the Politics of Discourse*, New York: Routledge, 1993.

Hermsen, Joke and Alkeline Van Lenning, eds *Sharing the Difference: Feminist Debates in Holland*, New York: Routledge, 1991.

Herschberger, Ruth [1948] *Adam's Rib*, New York: Harper & Row, 1970.

Hoagland, Sarah Lucia *Lesbian Ethics*, Chicago: Institute of Lesbian Studies, 1988.

—— and Julia Penelope, eds *For Lesbians Only*, London: Onlywomen, 1988.

Hole, Judith and Ellen Levine *Rebirth of Feminism*, New York: New York Times Books, 1971.

Holmes, Helen Bequaert and Laura Purdy, eds *Feminist Perspectives in Medical Ethics*, Bloomington: Indiana University Press, 1992.

hooks, bell *Ain't I a Woman: Black Women and Feminism*, Boston: South End, 1981.

—— *Feminist Theory: From Margin to Center*, Boston: South End, 1984.

—— *Talking Back: Thinking Feminist, Thinking Black*, Boston: South End, 1989.

—— *Yearning: Race, Gender, and Cultural Politics*, Boston: South End, 1990.

—— *Black Looks: Race and Representation*, Boston: South End, 1992.

Hull, Gloria *et al.*, eds *All the Women are White, All the Men are Black, But Some of Us are Brave*, Old Westbury, NY: Feminist Press, 1982.

Hunt, Mary E. *Fierce Tenderness: A Feminist Theology of Friendship*, New York: Crossroad, 1992.

Hynes, Patricia *The Recurring Silent Spring*, New York: Pergamon, 1989.

Irigaray, Luce *Speculum of the Other Woman*, Ithaca, NY: Cornell University Press, 1974.

—— *This Sex Which is Not One*, Ithaca, NY: Cornell University Press, 1977.

—— *The Irigaray Reader*, ed. Margaret Whitford, Oxford: Blackwell, 1991.

—— *Elemental Passions*, ed. Joan Collie and Judity Still, New York: Routledge, 1992.

—— *Ethics of Sexual Difference*, Ithaca, NY: Cornell University Press, 1993.

—— *Je, Tu, Nous: Toward a Culture of Difference*, New York: Routledge, 1993.

—— *Sexes and Genealogies*, New York: Columbia University Press, 1993.

Jaggar, Alison *Feminist Politics and Human Nature*, Totowa, NJ: Rowman & Allanheld, 1983.

—— ed. *Living with Contradictions: Controversies in Feminist Social Ethics*, Boulder, Col.: Westview, 1994.

—— and Paula Rothenberg, eds *Feminist Frameworks*, 2nd and 3rd edns., New York: McGraw Hill, 1978 and 1993.

—— and Susan Bordo *Gender/Body/Knowledge*, New Brunswick, NJ: Rutgers University Press, 1989.

James, Stanlie and Abena Busia, eds *Theorizing Black Feminisms*, New York: Routledge, 1993.

Janiewski, Dolores *Sisterhood Denied*, Philadelphia: Temple, 1985.

Jardine, Alice *Gynesis: Configurations of Woman and Modernity*, Ithaca, NY: Cornell University Press, 1985.

Jayawardena, Kumari *Feminism and Nationalism in the Third World*, London: Zed Books, 1986.

Jeffries, Sheila *The Spinster and Her Enemies: Feminism and Sexuality (1830–1930)*, London: Pandora, 1985.

—— *Anticlimax: A Feminist Perspective on the Sexual Revolution*, London: Women's Press, 1990.

Johnston, Jill *Lesbian Nation*, New York: Simon & Schuster, 1973.

Joseph, Gloria and Jill Lewis *Common Differences: Conflicts in Black and White Feminist Perspectives*, Boston: South End, 1981.

Kaye/Kantrowitz, Melanie and Irena Klepfisz, eds *The Tribe of Dina: A Jewish Women's Anthology*, Montpelier, Vt.: Sinister Wisdom, 1986.

Keller, Evelyn Fox *Reflections on Gender and Science*, New Haven Conn.: Yale University Press, 1985.

—— *Secrets of Life, Secrets of Death: Essays on Language, Gender and Science*, New York: Routledge, 1992.

—— and Marianne Hirsch, eds *Conflicts in Feminism*, New York: Routledge, 1990.

Kennedy, Ellen and Susan Mendus, eds *Women in Western Political Philosophy*, New York: St Martin's Press, 1987.

Keuls, Eva *The Reign of the Phallus: Sexual Politics in Ancient Athens*, New York: Harper & Row, 1985.

Kingston, Maxine Hong *The Woman Warrior*, New York: Vintage, 1977.

Kittay, Eva Feder and Diana Meyers, eds *Women and Moral Theory*, Totowa, NJ: Rowman & Littlefield, 1987.

Kitzinger, Celia *The Social Construction of Lesbianism*, London: Sage, 1987.

—— and Rachel Perkins *Changing Our Minds*, New York: New York University Press, 1993.

Klein, Renate and Deborah Steinberg, eds *Radical Voices*, New York: Pergamon, 1989.

Klepfisz, Irena *Dreams of an Insomniac: Jewish Feminist Essays, Speeches and Diatribes*, Portland, Oregon: Eighth Mountain, 1990.

Koedt, Anne *et al. Radical Feminism*, New York: Quadrangle, 1973.

Kournay, Janet A. *et al.*, eds *Feminist Philosophies*, Englewood Cliffs, NJ: Prentice Hall, 1992.

Kramarae, Cheris, ed. *Technology and Women's Voices*, New York: Routledge, 1988.

—— and Paula Treichler, eds *A Feminist Dictionary*, Boston: Pandora, 1985.

Krol, Sandera and Selma Sevenhuijsen, eds *Ethics and Morality in Feminism: An Interdisciplinary Bibliography*, Utrecht: Anna Maria van Schuurman Centrum, University of Utrecht, 1992.

Kuhn, Annette and AnnMarie Wolpe *Feminism and Materialism*, Boston: Routledge, 1978.

Ladner, Joyce *Tomorrow's Tomorrow*, New York: Doubleday, 1972.

Larrabee, Mary Jeanne *An Ethic of Care*, New York: Routledge, 1992.

Lather, Patti *Getting Smart: Feminist Research and Pedagogy With/In the Postmodern*, New York: Routledge, 1991.

Lederer, Laura, ed. *Take Back the Night*, New York: William Morrow, 1980.

Le Doeuff, Michèle *Hipparchia's Choice: An Essay Concerning Women, Philosophy, Etc.*, Oxford: Blackwell, 1991.

Leidholdt, Dorchen and Janice Raymond, eds *The Sexual Liberals and the Attack on Feminism*, New York: Pergamon, 1990.

Leighton, Anne T. *Scrapp*, Faultline, Cal.: Invent Books, 1994.

Lennon, Kathleen and Margaret Whitford, eds *Knowing the Difference: Feminist Perspectives in Epistemology*, New York: Routledge, 1994.

Lerner, Gerda *The Creation of Patriarchy*, New York: Oxford University Press, 1986.

Linden, Robin Ruth *et al.*, eds *Against Sadomasochism*, East Palo Alto, Cal.: Frog in the Well, 1982.

Lloyd, Genevieve *The Man of Reason*, Minneapolis: University of Minnesota Press, 1984.

Longino, Helen *Science as Social Knowledge*, Princeton, NJ: Princeton University Press, 1996.

Lorde, Audre *Zami*, Trumansburg, NY: Crossing, 1982.

—— *The Cancer Journals*, Iowa City: Aunt Lute, 1980.

—— *Sister Outsider*, Freedom, Cal.: Crossing, 1984.

—— *A Burst of Light*, Ithaca, NY: Firebrand, 1988.

Lowe, Marianne and Ruth Hubbard, eds *Woman's Nature: Rationalizations of Inequality*, New York: Pergamon, 1983.

Lugones, María *Pilgrimages/Peregrinajes: Essays in Pluralist Feminism*, Albany: State University of New York Press, 1994.

—— *Intimate Interdependencies*, Boulder Col.: Westview, 1994.

Macdonald, Barbara and Cynthia Rich *Look Me in the Eye: Old Women and Aging and Ageism*, Minneapolis: Spinsters Ink, 1991.

MacKinnon, Catherine *Sexual Harassment of Working Women*, New Haven, Conn.: Yale University Press, 1979.

—— *Feminism Unmodified*, Cambridge, Mass.: Harvard University Press, 1987.

—— *Toward a Feminist Theory of the State*, Cambridge, Mass.: Harvard University Press, 1989.

—— *Only Words*, Cambridge, Mass.: Harvard University Press, 1993.

McMillan, Carol *Woman, Reason and Nature*, Oxford: Blackwell, 1982.

McNaron, Toni, ed. *The Sister Bond*, New York: Pergamon, 1985.

Mahowald, Mary, ed. *Philosophy of Woman*, Indianapolis, Ind.: Hackett, 1978.

Mamonova, Tatyana *Russian Women's Studies*, New York: Pergamon, 1988.

Manning, Rita *Speaking from the Heart: A Feminist Perspective on Ethics*, Lanham, Md.: Rowman & Littlefield, 1992.

Marks, Elaine and Isabelle de Courtivron, eds *New French Feminisms*, Amherst: University of Massachusetts Press, 1980.

Martin, Jane Roland *Changing the Educational Landscape*, New York: Routledge, 1994.

Merchant, Carolyn *The Death of Nature*, New York: Harper & Row, 1980.

Meyers, Diana *Self, Society, and Personal Choice*, New York: Columbia University Press, 1989.

Midgley, Mary and Judith Hughes *Women's Choices*, London: Weidenfeld & Nicholson, 1983.

Milan Women's Bookstore Collective, The *Sexual Difference*, Bloomington: Indiana University Press, 1990.

Millett, Kate *Sexual Politics*, New York: Avon, 1969.

Minas, Anne *Gender Basics*, Belmont, Cal.: Wadsworth, 1993.

Minnich, Elizabeth Kamarck *Transforming Knowledge*, Philadelphia: Temple, 1990.

Mitchell, Juliet *Women's Estate*, New York: Pantheon, 1971.

—— *Psychoanalysis and Feminism*, London: Allen Lane, 1974.

Modeleski, Tania *Feminism Without Women: Culture and Criticism in a Postfeminist Age*, New York: Routledge, 1991.

Mohanty, Chandra Talpade *et al. Third World Women and the Politics of Feminism*, Bloomington: Indiana University Press, 1991.

Moi, Torril *Sexual/Textual Politics*, New York: Methuen, 1985.

—— ed. *French Feminist Thought*, New York: Blackwell, 1987.

Moraga, Cherríe *Loving in the War Years*, Boston: South End, 1983.

—— *The Last Generation*, Boston: South End, 1993.

—— and Gloria Anzaldúa, eds *This Bridge called My Back: Writings by Radical Women of Color*, New York: Kitchen Table, Women of Color, 1981.

Morgan, Elaine *The Descent of Woman*, New York: Stein & Day, 1972.

Morgan, Robin, ed. *Sisterhood is Powerful*, New York: Vintage, 1970.

—— *Anatomy of Freedom*, Garden City, NY: Anchor, 1992.

—— ed. *Sisterhood is Global*, Garden City, NY: Anchor, 1984.

Morrison, Toni, ed. *Race-ing Justice, En-Gendering Power: Essays on Anita Hill, Clarence Thomas, and the Construction of Social Reality*, New York: Pantheon, 1992.

Myron, Nancy and Charlotte Bunch, eds *Lesbianism and the Women's Movement*, Baltimore: Diana, 1975.

Nelson, Lynn Hankinson *Who knows: From Quine to a Feminist Empiricism*, Philadelphia: Temple, 1990.

Nicholson, Linda *Gender and History*, New York: Columbia University Press, 1986.

—— ed. *Feminism/Postmodernism*, New York: Routledge, 1990.

Noddings, Nel *Caring*, Berkeley: University of California Press, 1984.

Nye, Andrea *Feminist Theory and the Philosophies of Man*, New York: Routledge, 1988.

—— *Philosophia: The Thought of Rosa Luxemburg, Simone Weil, and Hannah Arendt*, New York: Routledge, 1993.

—— *Words of Power: A Feminist Reading of the History of Logic*, New York: Routledge, 1990.

Okin, Susan Moller *Women in Western Political Thought*, Princeton, NJ: Princeton University Press, 1979.

—— *Justice, Gender, and the Family*, New York: Basic Books, 1989.

Oliver, Kelly, ed. *Ethics, Politics, and Difference in Julia Kristeva's Writing*, New York: Routledge, 1993.

Olsen, Tillie *Silences*, New York: Delacorte, 1979.

Osborne, Martha Lee *Woman in Western Thought*, New York: Random House, 1979.

Parker, Pat *Movement in Black*, Ithaca, NY: Firebrand, 1989.

Patai, Daphne *The Orwell Mystique*, Amherst: University of Massachusetts Press, 1984.

Pateman, Carole *The Sexual Contract*, Stanford, Cal.: Stanford University Press, 1988.

—— *The Disorder of Women*, Oxford: Polity Press, 1989.

—— and Elizabeth Gross, eds *Feminist Challenges*, Boston: Northeastern University Press, 1986.

Pearsall, Marilyn, ed. *Women and Values*, 1st and 2nd edns, Belmont, Cal.: Wadsworth, 1986 and 1993.

Penelope, Julia *Speaking Freely: Unlearning the Lies of the Fathers' Tongues*, New York: Pergamon, Athene Series, 1990.

—— and Susan Wolfe, eds *The Coming Out Stories*, Watertown, Mass.: Persephone, 1980.

Pierce, Christine *How to solve the Lockheed Case*, New Brunswick, NJ: Transaction, 1986.

Piercy, Marge *Woman on the Edge of Time*, New York: Fawcett Crest, 1976.

Pitkin, Hanna Fenichel *Fortune is a Woman: Gender and Politics in the Thought of Niccolò Machiavelli*, Berkeley: University of California, Press, 1984.

Plant, Judith, ed. *Healing the Wounds: The Promise of Ecofeminism*, Philadelphia: New Society, 1989.

Plaskow, Judith and Joan Arnold, eds *Women and Religion*, Missoula, Mont.: Scholars, 1974.

—— and Carol Christ, eds *The Weaving Visions: New Patterns in Feminist Spirituality*, New York: Harper & Row, 1989.

Pratt, Minnie Bruce *Rebellion*, Ithaca, NY: Firebrand, 1991.

Rabinowitz, Nancy Sorkin and Amy Richlin, eds *Feminist Theory and The Classics*, New York: Routledge, 1993.

Ramos, Juanita, ed. *Compañeras: Latina Lesbians*, New York: Latina Lesbian History Project, 1987.

Raymond, Janice *A Passion for Friends: Toward a Philosophy of Female Affection*, Boston: Beacon, Press, 1986.

Redstockings *Feminist Revolution*, New York: Random House, 1978.

Reed, Evelyn *Women's Evolution: From Matriarchal Clan to Patriarchal Family*, New York: Pathfinder, 1975.

Reiter, Rayna, ed. *Toward an Anthropology of Women*, New York: Monthly Review Press, 1975.

Rich, Adrienne *Of Woman Born*, New York: Norton, 1976.

—— *On Lies, Secrets, and Silence*, New York: Norton, 1979.

—— *Blood. Bread, and Poetry*, New York: Norton, 1986.

Rosser, Sue *Feminism within the Science and Health Care Professions*, New York: Pergamon, 1986.

Rothschild, Joan, ed. *Machina Ex Dea: Feminist Perspectives on Technology*, New York: Pergamon, 198 ,.

Rowbotham, Sheila *Women, Resistance, and Revolution*, New York: Pantheon, 1972.

—— *Women in the Movement*, New York: Routledge, 1992.

Ruddick, Sara *Maternal Thinking: Toward a Politics of Peace*, Boston: Beacon Press, 1989.

Rush, Florence *The Best Kept Secret: Sexual Abuse of Children*, Englewood Cliffs, NJ: Prentice Hall, 1980.

Russell, Diana, ed. *Exposing Nuclear Phallacies*, New York: Pergamon, 1980.

—— and Nicole Van de Ven, eds *The Proceedings of the International Tribunal on Crimes Against Women*, Millbrae, Cal: Les Femmes, 1976.

Ruth, Sheila *Take back the Light: A Feminist Reclamation of Spirituality and Religion*, Lanham, Md.: Rowman & Littlefield, 1993.

Sabbah, Fatna *Woman in the Muslem Unconscious*, New York: Pergamon, 1984.

Sargent, Lydia, ed. *Women and Revolution*, Boston: South End, 1981.

337

Sawicki, Jana *Disciplining Foucault*, New York: Routledge, 1991.

Saxton, Marsha and Florence Howe, eds *With Wings: An Anthology of Literature by and about Women with Disabilities*, New York: Feminist Press, 1987.

Sayers, Janet *Biological Politics*, London: Tavistock, 1982.

Scheman, Naomi *Engenderings: Constructions of Knowledge, Authority, and Privilege*, New York: Routledge, 1993.

Schoenfielder, Lisa and Barb Weiser, eds *Shadow on a Tightrope: Writings by Women on Fat Oppression*, Iowa City: Aunt Lute, 1983.

Sedgwick, Eve Kosofsky *Between Men: English Literature and Male Homosocial Desire*, New York: Columbia University Press, 1985.

Shange, Ntozake *For Colored Girls who have considered Suicide/When the Rainbow is Enuf*, New York: Macmillan, 1975.

Sherwin, Susan *No Longer Patient: Feminist Ethics and Health Care*, Philadelphia: Temple, 1991.

Shiva, Vandana *Staying Alive: Women, Ecology, and Development*, London: Zed Books, 1988.

Shogan, Debra, ed. *A Reader in Feminist Ethics*, Toronto: Canadian Scholar's, 1992.

Shrage, Laurie *Moral Dilemmas of Feminism: Prostitution, Adultery and Abortion*, New York: Routledge, 1994.

Silvera, Makeda, ed. *Piece of My Heart: A Lesbian of Color Anthology*, Toronto: Sister Vision, 1991.

Simons, Margaret, ed. *Rereading the Cannon: Feminist Interpretations of Simone de Beauvoir*, University Park: Pennsylvania State University Press, 1994.

Singer, Linda *Erotic Welfare: Sexual Theory and Politics in the Age of Epidemic*, New York: Routledge, 1993.

Smith, Barbara, ed. *Home Girls: A Black Feminist Anthology*, New York: Kitchen Table, Women of Color Press, 1983.

Smith, Dorothy *The Everyday World as Problematic*, Boston: Northeastern University Press, 1987.

—— and Sarah David, eds *Women Look at Psychiatry*, Vancouver: Press Gang, 1975.

Snitow, Ann *et al.*, eds *Powers of Desire: The Politics of Sexuality*, New York: Monthly Review Press, 1983.

Solanas, Valerie *SCUM Manifesto*, London: Matriarchy Study Group, 1968, 1983.

Spallone, Patricia and Deborah Steinberg, eds *Made to Order: The Myth of Reproductive Progress*, New York: Pergamon, 1987.

Spellman, Elizabeth *Inessential Woman: Problems of Exclusion in Feminist Thought*, Boston: Beacon Press, 1988.

Spender, Dale *Man Made Language*, New York: Routledge, 1980.

—— *Women of Ideas and What Men have done to Them*, London: Ark Paperbacks, 1983.

Spivak, Gayatri Chakravorty *In Other Worlds: Essays in Cultural Politics*, New York: Methuen, 1987.

Spretnak, Charlene, ed. *The Politics of Women's Spirituality*, New York: Doubleday, 1982.

Stambler, Sookie, ed. *Women's Liberation*, New York: Ace Books, 1970.

Stanley, Liz and Sue Wise *Breaking Out Again: Feminist Ontology and Epistemology*, New York: Routledge, 1983, 1993.

Steady, Filomina Chioma, ed. *The Black Woman Cross-Culturally*, Cambridge, Mass.: Schenkman, 1981.

Stone, Merlin *When God was a Woman*, New York: Harcourt Brace Jovanovich, 1976.

Swirski, Barbara and Marilyn Safir, eds *Calling the Equality Bluff: Women in Israel*, New York: Pergamon, 1991.

Tanner, Leslie, ed. *Voices from Women's Liberation*, New York: New American Library, 1970.

Terborg-Penn, Sharon Harley and Andrea Benton Rushing, eds *Women in Africa and the African Diaspora*, Washington, DC: Howard University Press, 1978.

Thürmer-Rohr, Christina *Vagabonding*, Boston: Beacon Press, 1987.

Tong, Rosemary *Women, Sex, and the Law*, Totowa, NJ: Rowman & Allanheld, 1984.

—— *Feminist Thought*, Boulder, Col.: Westview, 1989.

—— *Feminine and Feminist Ethics*, Belmont, Cal.: Wadsworth, 1993.

Trebilcott, Joyce, ed. *Mothering*, Totowa, NJ: Rowman & Allanheld, 1984.

—— *Dyke Ideas*, Albany: State University of New York Press, 1993.

Trinh T. Minh-ha *Woman, Native, Other: Writing Postcoloniality and Feminism*, Bloomington: Indiana University Press, 1989.

—— *When the Moon waxes Red: Representation, Gender and Cultural Politics*, New York: Routledge, 1991.

—— *Framer Framed*, New York: Routledge, 1992.

Tronto, Joan *Moral Boundaries: A Political Argument for an Ethics of Care*, New York: Routledge, 1993.

Tuana, Nancy, ed. *Feminism and Science*, Bloomington: Indiana University Press, 1989.

—— *Woman and the History of Philosophy*, New York: Paragon House, 1992.

—— *The Less Noble Sex: Scientific, Religious and Philosophical Conceptions of Woman's Nature*, Bloomington: Indiana University Press, 1993.

Vance, Carol, ed. *Pleasure and Danger*, New York: Routledge, 1989.

Vetterling-Braggin, Mary, ed. *Sexist Language*, Totowa, NJ: Littlefield, Adams, 1981.

—— ed. *'Femininity,' 'Masculinity,' and 'Androgyny'*, Totowa, NJ: Littlefield, Adams, 1982.

—— *et al.*, eds *Feminism and Philosophy*, Totowa, NJ: Littlefield, Adams, 1977.

Waithe, Mary Ellen, ed. *A History of Women Philosophers*, vols 1–5, Boston: Martinus Nijhoff, 1987–94.

Walby, Sylvia *Theorizing Patriarchy*, Cambridge: Blackwell, 1990.

Walker, Alice *In Love and Trouble*, New York: Harcourt Brace Jovanovich, 1973.

—— *You can't Keep a Good Woman Down*, New York: Harcourt Brace Jovanovich, 1981.

—— *The Color Purple*, New York: Harcourt Brace Jovanovich, 1982.

—— *In Search of Our Mother's Gardens*, New York: Harcourt Brace Jovanovich, 1983.

—— and Pratibha Parmar *Warrior Marks: Female Genital Mutilation and the Sexual Blinding of Women*, New York: Harcourt Brace, 1993.

Walker, Barbara *The Crone*, San Francisco: Harper & Row, 1985.

Wallace, Michele *Black Macho and the Myth of the Superwoman*, New York: Dial, 1978.

Warhol, Robyn and Diane Price Herndl *Feminisms*, New Brunswick, NJ: Rutgers University Press, 1991.

Waring, Marilyn *If Women Counted: A New Feminist Economics*, New York: Harper & Row, 1988.

Warland, Betsy *InVersions: Writings by Dykes, Queers, and Lesbians*, Vancouver: Press Gang, 1991.

Warren, Karen, ed. *Ecological Feminist Philosophies*, New York: Routledge, 1994.

Weed, Elizabeth, ed. *Coming to Terms: Feminism, Theory, Politics*, New York: Routledge, 1989.

Weedon, Chris *Feminist Practice & Poststructuralist Theory*, New York: Blackwell, 1987.

White, Evelyn, ed. *The Black Women's Health Book*, Seattle, Wash.: Seal Press, 1990, 1994.

Whitford, Margaret *Luce Irigaray*, New York: Routledge, 1991.

Williams, Patricia J. *The Alchemy of Race and Rights*, Cambridge, Mass: Harvard University Press, 1991.

Wittig, Monique *Les Guérillères*, Boston: Beacon Press, 1969, 1985.

—— *The Lesbian Body*, New York: Avon, 1976.

—— *The Straight Mind*, Boston: Beacon Press, 1992.

—— and Sande Zeig *Lesbian Peoples: Material for a Dictionary*, New York: Avon, 1979.

Wolf, Margery and Roxane Witke, eds *Women in Chinese Society*, Stanford, Cal.: Stanford University Press, 1975.

Wolfe, Susan and Julia Penelope, eds *Sexual Practice, Textual Theory: Lesbian Cultural Criticism*, Cambridge: Blackwell, 1993.

Wright, Elizabeth, ed. *Feminism and Psychoanalysis: A Critical Dictionary*, Oxford: Blackwell, 1992.

Yeatman, Anna *Postmodern Revisionings of the Political*, New York: Routledge, 1993.

Young, Iris *Justice and the Politics of Difference*, Princeton, NJ: Princeton University Press, 1990.

—— *Throwing Like a Girl and Other Essays in Feminist Philosophy and Social Theory*, Bloomington: Indiana University Press, 1990.

Zita, Jacquelyn *Fleshing Out the Body*, Albany: State University of New York Press, 1994.

Journals

APA Newsletter on Feminism
Differences: A Journal of Feminist Cultural Studies
Feminist Studies
Hypatia: A Journal of Feminist Philosophy
Lesbian Ethics

Sage: A Scholarly Journal on Black Women
Signs: A Journal of Women in Culture and Society
Sinister Wisdom

CHAPTER 11

Philosophy of law

Calvin G. Normore

❧◈❧

The past forty years have seen a remarkable interpenetration of law and philosophy. Philosophical treatises like J. Rawls's *A Theory of Justice* (1971) have been studied with as much care by lawyers as philosophers while philosophically sophisticated works of legal theory like H. L. A. Hart and Tony Honoré's *Causation in the Law* (1959) have had an influence in areas of philosophy with no obvious connection to law. So deeply connected have the two subjects become that it is probably not possible any longer to say where the philosophy of law leaves off and the rest of philosophy or the rest of law begins. This essay discusses recent work in the areas usually treated as central in books and courses in the philosophy of law – fundamental jurisprudence, the theory of crime and punishment, and issues in responsibility and tort.

❧ FUNDAMENTAL JURISPRUDENCE ❧

Contemporary work in Anglo-American jurisprudence starts from H. L. A. Hart's *The Concept of Law* (1961). In that book Hart argues for a sophisticated legal positivism which finds the source of legal authority in the acceptance by a community of a system of rules. That system is grounded in a fundamental rule of recognition which determines what is to be included among the rules which are the ordinary laws ([11.9], 97 ff.) This picture has two essential aspects. First there is the role of acceptance. Unlike natural-law theories Hart's finds a crucial aspect of the binding force of law in its acceptance by a community as binding. Second there is the notion of a rule. Unlike earlier positivist theories, notably that of John Austin which focused on the idea that a law was a command (typically a threat) issued by a sovereign and backed by force, Hart's theory claims that laws are rules which serve as standards for guiding conduct. Deviations from these standards may well be punished and many people may be motivated to conform merely by the fear of such punishment but theirs is not the point of view from which these are standards and give rise to obligations. That point of view, rather, takes the law as a guide for behaviour and holds the fact that something is a law to be a reason for following it. Those who find or make themselves outsiders to the law may nonetheless act in accord with the law (out of fear of sanction or a desire not to stand out for example) but they do not follow it. Hart illustrates the difference between the two points of view by reflection on the difference between a typical attitude to the law – which is taken to obligate and is used as a guide to action – and to the threats of a gunman – which may oblige us but do not obligate us and with which we would not comply if we did not fear the consequences of non-compliance ([11.9], 80 ff.) Hart recognizes that a system of rules for guiding conduct could exist without officials of any kind but thinks that such a system will have obvious defects which can be overcome by supplementing the primary conduct-guiding rules with secondary rules governing the recognition, change and enforcement of the primary rules. A fully developed legal system will consist of rules of both kinds.

I began by describing Hart's position as sophisticated legal positivism and it is certainly the case that he distinguishes sharply between moral and legal obligation and refuses to ground either in the other. Nonetheless he recognizes an intimate connection between them which is itself grounded in what he takes to be the fact that both are systems of rules closely connected with human survival. For him this fact ensures that there will be a minimal content 'naturally' present in any plausible legal or moral system. Thus while he denies that the immorality of a rule automatically excludes it from the law he recognizes that some features of law are natural in the sense of being a part of any well-established legal system governing the behaviour of human beings in a world like our own. Prohibitions like 'Thou shalt not kill' and structural features like the attachment of sanctions to prohibitions are examples to which he points.

Hart's picture of the law opened new and wide avenues of communication between legal theory and philosophy. His conception of rules, of rule-following and of the relations among systems of rules was closely connected with ideas worked out by Wittgenstein and J. L. Austin and forcefully advocated by writers like P. Winch. His insistence on the need for thought about how the law could be normative connected him both with those writers and with others who were concerned with how norms could be part of a philosophy which took modern science seriously.

What distinguishes Hart most sharply from traditional positivist theories of law is his recognition that law has a normative aspect which cannot be reduced to anything like predictions or threats. The law 'claims' that we ought to obey it. What distinguishes him most sharply from traditional natural-law theorists is his insistence that the norms involved in the law are specifically legal norms which arise in the acceptance of a legal system by a community.

How norms could emerge from the combination of the existence of a practice and its acceptance has come to be seen as one of the deepest problems of contemporary philosophy. The problem's significance for legal theory was already recognized by H. Kelsen who in his *General Theory of Law and the State* (1961) arrived at the remarkable view that every legal system rests on a single norm (roughly of the form 'the laws of this system ought to be obeyed') which is presupposed in the operation of that legal system and in legal (as contrasted with sociological) study of that system. In effect Kelsen took the normativity of the law to be presupposed by the law. Hart's view, on the other hand, was that law was indeed normative but was nonetheless entirely constituted by the existence and acceptance of certain practices. Since to accept a rule is at least to treat it as a reason for action, it is not implausible that one's own acceptance of a legal system gives one reason to follow it but why the acceptance of such a system within your community should give you reason to follow it whether or not you accept it yourself is considerably more mysterious. In consequence at least one of the most notable of Hart's students, Joseph Raz, has been driven, in *The Authority of Law* (1979), to acknowledge that there is no general obligation to obey the law (in the sense of 'obligation' in which being under an obligation entails having a reason to act).

Contemporary jurisprudence is dominated by responses to Hart. Perhaps the most influential has been that by Ronald Dworkin. In a series of papers collected in *Taking Rights Seriously* (1977) Dworkin challenges key aspects of Hart's picture. First he argues that Hart has overemphasized the role of rules at law. Dworkin contrasts rules with what he calls 'principles'. They differ in that when a rule clearly applies to a case it dictates how the case is to be treated. Rules may conflict but such conflicts must be resolved by deciding which rule is to apply. Rules may be vague but such vagueness is resolved by deciding whether the rule applies. Hart had suggested that when such decisions are themselves not dictated by other rules a judge who makes them is simply legislating. Since conflict and vagueness seem inescapable in the law Hart thus recognized a realm of judicial discretion practically indistinguishable from legislation. Principles on the other hand have 'weight' for Dworkin. In *A Matter of Principle* (1985) he develops his earlier argument that different principles may clearly apply to a situation and may point in different directions. In such a case the decision should take all of them into account. Principles are (or provide) reasons for action and like reasons can conflict, override and be overridden, and serve as guides to the interpretation of statute and of precedent cases.

Having argued for the category of principles Dworkin applies it in two striking ways. He uses it first to provide a new model of adjudication and second to argue for a very close relation between law and morality.

Dworkin illustrates his model of adjudication through the figure of Hercules, a judge who knows every statute and every case and suffers no limitations of memory or cognitive capacity. Dworkin suggests that what Hercules must do to settle a case before him is to come up with a theory of the law as a whole and apply it. To generate such a theory of the law Hercules will treat precedent cases and existing statutes as data and will be guided by his current stock of principles. His aim is a theory which accounts for as much of the data as possible and gives each principle the range and weight which seems appropriate. In constructing such a theory Hercules may be led to the view that there are implicit in the law principles not previously noticed. To construct a sufficiently general and coherent theory he may also be forced to conclude that some earlier cases (those which he cannot fit into a satisfactory theory) were wrongly decided. Once he has such a global legal theory Hercules will apply it to the case before him. This case then serves as a further data point. Dworkin suggests that in a well-developed legal system there will be enough cases, statutes and already recognized principles to make the construction of such a global theory possible. Thus he thinks it at least very unlikely that judicial discretion in Hart's sense is ever called for.

In his magisterial *Law's Empire* (1986) Dworkin re-phrased the project in which Hercules is engaged as a project of providing an interpretation of the law by analogy to the way in which a director might interpret a play by Shakespeare. Dworkin regards the project of interpreting as a project of discovering the intention behind something – even in those cases in which we cannot suppose that what is being interpreted is a product of anyone's actual intention. Thus we can interpret a social practice (Dworkin's example is the practice of doffing one's cap in the presence of certain others) by treating it 'as if it were the product of a decision to pursue one set of themes or visions or purposes, one "point" rather than another' ([11.7], 58–9). This move illuminates Dworkin's project but it also makes it more controversial because, by appealing to the concept of interpretation and to literary and dramatic examples of its use, Dworkin opens jurisprudence up to the debates about interpretation which have raged among literary critics and philosophers of literary criticism for much of this century. This has had the sociological effect of giving literary critics employment in law schools and the theoretical effect of embroiling legal theory in the debates around deconstruction.

In *Law's Empire* and his more recent papers Dworkin develops his account of how cases, statutes, rules, principles and other elements are to be interpreted around the slogan 'Law as Integrity'. The integrity of the law is a matter of its internal coherence and the systematic application of its fundamental principles. To conceive of the law as having integrity involves first taking it to be an ideal of political practice that legislators try to make the law morally and politically coherent and second taking there to be a requirement on the part of judges to try to interpret the law as morally and politically coherent. Dworkin takes this demand for coherence to be of one piece with the requirement that the law be just and both substantively and procedurally fair. He argues that interpretive practice of judges must attempt to treat the law as though it flowed from principles of justice, fairness and procedural due process. This has the consequence of placing a theory of political practice (a rather hopeful liberal theory of political practice) at the heart of the theory of adjudication. Not surprisingly this has been highly controversial.

Dworkin argues for a much closer relation between law and morality than Hart admits. He claims, for example, that the Constitution of the United States of America appeals directly to moral principles and moral rights which thus become part of the law and have a legal weight which must be respected in deciding cases. He argues that fundamental moral values, fairness for example, have legal force and can be used both to determine what the law is and how it is to be applied. He has argued that in situations where it seems to a citizen that a statute violates a moral right for whose legal standing a substantial case can be made the citizen is under no obligation to obey the statute and that the state should take special care with such cases of civil disobedience and should be very reluctant to prosecute them.

Dworkin's relationship to the natural-law tradition is complex and subtle. His accounts of the legal force of moral principles and rights are put forward as claims about the best interpretation of the actual constitutional and legal systems of the North American and European democracies. He denies that what is to be properly called 'law' in any society at any time must respect even the fundamental aspects of morality as we conceive it – or even as that society at that time conceives it. He rejects, for example, the thought that Nazi law was not law at all. Nevertheless he also suggests that 'law' is what a Wittgensteinian might call a 'family-resemblance' concept and that Nazi law differs *as law* in significant ways from Anglo-American law – ways which might make it incapable of justifying coercion. He seems thus committed to the possibility that there might be valid law which did not provide anyone with a reason for acting.

Whether or not we count Dworkin as a natural-law theorist there has been a revival of natural-law theory in the work of philosophers and jurisprudents like Alan Donagan, John Finnis and Germain Grisez. At the centre of this movement has been Finnis's book *Natural Law and Natural Rights* (1980). Finnis begins with the claim that law is necessary for the provision of certain goods which are essential to human flourishing. Among those goods he counts life and health, knowledge, play, aesthetic experience, friendship and other forms of sociability, practical rationality and the contact with the larger order of things which he calls religion. Finnis claims that, properly understood, this is an exhaustive list and that the goods on it are each basic in the sense of being neither reducible to the others nor ranked with respect to them. They are incommensurable requirements for full human flourishing. What Finnis calls the 'common good' of a community is a complex of all these goods and their derivatives in the particular forms appropriate to the members of that community. It is, thus, itself very complex. Finnis reasons from this fact and from his reflections on the nature of the good of practical rationality itself to the conclusion that authority is necessary. Nor is authority necessary only to deal with those who put their own interests ahead of the common good. Even in a community of those striving to attain the common good there would be need for authoritative solutions to co-ordination problems. Such solutions can be found in custom, but, because custom is such an unwieldy instrument, are more likely to be provided by rulers and the legal systems they create. For Finnis the authority of a particular legal system is parasitic upon the fact that most of the community does in fact conform to the demands that legal system makes. This fact and the need for some legal system legitimize (*ceteris paribus*) the particular system in place. There is thus provided a reason for conforming to the demands of that legal system.

Whereas Dworkin conceives of law as an instrument of justice and Finnis conceives of it as an instrument of goodness, Richard Posner and the 'Law and Economics' movement of which he is a central figure conceive of it as an instrument of economic efficiency.

The Law and Economics movement began from Ronald H. Coase's paper 'The Problem of Social Cost' (1960). It received impetus through Guido Calabresi's analysis of the fault system in his *The Costs of Accidents* (1970 [11.30]) and through the analysis of entitlements in G. Calabresi and A. D. Melamed's 'Property Rules, Liability Rules and Inalienability: One View of the Cathedral' (1972 [11.31]). It achieved the status of a movement after the publication of Richard Posner's

Economic Analysis of Law (1973). Posner agues that the basic aim of law is to alter incentives. For example the law deters activity by raising the expected costs of that activity above the gains to be anticipated from it. Posner suggests that the basic formal structure of law – features such as that compliance must be possible, that like cases are treated alike and that law must be public – can be explained if we suppose that the point of the law is to give people incentives to do what is economically efficient and suppose that judges are implicitly attempting to determine what would promote that goal. He argues further that the descriptively most adequate theory of the common law treats it as a method for allocating responsibilities among interacting agents so as to maximize the joint value of their activity – that is so as to produce economic efficiency. In his seminal paper Coase showed that standard economic theory entails that if there are no costs to transactions among the interacting parties and if the parties are willing to bargain and trade then any assignment of entitlements among them will be efficient. If efficiency requires that one party have an entitlement it does not have then everyone would be better off if that party bought the entitlement from whoever does have it. If such buying and selling were costless and everyone was willing to buy or sell whenever it was in their interest, then the entitlements would end up wherever it was most efficient that they be. But these conditions are often not met. In particular transaction costs are often quite high. In such cases Posner argues that the law should 'mimic the market'. As he puts it 'Transaction costs are minimized *when the law (1) assigns the right to the party who would buy it ... if it were assigned to the other party instead and transaction costs were zero, or (2) places liability on the party who, if he had the right and transaction costs were zero, would sell it*' ([11.12], 18).

Although Posner thinks that his theory gives a good account of the common law he admits that it gives a poorer account of statute law. He argues that this too is explicable on his approach because an economic theory of legislatures will show that they may be expected to be much less concerned with efficiency than are markets or appellate judges. Markets produce efficiency directly and only redistribute wealth incidentally. Legislatures on the other hand have powerful economic incentives to be concerned primarily with the distribution of wealth and only incidentally in efficiency.

Posner ends *Economic Analysis of Law* by leaving as an exercise to the reader the problem '*Can the idea of "justice" as it is used in discussions of law and legal rules and institutions, be deduced from the economist's idea of efficiency? If not are justice and efficiency incompatible?*' ([11.12], 395). Almost all the critical discussion of the Law and

Economics movement has been concerned with precisely this question (cf. Coleman [11.2]).

All of the movements with which we have been concerned so far share the view that much, if not quite all, Anglo-American law is justifiable in some fairly full-blooded sense. This position is rejected by the Critical Legal Studies movement.

The Critical Legal Studies movement does not speak with one voice and both its supporters and its critics sometimes treat it rather as a political movement to which one does or does not belong than as a position to which one may or may not subscribe. One of the most central figures in the movement has been Roberto M. Unger, and I will focus on his formulation of its aims and methods. In *The Critical Legal Studies Movement* (1986) Unger describes the movement as having arisen out of a tradition concerned to criticize what he calls formalism and objectivism. Formalism is the view that legal decisions are not political decisions but can be justified by methods of legal reasoning which can be recognized as themselves justified from a standpoint within the law. Objectivism is the view that the legal system as a whole is not merely the resultant of power struggles among competing factions within the society but is justifiable as the embodiment of an objective order of some kind – usually conceived of as a moral or rational order. Unger argues that these two views are mutually supporting and suggests that once the idea that the law embodies objective morality or rationality has been rejected one can see clearly that the project of justifying particular legal decisions by uncontroversial methods must itself be rejected.

The Critical Legal Studies movement positions itself as the heir to the legal realism of Frank, Holmes and Llewellyn and the opponent of both the view which Dworkin represents (what Unger calls the 'rights and principles school') and the Law and Economics movement. Unger calls these watered-down versions of nineteenth-century juris-prudence motivated largely by the fear that if one accepted the critique of formalism and objectivism then legal doctrine and perhaps even the possibility of normative argument would be undermined. It is understandable that the verbal (and institutional) clashes between the Critical Legal Studies movement and its opponents have been unusually bitter.

It is significant that Unger does not think that Critical Legal Studies undermines either legal doctrine or normative argument. What it does, he suggests, is to continue the legal-realist programme of expanding legal doctrine by bringing both empirical social theory and debate about the right and feasible structure of society explicitly to bear upon the law and legal justification. One consequence of this, he thinks, is to separate political and legal ideals – like that of equality or market rationality – from current conceptions of these ideals, conceptions which treat contingent institutional arrangements as part of the ideal itself. This is to be done partly through detailed historical studies which show how the law typically contains opposing conceptions (principles and 'counter-principles') and show in detail how through political struggles and political deals they came both to be present. This process is illustrated in the law of contract where two conceptions are very much in evidence – one which emphasizes the freedom to choose both with whom to bargain and what terms to accept and another which emphasizes that unfair contracts, no matter how voluntary, are not enforceable. Each of these conceptions can be generalized to a complete theory of contract and each will then treat the core examples of the other as isolated limiting cases. Neither conception by itself can give an adequate account of the existing law of contract and once one sees this one sees also that the concept of contract is not tied to either conception.

The Critical Legal Studies movement sees the law as essentially contested and thinks it highly unlikely that the kind of interpretive project Dworkin proposes – which would yield a theory of the law as a coherent whole – could be carried out for even a very small branch of the subject. The basic reason for this is that the law of a society reflects the history of that society. Since the history of all the larger societies is a history of political and social conflict it is very likely that the law of these societies will itself reproduce these conflicts in the history of precedent cases and the history of statute. At a more abstract level Unger wants to insist (specifically against traditional Marxism) that history is not the working out of a deterministic process but reflects significant choices that could have been made differently. Law will reflect this indeterminism and to attempt retrospectively to impose on these legal choices an explanatory structure which treats the development of law as the unfolding of a single theory is deeply misguided.

It is at this point that the Critical Legal Studies movement intersects currents in contemporary literary theory and contemporary general philosophy. In developing his account of legal interpretation Dworkin appeals to the hermeneutical work of H.-G. Gadamer. In response his critics appeal to other parts of nineteenth- and twentieth-century German and French philosophy – to Hegel, Marx and Nietzsche, to Foucault and Derrida, and sometimes to Heidegger. Dworkin's analogy between legal and literary interpretation has been taken up by deconstructionist critics, lawyers and philosophers who argue that the best picture of texts is not one which treats them as though they were the product of a single coherent authorial intention but regards them instead as more like the field on which various forces and purposes play themselves out. If this is how it is with texts then if Dworkin's analogy holds it will be so with law, and rather than seeking a coherent theory of the law the jurisprudent should recognize its incoherence and its frankly political character. This will involve abandoning legal science as someone like Dworkin conceives it for something more like Unger's expanded doctrine. Philosophical support for these moves is found in Hegel's account of contradictions, in Nietzsche's genealogical account of morality, in Foucault's archaeology of concepts and in Derrida's deconstruction of text (cf. Cornell, Rosenfeld and Gray [11.3]).

❧ THE ENFORCEMENT OF MORALITY ❧

Excepting Law and Economics all of the schools of jurisprudence discussed above agree that there is a deep connection between morality and the sources of law.[1] They disagree fiercely over what that connection is. But morality can also enter the law in quite another way. The law can be called upon to apply legal sanctions to what are perceived to be immoral activities even when no issue of justice or fairness seems to be at stake. The issues involved here are not entirely distinct from the debates in fundamental jurisprudence canvassed above but they have given rise to another literature and another set of connections between law and philosophy.

The contemporary debate about the enforcement of morals at law began with Patrick Lord Devlin's 1958 Maccabean lecture to the British Academy which criticized the recommendation in the 1957 Wolfenden Committee Report that homosexual relations between consenting adults be de-criminalized. The Wolfenden Committee offered the ground that sexual relations between adults were a matter of private morality and that the state had no business regulating private morality. This recommendation echoed the views of the drafters of the Model Penal Code published just two years before in the United States and suggested a trend in Anglo-American jurisprudence. Against this line of thought Devlin argued that the distinction between private and public morality which it presupposed could not be sustained. In 1963 Hart entered the debate with his lectures published as *Law, Liberty and Morality*. Devlin replied in 1965 with his *The Enforcement of Morals*.

Hart's defence of the Wolfenden Report rested on an appeal to and defence of a principle which he found in Mill's *On Liberty* and which has become known as the 'harm principle'. In Mill's formulation it is that 'the only purpose for which power can be rightfully exercised over any member of a civilized community, against his will, is to prevent harm to others' (Mill [11.21]). Mill understood this principle as grounding both liberty of conscience and expression and liberty of tastes and pursuits. Hart agreed and argued that something very like the harm principle lay at the core of a liberal-democratic conception of law. Devlin, on the other hand, argued that such a principle neither could be found in the law as it stood (which criminalized not only homosexuality but also suicide and other self-regarding acts pretty clearly excluded by the principle) nor should be imported into it. At the core of Devlin's argument lay the view that whatever else it may be the law is a means whereby a community exhibits its shared values. Devlin argued that a society is justified in ensuring its own preservation (which is after all why treason is a criminal act). Therefore if the spread of immoral or offensive activity threatens the continued existence of the society the society may prohibit it even if no member of the society is harmed by such acts. An activity can threaten a society's existence in several ways. It can, for example, open a society to conquest or bring it to the brink of civil war. It can also threaten to transform the society in ways which would make it a different society sharing and exhibiting quite different values. A society has a right to protect itself against its destruction in any of these ways. Hart replied that the right of a society to preserve itself against being transformed into another society was much more limited than Devlin admitted. A society had the right to prevent its violent destruction but not the right to prevent its evolution by persuasion.

The Devlin/Hart debate not only reprised the debate between Mill and Stephen (as Hart himself made clear) but also brought into sharp focus the contrast between the liberal conception of the state (which both Mill and Hart accept) and the conception of the state which Hegel espouses in his *Philosophy of Right* and which Devlin and later conservative writers like Roger Scruton (in *The Meaning of Conservatism*) accept.

The debate next moved to the United States. The US Supreme Court, in a series of decisions from *Griswold* vs *Connecticut* (1965) (which struck down a Connecticut ban on contraceptives which extended to married couples) to *Roe* vs *Wade* (1973) (which found that a woman had the right to an abortion in the second trimester of a pregnancy), found in the US Constitution a previously unrecognized right to privacy, just the sort of right Hart had argued was essential to liberal democracy. Despite this line of cases courts in the US (and elsewhere) steadfastly maintained that the state was under no obligation to permit marriages between same-sex couples (which it was widely recognized were prohibited precisely because they were found immoral and offensive by a large segment of the population). Meanwhile debate over the banning of materials deemed obscene or pornographic continued to grow and to attract the attention of higher courts and controversy arose within some jurisdictions (notably the United States) about whether someone could be prohibited the use of a means to express views because those means were deeply offensive to some person or group (Nazi groups marching through public streets in Jewish neighbourhoods for example) and in other jurisdictions (notably Canada) about whether the dissemination of views which could not be reasonably held to be true and which would incite hatred could be prohibited. In all these issues the adequacy of the harm principle was directly at stake.

At the level of theory there was also considerable development. Eugene Rostow came to Devlin's defence in his *The Sovereign Prerogative* (1962). Dworkin entered the fray in 1966, arguing that there was no right held by a society to enforce a consensus of opinion no matter how deeply held unless that consensus could be defended as a moral consensus, and to be so defended it would have to be shown to be reasonable by the standards of rationality and reasonableness the society and its courts were willing to apply elsewhere. Mere unanimity of feeling did not, he claimed, amount to moral argument. But the most detailed work on this subject has been by Joel Feinberg and is systematically presented in his four-volume *The Moral Limits of the Criminal Law* (1984–8). Feinberg focuses on four principles which have been supposed to provide reasons for criminalizing behaviour. The first is the harm principle. The second is what Feinberg calls the offence principle – that an act's seriously offending others can be a reason to prohibit it. The third is legal paternalism – that an act's harming the agent can be a reason to prohibit it – and the fourth is legal moralism – that an act's profound immorality can be (by itself) a reason to prohibit it. Feinberg accepts both the harm principle and the offence principle but rejects both legal paternalism and legal moralism. In the case of legal moralism he thinks that there is no essential connection between something's moral status and someone's welfare in even the widest sense and so the mere fact that an act is morally reprehensible is no ground for prohibition. Feinberg wants to reject legal paternalism but admits that a person can, even voluntarily, undermine her own interests. This consideration is trumped he argues, by the interference with personal autonomy the prohibition of such acts would require. By accepting the offence principle Feinberg distances himself from Mill. He motivates this distance by having us imagine a 'ride on the bus' during which a remarkable set of very unpleasant incidents occur, all of them quite intentionally produced by others without any concern for their obvious unpleasantness to you. Feinberg argues that these are clearly evils for you, though evils of a sort he thinks different from harms, and that you are wronged by them. Hence the state may prohibit them.

Dworkin, Feinberg and Hart consider themselves to be articulating the attitude liberalism should take to the enforcement of morals but it is hard to find a principle which distinguishes them all from Lord Devlin. Dworkin's disagreement with Devlin is not about whether the community's morality counts but about what counts as the community's morality. Hart's disagreement with Devlin is about whether it is the community's morality as distinguished from 'such universal values as individual freedom, safety of life and protection from deliberately inflicted harm' (Hart [11.19], 70) which licenses prohibition. Feinberg's disagreement with Devlin is over whether anything which does not count as a harm or offence to another person could ground prohibition. These are such different grounds for argument that one is led to wonder whether they are unified by more than the conclusion that certain kinds of sexual conduct should not be criminal.

In recent years the discussion of the enforcement of morality has focused in the United States on whether pornography should be banned. Among the theoretical issues involved has been whether the harm principle justifies such prohibition. Some of this discussion has turned on whether pornography harms individual women or women as a class by increasing the incidence of violent sexual crimes but there have also been several attempts to argue for new categories of wrong and to extend the 'traditional' harm principle to them. For example Andrea Dworkin and Catherine MacKinnon [11.17] have argued that pornography harms women not by (or at least not simply) by causing acts of sexual violence but by creating a climate of values in which it is more difficult than it should be to see such acts as having the scope and gravity they should be seen to have. In more recent work MacKinnon [11.20] has argued that pornographic depictions should be conceived not merely as semantic vehicles but as acts with the power to harm.

❧ PUNISHMENT ❧

Perhaps the most basic question in the criminal law is what justifies punishment. This question can be understood either as asking for a justification of a penal system or as asking what explains how a society is justified in treating a criminal very differently from either a tortfeaser or someone who has innocently caused a harm.

Contemporary discussion of the first reading of the question begins from Calabresi and Melamed in 'Property Rules, Liability Rules and Inalienability' [11.31]. Calabresi and Melamed distinguish between a system of property rules and a system of liability rules. A system of property rules recognizes rights or entitlements which holders can transfer at will but of which they may not be deprived without their consent. A system of liability rules recognizes rights or entitlements may be taken from the holders provided the holders are fully compensated. Calabresi and Melamed point out that when the cost of obtaining a holder's consent is high it may be more efficient to have a system of liability rules than a system of property rules. Reflecting on this issue Robert Nozick (in *Anarchy, State and Utopia* [11.28]) raises the question why not simply have a system of liability rules. Since no one would take an entitlement and fully compensate the holder unless it improved their own situation and since the compensation guarantees that the holder is not made worse off any taking would be a Pareto-efficient move. Why not then encourage such takings?

Nozick points out that in economic terms such a system would be one which sets the price of every entitlement at the minimum the holder would take for it. It thus solves the problem of setting a 'just price' in a way that is systematically advantageous to the buyer. He suggests that this is unfair to the holders of goods – who could reasonably hope to do better if their consent were required and who, Nozick argues, have a natural right not to have their goods taken without that consent. (Except in unusual situations: Nozick seems uncertain about the rights of holders when the transaction costs are indeed prohibitively high.) Nozick's conclusion is that a system of property rights is necessary, not for the sake of efficiency but to protect the natural rights of holders. If 'thieves' were only required to compensate their victims they would have no incentive not to take first and compensate later so without punishment in addition to compensation a system of property rights would collapse into a system of liability rules. Hence a society which endorses property rights has an incentive to have punishments as well as compensation.

This ingenious argument does not immediately justify punishment in the sense of the second reading of our question. Even if a system of punishment is a necessary condition for a system of property another argument is required to show that this is not a *reductio* of the view that property rights are themselves justified. This argument has been surprisingly difficult to produce. The argument is required because punishment involves doing to the guilty what it would be impermissible to do to the innocent – depriving them of life or liberty or some of the means they might otherwise use to pursue happiness. But it is far from clear exactly how the mere fact that someone is guilty could justify such deprivation.

Contemporary justifications of punishment are usually classified as consequentialist, retributive or communicative – though these labels are ill-fitting Among consequentialist theories most focus on the uses of punishment either as a deterrent to crime or as a way of rehabilitating the criminal while others focus on such effects as the greater security punishment yields the innocent. Retributivist theories argue that punishment is deserved by the criminal and communicative or educative theories hold that a crime makes it appropriate to send the criminal a moral message and that punishment does this.

Theoretical work in the first part of this century was largely consequentialist and emphasized the benefits of criminal rehabilitation. In the early 1970s the influence of this approach began to wane. On the one hand behavioural psychologists argued that punishment was less effective than reward as a method of behaviour-modification and on the other rising crime rates and statistics which indicated that existing rehabilitation programmes were a failure combined to suggest that rehabilitation could not justify the existing penal system. At a more theoretical level there was increasing concern that some practices involved in rehabilitation, notably that of indeterminate sentencing, were unjust.

More recent discussions of consequentialist theory have focused on deterrence and on the benefits of keeping criminals off the streets. Here again there has been little clear evidence that the punishments Anglo-American jurisdictions apply deter crime (especially murder and other very serious crimes) and increasing evidence that the societies cannot afford to incarcerate (or legally execute) enough of those whom their policies classify as criminals to induce a sense of security in their cities. Moreover deterrence-based theories of punishment conflict as badly as do rehabilitative theories with the strong intuition that there should be some proportion between the crime and its punishment. If deterrence requires that the expected value of the crime be lower than the expected value of not committing it then one could anticipate that the punishment required for deterrence would vary inversely with the likelihood that the criminal would be caught. Since this likelihood seems to have no necessary connection to the seriousness of the crime then the punishment required for deterrence will have no such connection either.

Perhaps the most interesting recent theoretical work on deterrence theories of punishment has grown out of reflection on the general structure of deterrence. One deters an agent by instilling in that agent a fear of the consequences of his act. One way of doing that is to threaten the agent with harm. When then is one justified in threatening an agent with harm? Several authors (notably Warren Quinn and Dan Farrell) have seen a connection between such cases and cases of self-defence. Farrell has suggested that the right to self-defence can itself be grounded in a moral permission to distribute harms in such a way that they fall upon the agent who is acting wrongfully rather than upon her innocent victim. He suggests further that one has a moral permission to undertake a plan of action which would so redistribute the harms and therefore that one has a moral permission to undertake a plan of action which would threaten to redistribute the harms. But a plan of action which involved such threats but did not involve carrying them out would not be a credible plan and so would not redistribute the harms. Hence one has a moral permission to a plan of action which involves threatening to redistribute harm which would be wrongfully done one so that it falls on the wrong-doer instead and involves carrying out that threat. Just as I may knock out a thief who attempts to steal my purse so I may threaten to knock him out if he does steal my purse and I may carry out my threat. Such a theory has the advantage over other deterrence theories that it supplies a natural way of setting limits upon punishment parasitic upon the acceptable limits on the force one may use in self-defence. This approach to punishment builds upon a lively recent debate about deterrence sparked by work of Gregory Kavka.

Most of the theoretical work on the theory of punishment in the past quarter-century has been within the broad framework of retributivism theories. Retributive theories argue that by committing her crime the criminal deserves punishment. Most of the recent work on such theories has been done within rights-based ethical frameworks and so has had to face the question of how it is that the criminal no longer has the rights one ordinarily has within a system of property rules not to be killed, incarcerated or deprived of one's property without one's consent. Contractarians about morality have been tempted to the view that by his crime the criminal voids society's contract with him and so relieves others of their usual moral and legal obligations to him. This approach seems to share the difficulties traditional consequentialists have had in explaining why punishment should be proportional to the gravity of the crime. If something no longer has moral or legal standing then it would seem the issue of proportionality should not arise. But it seems clear that in criminal cases it does arise. Those among retributivists who hold that rights are natural have been less tempted to think that criminals forfeit them than that they are overridden by other considerations. The difficulty here has been to reconcile this with the idea that rights are in some sense absolute and cannot be balanced by other considerations.

Among the most interesting recent work on punishment has been the communicative theories advocated by R. A. Duff and J. Hampton. These theories owe something to Plato and Hegel and something also to Nozick. Hampton [11.26] argues that punishment is justified because a society has a moral right, and perhaps even a moral duty, to convey basic moral and legal principles to its members. Sometimes this can only be done or can be best done by a vehicle which will make a deeper impression than mere words would and perhaps especially conveying to them what it is like to be the victim of a crime. Punishment then is a kind of 'act speech' which communicates values in a striking way. Moreover, Hampton argues that it is the only kind of communication which is necessarily connected with the goal of moral education because it is the only kind of communication which shows the criminal both that her behaviour is wrong and what is wrong about it. Hampton's view is that the state may not use these methods upon all its citizens because the value of autonomy is a strong one which cannot be lightly overridden. The presumption has to be that a citizen understands the basics of morality and law and has the ability to apply them unless she shows otherwise by her behaviour. The latter is precisely what the criminal does. Hampton is insistent that this theory holds punishment to be education and not conditioning and must respect the autonomy of the criminal to the extent this is compatible with communicating the message. Thus she thinks the theory has the resources to explain the intuitive limits on punishment (related presumably to how morally blind and incapable the criminal, as evidenced by the crime, has shown himself to be). Hampton's is a general theory of punishment and her illustrations focus on the ways in which parents educate their children morally through punishment.

Part of what fuels both classical retributivist and communicative theories of punishment is the conviction that consequentialist theories are incapable of treating a criminal as someone who has voluntarily done wrong rather than as something more like a mechanism which has malfunctioned. Thus both retributive and communicative theories insist that the criminal's free choice in the commission of the crime must play a role in the account of punishment. The communicative theorists, for example, regard the criminal as a participant in a communicative situation who has herself spoken and who is being pressed to listen to a reply which she may or may not accept. This emphasis on the criminal's free choice plays an essential role in another theory of punishment which seems to escape the classifications offered above. John Finnis suggests (in *Natural Law and Natural Rights* [11.8]) that we can provide a satisfactory account of the justification of punishment by regarding it as a means to restore the balance of advantages between the criminal and the law-abiding which the criminal has disturbed by his crime. Part of this balance is restored by the ordinary methods of compensation and restitution but, Finnis argues, the criminal has stolen another advantage which is precisely that of exercising his free choice without regard for the consequences to others. To deprive the criminal of this advantage his free choice must be (at least temporarily) restricted beyond the scope permitted the law-abiding. Finnis thinks that it is this that punishment does and its doing so explains why it usually takes the forms of incarceration and deprivation of resources needed to exercise choice.

❧ CAUSATION, RESPONSIBILITY AND TORT ❧

The classic among contemporary works on causation and responsibility at law is H. L. A. Hart and Tony Honoré's *Causation in the Law* (1959). Hart and Honoré painstakingly analyse the concept of cause as that is used both by philosophers and by lawyers and apply their analysis to issues of legal responsibility. Hart and Honoré are concerned to chart a careful path between those whom they term 'causal minimalists' who in the extreme deny that the question of who caused a harm or loss is at all relevant to the issue of who should be held liable and 'causal maximalists' who argue in the extreme that issues of liability should be settled entirely by reference to causal criteria. Their own view is that the paradigm cases of liability are those in which that liability falls on the party which caused the harm or loss but that these cases by no means exhaust the subject. There are, they point out, clear cases in which a party may be liable though having no causal connection whatever to the act for which they are held liable – an insurer or guarantor may be liable for acts caused by the insured for example. There are also a variety of cases in which a party is liable though their conduct was not the cause of the harm in the ordinary sense of cause but at most an occasion or what lawyers and medieval theologians call a *sine qua non* cause. And there are cases, notably in the law of negligence, where an agent is merely an occasion but is held liable.

The connection between responsibility and causation is an issue in moral as well as legal theory and practice and has received considerable attention in both quarters since the publication of *Causation in the Law*. The entire contemporary debate has been conditioned by the difficulty of giving an adequate analysis of causation. Two recent philosophical analyses have received special attention. One is J. L. Mackie's treatment (in *The Cement of the Universe*, [11.37]) of a cause as an insufficient but necessary member of a minimal set of conditions jointly sufficient (but not necessary) to produce the effect. The other is David K. Lewis's analysis of 'A is a cause of B' as 'A and B and if it were not the case that A it would not be the case that B' [11.36]. Neither of these accounts distinguishes between what Hart and Honoré would consider causes and what they would consider occasions or *sine qua non* causes. Given that the most influential philosophical accounts of causation do not make that distinction it is not surprising that much legal theory has refused to do so. Since in a typical case of tort both parties will be *sine qua non* causes of the harm done and in a typical crime the behaviour of both criminal and victim will be *sine qua non* causes of the crime, then if the best analysis of causation cannot distinguish *sine qua non* causes from other causes, there will be no causal principle which will distinguish the roles of the parties. In that case the law will have to rely in general on something other than causation to settle liability. This position has long been advocated by Leon Green but has received important impetus on the one hand from the recent general willingness to treat 'factual' issues (like questions of who caused what) as being themselves partly normative issues, and on the other from the rise of the Law and Economics movement which claims that tort law (and the common law more generally) can be adequately interpreted as pursuing the goal of economic efficiency – a goal which does not require settling causal issues between the parties. One can then reconstruct the reasoning of Hart and Honoré's causal minimalists as follows: 'In almost any situation in which a harm occurs that harm would have been avoided by a different behaviour on the part of any of the parties. Thus the behaviour of each of the parties is a cause of the harm. We should then regard the harm as a joint product of the activity of the parties and treat the question before us as that of dividing the joint product between them. Since our best theories of causation give us no grounds for distinguishing the contribution of the parties to the joint product we must look for a non-causal (legal or moral) principle which does.' At this point we should expect causal minimalists to begin to disagree as they propose different normative bases on which to divide liability, and they do.

Although little of the recent work on causation would make one sanguine about using causal principles from outside law and morality to settle issues of liability or blame the revival of moral and legal theories which emphasize individual autonomy and agency points in a different direction. For example Alan Donagan's *The Theory of Morality* (1973) takes it as the standard case that one is morally responsible for exactly that for which one is causally responsible and then proceeds to discuss deviations from this standard case. R. A. Epstein maintains that one should be held liable for exactly what one causes according to a number of paradigmatic causal scenarios. Such theories presuppose an account of causation adequate to their needs.

❧ OTHER SUBJECTS ❧

The areas discussed above have been the most central and most active parts of the philosophy of law in recent years but they do not exhaust the subject. In particular there is the issue of group or collective rights. In several common-law countries (notably Canada and New Zealand) questions about the existence of collective moral and legal rights are of immediate legal and political importance and if the apparent trend towards multicultural and multilingual societies in the common-law countries continues these issues will become more widely pressing. At the theoretical level the philosophical issues involved have been recently explored by Will Kymlicka in *Liberalism, Community and Culture* (1994) and some of the legal issues involved have been treated in a special issue of *The Canadian Journal of Law and Jurisprudence* (1991 [11.38]) devoted to collective rights. There is every indication that this will be an increasingly important area of the philosophy of law in the near future.

❧ NOTE ❧

1 And one could argue that Law and Economics should not be excepted because economic efficency could be understood as a moral ideal.

❧ BIBLIOGRAPHY ❧

Jurisprudence

11.1 Coase, Ronald H. 'The Problem of Social Cost', *Journal of Law and Economics*, 3 (1960): 1–44.

11.2 Coleman, Jules L. *Markets, Morals, and the Law*, New York: Cambridge University Press, 1988.

11.3 Cornell, Drucilla *Beyond Accommodation: Ethical Feminism, Deconstruction and the Law*, New York: Routledge, 1991.

11.4 ——, M. Rosenfeld, and D. Gray *Deconstruction and the Possibility of Justice*, New York: Routledge, 1992.

11.5 Dworkin, Ronald *Taking Rights Seriously*, Cambridge, Mass: Harvard University Press, 1977.

11.6 —— *A Matter of Principle*, Oxford: Oxford University Press, 1985.

11.7 —— *Law's Empire*, Cambridge, Mass: Harvard University Press, 1986.

11.8 Finnis, John *Natural Law and Natural Rights*, Oxford: Oxford University Press, 1980.

11.9 Hart, H. L. A. *The Concept of Law*, Oxford: Oxford University Press, 1961.

11.10 Hegel, Georg W. F. *Philosophy of Right*, trans. with notes by T. M. Knox, Oxford: Clarendon Press, 1962.

11.11 Kelsen, H. *General Theory of Law and State*, New York: Russell & Russell, 1961.

11.12 Posner, Richard *Economic Analysis of Law*, Boston: Little, Brown, 1972.

11.13 Rawls, John *A Theory of Justice*, Cambridge, Mass: Harvard University Press, 1971.

11.14 Raz, Joseph *The Authority of Law*, Oxford: Clarendon Press, 1979.

11.15 Unger, Roberto M. *The Critical Legal Studies Movement*, Cambridge, Mass: Harvard University Press, 1986.

The enforcement of morality

11.16 Devlin, Patrick *The Enforcement of Morals*, Oxford: Oxford University Press, 1965.
11.17 Dworkin, A. and C. A. MacKinnon *Pornography and Civil Rights: A New Day for Women's Equality*, Minneapolis, Minn. (734 E. Lake St, Minneapolis 55407): Organizing Against Pornography, 1988.
11.18 Feinberg, Joel *The Moral Limits of the Criminal Law*, 4 vols, New York: Oxford University Press, 1984–8.
11.19 Hart, H. L. A. *Law, Liberty and Morality*, Stanford: Stanford University Press, 1963.
11.20 MacKinnon, Catherine A. *Only Words*, Cambridge, Mass.: Harvard University Press, 1993.
11.21 Mill, John S. *On Liberty*; with *The Subjection of Women*; and *Chapters on Socialism*, Cambridge: Cambridge University Press, 1989.
11.22 Rostow, Eugene V. *The Sovereign Prerogative: The Supreme Court and the Quest for Law*, New Haven, Conn.: Yale University Press, 1962.
11.23 Scruton, Roger *The Meaning of Conservatism*, Harmondsworth: Penguin, 1980.

Punishment

11.24 Duff, R. A. *Trials and Punishments*, Cambridge: Cambridge University Press, 1986.
11.25 Farrell, D. 'Deterrence and the Just Distribution of Harm', *Philosophy and Public Affairs*, 24 (1995): 220–40.
11.26 Hampton, Jean 'The Moral Education Theory of Punishment', *Philosophy and Public Affairs*, 18 (1989): 53–67.
11.27 Kavka, G. S. *Moral Paradoxes of Nuclear Deterrence*, New York: Cambridge University Press, 1987.
11.28 Nozick, R. *Anarchy, State and Utopia*, New York: Basic Books, 1973.
11.29 Quinn, W. 'The Right to threaten and the Right to punish', *Philosophy and Public Affairs*, 14 (1985): 327–73.

Causation, responsibility and tort

11.30 Calabresi, Guido *The Costs of Accidents*, New Haven, Conn.: Yale University Press, 1970.
11.31 ——and A. D. Melamed 'Property Rules, Liability Rules and Inalienability:

One View of the Cathedral', *Harvard Law Review*, 85 (April 1972): 1089–1128.

11.32 Donagan, Alan *The Theory of Morality*, Chicago: University of Chicago Press, 1973.

11.33 Epstein, R. A. 'A Theory of Strict Liability', *Journal of Legal Studies*, 2 (1973): 151–221.

11.34 Green, Leon *Rationale of Proximate Cause*, Kansas City: Vernon Law Book Co., 1927.

11.35 Hart, H. L. A. and Tony Honoré *Causation in the Law*, Oxford: Oxford University Press, 1959 (2nd edn, 1985).

11.36 Lewis, D. K. 'Causation', in D. K. Lewis, *Philosophical Papers*, vol. 2, Oxford: Oxford University Press, 1986: 159–213.

11.37 Mackie, John L. *The Cement of the Universe*, Oxford: Clarendon Press, 1974.

Multiculturalism

11.38 *Canadian Journal of Law and Jurisprudence*, 4(2) (1991).

11.39 Kymlicka, Will *Liberalism, Community and Culture*, Oxford: Clarendon Press, 1994.

CHAPTER 12

Applied ethics

Justin Oakley

❦

INTRODUCTION

Applied ethics is a branch of philosophy which employs ethical theory and the methods of philosophical reasoning to illuminate and resolve important practical problems. In so doing, applied ethics addresses issues which go beyond purely theoretical ethical concerns with the systematic justification of moral judgements, dealt with by normative ethics, and questions about the nature of moral statements, which is the province of meta-ethics. Instead of focusing on those theoretical issues, applied ethics takes as its subject matter the more immediate problems confronted in our lives and in the lives of those with whom we share the world. It does so by bringing the distinctive strengths of philosophical analysis and argument to bear on a variety of practical issues such as abortion, euthanasia, warfare and environmental pollution. These are the kinds of issues which feature prominently in our popular press, but the deeper ethical questions they raise receive scant if any attention there.

After many decades of neglect, applied ethics has flourished in the latter half of the twentieth century, and in fact, has probably undergone more growth during this time than has any other area of philosophy in the same period. It would be a mistake, however, to assume that philosophical activity in applied ethics is only a recent phenomenon, for many of our philosophical forebears were actively engaged with practical ethical questions in their writings. Indeed, the distinctions among meta-ethics, normative ethics and applied ethics reflect recent trends towards specialization, and earlier philosophers writing on ethics would have regarded themselves as addressing questions from all three of those domains. Many of the ancient Greek philosophers shared Aristotle's view that ethics is pre-eminently a *practical* enterprise, and this is clearly reflected in their discussions of the ethics of friendship, death and justice in public life. Medieval scholastics such as St Thomas Aquinas wrote dissertations on war and human sexuality, while several centuries later, David Hume, Immanuel Kant and Voltaire dealt with topics such as suicide and world peace. In the late eighteenth century, Jeremy Bentham applied his revisionary utilitarianism to the ethics of capital punishment, and in the nineteenth century John Stuart Mill developed his influential views on liberalism and on equality between the sexes. We can see, then, that representatives of the three main traditions in normative ethics – Aristotelian virtue ethics, Kantian deontology and utilitarianism – all believed it important to consider the ramifications of their theories for the ways we live our lives. This also gives some idea of the diversity of issues examined in applied ethics, and it illustrates the variety of approaches to ethics through which philosophers have attempted to cast light on important practical problems.

In view of this historical background, it is somewhat surprising that philosophers writing on ethics in the first half of the twentieth century did not share this belief in its practical importance and value. Influenced by the dominant positivist school of thought, according to which all inquiry was modelled on the empiricist methods of science, philosophers regarded normative ethics as speculative and unscientific, because ethics was thought not to be grounded in facts, and hence to be unphilosophical. The proper task of philosophy, it was argued, is to examine meta-ethical questions about the nature of moral judgements, and about how such judgements are to be classified. So in 1936 A. J. Ayer proclaimed that 'A strictly philosophical treatise on ethics should ... make no ethical pronouncements', and that 'ethics, as a branch of knowledge, is nothing more than a department of psychology and sociology' (Ayer [12.1], 103, 112). Thus was dispatched normative ethical theory from the province of true philosophy, and its companion, applied ethics, shared the same fate.

The reign of meta-ethics and the antagonism towards normative ethical theory set the agenda for philosophers until the late 1960s, when normative and applied ethics underwent something of a renaissance. The resurgence of applied ethics was a natural consequence of the renewed activity in normative ethics during the late 1950s, which itself grew out of increasing dissatisfaction with the sterility and insularity of the dominant concerns of meta-ethics. This disenchantment with an inward-looking meta-ethics, and the return of philosophers to an examination of substantive questions of normative ethics, was essentially stimulated by the profound and widespread social changes which began in the west in the 1960s. There was enormous questioning of the dominant moral codes of behaviour, and the study of substantive ethical questions began to be viewed as directly relevant to the broader concerns about equality and racial discrimination raised by the American civil-rights movement, and to issues about civil disobedience, pacifism and international justice, raised by the widespread student protests against US involvement in the Vietnam War. Normative ethics, as practised by academic philosophers, began to be seen as offering an important and distinctive perspective on these social developments, and philosophers started moving away from their preoccupation with meta-ethics and again engaged with substantive issues of broader public concern. Scholarly institutes devoted to the philosophical study of applied ethics began to be set up, pioneered by the establishment of the Hastings Center in New York State in 1969. The motivation for this renewed activity in applied ethics was the recognition of the value of ethics both in identifying the crucial issues at hand, and in lending the rigour of philosophical argument to the burgeoning discussions of those issues.

One of the earliest areas where dominant social values began to be widely questioned in this period was sexuality and personal relations, and here philosophers contributed articles challenging received views on the ethics of contraception, monogamous relationships and homo-sexuality. These debates fed into others which were beginning in related areas, such as the morality of the law, punishment and civil disobedience. For example, in the United Kingdom in the late 1950s, the Wolfenden Committee's influential report recommending the de-criminalization of homosexuality stimulated a lively debate between Lord Patrick Devlin and Oxford philosopher H. L. A. Hart on whether the law should aim to uphold our shared moral beliefs, or to prevent harm to others. Also, Pope Paul VI's 1968 condemnation of contraception, after an earlier papal commission had already supported the use of contraception in marriage, aroused much controversy among moral theologians. Around the same time, many states began to look afresh at whether or not to retain capital punishment, and ethicists discussed whether punishment should seek to exact retribution, or to deter future offenders – a question which had been addressed by philosophers since Bentham. Civil disobedience arose as a major issue in the civil rights debates of the early 1960s, and with the entry of the United States into the Vietnam War in 1961. Although the civil-rights movement made some headway with the introduction in 1964 of the US Civil Rights Act, continuing concerns about widespread discrimination, along with the activation of legislative provisions for civil conscription during the Vietnam War maintained the focus of many citizens on the issue of whether it is morally permissible to disobey the law, and philosophers began to take up these concerns in their writings.

The Vietnam War and the massive bombing raids which were thereby undertaken also raised renewed concerns about our treatment of the environment, which had been simmering since the Hiroshima and Nagasaki bombings of 1945, and had reached into new areas in 1962 with Rachel Carson's expose in *Silent Spring* of the effects of widespread use of insecticides such as DDT on delicate ecosystems. During the late 1960s and early 1970s, ethicists joined with biologists and anthropologists to protest against our unrestrained pollution and depletion of the world's natural resources, where the earth was regarded as an object to be plundered for our own purposes, rather than as worthy of respect in its own right. This led to discussions of questions of international justice raised by concerns about overpopulation and Third World poverty. What moral obligations, philosophers began to ask, do we owe to the victims of famine? To what degree are we morally responsible for these catastrophes?

Some philosophers and political scientists argued that a major factor in the occurrence of these tragedies was the single-minded drive of western transnational corporations towards profit, at the expense of human welfare of the citizens of the host countries. This led to a major upsurge of activity in an area which came to be known as business ethics. Philosophers began discussing whether, as economist Milton Friedman argued in 1962, the social responsibility of a business corporation was to concentrate single-mindedly on maximizing its profits, or whether private corporations could also be held accountable for the social and environmental consequences of their actions. Spurred on by these developments, ethicists began to reflect on the nature of professional ethics and their relation to ordinary ethical standards.

The relation of ordinary ethical standards of conduct to professional ethics also arose as a question within medical ethics, where doctors were beginning to deal with the novel and difficult ethical issues brought about by developments in modern medical technology. In this context, ethicists turned their attention to issues about death and dying, and about whether doctors and other health professionals have the right to override a patient's request for the withdrawal of medical treatment. These discussions took up older debates about the nature and moral significance of death and the morality of suicide.

The movement supporting equal rights for women raised new areas of debate about equality of employment opportunities and the justifiability of preferential hiring policies. The women's movement also brought questions about the morality of abortion out of the churches and into the public consciousness, where access to abortion became an issue of bitter public debate.

As this brief introduction indicates, the term 'applied ethics' encompasses a broad range of areas in public and private life. There is the ethics of national and international justice, environmental ethics, ethics of health care, reproduction and genetics, ethics in public policy, business ethics, police ethics, engineering ethics, media ethics and the ethics of the legal profession. Three areas of enduring interest in applied ethics are bioethics, environmental ethics and business ethics, and I shall discuss developments in each of these fields in detail. These areas have become more distinct as the study of applied ethics has flourished; however after an initial divergence, there has been something of a confluence of various sub-disciplines under the heading of 'professional ethics'. This has occurred because of the recognition that each field addresses certain common issues, such as whistle-blowing, conscientious objection and the limits of professional responsibility.

❧ BIOETHICS ❧

One of the earliest areas of resurgence in applied ethics was bioethics. Originally coined as a term describing the ethics of population and the environment, bioethics has come to refer to the study of ethical issues in health care, reproduction, biology and genetics. As such, it includes in its ambit medical ethics, nursing ethics and ethical issues raised in the other paramedical and welfare professions, such as psychiatric care and social work. Bioethics was at the forefront of the renaissance of applied ethics for several reasons. To begin with, advancements in disease control and the development of new medical technologies such as artificial respirators – which could prolong almost indefinitely the life of a comatose patient – led to a re-examination of received views about death, withdrawal of life-support, and the allocation of expensive medical resources. But the rise of bioethics was the result of social as well as scientific and technological factors, for in the 1960s there was an increasing move towards the recognition of patients' rights to due care and adequately informed consent. This movement began to broaden its agenda from initial concerns about experimentation on human subjects, which had been an issue since the Nuremberg Trials of 1947 and the subsequent ethical code of practice issued in 1949, to more general consumerist matters of informed consent and patients' rights to treatment without discrimination.

This consumerist movement towards greater recognition of patient rights intersected with the increasingly vocal women's movement of the late 1960s on the issue of access to abortion. After the de-criminalization of abortion by Britain in 1967, and by New York State in 1970, the most significant event for the pro-choice movement was the 1973 US Supreme Court decision in *Roe* vs *Wade*, which held that women have a constitutional right to an abortion in the first six months of pregnancy. Against this social and legislative background, philosophers turned their attention to the morality of abortion with renewed vigour, and this became one of the earliest issues in applied ethics to attain prominence. Before 1970, most twentieth-century discussions of the morality of abortion focused on whether a fetus has a right to life.[1] If this right could be established, it was argued, then abortion is immoral. However, the first issue of the pioneering journal *Philosophy and Public Affairs*, published in September 1971, carried a ground-breaking article on abortion by the American philosopher Judith Jarvis Thomson, which not only changed the face of the abortion debate, but became one of the most widely known and influential articles in applied ethics ever written.

Thomson rejected the premise that the morality of abortion revolves around the right to life of the fetus. By means of an ingenious analogy, Thomson convincingly demonstrated that granting a fetus a right to life does not entail that abortion is immoral. Thomson asks us to imagine that we awake after being kidnapped by the Society of Music Lovers to find our circulatory system connected to a famous concert violinist, who because of his defective kidneys requires the use of our kidneys for nine months in order to stay alive. In this case we would think, and quite correctly Thomson argues, that the concert violinist has no right to the use of our kidneys for that period, and that we could permissibly disconnect ourselves from him immediately, even knowing that this will result in his death. Having secured our assent to this claim, Thomson goes on to argue that the situation with pregnancy (at least when pregnancy is unchosen) is similar in the relevant respects. That is, the fetus, like the violinist, may well have a right to life, but a pregnant woman can nevertheless justifiably abort the fetus, just as we could justifiably unplug ourselves from the concert violinist (Thomson [12.28]).[2] The effect of Thomson's article was to shift the focus of the abortion debate away from the moral status of the fetus and onto the question of the extent of a pregnant woman's right to control her own body, which Thomson herself saw as the fundamental issue.

Thomson's article was seen as providing a solid philosophical basis for the growing pro-choice movement in favour of abortion on demand, and it spawned a whole industry of books and papers devoted to assessing her argument and its implications for the morality of abortion. One issue arising out of Thomson's argument which has been receiving increasing attention is whether a woman's right to bodily autonomy also gives her the right to fetal destruction. This has become important in the wake of advancements in life-supporting technologies for extremely premature infants, whereby progressively younger infants can be saved, for this means that abortion, at increasingly earlier stages of pregnancy, need not entail the death of the fetus. Also, the legalization of abortion itself raised new ethical questions about research on the aborted fetus.

Another early issue which continues to receive attention was the question of infanticide, especially in the case of severely disabled new-born infants. The most radical view on the morality of infanticide was advanced by Michael Tooley in a highly controversial paper published in *Philosophy and Public Affairs* in 1972. In this paper, Tooley argued that it is not only fetuses which lack a right to life, but new-born infants possess no such right either, and so infanticide shortly after birth is morally permissible. Tooley's argument for this extreme position is based on his contention that it is only persons, rather than human beings as such, which have a right to life. Tooley's central claim is that personhood requires the capacity for self-awareness, which new-born infants lack. The argument for this claim is premised on certain ideas about the nature of rights. Tooley begins by arguing that conferring rights on a being entails that we are obliged to treat that being in certain ways. The next (and most questionable) step in the argument is that we have obligations towards a being in regard to a certain feature only if it is capable of *desiring* that feature, and this in turn requires that it must be able to have a concept of that feature. Tooley then argues that no being can desire that it *continue* existing as a subject of experiences and mental states unless it believes that it is *now* such a subject. However, since infants are apparently incapable of conceiving of themselves as continuing subjects of experiences until at least three months after birth, Tooley concludes that it is not in itself wrong to kill them before they acquire such a capacity for self-awareness (Tooley [12.29]). For a variety of reasons, many rejected Tooley's specific conclusions about infanticide, although many philosophers found his distinction between the moral standing of humans and that of persons persuasive, and went on to apply it to arguments about severely disabled new-born infants, the elderly and ethical issues in our treatment of animals. For example, utilitarians such as Peter Singer and Helga Kuhse have appealed to Tooley's notion of personhood as a morally significant boundary which can be invoked in making non-treatment decisions about seriously disabled new-born infants (Kuhse and Singer [12.19]). However, others have argued that the moral significance of potentiality and parents' duties towards their offspring would rule out infanticide as immoral.

Moving from the beginning to the end of the life cycle, ethical issues in death and dying have been a major focus of discussion in bioethics from the very beginning of its resurgence in the late 1960s. Improvements in dealing with infectious diseases, in organ transplantation and in life-support systems at that time led philosophers and others to reflect anew on the meaning and moral significance of death, and on the ethics of care for the terminally ill. A question which has aroused great controversy is whether it is ever morally justifiable to bring about, by act or omission, the death of a patient at their request, when this is done for humane reasons. Advocates of voluntary euthanasia support the idea that bringing about the death of a patient in these circumstances is morally justifiable, given that the patient was competent when the request was made. Indeed, to hold otherwise, many argue, is to deny a person their right to 'die with dignity'. This position is put forward by both utilitarians (see Rachels [12.24]), who seek to maximize preference-satisfaction, and by some Kantians, who champion the importance of respect for patient autonomy. However, those opposed to voluntary euthanasia argue that a request to bring about death is an admission of defeat, and, moreover, involves usurping the will of God, who alone can decide when a person's time has come.

These debates re-engaged those discussions of the ethics of suicide which were prominent in the writings of some pre-twentieth-century philosophers, but modern medicine's unprecedented ability to sustain life brought hitherto unforeseen issues into the arena. One of the key events upon which much of the contemporary debate has focused is the 1976 New Jersey Supreme Court ruling on Karen Ann Quinlan, who had been lying comatose with respirator support since April 1975. The court supported Karen's parents' right to withdraw artificial life-support, so that Karen could die in peace. Even though after removal of the respirator, Karen actually survived in a persistent vegetative state until 1985, the court's decision provoked great controversy about the implications it was perceived as having for the obligations of health-care professionals to maintain life-sustaining treatment, especially in cases where the benefits of such treatment to the patient appeared to be negligible. Some ethicists have thought that the justification of voluntary euthanasia centres on whether death is brought about actively or rather by an omission to provide treatment, and they have argued that euthanasia is sometimes justifiable in the latter case, especially where the treatment withheld would be regarded as 'extraordinary means'. Others have argued that actions which bring about death as a foreseen but unintended consequence are morally permissible (see Steinbock [12.27]). Many utilitarians have responded that these arguments rely on morally irrelevant distinctions, and that the real issue is whether death would be on balance a benefit rather than a harm (see Glover [12.15]; Kuhse [12.18]), although some (e.g. Beauchamp [12.7]) have defended the moral relevance of the active/passive euthanasia distinction on utilitarian grounds.

The Quinlan case and others involving terminal care for conscious patients gave new momentum to the movement to legalize voluntary euthanasia, which had originated in Britain in the 1930s, to press for legal recognition of competent patients' refusals of medical treatment. Indeed, following the 1973 decision by the courts in the Netherlands not to prosecute doctors who provide voluntary euthanasia, ethicists have discussed at length the implications which such liberalization has for the common objection that such a legalized euthanasia leads inexorably down a slippery slope towards a Nazi-style systematic eradication of the 'socially undesirable'. Those who hold such a view also point to the recent advent of self-administered 'suicide machines' and manuals, which have received much media coverage, as further evidence for their claims. The Quinlan case also reopened an old debate about the definition of death, and contributed to a gradual shift away from the traditional heart-lung notion to the now widely accepted brain-death criterion.

The ethics of abortion and euthanasia were at the forefront of the rapidly emerging field of bioethics during the 1970s, but important scientific advances in new reproductive technologies in the late 1970s and early 1980s sparked a second wave of activity in bioethics, which dealt with the novel and fundamental ethical issues raised by those advances. Foremost among these developments was the birth in 1978 of the first baby from *in vitro* fertilization (IVF), where conception occurs in a test tube rather than inside a woman's body. Initial concerns about IVF surrounded the question of whether it is permissible to 'tamper with nature' in this way, or to usurp God's power to create human life (as arose in the euthanasia debate regarding the taking of human life). However, with the enormous growth in IVF programmes in many countries, later issues focused on whether public expenditure on this new procedure could be justified, against the competing claims of preventive health care, which arguably was far more cost-effective (see Singer and Wells [12.26]).

Early feminists such as Shulamith Firestone, who in 1970 proclaimed that 'pregnancy is barbaric', had eagerly anticipated new reproductive technologies like IVF, for their potential to emancipate women from the burden of reproduction (Firestone [12.13], 198). But the advent of these new technologies met with substantial opposition from many feminist ethicists, who argued that such procedures, carried out mainly by males, merely reinforced existing structures of oppression against women, and bring a range of serious risks which are often undisclosed to the women who participate in them. However, some feminist ethicists have recently come out in support of these technologies on the grounds that, when properly conducted, they actually enhance rather than undermine the autonomy of women (see Birke *et al.* [12.9]).

The apparent success of these reproductive technologies gave added impetus to biological and genetic research into embryo development, and the expertise of bioethicists was called on by government bodies in Australia, the UK and the USA to help draft legislation to regulate such research. This research and its obvious demonstrable benefits raised new questions about the permissible limits of embryo experimentation, and bioethicists turned their attention to discussions about the moral status of the early embryo.

Embryo research and advances in our knowledge about gene sequences also provided new opportunities for pre-natal screening of embryos for genetic diseases and other characteristics, such as sex. This, combined with progress in the Human Genome Project's attempt to map the entire human genome, has brought manipulation of human characteristics through genetic therapy and genetic engineering from the realms of fantasy into reality. These developments raise questions at the frontiers of applied ethics, and bioethicists have only just begun to respond to the call for further discussion of these unprecedented ethical issues. For example, bioethicists are turning their attention to questions about when genetic manipulation for therapeutic purposes might be justified, and whether eugenic genetic engineering is ever morally permissible. Also, the massive genetic data bank being created by the Human Genome Project has raised interesting new questions about the patenting and ownership of genetic sequences and life forms, and about confidentiality in relation to human genetic information.

This brief survey amply illustrates the diversity of issues addressed in bioethics, and indicates how, like many areas of applied ethics, discussions in bioethics draw on knowledge from a range of disciplines outside ethics and philosophy. However, underneath this apparent variety of topics yielded by the spreading branches of bioethics are some common fundamental questions which remain unresolved. For example, the debates on abortion, infanticide and euthanasia have all placed the traditional Christian notion of the sanctity of human life under critical scrutiny, and adherents of this view have been challenged to give an account of the extent, if any, to which quality-of-life considerations may be permitted to influence decisions to bring about the death of a human being. This challenge has been issued by writers who believe, contrary to the sanctity-of-life view, that different human lives may vary in value, as is suggested by our sense that death at certain stages of life may be significantly more tragic than it would be at other stages. For instance, dying just prior to the fulfilment of one's major goals is arguably more tragic than dying before the 'journey' of one's life has begun, or after it has been completed (see Singer [12.25]). Given that our greater technological capacity to sustain human life often comes at great expense, the question of justice in the allocation of health-care resources is also beginning to assume centre stage, especially in the wake of the widespread influence of economic rationalism in the late twentieth century. A range of bioethicists writing on justice in health care have drawn on the work of political philosophers such as John Rawls, in the Kantian tradition (see Veatch [12.30]; Daniels [12.11]), and Robert Nozick, in the libertarian tradition (see Engelhardt [12.12]), in order to provide the moral grounds of a system of health-care resource allocation, and this is an area where much work can be expected to be done in the future. Among other unresolved issues which arise in several contexts are questions about the value of privacy, and its implications for determining when the confidentiality of patients with HIV and other infectious diseases might justifiably be breached. Also, the increasing use of advance directives in health care raises questions about personal identity over time, and about the conditions under which paternalistic intervention in patient care may be justified, and further work remains to be done in this area.

A feature of the bioethics movement, however, is its capacity to reach consensus on certain fundamental points. Most notably, there is widespread agreement on the importance of personal autonomy for justifying decisions in patient care, and this concept plays a major role in the arguments of many writers in such areas as the ethics of repro-ductive decisions, medical experimentation and the permissibility of euthanasia. In particular, the rise of informed consent from a specific doctrine in medical experimentation to a general and virtually inviolable principle in patient care, is testimony to the priority given by bioethic-ists to the value of autonomy, upon which this principle is based. Indeed, the principle of informed consent has been supported by bio-ethicists from both the utilitarian and Kantian traditions (see Beauchamp and Childress [12.8]). There is also a significant degree of agreement on the point that the citizens of a just state have a right to a certain minimal level of health care, and that this care ought to be distributed at least partly according to the needs of the potential recipients.

We can see, then, that bioethics has been quite successful in ident-ifying, examining and in some cases resolving a variety of practical issues; however, bioethics is not simply the mechanical application of ethical theories to practical problems in health care. For the discussion of these practical issues has led in turn to a certain reorientation and re-examination of various aspects of ethical theory itself. This reflexive focus on theory has taken two different forms. First, there has been some adjustment in what are perceived to be the paradigmatic problems of moral practice against which any adequate ethical theory is to be tested. So, for example, the concept of personal autonomy has been accorded a great deal of moral weight in justifying decisions in health care, and so any ethical theory which seeks to be action-guiding in bioethics must be able to account for the importance of personal autonomy. The value of autonomy is naturally explained in Kantian ethics, with its emphasis on right action being determined by humans as self-legislating moral agents. Utilitarianism, however, has traditionally had difficulty in adequately capturing the moral value of individual autonomy, given utilitarianism's single-minded concern with maximization of overall well-being, although recent utilitarians have been making concerted attempts to give autonomy due recognition. Another case where practical issues have redirected the focus of ethical theory is in the renewed attention being paid to the nature and moral significance of personal identity, in light of debates about brain death.

The second way in which attention to issues in bioethics has influenced ethical theory is more fundamental. That is, the very concepts in terms of which these theories are defined and articulated have changed in some instances, as a result of difficulties in applying them to practical problems. For example, Bentham and Mill's classical formulations of utilitarianism in terms of maximizing subjective experiences of pleasure and happiness are regarded as vague by many modern utilitarians, and later writers cast utilitarian theory in terms of maximizing the satisfaction of interests or preferences (e.g. see Hare [12.16], [12.17]). This move has been made partly as a way of broadening the moral sphere to allow consideration to be given to the interests of beings who may not at that time be undergoing any experiences, such as future generations and the comatose, and it has also been influenced by applications of economic theory. Another example of such theoretical modification is the way in which modern Kantians such as Onora O'Neill have focused on the immorality of deceptive and coercive institutions, rather than on the direct application of Kant's categorical-imperative procedure itself (see O'Neill [12.21–3]). And finally, the initial move to subsume professional ethics within broader-based universalist ethical theories has provoked a contrary trend to revive a distinctive medical ethic, grounded in the particularities of the doctor–patient relationship, which modern formulations of virtue ethics and feminist ethics of caring have been thought by some as especially able to capture.

Thus, there is to some extent a dialectical relationship emerging between applied ethics and ethical theory, with each challenging and forcing amendments to the other, in response to their application to the kinds of practical problems discussed above. Also, there is some overlap in the underlying issues addressed by bioethics, on the one hand, and environmental ethics and business ethics, as we shall see.

❧ ENVIRONMENTAL ETHICS ❧

Turning from bioethics to environmental ethics, one may initially be struck by the differences between the kinds of issues addressed by these two fields of applied ethics. However, both these movements share common roots in the widespread challenges to popular conscious-ness during the 1960s, and both raise certain common underlying ethical issues which are difficult to resolve. Broadly speaking, environmental ethics deals with questions of rightness and value regarding our relation-ship with the rest of the natural world. As such, environmental ethicists discuss issues which arise in relation to pollution, the exploitation of natural resources, overpopulation, our attitudes towards and treatment of animals, and the value of ecosystems themselves. In doing so, dis-cussions in environmental ethics often proceed by identifying the kinds of values or features which are at issue, and by attempting to determine, in light of those values or features, what various ethical theories or principles would have us do.

The beginnings of environmental ethics in the twentieth century can be traced back as early as 1915, when Albert Schweitzer began to develop an ethics based on 'reverence for life', in which he included animals, insects and plants as well as human beings. This expansion of the realm of value was quite explicitly taken further during the 1930s and 1940s by the American ecologist Aldo Leopold, in his book *A Sand County Almanac* (1949), which promulgated a holistic 'land ethic', whereby value was attributed to the whole integrated biosphere of landscapes and ecosystems, rather than merely to individual life forms (Leopold [12.37]). This was a precursor to the 'deep-ecology' movement of later decades, which, as we shall see, developed a quasi-spiritual view of the intrinsic value of the biosphere.

However, activity in environmental ethics took a quantum leap during the 1960s, with mounting concerns about pollution, resource depletion and overpopulation. The watershed of the environmentalist movement was Rachel Carson's revelations in *Silent Spring* of wide-spread land degradation resulting from the use of chemical insecticides such as DDT (Carson [12.32]). The exposure by Carson of the pois-oning and fracturing of fragile ecosystems broadened existing public concerns about toxins in food and the environmental effects of nuclear fall-out. Carson's highly influential book, which she dedicated to Albert Schweitzer, forced many to reconsider their instrumentalist attitude to the natural world as an inexhaustible 'resource' which could be unthinkingly used for human edification.

This reassessment led to the formation of broad environmentalist movements, which began to gain a great deal of exposure through public events such as 'Earth Day' in 1970, where American Senator

Gaylord Nelson called for every American's 'inalienable right to a decent environment' to be enshrined in the constitution.[3] The word 'green' began to be used as a verb to denote the development of a commitment to environmental concerns. There was also discussion about whether pollution and overutilization of land violated the rights or interests of future generations to inherit a world which was still livable. Some ethicists argued that, as with spatial distance, temporal distance between populations is irrelevant to setting our moral obligations, and so decisions about the utilization of non-renewable resources must make allowance for our duties towards future inhabitants of Earth. This argument draws on intuitions shared by many about our duties to generations in the not-too-distant future, such as our children, but some philosophers objected to this argument because of the epistemic difficulties in foreseeing what the interests of generations in the distant future will actually be.

These concerns about environmental degradation took on a new urgency with the so-called 'energy crisis' in the 1970s, where many became aware that the known reserves of oil and other fossil fuels, on which much of the world's economy depends, were diminishing at an alarming rate. The recognition of the finiteness of these conventional energy sources inspired developments in alternative energies such as nuclear power, but these carried environmental problems of their own. Concerns about resource depletion also gave rise to a variety of theories which sought to explain this phenomenon. A controversial explanation, tracing the problem to demographics, was offered by Paul Ehrlich in his 1968 book *The Population Bomb*. Echoing Malthus's eighteenth-century views, Ehrlich argued that the environmental crisis was due to the burgeoning world population, which was doubling in size approximately every forty years, and to the resulting exponential increase in the consumption of non-renewable resources (Ehrlich [12.33]). Ehrlich's argument, which pointed to the increased consumption arising from the desire for higher living standards, also raised questions about the ethics of private corporations deriving profits from meeting desires induced by increasingly sophisticated methods of advertising, which I shall discuss later under business ethics. Ehrlich's claims also intensified the debate about the ethics of contraception, discussed in the previous section, for the widespread availability and use of contraception was championed by many as an answer to the dangers of overpopulation. The overpopulation argument also raised some fundamental questions about the extent of the western world's moral responsibility for and duties regarding the plight of populous but underdeveloped Third World countries stricken by famine and poverty.

The question of moral responsibility also arose in relation to scientists whose research had the potential for application in areas which carried hazards of environmental degradation and pollution, such as agriculture, genetics and weapons research. Here ethicists challenged the appeal to ignorance of consequences, or the attempt to diffuse responsibility over the research organization, which scientists often invoked as a way of excusing themselves from the burden of responsibility for the harmful environmental applications of their research. This led to increased attention being paid to questions about foreseeability, culpability and collective responsibility.

However, during the 1970s the early focus on the human impact of environmental destruction began to be regarded as too narrow and 'anthropocentric', and started to be supplanted by an ever increasing expansion of the ethical sphere to include animals, plants and eventually all life forms. This move was being driven largely by philosophers, whose concerns about the environment led them to reconsider traditional assumptions about the boundaries of moral value and moral recognition, and it was really only with the advent of systematic reflection on these deeper considerations that a distinctive and recognizable movement in environmental ethics began to take shape. An indication of this coalescing of concerns was the appearance in 1979 of the first issue of the international journal, *Environmental Ethics*.

One of the earliest issues in this expansionist movement, which bore clear philosophical roots in ethical theory, was the call to include animals in the moral domain. Thus, drawing on the civil-rights movement's rationale for extending proper moral consideration to blacks and women, Australian philosopher Peter Singer's 1975 book *Animal Liberation* presented a powerful argument in favour of granting adequate recognition to the moral status of animals. Condemning common practices in animal farming and experimentation, Singer argued in favour of vegetarianism on utilitarian grounds, and in doing so brought applied ethics to the dinner table, where our eating habits became a matter of ethics rather than simply of etiquette. Singer argued that the principle of equal consideration of interests underlying arguments against racism and sexism entails that discrimination against beings solely on the basis of their species, or *speciesism*, is also unjustifiable. For any being which has the capacity to suffer thereby has interests which, opponents of racism and sexism must in all consistency agree, ought to be given equal consideration. Therefore, since all animals (except perhaps molluscs and some other invertebrates) have the capacity to suffer, and to experience suffering in much the same ways as humans (given the physiological similarity and common evolutionary origin of their respective nervous systems), all such animals are entitled to equal moral consideration. And if we accept that causing such suffering is morally wrong, then we ought to reform our attitudes towards and treatment of animals (Singer [12.46]). *Animal Liberation* touched the lives of many people, and lit the candle of the animal-liberation movement. Some ethicists extended Singer's arguments to campaign in their writings against zoos and animal blood sports, and began to investigate different approaches to establishing why and to what extent animals can justifiably be included in the moral sphere.

With the rapid diminution and extinction of plant as well as animal species occurring during the 1970s due to industrial, transportation and urban-land developments, the environmental movement lobbied successfully for legislative changes to protect endangered species, which resulted in the Endangered Species Act being passed in the United States in 1973. These popular and legislative moves led some ethicists to fix their gaze more broadly, and they began to focus on the difficult question of why, if at all, we ought to preserve diversity of species. This broke new ground in applied ethics in two ways. First, the variety-of-species question was taken up in a *general* way, without giving the human species undue priority, and it took the preservation of orchids and other plant species to be an ethical issue. But second, and more fundamentally, the *reasons* which environmental ethicists began to offer for the importance of maintaining species diversity went beyond the value of species to us as humans. That is, while some ethicists argued for preserving biological diversity by appealing to the value of natural variety in enhancing our understanding and appreciation of nature, others argued that whole ecosystems themselves have intrinsic value, and that the value of a particular species could be seen in terms of its importance for maintaining the integrity of that ecosystem (see Norton [12.42]).

This embracing of ethical value in aspects of nature itself found inspiration in the earlier ethics of Schweitzer and Leopold, and was taken even further in the 'deep-ecology' movement, which began in 1972 with a landmark article by Norwegian philosopher Arne Naess, who drew a distinction between shallow and deep approaches to eco-logical ethics. Naess argued that environmental movements which were motivated by 'shallow' ecological concerns were inadequate, since they operated within the traditional anthropocentric framework, whereby the environment had value because of its contribution to human well-being. A 'deep' ecological movement, on the other hand, was committed to maintaining the intrinsic value of the whole biosphere for its own sake, rather than simply for our human edification (Naess [12.39]). There are several varieties of deep ecological theories, grounded in a range of different metaphysics. Some deep ecologists, who regard nature as an extension of themselves, have been criticized as chauvinistic by writers such as Richard Sylvan, who argues that such approaches fail to recognize the otherness of nature and its profoundly non-personal character (Sylvan [12.48]).

This notion of an environmental ethic grounded in the intrinsic value of all nature inspired many writers to go on and develop their own variants of a life-centred or biocentric ethics, and some went beyond this by arguing that even *inanimate* nature has its own independent standing or its own intrinsic value. For example, in a highly influential 1972 paper, legal philosopher Christopher Stone argued that trees, forests, rivers and oceans ought to be recognized as having legal rights. Stone's argument for this claim begins by making explicit the criteria for an entity to have legal rights, which include the provision that legal actions can be instituted *on its own behalf*, having injuries *to it* taken into account by the courts in determining legal relief, and having compensation awarded *to its own benefit* (and not merely to a guardian). Stone then offers a systematic critique of the prevailing legal position on the environment, arguing that there are no good reasons for holding that natural objects cannot fulfil these criteria. Stone suggests that the legal problems of a natural object can be handled by appointing a guardian to act as an advocate for its needs and interests, as is done with persons who have become legally incompetent, and he argues that the cost of 'making the environment whole' (e.g. through reseeding a logged forest, repairing its watersheds and restocking its wildlife) should be the guiding principle in determining the amount of compensation awarded to it (Stone [12.47]). In the early 1980s the philosophical foundations of this approach were further developed by Kantian philosopher Paul Taylor, who argued for a kind of egalitarian environmental ethics, whereby every living thing is entitled to equal respect as a member of the 'community of life' (Taylor [12.49], [12.50]).

However, other ethicists, such as J. Baird Callicott and Holmes Rolston III, rejected the individualism or atomism prevalent in many theories of environmental ethics. In contrast to these approaches, which emphasized the flourishing of individual members of species, Callicott and Rolston were inspired by the earlier ethics of Leopold to attribute value to the entire community of life forms, land forms and ecosystems as an integrated whole, which was given greater weight than any of its component parts. Thus, in Callicott's ethics, oceans and lakes, mountains, forests and wetlands are assigned a greater value than individual animals, and even viruses and bacteria are included in the realm of value (see Callicott [12.31]). Indeed, Rolston argued that entities such as stalactites, crystals and even entire planetary systems have intrinsic value (Rolston [12.45]). However, some philosophers, such as animal-rights advocate Tom Regan, have argued that this holistic ecocentrism is really just a form of 'environmental fascism', in its indefensible requirement that the rights of individuals must sometimes be sacrificed to the good of the ecosystem as a whole.

Certain writers have recently sought to give this holistic approach to environmental ethics a metaphysical basis. For example, the Australian philosopher Freya Mathews argues for a Spinozistic 'ethic of interconnectedness', whereby the apparently different features of the natural world are regarded as attributes of the same underlying substance. Mathews endorses English biochemist James Lovelock's claim, in his influential book *Gaia: A New Look at Life on Earth*, that the biosphere consists in systems of self-realizing beings. Recalling Spinoza's notion of *conatus* (or the drive to self-realization), Mathews goes on to argue that these self-realizing beings have equal intrinsic value, although she does allow that some degree of species loyalty is morally permissible. Further, in developing our commitment to our own self-realization, Mathews argues that we come to identify with this *conatus* in other beings, and so become properly disposed both emotionally and practically to safeguard Nature in all its manifestations. (Mathews [12.38]).

The move by ethicists towards a larger picture has also been reflected in a shift in the environmental movement during the 1980s away from an exclusive focus on narrower local issues, such as the preservation of a particular species, towards a more global outlook, with the advent of problems in ozone-layer depletion, the 'greenhouse effect' and consequent global warming. This broader perspective has raised new and challenging ethical issues about international environmental justice, and has brought out interesting tensions between environmental values and the claims of social justice. One example of this tension between competing values which is beginning to receive attention concerns the question of the extent to which it is justifiable for affluent western nations to compel impoverished Third World states to preserve wilderness areas, when the economies of those states are so dependent on exploitation of the land for farming and other activities. The question of moral responsibility for this potential conflict also arises, since some writers argue that western nations have helped to bring about a situation of Third World dependence such that wilderness areas in those countries are now under threat.

In summary then, the movements in the intellectual landscape of environmental ethics can be portrayed as a progressive broadening of our concern for different life forms, corresponding to a gradual deepening in our views of what is valuable. But exactly how far we must extend our ethical concerns in these directions remains a hotly debated issue, and the boundaries between the diverse camps in environmental ethics can by and large be drawn according to the different answers they give to this question.

However, it should not be thought that the proper limits to extending the moral domain can be found simply by rigorously applying the particular ethical theory one is already committed to. For as we saw with bioethics, environmental ethics also has a reflexive aspect, where the application of ethical theory to practice has led to new issues and problems for ethical theory itself. For example, ethicists who had adopted the discourse of rights have had some difficulty in capturing the moral status of animals, plants and landscapes in those terms, and some have subsequently abandoned rights talk in favour of the broader notion of 'interests', which they think is better able to accommodate environmental values (on rights and interests, see Feinberg [12.36]). Others, such as John Rodman [12.44], have reformulated Kant's well-known categorical imperative urging us to treat people as ends in themselves, rather than using them as mere means, and have argued that this principle applies to all living things and natural systems which have ends of their own. More fundamentally, the application of ethical theory to environmental issues has also cast debates about the nature and importance of intrinsic and instrumental values into a new arena, and has led to some clarification of how candidates for intrinsically valuable entities, such as ecosytems, are related to our valuing them. These debates have connected in interesting ways with other, broader, debates in meta-ethics, such as that between Humean projectivism and moral realism.

Another way in which discussions in environmental ethics have raised deeper issues is in the ecofeminist critique of the very idea of an environmental ethic based on a 'theory' at all. Ecofeminists reject the need for theory as a masculinist prejudice which ignores the reality and plurality of experience, and especially of women's experience. In support of this approach, some writers point to the similarities between man's quest for domination over nature, and his attempts to subordinate women (see Warren [12.52]). Other writers argue that historically, women have experienced a close emotional identification with nature (see Ortner [12.43]), and that women are characteristically more sensitized than men to the particularities and the contextual features of situations. While such large claims cannot be evaluated here, we can nevertheless see that issues similar to those raised in feminist critiques of new reproductive technologies and of abstract ethics, which we noted above in discussing bioethics, are beginning to receive much attention in environmental ethics also.

❧ BUSINESS ETHICS ❧

A third area which has emerged as a distinct and active sub-discipline of applied ethics is business ethics. Generally speaking, business ethics is the study of ethical issues in private enterprise and the conduct of commercial affairs. A variety of ethical issues arises in those contexts, but the attention of ethicists has centred mainly on questions concerning the social responsibilities of private corporations, collective responsibility for environmental pollution and other harms, the morality of bribery and extortion, and the justifiability of whistle-blowing against one's colleagues. The orientation of business ethics differs from those of both bioethics and environmental ethics in several respects. To begin with, since business ethics is really a sub-division of professional ethics, it is comparable to such fields as medical ethics and legal ethics. For like those fields, business ethics deals with issues which are somewhat narrower than those addressed in bioethics and environmental ethics, which raise fundamental questions about the moral status of human beings and the value of life itself. Also, unlike philosophers engaged in bioethics and environmental ethics, philosophers writing on business ethics have on the whole not made deliberate attempts to formulate unified theories or world-views within which to explain and resolve the distinctive problems which arise in studying the activities of private corporations. Of course, discussions in business ethics do involve applications and examinations of traditional utilitarian, Kantian, and Aristotelian ethical theories, and there is also some scrutiny of broad political and economic theories such as liberalism, capitalism and socialism. However, philosophers have not by and large tried to develop a distinctive 'business ethic', in any sense analogous to either a philosophical medical ethic, or an environmental ethic such as deep ecology. Indeed, the absence of attempts to articulate an overall business ethic is not surprising, given the variety of different commercial enterprises which business ethicists take as their cases in point, and the absence in business of any general traditional professional ethic, akin to the Hippocratic Oath of the medical profession.

The ethics of business and commerce have been discussed by philosophers since the ancient Greeks and Romans, and such concerns also figure prominently in the Christian tradition of moral theology. But the groundwork for many modern discussions of ethical issues in business was laid by the eighteenth-century Scottish philosopher–economist Adam Smith in his classic text on political economy, *The Wealth of Nations* (1776), which argued that a nation's wealth is maximized by permitting individuals to pursue their own interests, rather than through political intervention to secure some notion of the common good. Despite these historical antecedents however, it was really only in the late 1970s that the somewhat disparate range of concerns addressed in business ethics were brought together as a unified field of study. The seeds of this emerging field were planted in America during the late 1950s and early 1960s, when the behaviour of private corporations came under closer public and government scrutiny. This increased attention was due to a number of factors, such as the growing consumerist and civil-rights movements during that period, but there was also a significant move within certain corporations themselves to examine conventional business practices, in response to their desire to remain competitive with the resurgent economies of Japan and Germany. These movements raised concerns about such issues as industrial pollution, unjust discrimination, corrupt business practices and the extent to which weapons manufacturers gave impetus to US involvement in the Vietnam War.

It is common to distinguish between three levels of analysis in business ethics. The first and most fundamental level deals with the values arising out of the broad social, cultural, political and economic environment in which the activities of corporations are set, and addresses underlying questions about issues such as the compatibility of the free market with considerations of justice and general welfare. The second level of analysis examines the ethics of corporate behaviour directly, in light of certain background assumptions about the distinctive institutional norms of private corporations, while the third level concentrates on the rights and obligations of individuals within a particular business organization.

Following the concerns raised by the environmental and civil-rights movements in the early 1960s, one of the first debates in business ethics concentrated on the fundamental question of whether private corporations have any broader social responsibilities, such as maintaining the environment, or alleviating poverty and suffering, or whether it is morally permissible for corporations to focus exclusively on maximizing returns to their shareholders. One of the principal proponents of the latter view was the well-known American economist Milton Friedman, in his 1962 book *Capitalism and Freedom*. Reacting against what he saw as the rising tide of support for the idea that private corporations have greater social responsibilities, Friedman argued that a corporation is purely an instrument of the shareholders who own it, and so its obligations are owed exclusively to them, rather than to the members of society at large, who have no legitimate claims on it. In Friedman's view, the responsibility for dealing with broader social problems falls into the hands of governments themselves, who already exact contributions from private corporations for broader social purposes in the form of corporate taxation. Friedman also supported his position by invoking Adam Smith's argument that social welfare is in any case often best promoted by allowing private corporations to pursue their own interests, since such activity will be indirectly led by an 'invisible hand' to promote social welfare in ways which are often more effective than any corporate activity which aims more directly at this goal (see Friedman [12.61]).

However, this Friedmanesque plea for laissez-faire capitalism and free-market corporate behaviour was hotly contested on a variety of grounds. Many argued that this approach took a far too narrow and atomistic view of private corporations, since their activities affected not only their company shareholders, but also what are sometimes called their 'stakeholders', such as their employees, clients, consumers and the broader community who live near them (see Solomon [12.68]). This raised the question of whether the realm of interests which must be considered in evaluating the activities of businesses can be justifiably expanded in such ways, and this has become one of the central issues of business ethics. Others expressed scepticism about Friedman's empirical claim regarding the effects of the invisible hand on social welfare, and argued instead that an unregulated laissez-faire market would often have significant undesirable consequences for social welfare.

Another branch of opposition to Friedman's view focused not so much on the general question of whether a corporation's neglect of broader social obligations in concentrating on maximizing profits is wrong in itself, but instead challenged a specific implication of that view in regard to environmental and other public harms, in cases where a clear causal link could be established between a corporation's activities and those broader ill-effects. This kind of criticism arose largely in response to widespread public concerns about the environmental effects of industrial pollution, and about the safety of food additives and pharmaceuticals, especially with the emergence of the devastating side-effects of certain drugs, such as Thalidomide. Philosophers started to take up these public concerns, and began to debate conceptual and ethical questions about corporate moral responsibility, and about the extent, if any, to which a body of people (a corporation) could meaningfully be held responsible for wrongdoing. Many argued that where social and environmental harms could be shown to be the direct result of business activities, as in industrial pollution and the manufacture of hazardous products, there is a clear case for holding corporations accountable for those consequences (see Arrow [12.55]). However, other writers, influenced by sociological and legal views of the nature of organizations and their limited liability, argued that the idea of a corporation being held morally responsible for harmful outcomes is incoherent, and contended that the notion of moral responsibility is properly applicable only to individuals.

This debate led to discussions among business ethicists and philosophers about the kinds of entities which moral responsibility can be legitimately attributed to, and they examined whether the organizational decision-making structures involving corporate reasons for actions are sufficiently analogous to those of individual persons to treat corporations as accountable moral agents (see French [12.60]). Some have conceded that corporations can bear *collective* moral responsibility for wrongdoing and be liable to sanctions as a result, but have insisted that they cannot be allocated *distributive* moral responsibility for such consequences, and so responsibility and blame cannot be meted out to individual employees. However, others have argued that in the process of incorporating and co-ordinating the disparate actions of individual employees into a structure of power and responsibility, corporations themselves often have a relatively clear idea of how responsibility is distributed over the organization. Indeed, some have pointed out that a refusal to make these structures explicit has enabled corporations to 'shield' guilty parties from appropriate legal and moral sanctions for their contribution to great human and environmental disasters (see Wells [12.70]). One widely supported suggestion often made in this context is that corporations should develop clearer organizational structures so that individual employees can know what they are and what they will be held responsible for. Many corporations are beginning to take such measures, and this suggestion has also had an impact on professional business-ethics education. However, questions remain about what share of moral responsibility it is justifiable to allocate to individual members of large corporations, in cases where social and environmental harms are clearly the result of the activities of the corporation which employs them. This also raises issues about conscientious objection, conflicting loyalties and whistle-blowing, which we shall turn to later.

The publicity surrounding the harmful social and environmental effects of certain corporate activities also raised deeper questions about the relationship between ordinary and professional standards of morality, which we saw also arose in the context of medical ethics. On the Friedman view, the appropriate guiding norms of business are given content entirely by reference to its overriding single goal of maximizing profits for shareholders. In response to protests from those who sought to demonstrate the wider moral responsibilities of business in a democratic pluralist society, supporters of the Friedman approach drew on the common analogy between business and sports, which have their own internal systems of rules, and where ordinary moral standards are somewhat attenuated. The rejoinder to this, however, has been to point out that even in those seemingly extra-moral enclaves, ordinary moral and legal requirements are not suspended altogether. So, for example, a footballer who uses excessive violence during a match can still be charged with assault. Thus, neither a sportsman nor a businessman can properly be regarded as 'a law unto themselves'. Indeed, some writers, such as environmental lawyer and ethicist Christopher Stone (familiar from the previous section for his argument that trees should have legal rights), turned Friedman's question around, and asked instead why there is any reason to believe that corporations ought to be *exempted* from the ordinary moral obligations of non-maleficence and beneficence which apply to all members of our society. How can a corporate executive, just in virtue of the role he or she occupies, properly regard himself as immune from ordinary moral obligations in respect to his behaviour in his corporate capacity (Stone [12.69])? This kind of argument drew on interesting work in the morality of roles and their attendant obligations, which some philosophers have argued offers a framework better able to capture the distinctive moral position of a company employee than is provided by analyses in terms of the dichotomy between individual and corporate responsibility. For, as R. S. Downie argued, 'an individual person can act in a public or official capacity ... [and] in accepting the role he adds to his share of rights and duties those which go with the role' (Downie [12.59]). This also raised questions about the concept and moral basis of professionalism, and about the limits of professional autonomy, which also arise in medical, legal and other areas of professional ethics.

Another early issue which has received much attention by business ethicists is the ethics of advertising, which became prominent as a result of the massive spread of television and its enormous expansion of markets during the 1950s. An initial skirmish in the early 1960s between influential American economists J. K. Galbraith and F. A. Hayek, on the relationship between advertising and consumer demand, brought out one of the key issues in the debate. Galbraith argued that the effects of television advertising confounded traditional justifications of the free market based on its alleged efficiency in meeting existing consumer demand, because of what he called 'the dependence effect'. This is the phenomenon whereby increases in an individual's wants are directly responsive to increases in the levels of production and consumption, since the production which satisfies existing consumer demand itself often results in the creation of new wants (see Galbraith [12.62]). In other words, as a society becomes better off and more productive, and corporations acquire greater access to advertising, individuals come to develop new desires for material goods, through the influence of advertising and their desire to emulate the affluence of others. James Joyce was aware of this long ago: 'Mass seems to be over. Could hear them all at it. Pray for us. And pray for us. And pray for us. Good idea the repetition. Same thing with ads. Buy from us. And buy from us.'[4] Galbraith argued that the creation of these artificial wants, which could be met only through acquiring more goods, simply increased the spiral of consumption, and he argued that we should concentrate instead on meeting those wants which individuals would experience in the absence of those seductive influences. The creation of wants by advertising illustrated another dimension to the social responsibilities of corporations, and aroused important debates in ethical theory about the moral status of different kinds of preferences.

In response to this, Hayek contended that Galbraith's emphasis on meeting original desires uninfluenced by the existence of products which society makes available is a fruitless search for a chimera, since most of our desires, including those for literature, music and other cultural pursuits, are influenced in some way by socialization. Hayek also argued that the producers of goods are not themselves able to determine what consumers will come to want, since people are able to make free choices about such matters for themselves (Hayek [12.64]), and indeed, advertising arguably performs a useful function in informing people of what products are available. However, as others have pointed out, advertising can properly perform this informative function only if it is honest about the products it promotes, but this may well not be the case, since lying or concealing the truth may often serve the company's interests in selling its products and maximizing its profits. This has led to debates about what level of honesty advertisers are morally obliged to uphold, and whether there ought to be legislative provisions against false advertising to protect the rights of consumers (see Goldman [12.63]).

All these issues have been discussed since the early 1960s by a variety of groups, such as economists, political theorists, corporate executives and the public at large. However, it was not really until the late 1970s that philosophers began to engage in sustained discussions of these ethical issues, and this upsurge of activity is evident in the many anthologies on business ethics which began to appear then (see Bibliography, p. 396). With the publication of the inaugural issue of the *Journal of Business Ethics* in 1982, business ethics became the latest of the three main fields of applied ethics to emerge as a recognizably distinct area of study.

Since becoming involved in business ethics, philosophers have developed the early discussions of broad questions much further, and they have also written extensively on specific issues which arise in the context of the individual employee's relationship with his or her corporation. There has been much recent discussion of the morality of various forms of corruption, such as bribery, extortion and insider trading, and also of the moral responsibilities of individual employees who become aware of such activities within their organization.

Business ethicists have taken an interesting approach to discussing the morality of bribery and extortion. Instead of simply issuing blanket condemnations of these practices, business ethicists have argued that there are various circumstances where such practices may be justified. For instance, since bribery is aimed at influencing a person to violate his or her institutional duties or expected roles, one situation where bribery has been claimed to be morally justified is where the institutional duties or roles of the person bribed are themselves already morally unjustifiable. Some writers also argue that the distinction between bribery and extortion is morally significant, since bribery takes the form of inducements for the provision of special favours, whereas extortion (or, as it is more commonly called, blackmail) involves receiving payment for something one is already supposed to do, but which one threatens not to do unless one receives a certain payoff (see Philips [12.67]). Since bribery involves an inducement to violate impartiality, it has been regarded by many as much more difficult to justify than extortion, which does not involve such a violation, and which utilitarians argue is justifiable in cases where such action would prevent great harm. Another kind of situation where bribery and extortion have been defended is where such practices are an integral part of the customs of a particular country in which one is a guest. This has raised interesting meta-ethical questions about the validity of cultural relativism, but many ethicists reject the relativist position, and so argue that it cannot be used to justify acts of bribery and extortion.

With the enormous profits being made during the stock-market boom of the 1980s, and the equally large losses incurred in the stock-market collapse of 1987, business ethicists turned their attention to questions about whether practices such as 'insider trading' in company shares are ever morally justifiable. Insider trading involves buying large numbers of shares in a company which one knows through 'inside' information is about to be the target of a takeover bid, and then selling these shares at an inflated price to the company making the takeover bid. Insider trading raises ethical issues because it is a practice whereby employees make a personal profit from confidential information about their company's intentions which they have been entrusted with. Insider trading has been portrayed by some as ethically unobjectionable, on the grounds that it is just another example of the spirit of entrepreneurship upon which the business world is built. Nevertheless, ethicists have argued that insider trading is immoral, for a variety of reasons. For example, Gary Lawson argues that the shareholders of the target company are being deceived into making an unfair trade, since they are selling their shares without knowledge of the impending takeover, and so without knowledge of their true market value. Lawson also argues that insider trading may be thought wrong on the grounds that employees are thereby breaking their promise to their employers not to use their position to seek undeserved personal advantage, and that it may be tantamount to stealing information which rightly belongs to their employers (see Lawson [12.66]).

However, since these practices clearly do take place within the modern corporate world, what have business ethicists advised an employee to do where he is aware of such practices occurring, or is being told to participate in these or other immoral practices himself? These situations are extremely difficult for individuals, especially since the burgeoning numbers of unemployed are likely to make many reluctant to take any action. One course open to employees asked to participate in the immoral actions of a corporation which is, say, causing serious environmental damage, would be to refuse on conscientious grounds to carry out their duties. This kind of situation also occurs in the context of nursing and patient care, and it raises important questions about the moral significance of personal integrity, which has received much recent attention in debates about ethical theory. However, where an employee is aware of wrongdoing within their organization but is not themselves participating in it, under what circumstances would they be morally obliged to 'blow the whistle' on their colleagues? This question about the justifiability of whistle-blowing arises in many areas of professional ethics, and ethicists have given different reasons in support of such action being taken. Kantians argue that whistle-blowing is justified because one's duties to prevent harm and injustice to others override one's institutional duties, while utilitarians have defended such action in cases where the harms one is calling attention to are worse than the harms which occur as a result of one's blowing the whistle (see James [12.65]). These kinds of situations often raise difficult questions about conflicting loyalties, and their resolution may well weigh heavily on the individual who has carried out the whistle-blowing (see Wren [12.71]).

We can see then, that business ethics often brings out vexed questions which require deeper analysis in terms of ethical theory before they can be resolved. Nevertheless, business ethics does not generally raise ultimate questions about the nature and value of life itself, and so the reflexive focus back on issues of theory has been less apparent in this field than it is in bioethics and environmental ethics. Nonetheless, the rise of international business and the variations in customs regarding gifts, payments and bribes has led to some revival in discussions of cultural relativism, which had been dismissed by many earlier philosophers. And more importantly, the recognition of the role which the profit motive plays in business affairs has led some business ethicists to raise interesting questions about moral motivation, and about their implications for professional business-ethics education.

❧ CONCLUSION ❧

In this broad sweep over the terrain of applied ethics I have sought to demonstrate both the diversity of issues which have been discussed within its various sub-disciplines, and also how the application of different ethical theories allows some progress to be made in resolving these issues. There are many smaller fields within applied ethics which have made significant progress during the period we have been dealing with, but it is beyond the scope of this chapter to discuss these in any detail. Some of these, such as legal ethics, and computer ethics, may well go on to become highly active fields in their own right. In any case, as we approach the end of the twentieth century, what emerges from this brief survey is that the field of applied ethics has transcended its origins in the popular movements of the late 1950s and early 1960s, and has gone on to become perhaps the most flourishing of all branches of philosophy. In doing so, it has added depth and rigour to popular debates about the most pressing issues in our lives, and has set new challenges for ethical theory. It has also developed the interdisciplinary aspect of ethics, which has always been one of philosophy's great strengths. Let me say a little in closing about what I believe the future directions and issues in applied ethics are likely to be.

In environmental ethics, the rise of globalism and the move towards a new world order in the 1990s seems likely to usher in a greater interventionist role for the United Nations in environmental protection, and since environmental values may diverge from what social justice requires of us in regard to the survival of those in under-developed countries, we can expect further discussion of what kinds of trade-offs between justice and environmental values might be justifiable. This issue also looks likely to arise in regard to the international behaviour of transnational corporations. In bioethics, new advances in reproductive technologies may lead to a questioning of women's responsibilities with regard to child-bearing, and the continued march of the patient-rights movement will intensify debates over both the morality of voluntary euthanasia and its possible legalisation. Justice in health-care resource allocation and its implications for patients' rights to adequate access to and delivery of care will be another subject of continued debate, especially in the wake of our ageing populations, and the widespread moves by many governments to further ration health-care expenditure. Also, progress in gene-mapping coupled with increasing sophistication in pre-symptomatic genetic screening techniques will raise new questions about the desirability and use of such measures both in reproduction and in the workplace. In business ethics, affirmative-action programmes for increasing the participation of women in the workforce will ensure further discussions of justice and fairness in employment policies, and there seems likely to be a greater focus on the moral responsibilities of individual employees in cases where they are acting in an official capacity.

On a deeper level, there are already signs that the renaissance of applied ethics is spawning a satellite industry of philosophers and others engaged in a reflexive critique of the very enterprise of applied ethics, its influences, its methodology and its relation to ethical theory.[5] For example, some writers have recently argued that bioethics is overly dominated by an ideology of individualism, where the value of personal autonomy has too often been allowed to reign supreme over values of beneficence and community (see Callahan [12.10]). There also promises to be further discussion of the distinction between professional and ordinary morality, and of the special rights and duties which an employee's role confers on him. This might have implications for ethical theory, for it might suggest that there are important limitations on the capacity of the traditional partiality/impartiality framework to capture role-based values and obligations (see Blum [12.2]). The focus on professional roles might also pave the way for stronger connections between applied ethics and moral psychology, where questions about the importance of psychological notions such as 'identification' may arise in relation to the concept of a profession as a 'vocation'. Thus, we may begin to see the development of fields such as applied moral psychology.

The importance of psychology for applied ethics may also become apparent in the context of professional ethics education, where after more than a decade of teaching such courses, philosophers are beginning to ask deeper questions about what the aims of such courses are. For example, ought we to be trying to teach doctors and businessmen just to be good reasoners, ought we be trying to develop their sense of conscience, or ought we be aiming to bring about fundamental changes in their characters? These questions cannot be adequately answered without returning to the nature of ethical theory itself, and the role which different theories give to the importance of character development in acting rightly. This has also raised the question of whether there can be any 'moral experts', which some writers regard as an oxymoron, and on which we can expect to see a good deal of further debate in the future.

John Dewey once said that philosophy should be judged by its capacity to meet the challenge of the very conditions which give rise to it. Applied ethics has helped rescue moral philosophy from the intellectual doldrums of the earlier twentieth century, and it is vital to the future of the discipline, for the disengagement of philosophy from practice can only abet the case for the prosecution.[6]

❧ NOTES ❧

1 The idea that the immorality of abortion follows from the moral status of the fetus is largely a twentieth-century phenomenon. Prior to that, purposes was widely regarded as morally permissible, unless sought for certain purposes, such as convenience or sex selection (see Luker [12.20]).

2 This article has probably been more widely anthologized in applied-ethics collections than any other single article, and that alone indicates a measure of its influence.

3 See *Newsweek*, 4 May 1970: 76.

4 James Joyce, *Ulysses*, (London: Bodley Head, 1960), p. 492. (Originally published in 1922.)

5 For example, on the implications of applied ethics for ethical theory, see Rosenthal and Shehadi [12.4], Winkler and Coombs [12.6]; and on major influences on American bioethics, see Fox [12.14].

6 I would like to thank Lynn Gillam, Peter Singer, Chin Liew Ten and, especially, Robert Elliot, for helpful discussions and comments on previous drafts of this chapter.

❧ BIBLIOGRAPHY ❧

General

12.1 Ayer, A. J. [1936] *Language, Truth, and Logic*, London: Gollancz, 1970.

12.2 Blum, Lawrence A. 'Vocation, Friendship, and Community: Limitations of the Personal–Impersonal Framework', in Owen Flanagan and Amelie O. Rorty, eds, *Identity, Character, and Morality: Essays in Moral Psychology*, Cambridge, Mass.: MIT Press, 1990.

12.3 Rachels, James *Moral Problems*, New York: Harper & Row, 1971.

12.4 Rosenthal, David M. and Fadlou Shehadi, eds *Applied Ethics and Ethical Theory*, Salt Lake City: University of Utah Press, 1988.

12.5 Singer, Peter, ed. *Applied Ethics*, Oxford: Oxford University Press, 1987.

12.6 Winkler, Earl R. and Jerrold R. Coombs, eds *Applied Ethics: A Reader*, Oxford: Blackwell, 1993.

Bioethics

12.7 Beauchamp, Tom L. 'A Reply to Rachels on Active and Passive Euthanasia', in Tom L. Beauchamp and Seymour Perlin, eds, *Ethical Issues in Death and Dying*, Englewood Cliffs, NJ: Prentice Hall, 1978.

12.8 —— and James F. Childress *Principles of Biomedical Ethics*, 3rd edn, New York: Oxford University Press, 1989.

12.9 Birke, Lynda, Susan Himmelweit and Gail Vines *Tomorrow's Child: Reproductive Technologies in the 90s*, London: Virago, 1990.

12.10 Callahan, Daniel, 'Autonomy: A Moral Good, Not a Moral Obsession', *Hastings Center Report*, 11(5) (1984): 40–2.

12.11 Daniels, Norman *Just Health Care*, New York: Cambridge University Press, 1985.

12.12 Engelhardt, H. Tristram *The Foundations of Bioethics*, New York: Oxford University Press, 1986.

12.13 Firestone, Shulamith *The Dialectic of Sex*, New York: Bantam Books, 1970.

12.14 Fox, Renee C. 'The Evolution of American Bioethics: A Sociological Perspective', in George Weisz, ed., *Social Science Perspectives on Medical Ethics*, Dordrecht: Kluwer, 1990.

12.15 Glover, Jonathan, *Causing Death and Saving Lives*, Harmondsworth: Penguin, 1977.

12.16 Hare, R. M. *Freedom and Reason*, Oxford: Oxford University Press, 1963.

12.17 —— *Moral Thinking*, Oxford: Oxford University Press, 1981.

12.18 Kuhse, Helga *The Sanctity-of-Life Doctrine in Medicine: A Critique*, Oxford: Oxford University Press, 1987.

12.19 —— and Peter Singer *Should the Baby Live?* Oxford: Oxford University Press, 1985.

12.20 Luker, Kristin *Abortion and the Politics of Motherhood*, Berkeley: University of California Press, 1984.

12.21 O'Neill, Onora 'Paternalism and Partial Autonomy', *Journal of Medical Ethics*, 10 (1984): 173–8.

12.22 —— *Faces of Hunger*, London: Allen & Unwin, 1986.

12.23 —— *Constructions of Reason: Explorations of Kant's Practical Philosophy*, Cambridge: Cambridge University Press, 1989.

12.24 Rachels, James *The End of Life: Euthanasia and Morality*, Oxford: Oxford University Press, 1987.

12.25 Singer, Peter, 'Life's Uncertain Voyage', in P. Pettit, R. Sylvan and J. Norman, eds, *Metaphysics and Morality*, Oxford: Blackwell, 1987.

12.26 —— and Deane Wells *The Reproduction Revolution*, Oxford: Oxford University Press, 1984.

12.27 Steinbock, Bonnie, ed. *Killing and Letting Die*, Englewood Cliffs, NJ: Prentice Hall, 1981.

12.28 Thomson, Judith Jarvis 'A Defense of Abortion', *Philosophy and Public Affairs*, 1(1) (1971): 47–66.

12.29 Tooley, Michael 'Abortion and Infanticide', *Philosophy and Public Affairs*, 2(1) (1972): 37–65.

12.30 Veatch, Robert M. *A Theory of Medical Ethics*, New York: Basic Books, 1981.

Environmental ethics

12.31 Callicott, J. Baird *In Defense of the Land Ethic: Essays in Environmental Philosophy*, Albany: State University of New York Press, 1989.

12.32 Carson, Rachel *Silent Spring*, Boston: Houghton Mifflin, 1962.

12.33 Ehrlich, Paul *The Population Bomb*, New York: Ballantine, 1968.

12.34 Elliot, Robert 'Environmental Ethics', in Peter Singer, ed., *A Companion to Ethics*, Oxford: Basil Blackwell, 1991.

12.35 —— and Arran Gare, eds *Environmental Philosophy: A Collection of Readings*, St Lucia: University of Queensland Press, 1983.

12.36 Feinberg, Joel 'The Rights of Animals and Unborn Generations', in William T. Blackstone, ed., *Philosophy and Environmental Crisis*, Athens: University of Georgia Press, 1974.

12.37 Leopold, Aldo *A Sand County Almanac*, New York: Oxford University Press, 1949.

12.38 Mathews, Freya *The Ecological Self*, London: Routledge, 1991.

12.39 Naess, Arne 'The Shallow and the Deep, Long-range Ecology Movement: A Summary', *Inquiry*, 16 (1973): 95–100.

12.40 Nash, Roderick *Wilderness and the American Mind*, 3rd edn, New Haven, Conn.: Yale University Press, 1982.

12.41 —— *The Rights of Nature*, Sydney: Primavera Press, 1990.

12.42 Norton, Bryan G. *Why Preserve Natural Variety?* Princeton, NJ: Princeton University Press, 1987.

12.43 Ortner, Sherry B. 'Is Female to Male as Nature is to Culture?', in Michelle Rosaldo and Louise Lamphere, eds, *Woman, Culture and Society*, Stanford, Cal.: Stanford University Press, 1974.

12.44 Rodman, John 'Four Forms of Ecological Consciousness Reconsidered', in Donald Scherer and Thomas Attig, eds, *Ethics and the Environment*, Englewood Cliffs, NJ: Prentice Hall, 1983.

12.45 Rolston III, Holmes *Environmental Ethics: Duties to and Values in the Natural World*, Philadelphia: Temple University Press, 1988.

12.46 Singer, Peter *Animal Liberation*, London: Jonathan Cape, 1975.

12.47 Stone, Christopher D. 'Should Trees have Standing? Toward Legal Rights for Natural Objects', *Southern California Law Review*, 45 (1972): 450–501.

12.48 Sylvan, Richard *A Critique of Deep Ecology*, Discussion Papers in Environmental Philosophy, no. 12, Canberra: RSSS, Australian National University, 1985.

12.49 Taylor, Paul W. 'The Ethics of Respect for Nature', *Environmental Ethics*, 3(3) (1981): 197–218.

12.50 —— *Respect for Nature: A Theory of Environmental Ethics*, Princeton, NJ: Princeton University Press, 1986.

12.51 Vandeveer, D. and C. Pierce, eds, *People, Penguins and Plastic Trees: Basic Issues in Environmental Ethics*, Belmont, Cal.: Wadsworth, 1986.

12.52 Warren, Karen J. 'The Power and Promise of Ecological Feminism', *Environmental Ethics*, 12(3) (1990): 125–46.

12.53 Zimmerman, Michael E., J. Baird Callicott, George Sessions, Karen J. Warren and John Clark, eds *Environmental Philosophy: From Animal Rights to Radical Ecology*, Englewood Cliffs, NJ: Prentice Hall, 1993.

Business ethics

12.54 Applebaum, David and Sarah V. Lawton, eds, *Ethics and the Professions*, Englewood Cliffs, NJ: Prentice Hall, 1990.

12.55 Arrow, Kenneth 'Social Responsibility and Economic Efficiency', *Public Policy*, 21 (1973): 303–18.

12.56 DeGeorge, Richard and Joseph A. Pichler *Ethics, Free Enterprise, and Public Policy*, New York: Oxford University Press, 1978.

12.57 Donaldson, Thomas *The Ethics of International Business*, New York: Oxford University Press, 1989.

12.58 —— and Patricia Werhane *Ethical Issues in Business*, Englewood Cliffs, NJ: Prentice Hall, 1979.

12.59 Downie, R. S. 'Responsibility and Social Roles', in Peter A. French, ed., *Individual and Collective Responsibility*, Cambridge: Schenkman, 1972.

12.60 French, Peter A. 'The Corporation as a Moral Person', *American Philosophical Quarterly*, 15(3) (1979): 207–15.

12.61 Friedman, Milton *Capitalism and Freedom*, Chicago: University of Chicago Press, 1962.

12.62 Galbraith, J. K. *The Affluent Society*, London: Hamish Hamilton, 1958.

12.63 Goldman, Alan 'Ethical Issues in Advertising', in Tom Regan, ed., *Just Business*, Philadelphia: Temple University Press, 1983.

12.64 Hayek, F. A. 'The Non Sequitur of the Dependence Effect', in Tom L. Beauchamp and Norman E. Bowie, eds, *Ethical Theory and Business*, Englewood Cliffs, NJ: Prentice Hall, 1979.

12.65 James, Gene G. 'In Defence of Whistleblowing', in Joan C. Callahan, ed., *Ethical Issues in Professional Life*, New York: Oxford University Press, 1988.

12.66 Lawson, Gary 'The Ethics of Insider Trading', *Harvard Journal of Law and Public Policy*, 11 (1988): 727–83.

12.67 Philips, Michael 'Bribery', *Ethics*, 94 (1984): 621–36.

12.68 Solomon, Robert C. 'Business Ethics', in Peter Singer, ed., *A Companion to Ethics*, Oxford: Basil Blackwell, 1991.

12.69 Stone, Christopher D. *Where the Law Ends: The Social Control of Corporate Behaviour*, New York: Harper & Row, 1975.

12.70 Wells, Celia 'The Hydra-headed Beast', *Times Higher Education Supplement*, 11 January 1991, p. 16.

12.71 Wren, Thomas E. 'Whistleblowing and Loyalty to One's Friends', in William C. Heffernan and Timothy Stroup, eds, *Police Ethics*, New York: John Jay Press, 1985.

CHAPTER 13

Aesthetics

George Dickie

❧ INTRODUCTORY REMARK ❧

Aesthetics in the English-speaking world during the twentieth century, with regard to its central problems, falls into three relatively distinct periods: the psychological, the analytic and the contextual.

Until the 1950s, philosophers attempted to resolve aesthetics' central questions – the nature of the experience of art and the nature of art – by using notions of *individual psychology*, notions of what persons do or undergo as individuals. The attempt to define 'art' as the expression of emotion is an example of the use of such a concept. These notions of individual psychology contrast with social notions of what persons do or undergo as members of groups, for example, a person scoring during a game or receiving a degree from a university.

During the 1950s and 1960s aesthetics was impacted by the two strains of analytic philosophy. One strain is of a formal and stipulative sort. The principal figures in this tradition, Monroe Beardsley and Nelson Goodman, have much in common with the philosophers of the psychological period.

The second strain of influence from analytic philosophy derives from Wittgenstein and the ordinary-language philosophers. Philosophers in this tradition deny that 'art' can be defined and generally advocate a non-essentialist approach in aesthetics. These philosophers, unlike Beardsley and Goodman, break sharply with the methods of the psychological period.

From the early 1960s, a number of philosophers have attempted to resolve the central problems of aesthetics with *contextual* theories. Philosophers during this most recent period have done three things. One, they attacked the use of the notions of individual psychology. Two, they ignored or attacked the anti-essentialist approach of the

Wittgensteinians. Three, they attempted to describe the experience of art and/or to define 'art' in terms of artworks' contexts.

I shall discuss relatively few philosophers in order to give more complete accounts of their views. Even so, the accounts may not be complete enough to give a full sense of why the theories of these philosophers were so persuasive and influential at the times they were set forth. The Bibliography, structured with the headings used in the text, lists other works related to the views discussed.

❧ THE PSYCHOLOGICAL PERIOD ❧

Aesthetic experience

Edward Bullough

Schopenhauer, in the nineteenth century, was the first to present a full-blown aesthetic-attitude theory, a theory that places disinterested cognition and a detached state of mind at the centre of aesthetic theorizing. This way of theorizing has been enormously influential. Bullough's article on psychical distance (1912 [13.1]) presents the earliest of the well-known, twentieth-century, aesthetic-attitude theories. Bullough, following Schopenhauer, seeks to allay the philosophical fear that people, unless psychologically restrained, will behave practically towards natural scenes and behave towards art in the practical way they behave towards reality.

Bullough claims that to appreciate aesthetic qualities, one must be psychically distanced, a state that puts one 'out of gear with practical needs and ends' and blocks practical thoughts and actions. This state detaches the experience of aesthetic qualities from the rest of experience. Ethel Puffer, Bullough's contemporary with a similar theory, claims that the description of aesthetic detachment 'constitute[s] a theory and a definition of hypnotism'.

Bullough illustrates psychical distance with two cases: someone in a fog at sea and a jealous husband at *Othello*. Supposedly, a distanced person would be able to appreciate aesthetic features because his state of being distanced would prevent him in the one case from being consumed with thoughts of dangers at sea or in the other case with thoughts of an unfaithful spouse. Bullough generalizes from such cases and concludes that all appreciation of aesthetic features requires being psychically distanced. He even claims that being psychically distanced makes stage characters fictional for audience members; gallant, undistanced spectators will attempt to rescue stage actresses from stage villains.

There is a certain plausibility to the view that persons in desperate straits, say, in a fog at sea, must be psychologically restrained in order to appreciate aesthetic features. Most aesthetic situations – looking at a still-life in a museum, for example – are not desperate and do not suggest the need for psychological restraint. It is a mistake to generalize from desperate cases to non-desperate ones. Even in the desperate cases there is no reason to think that psychological restraint occurs or is needed. Worrying about dangers at sea or a wife's suspicious behaviour are just ways of being distracted from the aesthetic qualities of the fog or the action of the play, not ways of being free of psychological restraint. If one's fear or suspicion are allayed, one can attend to aesthetic qualities or a play's action.

That the experience of art requires a detached state has led to the condemnation of certain artistic techniques. One Bullough follower (Dawson [13.2]) condemned Peter Pan's appeal for applause to save Tinker Bell's life because it would supposedly destroy psychical distance and make children unhappy. Should these imaginary, theoretical children be taken seriously? Multitudes of children over the years have responded enthusiastically to the appeal! Incidentally, an actor addressing the audience is an old and common device.

Aesthetic-attitude theorists think that threatening situations, certain theatrical devices, and (if attended to) the intellectual, moral and referential content of art can destroy the detached state that makes aesthetic experience possible. They believe, however, that being psychically distanced can block attention to art's content and allow it to be properly experienced – as the object of aesthetic experience.

David Prall

In *Aesthetic Judgment* (1929), Prall continued the aesthetic-attitude tradition. He begins by declaring that art and the experience of it 'do not contribute to the interested practical and social activities of men' [13.4]. The proper experience of art is of its 'aesthetic surface', colour, sound, spatial order, rhythm, and the like, features that are appreciated independently of anything they are related to. If one attends to the intellectual, moral or referential content of art rather than merely to its aesthetic surface, one 'depart(s) from the ... aesthetic attitude'. Prall devotes much space to detailed discussions of aesthetic surfaces. Late in his book, he has second thoughts about art's content. Of literature, he says we experience 'the vast possibilities of life, of human passion and emotion, ... and all the thousand relations that men bear to each other'. He then tries to link aesthetic surface to content by 'thickening' aesthetic surface to encompass art's intellectual, moral, and referential content. He first defined aesthetic surface as a perceptual quality experienced as *unrelated* to anything else, but now he wants to *relate* it to what it can represent, describe, state and refer to. Prall ends in a contradiction, trying to give both the content of art and aesthetic surface the weight they deserve.

Jerome Stolnitz

The staying power of the aesthetic-attitude tradition is shown by the fact that Stolnitz claims in 1960 [13.5] that *attending disinterestedly* detaches aesthetic experience from the rest of experience. Stolnitz contrasts disinterested attention with interested attention. He claims, for example, that a critic attending a concert to write a review attends to music *interestedly*, while a person with no such ulterior motive attends *disinterestedly* and has an *aesthetic* experience. The difference between the critic and the non-critic is, however, one of motives, not attention. Motives can affect attention – distract it, focus it – but if the critic and the non-critic attend to the music, despite their motives, their attentions will not be of different kinds. Attending in order to write a review is not a kind of attending, although the prospect of writing a review might focus attention sharply. The critic case and other cases that Stolnitz calls 'attending interestedly' do not involve a kind of attending but simply attending with a particular motive. Some of his cases of 'attending interestedly' turn out to be cases of inattention.

John Dewey

Dewey's theory of aesthetic experience is discussed out of chronological order because it acts as a corrective for the highly influential aesthetic-attitude theories. Dewey begins *Art as Experience* (1934 [13.3]) with a promising account of the experience of art, focusing on the experience of an organism within its environment. In speaking of art *as experience*, he is emphasizing the distinction between what he calls 'the art product', for example, a canvas covered with paint and what he calls 'art', the art product when properly experienced. Dewey understands the experience of art to be a development out of ordinary experience, and it is not seen as detached from life.

    Dewey envisages the experience of art as aesthetic experience, which he sees as a development out of the aesthetic experience of natural things. He explicitly rejects the conception of aesthetic experience that flows from Schopenhauer through Bullough to Prall. He sees aesthetic experience not as detached and contemplative but simply as experience with a substantial degree of internal coherence; it is for him the kind of thing we note as being '*an* experience', experience in which the elements cohere into a consummatory unity and stand out from the flow of experience.

Dewey does not say much about the referential aspects of art. Reference is troublesome for aesthetic-attitude theorists because features of art that refer from *inside* a supposedly detached and self-contained aesthetic experience to something outside it are thought of as disruptive of aesthetic experience. Referential features of art are not a problem for Dewey. The elements of aesthetic experience, for him, cluster together but they are not detached and isolated from the rest of experience.

The philosophy of art

George Santayana

While Santayana's *Reason in Art* (1905 [13.11]) is perhaps the earliest of the twentieth-century philosophies of art in English, its philosophical theses are neither developed nor argued for. The book is largely devoted to art criticism.

Santayana begins with a discussion of the place of art within his philosophical naturalism. By 'art' he means technology. Santayana then moves to the *fine* arts, defining them as 'productions in which an aesthetic value is or is supposed to be prominent'. He notes that fine art 'has many non-aesthetic functions and values', a thesis that recurs frequently to emphasize the continuity of art with life. Santayana's definition and his repeated thesis are never defended, and the holders of opposing views are not mentioned. The philosophical topics appear merely to be prologue to the art criticism.

Clive Bell

Bell's *Art* (1914 [13.6]) presents what is generally regarded as a formalist philosophy of visual art. The foundation of Bell's theory is 'the aesthetic emotion', an emotion distinct from the ordinary emotions of life such as pity and fear. All *sensitive* persons, he says, can experience and identify this emotion. He then asserts, 'The objects that provoke this emotion we call "works of art".' The next step is to discover what works of art have in common as their essential quality. He assumes that only *one* thing causes aesthetic emotion. His answer is that the essential quality of art is *significant form*. He means by 'form' the relations of line and colours in visual art, and by 'significant form' he means the sub-set of these forms that evoke aesthetic emotion. Bell denies that representation as such in art has any artistic value.

Bell's view is not really a philosophy of art because it excludes many objects ordinarily viewed as works of art. He asserts that the great bulk of paintings, statues and the like are not works of art; they do not provoke aesthetic emotion. Another reason his theory is not a philosophy of art is that he says significant form, art's essential quality, sometimes occurs in natural objects – he cites a butterfly wing. Bell's class of works of art includes objects that no one regards as art!

Bell's theory is really an instrumentalist theory for the *evaluation* of visual art, that is, a theory about what in visual art is instrumental in producing valuable experience (aesthetic emotion). It seems unlikely that there are aesthetic emotions, although valuable experiences are produced by art. The psychological content of Bell's theory is suspect, but as an evaluational theory, its instrumentalist structure is promising.

John Dewey

The expressionist theory of art arose in the nineteenth century and remained a powerful influence well into the present century. In *Art As Experience* (1934 [13.8]), Dewey presents one of the earliest of the twentieth-century expressionist theories. He launches into an account of art as the expression of emotion without any argument, seeming to regard it as obviously true, as did many others of the time. Dewey distinguishes the mere venting of emotion from the expression of emotion, the latter requiring the conscious ordering of a medium. This distinction allows him to exclude some emotional behaviour (venting) from the domain of art.

Although he writes at length about expression and expressive objects, it is not clear whether he identifies the expression of emotion with art, or whether he thinks expression is just a necessary condition of art.

Art frequently has expressive qualities, but affirming the expression theory of art is another matter entirely. The expression theory has received effective criticism in recent years; few today believe that every work of art is an expression of emotion of its creator or that every expressive quality of a work of art is an actual expression of an emotion.

Dewey claims that the expressiveness of art entails that each art form is a language for a kind of communication. Whether every art form is a language and a means of communication is very doubtful and that this follows from being expressive is even more doubtful.

Despite the difficulties of Dewey's theory of art, much of what he has to say about expression and expressive qualities is quite sound. He also shows a very considerable knowledge of the arts, especially the visual arts.

R. G. Collingwood

In *Principles of Art* (1938 [13.7]), Collingwood, also following the expressionist tradition, claims that what he designates 'art proper' is *identical* with the expression of emotion. He gives an argument of sorts to support his claim: he is making clear how words are used in English. The meanings of 'art (proper)' and 'craft' are completely distinct. A craft object is a preconceived product produced by the application of a skill to a raw material, while art is a completely spontaneous, unplanned thing. Crafts may be involved in the conveying of art to its audience, but art and craft are distinct.

Collingwood asserts without argument that 'Art has something to do with emotion', i.e. that art and emotion are necessarily connected. He assumes two possibilities: something can express emotion or something may be designed to evoke emotion. The latter would involve a preconceived end (the evoking of emotion) and would, therefore, be a craft product. Expressing emotion is spontaneous. He concludes that art, which he believes to be spontaneous and unplanned, is identical with the spontaneous phenomenon of expressing of emotion. Even if his premises were granted and it were agreed that art is necessarily connected to the expression of emotion, it does not follow that art is *identical with* the expression of emotion.

Collingwood's conclusion appears to make rages and the like into art. He tries to avoid this difficulty by saying that such behaviours are not art because they are betrayals rather than expressions of emotion, which, he claims, are controlled actions. This move narrows the ordinary meaning of 'expression of emotion'.

Collingwood claims people sometimes confuse art proper with the crafts he calls 'magical art' and 'amusement art'. Magical art, for example, patriotic and religious art, is craft because it is designed to evoke emotions to sustain certain life activities, and amusement art is craft because it is designed to evoke emotion for enjoyment. He suggests that because they were designed to evoke emotion in Elizabethan audiences, Shakespeare's plays are not art!

The expression of emotion is an act of the imagination in that it brings something into consciousness. Collingwood takes this to mean that an act of expression, i.e. art, is imaginary and takes place in the mind only and is purely mental. Thus, for Collingwood, paintings, statues and the 'noises' musicians make are not art; they are craft objects that enable others to re-create art in their own minds. This means that what are ordinarily understood to be artworks are understood by Collingwood to be craft objects, and that what are ordinarily understood to be the conceiving of and the understanding and appreciation of art are understood by Collingwood to be artworks.

There are several difficulties with Collingwood's theory. First, it excludes many things that almost everyone thinks of as art, namely works with no emotional content. His response is that a product of serious activity always retains an element of emotional expressiveness. He cites Eliot's *The Waste Land* as an example of art. This work is the result of serious activity and has emotional content, but it is not clear that a serious activity must always have an emotional element. It is also not clear that the creation of art is always a serious affair. Second, his theory is also flawed if, as he apparently thinks, it excludes Shakespeare's plays from the domain of art. The third difficulty is that his *identification* of art with the expression of emotion would turn into art many things that no one thinks are art. When a parent says in a controlled but exasperated tone, 'Turn off the television and do your homework', that parent is expressing emotion but not thereby creating a work of art.

Suzanne Langer

In *Feeling and Form* (1953 [13.9]), Langer, continuing the focus on emotion, defines 'Art' as 'the creation of forms symbolic of human feeling'. She is claiming that every artwork *as a whole* is a symbol. She explains that art symbolizes by abstraction; for example, 'Music is a tonal analogue of emotive life.' Art symbolizes by abstract resemblances. She is not talking about the resemblance involved in representation; both non-objective and representational art allegedly symbolize. Art for Langer is an iconic symbol, i.e. a symbol that resembles what it symbolizes. The main difficulty with her account is that it ignores the *conventional* basis of symbols. Iconic symbols do not function merely in virtue of a resemblance; as all symbols must, they have to be *established* as signifying what they do. In *Problems of Art* (1957 [13.10]), Langer accepted this criticism which reduces her theory to the view that art is the creation of forms that resemble human feeling.

Does every work of art resemble human feeling? Some music is a tonal analogue of emotive life and some visual art does resemble human feeling. Many works of art – non-objective and representational – however, just do not resemble human feeling; Langer overgeneralizes from what is true of some cases.

General Comment

The central ideas of all the foregoing theories are notions of individual psychology. Psychical distance and disinterested attending would both be phenomena that individuals do or undergo as individuals. Aesthetic surface, aesthetic qualities and significant form are or would be objects of perception, and perceptual discrimination is an ability that individuals exercise as individuals. Dewey's conception of the aesthetic experience as *an* experience of consummatory unity is something an individual undergoes as an individual. The expression of emotion *is* something an individual does as an individual, and aesthetic emotion *would be* a kind of thing that an individual would do as an individual. Langer's basic notion – noting resemblance – is something individuals do as individuals. Two of these notions fall under the category of awareness, two fall under the category of affect, and six fall under the category of perception.

THE ANALYTIC PERIOD

The experience of art

Monroe Beardsley

Beardsley's *Aesthetics* (1958 [13.12]) describes its subject as 'metacriticism', the analysis of concepts involved in describing, interpreting and evaluating art. Beardsley begins by trying to characterize the proper objects of criticism, which he calls 'aesthetic objects' (the aesthetic aspects of artworks). His focusing on *aesthetic* objects shows that he is continuing the earlier tradition of focusing on the aesthetic aspects of art. His first step is to argue that artists' intentions are distinct from artworks and, thus, not aspects of their aesthetic objects. His second step is to distinguish between the *perceptual* aspects of art (those perceptible *under the normal conditions for experiencing art*) and the *physical* aspects of art (those aspects not perceptible under normal conditions). This second step is supposed to eliminate certain aspects of art that are not proper objects of criticism – (1) physical aspects such as sound waves and light waves that are not experienced at all and (2) aspects such as the colour of the back of a painting and the actions of unseen stage-hands that are not experienced under normal conditions. The second step does not eliminate perceptible things such as print marks used to inscribe a poem and the colour of a painting's frame, but Beardsley's third step is supposed to do this. This third step – the consideration of the properties of various perceptual domains – concludes with the definitions of 'visual design', 'musical composition' and 'literary work', which are supposed to eliminate the remaining improper elements. I shall consider only 'visual design', which is defined as 'a bounded visual area containing some heterogeneity'. The colour of a painting's frame is *not*, however, eliminated by the third step; it is perceptible and is part of *a* bounded, heterogeneous visual area, and there are analogous problems in other visual-art cases. Moreover, the perceptual/physical distinction would eliminate important aspects of some aesthetic objects – the non-perceptible meaning of literary works, for example. The second and third steps of Beardsley's account of aesthetic objects both fail; his understanding of the objects of criticism throughout his book is not, however, hampered by this. The initial question of whether artists' intentions are relevant to interpretation is still a hotly debated topic.

Beardsley concludes that *the* function of aesthetic objects is the production of aesthetic experience, and he works out an account of such experience that owes something to Dewey and something to Bullough and others. According to Beardsley, every aesthetic quality (gracefulness, delicacy, and the like) of an aesthetic object is an instance of one of three primary aesthetic properties: unity, intensity or complexity. These three primary properties when perceived can supposedly *cause* a person's experience to have certain affects, namely, to be unified, intense and complex. Aesthetic experience, thus conceived, consists of (1) the experience of the three primary perceptual properties of aesthetic objects and (2) the affects (felt unity, intensity and complexity) that are caused by these primary perceptual properties. In addition, he alleges that aesthetic experience has a *detached* nature deriving from its unity which supposedly insulates and detaches the experience from things outside it. Beardsley agrees with Dewey that aesthetic experience is highly unified. He, however, accepts Bullough's contention that aesthetic experience is detached, a view Dewey explicitly rejects.

Beardsley concludes that any content of art that refers to something outside the aesthetic experience – say, its cognitive or moral content – is nullified by the *detached* nature of aesthetic experience. On his view, only the non-referential aspects of art – the aesthetic qualities of unity, intensity and complexity – contribute to aesthetic experience. Because Beardsley conceives of aesthetic experience as detached, his theory has no way to account for the functioning of whatever referential content art has. This signals that the notion of the experience of art as detached is flawed; Beardsley should have followed Dewey more closely.

Nelson Goodman

In *Languages of Art* (1968 [13.16]), Goodman agrees with Beardsley that the function of art is to produce aesthetic experience, but his conception of such experience is radically different. Goodman claims that the aesthetic experience of art is not a matter of the appreciation of aesthetic qualities, is not detached and is cognitive in nature. He, thus, breaks sharply with the tradition followed by Bullough, Prall, Stolnitz and Beardsley.

Goodman claims that every work of art is a symbol that symbolizes by description, representation, expression, exemplification or some combination of the four. He asserts that the purpose of symbols and, hence, art, is cognition and that art is to be evaluated by how well it serves its cognitive purpose. Art's cognitive purpose is served by 'the delicacy of its discriminations ... the way it works in grasping, exploring, and informing the world ... how it participates in the making, manipulation, retention, and transformation of knowledge'.

Many works of art are symbolic, but are they all? In the section on the evaluation of art at the end of this article (pp. 421–5), it will be argued that some artworks (most non-objective art and instrumental music) are not symbolic.

Frank Sibley

Sibley's 'Aesthetic Concepts' (1959 [13.17]) began an important discussion of aesthetic qualities and has generated a large literature. He begins his article by distinguishing aesthetic terms, concepts and qualities from non-aesthetic terms, concepts and qualities. 'Red' and 'square' are examples of non-aesthetic terms, and redness and squareness are examples of non-aesthetic qualities. The application of non-aesthetic terms and the discernment of non-aesthetic qualities requires only 'normal eyes, ears, and intelligence'. 'Fiery' and 'delicate' are examples of aesthetic terms and fieriness and delicacy are examples of aesthetic qualities. The application of aesthetic terms and the discernment of aesthetic qualities requires more than normal perception and intelligence, they require 'the exercise of taste, perceptiveness, sensitivity'. For Sibley, an aesthetic term is *identified* as one whose application requires an exercise of taste, and an aesthetic quality is *identified* as one whose discernment requires an exercise of taste. For Sibley, terms are not aesthetic or non-aesthetic as such; some terms may always be used aesthetically, but some may be used aesthetically and non-aesthetically, depending on context. Thus, for Sibley, taste is the most basic category; taste identifies which use of a term is an aesthetic use and identifies which features are aesthetic features.

Aesthetic qualities, he claims, depend on non-aesthetic features. What is the nature of this dependence relation? Non-aesthetic qualities such as squareness have necessary and sufficient conditions, in this case, having four equal sides and four right angles. Sibley denies that aesthetic qualities have necessary and sufficient conditions because, for example, one object is delicate because of one set of non-aesthetic features and another object is delicate because of a different set of non-aesthetic features. In addition, he also denies there are *logically sufficient* conditions for aesthetic qualities. In a particular case of, say, delicacy, its non-aesthetic conditions do suffice to produce delicacy, but the occurrence elsewhere of those same non-aesthetic conditions is not, he claims, always sufficient to produce the occurrence of delicacy. It is true that certain non-aesthetic features may count only towards and not against the occurrence of a certain aesthetic quality, but the occurrence of such non-aesthetic features cannot guarantee the occurrence of a particular aesthetic quality. Also, some aesthetic qualities may be governed *negatively* by non-aesthetic conditions; for example, a painting consisting only of pale pastel colours could not be garish. Sibley's view is that aesthetic qualities depend on non-aesthetic features but that they are not positively condition-governed and that, consequently, the applications of aesthetic terms are not rule-governed.

That there are aesthetic qualities and that they depend on non-aesthetic qualities is widely accepted. Many also accept Sibley's contention that aesthetic qualities are not condition-governed. The chief difficulty with Sibley's view is his notion of taste and its use in identifying what counts as an aesthetic quality. This difficulty is brought out by Ted Cohen (1973 [13.14]) who focuses on the perception of aesthetic qualities in simple cases. Consider the perception of *gracefulness* in a female ballet dancer's movements or the *awkwardness* in the walking of a year-old child. Cohen asks, does it take anything other than normal eyes and intelligence to note these two aesthetic qualities? He answers in the negative, and if that is so, then taste does not identify what counts as an aesthetic quality in simple cases. Perhaps to try to forestall this argument, Sibley claimed in 'Aesthetic Concepts' that virtually everyone can exercise taste to some degree in some domains. But if normal sense faculties and intelligence *and* taste are almost always present at the same time, how can we know in simple cases whether it is normal perceptive capacities or taste that discerns aesthetic qualities. Or, consider complicated cases in which one person discerns and another person fails to discern an aesthetic quality. Perhaps the person who fails to perceive does so because his normal perceptive capacities are a bit limited and the person who does perceive has slightly greater normal perceptive capacities. It does not seem that we can be assured in either simple or complicated cases that there is taste in Sibley's sense, and, hence, we cannot be assured that Sibley has a way of identifying what counts as an aesthetic quality.

The philosophy of art

Paul Ziff

Ziff in 'The Task of Defining a Work of Art' (1953 [13.25]) was the first to apply the anti-essentialism that began sweeping through philosophy in the 1950s to the philosophy of art. He claims usage of the expression 'work of art' shows there is no necessary condition for being art, not even being an artifact. A naturally formed stone that looks like a sculpture and is worth contemplating can, for example, be said to be a work of art. This is supposedly so because the stone *sufficiently* resembles a characteristic case of art. The many different usages of 'work of art' supposedly show that many different sufficiency definitions are possible. Each such definition has a characteristic case, say, Rembrandt's *Night Watch*, and anything that sufficiently resembles it is a work of art. Even if a characteristic case is an artifact, members of the class of objects it generates do not need to be artifacts, they need only to resemble the characteristic case sufficiently. No rule can be given, he says, as to what constitutes sufficient similarity. Ziff says that novels, poems and musical compositions are so different from paintings that they cannot be included in the class of objects that sufficiently resembles *Night Watch*. They can, however, be called works of art because they sufficiently resemble other characteristic cases. On Ziff's view, there are as many different definitions of 'work of art' as there are different uses of the term.

Morris Weitz (1956 [13.24]) and William Kennick (1958 [13.23]), influenced by the anti-essentialism of the period, drew similar conclusions about the definition of 'art'. These three articles brought attempts to define 'art' to a virtual halt during the analytic period. Sibley's claim that aesthetic qualities are not condition-governed is in the same anti-essentialistic tradition that Ziff is in.

A naturally formed stone *can* be said to be a work of art and a class *can* be constructed that includes sculptures plus such a stone. Should these two facts cause philosophers to abandon the traditional claim that artifactuality is a necessary condition for art? I think not. Philosophers of art need take no interest in such usage or in a class so constructed, because they have always theorized about a class of human artifacts. Artifactuality is a built-in feature of their activity; their real problem has always been to discover the other defining feature or features of these artifacts. Moreover, there is solid agreement about which artifacts belong to the class of objects they theorize about – paintings, poems, plays, and so on.

Nelson Goodman and Monroe Beardsley

Because of the powerful influence of anti-essentialism, theorizing about art was not a popular activity among philosophers in the analytic period. Whether Goodman's claim that all works of art symbolize is put forth as a partial definition of 'art' or simply as a universal generalization is unclear; either way his claim fails because of his theory's inability to deal with non-objective art and instrumental music.

Beardsley did not turn his attention to the definition of 'art' until 1979. He writes then, 'an artwork can be usefully defined as an intentional arrangement of conditions for affording experiences with marked aesthetic character' [13.21]. This definition, which continues Beardsley's emphasis on aesthetic features, was put forth in explicit opposition to contextual theories of the late 1960s and the 1970s that take the domain of art to include Duchamp's *Fountain*, dadaist works generally and similar artworld creations – works that have little or no capacity to afford aesthetic experience as Beardsley conceives it. Beardsley's ruling out of such avant-garde works in order to make aesthetic considerations *necessary* is a stipulatory move characteristic of his wing of analytic philosophy. Also, since Beardsley's definition of 'artwork' depends on his notion of detached aesthetic experience, his definition inherits all the difficulties involved in the idea of detachment.

General Comment

Many philosophers of the analytic period continued to try to solve the problems of aesthetics with concepts of individual psychology. Beardsley's use of *perceptibility* and the *properties of perceptible domains* to try to distinguish aesthetic objects are uses of such concepts. Perception is an activity a person does as an individual. Similarly, his notion of aesthetic *experience* with its content of aesthetic qualities and their affects and its detachedness is something a person undergoes as an individual. Goodman's claim that the aesthetic experience of art is an *experience* of the reference of symbols involves something persons undergo as individuals. Ziff's notion of *noting sufficient resemblance* is a notion of something that a person does as an individual. Finally, Sibley's attempt to distinguish aesthetic from non-aesthetic features on the basis of what *normal eyes, ears and intelligence* can discern and what *taste* can discern is clearly the use of notions of capacities persons exercise as individuals.

❧ THE CONTEXTUAL PERIOD ❧

Introductory Remark

Contextualist theorists break sharply with the traditions of the two earlier periods. One or more of the three hallmarks of the contextual period – the rejection of concepts of individual psychology, the rejection or ignoring of the prevalent anti-essentialism and the use of the contexts in which artworks are embedded – were enunciated independently in five articles by four philosophers during the period 1962–5. In 'Is Psychology Relevant to Aesthetic?' (1962 [13.27]), I claimed that the thought and behaviour of art's audiences are not controlled by the psychological phenomenon of psychical distance but by rules of artwork contexts. In 'Aesthetic Essence' (1965 [13.26]), Marshall Cohen attacked a number of individual psychology notions, including psychical distance as a controller of spectator behaviour. Concerning the contextual control of behaviour, Cohen mentioned the *learning* of how artworks are to be experienced. In 'The Myth of the Aesthetic Attitude' (1964 [13.28]), I attacked Bullough and the aesthetic-attitude theories of Jerome Stolnitz and Eliseo Vivas. In 'The Artworld' (1964 [13.37]), Arthur Danto, ignoring the prevalent anti-essentialism, set forth the first contextualist account of the nature of art. In 'Family Resemblances and Generalization concerning the Arts' (1965 [13.48]), Maurice Mandelbaum directly attacked the anti-essentialism of Ziff and Weitz. Mandelbaum also recommended a contextual approach to generalizing about art without attempting to work out the details.

The positive insights of these five articles were developed along two lines: accounts of the contextual control of experiences of art and accounts of the contextual nature of art.

The experience of art

Marshall Cohen and George Dickie

The criticisms Cohen and I made of the mechanisms of individual psychology supposedly involved in the proper experience of art were incorporated into my earlier criticisms of aesthetic-attitude theories and of Beardsley's account of aesthetic object and require no further comment.

Aesthetic-attitude theorists claimed that a particular psychological state (variously described) controls the thought and behaviour of the experiencers of art; jealous husbands can attend to *Othello* if psychically distanced, children are disturbed by Peter Pan's request for applause because it destroys their psychical distance, and gallant spectators do not attack stage villains if they are psychically distanced. If, however, there are no such psychological states, what does control thought and behaviour in the face of artistic phenomena?

Samuel Johnson's eighteenth-century answer was 'The truth is, that the spectators are always in their senses, and know, from the first act to the last, that the stage is only a stage, and that the players are only players' [13.30]. One's knowledge of the nature of an artistic activity, alluded to by Cohen [13.26] and myself [13.27], is what controls spectator's thoughts and actions.

A more extensive, if somewhat piecemeal, account of the contextual control of the experience of art is found in my *Art and the Aesthetic* (1974 [13.29]). Consider the cases of the attacker–spectator and Peter Pan's appeal. There is a general *rule* or *convention*, understood by all, that audience members do not interact with a play's action. A gallant spectator who attacked a stage villain would be someone who flouts this convention out of ignorance of theatre art or because of insanity. Such a spectator would not be someone who had lost the aesthetic attitude, although he could be someone who had lost his mind. When Peter Pan appeals for applause, it signals that the usual convention is being set aside and that a different convention is being put in place. Children catch on right away that there has been a convention shift, even if some aestheticians don't. A convention is by definition something that can be done in more than one way, and different plays have different conventions governing spectator participation. Reflection will reveal that there are many conventions involved in the presentation of the arts to their publics. Although the jealous-husband-at-*Othello* case does not involve being in or losing the aesthetic attitude any more than the other two cases do, it does not directly involve theatre convention either; the husband is just someone whose thoughts of his wife may cause him not to pay attention to the play.

Aesthetic-attitude theorists claim that being in the aesthetic attitude reveals which characteristics of art belong to the aesthetic object of works, i.e. which characteristics are to be appreciated and criticized. Beardsley makes a similar claim for perceptibility and other criteria. Both claims fail. What does direct attention to aesthetic objects of works of art? It is the background knowledge of theatre – its nature and conventions – that isolates the aesthetic objects of plays. The situation is the same in the other arts; it is the background knowledge of painting, literature, and the like, not the functioning of mechanisms of individual psychology, that guides people to the characteristics of art that are to be appreciated and criticized.

Kendall Walton

I turn from the question of what controls those who experience art to the consideration of the aesthetic content of art. Sibley concluded that aesthetic qualities depend on non-aesthetic qualities. In 'Categories of Art' (1970 [13.31]), Kendall Walton, Sibley's student, goes a step further, concluding that the aesthetic qualities of *artworks* depend also on the historical contexts of the artworks. He challenges the view that artworks' aesthetic qualities can be discovered by *merely* perceiving them. Walton notes that artworks are perceived as members of categories – as statues, as paintings, as cubist paintings. Each category has *standard* features, those features that make for belonging to that category. Flatness, motionlessness and the use of shapes are among the standard features for the category of painting. Flatness, motionlessness and use of *multiple squarish* shapes are standard features for the category of cubist painting. Being the colour of marble and not representing the body from a point just below the shoulders are standard features for Roman marble busts. Each category also has *variable* features, features that may be different in different works of the category and which have nothing to do with works belonging to a category. *Particular* shapes and colours are variable for the category of paintings, and *particular* colours are variable for the category of cubist paintings. A feature is *contra-standard* for a category if its presence tends to disqualify a work with that feature from the category. A protruding, three-dimensional object would be contra-standard for the category of paintings.

Categories are involved in visual representation. Standard features are ordinarily irrelevant to representation. A painting's being flat and motionless does not prevent it from representing a three-dimensional object in motion. A Roman bust's being made of white marble and not representing the body from just below the shoulders does not make it portray a very pale person who has been severed at the chest. In contrast, variable features *are* involved in representation – the particular shapes and colours of a painting and the particular shapes of a Roman bust represent by means of resemblance.

Categories are involved in determining the *aesthetic* qualities of artworks. A person unfamiliar with the category of cubist painting might find a cubist painting to have the aesthetic quality of jumbledness. He would be looking at the painting under the category of ordinary representational painting, taking its multiple squarish shapes to be variable and representative of, say, a rather chopped-up looking man. A person looking at the painting under the category of cubist painting, taking its multiple squarish shapes to be standard, would see the painting to be just a representation of a man and not jumbled. Moreover, when the repeated squarish shapes are taken as standard and not as representative, their repeatedness may impart an aesthetic quality of orderliness to the surface of the painting.

An artwork can thus have one set of aesthetic properties when viewed as a work in one category and another set when viewed as a work in another category. An artwork's *actual* aesthetic properties are the ones it is perceived to have when it is perceived *correctly*. How is correctness determined? Walton cites four considerations that count towards determining correct categories.

1   An artwork's having a relatively large number of features standard and few or no contra-standard features for a category make for that category's being correct for the artwork. This condition alone does not suffice; certain works of Cézanne would appear to fit into the category of cubist paintings, but they are not cubist paintings.

2   An artwork's being better when perceived in a particular category rather than in others makes for that category's being correct. The two conditions do not suffice; given a mediocre work that obviously fits into a particular category, it would always be possible to invent a new, outlandish category in which the work would be better.

3   An artwork's fitting into a well-established category makes for that category's being correct. This historical condition will not resolve every problem; important, new works and categories are sometimes invented – Walton cites Schoenberg's twelve-tone music.

4   An artwork's being intended by its maker to be perceived in a category makes for that category's being correct. This historical condition will not resolve every case; artists' intentions are frequently unknown or unclear.

These conditions establish the correct category for many cases but leave undecidable cases. Walton cites Giacometti's sculptures. If they are seen as sculptures, their limbs look frail and wispy. If they are seen as thin metal sculptures, their limbs do not look frail but just expressive. It is not incorrect to perceive the sculptures either way, and thus it cannot be said what the actual aesthetic properties of the works are. Walton does not regard the existence of undecidable cases to be a bad thing.

The philosophy of art

Arthur Danto

Danto followed 'The Artworld' [13.37] with a series of publications. In these publications, Danto begins by conceiving of an artwork and a non-art object that are visually indistinguishable: Duchamp's *Fountain* and a urinal that looks exactly like it, Rembrandt's *The Polish Rider* and a randomly produced non-art object that looks exactly like it, and so on. Such pairs show that it is not its exhibited, perceptible properties that make something art but a context in which it is embedded.

What was new for twentieth-century aesthetics is that the context that Danto envisaged involves *cultural* concepts rather than notions of individual psychology. In contrast, the expression theory envisaged artworks embedded in a context involving the expressing of an emotion.

Danto gives two different accounts of the cultural context that makes something an artwork. In 'The Artworld' he claims that the prevailing *art theory* provides the context that enables artifacts to be works of art. Once the prevailing, enabling theory was the 'Imitation Theory of Art', and now it is what he calls the 'Real Theory of Art'. In 'Artworks and Real Things' (1973 [13.38]), Danto claims *being a statement* makes something an artwork – this alleged art-making context is a linguistic one rather than an art-theory one. In 'The Transfiguration of the Commonplace' (1974 [13.39]) and in his book of the same name (1981 [13.40]), he continues to speak of a linguistic context, claiming that being *about* something and therefore being *subject to interpretation* is what makes something an artwork.

At the beginning of his third article [13.39] he makes a less than universal claim about aboutness. Danto conceives of an artist who exhibits a square of primed canvas he entitles *Untitled* and who declares that it is not about anything. Danto then says,

> Our artist has produced something which is of the right sort to be about something, but in consequence of artistic fiat it happens only not to be about anything. . . . Artworks may indeed reject interpretation, but are of the right sort to receive them.

Danto is saying that artworks are the sorts of thing that are typically about something but that it is possible for artworks not to be about anything and thus not interpretable. Aboutness is not, therefore, a universal property of artworks. However, at the end of this article, Danto writes,

> As for the somewhat empty works [including presumably *Untitled*] with which I launched this discussion, I have this to say, what they are about is aboutness, and their content is the concept of art.
>
> [13.39]

Danto originally claimed that the artist's declaration that *Untitled* was not about anything made it not about anything. Is *Untitled* about aboutness or is it merely 'the right sort to be about something'? In any event, there is no reason to think that many present-day non-objective paintings are about anything, even if some non-objective paintings such as *Untitled* are about something. Retreating to an earlier time, a typical piece of eighteenth-century instrumental music is not about anything either. There appear to be counter-examples to Danto's claim, if it is the claim that all artworks are about something. He may, however, be making the weaker claim that artworks are the sort of thing that *can be* about something.

Even if all artworks were about something and subject to interpretation, Danto would not have a theory that picks out only the class of works of art. Statute laws, directions for assembling a bicycle and many other non-artworks are about something and are subject to interpretation.

Danto appears to claim that artworks are about something and subject to interpretation; these two ways of talking about *meaning* point in different directions. Saying that an artwork is about something points to an artist who creates an object. Saying that an artwork is subject to interpretation implies that its meaning can be understood by members of an artworld *public*. Although some earlier philosophies of art have referred to art's audience as necessary, Danto's was one of the first to indicate that the necessary audience is an artworld public – a cultural phenomenon. Danto is right that artworks are bearers of meaning embedded in a context or framework between artist and public; he is not right if he thinks the meaning borne is always aboutness.

Maurice Mandelbaum

In 'Family Resemblances and Generalization concerning the Arts' [13.48], Mandelbaum criticizes the view of Weitz and others that 'art' cannot be defined. These philosophers had claimed that artworks have no common characteristic, just overlapping similarities; they called the concept of such a class a 'family-resemblance' concept. Mandelbaum notes that *family* resemblances literally occur among persons with a genetic tie; no one of the overlapping visible resemblances exhibited by family members may be shared by all, but all *family* members share an underlying genetic connection. He suggests that the defining features of art may be discoverable, if instead of looking at the perceptible characteristics exhibited by art, one looks for underlying relational features, namely, relationships that can be discovered among art object, artist and contemplator. Mandelbaum does not attempt such a theory.

George Dickie

Danto revealed art's cultural context and implied that artists and publics are necessary. Mandelbaum recommended attention to the relationships among art object, artist and contemplator. Guided by these ideas, beginning with 'Defining Art' (1969 [13.42]) and concluding with *Art and the Aesthetic* (1974 [13.29]), I worked out the earlier of the two versions of the *institutional* theory of art. In both versions 'institutional' refers to a cultural *practice* – the set of practices involved in producing the various arts – not an organization of persons that has meetings and acts as a group. In the earlier version, an artwork is defined as an artifact that has had candidacy for appreciation conferred on some of its features (its aesthetic object) by some person or persons who act on behalf of the artworld. I maintained that artifactuality could be achieved in the usual way by working with artistic media. I, however, also maintained it could be conferred on an object; I argued that *Fountain* and such works had had artifactuality conferred on them. According to this earlier version of the theory, to be an artwork is to have acquired a status within a rather formally described institutional structure as the result of an artist's or artists' action.

Ten years later in response to the criticism of Beardsley and others, I presented in *The Art Circle* (1984 [13.43]) a greatly revised and more informal institutional theory. I dropped the formal terminology – *acting on behalf of* the artworld and *conferring* of candidacy and artifactuality – and spoke instead of artists working with their materials against the background of the artworld. Also, in *The Art Circle*, instead of defining just 'art', I gave five interrelated definitions, which provide the leanest possible account of the new version.

> An artist is a person who participates with understanding in the making of a work of art.

> A work of art is an artifact of a kind created to be presented to an artworld public.

> A public is a set of persons the members of which are prepared in some degree to understand an object which is presented to them.

> The artworld is the totality of all artworld systems.

> An artworld system is a framework for the presentation of a work of art by an artist to an artworld public.

Note that the last definition makes use of the key terms of the other definitions. The definitions are obviously circular – but not viciously so. Circularity is vicious if one is confronted with a circular account of an alien phenomenon of which one is ignorant. The making and appreciating of art, however, is a cultural phenomenon people are involved with from early childhood; the meanings of the key terms of this interconnected system are well known to everyone. We learn about the concepts of this circular set at the same time; one cannot be taught what a work of art is without being taught what an artist, an artworld public and an artworld system (painting, theatre, and the like) are. None of the key notions serves as a foundation for the rest. (By the way, new artworld systems – for example, happenings – are introduced from time to time.)

The institutional definition of 'work of art' is value-neutral – it covers good, bad and indifferent art. The definition of 'art' has to be about all art, not just valuable art or any other sub-set. What artworks have in common is not value but a *status* within the artworld. By the way, the definition of 'work of art' refers to the basic or primary items presented to artworld publics, not things like playbills, programme notes, and the like which are parasitic on the primary items.

The notion of *understanding* is used in the definitions of 'artist' and 'public'. What both an artist and a member of an artworld public understand is the general idea of art, i.e. that they are engaged in a certain, specific kind of activity. What in addition an artist must also understand is the particular medium in which he is working. Also, the definition of 'work of art' speaks of an artifact *of a kind* created to be presented to an artworld public. The 'of a kind' qualification is made in order not to exclude works of art that are created but, for whatever reason, are never presented.

The institutional theory does not mention certain highly valued features of art – representational, expressive, symbolic and aesthetic features. Important as such features are, when they occur in art, they are not universal features of art and, hence, cannot be defining characteristics. Art is a cultural invention that can incorporate all these features and others, but it does not have to involve any of them.

In *Definitions of Art* (1991 [13.41]), Stephen Davies surveys and analyses theories of art presented since the 1950s; he distinguishes between functional and procedural accounts of art. Functional accounts see art as having a specific function – to express emotion, to produce aesthetic experience, to be about something. The institutional account of art is procedural, i.e. defines 'art' in terms of certain cultural procedures. A procedural theory places no limits on what artworks can function to do, but it claims that none of the functions is universal and defining. Davies also discusses a number of recent definitions of 'art' which in one way or another resemble the institutional theory; he characterizes these theories as *historical, narrative* or *intentional*. Works on these theories and on theories not discussed by Davies are listed in the Bibliography: see T. Diffey [13.44]; J. Margolis [13.49]; T. Binkley [13.32–3]; J. Levison [13.47]; M. Eaton [13.45]; L. Krukowski [13.46]; and N. Carroll [13.34].

❧❧ INTERPRETING AND EVALUATING ART ❧❧

Interpretation

Monroe Beardsley

Beardsley argues that to interpret an artwork is to understand its meaning. Interpreting the words, sentences, representations, motives of characters, and the like in artworks is not different from understanding parallel things in real life.

Suppose in a conversation about where people are from, someone says, 'He was born in a small town in the state of New Jersey, USA.' The hearer will easily understand (i.e. correctly interpret) the remark. Similarly, there are cases in which it is understood without a doubt what someone's motive is. Some statements and actions are easy to interpret. If someone utters a truly ambiguous sentence, the hearer can not understand it because it does not have *a* meaning, although it suggests two or more meanings; the remark will not be interpretable. If someone utters a garbled string of words, the utterance cannot be interpreted either. Similarly, sometimes we have no idea what motivates a person's action.

The interpretation of artworks, on Beardsley's view, parallels interpretation in real-life situations. A novel that begins 'He was born in a small town in New Jersey, USA' and continues with sentences that are just as straightforward could be easily understood, i.e. easily interpreted. Critics and philosophers, however, are not usually concerned with simple and easily interpreted works but with questions about complicated cases such as 'Is there a hint of pantheism in "A Slumber did My Spirit Seal"?', 'Are the ghosts in "The Turn of the Screw" real or imaginary?', 'Is Lear senile or sane?' and 'Is the woman in *American Gothic* the farmer's wife or daughter?' On Beardsley's view, in simple and complicated cases alike, there are three possibilities: a correct interpretation that takes account of everything in an unambiguous work, a misinterpretation that does not take account of everything in a work, or no interpretation at all. There may be different reasons why an interpretation cannot be given – for example, a poem may exhibit no clear evidence for or against, say, pantheism, a play may exhibit some evidence, say, for a character's sanity and some for his senility and be inconclusive, and so on. For Beardsley, an artwork may be misinterpreted because something in the work is missed or misunderstood or because someone reads something into the work that is not there.

Joseph Margolis

Margolis and others hold a view of interpretation that seems opposed to Beardsley's. Margolis claims that incompatible interpretations of an artwork can be jointly confirmed as plausible, that is, that a person can justifiably accept incompatible interpretations of an artwork as jointly plausible.

Notice that Margolis's account, unlike Beardsley's, is cast in terms of plausibility. Even so, there seem to be problems. Could it ever be jointly confirmed as plausible that Lear is senile *and* plausible that he is sane? The closest that one could come to this would be if the evidence in the play for Lear's senility and his sanity were equal. We would then say that it is just as plausible that Lear is senile as it is that he is sane, but this is very different from saying that it is plausible that Lear is senile *and* sane.

As it turns out, Beardsley and Margolis are not talking about the same thing. Beardsley is talking about the interpretation of the meaning of words, sentences, representations, motives of characters, and the like in artworks. He is concerned, for example, with the questions of whether word order in a poem hints at a pantheistic or mechanistic universe and whether Lear's words and actions are evidence of senility. Margolis is not talking about the discovery *in* artworks of subtle or difficult meanings, he is talking about what Beardsley calls the 'superimposition' of grand schemes such as Marxism and Freudianism onto artworks. Beardsley agrees that artworks – his example is 'Jack and the Beanstalk' – can be read in the light of, or taken as illustrating elements of, Marxism, Freudianism, and the like. Such viewings, however, do not reveal meaning *in* artworks, although they may impose meanings on them. Incompatible superimpositions of an artwork may perhaps be jointly acceptable as plausible, if they can be fitted onto the artwork.

Deconstruction

If Margolis's view is not inconsistent with Beardsley's, the position of the deconstructionists is. This theory did not orginate in the English-speaking world but its influence has certainly reached it. The deconstructionists maintain that because of the nature of signs and language, correct interpretations of artworks are not possible. The deconstructionists conclude that since correct interpretations of artworks (and even of ordinary communications) are not possible, one is free to put any interpretation on artworks that one wishes; indeed one's only option is to understand in this 'free' way.

It is true that even simple communications sometimes fail. But simple communications are not *always* not possible or language would not exist. Language use would never have evolved if communication always were not possible. Cities, airplanes and anything more advanced than a mud hut would not have come into existence if communication were not possible. The fact is that we know how to communicate; we know how to remove ambiguities and obscurities by asking questions and offering clarifications and the like.

Artworks are of course not simple communications. We misinterpret or fail to interpret artworks with some frequency because they are complicated and because some artworks are ambiguous or intractably obscure. Artworks, however, like simple communications, would not exist if the understanding or interpretation of them were not generally possible. The fact is that we know how to interpret artworks and correctly do so with considerable frequency.

If the deconstructionists are right, it is hard to see how they could have been so successful in communicating their view among themselves and to others. The philosophical conclusion that correct understanding or interpretation is not possible is a curious and paradoxical affirmation.

Evaluation

J. O. Urmson

It is most promising to evaluate art instrumentally, i.e. according to its capacity to produce valuable or valued experience. Urmson's 'On Grading' (1950 [13.64]), although not focused on art, is an early account of instrumental evaluation. Urmson's example of grading Red Delicious apples is instructive. There are agreed-on criteria: dark-redness, lack of wormholes, firmness, sweetness, etc. The best apples are dark-red, unblemished, firm and quite sweet, and the remainder sort out below the best. Dark-redness is an aesthetic criterion, firmness and sweetness are taste criteria, and lack of wormholes is indicative of taste quality and is aesthetic as well. All the criteria involve capacity to produce valued experiences – aesthetic or taste.

Applying instrumentalist grading to artworks involves several questions. Are there agreed-on criteria so that relativism can be avoided? How many criteria are there? Are there evaluational principles, and if so, how are they formulated?

Monroe Beardsley

Beardsley believes that *the* function of artworks is to produce aesthetic experience. Since aesthetic experience is valuable, his instrumentalist conclusion is that artworks are to be evaluated according to their capacity to produce this valuable kind of experience.

Beardsley believes that aesthetic experience is detached from the remainder of experience. He, therefore, concludes that the referential aspects of art (those aspects that relate art to the world outside aesthetic experience) are irrelevant to the evaluation of art as art. On his view, only art's aesthetic characteristics are relevant to its value.

As noted earlier, Beardsley thinks all aesthetic qualities are subsumable under unity, intensity and complexity, and he sees these three as the criteria of artistic value. There are, according to him, three corresponding evaluative principles: each principle has one of the three criteria as its subject: for example, 'Unity in an artwork is always valuable (for producing aesthetic experience).' Beardsley's three principles plus complete information about an artwork's unity, intensity and complexity can never logically entail specific, narrowly focused evaluations such as 'This artwork is *good*' or 'This artwork is *excellent*.' In fact, his three principles can entail only unspecific evaluations such as 'This artwork is *valuable to some degree*.'

Beardsley failed to see that on his theory there are principles that have aesthetic experience as their subjects that *would* logically entail specific, narrowly focused evaluations. An example of such a principle is 'Aesthetic experiences of a fairly great magnitude are always good.' This principle, together with the information that an artwork can produce an aesthetic experience of fairly great magnitude, entails that the artwork can produce a *good* aesthetic experience. If an artwork can produce a *good* aesthetic experience, then the artwork itself is *instrumentally* good.

Beardsley avoids relativism because, on his theory, there can be no disagreement over whether an artwork's characteristics produce one kind of value experience in one person and a different kind in another person. For Beardsley, an artwork can produce instrumentally valuable aesthetic experience which in turn is instrumentally valuable for producing mental health, and whether aesthetic experience produces mental health is an empirical matter.

If Beardsley's theory were correct, there would be evaluational criteria and corresponding evaluational principles. The question of *agreeing on* criteria would not arise because unity, intensity and complexity are just properties that produce aesthetic experience. Furthermore, the value of every artwork could be compared with that of every other work because artworks' values are determined by their capacity to produce one kind of thing – aesthetic experience.

Unfortunately, there is good reason to think that Beardsley's conception of aesthetic experience is defective and that the valued experiences that are relevant to the instrumental evaluation of art are more complicated than he envisaged. Relativism is still a possiblity.

Frank Sibley

According to Sibley in 'General Criteria and Reasons in Aesthetics' (1983 [13.63]), Beardsley desires to require that the presence in an artwork of any one of his criteria – unity, intensity, complexity – must always contribute positively to an artwork's overall value. Thus, for Beardsley, a critical principle must have the form: '——— in an artwork is always valuable' with 'valuable' being understood to entail 'contributes to overall value'. Sibley argues that Beardsley's desired requirement cannot be maintained because *interactions* among his three criteria are possible; for example a work's complexity may cause a work to be disunified. The presence of a valuable property *a* in a particular degree in a given work may interfere with achievement of a particular degree of another valuable property *b* in that work and cause the work's overall value to be less than it would be if the degree of *a* were of some other magnitude.

Sibley also maintains that there are many aesthetic properties of artworks that are not subsumable under unity, intensity and complexity. He claims there are *positive* aesthetic properties besides unity, intensity and complexity – for example gracefulness, delicacy. He also claims that there are many negative aesthetic properties – garishness, insipidness, and the like.

On Sibley's view, there will be as many critical principles as there are aesthetic properties – positive and negative. Since any one of the aesthetic properties can interact with non-aesthetic or other aesthetic properties in an artwork to reduce (or enhance) overall value, critical principles must be formulated in a way that reflect this fact. Principles of the kind Sibley has in mind would have to have the form: '——— in an artwork, in isolation from the other properties of the work, is always valuable.' This says that, for example, gracefulness is a valuable property but that it cannot be fitted in everywhere. The application of such principles to artworks always requires qualifications about interactions among the various properties of artworks. Sibley's principles can entail only unspecific evaluations of artworks such as 'This artwork is valuable to some degree.'

For Sibley, artworks are instrumentally valuable because they can produce valuable experiences, but he does not claim, as Beardsley does, that artworks produce a single kind of instrumentally valuable experience. Thus, on his view, it is possible that persons can derive different value-experiences from an artwork and relativism is not ruled out.

Nelson Goodman

Goodman disagrees with Beardsley (and Sibley) that it is the possession of aesthetic qualities that makes art valuable, claiming that art's value is a function of the symbolizing or reference of its cognitive aspects. He agrees that art is to be evaluated by its capacity to produce aesthetic experience, but he claims that aesthetic experience is cognitive in nature and not a matter of aesthetic qualities.

The cognitive aspects of art are frequently valuable. The crucial cases for Goodman, however, are non-objective paintings and instrumental music. He claims such works are valuable because their dominant characteristics symbolize themselves (by *exemplification*), that is, that the characteristics are valuable because they are *samples* of themselves, like paint chips at a paint store.

Consider a non-objective painting entitled #3 that is uniformly painted a brilliant red. Does it function like a paint chip? One could use it as an example of the colour one desires for a car, but this is not the typical way we use such paintings. Non-objective paintings as they are typically experienced do not exemplify. (So, all artworks do not symbolize.) Paint chips *are* valuable because they are samples, but the colours they exemplify are or can be non-referentially valuable. Valuable non-objective paintings are typically valuable in a similar non-referential way.

Similarly, the brilliant red of a sunset is a paradigm of aesthetic value and of course it does not typically exemplify anything. Assume #3 to be the same shade of red as this sunset; typically such a painting will be valuable in the way that the sunset's colour is even if it were valuable because it is a sample.

Goodman is right that the cognitive content of art can have artistic value, but Beardsley is right that the possession of aesthetic qualities can have artistic value. Both neglect a valuable aspect of art.

Bruce Vermazen

Beardsley and Goodman attempt to evaluate artworks on the basis of *one* complex property, namely an artwork's capacity to produce a particular kind of valuable experience. This would make the values of artworks the function of a single property and make every artwork's value comparable to that of every other. Unfortunately, their conclusions are not proven.

Vermazen in 'Comparing Evaluations of Works of Art' (1975 [13.65]) claims persuasively that artworks' values are a function of multiple independently valuable properties. If two artworks have different independently valuable properties, it will be impossible to compare their value – it is an apples-and-oranges situation. If two artworks each have the same independently valuable property and only that one valuable property, then their values can be compared and ranked. Vermazen then shows that if two artworks have the same independently valuable properties but have two or more such properties, it will be possible to compare and rank the values of the two artworks if the values of the properties are of a certain sort but that it will not be *generally* possible to compare and rank the values of all such pairs of artworks. Vermazen's article shows that the kind of evaluational programme Beardsley and Goodman have in mind will not work.

For a more extensive discussion of the evaluation of art, see my *Evaluating Art* (1988 [13.60]).

❧ BIBLIOGRAPHY ❧

The psychological period

Aesthetic experience

13.1   Bullough, E. ' "Psychical Distance" as a Factor in Art and as an Aesthetic Principle', *British Journal of Psychology*, 1912: 87–117.
13.2   Dawson, S. ' "Distancing" as an Aesthetic Principle', *Australasian Journal of Philosophy*, 1961: 155–74.
13.3   Dewey, J. *Art as Experience*, New York: Capricorn Books, 1934.
13.4   Prall, D. *Aesthetic Judgment*, New York: T. Crowell, 1929.
13.5   Stolnitz, J. *Aesthetics and the Philosophy of Art*, Boston: Houghton Mifflin, 1960.

The philosophy of art

13.6   Bell, C. *Art*, London: Chatto & Windus, 1914.
13.7   Collingwood, R. G. *Principles of Art*, Oxford: Clarendon, 1938.
13.8   Dewey, J. *Art as Experience*, New York: Capricorn Books, 1934.
13.9   Langer, S. *Feeling and Form*, New York: Scribner's, 1953.
13.10   —— *Problems of Art*, New York: Scribner's, 1957.
13.11   Santayana, G. *Reason in Art*, New York: Scribner's, 1946.

The analytic period

The experience of art

13.12 Beardsley, M. *Aesthetics: Problems in the Philosophy of Criticism*, New York: Harcourt, Brace, 1958; 2nd edn with postscipts, Indianapolis: Hackett, 1981.

13.13 —— *The Aesthetic Point of View*, Ithaca, NY: Cornell University Press, 1982.

13.14 Cohen, T. 'Aesthetic/Non-aesthetic and the Concept of Taste: A Critique of Sibley's Position', *Theoria*, 39 (1973): 113–52.

13.15 Fisher, J., ed. *Essays on Aesthetics: Perspectives on the Work of Monroe C. Beardsley*, Philadelphia: Temple University Press, 1983.

13.16 Goodman, N. *Languages of Art*, Indianapolis: Bobbs-Merrill, 1968.

13.17 Sibley, F. 'Aesthetic Concepts', *Philosophical Review*, 68 (1959): 421–50.

13.18 —— 'Aesthetic and Nonaesthetic', *Philosophical Review*, 74 (1965): 135–59.

The philosophy of art

13.19 Aagaard-Morgensen, L., ed. *Culture and Art*, Atlantic Highlands, NJ: Humanities Press, 1976.

13.20 Beardsley, M. 'The Definitions of the Arts', *Journal of Aesthetics and Art Criticism*, 20 (1961): 176–87.

13.21 —— 'In Defense of Aesthetic Value', *Proceedings and Addresses of the American Philosophical Association*, 52 (1979): 723–49.

13.22 Goodman, N. *Languages of Art*, New York: Bobbs-Merrill, 1968. ——*Ways of Worldmaking*, Indianapolis: Hackett, 1978.

13.23 Kennick, W. 'Does Traditional Aesthetics rest on a Mistake?', *Mind*, 67 (1958): 317–34.

13.24 Weitz, M. 'The Role of Theory in Aesthetics', *Journal of Aesthetics and Art Criticism*, 15 (1956): 27–35.

13.25 Ziff, P. 'The Task of Defining a Work of Art', *Philosophical Review*, 62 (1953): 58–78.

The contextual period

The experience of art

13.26 Cohen, M. 'Aesthetic Essence', in *Philosophy in America*, ed. M. Black, London: Allen & Unwin, 1965: 115–33.

13.27 Dickie, G. 'Is Psychology Relevant to Aesthetics?', *Philosophical Review*, 71 (1962): 285–302.

13.28 —— 'The Myth of the Aesthetic Attitude', *American Philosophical Quarterly*, 1 (1964): 56–65.

13.29 —— *Art and the Aesthetic*, Ithaca, NY: Cornell University Press, 1974.

13.30 Johnson, Samuel *Johnson on Shakespeare*, ed. Walter Raleigh, London: Oxford University Press, 1959.

13.31 Walton, K. 'Categories of Art', *Philosophical Review*, 79 (1970): 334–67.

The philosophy of art

13.32 Binkley, T. 'Deciding about Art', in L. Aagaard-Mogersen, ed., *Culture and Art*, Atlantic Highlands, NJ: Humanities Press, 1976.

13.33 —— 'Piece: Contra Aesthetics', *Journal of Aesthetics and Art Criticism*, 35 (1977): 265–77.

13.34 Carroll, N. 'Art, Practice, and Narrative', *The Monist*, 71 (1988): 140–56.

13.35 Carney, J. 'Defining Art', *British Journal of Aesthetics*, 15 (1975): 191–206.

13.36 Cohen, T. 'The Possibility of Art: Remarks on a Proposal by Dickie', *Philosophical Review*, 82 (1973): 69–82.

13.37 Danto, A. 'The Artworld', *Journal of Philosophy*, 6 (1964): 571–84.

13.38 —— 'Artworks and Real Things', *Theoria*, 39 (1973): 1–17.

13.39 —— 'The Transfiguration of the Commonplace', *Journal of Aesthetics and Art Criticism*, 33 (1974): 139–48.

13.40 —— *The Transfiguration of the Commonplace*, Cambridge, Mass.: Harvard University Press, 1981.

13.41 Davies, S. *Definitions of Art*, Ithaca, NY: Cornell University Press, 1991.

13.42 Dickie, G. 'Defining Art', *American Philosophical Quarterly*, 6 (1969): 252–8.

13.43 —— *The Art Circle*, New York: Haven, 1984.

13.44 Diffey, T. 'The Republic of Art', *British Journal of Aesthetics*, 9 (1969): 145–56.

13.45 Eaton, M. *Art and Nonart*, Rutherford, NJ: Fairleigh Dickinson University Press, 1983.

13.46 Krukowski, L. *Art and Concept*, Amherst, Mass.: University of Massachusetts Press, 1987.

13.47 Levison, J. 'Defining Art Historically', *British Journal of Aesthetics*, 19 (1979): 232–50.

13.48 Mandelbaum, M. 'Family Resemblances and Generalization concerning the Arts', *American Philosophical Quarterly*, 2 (1965): 219–28.

13.49 Margolis, J. 'Works of Art as Physically Embodied and Culturally Emergent Entities', *British Journal of Aesthetics*, 14 (1974): 187–96.

13.50 Tilghman, B. *But is It Art?*, Oxford: Blackwell, 1984.

13.51 Walton, K. 'Categories of Art', *Philosophical Review*, 79 (1970): 334–67.

13.52 Wollheim, R. *Art and Its Objects*, London: Cambridge University Press, 1980.

Interpreting and evaluating art

Interpretation

13.53 Barnes, A. 'Half an Hour before Breakfast', *Journal of Aesthetic and Art Criticism*, 34 (1976): 261–71.

13.54 Beardsley, M. *The Possibility of Criticism*, Detroit: Wayne State University Press, 1970.

13.55 Eaton, M. 'Good and Correct Interpretations of Literature', *Journal of Aesthetics and Art Criticism*, 29 (1970): 227–33.

13.56 Hampshire, S. 'Types of Interpretation', in *Art and Philosophy*, ed. W. Kennick, 2nd edn, New York: St Martin's Press, 1966.

13.57 Margolis, J. *The Language of Art and Art Criticism*, Detroit: Wayne State University Press, 1965.

13.58 Norris, C. *Deconstruction: Theory and Practice*, London: Methuen, 1982.

Evaluation

13.59 Beardsley, M. 'On the Generality of Critical Reasons', *Journal of Philosophy*, 59 (1962): 477–86.

13.60 Dickie, G. *Evaluating Art*, Philadelphia: Temple University Press, 1988.

13.61 Isenberg, A. 'Critical Communication', *Philosophical Review*, 58 (1949): 330–44.

13.62 Savile, A. *The Test of Time*, Oxford: Clarendon Press, 1982.

13.63 Sibley, F. 'General Criteria and Reasons in Aesthetics', in *Essays on Aesthetics: Perspectives on the Work of Monroe Beardsley*, ed. J. Fisher, Philadelphia: Temple University Press, 1983: 3–20.

13.64 Urmson, J. O. 'On Grading', *Mind*, 59 (1950): 145–69.

13.65 Vermazen, B. 'Comparing Evaluations of Works of Art', *Journal of Aesthetic and Art Criticism*, 34 (1975): 7–14.

13.66 Wolterstorff, N. *Art in Action*, Grand Rapids, Mich.: W. B. Eerdmans, 1980.

13.67 Yanal, R. 'Denotation and the Aesthetic Appreciation of Literature', *Journal of Aesthetics and Art Criticism*, 36 (1978): 471–8.

13.68 Ziff, P. 'Reasons in Art Criticism', in *Philosophy and Education*, ed. I. Scheffler, Boston: Allyn & Bacon, 1958.

CHAPTER 14

Philosophy of religion

Edward R. Wierenga

—◦❖◦—

Philosophy of religion is critical reflection on philosophical issues that arise in religion. Sources of such issues include religious *claims* (for example, that God exists, about which it can be asked what it means, whether it is true or whether it is reasonable to accept), *concepts* (for example, omniscience or immutability, about which it may be asked how they are to be analysed or whether they are compatible with each other) and *practices* (for example, prayer, about which it may be asked whether it is sensible to express a thought or desire that God already knows one to have). Although all religions suggest topics for philosophical scrutiny, philosophers writing in English in the twentieth century have focused their attention primarily on philosophical issues raised by theism, no doubt because Christianity was the religion with which the majority were most familiar. Theism may be defined, as it was by Robert Flint in his book of that name [14.3], as 'the doctrine that the universe owes its existence, and continuation in existence, to the reason and will of a self-existent Being, who is infinitely powerful, wise, and good'. Philosophy that considers the existence and attributes of such an infinitely powerful, wise and good being, that is, God, is often called philosophical theology. Other topics that philosophers of religion have addressed include mysticism and the nature of religious experience, the relation between religion and science, religious language, the nature of religion and immortality. In addition, in the final decades of the century some philosophers of religion have begun again to work on more specifically theological topics, such as the Christian doctrines of the incarnation, atonement and original sin.

There is perhaps no other specialty of philosophy that is so closely intertwined with work in other areas of philosophy. Philosophy of religion reflects, reacts to, and borrows from the rest of philosophy. In the early years of the century, when idealism and metaphysical system-building were fashionable, philosophers of religion attempted to incor-

429

porate such religious claims as were amenable into a comprehensive metaphysical framework. In the middle years of the century philosophers of religion attempted to respond to the logical-positivist attack on metaphysics and religion. Philosophers party to these disputes debated not about whether religious claims are true or justified but about whether they are so much as meaningful. In the final third of the century philosophy of religion has become more technical and specialized, borrowing insights from work in philosophical logic, for example, and applying them to some of the traditional arguments for and against God's existence.

❦ IDEALISM ❦

Many of the most distinguished philosophers of religion have been invited to give the Gifford lectures, a series of lectures held each year at one of the Scottish universities (Aberdeen, Edinburgh or Glasgow) to promote 'the study of Natural Theology in the widest sense of the term – in other words, the knowledge of God'. In 1900 those lectures were given for the first time by an American, Josiah Royce, of Harvard University. Royce was the foremost American exponent of absolute idealism, a speculative philosophical view according to which there is one spiritual, self-conscious being – the Absolute – and everything that is real is so by virtue of its participation in the Absolute. Royce himself seems to have come to this view through the influence of the German idealists, in particular, Hermann Lotze. However, absolute idealism was also the dominant doctrine in British philosophy at the beginning of the century, represented by such defenders as Edward and John Caird, as well as by T. H. Green.

Royce's Gifford lectures, published as *The World and the Individual* [14.7], employed an argument that Royce developed in several places, namely, that the possibility of error can be used to show the existence of the Absolute. Royce held that the 'external meaning' of an idea depends upon what it is intended to mean. Furthermore, that an idea fails to correspond to what is intended – that an idea is in error – therefore depends on there being an intelligence that grasps both the idea and its intended object. Finally, since there are infinitely many possibilities for error, there must be an infinite intelligence – the Absolute – that understands them all.

Andrew Seth Pringle-Pattison, in his Gifford lectures of 1912–13, *The Idea of God in the Light of Recent Philosophy* [14.4], agreed with Royce's idealism, holding that 'self-conscious life [is] organic to the world', but he denied that all consciousness is unified into a single self. God is thus not to be identified with the Absolute. This personal idealism was also defended by Hastings Rashdall in his *Philosophy and Religion* [14.5].

❧ WILLIAM JAMES AND PRAGMATISM ❧

An alternative to the speculative metaphysics and grand system-building of the absolute idealists (and of the later Whiteheadians) was the problem-driven, piecemeal approach to philosophy practised by William James and other pragmatists. In 'The Will to believe' [14.9] James took up the challenge of W. K. Clifford [14.58] that 'it is wrong always, everywhere, and for every one, to believe anything upon insufficient evidence'. Conceding that there was insufficient evidence in favour of religious belief, James attempted to provide a justification of faith. He distinguished between the intellectual duty to believe truths and the duty to avoid falsehoods, noting that emphasizing the latter obligation would encourage one to withhold assent to a proposition when the evidence for it was not compelling. James urged allegiance instead to the more venturesome obligation to acquire true beliefs. He thought that this provided a justification for choosing to believe a proposition in cases in which one was forced to make a choice, in which the choice made a difference to one's life, and in which the choice could not be decided on intellectual grounds. James held, in particular, that accepting the religious hypothesis, believing that God exists, is permitted by this principle.

In 1901 and 1902 James delivered his *The Varieties of Religious Experience* [14.10] as the Gifford lectures. James defined religion as 'the feelings, acts and experiences of individual men in their solitude, so far as they apprehend themselves to stand in relation to whatever they may consider the divine'. James went on to discuss repentance, conversion and saintliness, but, given the primacy he attached to experience, it is natural that he focused on mysticism. Drawing on the writing of mystics, James characterized mystical experience as ineffable, that is, it defies expression, as having noetic quality, that is, as seeming to its subjects as states of insight into truth, and as transient and passive. James concluded that such states were authoritative for those who had them but they had no evidential value for those who do not have them beyond pointing to the 'possibility of other orders of truth'.

James inaugurated a tradition of investigating the phenomenology and evidential value of mystical experience which continued throughout the century, with the work of W. T. Stace and Nelson Pike being especially noteworthy.

⁓ ALFRED NORTH WHITEHEAD AND ⁓ PROCESS PHILOSOPHY

In 1927–8 the Gifford lectures were delivered by Alfred North White-head. Whitehead had begun his career as a mathematician, co-authoring in 1910–13 with Bertrand Russell the monumental *Principia Mathematica*. By the 1920s Whitehead had moved to America and was attempting to develop a speculative metaphysical system inspired by scientific cosmology. The notoriously obscure language of his Gifford lectures, published as *Process and Reality* [14.15], makes them difficult to interpret. Whitehead elaborated a 'dipolar' concept of God. In his 'primordial nature', God is part of the process of the natural world – not the creator and devoid of consciousness – who nevertheless contributes to the order of the world. By contrast, the 'consequent nature' of God is a consciousness that grows as it incorporates the values that arise as things continually change. Whitehead summarized these apparently conflicting strains with a series of aphorisms such as, 'It is as true to say that God creates the World, as that the World creates God.'

Whitehead's rejection of the classical conception of God as immutable, eternal, absolute, omnipotent, and so forth, was found congenial by others who developed his views. Charles Hartshorne, for example, defended a dipolar view of God, and such 'process theologians' as John Cobb attempted to give an explicitly Christian development of Whitehead's thought.

⁓ THEOLOGICAL LANGUAGE: ⁓ VERIFIABILITY AND MEANING

Interest in developing speculative metaphysical systems declined under the influence of logical positivism. This was a school of philosophy developed by Morris Schlick, Rudolf Carnap and other members of the Vienna Circle. It was introduced to English-speaking philosophers by A. J. Ayer in his *Language, Truth, and Logic* [14.16]. The centrepiece of logical positivism was the verifiability criterion of meaning. According to this view a sentence is meaningful only if it is either analytic or empirically verifiable. A satisfactory statement of what was required for a sentence to be verifiable was never found; roughly, however, the idea was that a sentence is verifiable just in case it could at least in principle be established or falsified by empirical observation. Ayer wielded the principle of verification to yield the conclusion that the sentences of traditional metaphysics, of ethics, and of religion are all meaningless. He held that such claims were not analytically true and that there was no conceivable observation that would confirm or refute them. Accordingly, Ayer concluded that these sentences were neither true nor false but meaningless, in particular, 'no sentence which purports to describe the nature of a transcendent god can possess any literal significance'.

Ayer's case was bolstered by a famous example published in the mid-1940s, around the same time that *Language, Truth, and Logic* came out in a second edition. In his essay, 'Gods' [14.20], John Wisdom described an example of two people who observe an apparently untended garden. One thinks that there is a gardener; the other does not. All attempts to detect the gardener fail, yet the one person continues to believe that there exists an unseen and unheard gardener who is manifested only in his works. Although Wisdom held merely that the difference between the two observers 'has ceased to be experimental', other philosophers drew the conclusion that, since no observation would falsify the believer's claim, that claim, that there is an unseen and unheard gardener, is meaningless. Antony Flew, for example, claimed that 'if there is nothing which a putative assertion denies then there is nothing which it asserts either: and so it is not really an assertion' [14.18]. Flew then suggested, with respect to a version of Wisdom's story he elaborated, that 'when the Sceptic in the parable asked the Believer, "Just how does what you call an invisible, intangible, eternally elusive gardener differ from an imaginary gardener or even from no gardener at all?" he was suggesting that the Believer's earlier statement had been so eroded by qualification that it was no longer an assertion at all.' Flew held that theological utterances generally, since they cannot be falsified, are similarly vacuous.

This idea, that the central challenge to religious belief was not that such beliefs are false but that they are not even meaningful, continued to dominate the philosophy of religion into the 1950s. It was shared by most of the contributors to what was the leading collection of essays in philosophy of religion of the decade, *New Essays in Philosophical Theology*, a volume that included, in addition to Flew's piece, essays by R. M. Hare, Basil Mitchell, P. H. Nowell-Smith, and others.

The verificationist challenge to the meaningfulness of religious belief was so widely accepted that even many theistic philosophers and theologians felt compelled to offer reinterpretations of traditional religious assertions that would permit them to pass the verifiability test of meaningfulness. A typical and well-known example of such a response is R. B. Braithwaite's *An Empiricist's View of the Nature of Religious Belief* [14.17]. According to Braithwaite, the Christian's apparent claim that God is love is not a claim about a supernatural reality, but is rather merely an expression of the believer's intention to follow an agapeistic way of life. Other religious utterances are to be understood similarly as expressions of emotion or as declarations of an intention to act in a certain way.

As long as the very meaningfulness of religious utterances was in question relatively little attention was given to other issues in the philosophy of religion. Eventually, however, commitment to the verifiability criterion of meaning waned. This was due primarily to the problems, first, of saying why the criterion should not be applied to itself – for it seemed to be unverifiable – and, second, to the problem of formulating the principle in a way that ruled out sentences of metaphysics and religion without also ruling out clearly meaningful sentences such as sentences of science. The history of this latter problem is detailed by Carl Hempel in 'Problems and Changes in the Empiricist Criterion of Meaning' [14.19].

⮞⮞ WITTGENSTEINIAN FIDEISM ⮜⮜

A similar preoccupation with religious language was channelled in a somewhat different direction by Ludwig Wittgenstein and his followers. Wittgenstein's most explicit discussion of religion is to be found in his *Lectures and Conversations* [14.25], student notes of lectures he gave in 1938. There he held that the religious believer's use of language is so different from that of the non-believer that the non-believer is unable to contradict the believer. Wittgenstein does not draw the conclusion, however, that the believer's assertions are meaningless. Rather, what the believer means is determined by a 'picture' or way of looking at life that the non-believer does not share.

Employing locutions that Wittgenstein used elsewhere, we can put this view as the claim that the meaning of religious terms depends upon their role in a 'language-game' or in a 'form of life'. Thus, terms such as 'God' or 'judgement day' have a meaning for a believer that depends upon their use in a range of practices in which the believer participates. It does not make sense, then, to attempt to find evidence or justification for religious assertions, for that inquiry is outside the religious form of life in which such assertions have a meaning. Followers of Wittgenstein such as Norman Malcolm and D. Z. Phillips emphasized versions of fideism according to which it is misguided to seek rational grounds for religious belief. On their view, religious belief is groundless; within religious practice it is not a hypothesis for which evidence may be sought, but there is no external perspective from which the religious form of life may be evaluated. Critics, such as Kai Nielsen, have objected that a single conceptual structure may include both science and religion, in which case the demand for evidence is in order, and, in any event, whole forms of life (e.g. witchcraft) are open to appraisal.

❧ THE PROBLEM OF EVIL ❧

An exception to the prevailing philosophical climate in the 1950s, according to which religious claims were either meaningless or logically isolated to the language-game in which they were used, came in the form of an attack on the truth of theism. In 1955 J. L. Mackie inaugurated a period of intense interest in the problem of evil by presenting a forceful challenge to theism. H. D. Aiken, Antony Flew and H. J. McCloskey also published versions of this objection. According to Mackie, theism is not merely false, but inconsistent, because its central tenets could not possibly all be true. Theists hold that (1) *God is omnipotent*, (2) *God is wholly good* and (3) *There is evil*. According to Mackie, these propositions are contradictory in the sense that if any two are true, the remaining one would have to be false. This is what has since become known as the *logical problem of evil*. Mackie noted that in order to demonstrate that the theistic beliefs are contradictory one would have to find some necessarily true propositions – he called them 'quasi-logical rules' – connecting the concepts of omnipotence, goodness and evil in such a way that in conjunction with the theistic beliefs an explicit contradiction is deducible. Mackie's candidates for the requisite necessary truths were (4) *There are no limits to what an omnipotent being can do* and (5) *A good being eliminates evil as far as it can*. Critics such as Nelson Pike and Alvin Plantinga pointed out that, since a good person could permit evil if the person had a good reason, (5) is not a necessary truth. Subsequent attempts to substantiate Mackie's charge failed to uncover variants of (4) and (5) with the twin features of being necessarily true and of entailing, in conjunction with the theistic beliefs, an explicit contradiction. That leaves it open, however, that the theistic beliefs are inconsistent, even if it has not been shown that they are. Accordingly, a sizeable body of literature has been produced in the attempt to show that theism is consistent.

Plantinga defined a *defence* against evil as the attempt to show that the existence of God and the existence of evil are logically consistent with each other. By contrast, a *theodicy* is the attempt to say what the real reason or correct explanation for evil is. A defence, therefore, can succeed if it provides a logically possible scenario in which God and evil co-exist. The free-will defence was supported in a short reply to Mackie by S. A. Grave and developed with great ingenuity by Alvin Plantinga. Its main idea is that it is possible that God valued having free creatures but was unable, despite his omnipotence,

435

to create such creatures who only do what is right; since, if God causes someone to do what is right, that person does not do it freely. If this scenario is possibly true, then it is possible both that God exists and that there is evil.

The free-will defence explicitly addresses so-called moral evil, that is, evil that results from the free actions of created agents. Critics have noted that there is also the question of the compatibility of God's existence with natural or physical evil, such as suffering due to earthquakes or floods. Plantinga's response is that it is possible that all evil is moral evil, since it is possible that apparently physical evil is caused by non-human agents. Despite this being only a claim of possibility, it has been controversial. Other philosophers, for example Richard Swinburne and Peter van Inwagen, have suggested that natural evil is due to the regular operation of physical laws and that the value of having physical laws outweighs the resulting evil.

An alternative to the free-will defence, promoted by John Hick, emphasizes the value of evil for the growth of people's characters. According to Hick, evil provides an opportunity for 'soul-making' or spiritual development, which is required for people to become fit for a relationship with God; evil is thus not simply an unfortunate consequence of having creatures with free will. Hick derived this view from Irenaeus (120–202), and Hick regarded it a virtue of this account that it avoids the Augustinian doctrine of the Fall and the consequent problem of explaining how the good creation of a perfect God could become evil. Hick clearly intended his account to be a theodicy, but, if it is possibly right, it also provides a defence against the logical problem of evil.

Thus far the discussion focused on the logical problem of evil, but as philosophers became convinced that an adequate defence could be made against it, a second problem, *the evidential problem of evil*, began to attract attention. According to William Rowe, among others, the existence of evil, while not logically incompatible with the existence of God, is nevertheless evidence against God's existence; given the evil that there is in the world, the reasonable conclusion is that God does not exist. One response, defended by William Alston, is to hold that we are not in a position to know whether evil that appears to be gratuitous or unjustified really is; if there were a God he would likely have reasons for permitting evil that human beings could not even grasp. A second response, developed by Plantinga, concedes that *God exists* is improbable given *There is evil* but holds that *God exists* need not be improbable on a theist's total body of evidence. The issues here have to do with religious epistemology, to be discussed below.

❧ THE ONTOLOGICAL ARGUMENT ❧

A period of intense activity in philosophy of religion was inaugurated in 1960 when the *Philosophical Review* published an article by Norman Malcolm [14.41] in which Malcolm claimed to have found a sound version of Anselm's ontological argument for God's existence. Anselm (1033–1109) had held that God, understood as the being than which nothing greater can be conceived, must exist; for the assumption that God does not exist leads to the absurdity that it is conceivable that there is something which is greater than the being than which nothing greater can be conceived. Malcolm was willing to concede, as most philosophers at the time thought, that this version of the argument was refuted somehow by Immanuel Kant's (1724–1804) claim that 'existence is not a predicate'. Malcolm held, however, that there was a second argument in Anselm's *Proslogion*, one according to which *the logical impossibility of non-existence* is a perfection. Thus, if God is a being than which a greater cannot be conceived, he must exist necessarily, if at all. So either God's existence is necessary or it is impossible. According to Malcolm, God's existence is impossible only if the concept of God is self-contradictory or nonsensical. Malcolm denied that the concept of God is in this way impossible; accordingly, God exists necessarily.

Charles Hartshorne had presented a similar argument twenty years earlier, but his work had not attracted the same attention. By contrast, more than a hundred articles were submitted to the *Philosophical Review* in response to Malcolm's piece, of which the journal published a handful before enforcing a moratorium on the topic. Work on the argument continued, nevertheless. David Lewis applied insights derived from possible-world semantics for modal logic – an interpretation of claims about necessity and possibility in terms of logically possible worlds – to a version of Anselm's argument, a version that Lewis claimed to be defective. Alvin Plantinga proposed another modal version, which, though he claimed it to be sound, he conceded did not succeed as a proof. Nevertheless, Plantinga insisted that such an argument could demonstrate the rationality of belief in God, since someone could rationally believe its premise and rationally recognize that the conclusion that God exists follows from it.

❧ ANALYTIC PHILOSOPHY OF RELIGION ❧

Just as discussion of the ontological argument ushered in a period of renewed interest in the philosophy of religion, it also marked the introduction of greater rigour and more technical methods into the field. Signs of interest in the field included the founding of several journals devoted to the philosophy of religion. *Sophia*, committed to discussion of philosophical theology, was inaugurated by the University of Melbourne in 1962; *Religious Studies*, published by Cambridge University Press, began in 1965; and the *International Journal for Philosophy of Religion*, edited in the United States and published in the Netherlands, commenced in 1970. Increased rigour resulted in part from a more careful attention to arguments. It was due, in addition, to the fact that philosophers of religion appealed to insights from other areas of philosophy, which were also becoming more technical. Thus, as noted above, work on the ontological argument drew on work in modal logic. Other areas of philosophical logic, for example, theories of counter-factual conditionals, came to figure in treatments of the problem of evil; metaphysical doctrines about the fixity of the past were applied to the topic of foreknowledge and free will; and probability theory was applied to arguments for and against God's existence.

The most influential work in analytic philosophy of religion in the 1960s was Alvin Plantinga's *God and Other Minds* [14.48]. In it Plantinga applied the techniques of analytic philosophy to the traditional arguments for God's existence as well as to arguments against God's existence, notably the problem of evil. Plantinga claimed that these arguments are all unsuccessful. However, he then examined the analogical argument for the existence of other minds – an argument for the conclusion that other people have mental states that appeals to the premise that their behaviour is analogous to one's own behaviour when one is in certain mental states. Plantinga held that this argument, though unsuccessful, is the best argument we have for the existence of other minds. He claimed, furthermore, that its defect is the same as the defect he had uncovered in the argument from design for God's existence. He concluded that since it is nevertheless rational to believe in other minds, it is also rational to believe in God.

Another topic to attract attention was that of the attributes of God. In his Wilde Lectures in 1970–2, later revised as *The God of the Philosophers* [14.44], Anthony Kenny took up such topics as divine omniscience, omnipotence, and immutability. Drawing on the work of Arthur Prior and Norman Kretzmann, he argued that if God is omniscient then he is not immutable. He further claimed if God has infallible knowledge then determinism is true and God is responsible for human wickedness. Kenny concluded that 'there cannot . . . be a timeless, immutable, omniscient, omnipotent, all-good being'. By contrast, Richard Swinburne in *The Coherence of Theism* [14.52], the first volume of his important trilogy in philosophical theology, attempted to describe 'what it means to claim that there exists eternally an omnipresent spirit, free, creator of the universe, omnipotent, omniscient, perfectly good, and a source of moral obligation', and he endeavoured to show that this central claim of theism is 'coherent'. Swinburne's presentation involved attenuating certain of the attributes somewhat. For example, on the assumption that God is contingent, omniscience requires, not knowledge of all truths, but, at any given time, knowledge of every true proposition about that time or an earlier one and knowledge of only those propositions about future times that report events that are physically necessitated at the earlier time. And for Swinburne divine eternity meant being everlasting, rather than the more traditional, Boethian, idea of a simultaneous, timeless grasp of an illimitable life. On the other hand, if God is a necessary being, then, according to Swinburne, the theist needs to use some predicates of God *analogically* rather than literally.

In the decade following the publication of these seminal works, Edward Wierenga attempted in *The Nature of God* [14.54] to provide philosophically defensible accounts of several of the divine attributes, accounts that he claimed were adequate to the demands of classical theism as well as immune to the kinds of objections raised by Kenny. The question of whether divine foreknowledge is compatible with human free action attracted considerable attention. Many philosophers felt compelled to point out, as Aquinas had done much earlier, that a certain simple argument for incompatibility is fallacious. That argument is: (1) If God knows in advance that a person will perform a certain action, then the person must perform it. (2) If a person must perform a certain action, then the person does not do so freely. Therefore, (3) if God knows in advance that a person will perform a certain action, then the person does not do so freely. The first premise is ambiguous. It can be taken as the truth (1') Necessarily, if God knows that a person will perform a certain action, then the person will do so; but so taken the conclusion does not follow. The conclusion does follow if the premise is understood as (1'') If God knows that a person will perform a certain action, then the proposition that the person will perform that action is necessarily true; but under this interpretation the premise is false.

A considerably more vexing argument for the incompatibility of divine foreknowledge and human free action appeals to the apparent fixity or necessity of the past. According to this argument, what God in the past believed about the future is now part of the past and thus fixed or unalterable. Also, what follows of necessity from what is thus fixed is itself fixed or unalterable. But it follows of necessity, given God's (essential) omniscience, that if he knew in the past that someone would perform a certain action tomorrow that that person will perform the action. So the proposition that the person will perform that action is fixed or unalterable. Then, however, it is not up to the person whether he or she performs the action; so the action is not free. A version of this argument was presented by Nelson Pike in *God and Timelessness* [14.47]. In *God, Time, and Knowledge* [14.43] William Hasker argued that the standard defences of the compatibility of divine foreknowledge fail. In particular he objected to the Ockhamist response, which holds that propositions about God's past foreknowledge are not strictly about the past, and he objected to the eternalist response, according to which God is outside time. Hasker claimed that solutions to the problem require that we have a power over the past that in fact no one has. Linda Zagzebski also took up this topic in *The Dilemma of Freedom and Foreknowledge* [14.55]. Although sharing Hasker's scepticism with respect to the traditional responses, she argued that two assumptions of the above argument, namely that fixity is transferred by entailment and that actions fixed in the relevant sense are not free, may both be rejected.

In addition to the ontological argument, discussed above, analytic philosophers of religion have discussed other arguments for God's existence. In *The Cosmological Argument* [14.50], William Rowe examined versions of the argument that derives from the assumption that contingent things exist now the conclusion that there was a first cause, namely God, of what exists. Rowe claimed that this argument failed as a proof of theism but concluded that it may show the reasonableness of theistic belief. Richard Swinburne considered a variety of theistic arguments in *The Existence of God* [14.53]. Swinburne emphasized the explanatory power of the theistic hypothesis and claimed that the cumulative case of several arguments taken together renders the proposition that God exists more probable than not. In this conclusion, if not in the detailed way he arrived at it, Swinburne's position resembled that of Basil Mitchell, his predecessor as Nolloth Professor of Philosophy of the Christian Religion at Oxford University.

RELIGIOUS EPISTEMOLOGY

Just as at the beginning of the century William James had responded to W. K. Clifford's dictum that it is always wrong to believe a proposition on insufficient evidence, so in the final third of the century was interest in religious epistemology rekindled by the evidentialist challenge to the rationality of theistic belief. As Antony Flew put it,

> If it is to be established that there is a God, then we have to have good grounds for believing that this is indeed so. Until or unless some such grounds are produced we have literally no reason at all for believing; and in that situation the only

reasonable posture must be that of either the negative atheist or the agnostic.

([14.59], p. 22)

This objection may be put as an argument: (1) It is rational to believe that God exists only if there is sufficient evidence for God's existence. (2) There is not sufficient evidence for God's existence. Therefore, (3) it is not rational to believe that God exists.

Alvin Plantinga suggested that this demand for sufficient evidence appeals to classical foundationalism. According to the latter doctrine, some propositions may be rationally believed without being based on other beliefs. Such 'properly basic propositions', according to Plantinga's construal of classical foundationalism, either are self-evidently true, are ones that a person could not possibly believe without their being true, or are evident to the senses. Any other proposition may be rationally believed only if it is justified by, supported by or evident with respect to properly basic propositions. The evidentialist objection may then be reformulated as: (1') It is rational to believe that God exists only if the proposition that God exists is properly basic or evident with respect to propositions that are properly basic. (2'a) The proposition that God exists is not properly basic. (2'b) The proposition that God exists is not evident with respect to propositions that are properly basic. Therefore, (3') it is not rational to believe that God exists. Plantinga claimed, first, that it is at least dubious that the proposition that God exists is not properly basic – perhaps classical foundationalism's standards for what counts as properly basic are mistaken. Second, however, if those criteria for what it takes to be properly basic are correct, then it is not rational to believe the first premise of the argument; for (1'), itself, is neither properly basic nor evident with respect to propositions that are. The argument is therefore defective: if the second premise is false, the argument is unsound, but if the second premise is true, then it is not rational to accept its first premise.

Not content with merely rebutting the evidentialist objection to theistic belief, philosophers turned their attention to providing epistemological theories according to which theism was justified. Plantinga himself defended a view according to which a person's belief in a proposition is justified just in case the belief is produced by that person's epistemic faculties functioning properly (in circumstances for which they were designed). Plantinga's preferred account of a person's faculties functioning properly is that they function in the way God intended them to function. A theist, furthermore, might think that God would design people in such a way that they came to hold a belief in his existence; if so, such a belief would be justified.

William Alston claimed that beliefs should be evaluated by refer-

441

ence to the epistemic practice within which they arise. He then noted the difficulty of justifying, in the sense of providing good evidence in favour of, the perceptual epistemic practice in which our ordinary beliefs about the world arise. Alston suggested that our perceptual practice is justified only in a weaker sense according to which there are no good objections to it or it is not irrational to participate in it. Finally, Alston argued that what he called Christian mystical practice, which yields beliefs about God in the presence of religious experience, is in striking respects analogous to perceptual practice. In particular, it is 'rationally engaged in since it is a socially established doxastic practice that is not demonstrably unreliable or otherwise disqualified for rational acceptance'.

THEOLOGICAL TOPICS

At the close of the twentieth century, two trends appeared to emerge in the philosophy of religion. One was an expansion of the field to include or at least border on any philosophical work that takes an explicitly theistic perspective. For example, the divine-command theory of ethics, a meta-ethical theory which holds that God's commands determine the moral status of actions, came to be treated in the textbook anthologies of philosophy of religion. In addition, philosophers of religion took notice of such work as that of the authors collected in *Christian Theism and the Problems of Philosophy* [14.62], philosophers who appealed to tenets of theism in their work in metaphysics and epistemology.

A second trend was for philosophers of religion to direct their attention, often sympathetically, to explicitly theological topics, especially to the doctrines of Christian theism. For example, in *The Logic of God Incarnate* Thomas Morris used the tools of analytic philosophy to defend the doctrine of the incarnation, the belief that Jesus was both fully God and fully human. Morris was particularly concerned to rebut such critics as John Hick, who objected that this doctrine was incoherent by claiming that the properties essential to divinity and the properties essential to humanity are incompatible with each other. Other topics to attract attention were the Christian doctrines of the Trinity – that God is three persons in one – and of the atonement – that Christ's sacrifice restores sinful people to a right relationship with God. Philip Quinn wrote a series of papers detailing and criticizing the theories of the atonement proposed by Aquinas, Abelard and Kant. Richard Swinburne took up the topic in the first volume of a series on theological issues; the second volume, on revelation, addressed another issue of theological interest.

❧ BIBLIOGRAPHY ❧

Primary sources

Nineteenth-century background

14.1 Caird, Edward *The Evolution of Religion*, 2 vols, Glasgow: J. MacLehose, 1894.
14.2 Caird, John *An Introduction to the Philosophy of Religion*, Glasgow: J. MacLehose, 1880.
14.3 Flint, Robert *Theism*, New York: C. Scribner, 1876; 7th edn, rev., 1889.

Idealism

14.4 Pringle-Pattison, Andrew Seth *The Idea of God in the Light of Recent Philosophy*, New York and London: Oxford University Press, 1917.
14.5 Rashdall, Hastings *Philosophy and Religion*, London: Duckworth, 1909.
14.6 Royce, Josiah *The Religious Aspect of Philosophy*, Boston: Houghton, Mifflin, 1885.
14.7 —— *The World and the Individual*, 2 vols, New York and London: Macmillan, 1900–1.

James and pragmatism

14.8 Clifford, W. K. *Lectures and Essays*, London: Macmillan, 1879.
14.9 James, William, 'The Will to believe', *New World*, 5 (1896): 327–47.
14.10 —— *The Varieties of Religious Experience*, New York: Longman's, Green, 1902.
14.11 Pike, Nelson *Mystic Union: An Essay in the Phenomenology of Mysticism*, Ithaca, NY: Cornell University Press, 1992.
14.12 Stace, Walter T. *Mysticism and Philosophy*, Philadelphia: Lippincott, 1960.

Whitehead and process theology

14.13 Cobb, Jr, John B. *A Christian Natural Theology: Based on the Thought of Alfred North Whitehead*, Philadelphia: Westminster Press, 1965.
14.14 Hartshorne, Charles *The Divine Relativity: A Social Conception of God*, New Haven, Conn.: Yale University Press, 1948.
14.15 Whitehead, Alfred North *Process and Reality: An Essay in Cosmology*, New York: Macmillan, 1929.

Verifiability and meaning

14.16 Ayer, A. J. *Language, Truth, and Logic*, New York: Dover, 1936.
14.17 Braithwaite, R. B. *An Empiricist's View of the Nature of Religious Belief*, Cambridge: Cambridge University Press, 1955.

14.18 Flew, Antony and Alasdair MacIntyre, eds *New Essays in Philosophical Theology*, New York: Macmillan, 1955.
14.19 Hempel, Carl 'Problems and Changes in the Empiricist Criterion of Meaning', *Revue Internationale de Philosophie*, 4 (1950): 41–63.
14.20 Wisdom, John 'Gods', *Proceedings of the Aristotelian Society*, suppl. vol. 45 (1944–5): 185–206.

Wittgensteinian fideism

14.21 Hudson, W. D. *Wittgenstein and Religious Belief*, London: Macmillan, 1975.
14.22 Malcolm, Norman 'The Groundlessness of Religious Belief', in Stuart Brown, ed., *Reason and Religion*, Ithaca, NY: Cornell University Press, 1977.
14.23 Nielsen, Kai 'Wittgensteinian Fideism', *Philosophy*, 52 (1967): 191–201.
14.24 Phillips, D. Z. *Religion without Explanation*, Oxford: Basil Blackwell, 1976.
14.25 Wittgenstein, Ludwig *Lectures and Conversations on Aesthetics, Psychology, and Religious Belief*, ed., Cyril Barret, Berkeley: University of California Press, 1967.

The problem of evil

14.26 Aiken, H. D. 'God and Evil: A Study of Some Relations between Faith and Morals', *Ethics*, 48 (1958): 5.
14.27 Alston, William P. 'The Inductive Argument from Evil and the Human Cognitive Condition', *Philosophical Perspectives*, vol. 5: *Philosophy of Religion*, ed. James Tomberlin, Atascadero, Cal.: Ridgeview, 1991: 29–67.
14.28 Grave, S. A. 'On Evil and Omnipotence', *Mind*, 65 (1956): 259–62.
14.29 Hick, John *Evil and the God of Love*, New York: Harper & Row, 1966; 2nd edn, 1978.
14.30 Mackie, J. L. 'Evil and Omnipotence', *Mind*, 64 (1955): 200–12.
14.31 McCloskey, H. J. 'God and Evil', *Philosophical Quarterly*, 10 (1960): 97–114.
14.32 Pike, Nelson 'God and Evil: A Reconsideration', *Ethics*, 48 (1958): 116–24.
14.33 Plantinga, Alvin *God and Other Minds*, Ithaca, NY: Cornell University Press, 1967.
14.34 —— *God, Freedom, and Evil*, New York: Harper & Row, 1974.
14.35 Rowe, William 'The Problem of Evil and Some Varieties of Atheism', *American Philosophical Quarterly*, 16 (1979): 335–41.
14.36 Swinburne, Richard *The Existence of God*, Oxford: Oxford University Press, 1979.
14.37 van Inwagen, Peter 'The Magnitude, Duration, and Distribution of Evil: A Theodicy', *Philosophical Topics*, 16 (1988): 161–81.

The ontological argument

14.38 Alston, William 'The Ontological Argument Revisited', *Philosophical Review*, 69 (1960): 452–74.
14.39 Hartshorne, Charles *Man's Vision of God*, New York: Harper & Row, 1941.
14.40 Lewis, David 'Anselm and Actuality', *Noûs*, 4 (1970): 175–88.

14.41 Malcolm, Norman 'Anselm's Ontological Arguments', *Philosophical Review*, 69 (1960): 41–62.
14.42 Plantinga, Alvin *The Nature of Necessity*, Oxford: Oxford University Press, 1974.

Analytic philosophy of religion

14.43 Hasker, William *God, Time, and Knowledge*, Ithaca, NY: Cornell University Press, 1989.
14.44 Kenny, Anthony *The God of the Philosophers*, Oxford: Oxford University Press, 1979.
14.45 Kretzmann, Norman 'Omniscience and Immutability', *Journal of Philosophy*, 63 (1966): 409–21.
14.46 Mitchell, Basil *The Justification of Religious Belief*, New York: Seabury, 1974.
14.47 Pike, Nelson *God and Timelessness*, London: Routledge & Kegan Paul, 1970.
14.48 Plantinga, Alvin *God and Other Minds*, Ithaca, NY: Cornell University Press, 1967.
14.49 Prior, Arthur 'The Formalities of Omniscience', *Philosophy*, 32 (1960): 121–57.
14.50 Rowe, William *The Cosmological Argument*, Princeton, NJ: Princeton University Press, 1975.
14.51 Stump, Eleonore and Norman Kretzmann, 'Eternity', *Journal of Philosophy*, 78 (1981): 429–58.
14.52 Swinburne, Richard *The Coherence of Theism*, Oxford: Oxford University Press, 1977.
14.53 —— *The Existence of God*, Oxford: Oxford University Press, 1979.
14.54 Wierenga, Edward *The Nature of God*, Ithaca, NY: Cornell University Press, 1989.
14.55 Zagzebski, Linda *The Dilemma of Freedom and Foreknowledge*, New York: Oxford University Press, 1991.

Religious epistemology

14.56 Alston, William P. 'Christian Experience and Christian Belief', in A. Plantinga and N. Wolterstorff, eds, *Faith and Rationality*, Notre Dame: University of Notre Dame Press, 1983.
14.57 —— *Perceiving God: The Epistemology of Religious Belief*, Ithaca, NY: Cornell University Press, 1991.
14.58 Clifford, W. K. 'The Ethics of Belief', in W. K. Clifford, *Lectures and Essays*, ed. F. Pollock, London: Macmillan, 1879.
14.59 Flew, Antony *The Presumption of Atheism*, London: Pemberton, 1976.
14.60 Plantinga, Alvin 'Is Belief in God Rational?', in *Rationality and Religious Belief*, ed. C. F. Delaney, Notre Dame: University of Notre Dame Press, 1979.
14.61 —— 'Reason and Belief in God', in A. Plantinga and N. Wolterstorff, eds, *Faith and Rationality*, Notre Dame: University of Notre Dame Press, 1983.

14.62 —— *Warrant and Proper Function*, Oxford: Oxford University Press, 1992.

Theological topics

14.63 Beaty, Michael, ed. *Christian Theism and the Problems of Philosophy*, Notre Dame: University of Notre Dame Press, 1990.

14.64 Feenstra, Ronald and Cornelius Plantinga, Jr, eds, *Trinity, Incarnation, and Atonement*, Notre Dame: University of Notre Dame Press, 1989.

14.65 Hick, John 'Jesus and the World Religions', in J. Hick, ed., *The Myth of God Incarnate*, London: SCM Press, 1977.

14.66 Morris, Thomas V. *The Logic of God Incarnate*, Ithaca, NY: Cornell University Press, 1986.

14.67 Quinn, Philip L. 'Christian Atonement and Kantian Justification', *Faith and Philosophy*, 3 (1986): 440–62.

14.68 Stump, Eleonore 'Atonement according to Aquinas', in Thomas V. Morris, ed., *Philosophy and the Christian Faith*, Notre Dame: University of Notre Dame Press, 1988.

14.69 Swinburne, Richard *Responsibility and Atonement*, Oxford: Oxford University Press, 1989.

14.70 —— *Revelation*, Oxford: Oxford University Press, 1992.

Secondary sources

14.71 Lewis, H. D. 'The Philosophy of Religion 1945–1952', *Philosophical Quarterly*, 4 (1954): 166–81, 262–74.

14.72 Sell, Alan P. F. *The Philosophy of Religion: 1875–1980*, London: Croom Helm, 1988.

14.73 Wainwright, William J. *Philosophy of Religion: An Annotated Bibliography of Twentieth-Century Writings in English*, New York and London: Garland, 1978.

14.74 Wieman, Henry Nelson and Bernard Eugene Meland, eds, *American Philosophies of Religion*, Chicago and New York: Willett, Clark, 1936.

14.75 Zagzebski, Linda 'Recent Work in the Philosophy of Religion', *Philosophical Books*, 31 (1990): 1–6.

Glossary

꧁꧂

absolute idealism – a school of philosophy in both Britain and the United States in the late nineteenth and early twentieth centuries. Influenced by Hegel, F. H. Bradley was its main exponent. It stressed the unreality of space, time and physical objects and held that reality was indivisible and spiritual. There is one spiritual, self-conscious being – the Absolute – and everything that is real is so by virtue of participation in the Absolute.

accident – a property that does not apply to an object necessarily, to be contrasted with essential properties.

actual world – the possible world at which all actual truths obtain.

actuality – the feature that distinguishes our possible world from the others and real things from those which are merely possible.

analytic – *see* analytic truth.

analytic truth – a statement that is true just in virtue of the meanings of its constituent terms. Contrasts with 'synthetic truth'.

anti-realism – a metaphysical position which denies realism, the view that there is a mind-independent world with which assertions must correspond in order to be true.

a posteriori **knowledge** – knowledge that depends on a specific sensory or perceptual experience.

a priori **knowledge** – knowledge that does not depend on any specific sensory or perceptual experience.

argument from design – an argument for the existence of God that appeals to the evidence of design in the universe as a reason for thinking that there is a designer.

Äusserungen – a term of art in Wittgenstein for certain first-person psychological utterances such as 'I am afraid.' Their characteristic feature is that they are not *descriptions*, and in particular not descriptions of the inner. *Äusserungen* have the same function as more primitive reactions or expressions which they replace; for example 'I am afraid' may be functionally equivalent to a groan of fear.

being – in Meinong's theory, the widest category of objects, only some of which have the property of existence.

binary function – a function relating two arguments to a value (the way, for example, addition is a function of two numbers having their sum as the value of the function for those arguments). Gottlob Frege interpreted relations between objects as binary functions with truth values, the true or the false, as their values.

brain in a vat – a thought experiment described by Hilary Putnam, according to which we might just be brains kept alive by a mad scientist in a vat of nutrients.

causal theory of names – what a name refers to on some occasion is determined by the causal chain between that use and previous uses of the name to refer to some object.

common law – a system of law originating in England after the Norman conquest consisting of decisions made by courts in cases where there is no controlling legislation. One of its fundamental principles is that courts have an obligation to follow precedent and treat like cases alike and so earlier decisions become a source of law for later ones. Today common law is usually divided into three branches – contract, property, and tort. Although many jurisdictions now have codes of criminal law important aspects of criminal law remain common law. The common law spread to many parts of the British Empire and forms the basis of law in such countries as Australia, Canada and the United States.

common-sense view of the world – a view, espoused by G. E. Moore in his 'Defence of Common Sense' (1925). It rejected any philosophical proposition that conflicted with certain common beliefs of ordinary life.

consequentialism – at their simplest, consequentialist theories of right and wrong locate these moral characteristics of acts in the comparative goodness or badness of their consequences: the better or worse its consequences, the more right or wrong the act. In more complicated forms of consequentialist theory, the connection between actions and morally significant consequences is indirect. Acts are not right or wrong according to the relative merit of their own immediate consequences, but rather, according to the more general consequences of those moral practices or aspects of moral character to which actions of the kind in question might be attached. An act which by itself produces good consequences might thus be a very bad way of acting. Moore's view that for epistemological reasons we ought to abide by the dictates of the rules of common sense is one form of indirect consequentialism.

cosmological argument – an argument for the existence of God that derives from the assumption that contingent beings exist the conclusion that there is a First Cause, namely, God.

counterpart – in David Lewis's modal theory objects do not exist in more than one possible world. Statements attributing an essential property to an object really attribute it to the object and all of its counterparts in other worlds, the objects in those worlds most similar to the original.

criterion – in the later Wittgenstein a criterion is a test, holding in virtue of a rule of language, for the truth of a judgement. So the criterion for being an international grandmaster in chess is that one have such and such a numerical rating gained in such and such a way, as dictated by an explicit rule.

de dicto **necessity** – necessity of the *dictum* or proposition, a general necessary truth, contrasted with those that attribute a property necessarily to an object. (*See de re* necessity.)

de re **necessity** – necessity of the thing. (*See de dicto* necessity.)

definite description – a phrase that begins with the word 'the' followed by a noun or noun phrase, for example, 'the present King of France' and 'the oak table with the Limoge vase'.

deontological ethics – deontological theories take right and wrong, rather than good and bad, as the primary notions of morality. Etymologically, 'deontology' comes from the Greek words *deon* (duty) and *logos* (science). Deontological approaches to ethics are non-consequentialist in denying that questions of duty, or of the right, are necessarily parasitic on questions of the good. What one ought to do is not simply a matter of what will produce the best consequences, but primarily a question about what kinds of acts one ought or ought not perform.

domain – in logic, the range of interpretation of the quantifiers, 'there are' and 'for all'. The domain of a possible world is the class of objects which exist at, or according to, that world.

doxastic – belief-oriented. A psychological state is doxastic if and only if it includes belief as an essential component.

Duhem, Pierre – a prominent French physicist and philosopher of science (1861–1916). He is best known among philosophers of science for his version of epistemic holism according to which a scientific hypothesis is always tested on the basis of other hypotheses, so that confirmation and falsification are conditional on accepted hypotheses.

emotivism – a kind of non-cognitivism, emotivism holds that moral claims, such as 'lying is wrong', merely serve to vent a speaker's emotional reaction to his or her subject matter, or perhaps evoke a similar emotional reaction in the speaker's audience. On this view of moral discourse, moral claims do not make statements about anything at all, not even the speaker's own emotional state; instead, they function as actual expressions of a particular emotional response to whatever it is they purport to be about.

empiricism – the evidence of the *senses* – e.g. visual, auditory, tactile or gustatory experiences – is a sort of evidence appropriate to genuine knowledge. (Strict empiricism: *only* the evidence of the senses is appropriate to genuine knowledge.)

epistemic coherentism – all justification is inferential and systematic in virtue of coherence relations among beliefs.

epistemic contextualism – justification has a two-tier structure in that some beliefs are 'contextually basic' – i.e. taken for granted in a context of inquiry – and all inferentially justified beliefs depend on such contextually basic beliefs.

epistemic foundationalism – justification has a two-tier structure in that some instances of justification are non-inferential, or foundational, and all other instances of justification are inferential, deriving ultimately from foundational justification.

epistemic holism – *see* epistemic coherentism.

epistemic infinitism – regresses of inferential epistemic justification are endless, or infinite.

epistemology – the theory of knowledge, the philosophical study of the nature, origin and scope of knowledge.

essential property – a property an object has necessarily, that is, in every possible world.

essentiality of origin – the thesis that the origins of an object, what it is originally made from, for example, in the case of an artifact, is an essential property of it.

ethical intuitionism – ethical intuitionism supposes that the human mind includes a cognitive faculty that enables it to apprehend, in a direct sort of way, the presence or absence of moral properties as they actually exist in the objects of moral thought. Although intuitionism is, strictly speaking, an epistemological theory, it is often presented as a form of ethical objectivism.

ethical naturalism – ethical naturalism, a kind of objectivism, holds that moral claims are true or false depending on the way in which the natural world is actually configured. It should not be confused with naturalized ethics, which represents a more contemporary, positivistic effort to account for ethical thought and behaviour on the basis of certain natural aspects of human psychology and social interaction. Unlike the earlier naturalism of Dewey or Perry, which is also based on natural facts related to human psychology and society, naturalized ethics is typically advanced as a form of ethical subjectivism or non-cognitivism. For representative examples of each see Harman [5.26] and Gibbard [5.21].

ethical non-cognitivism – ethical non-cognitivism comprises those metaethical theories which hold that moral claims are not propositional: moral claims do not express statements which are either true or false, depending on the way the world is. Loosely put, there are no moral properties, subjective or objective, of which the human mind might enjoy any sort of cognitive awareness.

ethical non-naturalism – ethical non-naturalism, a kind of objectivism, holds that moral claims are true or false depending on the way in which certain non-natural aspects of the world are actually configured. Advanced by G. E. Moore in 1903, this view has remained an historical anomaly.

ethical objectivism – objectivists about morality hold that moral claims express propositions, and that what makes these propositions true or false are features of the world that exist independently of human beliefs about morality.

ethical subjectivism – subjectivists about morality also hold that moral claims express propositions, but think that what makes these propositions true or false are the moral responses of the speaker or his or her community to whatever it is that the claims are about. In saying that lying is wrong, for example, I make a statement about my own moral beliefs, or perhaps my community's moral beliefs.

extension – the set of objects of which a predicate is true is its extension. Properties are also said to have as an extension the set of their instances.

fallibilism about justification – there can be false justified beliefs.

family resemblance – Wittgenstein holds that the items belonging to the extension of a given term such as 'game' may fail to share necessary and sufficient features in virtue of which they fall under the term. Rather properties may be distributed among the class of items in a way analogous to the manner in which features are allocated among the various members of a family. A and B may share the family hair colour but not the family nose, B and C the family nose but not the hair colour, and so on.

first-order logic – logic where quantifiers 'all' and 'some' range only over individuals and not higher-order entities such as properties or predicates.

free-will defence – the attempt to show that God's existence is compatible with the existence of evil by appealing to the value of creatures with free will.

functionalism – theory in the philosophy of mind by which mental notions such as pain are to be defined by the causal role or function they perform mediating between sensation and action.

Gettier problem – the problem of finding a modification of, or an alternative to, the standard justified-true-belief analysis of knowledge that avoids difficulties from counter-examples to that analysis inspired by Edmund Gettier in 1963.

grue – Goodman's fabricated predicate, true of those things that are examined before the year 2000 and found to be green, otherwise blue things.

haecceitism – the thesis that one object can occur in different possible worlds, without requiring that they have any distinctive individual essence that grounds that identity.

haecceity – the non-qualitative ground of identity of an object across possible worlds, as a 'thisness' contrasted with a qualitative quiddity, or 'suchness'.

historical theory of names – *see* causal theory of names.

idealism about something, x – the existence of x depends on the intellectual or perceptual processes of a conceiver.

immanent universals – the view that universals are located (wholly) in each of their instances, and depend on them ontologically. Thus there can be no uninstantiated immanent universals.

indexical – an expression such as 'I', 'now', 'here', 'this' and 'that' which depends for its interpretation on the context of utterance.

individual – entity of basic ontological category. Concrete particulars, spatio-temporally located physical objects are model individuals, although other sorts, including abstract entities, may be included. Defined in logic as objects of the lowest logical type.

individual essence – essential property had by at most one object.

individuation – process by which an entity is distinguished from its environment at one time and through time.

inferential justification – the justification of one belief depends on another belief or set of beliefs.

inherence – variously, relation or non-relational tie between a property or universal and its instances.

intensionality – semantic characterization of an expression in which expressions with the same reference or same extension cannot be substituted for each other. Contrasts with extensionality.

internal relations, doctrine of – a metaphysical principle, espoused by F. H. Bradley, which held that relational properties are reducible to intrinsic properties and, ultimately, unreal.

intrinsic – property internal to an object, independent of its relations with any other object.

lambda-operator – the lower-case Greek letter *lambda* used as a variable-binding operator for generating function-expressions from other expressions. It was used in this way to characterize the notion of an algorithm (recursive function) by Alonzo Church in his *The Calculi of Lambda-Conversion*, and also in his simple type theory to generate complex expressions for functions (including concepts as functions from objects to truth values). Rudolf Carnap, Richard Montague and others followed Church in this use of the lambda-operator.

language-game – a term from Wittgenstein's later philosophy denoting a custom-regulated pattern of interaction in which words play a role. For instance in the language-game of the builders in §2 of the *Philosophical Investigations* the role of the word 'slab' is to indicate the type of building block the helper is to bring in response to the call 'Slab!'

legal positivism – the view that no moral judgement need be involved in deter-mining what the law is. It is usually contrasted with natural law theory (q.v.). It is especially associated with John Austin (1790–1859) who spoke of law as the command of a sovereign to that sovereign's subjects backed up by a threat sanction. Modern legal positivism speaks of the acceptance of law by a community rather than the command of a sovereign.

logical atomism – a philosophy defended by Bertrand Russell in his 'The Philo-sophy of Logical Atomism'. It held that all meaningful propositions were truth-functions of elementary or atomic propositions which, in turn, charac-terized metaphysically basic facts.

logical constructionism – a philosophical strategy, developed by Bertrand Russell, which treated philosophically troublesome entities (e.g. numbers, physical objects) as analysable in terms of – or 'logically constructed out of' – less troublesome entities (e.g. sets, sense data).

logical empiricism – *see* logical positivism.

logical positivism – the view of the Vienna Circle that philosophy should use modern logic (deriving from Frege and Russell), various analytical techniques and the verification principle to restrict philosophical pursuits to the advance-ment of 'scientific' knowledge, thereby banishing metaphysical concerns from philosophy.

logical type – classification of logical expressions into objects, predicates, etc., depending on their logical category.

mass terms – terms such as 'water' or 'food' that stand for quantities of stuff, rather than distinct individuals.

Meinongian – view characteristic of Alexius Meinong, chiefly the view that there is a distinction between what there is (what has 'being') and what exists.

mereological sum – object that has arbitrary other objects as its parts. Defined formally as the object that overlaps exactly those other objects.

mereology – study of the part–whole relationship.

meta-ethics – while substantive ethics concerns itself with theories of right and wrong and good and bad, meta-ethics concerns itself with the more general question of what, exactly, ethical theories are theories of. Answers range from that simple, undefinable, non-natural object of thought, goodness, to nothing at all.

meta-language – a language used to talk about another, 'object-' language.

metaphysical realism – generally, the view that a particular class of entities, such as universals, exists. More recently identified as the view that truth consists of a correspondence with a mind-independent reality and that truth is 'non-epistemic', that is, is independent of our knowledge.

modal logic – that branch of logic that deals with the concepts of necessity and possibility.

modal operator – expression such as 'necessarily' or 'possibly' that expresses a modality, or mode of truth.

modal realism – the view that possible worlds and possible but non-actual entities exist. Contrasted with actualism.

naive realism – things are just as they seem to be in ordinary perceptual experience.

naming theory of meaning – the meaning of a name is the object it directly denotes or picks out.

natural kind – class of objects that share a common essence, or genuine property.

naturalism – project to reduce the notions and ontology of a field of study to those necessary for the study of the natural world, that is those of science.

naturalistic fallacy – specifically, the naturalistic fallacy refers to a logical error that Moore believed himself to have discovered in the work of those earlier moral philosophers whom he believed to have defined goodness in terms of some other, natural property, something which Moore thought could be logically ruled out by appeal to the open question argument. More generally, the naturalistic fallacy has come to refer to the questionable legitimacy of any move to base claims about what ought to be on claims about what naturally is.

natural-law theory – the view that there are principles or values which are independent of any human institution and to which any human legislation or decision must conform if it is to have the force of law

neutral monism – a metaphysical view, first expressed by William James, and later by Bertrand Russell. It viewed both minds and physical objects as metaphysically secondary entities, holding that both should be regarded as constructions out of immediate experience – which, in turn, was viewed as the ultimate 'stuff' of reality.

nominalism – thesis that all that exists is particular, there are not general or universal entities. Also identified with the rejection of abstract entities such as sets and numbers.

norm – a standard which guides action by making it appropriate to claim that that action ought to be done. Ordinarily, at least, the acceptance of a norm involves recognizing that one thereby has a reason to conform to it

object theory – term used by Meinong for the most general study of objects, existent and not.

ontological argument – an argument for the existence of God which derives the conclusion that God exists just from the concept of God as 'that than which nothing greater can be conceived' or as the greatest possible being.

ontological commitment – relation of a theory to those objects that one asserting the theory believes to exist.

ontology – the philosophical study of existence in general, e.g. of the kinds of things that exist.

opacity, referential – a grammatical context occurring in a sentence and containing a nominal expression (a name, definite description or quantifier phrase) is said to be referentially opaque if the substitution of a co-referring expression, in the case of a name or definite description, or the exportation of a quantifier phrase, can change the truth value of the sentence. Thus, the fact that 'Jones believes that Cicero denounced Cataline' can be true and 'Jones believes Tully denounced Cataline' can be false, even though 'Cicero' and 'Tully' are co-referring nominal expressions (a fact that Jones does not know), indicates that the grammatical context following 'believe' is referentially opaque. Similarly, the fact that 'Jones seeks a unicorn' can be true even though the result of exporting the quantifier phrase, 'a unicorn', as in 'A unicorn is such that Jones seeks it', is false (because there are no unicorns) indicates that the grammatical context following 'seek' is referentially opaque.

open question argument – by means of the open question argument, Moore thought that he could prove that 'good' was undefinable. If we substitute any proposed definition, x, into 'but is x good?', the question is an open one, which shows, according to Moore, that 'x' and 'good' can't mean the same thing.

ostensive definition – conveying the meaning or referent of a term by pointing out one of its exemplars, as in: 'That [*pointing*] is [what we count as] red.' In the later Wittgenstein ostensive definition is distinguished from what he calls ostensive teaching. In the latter case a learner is encouraged to call out the right name when a certain type of object is pointed to; but the learner has not yet mastered the use of the expression 'What is that called?' In the former case the learner has mastered a language-game for asking what a given thing is called.

Pareto efficiency – one situation a Pareto-dominates another b if it is possible to move from b to a making at least one party better off and no parties worse off. A situation is Pareto-efficient if no situation Pareto-dominates it. The concept is named after the late nineteenth-century social theorist Vilfredo Pareto.

phenomenalism – the philosophical view which attempts to analyse the physical world as a construction out of immediate experience or phenomena.

picture theory of meaning – the view, expressed by Ludwig Wittgenstein in *Tractatus Logico-Philosophicus*, that the basic or atomic propositions of language function as pictures of basic facts, which, in turn, were viewed as arrangements of absolutely simple objects.

platonic realism – view that abstract entities, in particular, universals, exist and do not depend on concrete instances for that existence.

possibilia – merely possible individuals distinct from any actual thing.

possible world – way things might have been, either an abstract or concrete entity in different theories.

pragmatism – a school of philosophical thought, originally formulated by C. S. Peirce in the late nineteenth and early twentieth centuries, and developed in various ways by William James, John Dewey, and others. The Pragmatists agreed that every meaningful thought or proposition must have practical – and, therefore, observable – consequences in human life.

problem of evil – the problem of reconciling the existence of God with the existence of evil. The logical problem of evil is the claim that the existence of an omnipotent, omniscient, perfectly good being is logically incompatible with the existence of evil. The evidential problem of evil is the claim that the existence of evil is good evidence against the existence of God.

proper name – a word that names or denotes an individual object; Russell distinguished between ordinary proper names, such as 'Socrates' and 'Fido', which are disguised or abbreviated definite descriptions, from logically proper names, such as 'this' and 'that', which denote their object without any mediating descriptive content. Other philosophers, such as Donnellan and Kripke, have argued that ordinary proper names actually function the way that Russell thought logically proper names do.

quiddity – 'suchness', qualitative individual essence.

radical interpretation – determining the conditions under which a speaker's utterance is true without relying upon previous knowledge about what the speaker believes or what language he or she speaks.

rationalism – some knowledge does not depend on the evidence of the senses. (Strict rationalism: no knowledge depends on the evidence of the senses, and genuine knowledge does exist.)

realism about something, *x* – the existence of *x* does not depend on the intellectual or perceptual processes of a conceiver.

rigid designator – expression that designates the same entity in every possible world. Contrasted with definite descriptions which may not be rigid.

scientific realism – thesis that the entities and properties postulated by science are real.

scientism – perjorative term for the excessive veneration or respect for science.

semantic holism – the meaning of any statement depends on the meaning of some other statement(s).

set – a group or collection of individuals itself viewed as an individual.

ship of Theseus – a legendary ship which was replaced plank by plank until it had no plank in common with its original constitution.

singular term – a proper name, definite description, singular personal pronoun, or demonstrative pronoun.

situational ethics – situational ethics is the view that no theories of ethics are possible because any action's rightness or wrongness depends entirely on the situation in which it is performed, and all situations are unique.

sortal term – a general term for a sort or kind of individual thing, e.g. 'table', 'lion' or 'number', as opposed to mass terms like 'water', or adjectives like 'blue'.

statutory law – a statute is an act of a legislature commanding or forbidding something. Unlike common law which consists of decisions of courts, statutory law consists of statutes.

substantive ethics – in the early twentieth century, this branch of philosophy concerned itself with the general question of what makes actions right or wrong. Some answers to this question proposed a single, general principle, such as 'those acts are right which produce the best consequences', while others proposed a number of such principles, such as Ross's list of *prima facie* duties. But according to the situational view of ethics espoused by Carritt, substantive ethics was, strictly speaking, impossible; there simply was no general answer to the question of what it is that makes acts right or wrong.

synthetic truth – a statement that is true in virtue of considerations other than the meanings of the constituent terms.

temporal part – an object at a moment or through an interval seen as an individual in its own right.

theodicy – the attempt to explain what justifies evil or what is the reason for evil.

token/type – a distinction between particular occurrences of a kind and the kind itself. The distinction is usually applied to linguistic entities. Thus in the sentence 'The man bit the dog' there are two tokens of the type *the*; on the other hand there are only four word types in the sentence. So if we ask how many words there are in the sentence we will get a different answer depending on whether we mean word types or word tokens.

truth-function – a given proposition, *p*, is a truth-function of the propositions which make up a certain set, *s*, if and only if the truth-value (i.e. the truth or falsity) of *p* is completely determined by the truth-values of the propositions in *s*. Russell and Wittgenstein were attracted to the view that all of the propositions of language are truth-functions of a set of elementary propositions about elementary facts. Russell never embraced this view without reservation, but Wittgenstein defended it in the *Tractatus Logico-Philosophicus*.

utilitarianism – a kind of consequentialism, utilitarianism ties the rightness of acts to the maximization of utility; 'utility' may simply refer to pleasure, or it may include such goods as personal affection and knowledge, as in Moore's ideal version of the theory. In more current usage, however, 'utility' is usually confined to either pleasurable mental states or satisfied preferences, and so Moore's theory would now be designated as a non-utilitarian form of consequentialism.

variable, bound – in symbolic logic, a variable such as *x* or *y* that is preceded by a quantifier 'For all *x*, . . .' or 'For some *y*, . . .', as opposed to a free variable, which is not.

verification principle – a principle espoused by the members of the Vienna Circle which held that a meaningful non-logical proposition must be capable, in principle, of empirical verification. Various formulations of the principle were offered with none winning general acceptance. The principle was used to discredit traditional metaphysics.

Vienna Circle – a group of philosophers, many with scientific or mathematical training, who came together in Vienna under the leadership of Moritz Schlick during the 1920s. The group espoused the philosophy of logical positivism, which proved to be both influential and controversial for two decades both on the European continent and in the English-speaking world.

Zeno (of Elea) – a pre-Socratic Greek philosopher (born about 490 BC) who is best known for formulating what have come to be known as 'Zeno's paradoxes'. These are arguments, still objects of respectful scrutiny in the twentieth century, designed to prove that change, in the form of physical motion, is impossible. Zeno also argued that the concepts of plurality and spatial location are deeply incoherent and so have no application to reality. He believed that reality, properly understood, is an unchanging, undivided whole. As such, there are interesting parallels between Zeno's thought and that of the absolute idealists of the late nineteenth and early twentieth centuries.

Index